Research Methods for Communication Science

James H. Watt
University of Connecticut
and
Sjef A. van den Berg
University of Connecticut

Allyn and Bacon
Boston • London • Toronto • Sydney • Tokyo • Singapore

Series Editor: Carla Daves
Marketing Manager: Joyce Nilsen
Production Administrator: Marjorie Payne
Editorial Assistant: Mary Visco
Composition/Prepress Buyer: Linda Cox
Manufacturing Buyer: Megan Cochran
Editorial-Production Service: Chestnut Hill Enterprises, Inc.

Library of Congress Cataloging-in-Publication Data

Watt, James H.
    Research methods for communication science / James H. Watt and
Sjef van den Berg.
        p.   cm.
    Includes index.
    ISBN 0-205-14026-2
    1. Communication–Research–Methodology. I . Berg, Sjef van den.
    II. Title.
P91.3.W38   1995
302.2'072–dc20   94-32092
                                                                          CIP

Printed in the United States of America

10   9   8   7   6   5   4   3   2   1   99   98   97   96   95

Contents

Preface

The authors of this book have a combined 80 semesters experience in teaching research methods to undergraduate and graduate communication students. Or, put another way, they have had the same experience 80 times. And that should permit some generalization. At the beginning of each semester the classroom is filled with students who believe (to make another statistical generalization) that science is done across campus in those buildings, not here; that learning to do research is an alien activity that requires initiation rites that communication students can only imagine in dark dreams; and that communication research is an oxymoron.

Over the course of a semester, a few of these students experience the transformation that warms the heart of every professor: by the end of the semester the "deer in headlights" expressions have turned into genuine appreciation for the simplicity, cleverness, and occasional beauty of the research enterprise. For most students, communication research has at least been demystified and the student can take away an important professional skill. But in selecting a text to teach research methods, we've had some of the same frustrations for 80 semesters, too.

There are plenty of research methods texts for students of sociology and psychology. There are even a few for mass communication and interpersonal communication. But none of these focus on communication research as an activity that includes mass communication, interpersonal communication, group communication, organizational communication, marketing communication, and information campaigns. Also, to exaggerate a bit, the texts that we have used in the past seemed to have been aimed at one of two audiences: the lay person (*Statistics for Someone Even As Dumb As You*) or the High-Priest-in-Training (*Techniques for Folding Questionnaires (Matrix Algebra Edition)*).

Another consistent problem in methods texts has been the focus on the procedures of research, without a good explanation of *why* it should be done the way it is. Of course, we could always assign a supplementary philosophy of science text (*The Epistemology and Ontology of Phenomenology: An Apology*), but few of those exhibit any interest at all in discussing the *how* of conducting inquiry. And we're already in enough trouble with students for assigning problem sets. Of course, we could rely on the prevailing culture which makes scientific-like approaches to acquiring knowledge almost seem like common sense, but there are too many examples of sincere belief in pseudo-scientific procedures (even among our students) to make us comfortable in that approach.

What we thought was needed is a text aimed at communication students that integrates the basic rules of science with the research procedures that follow these rules. It's not enough to tell students they need a random sample; we must also say why they need it, and then follow that up by showing how to get one. This means integrating basic philosophy of science, statistics, research design, and investigatory procedures.

This text is the product of our struggle to put all these elements together. In designing the text, we started with a reasonable assumption: Communication students are as intelligent as the people over there in the science and math buildings.

That assumption has two implications. First, we do not have to "dumb down" the discussions of the scientific method and empirical procedures. The logic of research is accessible to all students, because they behave like scientists most of the time. Even statistics, given a good reason for their existence, are understandable and useful, if not totally enjoyable.

Second, students are perfectly capable of expanding their knowledge of specialized research skills on their own after they have been introduced to the general logic of scientific investigation. We do not have to be exhaustive in discussing research design or statistics or interviewing techniques. If we point the student in the right direction, mention the key term, and kick about the intellectual territory a bit, they'll be able to find other sources that will explain the intricacies and cul-de-sacs of research in much more detail than our editor (and our energy) will permit in this volume. For each chapter we've come up with a number of sources that are good places to look further.

As a result of our goals and assumptions, this book has its easy and its difficult sections. Life is like that. While we expect some creaking and groaning as students' cognitive structures expand a little, over 20 years we have collected 2893 pieces of evidence that tell us communication students can become competent scientists.

The book is divided into three sections. The first lays out the elements of the scientific method, and the requirements that playing by the rules of science places on the researcher.

The second section focuses on ways of describing relationships and inferring their presence from limited observation. (All right, it's sampling and statistics.) Again, the reasons for using statistics refer back to the rules of science.

The final section lays out the elements of research design and presents some typical research procedures. The material covered in the first two sections provides the basis for design decisions. There are also extended examples of classic or particularly interesting communication research studies that place the abstract design principles in some concrete context.

We've used examples from various communication subdisciplines as a way of engaging the interest of a wide range of communication students. Whenever possible, we've tried to include detailed examples to show calculations or the implications of research decisions. The emphasis on examples prompted one reviewer to summarize our manuscript with the succinct phrase "…there are a lot of words in there." We plead guilty, but we think detailed description with many examples is a superior way to understand the more difficult material.

The book is suitable for undergraduates and as a first research methods text for graduate students. Although all the examples are drawn from communication research, the book could be used in most behavioral or social science research methods courses. We hope it will be.

Acknowledgments

It is traditional to acknowledge the aid of spouses and family members in the preparation of a book. Who are we to flout tradition? Antonia Brancia and Alicia Welch put up with unmowed lawns and unfixed plumbing and periodic bouts of grouchiness as we struggled to cram all the neat and important stuff into some form that would be useful to someone other than the two of us and that strange little graduate student who later founded the multimillion dollar corporation. Likewise, Ian and Pieter and Jesse were good about overlooking discussions of the Central Limit Theorem at soccer games and birthday parties. We found they were perfectly capable of finding the beach while our faces reflected the blue glare of the computer monitors.

The manuscript was seriously improved by the comments and gentle editing of Erica Weigel and Nancy Menelly, who transcended their station as graduate students to become collaborators. In addition, the comments of the following reviewers have helped to refine this text: Cam Brammer, Marshall University; Joanne Cantor, University of Wisconsin; Timothy Edgar, University of Maryland; Ronald Faber, University of Minnesota; Robert Gass, California State University; Michael Mayer, Arizona State University; Calvin Morrill, University of Arizona; Clifford Nass, Stanford University; Mary Hinchcliff, Southern Illinois University; Brian Spitzberg, San Diego State University. We would also like to thank Stephen Hull and the other people at Allyn & Bacon for their encouragement and tolerance of our mid-course corrections and naive time estimates.

We must also acknowledge our debt to the people who taught us research methods at the University of Wisconsin way back when: Jack MacLeod, Steven Chaffee, Jerold Hage, and James Tankard. They may not agree with everything that's in this book, but they are responsible for large parts of it.

Part I

Philosophy of Science, Empiricism, and the Scientific Method

The whole of science is nothing more than a refinement of everyday thinking.—ALBERT EINSTEIN
GERMAN-AMERICAN PHYSICIST [1879–1955]

There are in fact two things, science and opinion; the former begets knowledge, the latter ignorance.—HIPPOCRATES
GREEK PHYSICIAN [C. 460–370 BC]
LAW, BK. IV10

Science is built up with facts, as a house is with stones. But a collection of facts is no more a science than a heap of stones is a house.
—JULES HENRI POINCARÉ
FRENCH MATHEMATICIAN AND PHILOSOPHER [1854–1912]

Skepticism is the chastity of the intellect.—GEORGE SANTAYANA
AMERICAN POET AND PHILOSOPHER [1863–1952]

Chapter *1*

Nature and Utility of Scientific Theory

All humans spend time puzzling about the world around them and wondering why and how things happen. In fact, this curiosity and thought really define what we call human consciousness. We wonder about the way that things work, and we speculate about the causes of interesting events. One way or another, we come up with a reason or an explanation about the nature of reality, or at least the part of reality which interests us. In many cases, our observations of events have provided the evidence that forms the basis of our explanations.

Naive Science and Theory

When we act in this way, we are behaving like scientists. Our goals as inquisitive human beings are identical to those of the scientist: We are interested in understanding how things work, in finding explanations and in predicting outcomes. Since we are not acting with awareness of the rules of science, we'll call our activities *naive science*. The major difference between ordinary thought and scientific investigation is in the more stringent requirements for scientific study. But this is a very important difference, as we'll see later.

As naive scientists, we try to understand some interesting situation in a way that will predict or explain its operation. This understanding is a kind of theory. The word *theory* is sometimes used to mean a wild speculation ("It's only a theory, but could ancient spacemen have landed in mid-town Manhattan?"). That's not what we refer to when we speak of theory. We'll use the term to mean a simplified explanation of reality.

Kerlinger, in the classic textbook *Foundations of Behavioral Research* (1986), gave this definition of theory:

> *A theory is a set of interrelated constructs (concepts), definitions, and propositions that present a systematic view of phenomena by specifying relations among variables, with the purpose of explaining and predicting the phenomena.*

On the face of it, this looks like a rather formidable (and properly scientific) definition. But let's take it apart and look at what it says.

First of all, the purpose of theory is to explain and predict events. If we can predict an event, we may be able to avoid the danger it poses, or to profit from its occurrence. And if we can understand something well enough to explain it, we have the additional possibility of controlling it to our benefit or even changing it. Early naive scientists developed a theory of fire which predicted the consequences of sticking one's hand in the bright flames; later scientists developed a theory of oxidation which allowed them to make the fire hotter or cooler by regulating the flow of oxygen to the flames.

A theory achieves prediction and explanation by stating relationships between *concepts* which are defined as *variables*. So what are variables? Variables are things that *vary*— that is, take on different intensities, values, or states. We're only interested in predicting or explaining things that change. While we can describe something that never changes, predicting its behavior is trivial: It'll be the same tomorrow as it is today, and the same for all days after that, and nothing will produce any change in it. And there's no need to explain its relationship to other variables, as they cannot affect it. Therefore, we have no need for a theory about nonvariables. In developing a theory of fire, our naive fire scientist probably observed that a fire could be very small (a smoldering ember), bigger (a camp fire), or huge (a forest fire). "Size of fire" is thus a variable, and it can be theoretically related to other variables like "Time it takes to cook a mastodon."

So what are concepts or constructs? They are the mental image of the thing which varies. In the example above, "fire" is the concept, while "size of fire" is the variable based on the concept. Concepts are described in language through definitions. If able to do so, primitive humans might have passed on to a neighbor a definition of the concept of a fire: "occurs on wood, gives off flickering light, is hot...." A later scientist might have defined this concept of the same situation somewhat differently ("electromagnetic radiation in the infrared through visible light region given off by the exothermic combination of oxygen with another element or compound"). In both cases, however, these people have described the concept of fire using words they understand.

Humans, as naive scientists, just naturally try to explain and predict ordinary events in their world. We are uncomfortable with unexplained phenomena, and we have a very basic drive to explain things. Although we'll be talking about theory in the context of human communication for the remainder of this book, let's take another look at a very ordinary example of naive science in the physical world to illustrate the process of building a theory.

Francine Brown decides to take her vacation at a popular ocean resort. The first day at the beach, the water is warm and wonderful for swimming. The second day, the water is very cold. The next day, the water is again very warm. Now this *phenomenon* (variability of the water temperature) interests her, because she likes to swim, and she doesn't like cold water.

What could be causing this day-to-day variation? The sun has been out every day, so that can't be the cause of different water temperatures. Since the sun itself is not variable, she doesn't need to include it in her theory. She begins to observe the water very carefully each day, and she notices that the water is clearer on the days that it is cold, and murkier on the days that are better for swimming.

Francine now can predict whether swimming will be good or not by observing the clarity of the water. She can therefore avoid the shock of diving into frigid water. But this still does not explain *why* the water temperature should shift. In other words, she can *predict* the phenomenon, but she can't yet *explain* it.

After several more days of observation, she notices a relationship between variations in the direction of prevailing winds on the previous day and the water temperature the next day. Days in which the winds are out of the northeast are followed by days with cold water. Days in which the wind is from another direction are followed by warm water. Now Francine has another way of predicting the water temperature: If the winds are out of the northeast today, the water will be too cold to swim tomorrow.

Why should the wind direction affect water temperature, she wonders? After looking at a map, she improves her theory by adding some *process* or *mechanism* to explain why things should be working this way. To the northeast lies open ocean, while the bay in which she is swimming is protected on all other sides by land. Thus northeast winds may blow colder, deep ocean waters (which are clearer, as less algae grow in cold temperatures) into the bay.

What Francine has done is to identify variables (bay water temperature, bay water clarity, and wind direction) and to specify relationships among them. In fact, she will probably call one of these variables (wind direction) the *cause,* and the other two variables the *effects*: prevailing northeast winds will cause bay water to become colder and clearer. Causality will be discussed in more detail later in this book, but Francine has an intuitive idea of what constitutes a *causal relationship*: it's a specific condition of a variable (northeast wind) which occurs earlier in time than a corresponding condition of another variable (such as cold water), combined with some reasonable explanation for the relationship between these two variables (the nature of the geography of the region).

However, the utility of Francine's theory is limited by the extent to which she is confident that it reflects reality. Do things always work this way? Maybe it was just a coincidence that the wind happened to be from the northeast before cold swimming days. Francine's theory is no good for making decisions about swimming if there is no real relationship between wind direction and water temperature.

Her next logical step is to collect more evidence. Being a really committed naive scientist, Francine extends her vacation two weeks, and observes the wind direction and water temperature each day. Her logic here is very straightforward. If the phenomenon operates the way she thinks it should, then the direction of the wind today is always going to determine the water temperature tomorrow. Each additional day that this prediction proves correct provides Francine with more evidence that her explanation is the correct one and that her theory can be used to make decisions about swimming the following day. Francine realizes that more evidence can improve the *probability* that her theory is true. With each additional confirming observation, she is more certain that the relationship between the variables is not just a coincidence.

Francine has carried out all the major steps of a scientific study: She has sought out relevant constructs that vary, observed their values (e.g., water is cold or warm; wind is from the northeast or south), created a theory which contains a testable prediction, and collected evidence to see if her predictions are probably correct. She has done this without really being conscious of it, because that's the way humans learn about their world.

But humans are also often somewhat sloppy in their reasoning, and sometimes create incorrect naive theories. The process of developing explanations for phenomena and for testing whether the explanations are probably true or false has many opportunities for error. To overcome this, the *scientific method* has evolved as a highly formalized, systematic and controlled version of the innate human activity of collecting and summarizing information into naive theories.

Naive Inquiry Versus Scientific Method

The main difference between science and naive inquiry is the awareness that our observations and reasoning are error-prone, and that we must employ strategies to help us guard against committing error. Kerlinger (1986) emphasizes five points on which science and naive inquiry differ: (1) development of theories, (2) testing of theories, (3) control of alternative explanations, (4) nature of relationships, and (5) testing theories with observable evidence. These points, which are summarized below, offer striking illustrations of the differences between formalized, systematic, and controlled inquiry ("science") and naive inquiry.

Development of Theories

A theory presents us with an explanation of a phenomenon: It consists minimally of a concept considered to be a cause, a concept considered to be an effect, and a statement about how and why the two should be related. More formally, a theory is a set of two or more concepts interrelated by one or more hypothetical or theoretical propositions. A theory represents a statement about what *might* logically be happening.

Science and naive inquiry differ greatly in the way in which the concepts of inquiry are selected for study. The scientist will systematically select all the concepts which can be reasonably thought to be possible causes of a phenomenon. The scientist will also eliminate from the theory all other concepts considered to be irrelevant. This process of selection and elimination continues until the total set of available concepts has been reduced to those that are determined by the scientist to be relevant to the problem. This process is accomplished in part via a thorough review of the published research literature, which tells the scientist which concepts have or have not been found to be linked to the phenomenon to be investigated. The scientist relies on the previous work of others to justify using the concepts, and to explain the cause-effect sequence in their relationships.

But the scientist also realizes that the concepts previously used by other researchers may not exhaust all possible causes or effects. Researchers may have overlooked the "real" cause simply because they were not aware of its existence. For example, for all the time that physicians were not aware of the existence of bacteria, they could not consider them as causes of disease. Consequently, by logic, insight, or observation, the scientist may add new concepts to the theory. The scientist is always considering alternative concepts and processes to see if they might more clearly explain the phenomenon being studied.

The naive scientist, on the other hand, does not go through this systematic review process, looking at the work of others, and considering alternative concepts. Rather, guided by biases or convictions, a concept may be selected as a cause simply because it is appealing. Similarly, a naive scientist may latch onto a concept as being a possible cause simply because he or she would *like* it to be the cause, not necessarily because there is a logical reason for it to be so. In this way, moral decay has been held up as the "cause" of natural disasters; the color of a person's skin has been believed to predict one's willingness to work; and God's wrath has been seen as the cause of disease.

In other cases, however, naive scientists like Francine Brown base their explanation of phenomena on their own observation of reality. In this way they are like true scientists who also may use personal observation to help develop theories. The difference is this: The naive scientist will probably consider personal observations to be sufficient to construct a completed theory. For the true scientist, however, personal observations are only a preliminary step in the process of scientific investigation.

The naive scientist selects concepts based on their *appeal* rather than their *relevance*. This constitutes a decidedly nonsystematic method of constructing theories, and the resulting theories are often wrong. Naive scientists do not critically examine alternative explanations for phenomena, and thus may include irrelevant concepts, fail to include important concepts, and miss the true relationships among concepts.

Testing of Theories

Naive science and science differ dramatically in their demand for evidence that supports the truth of a theory. The naive scientist will frequently be satisfied a theory is correct if its truth is obvious, and will conclude that no further support is needed. The theory is thought to be correct because it is "self-evident," "common sense," "is what any reasonable person would conclude." If evidence is obtained at all, the naive scientist's own, informal, personal observations are usually considered sufficient. Often, if more objective evidence is sought, it is frequently done in such a way as to provide more information that is consistent with the existing theory and to ignore any conflicting information.

For instance, some media critics believe television crime programs cause viewers to commit similar crimes. As evidence, they cite the example of the broadcast of a program depicting a distinctive crime, which is then followed by the commission of several similar crimes the next day. However, they ignore the millions of people who watch the same program and do not commit the crime, and those persons who did not watch the program but yet committed the same kind of crime.

This is not necessarily conscious behavior; all of us tend to select certain evidence because it is consistent with our preconceptions, and to ignore other evidence because it is not. This is basic human psychology, but it is also bad science, and we must guard against it.

Unlike the naive scientist, the true scientist is not satisfied by the mere fact that a theory conforms to common sense or personal observation. A true scientist insists on obtaining objective evidence before making judgments about the probable truth or falsehood of the theory. *Objective* means that the evidence can be collected by any other person (the evidence is reproducible), and that it is not biased toward proving the theory either true or false. Furthermore, the true scientist is aware of the human tendency toward the selective use of evidence and will try mightily to guard against preconceptions or biases affecting his or her research. The scientist does this by giving alternative explanations of the phenomenon, many of which may be quite different from one's own theory, an equal chance to be proven true. The true scientist also publishes research procedures, so that unconscious bias can be detected by others. This adds the benefit of enabling other researchers to reproduce the observations.

There are many other procedures to ensure against biased testing of theories, such as using randomly selected subjects, using persons who do not know the purpose of the research study to administer tests, and so on. Some of these will be covered later, but there are three key ideas to be remembered: (1) theories must be tested objectively, rather than just assumed to be true or false; (2) all information must be considered on an equal basis, rather than selected just to support the theory; and (3) testing of theories must be done under conditions which will minimize the possibility of conscious or unconscious subjective biases of the researcher.

Control of Alternative Explanations

This point is very closely related to the development of theories. Recall that the scientist systematically eliminates any concepts that are irrelevant to the phenomenon to be explained, and includes all relevant concepts. This process will, in all likelihood, leave the scientist with a number of possible competing "causes" for any phenomenon ("effect"). If several concepts produce the same effect, how can we distinguish among them?

The answer lies in the *control* of competing causes. In order to measure the effect of any single causal variable on the effect variable, the scientist will have to control for all other potential causal variables. By doing this, the scientist will be able to guard against confusing one causal relationship with another. In other words, the scientist will be able to design a study in such a way that it can be unequivocally stated that this particular variable causes this particular effect, *independent* of all other causal variables.

The naive scientist is neither systematic nor thorough in investigations. Consequently, control over other confounding causal variables is not possible, because other relevant concepts may not have been identified. A particular cause and an effect may appear to be linked together, but we cannot say that this particular cause truly brought about this effect, because we do not know whether other causes may have been operating simultaneously.

The key idea here is that the scientist will control the research situation so that it can be stated with confidence that whatever effect is observed is in fact due to a particular cause, *and not to competing causes*. This statement can be made because other known causes have been eliminated or controlled in some way. The particular methods used for control will be described in detail later in this book.

Nature of Relationships

There are three possible relationships between two concepts. First, the relationship might be *null*. This means that there is no relationship at all—the concepts operate independently of each other. We may observe that children who watch more televised violence are no more nor less aggressive than other children. In other words, there is no relationship between viewing violence and acting aggressively.

A second type of relationship is *covariance*, where the concepts vary together, but one is not the cause and the other the effect. The price of rum and the size of professors' salaries vary together quite consistently (as one goes up, so does the other), but we could not reasonably state that one causes the other. A covariance relationship can be *positive* or *negative*. If we see more of one variable (price of rum) associated with *more* of the other (professors' salaries), the relationship is positive. If more of the first variable (say, consumption of rum) is associated with *less* of an associated variable (accuracy in doing math problems), the relationship is negative.

Finally, the concepts might have a *causal* relationship. In this case the concepts covary (are related) and changes in one concept precede changes in the other concept, and the causal relationship between the two can be justified logically. We can say that changes in the inflation rate cause changes in the price of rum. The inflation rate changes first, and then, by the process of devaluation of currency, the price of rum increases. Causal relationships can be positive or negative, just like covariance relationships.

It is absolutely essential that theories distinguish among these kinds of relationships. If null relationships are confused with covariance or causal relationships, we fail to explain reality correctly with our theory. If covariance relationships are confused with causal relationships, we may make serious errors in applying our theory. For example, if we state that changes in the price of rum cause changes in professors' salaries, we might conclude that the way to improve compensation to academics is by enacting a large tax on rum!

The scientist applies the rules of mathematics and statistics to distinguish between null and non-null relationships. One can subsequently apply the conditions of causality to non-null relationships to distinguish between covariance and causal relationships. The techniques of research design are used to establish covariation and causal relationships. Again, these techniques will be discussed later.

In contrast, the naive scientist is likely to capitalize on the joint occurrence of two phenomena and to assume them to be linked in a cause-and-effect fashion, particularly if this fits his or her preconceptions or beliefs. A naive scientist whose nephew is arrested for drug possession may conclude that his antisocial behavior is caused by his habit of listening to rock music. After all, many drug users also listen to lots of rock, and some lyrics can be interpreted as advocating drug use. A true scientist will apply more stringent tests of evidence and causality before reaching such a conclusion.

Testing Theories with Observable Evidence

Science requires objective evidence before making decisions about the truth or falsehood of a theory. Answering scientific questions demands unbiased observation and testing. This requires that the search for relevant concepts be limited to those concepts which can be translated into variables that are *observable* by any person. The scientist cannot be concerned with unobservable events, or events that are observed in one fashion by one person, and in another way by someone else. This requirement limits the areas for scientific investigation. For example, there can be no real scientific investigation of morality, as this concept cannot be objectively observed. What is perceived as moral behavior for a Shiite Muslim may be quite immoral for a Methodist, and vice versa. Morality is thus a concept which is not objectively observable, and cannot be included in a scientific theory.

Similarly, science will never be able to determine the number of angels that can dance on the head of a pin, as most persons cannot observe angels.

But the naive scientist is often not concerned with such rules of evidence. A naive theory is accepted as true if its truth is obvious to any reasonable person; observable evidence is not required. Likewise, if the naive scientist assumes that everyone observes concepts just as he or she does, then the resulting theory will apply only to people who think similarly.

There are many areas of human concern which are worthy of thought and debate, but which are off-limits to scientific investigation. A naive scientist is less likely to distinguish between these areas and those which may be properly investigated with the scientific method. There are different methods of acquiring knowledge about what is or is not real. Science is only one of them.

Methods of Knowing

As the previous discussion has shown, a distinguishing characteristic of science is the method by which we *know* something to be true. This can be highlighted by contrasting science to other methods of knowing reality. Charles Peirce (in Kerlinger, 1986) classified methods of knowing, or as he called them, methods of "fixing belief" into four categories: the *method of tenacity*, the *method of authority*, the *a priori method* and finally, the *method of science*. These four categories will be presented in a hierarchy, because each level can be seen as having introduced additional safeguards to assure truth.

Probably the least sophisticated method for fixing belief is the *method of tenacity*. This method determines truth, or establishes explanations, by asserting that something is true simply because it is commonly known to be true. Period. This sometimes fanatical adherence to a set of beliefs is exemplified in racial or ethnic stereotypes. In the method of tenacity, the process of formulating beliefs occurs entirely within a given individual and is entirely subject to that person's beliefs, values, and idiosyncrasies. Although it is the most primitive, this method of forming beliefs about what is true and what is false is very commonly used. Remarkably, people often sustain belief even in the face of contrary evidence. For instance, a person who tenaciously holds to the view that the portrayal of sexual themes in motion pictures causes sex crimes would probably never be convinced by any number of research studies which indicate no evidence for such a relationship.

The second method is the *method of authority*. In this method, truth is established when someone or something for which I have high regard states the truth. I may accept my physician's diagnosis of my illness as truth because my physician has been correct in the past, or because I have been taught that physicians are expert in what they do. Or I may regard a religious text or a political tract as the distillation of truth, because they are sources of authoritative statements.

This method has an advantage over the method of tenacity because it often relies on the testimony of experts. If the source is indeed expert, adopting the expert's advice may be beneficial. In the case of medical problems, for instance, it would be better if a patient followed a doctor's expert advice rather than clinging to the personal belief that a medical condition was the consequence of the wrath of a vengeful god and not subject to cure.

The method of authority is quite widespread and has both its uses and abuses. The number of people who make a living as consultants, or purveyors of expertise, testifies to its popularity. The method is also used in advertising, as products are ringingly endorsed by people who "ought to know," such as a champion tennis player endorsing a racquet. But this method is dangerous when the purported expert is really not knowledgeable (such as a medical "quack"), or when persons with expertise in one area give advice in an unrelated area (a movie star endorses a political candidate).

The third method of knowing is variously known as the *a priori method* or the *method of reasonable men*. This method rests on the idea that the propositions submitted are self-evident, that is, they agree with reason. The criterion for fixing belief thus lies in the reasonableness of the argument, which is to be furthered by the unfettered exchange of information among people. The idea of a "marketplace of ideas" applies here, as the truth would ostensibly emerge after each proposition was examined for its logical consistency and reasonableness. There are again some advantages over the previously discussed method of authority. Whatever emerges as truth will at least have been able to withstand scrutiny by a number of people who evaluate its logical consistency, quality of reasoning, and so on. In this respect, whatever is held to be true will be the product of a social process involving many authorities, rather than the statement of a single authority.

The problem with this method lies in the definition of *reasonable*, or, more properly, who gets to define what is reasonable. The same facts presented to a number of reasonable people could lead to vastly different conclusions. For example, a set of regulations on communication technology may be evaluated by one government official as a prescription for economic development, while being dismissed by another official as stifling the free flow of information. Furthermore, the test for truth is that statements *agree with reason*, but *not necessarily that they agree with observable fact* or experience. By starting with a faulty premise, one can deduce a whole array of logical, but incorrect, conclusions.

The final method for fixing belief is the *method of science*. This method constitutes a critical shift in perspective. The previous three methods are focussed inward: With the method of tenacity, what we believe is determined by what we have believed all along and it may be completely idiosyncratic; with the method of authority, what we believe is determined by our evaluation of the credibility of the source of the knowledge; with the a priori method, truth is determined by whatever criteria we personally wish to establish for reasonableness. *Science shifts the locus of truth from single individuals to groups, by establishing a set of mutually agreed upon rules for establishing truth.* This establishes, in Peirce's words, an "external permanency" which transcends the belief systems of any single individual.

Scientific truth still demands logical consistency, like the a priori method. But the logical deductions must also be tested against an external reality that can be perceived by any person, and is not just the property of a single individual or group.

Contrasting the Methods of Knowing

It is interesting to consider the relationship between beliefs that are accepted as truth by each of the above three methods and TRUTH, the objective reality that exists "out there."

Of course, it can be argued that there is no such thing as objective reality. But if one accepts such an argument, one cannot use the method of science, which requires at least some common experience of reality that can be shared among individuals.

The method of tenacity is a complete roll of the dice. Tenaciously held beliefs may well agree with objective reality or may be far removed from it, but there is no way of knowing which is the case. The method of authority eliminates some of the more outrageous propositions that otherwise might arise. However, there is no guarantee that what is considered an outrageous proposition today might not in fact prove to be true tomorrow. The a priori method might eliminate idiosyncratic beliefs held by a single individual by submitting them to the scrutiny of the marketplace of ideas. Beliefs subjected to this method may be logically consistent, reasonable, and popular, but may still be incorrect.

Science states that there is an objective reality and that our ideas about it (our theories) do not alter that reality. The next step then is plainly obvious: In order to establish our theories as true, we must see how closely our vision of the way the world works corresponds to the way the world *actually* works. Unlike any of the other methods of knowing, science demands that we support our internal beliefs with external evidence.

Herein lies the strong suit of science. By imposing on the scientist the requirement that theories be tested against some observable reality, science has one attribute that the other ways of knowing do not: It is self-correcting. We may take a tenaciously held belief, elevate it by finding an authority who will vouch for it, and further justify it to reasonable people by showing its logic. But if the theory will not predict commonly observed reality, we must reject it and replace it with a corrected theory.

Because science requires we determine the extent to which our theories about the real world agree with how the real world actually operates, we need a method for testing the theoretical predictions against the observed reality. The supreme requirement imposed by this method is that all persons subscribing to it will agree about the truth or falsity of a theory when they are presented with the same information.

Scientific Method

The remainder of this chapter will outline the basic requirements of the scientific method. We need to meet these requirements to achieve the advantages that make science superior to other methods of fixing belief. These requirements provide the rigor that differentiates true science from naive science. These rules will be briefly introduced here, and they will be extensively discussed in the chapters to come.

Use and Selection of Concepts

We begin by conceptualizing the cause-and-effect phenomena, that is, by developing a verbal description or name for the events. By using the scientific method, we seek to explain phenomena by linking a concept called a cause to another concept called an effect. Whereas naive science may select as the cause a concept that has some innate appeal, science will consider as causes only those concepts that can be reasonably argued to be related to the effect. Scientists arrive at causally related concepts through a thorough review of previous research, by using logical deduction, and by insight and personal observation.

Linking Concepts by Propositions

If we are interested in explaining a phenomenon, we need to specify the functional mechanism whereby a cause brings about an effect: We need to state why changes in some variable A should lead to changes in some variable B. Such a functional statement distinguishes between causal relationships (which have such an explanation) on the one hand and mere covariance relationships (which do not) on the other.

Testing Theories with Observable Evidence

This means that any theory will not be regarded as probably true until we have had a chance to test it against some observable reality. It means we will withhold judgment about the truth or falsehood of a theory until we can determine the extent to which predictions derived from or consistent with our theory mirror observed reality.

Definition of Concepts

Testing theory with some observable evidence generates another requirement of science. Observing the real world brings with it the need to bridge the gap between theory, which is stated at a high level of abstraction, and observation, which takes place at a very concrete level. Bridging this gap is accomplished through a process of defining both the meanings of concepts and the indicators or measures that will be used to capture those meanings. We need to make very clear what the concept means and what it looks like, in concrete terms, when we observe it in the real world.

Publication of Definitions and Procedures

Because the scientific method is public, all other researchers need to have the ability to carry out the same procedures in order to arrive at the same conclusions. This requires that we be as explicit and objective as possible in stating and publicizing definitions and procedures. There should be no mystery in scientific procedures. This allows research studies to be replicated by independent scientists. It also facilitates the resolution of inconsistencies in research findings which involve the same phenomenon.

Control of Alternative Explanations

Scientific studies have to be designed in such a way that we can rule out alternative causes. When a relationship between two variables is studied, we must be able to isolate the effect of the single causal variable from the effects of all other possible causes. Isolating a true causal variable means that these other *confounding variables* have to be identified and their effects eliminated or controlled.

Unbiased Selection of Evidence

The decision to accept a theory as probably true or probably false will be based on the observation of limited evidence. For example, there are many studies of the concept of communication apprehension (fear when confronted with speaking in public, for example) that use observations of the behavior of a few hundred college students. Since the researcher will wish to generalize beyond this limited sample, science requires that the evidence be selected in such a way as to eliminate biases and thereby be representative of the greater population. In the case of the communication apprehension studies, if the students have been selected in an unbiased way, then the results may be extended to all college students, not just those few hundred who participated in the studies.

Reconciliation of Theory and Observation

The degree of agreement between what theory predicts we *should* observe and what we actually *do* observe is the basis of the self-correcting nature of the scientific approach. Any disagreement will have to result in careful scrutiny of the method used or in the revision of the original theory. This will lead to the generation of new predictions which will again be subjected to a new observational test. This process furthers theory by providing refinements to existing theories, or by substituting a new theory which better explains observed reality than did the old theory.

Limitations of the Scientific Method

The scientific method cannot be used to study all questions. We cannot employ the scientific method when objective observation is not possible. In this case, we must use other methods of fixing belief. For example, if we want to determine whether a social policy is good or bad, we may well want to yield to an authority such as the Bible or the Koran, because objective measurement of good and bad is not possible.

Basic beliefs or assumptions are not testable propositions, as they can never be disproved, and thus they cannot be investigated scientifically. The statement that "We take these truths to be self evident ... that all men are created equal...." is a wonderful statement of personal truth, but it lies outside the realm of scientific investigation.

The limits of science are clear; the limits of belief are not.

Summary

In this chapter we have distinguished between naive inquiry and the scientific method. Naive scientists are all people who try to understand the world around them by observing phenomena and making logical deductions about causes and effects. True scientists have further requirements.

Both true and naive scientists create *theories*, which are verbal representations of the reality of some *phenomenon*. These theories involve *concepts or constructs* which are verbal descriptions of the object or elements of the theory; *variables* which quantify the amount or state of the concept which is present in some instance; and *relationships* which link the concepts and variables together.

The true scientist must adhere to a more stringent set of rules in testing a theory than does the naive scientist. The true scientist's theory must include all the concepts that might be involved in a phenomenon and must exclude irrelevant concepts; the naive scientist often selects a set of concepts that are simpler and personally attractive. The true scientist must define concepts so that others can agree upon their meaning and can measure them objectively; the naive scientist defines concepts in a way which may make sense only to himself. The true scientist must make unbiased measurements and consider all evidence, whether it favors the theory of the scientist or not; the naive scientist often makes inadequate or incomplete measurements, and selects only supporting evidence.

The reward for adhering to the more stringent set of rules which the scientific method requires is a reduced chance of drawing the wrong conclusions. Since a scientific theory is based on objectively observable evidence, and it can be shared and tested by a group of persons, scientific theory is self-correcting. Incorrect or inadequate theory can be detected by other scientists, and so it can be rejected.

The basic requirements of science will be discussed in great detail in the following four chapters. In these chapters we will present specific strategies for responding to the requirements of the scientific method.

References and Additional Readings

Agnew, N. & Pike, S. W. (1969). *The science game: An introduction to research in the behavioral sciences.* Englewood Cliffs, NJ: Prentice-Hall.

Babbie, E. R. (1992). *The practice of social research* (6th ed.). Belmont, CA: Wadsworth (Chapter 1, "Human Inquiry and Science").

Chaffee, S. H. & Berger, C. R. (1987). What communication scientists do. In S. H. Chaffee & C. R. Berger (Eds.) *Handbook of communication science* (pp. 99–122). Newbury Park, CA: Sage.

Kerlinger, F. N. (1986). *Foundations of behavioral research* (3rd ed.) New York: Holt, Rinehart and Winston (Chapter 1, "Science and the Scientific Approach").

Krathwohl, D. R. (1985). *Social and behavioral science research.* San Francisco: Jossey-Bass (Chapter 1, "What Is Social and Behavioral Science Knowledge?").

Kuhn, T. S. (1970). *The structure of scientific revolutions* (2nd ed.). Chicago: University of Chicago Press.

Medawar, P. B. (1979). *Advice to a young scientist.* New York: Harper and Row.

Chapter *2*

Elements of Scientific Theories: Concepts and Definitions

In this chapter we will discuss the basic building blocks of a scientific theory: the concepts which represent the "real world" phenomena being explained by the theory. The scientific method requires that the nature of these concepts be unambiguously communicated to others. This requirement mandates the creation of *theoretical definitions*. A theoretical definition explains what is meant by the concept.

Concepts must also be capable of being objectively observed. This requires that we create *operational definitions*, which translate the verbal concepts into corresponding variables that can be measured. We will elaborate on each of these topics in this chapter. In the next chapter, we'll see how the defined concepts and their associated variables are related to each other to form complete theories.

Concepts and Constructs

The basic building blocks of theories are concepts. A *concept* is a verbal abstraction drawn from observation of a number of specific cases. The critical term here is "observed," because it means that there is a direct link between the concept (the abstraction) and its referents (the reality). For instance, we can observe a number of particular instances where individuals receive varying amounts of money for the work they have done over a given period of time. From these particulars we distill an abstraction and label it "income." Similarly, we observe individuals and find some of them short, some tall, and more of them in between; from these observations we generate the concept "height."

A construct serves the same function as a concept, but it is more abstract. It is not characterized by a direct link between the abstraction and its observed manifestations. For instance, "source credibility" is a construct that has been used in studying persuasion.

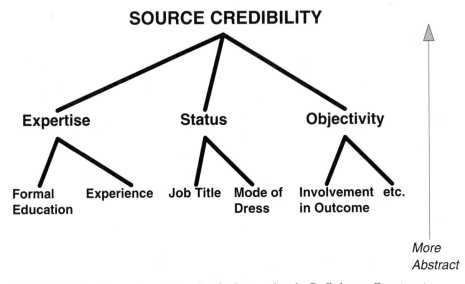

FIGURE 2-1   **Hierarchy of Levels of Abstraction in Defining a Construct**

This term can be used in the same way as a concept, but we should recognize that we cannot directly observe different levels of source credibility in individuals. However, we can observe the various parts which make up the construct individually, and then combine them to get some overall summary. Constructs are built from the logical combination of a number of more observable concepts. In the case of source credibility, we could define the construct as the combination of the concepts of expertise, objectivity, and status. Each of these concepts can be more directly observed in an individual. Of course, we might also consider some of these terms to be constructs themselves, and break them down into combinations of still more concrete concepts, as illustrated in Figure 2-1. What results is a set of constructs at decreasing *levels of abstraction*. Only at the bottom of this hierarchy are directly observable concepts.

From a practical point of view, it matters little whether we call the verbal building blocks concepts or constructs. It is more useful to consider every concept to be at some particular level of abstraction. This level is determined by the distance of the concept from the directly observable ideas at the bottom of the hierarchy. To simplify discussion, in the future we will use the term *concepts* to refer to either concepts or constructs, recognizing that any concept can really be a very abstract idea built from the combination of many less abstract (more concrete) concepts.

Definitions

A scientific concept really consists of three parts: a label, a theoretical definition, and an operational definition. We'll examine each of these elements separately.

Concept Labels

One of the requirements of a theory is that it be in a form which can be communicated to any interested person in an unambiguous fashion, so that it may be tested and evaluated by others. A great advantage of using concept labels is that they facilitate communication. It is vastly more convenient and efficient to refer to people's "income" than to refer to "the amount of money people receive in return for having made their labor or their knowledge available to another." It is also very easy, at this level of abstraction, to link one concept to another. If we are asked what interests us most in the field of communication, we might answer that our research focuses on the effect of "environmental change" on "task-oriented communication" in organizations.

But a label, particularly for abstract concepts like "task-oriented communication," is usually not sufficient to communicate the full meaning of the concept unambiguously. We need additional explanation.

Theoretical Definitions

The theoretical definition specifies the verbal *meaning* that is attached to the concept label. We need this explanation because the scientific method requires that others understand our theory and be able to criticize and reproduce our observations. If we fail to specify the meaning represented by a particular concept label, we leave room for misunderstanding. As we'll see below, the more abstract the concept that we're using, the worse this problem becomes.

To illustrate this, suppose that you ask a group of people to write down on an index card their explanation of the concept of a person's "age." You'll probably find that most of the definitions mention things like "how long someone has been alive," "the amount of time which has passed since birth," and other similar statements. The amount of overlap among these definitions probably will be very high, indicating high shared meaning.

Now suppose you repeat this procedure, but this time you ask people to define the term "media use." You'll probably get very different results. You might find, for instance, that half of the definitions have a central theme of time (for instance, "the amount of time people spend with media") and that the other half might focus on purpose (for instance, "whether people use media for entertainment, information, escape, and so on"). The amount of overlap among these definitions is much lower than the overlap for age.

Figure 2-2 illustrates the relationship between abstraction and meaning overlap. Age is a more concrete concept, so the concept label itself communicates the meaning of the concept almost as well as the definitions. Thus there is high overlap. Media use is more abstract, and can be constructed in many different ways from the combination of a large number of more concrete ideas. This produces many differences in the kinds of definitions which different individuals spontaneously produce.

We call self-defining concepts like age *primitive terms*. Primitive terms are adequately defined by their attached concept labels. These are the labels which appear at the bottom of the level of abstraction hierarchy. Probably only a small number of concepts that we are likely to use in communication research have such a high degree of shared meaning that they are primitive terms. And even then, the high degree of shared meaning might

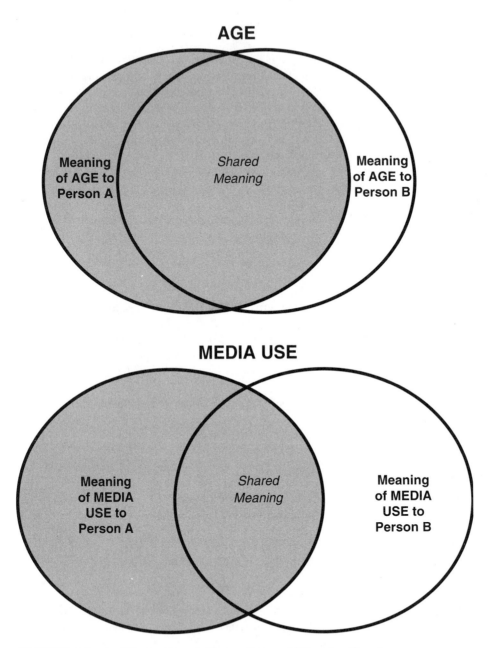

FIGURE 2-2   An Illustration of Abstraction and Meaning Overlap

only exist within a particular group, but may not be shared with other groups. "Communication apprehension" might be well-understood by communication researchers, but poorly understood by psychologists. Consequently, we always risk being on thin ice if we use primitive terms and assume that shared meanings exist.

The conservative approach (and therefore the recommended one) is to explicitly specify the meaning associated with each concept, regardless of the extent to which we think the meaning is shared. We do this because the rules of science demand that we use concepts understood by the whole community of researchers. We must have high meaning overlap, particularly for abstract concepts that are not self-defining. To achieve this, we must construct a theoretical definition for each concept in our theory.

The procedures for creating theoretical definitions are summarized in Exhibit 2-1, along with an example of the process. We've deliberately chosen an abstract concept that is not commonly used in communication research to illustrate the value of theoretical definitions.

Operational Definitions

We now have a concept label whose meaning is explained by a theoretical definition. But the rules of science demand that this concept be capable of being *unambiguously and objectively* observed by anyone. This means that we must create another type of definition, called an operational definition. An operational definition translates the verbal meaning provided by the theoretical definition into a prescription for *measurement.* Although they may be expressed verbally, operational definitions are fundamentally statements that describe measurement and mathematical operations.

An operational definition adds three things to the theoretical definition.

1. An operational definition describes the *unit of measurement.* (We'll discuss measurement in much more detail in Chapter 7.) Examples of units of measurement are minutes (to measure time), word counts (to measure newspaper coverage of a particular event), percentage of correct responses, etc.

2. An operational definition specifies the *level of measurement.* (Again, we'll cover this in much more detail in Chapter 7.) Levels of measurement can range from the simple nominal variables which only make distinctions between categories like "present or absent" or "yes or no" ; to ordinal variables which contain some information about the quantity ("more or less") of the concept present, but have no real measurement scales; to continuous variables which have real scale points which are equally spaced, and which can take on any value.

3. In the case of anything other than a primitive term, an operational definition provides a mathematical or logical statement that clearly states how measurements are to be made and combined to create a single value for the abstract concept. For example, when an operational definition is made of the concept in Figure 2-1, the operational definition will describe how "formal education" and "experience" are to be measured, and define the mathematical operations necessary to combine these measurements into a value for "expertise." Further operational definitions will describe how to mathematically combine the values for "expertise," "status," and "objectivity" to produce a value for "source credibility."

EXHIBIT 2-1   Procedure for Creating a Theoretical Definition

1. Select a summary label.

   media use efficiency

2. List the labels of all the more concrete concepts that are encompassed by the label.

   time spent with media
   money spent on media

3. Combine these labels into a verbal statement that defines the summary label.

   Media use efficiency is defined by the ratio of the time spent with media to the money spent on media.

4. Look at each label on the right-hand side of the definition (these are the labels developed in step 2). Unless the label is self-defining, make another list of more concrete concept labels which are encompassed by the label.

   time spent with media
    time spent using radio
    time spent using television
    time spent using newspapers
    time spent using magazines
    time spent using motion
     pictures
    time spent using video
     cassettes
   money spent on media
    per capita spending for
     advertising
    subscription costs
    rental costs
    money spent on radio
    money spent on television
    money spent on newspapers
    money spent on magazines
    money spent on motion
     pictures
    money spent on video
     cassettes

5. Combine these more concrete labels into definitions of the more abstract labels.

   Time spent with the media is defined by the sum of time spent with radio, television, newspapers, magazines, motion pictures, and video cassettes. Money spent with the media is defined by the sum of money spent on advertising in media (per capita), subscriptions, purchases, and rentals of media.

6. Continue this process of breaking down more abstract definitions into a series of concrete definitions, until all terms in the final definition are concrete, self-defining concepts which can be observed directly.

   The defining terms for "time spent with media" (time spent with radio, television, and so on) are primitive terms. No additional definition is needed.
   money spent on advertising (per capita)
    money spent on radio
     advertising
    money spent on television
     advertising
    money spent on newspaper
     advertising
    money spent on magazine
     advertising
   money spent on subscriptions
    money spent on magazine
     subscriptions
    money spent on newspaper
     subscriptions
    money spent on cable system
     subscriptions
    money spent on rentals
     money spent on rentals of
      videocassettes

EXHIBIT 2-1 *Continued*

Money spent on advertising is defined by the sum of per capita expenditures for radio, television, newspaper, and magazine advertising.

Money spent on subscriptions is defined by the sum of the money spent for magazine, newspaper, and cable system subscriptions.

Money spent on rentals is defined as the money spent on rentals of video cassettes.

No further breakdowns are necessary. All defining terms in these definitions are primitive terms.

The combined set of verbal definitions make up the formal theoretical definition for media efficiency. Note how much more clear and unambiguous the meaning of the concept has become.

The operational definition must be very closely associated with the theoretical definition. It must state clearly *how* observations will be made so they will reflect as fully as possible the meaning associated with the verbal concept or construct. The operational definition must tell us how to observe and quantify the concept in the real world. This connection between theoretical and operational definitions is quite critical. This connection establishes the *validity* of the measurement. The amount of validity in measurement is proportional to the extent to which we *actually* measure what we *intend* to measure, that is, the degree to which the operational definition and the theoretical definition correspond.

Table 2-1 shows some examples of the operational definitions of concepts which we have already used in earlier examples.

Units of Measurement

All the operational definitions in Table 2-1 set up some units of measurement. For "age," this is years. Without an operational definition to establish this unit, we could just as well think of age in months, days, or position in the life cycle (e.g., teenager, young married, senior citizen). For "Media Use Efficiency," the unit is hours per dollar, as the variable is defined as a ratio of time in hours to money in dollars. For "Satisfaction with Marital Communication," the unit is some relative degree of satisfaction.

Level of Measurement

The level of measurement specified in the operational definition will affect our observations. For example, both age and media use efficiency definitions set up scales which can take on any value (continuous interval scales), and thus allow the respondent to reply freely. But the satisfaction with marital communication definitions prescribe different levels of measurement. The first definition sets up a nominal scale. A respondent is really

TABLE 2-1 Examples of Operational Definitions

A Primitive Term

Theoretical Label: AGE
Operational Definition:
    AGE is operationally defined as the number of years since birth.

A More Abstract Concept

Theoretical Label: MEDIA USE EFFICIENCY
Operational Definition:
    MEDIA USE EFFICIENCY is operationally defined by the sum of the number of
    hours per week spent using radio, television, newspapers, magazines, motion pictures,
    and video cassettes divided by the dollar sum of national annual per capita
    expenditures for radio advertising, television advertising, newspaper advertising,
    magazine advertising and the respondent's yearly spending for magazine
    subscriptions, newspaper subscriptions, cable system subscriptions, and rentals of
    video cassettes.

An Example of Alternate Levels of Measurement

Theoretical Label: SATISFACTION WITH MARITAL COMMUNICATION
    Operational Definition 1 (nominal level measurement):
    Response to the question:
        "Generally speaking, do you feel that your communication with your spouse is
        satisfactory?"
            a. YES
            b. NO
    Operational Definition 2 (ordinal level measurement):
    Response to the question:
        "Generally speaking, do you feel that your communication with your spouse is"
            a. VERY SATISFACTORY
            b. SOMEWHAT SATISFACTORY
            c. NEITHER SATISFACTORY NOR UNSATISFACTORY
            d. SOMEWHAT UNSATISFACTORY
            e. VERY UNSATISFACTORY

answering a simple yes-no question: Are you satisfied? Put another way, satisfaction is measured as being either present or absent, with no amount or degree of satisfaction attached. The second definition sets up an ordinal scale: Respondents can be satisfied to either a greater or lesser degree.

The responses to these alternate definitions are not likely to be the same. The first question requires all respondents to take a stand as being either satisfied or unsatisfied, including those whose feelings are perilously close to neutrality. If a respondent is at least a little satisfied with his or her communication, he or she would probably check the first response. The second question allows for the expression of ambiguity. The consequence of adding additional categories that allow the respondent to report some *degree* of presence of the concept will be a more sensitive and accurate picture of the person's actual satisfaction, as those who are only minimally satisfied or unsatisfied can opt for the middle categories. The point to be recognized here is that the operational definition will critically affect the sensitivity of our observations. They must be constructed very carefully. We'll spend more time discussing this in Chapter 7.

Statements of Combination

For abstract constructs like media use efficiency, the operational definition must also specify the mathematical procedure used to combine the measured elements of the concept into one value. Note that this definition describes two addition operations (one for time using media and one for the cost of media) and one division operation. As an alternative to the verbal operational definition in Table 2-1, we could also express this operational definition with a mathematical formula.

This statement of the method of combination of concrete measurements is critical to our objective of clearly communicating our research procedures. Without it, other researchers cannot understand our measurements well enough to judge their value, nor can they reproduce our research.

Variables

Once the measurement system has been specified by the operational definition, different values of the concept can be observed. The concept can now be referred to as a *variable,* since it can respond to differences in the real world by taking on varying values, as specified in the operational definition. For example, some people are older than others. Likewise, some people undoubtedly show higher efficiency than others in terms of the ratio of time spent with the media, relative to their cost. We use variables to empirically test theories, as we'll discuss in Chapter 4.

Definitions and Validity

Throughout the discussion of concepts and definitions, we have really been talking about three different worlds: the real world, where events and phenomena actually occur; the verbal world, where these phenomena are distilled into concepts which are expressed verbally in theoretical definitions; and the measurement world where the concepts are observed as variables which are described by operational definitions. The theoretical definition mediates between the real world and the verbal world, and the operational definition mediates between the verbal world and the measurement world (see Figure 2-3).

The translations provided by definitions are imperfect. It's impossible to perfectly summarize the wild variety of the real world in a theoretical definition, or the rich meaning of a theoretical definition in the mathematical expression of an operational definition. But, like any creative endeavor, we may do a better or worse job in constructing these

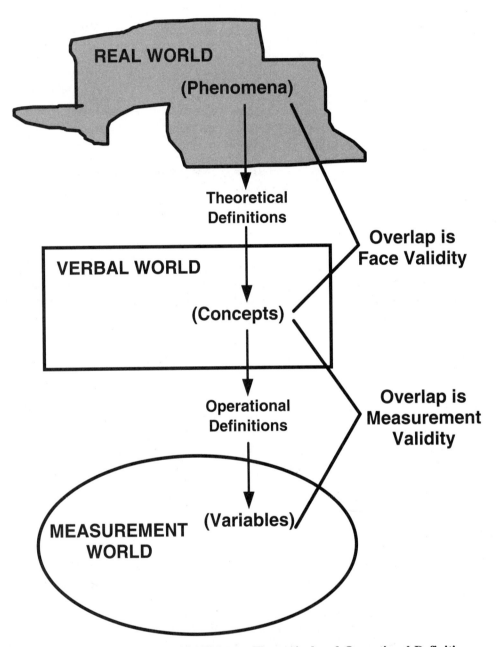

FIGURE 2-3   The Relationship Between Theoretical and Operational Definitions and Face and Measurement Validity

translations. The degree to which we match one world to another determines the validity of our definitions.

The match of the real world with the theoretical definition is called *face validity*. If the theoretical definition of a concept does not match observed reality, then we have poor face validity, and any theory using this concept will be flawed. Likewise, if the operational definition does not specify measurement which adequately represents the meaning contained in the theoretical definition, we have poor *measurement validity*.

As an example, let's suppose we ask a group of people to write down their own ideas of what "television viewing" means. To do this, they will recall their observations of the real world, and distill them into fragmentary concepts, which they will write down on index cards. If we put all these cards together, we have a verbal approximation of the real world phenomenon of television viewing. Looking at the cards, we see that two major themes are represented: time spent viewing television and the type of content viewed.

Now let's look at one of the cards. It says "television viewing is the amount of time you spend looking at television." If we take this as a theoretical definition of the concept of television viewing, it has poor face validity. It captures in words only half of the real world phenomenon, which includes the kind of content viewed, as well as the time spent viewing.

To improve the face validity of this definition, we might narrow the focus of our interest from "television viewing" to "amount of television viewing." Now the theoretical definition has good face validity. It captures most of the essence of the (more specific) real world phenomenon.

Alternatively, we could enlarge the theoretical definition of "television viewing" to read "television viewing is the amount of time spent viewing each type of content." With further development, this theoretical definition could also have good face validity, as it represents both major themes observed in the real world.

Let's extend this imaginary experiment. We now ask the people to provide some items for a questionnaire which will measure their idea of "television viewing." Since we had both time and content themes in the theoretical definitions, we will get similar results in the measurement items. A representative list of items is presented below in Table 2-2.

All of these items are good operational measurements of "television viewing," but they measure very different things. If we do not have a theoretical definition of the concept to guide us, then we have not given ourselves any criterion for distinguishing valid measurement items, that is, those which provide the best coverage of the meaning of the concept.

The measurement validity of a variable comes from the crucial overlap between its theoretical and operational definitions, so we need a theoretical definition before we can make any decisions about measurement validity. Suppose we use the less general theoretical definition which we developed above: "amount of television viewing is the amount of time spent looking at television." Then items *b* and *d* from the list simply will not be considered. They have no measurement validity, as they measure the content of viewing, not the amount of viewing. Items *a*, *c*, and *e* are valid items, as they represent measurement of the verbal meaning of the theoretical definition. Item *f* is partially valid, as it represents measurement of the amount of viewing, but only of a specific type of

---

TABLE 2-2   Alternative Operational Definitions for Television Viewing.

---

a. "Approximately how many hours a day do you spend watching television?"

_____ Hours

b. "Please indicate below why you watch television. Choose only one."

_____ entertainment exclusively

_____ entertainment mostly; some information

_____ equally entertainment and information

_____ information mostly; some entertainment

_____ information exclusively

c. "On a scale from 0 to 10, where 0 means never watching TV and where 10 means watching TV all the time, how would you rate the your television viewing?"

Response: _____

d. "Of the program types listed below, mark the ONE program category that you like to watch the most."

_____ news programs_____ sports _____ movies
_____ public affairs _____ sitcoms_____ dramatic series
_____ musical/variety   _____ other

e. "Which of the following two labels would you apply to yourself?"

_____ Heavy TV Viewer   _____ Light TV Viewer

f. "Of all the time you spend watching TV, about what percentage is devoted to watching news and public information programs?"

_____

---

content. That is, it is not exhaustive of the full meaning contained in the theoretical definition.

But if we choose the more general definition of viewing ("television viewing is the amount of time spent viewing each type of content"), then items *a* and *c* alone represent only partially valid measurement. They measure amount of viewing, but not type of viewing. We need a set of items which measures both amount of viewing and the content viewed. We can get this by combining responses to questions about *amount* with those that address *type* of viewing (by combining items *a* and *d*, for example), or by creating items which ask about amount of viewing of each type, like item *f*.

Making a decision about a theoretical definition imposes a constraint upon the operational measures. We are steered toward certain operational measures and away from others. The constraints operating in this example are represented in Figure 2-4. This figure illustrates the fact that certain operational definitions go with a particular theoretical definition, or one part of the definition, because they yield the concrete measurement of the meaning that has been specified in the theoretical definition.

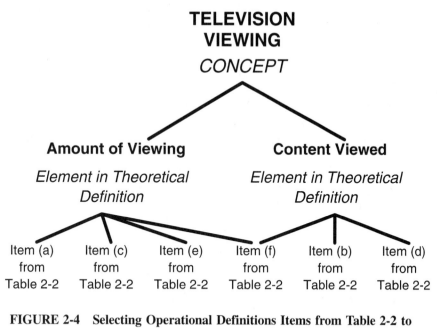

FIGURE 2-4   **Selecting Operational Definitions Items from Table 2-2 to Match Theoretical Definitions**

Benefits of Using Definitions

The rules of science require that we have theoretical and operational definitions for all concepts, so that anyone can examine our concepts, and reproduce our measurements. We can't conduct a scientific investigation without definitions. But you may read research reports which do not explicitly state the theoretical or operational definitions. Does this mean that the authors of these studies are unscientific? Or that the definitions are not really necessary? No and No. If you read carefully, you can usually figure out what the author really intended. But it's a much better practice to save the reader of a research report such hard work by providing both theoretical and operational definitions as part of the report of your research.

Here are some of the benefits of spending time developing good theoretical and operational definitions, and stating them explicitly.

Following the Rules

The rules of science require that we make all our ideas available to others, so that they may critically examine them. Furthermore, anyone who wants to repeat our investigations should be able to do so. A good theoretical definition makes the meaning of our concepts clear. A good operational definition allows the reader to understand how we have gone about measurement. It also allows others to repeat our measurements, to make sure that our conclusions are correct.

Better Validity

Thinking methodically about the varieties of real world phenomena which should be encompassed by our concept label will often suggest improvements to the theoretical definition. This will improve face validity. Likewise, stating the meaning of the concept verbally is extremely helpful in the specification of the operational definitions, especially the specific measurement indicators that we will use to reflect the meaning associated with the concept. This improves measurement validity.

The process of creating theoretical and operational definitions is interactive. For example, the act of creating an operational definition may suggest improvements to the theoretical definition, or vice versa. Any changes in the theoretical definition imply corresponding changes in the operational definition, and vice versa.

Improving Conceptualization and Measurement

A good theoretical definition will aid us in selecting valid operational measurement items, as we mentioned above. But we can use the definitions of other researchers to improve our own measurement and conceptual scheme, too. Generally you will not be the first or only researcher to be interested in a given phenomenon. One of the first courses of action to take when you become interested in a particular problem is to see what other researchers have done previously by conducting a thorough review of research literature.

Let's use the television viewing example one last time. Suppose that you originally think of television viewing exclusively in terms of the amount of exposure to television. However, as you review the literature, you are likely to encounter a large number of theoretical and operational definitions of television viewing which include the idea of the content or type of programming viewed. The fact that other people are defining and measuring the concept in a way different from the way you are thinking about it may convince you to expand your definitions of television viewing, and to include new measurement items to tap the more general definition.

Connecting Our Research to the Work of Others

The fourth reason for including definitions is that it allows us to account for conflicting findings in different studies focusing on the same phenomenon. As an example, consider a research project you carry out on the relationship between level of education and media use. Again, media use is defined as the purpose for which people use the media. In your research project you might find that education has an effect; specifically, people who have higher levels of education are observed to use the media more for information purposes and less for entertainment. The reverse holds, you find, for people with relatively lower levels of education; they use the media more for entertainment, less for information.

Later you come across another study that looked at the same phenomenon. The results from this study indicate that there is no relationship between education and media use. There is a conflict between these findings and the results of your study. Who is right?

This conflict might be resolved, if you find that media use in the other study had been defined as the amount of time people spend with the media, rather than the type of media that they use. In this case, there is no contradiction between the two sets of results. Although both you and the other researcher have used the label media use, it really represents somewhat different concepts.

The important fact to notice here is that, in the absence of definitions for the concepts, no explanation could have been made for the different results found in the two studies. The apparent contradiction could not be resolved.

Summary

Definitions link the real world in which phenomena actually occur with the verbal world in which we simplify and describe the phenomena and with the measurement world in which we make systematic observations.

A *theoretical definition* clearly states the meaning of the concept. This allows others to understand the researcher's vision of the concept, and to criticize it, if they disagree. The degree to which the verbal world theoretical definition captures the essence of the real world phenomenon which it describes is called *face validity*.

Operational definitions define the way in which the phenomenon is to be observed within the measurement world. They describe the units in which the measurement is to be made (like minutes, amount of satisfaction, etc.) and the level of measurement to be used (response in unordered categories (nominal); ordered categories (ordinal); or equally spaced categories or scales (interval). Operational definitions convert verbal concepts into measurable variables. The degree to which the operational definition reflects the meaning of the theoretical definition is called *measurement validity*.

Good theoretical and operational definitions allow researchers to communicate their concepts to others, so that they may be critically evaluated. The process of creating definitions improves both the face and measurement validity, as it forces the researcher to think critically about his concepts and measurements. Published definitions are a source of ideas about how communication phenomena may be described and measured. They also aid in resolving seemingly contradictory research results which occur when researchers attach similar labels to different concepts.

References and Additional Readings

Carmines, E. G. & Zeller, R. A. (1979). *Reliability and validity assessment* (Sage university papers series on quantitative applications in the social sciences, 07–017). Beverly Hills, CA: Sage.

Hage, J. (1972). *Techniques and problems of theory construction in sociology.* New York: Wiley (Chapter 1, "Theoretical Concepts"; Chapter 3, "Specifying the Definitions").

Kerlinger, F. N. (1986). *Foundations of behavioral research* (3rd ed.) New York: Holt, Rinehart and Winston (Chapter 3, "Constructs, Variables, and Definitions").

Zeller, R. A. & Carmines, E. C. (1980). *Measurement in the social sciences: The link between theory and data.* London: Cambridge University Press (Chapter 1, "Introduction to Measurement"; Chapter 3, "Reliability"; Chapter 4, "Validity").

$Chapter$ *3*

Elements of Scientific Theories:
Relationships

In the previous chapter, we covered the process of selecting and defining concepts. In this chapter, we will take the next step in creating a scientific theory: linking these concepts together in ways that predict and explain the operation of the "real world."

We'll begin by discussing the kinds of relationships that can be present between concepts. At the same time we'll introduce some graphical conventions that will help us to describe the relationships. These conventions have become fairly standard in social and behavioral research.

Types of Relationships

The smallest theory possible is made up of one relationship between two concepts. For instance, we state that a concept such as "income" is related to another concept, such as "newspaper readership." But there are three different ways that these two concepts can be related, and we need first to decide what the nature of the relationship is.

Null Relationships

One way the concepts might be related is to say that they have no relationship at all. This is not a contradiction in terms: The absence of a relationship is just as important to a theory as the presence of one. We call a statement of the absence of a relationship a null relationship. If we say that two concepts have a null relationship, we've stated that they operate completely independently, and that neither affects the other in any way. If we believe that newspaper readership and income operate in the real world as completely independent concepts, we can diagram the situation as shown in Figure 3-1(a).

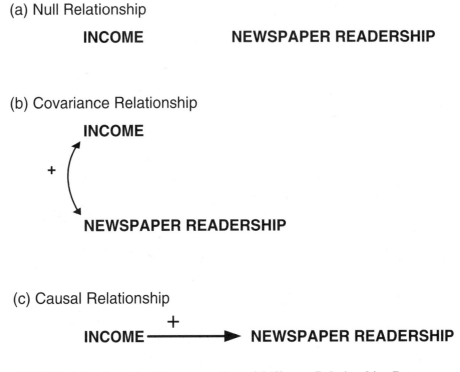

(a) Null Relationship

INCOME   **NEWSPAPER READERSHIP**

(b) Covariance Relationship

INCOME

+

NEWSPAPER READERSHIP

(c) Causal Relationship

+

INCOME ———→ NEWSPAPER READERSHIP

**FIGURE 3-1   Graphical Representation of Different Relationships Between
Two Concepts**

In this simple diagram, the concepts being related are represented by their labels. The null relationship is conventionally represented by the absence of any connecting line between the two concepts.

Covariance Relationships

A second way that concepts can be related is with a covariance relationship. In a covariance relationship, changes in the values of one variable (the measured concept) are associated with changes in the values of the other variable. That is, the variables shift values simultaneously, or covary. This does not mean that one concept is the cause and the other is the effect. A cause-effect relationship between concepts requires more than just covariance, as we'll see shortly.

A covariance relationship is typically diagramed with a curved, double-headed arrow between the concepts, as shown in Figure 3-1(b).

In this diagram, we've stated that changes in a person's income will be *associated* with changes in the person's level of newspaper readership. We've not said that more income *causes* more newspaper readership; nor have we said that reading the newspaper

TABLE 3-1   Covariance Relationships Between Two Variables: Income and Newspaper Readership

	Nature of Covariance		
	No (Null) Relationship	Positive Relationship	Negative Relationship
	Hrs/day reading	Hrs/day reading	Hrs/day reading
High Income	2	4	1
Low Income	2	1	4

Note that describing relationships as positive and negative is meaningful only when the covariance between the two variables is linear or proportional—that is, a specified increase in one variable always leads to the same amount of change in the other variable. If the relationship is more complex, we may be able only to distinguish between null and non-null relationships.

more frequently causes a rise in income. The covariance may be due to the action of other variables, something we'll expand upon soon.

The job of establishing covariance falls to statistics. For all their seeming complexity, statistics are really just a systematic way of organizing our observations so that we can make sound judgments. So what observations do we have to make in order to establish a covariance relationship? Formally, in order to determine whether a change in some variable A is associated with a change in some variable B (in other words, A covaries with B), we must observe the values of variable B when two or more different values of variable A occur. If changes in B are seen to occur systematically with each of the levels of A, then covariance is present.

For example, to determine whether newspaper readership is really associated with income, we would have to observe newspaper readership under at least two levels of income, such as high income and low income. Remember that a variable needs to have at least two levels to be called a variable (otherwise it would be a constant); and we need to see it operating with at least two of its levels, in order to determine whether it is related to some other variable. Two variables which are related proportionally can covary either *positively* or *negatively*. These relationships are shown in the examples in Table 3-1.

In the process of measuring one variable (like newspaper readership) under various levels of some other variable (like income), we may find that the same level of the measured variable is observed regardless of the level of the other variable. For instance, while observing the number of hours spent reading newspapers for two groups of readers—high income and low income—we might note that the average number of hours is the same for both groups (see the first column in Table 3-1). In this case we would conclude that newspaper readership and income are not related to one another. It makes no difference what income level people are; they all read newspapers for the same amount of time. To put it another way, knowing a person's income does not allow us to make any prediction about that person's level of newspaper readership; so we observe a null relationship.

But we might observe that higher levels of readership are observed under the condition of high income than under the condition of low income, as in the second column of Table 3-1. If this situation is found, we will conclude that the two variables are indeed related to one another, because higher values of income are associated with higher values of newspaper readership. We characterize the relationship as a positive one, because high values on one variable are associated with high values on the other, and low levels of both variables also are observed together. This covariance gives us some predictive power. Knowing a person's income provides information about that person's newspaper readership, and vice versa. If we know the value of one variable, we can predict the value of the other. The prediction may not be perfectly accurate, but it will be better than we could do by ignoring the person's income and just guessing about his or her readership.

The third column of Table 3-1 shows an inverse, or negative, relationship. Here the number of hours of readership per day is highest for the low income group and lowest for the high income group. High values on one variable are observed in association with low values on the other variable, and vice versa. Although the direction of the covariance relationship is reversed, we can still make predictions about a person's newspaper readership from that person's income level, or predictions about income from observations of newspaper readership. Consequently we say that there is a relationship between these two variables but that the relationship is a negative one. A commonly observed example of a negative relationship is the one between the frequency of communication between spouses about important issues in the relationship, and the amount of conflict between the spouses. More communication is generally (but not perfectly) associated with less discord.

Sometimes completely unexplained covariance relationships can be found. One of the authors once was a student in a class where the instructor showed a relationship between students' last names and the grade the student received on an examination. Students whose last names started with the letters nearer the end of the alphabet (N through Z) received higher grades on their examination than those students whose names began with the letters A through M. Covariance was established, but we would be hard-pressed to state that a causal relationship existed between these two variables; we simply can't think of a reason why a person's name should cause a difference in academic performance, even if we can show covariance.

While covariance relationships can provide *prediction*, they can't provide *explanation* of the relationship. But there are three basic reasons why we might include covariance relationships in a theory, even when they don't provide explanation.

One reason is that we *don't care* about the nature of the process relating the two variables. For example, we might observe that the variables age and income are positively related: Older individuals tend to have larger incomes than younger individuals. Suppose our theory concerns the effects of age and income on the communication patterns of a member of a small group. Our primary interest is in understanding differences in communication patterns. In this case we may not care to explain all the many ways that increasing age may produce increasing income. We're just content to say that the two covary, since we know this to be true from previous observations of the two variables.

Another reason for including covariance relationships in a theory is *ignorance*. As you'll see below, a statement of a cause-and-effect relationship requires more than simple covariance. If we lack the extra knowledge required to make a cause-and-effect statement, we may be forced to consider a relationship as covariance, rather than as causal. If the relationship is important to our theory, we will still have to include it.

For instance, we may observe that children who play more aggressively with other children are also more likely to watch violent television programs. But is this because violent television programs cause children to be aggressive, or is it because aggressive children prefer to watch violence? If we can't confidently propose the time ordering of cause and effect, we are forced to limit any description of the relationship to a simple statement of covariance. Likewise, if we can't explain why one variable should cause a change in another variable (like a person's name affecting a grade), then we must restrict statements about the relationship to simple covariance.

The third reason for including a covariance relationship in a theory is that it really represents a *spurious* relationship. The idea of a spurious relationship is the essence of the example from Chapter 1 of a positive covariance between the price of rum and professors' salaries. Although our statistics will show a very strong covariance between these variables, we know that both are the result of the action of a third variable: the performance of the whole economy.

To generalize, two variables may covary because they are both the effects of a common cause. If this common cause is difficult or impossible to measure, we may choose to summarize its effect by stating its outcome: a covariance between the two effect variables. Another example of this is seen in Figure 3-2. In this figure, we see a positive covariance relationship between social status and language complexity. Higher status persons use more complex language than lower status persons. But this covariance might be the result of a common, but unmeasured, causal variable. The amount of education received by the individual may produce higher social status, as the individual can advance in a career more quickly. Education may also produce more complex language usage, as formal education stresses this skill. Thus, there is no real relationship between social status and language complexity, although they covary. The unobserved, but real, causal variable (amount of education, in this case) is sometimes called a *confounding variable*, since it may mislead us by producing the appearance of a relationship between the observed variables. We'll deal with ways to handle confounding variables in the next chapter.

Causal Relationships

The third kind of relationship between variables is *causal*. This relationship has the most demanding criteria. Causality means that a change which occurs in one variable (the cause) brings about a change in another variable (the effect). Alternative terms for cause-and-effect variables are *independent variable* and *dependent variable*. This terminology is based on the logic that in a causal relationship the state of one variable (the effect) depends on the state of the other (the cause). The state of the cause is independent of the state of the effect variable.

There is a critical difference between covariance and causality: Covariance means that a change in one variable is *associated* with a change in the other variable; causality requires that a change in one variable *creates* the change in the other. In other words, *covariance alone does not imply causality.* Covariance is only one of four conditions

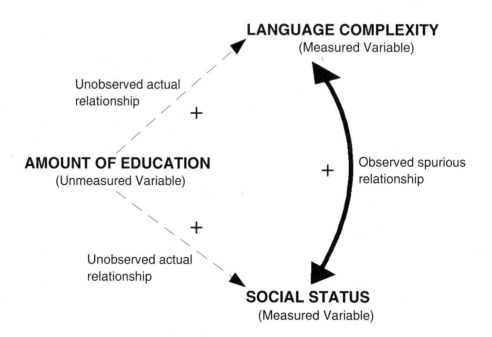

FIGURE 3-2   Illustration of a Spurious Relationship

which must be met before we can state that a relationship is causal. We will outline these conditions below.

Spatial Contiguity

The condition of spatial contiguity requires that the concepts must be connected "in the same time and space," as a logical system. This condition rules out magical effects by requiring a physical connection between the cause and effect. If I stick a needle in your arm, you would be inclined to say the that the needle causes pain. The needle and your arm exist in the same physical space. But if I stick a needle in the arm of a voodoo doll bearing your image, and for some reason you experience pain in your arm, you would not be likely to call the needle the cause of your pain. There is no physical connection between the arm of the doll and your arm, so you would probably seek other explanations for the pain in your arm (unless you believe in magic, in which case the scientific method is not going to help you understand reality). Spatial contiguity sets the basic conditions under which two variables can be connected in a relationship. This condition is sometimes called the "anti-magic" clause of the scientific method, since it rules out all magical effects by requiring a physical connection between cause and effect.

In our newspaper readership example, a person's income and a person's newspaper readership are spatially contiguous; they exist together as concepts which can be applied to the same physical person at a given time. They can be related by some rational process which does not involve magic.

In fact, we often meet the condition of spatial contiguity when we specify the *unit of analysis*. This is the basic unit which we observe in the real world when we begin extracting concepts to create our theory. A unit of analysis might be an individual, a work group, a corporation, a society, a message, or any unit which can be unambiguously defined and observed.

When we define the unit of analysis as an individual, we can talk about the income of the individual and the amount of newspaper readership of the individual. Since both these concepts are located within the same physical space occupied by the individual, we have met this condition of causality by the definition of the unit of analysis.

Covariance

It is obvious that the values of two variables must shift together in some systematic way, before we can say that they are causally related. In other words, a covariance relationship must exist between the cause-and-effect variables. We can see that covariation is a necessary but not sufficient condition for causation.

If income covaries positively with newspaper readership, we are saying that by knowing a person's income, we can infer newspaper readership. Since the relationship is positive, we predict that higher levels of income will be associated with higher levels of newspaper readership. Establishing the truth or falsity of this condition is the task of research design and statistics, and is addressed more fully in the following chapters.

Temporal Ordering

The third requirement for causality is temporal ordering. This means that a change in the variable which we call the cause must happen *before* the related change in the effect variable. But any modification of the effect variable must not change the cause variable. For instance, if we say that a person's income causes newspaper readership, changes in income must occur before any corresponding changes in newspaper readership, *and not vice versa.* Suppose a person gets a raise. If the theory is correct, we should see an increase in the amount of the person's newspaper reading, after some time lag. But if the newspapers go on strike and the person's readership is reduced, we would not expect to see a subsequent decrease in the person's income.

We can either observe this temporal ordering of cause and effect, or we may directly manipulate it with experimental designs, as we will see later.

Necessary Connection

If we think about the earlier example of the observed relationship between the first letter of a person's last name and that person's exam grade, we find that the relationship meets the requirements of spatial contiguity (the name and the exam score both exist within the same physical person), covariance (persons whose names begin with letters A through M scored lower than the others) and temporal ordering (a person's last name was established long before any examination was taken). But we nonetheless feel quite uncomfortable about considering this to be a causal relationship. We just can't think of any sensible reason why one's last name should create different levels of performance on an examination.

This intuitive feeling brings us to the fourth and last requirement for establishing causality: a "necessary connection" that exists between cause and effect. This necessary connection is a statement which specifies *why* the cause can bring about a change in the effect. It is the logical statement of the process or mechanism by which the two variables are related to one another in a cause-and-effect relationship.

Using the income and newspaper readership example, we might state that more income produces increases in newspaper readership by providing the individual with more money to purchase newspapers and with more leisure time to spend reading them. This statement gives a plausible explanation for the connection between the cause and effect. *It is important to understand that the necessary connection is a verbal statement, and it can never be directly tested*, as we are not observing the concepts involved in the process being described. In our simple theory, we are observing only income and the amount of newspaper readership, not the number of different newspapers purchased, or the amount of leisure time. (If we wish to observe the concepts stated in the necessary connection, our theory will become more complicated, as we will have added two new concepts. The number of necessary connections will actually increase as we add relationships among these new observed concepts.)

The idea of necessary connection emphasizes the importance of well-stated verbal theory, because it is only through theory that we can effectively make a case for a causal relationship between two variables. Even if we establish spatial contiguity, covariance, and temporal ordering, we still must justify the cause-effect relationship with a verbal statement. If we cannot suggest a plausible connection between the cause and effect, we have no option but to consider the relationship as simple covariance, as we mentioned above.

We symbolize a causal relationship which meets all four of the conditions by drawing an arrow from the cause variable to the effect variable, as shown in Figure 3-1(c). In the figure, the causal relationship diagramed states that income causes newspaper readership. This is a very strong statement, as all the conditions of causality are assumed to hold.

More complicated theories are built by combining null, covariance, and causal relationships, as illustrated in Figure 3-3. This diagram contains some very detailed statements about the nature of the relationships among the four concepts in this theory. Let's look at each of the relationships separately.

Gender–Income.   This is a covariance relationship. We expect to see some orderly pattern relating a person's gender and his or her income. We're not specifying any necessary connection between the concepts, so we are not saying that being male causes a person's income to be higher (or vice versa).

Gender–Age.   This is a null relationship. We expect no systematic relationship between a person's gender and his or her age.

Age–Income.   Here we expect to see some relationship between a person's age and his or her income. In fact, we expect older persons to make more money. This is symbolized by the "+" sign next to the curved arrow. But we are not stating that growing older causes a person to become wealthier, or that more wealth causes aging. We're just saying that we are likely to observe that older persons have more money, for unspecified reasons.

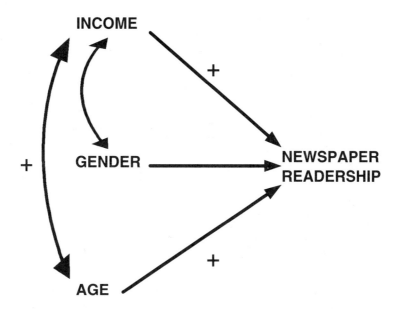

FIGURE 3-3   Example of a Diagram of a More Complex Theory

Income–Newspaper Readership.   This is the causal statement discussed above. We expect persons with higher incomes to read more newspapers (covariance) because the income provides the purchasing power and leisure time for such readership (necessary connection).

Gender–Newspaper Readership.   This is another causal statement. We might expect males to read more newspapers (covariance) because males tend to be less involved with household responsibilities, and thus have more time for reading (necessary connection).

Age–Newspaper Readership.   The final causal statement leads us to expect that older persons will read more newspapers (covariance) for two reasons: They have fewer children at home, and thus more leisure time; and they developed the habit of reading before the dominance of television news (necessary connection).

Theoretical and Operational Linkages

The statements of necessary connection in the above example are required to establish a causal relationship. These statements are also sometimes called *theoretical rationales* or theoretical linkages. They belong within the "verbal world" of theory, and they can be thought of as a kind of analog of a theoretical definition. The theoretical definition explains the nature of a single concept; the theoretical linkage explains the nature of a relationship between two concepts. The theoretical linkage is the product of a rational process; we propose what we think is the logical process which links the two concepts.

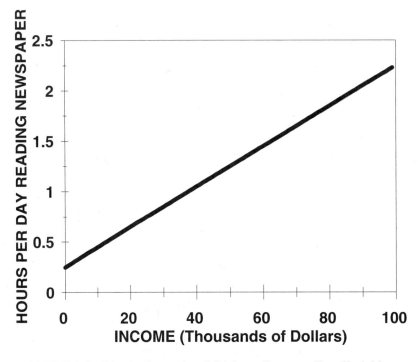

**FIGURE 3-4   Linear Operational Linkage Between Two Variables:
Income and Newspaper Readership**

A theoretical linkage alone is similar to the a priori or rational man approach to knowledge discussed in Chapter 1. But unlike the a priori approach, we go beyond the verbal statement of the process linking the two concepts, and add another linkage which operates between variables in the "measurement world." This *operational linkage* provides the means of testing the probable truth or falsity of the relationship. This distinguishes a scientific relationship, which must be shown to be true in the "measurement world" of observations, from an a priori relationship, which is *always* assumed to be true.

The operational linkage allows us to determine objectively if two concepts covary, by telling us *how* measured changes in one variable should be associated with measured changes in the other. By determining if the two variables covary in the way described by the operational linkage, we can test the probable truth of the relationship. An example of an operational linkage for one of the relationships in the newspaper readership example is shown in Figure 3-4. This operational linkage shows that a linear, positive relationship will be observed between the two concepts: As income increases, newspaper readership will increase at a steady rate. The shape of this operational linkage must correspond to the verbal description of the process. Our statement of necessary connection explained the process as a steadily increasing one, and the operational linkage reflects this explanation.

Just as each theoretically defined concept has a corresponding operational definition which describes the concept as a variable in the "measurement world," so each relationship between two variables has a corresponding operational linkage which tells us how two variables are related in the "measurement world." Furthermore, just as the theoretical definition and the operational definition must match in order to have good measurement validity for a concept, the theoretical linkage and operational linkage must match in order to have a valid test of a relationship.

Operational linkages are essentially mathematical functional statements. The linkage shown in Figure 3-4 can be written as the formula for a straight line:

$$\text{Newspaper readership} = m \cdot \text{Income} + b \tag{3.1}$$

where m is the slope of the line (amount of change in the Y-axis variable divided by the amount of change in the X-axis variable) and

b is the intercept of the line

The formula is identical in meaning to the graph in Figure 3-4. Linear operational linkages like the one above are the most common in communication research, possibly because they are the simplest way in which two variables can be related. But a linear linkage is only one of a number of possible ways in which two concepts can be related to one another.

Stating a theoretical linkage determines the nature of an operational linkage, as both linkages represent statements about the same real world relationship. The verbal world statement of the theoretical linkage cannot contradict the measurement world statement of the operational linkage.

For example, suppose that we have a theoretical linkage between age and newspaper readership that is stated like this: "Newspaper readership will increase with age because older persons will be more interested in world affairs, and will have more leisure time; but after a certain age, readership will decline as eyesight and mental faculties deteriorate." This theoretical linkage now demands something other than a linear operational linkage, as the linear linkage implies that readership will always go up as age increases, and this contradicts our theoretical linkage. To translate the verbal meaning of the theoretical linkage into measurement terms, we might use a linkage like that shown in Figure 3-5. This is called a *curvilinear operational linkage*, and it is somewhat harder to verify than a linear linkage. But if our theory demands it, we must seek out ways of testing nonlinear linkages.

Each type of linkage has a different function. A theoretical linkage alone states *why* a relationship might exist, but does not specify *how* the variables are related. An operational linkage alone tells us how the measured variables are related, without telling us *why* the relationship exists.

Both theoretical and operational linkages are required for a causal statement. We must have both the verbal world explanation which establishes the necessary connection (theoretical linkage), and the measurement world linkage which tells us specifically how the covariance operates (operational linkage). Understanding the relationship means that we can describe the mechanism whereby a change in one concept brings about a change

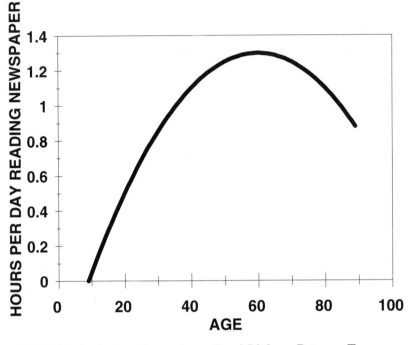

FIGURE 3-5   A Curvilinear Operational Linkage Between Two Variables: Age and Newspaper Readership

in the other, and that we can describe the covariance of the corresponding variables in measurement terms.

The covariance relationship requires only an operational linkage, as a covariance relationship provides only prediction. Prediction means that by knowing the state of one variable, we can predict the state of another variable. Looking at the relationship between income and newspaper readership shown in Figure 3-4, we see that we can predict an individual's level of newspaper readership by knowing that individual's income, and vice versa. If a person has a high income, we predict that the person will spend more time reading newspapers. Likewise, if we know that a person has low newspaper readership, he or she will also be likely to have a lower income.

All that is required to make a prediction is that we know *how* the two variables are related to one another, such as by the linear, positive relationship shown in Figure 3-4. We do not need to know *why* the two variables are related to one another. So we must have an operational linkage for prediction, but we do not require a theoretical linkage.

A null relationship, of course, needs neither type of linkage. The null relationship states that the concepts are independent, so that there is no need for any statement that explains the relationship (theoretical linkage) or tells how the measured variables covary (operational linkage).

The prediction provided by operational linkages and the explanation provided by theoretical linkages can also be seen as standing in a hierarchical relationship. The ability to formulate a prediction does not imply or require that we understand why the prediction might work! We may well be able to predict the severity of an upcoming winter from the density of hair on certain types of caterpillars without knowing why such a relationship might exist. But explanation *does* include prediction. Understanding how something works implies that we should be able to formulate a prediction, in addition to describing the process.

This hierarchical situation may be clearer if we review the requirements for covariance and causal relationships. All the conditions for the covariance relationship are also required for the causal relationship, so both relationships provide prediction. But the causal relationship adds the requirement of necessary connection, which is provided by the theoretical linkage. This adds explanation to mere prediction, and so a causal statement represents a theoretically stronger pronouncement.

Theory and Hypotheses

In this chapter and in the preceding one we have: (1) developed set of *concepts,* with (2) a *theoretical definition* for each which describes in detail the meaning of the concept. We also have developed a corresponding (3) *operational definition,* which specifies the measurement indicators and, if necessary, the ways in which they are to be combined. The operational definition serves as the observable measure of the meaning in the theoretical definition. Furthermore, our theory contains (4) a specification of the *theoretical linkages* between all concepts that are causally related. These theoretical linkages provide the rationale for the necessary connection of concepts connected with a causal relationship, that is, the explanation of *why* they are connected. All non-null relationships also contain (5) *operational linkages,* which provide a description of the specific manner in which the concepts are associated with one another.

But the rules of science now require that we test the theory against the observable real world, to see if it accurately describes objective reality. In this section, we will outline the next step in the scientific process: the formulation and testing of hypotheses derived from our theories.

Observation and Hypotheses

The first thing we need to be aware of is this: While the theoretical linkage is not testable, the operational linkage is. The theoretical linkage exists only in the "verbal world," and its test of truth is logical deduction. But the operational linkage predicts the way in which the measured variables should behave. Its test of truth goes beyond simple logical deduction, and must include observation of the real world. The vehicles for this observation are the operational definitions of variables in the measurement world.

We derive hypotheses from the operational linkages. Hypotheses are verbal statements that specify how the variables, as defined by operational definitions, should be associated with one another if the theoretical linkage is, in fact, correct.

Let us return to our running example. Assume that the operational definition of income is: "The total adjusted gross income in thousands of dollars as reported to the IRS in the most recent year" and that newspaper readership is defined as the response to the question: "Rounded to the nearest hour, how many hours do you spend reading newspapers on an average day?"

Using these definitions and the operational linkage shown in Figure 3-4, we can produce this hypothetical statement: "The greater the adjusted income of an individual, the more hours per day are spent reading newspapers." Note that this is just a verbal restatement of the operational linkage.

But when the statement is treated as a hypothesis, it has an additional, and very important, characteristic: It may be true, or it may be false. A hypothesis can be tested by observing the behavior of a number of units of analysis (like individuals or groups) and can be shown to be (probably) true or false. This is the critical element which the scientific method adds to the other methods of knowing reality. The decision about whether a hypothesis is (probably) correct is separate from our individual values or opinions, because it is based on a set of agreed-upon rules for determining truth or falsity.

All hypotheses *must* have the possibility of being shown to be either true or false. This is sometimes called the requirement of *falsifiability*. If the results of observation cannot be used to determine the probable truth or falsity of a statement, it is not a scientific hypothesis. For example, the statement "More time spent communicating can produce either no change, or produce increases in positive or negative feelings of intimacy between friends" is not a hypothesis, as observation of communication levels between pairs of friends cannot be used to determine whether the statement is probably true or false. As expressed, the statement will always be confirmed by observation (feelings of intimacy will either stay the same, go up, or go down—all of which are predicted by the statement). It is not falsifiable, so it cannot be tested scientifically.

You'll note that we have qualified the truth or falsity of hypotheses by saying "(probably) true or false." This is another important facet of hypotheses and of the scientific method: There is no absolute truth or falsity. We may be *more or less confident* of truth or falsity, but we can never be *totally* sure of either. As we'll see in the sections on statistics, we can increase this confidence with more and more observation, but we can never prove the absolute truth of a theoretical statement beyond any hint of a doubt. This is why a hypothesis is never said to be "proved" true. Absolute truth can exist only in the abstract logic of the verbal world, while hypotheses are tested by observations made in the real world. All observations have the possibility of error, and we will cover some of the sources of error later in Chapters 5 and 6.

Is this inability to find absolute truth a flaw of the scientific method? No, it's a strength. The book is never closed on any scientific truth—all theory is open to further investigation and revision, and all measurements are subject to critical review and reinterpretation. This continual revision and questioning of scientific theory leads theory to closer and closer approximations of real world reality.

Since hypotheses are the vehicle for the investigation of a theory's adequacy, we'll look at them in greater depth. Hypotheses can be classified in a number of different ways. We'll discuss some of the common distinctions made among hypotheses to provide a basis for the material covered in later chapters.

The most common distinctions made are these: comparative hypotheses versus relationship hypotheses; directional versus nondirectional hypotheses; and, finally, alternative or research hypotheses versus null hypotheses.

Relationship versus Comparative Hypotheses

A *relationship hypothesis* states the existence of a specific functional relationship between two variables (like the straight line function shown in Figure 3-4). · It is tested directly by observing the two variables involved in the relationship. For example, the hypothesis derived from the operational linkage shown in Figure 3-4 states that the two variables are positively related to one another. Verbally, the hypothesis is: "As income increases, newspaper readership increases proportionally." Such a hypothesis is called a relationship hypothesis, as it is stated in terms of the relationship between the measured variables. It can be diagramed as shown in Figure 3-1(c), if the relationship is a causal one, or 3-1(b) if it is a covariance relationship. The plus sign indicates that a positive relationship is expected.

To test for the probable truth or falsity of this hypothesized relationship, we directly observe the variables in a number of individuals, and look for covariance of the variables. We should find that most individuals who have high income spend large amounts of time reading newspapers daily; that most of those with low incomes spend small amounts of time reading newspapers; and that most of those with moderate incomes spend a moderate amount of time reading.

There is an alternative way of testing the same relationship. This alternative way provides an indirect test of the relationship by categorizing all the units of analysis into *groups*, according to their levels of one variable (in a causal relationship, the cause variable). The groups' average levels of the second variable are then contrasted. If the groups' averages differ, then the individuals in the groups must differ on the second variable in a consistent fashion, and the requirement of covariance is met.

For example, we could test the income–readership hypothesis by placing each person whom we observe in one of two groups, depending on the person's income level. The high income group could then be compared with the low income group in terms of their newspaper readership. We would expect that those in the high income group would spend more time reading newspapers, on average, than people in the low income group. This type of hypothesis is called a *comparative hypothesis,* because it involves comparing at least two groups (where each group represents a level of a variable) on some criterion variable. We can write this comparative hypothesis like this:

$$\text{Mean hours newspaper readership for low income group} < \text{Mean hours newspaper readership for high income group}$$

where < means "less than."

After we observe a number of individuals in each group, we can determine how correct our hypothetical statement is. If the low income group actually does spend less time reading newspapers than the high income group, we infer that income and newspaper readership covary in a positive fashion.

For reasons that will be made clearer in later chapters, we recommend that comparative hypotheses be avoided whenever possible. However, there are probably many instances where the option of using relationship hypotheses simply is not available. For instance, suppose we want to determine whether the gender of the newspaper reader is associated with the amount of time spent reading. While income has an underlying dimension that allows us to think of having "more or less" of this concept, the variable gender does not. We can speak of increases and decreases in income and newspaper readership; we cannot speak of increases or decreases in male or female in the same way. Variables whose operational definitions do not have an underlying dimension which can take on gradations of values (that is, nominal variables like gender) do not lend themselves to relationship hypotheses. This leaves comparative hypotheses as the only option.

Directional versus Nondirectional Hypotheses

Another distinction between types of hypotheses concerns the detail of the prediction that the hypothetical statement provides. The hypothetical relationship between income and newspaper readership shown in Figure 3-4 is very specific about the nature of the relationship between the two variables. It specifies a direct, positive relationship.

A *directional hypothesis* states that we should see covariance with a particular direction (either positive or negative) between the variables.[1] In contrast, a *nondirectional hypothesis* simply states that a relationship will be observed, without specifying the direction of the relationship. That is, we expect to observe *either* a positive *or* a negative relationship. Alternative directional and nondirectional hypotheses are diagramed in Figure 3-6.

Note that all we expect to observe in the nondirectional comparative hypothesis is a difference between the two income groups. We expect the two groups to spend different amounts of time reading newspapers, but we're not predicting whether the low income or the high income group will spend more time reading.

The reason we write nondirectional hypotheses is purely because we lack knowledge. We may simply not know enough about the phenomenon under study, and therefore about the nature of the relationship between the two variables, to be able to predict *how* they are related; we merely think that they *will be* related.

For instance, if an employer were to conduct an information campaign, urging all employees to increase their current contributions to the United Way, we might not know how to predict what they will do: The employees may respond favorably to the appeal and increase their contributions, or they may resent the intrusion into what they consider to be their private affairs and possibly reduce their contributions. In this case we simply do not have insight to predict the result, but we can contrast it to the null relationship, where we observe no change in their contributions as a result of the employer's communication.

Nondirectional hypotheses generally are associated with newly developing areas of research. Once a number of studies have been carried out in a given area, the results will usually provide enough information about the relationship to permit directional hypotheses. For example, in the 1960s there was a heated debate about the effects of televised violence on children's aggressiveness. Some researchers predicted a positive relationship, due to learning from television; others predicted a negative relationship due to the release of internal hostilities in fantasy form. In this situation, a nondirectional hypothesis is appropriate. However, after several hundred studies found a positive covariance between televised violence and aggression, and only a few found a negative relationship, a positive directional hypothesis became appropriate.

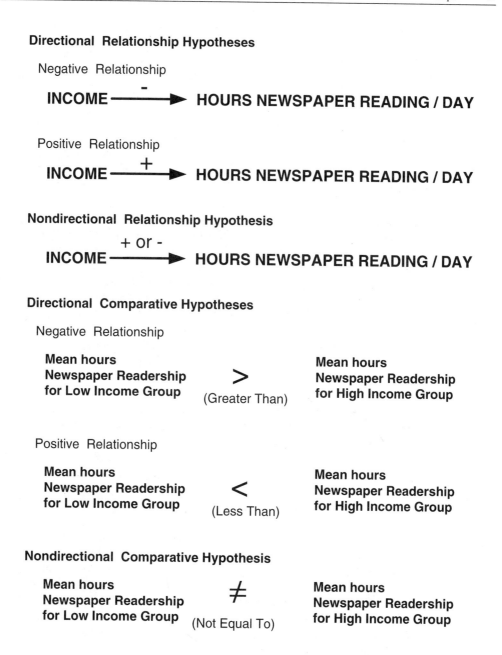

Directional Relationship Hypotheses

Negative Relationship

INCOME ——— HOURS NEWSPAPER READING / DAY

Positive Relationship

INCOME ——— HOURS NEWSPAPER READING / DAY

Nondirectional Relationship Hypothesis

INCOME ——— HOURS NEWSPAPER READING / DAY

Directional Comparative Hypotheses

Negative Relationship

| Mean hours Newspaper Readership for Low Income Group | > (Greater Than) | Mean hours Newspaper Readership for High Income Group |

Positive Relationship

| Mean hours Newspaper Readership for Low Income Group | < (Less Than) | Mean hours Newspaper Readership for High Income Group |

Nondirectional Comparative Hypothesis

| Mean hours Newspaper Readership for Low Income Group | ≠ (Not Equal To) | Mean hours Newspaper Readership for High Income Group |

FIGURE 3-6   **Examples of Directional and Non-Directional Hypotheses**

A nondirectional hypothesis is conservative, but that safety carries a penalty. Statistically, it is harder to distinguish a nondirectional relationship from a null relationship than it is to discriminate between a directional relationship and the null. We'll cover this fact in more detail when we talk about statistical power in Chapter 12.

Null versus Alternative Hypotheses

The alternative to either a positive or negative relationship is no relationship at all: a null relationship. In the context of a relationship hypothesis, this means that we find no covariance between variables. Similarly, with a comparative hypothesis, we find no difference at all between groups.

This brings us to a very simple but very powerful idea: We can decide whether a particular prediction is (probably) true if we can eliminate all competing predictions. If the statement "two variables are not related" is (probably) false, then it follows that the statement "the two variables are related" has to be (probably) true.

Hypothesis testing is thus reduced to a competition between two conflicting hypotheses: the *null hypothesis,* which states that there is no relationship between two variables, or that there is no difference between groups; and the *alternative hypothesis* (sometimes also called the research hypothesis), which is the statement of the non-null relationship between two variables or groups taken from the theoretical and operational linkages developed in our theory. The null hypothesis is often referred to as H_0 and the alternative or research hypothesis as H_a or H_r, or by a hypothesis number (i.e., H_1 is a non-null statement of hypothesis 1, H_2 of alternative hypothesis 2, etc.).

Obviously the null and the alternative hypotheses cannot be simultaneously true. The null hypothesis for the relationship between income and newspaper readership is: "There is no covariance between income and newspaper readership," while a competing nondirectional hypothesis might be "income covaries with newspaper readership." Only one of these statements can be true. Many of our statistical tests are designed to pit the null hypothesis against an alternative, non-null hypothesis. If we can reject the null hypothesis on the basis of our observations, it follows that we can accept the alternative hypothesis as (probably) true.

If we have a directional alternative hypothesis, however, we must do more than reject the null hypothesis. If our alternative hypothesis predicts a positive relationship, we must also show that the covariance is in the right direction before we can accept the alternative hypothesis. In this case, we need to eliminate both the null prediction, and the prediction that the relationship between the two variables is negative. If we find that persons with higher incomes spend less time reading newspapers, we cannot support the directional hypothesis that income and newspaper readership are positively related.

Although this example is for a relationship hypothesis, the same logic holds for covariance in comparative hypotheses. Group averages are examined rather than functional relationships, but the reasoning is identical: If we can reject the null hypothesis that the group averages do not differ, then we can establish the probable truth of the alternative hypothesis (that they *do* differ, so there is some systematic covariance). If the alternative hypothesis is directional, we must then also establish that differences between the groups are in the predicted direction before we can claim support for the alternative hypothesis (e.g., that the average time spent reading newspapers is higher for the high income group than it is for the low income group).

Summary

In this chapter we have outlined three different types of relationships that can be used to associate concepts in a theory. In *null relationships,* the variables representing the two concepts do not covary, and the concepts have no theoretical process which links them. In *covariance relationships,* the two variables covary systematically, but we cannot state that one variable causes the other. Covariance relationships may be used when we don't care about the nature of the relationship between the variables (probably because it is peripheral to our central theory), or when the covariance is the result of the spurious effect of another confounding variable, or when we simply don't know if the relationship meets all the criteria for a causal relationship. A *causal relationship* is the strongest theoretical statement, as it must meet four criteria: *spatial contiguity* (the cause and effect must be linked by some physical process); *covariance* (the variables must vary systematically, as in a covariance relationship); *temporal ordering* (changes in the cause must occur before changes in the effect, and not vice versa); and *necessary connection* (the cause must be linked to the effect by a rational, reasonable process).

In causal relationships, the condition of necessary connection is met with a *theoretical linkage,* which describes the process by which the two concepts are connected. In both covariance and causal relationships, the nature of the relationship between the operationally defined variables is described in measurement terms by an *operational linkage.* The theoretical linkage explains the make-up of the process linking the concepts, so it belongs to the "verbal world" of theory. The operational linkage tells us how the variables which represent the concepts are related in the "measurement world."

Scientific relationships are stated as testable *hypotheses.* A hypothesis predicts the behavior of variables, and it must be confirmed by observations made in the real world. A hypothesis can only be confirmed as *probably* true or *probably* false—absolute proof or confirmation is not possible. Furthermore, any hypothesis must be capable of being shown, by real world observation, to be either probably true or probably false.

There are several kinds of hypotheses that we can use to test relationships. *Relationship hypotheses* directly test the functional relationships between measured variables. *Comparative hypotheses* test relationships indirectly by summarizing the behavior of variables in groups of observations. *Directional hypotheses* predict the direction of the covariance between two variables (either positive or negative). *Nondirectional hypotheses* predict only that covariance exists, but do not forecast its direction. *Null hypotheses* and *alternative* or *research hypotheses* are competing statements about the same relationship. A null hypothesis states that the relationship does not exist; the alternative hypothesis states that it does. By providing evidence from observation about the probable truth of one of these hypotheses, we can eliminate the other, since both can't be simultaneously true. This is the basis for statistical hypothesis testing.

In the following chapter we will consider the next step in the scientific method: observing the variables in the real world in such a way that we can adequately test our hypotheses.

Notes

[1] Characterizing a relationship as positive or negative only has meaning if the operational linkage is linear. If two variables have a nonlinear operational linkage, we can't talk about directional hypotheses, as the direction of the relationship is different for different levels of the variables. See Figure 3-5 for an example of this. However, since most of the operational linkages used in communication science are linear, the directional/nondirectional distinction is important.

References and Additional Readings

Babbie, E. R. (1992). *The practice of social research* (6th ed.). Belmont, CA: Wadsworth (Chapter 3, "The Nature of Causation").

Hage, J. (1972). *Techniques and problems of theory construction in sociology.* New York: Wiley (Chapter 2, "Theoretical Statements" ; Chapter 4, "Specifying the Linkages").

Heise, D. R. (1975). *Causal analysis.* New York: Wiley (Chapter 1, "Causality and Causal Analysis"; Chapter 2, "Causal Diagrams and Flowgraph Analysis").

Kenny, D. A. (1979). *Correlation and causality.* New York: Wiley. (Chapter 1, "Structural Modeling").

Krathwohl, D. R. (1985). *Social and behavioral science research.* San Francisco: Jossey-Bass. (Chapter 9, "Causal Explanation: Possible Complexities").

Chapter 4

Testing Hypotheses: Confounds and Controls

In this chapter we will outline how we test the hypotheses generated from our theory. The scientific method requires that we test our theories by comparing what they predict we will observe to actual observations made in the real world. If our hypotheses are any good, they should predict what we actually see.

Multiple Variables and Confounds

It would make our life simpler if every effect variable had only one cause, and it covaried only with one other variable. Unfortunately, this is hardly ever the case. Virtually every communication variable we can think of is associated with a number of other variables either in causal relationships or in covariance relationships. For example, the amount of time we spend watching television is determined not only by our income, but also by our age, level of education, our interests, the number of children we have, the variety of programming available to us, alternative ways of spending our leisure time and a host of other variables. Our level of public communication apprehension can be affected by age, training in public speaking, amount of experience in public communication, ego strength, status differences between ourselves and the audience, and many other factors.

If we have a number of interrelated variables, then it becomes difficult to sort out how variables affect each other. It's far too easy to confuse one cause with another, or to attribute all change to a single cause when many causal factors are operating. Similarly, having multiple variables related to each other obscures the nature of covariance relationships: If we observe covariance between two variables, we must question whether they covary because of some real relationship between the variables, or whether the covariance is merely due to the spurious effect of a third confounding variable, as was illustrated in the

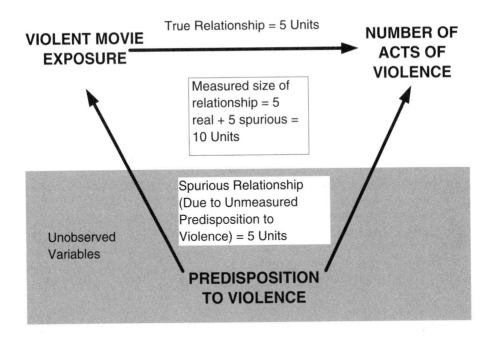

FIGURE 4-1   Multiple Variable Confound: Misestimation of the Size of a Relationship

previous chapter. Before we can establish that a relationship exists between two variables, we have to be able to sort out the effects of all the other variables which also may be related to the two.

The process of determining whether a relationship exists between two variables requires first that we establish covariance between two variables, as we discussed in the previous chapter. In addition to verifying that the two variables change in predictable, nonrandom patterns, we must also be able to discount *any other variable or variables* as sources of the change. To establish a true relationship, we must be able to confidently state that we observed the relationship in the real world under conditions which eliminated the effects of any other variables.

For example, if we are interested in determining whether there is a real relationship between exposure to movie violence and the the number of violent acts committed by adolescents, then we must observe these two variables covarying, while simultaneously eliminating the possibility that this covariance was produced by other factors. An example of a confounding factor for this relationship might be the adolescent's predisposition to aggressive behavior. Adolescents inclined toward aggression may choose to watch more violent movies than adolescents who are less aggressive, and they may also be more strongly affected by violent images. In order to conduct a legitimate test of the hypothesis which links two variables, we must find ways of controlling for the effects of the confounding variables.

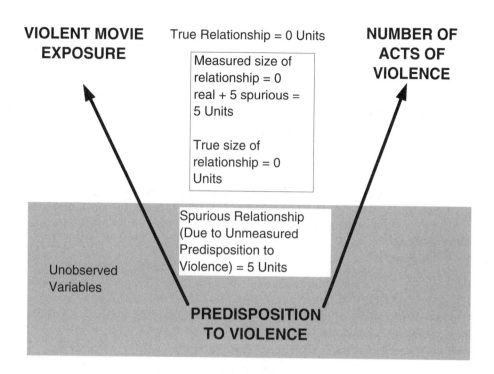

FIGURE 4-2   Multiple Variable Confound: Erroneous Inference

Graphical examples of the problem are shown in Figures 4-1 and 4-2. In Figure 4-1, we see that there are two ways that a person's exposure to movie violence can covary with number of acts of violence committed by that person. There is a direct causal relationship, with movie violence viewing causing an increase in the number of acts of violence. This is the hypothesis that we're interested in testing. In this hypothesis, exposure to movie violence is the independent variable and number of acts of violence is the dependent variable.

But there is also a spurious relationship between such exposure and violent acts, which is produced by the confounding variable of predisposition to violence. Adolescents who are generally more violent are also more likely to select violent movies for viewing. This produces a spurious covariance between the independent and dependent variables.

Since we are observing only the independent (exposure) and dependent (number of acts of violence) variables, we will overestimate the strength of relationship between them. If the true relationship is five units and the spurious relationship is also five units, we will conclude that the independent and dependent variables covary by ten units. In truth, the real relationship is much smaller. If we ignore the confounding variable, we will erroneously conclude that *all* change in number of acts of violence is due to the direct action of exposure to movie violence. We erroneously conclude that we have strong support for our hypothesis.

Figure 4-2 illustrates an extreme way that an unobserved third variable can mislead us. Here, our original hypothesis is false—there is no relationship between exposure to movie violence and number of acts of violence. All covariance between the two is the result of the confounding variable predisposition to violence. Since we observe only the exposure and the acts of violence variables, it appears that they are covarying, so we will incorrectly conclude that we have a modest causal relationship between viewing and violence, when we should conclude that there is no relationship.

We obviously must take steps to control all confounding variables, in order to avoid making misestimates of the size of relationships, or even drawing the wrong conclusions from our observations. If we do not do so, we risk lending the appearance of scientific truth to falsehoods. Failure to properly control for confounding variables is a common error found in poorly conducted science. Critical reading of popular press accounts of "dramatic scientific breakthroughs" often reveals this error. As true scientists, you must always be skeptical of the results of *any* study. And the first thing you should speculate about when you read a scientific report (in the professional journals as well as in the popular press) is the possible presence of confounding variables that may have confused the researcher's results.

Controlling for Confounding Variables

We'll introduce another example to illustrate the process of determining what variables to control, and how to control them. Let's suppose that we are studying the development of children's language. We know that the age of the child and a whole variety of family interaction variables will affect both the child's vocabulary size and the complexity of the child's reasoning processes (which we'll label cognitive complexity). However, we're primarily interested in the relationship between cognitive complexity and vocabulary size, and not in family interaction variables.

Identifying Control Variables

Let's start with a very wide view, and consider the idea that *any* given variable could potentially be included in our theory. We can first organize this universe of variables and reduce it enormously by classifying every variable into one of two categories: relevant or irrelevant to the phenomenon being investigated. This is the top stage illustrated in Figure 4-3.

The *relevant variables* are those which have already been shown to be important to understanding the phenomenon, or those for which a reasonable case can be made. For instance, if the research literature on this topic tells us that vocabulary size has been repeatedly observed to be associated with the age of the child, then we will consider age to be a relevant variable. And although no researcher may have reported it, we feel that the number of hours per week that the child spends outside the home should also be included in our theory. We'll have to justify classifying this variable as relevant, however. For the purposes of our example, let's argue that we think the additional exposure to other adults and children during the time spent outside the home should provide the child

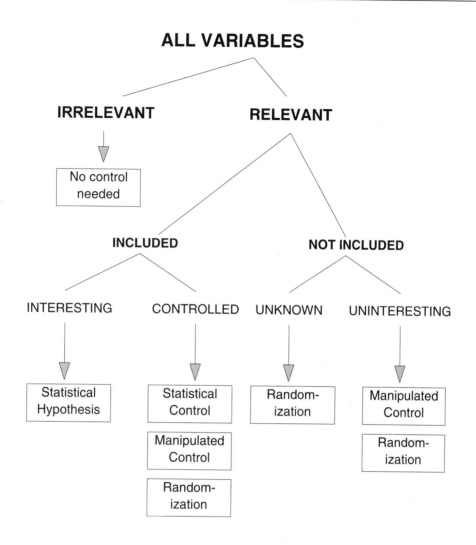

FIGURE 4-3   Methods of Controlling for Confounding Variables

with exposure to new words, and thus expand the child's vocabulary. (Note that we just provided a theoretical linkage for these two variables.)

We've already covered the process of isolating and defining relevant concepts and putting them together in hypothetical relationships in Chapters 2 and 3, so we'll not spend any additional time talking about the procedure of including concepts and variables in a theory. But the *exclusion* of many concepts from consideration brings up a critical point. If we have not included a concept and its related variable in our theory, it can be because of several different reasons, and each of these reasons has important implications for the control of confounding variables.

One reason we might choose to exclude a variable is because we consider it to be irrelevant to the phenomenon we are investigating. If we classify a variable as *irrelevant,* it means that we are willing to assume that it has no systematic effect on any of the variables included in our theory. The temperature on the day that each child in our language study was born is a real variable, but we will conclude that it has no bearing on the phenomenon of children's language, and thus it will have no effect on any of the variables which we deem relevant. Irrelevant variables require no form of control, as they are not systematically related to any of the variables in our theory, so they will not introduce any confounding influences.

Relevant variables can be further classified into two categories: those which are explicitly measured and included in the theory, and those which are not (as shown in Figure 4-3). It's quite clear why we would include relevant variables, but why would we *not* include them? Again, there are two basic reasons.

First, the variables might be unknown. We, along with other researchers, might have overlooked some relevant variables. But the fact that we have missed these variables does not mean that they have no effect. So we must take precautions that ensure that these unobserved, but relevant, variables do not confound our hypothesis tests. It is imperative that we take appropriate steps to ensure that the effects of any unknown variables are not *systematically* associated with any values of the relevant variables. If they are, we will make the kinds of errors illustrated in Figures 4-1 and 4-2.

Another reason for excluding relevant variables is because they are simply not of interest. The researcher might know that the variable affects the phenomenon being studied, but does not want to include its effect in the theory. For example, we might decide that the effect of age on children's cognitive complexity and vocabulary is relevant—increasing age affects both variables positively—but it is not the central question being studied. We can't ignore age, however, so we must take some positive steps to control for its effect. We'll discuss methods for controlling relevant but uninteresting variables in the next section.

There remain two kinds of variables that are explicitly included in our hypothesis tests. The first of these are the relevant, interesting variables which are directly involved in our hypothesis test. In our example, size of vocabulary and cognitive complexity are these variables. There is also another kind of included variable called a control variable. It is explicitly included in the hypothesis test, because it affects the interesting variables. But it is included only in order to remove or control for its effect on the interesting variables. The child's age is an example of this kind of control variable.

Internal Validity, External Validity, and Information

Knowing what variables you need to control is important, but even more important is the way you control for them. Several ways of controlling variables exist, but before we discuss them it is important to understand the criteria that are used to choose among them. We will take some time to define and describe two types of research validity prior to discussing the pros and cons of different types of control for confounding variables. Each method of control can be evaluated in terms of these validities, as well as by the amount of information about the action of control variables that is lost or gained in each method.

Internal validity is the degree to which we can be sure that no confounding variables have obscured the true relationship between the variables in the hypothesis test. It is the confidence that we can place in the assertion that the variables we have called causes or independent variables actually produce the observed effects. Internal validity is thus very closely associated with the amount of control which we exert over confounding variables. In a poorly controlled study, confounding variables may mislead us with spurious relationships. In Figure 4-2, the confounding effect of the uncontrolled variable predisposition to violence makes this study one that we characterize as having poor internal validity. Internal validity is also associated with the success with which we manipulate the independent variable in an experimental study. (An experimental study is one in which the independent variable or variables are deliberately manipulated by the researcher. We'll cover such studies in more detail in Chapter 14.)

External validity describes our ability to generalize from the results of a research study to the real world. If we have established that a relationship between two variables exists, it describes the degree to which this relationship can be generalized to groups, subjects, and conditions other than those under which the research observations were made. Unfortunately, control for the effect of confounding variables, which increases internal validity, often simultaneously reduces external validity. By exercising careful control over confounding variables, we may create a research environment that allows an unambiguous determination of the relationship between two variables, but at the same time creates an artificial situation in which any generalization to that real world is very difficult to justify.

The third criterion used to evaluate methods of control is the *amount of information* that we can obtain about any confounding variable and its relationship with the relevant variables. We are often at least marginally interested in describing the effects of confounding variables, and some methods of control provide us with information about the action of the confounding variables on the relevant variables.

Methods for Controlling Confounding Variables

The effects of confounding variables can be controlled with three basic methods, as shown in Figure 4-3. The methods are *manipulated control, statistical control,* and *randomization.* Each method has its advantages and disadvantages. This means that they should not be used interchangeably and that the decision about which of these methods to use should be made after some thought. Internal validity, external validity, and the amount of information that can be obtained about confounding variables differs for each of these methods. An example of each of the three methods for controlling the confounding variable can be seen in Table 4-1.

In this example our interest lies in studying the relationship between the method of communication used in teaching and student achievement. We want to contrast students in traditional lectures to students who are using computer-based instruction to see if there are differences in their performance. We speculate that the students in the computer-based group will be able to control the pace at which they learn and adapt it to their own abilities. Consequently we expect them to perform better than their colleagues who hear lectures, as these students cannot control the flow of information. Our hypothesis is that

TABLE 4-1   Examples of Control Methods

Manipulated Control

Previous Exposure	None		Some	
Teaching Method	Computer	Lecture	Computer	Lecture
Performance (% correct on exam)	85	75	NO DATA COLLECTED	
Effect of Teaching Method	$(85 - 75 = 10\%)$			

Statistical Control

Previous Exposure	None		Some	
Teaching Method	Computer	Lecture	Computer	Lecture
Performance (% correct on exam)	85	75	95	85
Effect of Teaching Method	$(85 - 75 = 10\%)$		$(95 - 85 = 10\%)$	
Effect of Previous Exposure	Computer	$(95 - 85 = 10\%)$		
	Lecture	$(85 - 75 = 10\%)$		

Randomization Control

Previous Exposure	Random Assignment	
Teaching Method	Computer	Lecture
Performance (% correct on exam)	90	80
Effect of Teaching Method	$(90 - 80 = 10\%)$	

teaching method will affect performance: specifically that the computer-using group will outperform the lecture group.

Suppose that our review of the literature has identified a variable called previous exposure to the material. This variable has been shown to have a positive effect on performance in past research studies. This classifies it as a confounding variable to control so that it will not jeopardize our hypothesis test. It is controlled in three different ways in Table 4-1.

Manipulated Control

Manipulated control essentially changes a variable into a constant. We eliminate the effect of a confounding variable by not allowing it to vary. If it cannot vary, it cannot produce any change in the other variables. If we use manipulated control, we will select subjects for the two conditions so they are as similar as possible on previous exposure. This may mean that we will select only subjects who have no previous exposure to the course material, or we may choose only students who have already had one course in the particular subject matter. Any other variables that confound the hypothesis test can be treated in the same manner. If we can hold all confounding variables constant, we can be confident that any difference in performance observed between the two groups is indeed due to the different teaching methods, as it could not have been due to the confounding variables. This gives us high internal validity for the study.

We can exert manipulated control outside of a laboratory or experimental setting, too. For example, suppose we are going to conduct a survey to determine whether there might be a relationship between the amount of information that a person recalls from Army recruiting commercials and his or her willingness to enlist. An obvious confounding variable in this relationship is age. This variable is probably related to recall of recruiting appeals because older audience members are less likely to watch such commercials (they are irrelevant to a senior citizen), so they will be less likely to remember information from them, as well as being less likely to enlist. Furthermore, younger viewers might be more willing to give up several years to serve in the Armed Forces, and they may also pay more attention to the commercials. If these things happen, we will confuse the effect of age with the effect of the commercials. To prevent this, we might control the confounding variable age by selecting only 17- to 19-year-olds to participate in our survey.

Another form of manipulated control is called *matching subjects.* Subjects are placed into research groups on the basis of equality on a number of characteristics, like age, sex, income, marital status, or any other set of variables which we think might confound the hypothesis tests. This ensures there are equal proportions of high and low income, married and unmarried, female and male participants in all research groups. By forcing all groups to be identical on the matched characteristics, the effects of these variables are made constant in all research groups, and thus cannot confound the relationship being tested.

Manipulated control favors internal validity. But as the number of variables that we control increases, external validity generally decreases. In the computer instruction example, if the previous exposure variable is controlled at "one previous course" and we find positive results for computer-based instruction, we can't say with any confidence that the same difference would exist for students with "no previous exposure" or "two previous courses." We can't generalize the results of our research as widely, so external validity is reduced. Likewise, if we find certain advertising appeals associated with intention to enlist for 17- to 19-year-olds, we can't be sure that the same appeals will stimulate enlistment among 21-year-olds.

Manipulated control prevents the controlled variables from having any effect on the dependent variable. As a consequence we will not find out what magnitude of effect (if any) these variables will have on the dependent variable. We will not find out, for instance, whether previous experience *really* affects academic performance in computer-based instruction. We have done the proper thing and controlled for it, since we suspected that it might confound our results, but we don't know whether or not it has an effect in the real world.

Statistical Control

With this method of control, we build the confounding variable into the research design as an additional measured variable, rather than forcing its value to be a constant. When we test the hypothesis, we do so with three (or more) variables, not two: the independent and dependent variables, plus the confounding (or control) variable or variables. The effect of the control variable is mathematically removed from the effect of the independent variable, but the control variable is allowed to vary naturally. We do not hold it constant by deliberately setting its value, as we would with manipulated control.

This process yields additional information about the relationship between the control variable and the other variables. In our computer-based instruction example, we could allow students to participate in our study without imposing any requirements about their previous exposure to the material we are going to teach. Rather than holding this variable constant at some chosen level, as with manipulated control, we will *measure* previous exposure for each subject and use statistical procedures to estimate its effect on student performance, and then to remove this effect from the estimate of the effect of the independent variable.

Table 4-1 shows some hypothetical data from our teaching method example. Statistical control allows us to determine whether a relationship exists between teaching method and achievement by contrasting the two groups which have instructional methods in common (the two computer groups) to the two other instructional method groups (the two lecture groups). The data in Table 4-1 show that students in the computer groups outperform the students in the lecture groups *regardless* of the level of previous exposure. In other words, teaching method has an effect *of its own* on the achievement of students. But we also see that the groups with "some" previous exposure performed at a higher level than the two groups with no previous exposure, and that they do this regardless of instructional method.

Statistical control thus provides us with information about the control variable. In this case, evidence about the relationship between the confounding variable of previous exposure and the dependent variable performance is obtained by contrasting the two "none" groups to the two "some" groups.

We can conclude that previous exposure (the control variable) is related to performance (the dependent variable) and that the nature of the relationship is positive as higher levels of previous exposure are associated with higher levels of performance. The size of the effect of previous exposure, which reflects the strength of the relationship, is the same as the effect size of teaching method. Computer groups scored 10 percent higher on exams than did lecture groups, regardless of previous exposure, and students with more previous exposure scored 10 percent higher than those with none, regardless of the teaching method.

If we used statistical control with our other example of research on reactions to recruitment advertising, we would ask audience members to state their age. The answers could then be used to determine whether age is indeed related to recall of advertising themes and to the inclination to enlist, as we suspected.

Statistical control not only provides additional information about the confounding variables, but also it has some real advantages over manipulated control in external validity. External validity is improved, because the confounding variables are allowed to vary naturally, as they would in the real world. In our computer-based instruction experiment, we don't need to guess whether any relationship we find holds for students with different levels of previous exposure because we have the answer in front of us in numerical form. We can see that the results generalize to students with different levels of previous exposure.

Internal validity is not compromised to achieve this advantage. We have still accounted for the effect of the confounding variable, so we will not confuse the effect of previous exposure with the effect of teaching method.

In general, statistical control provides much more information about our research problem than does manipulated control. But most advantages in one area usually have a cost in another, and this is no exception. An obvious large drawback of the method lies in the increased complexity of the measurement and statistical analysis which will result from the introduction of larger numbers of variables.

Randomization

The third method of controlling for confounding variables is to randomly assign the units of analysis (research subjects) to research groups or conditions. The rationale for this approach is quite straightforward: Any confounding variables will have their effects spread evenly across all groups, and so they will not produce any consistent effects that can be confused with the effect of the independent variable. This is not to say that the confounding variables produce *no* effects in the dependent variable—they do. But the effects are approximately equal for all groups, so the confounding variables produce *no systematic* effects on the dependent variable.

This can be easily illustrated by using some numbers. Assume that 100 students are to be assigned to the two teaching conditions in our teaching methods experiment. Of these 100 students, 50 have never taken a course in the same area before; the other 50 have taken at least one course. In order to assign students to one of the two conditions we are going to flip a coin: tails, to the computer-based group; heads, to the lecture hall. If a student stands before the experimenter waiting for the coin to be flipped, he or she has a 50 percent chance of going into the computer-based group and a 50 percent chance of attending lectures. Now, if the coin flipping experiment works perfectly, 50 students will be assigned to each of the two groups (because heads will occur just as frequently as tails). Because each student assigned to a group is just as likely to have had some previous exposure as to have had no previous exposure, we would expect half of the 50 students in each group to have had some exposure and the other half to have had none. The conditions are balanced, and prior exposure will have the same effect on the performance of both groups, so it will not be confused with the effect of teaching method.

Randomization techniques are also used in nonexperimental, or observational research (research in which the values of the independent variable are only observed by the experimenter, and are not manipulated), but not to the same extent as in experimental research. In telephone interviewing, for instance, once a number has been reached, we may flip a coin to decide whether we should talk to the male or female head of the household. If we did not do this, we would be likely to interview more females than males, since women tend to answer the phone more often than men in most households. This would introduce a systematic bias in the information we obtain. Flipping the coin introduces a random element that removes systematic effects of unmeasured confounding variables like the gender of the respondent.

The key difference between randomization and the other two techniques is that randomization does not involve identifying or measuring the confounding variables. If we use manipulated control, we must identify and measure the level of the confounding variable in order to hold it constant or ensure that it is matched across groups. Statistical control likewise requires explicit measurement of the confounding variable. But randomization works for *all* variables which are related to the relevant variables, as it will equalize all systematic covariation. Randomization is the only control method in which all confounding variables are controlled, without our even having to be aware of them.

Let's look at our computer-based instruction experiment again. Since the same effects of any confounding variable are represented in the two experimental groups in the same proportions, we know that any effect of the confounding variables will be the same in both experimental conditions. Consequently, any difference in performance observed between the two experimental groups is due only to differences in teaching method. Since half the students have some previous exposure, they will score an average of 95 in the computer group and 85 in the lecture group. But half of each of these groups will also be made up of students with no previous exposure, who will score 85 and 75, respectively (10 percent lower, due to the effect of previous exposure). So the average score for the computer group will be the average of 25 students who score 95 and 25 students who score 85, for an overall average score of 90. The overall average score for the lecture group will be the average of 25 students who score 85 and another 25 who score 75, or 80, as is illustrated in Table 4-1.

The major advantage of randomization is that we can assume that all confounding variables have been controlled. Even if we fail to identify all the confounding variables, we will still control for their effects. As these confounding variables are allowed to vary naturally, as they would in the real world, external validity is high for this method of control.

It might appear that randomization also results in high internal validity, but randomization is actually the weakest of the three control methods in this regard. This is the result of an assumption that we are forced to make. Since we don't actually measure the confounding variables, we assume that randomization produces identical effects from *all* confounding variables in all groups, and that this thus removes any systematic confounding effects of these variables.

But any random process will result in disproportionate outcomes occasionally. If we flip a coin 100 times, we will not always see exactly 50 heads and 50 tails. Sometimes we will get 60 heads and 40 tails, or even 70 tails and 30 heads. (We'll cover this in more detail in the next chapter.)

Consequently, we have no way of knowing with absolute certainty that the randomization control procedure has actually distributed identically the effects of all confounding variables. We trust that it did, even though it might not have. By pure chance alone, the coin flip may have placed more students with prior exposure in the computer group of our experiment, for example. If this happened, the confounding variable will exert a systematic influence on the dependent variable of performance. This situation gives us a weaker confidence in the internal validity of our results. With manipulated control and statistical control, we can be completely confident that the effects of the confounding variables have been distributed so that no systematic influence can occur, because we can observe the confounding variable directly. There is no blind chance involved.

A further disadvantage of randomization is that it produces very little information about the action of any confounding variables. We assume that we have controlled for any effects of these variables, but we don't know what the variables are, or the size of their effects, if, in fact, there are any. As we'll see in Chapter 12, this lack of information makes our hypothesis test more difficult. The general problem is this: We assume that we've eliminated the *systematic* effects of the confounding variables by ensuring that these effects are distributed across all values of the relevant variables. But we have not actually measured or *removed* these effects—the confounding variables will still produce change in the relevant variables. This makes it harder for us to observe the true covariance between the variables in the hypothesis test, since chance processes may not have distributed the effects of the confounding variable equally, and the size of the confounding effects may obscure the real effects of the independent variable.

Summary

Most communication phenomena have more than one cause for any single effect. This means that more than one cause variable is usually involved in determining the level of any dependent (effect) variable. However, we are usually interested in describing the effect of a single cause variable isolated from other confounding variables. If we blindly test for a relationship between a cause and an effect variable without controlling for the effects of the other cause variables which also affect the dependent variable, we will probably reach the wrong conclusions about the nature and strength of the true relationship. We must control for the effects of *all* variables which produce changes in the dependent variable before we can accurately describe the relationship between any one of these variables and the dependent variable.

There are three methods to control for confounding cause variables. The researcher may measure the levels of the confounding variables and design research so that the confounding variables are held constant. This is *manipulated control.* Alternatively, one might measure the variables and use mathematical manipulations to remove their effects from the estimate of the true relationship between the independent variable and the dependent variable. This is *statistical control.* Finally, one can use research procedures to ensure that the effects of all confounding variables are randomly distributed across all levels of the independent variable. This is *randomization control.*

Each of these control methods has advantages and disadvantages when we consider the internal validity, external validity, and amount of information about the controlled variables that the method produces.

Studies with high *internal validity* are those in which we can be sure that the true relationships between the independent and dependent variables are not obscured by the confounding variables. Manipulated and statistical control give high internal validity, while randomization control is a bit weaker. However, randomization control has a distinct advantage over the other methods because the confounding variables do not have to be described or measured.

Studies with high *external validity* are those in which the results can be correctly generalized to the external world. Manipulated control is weak in external validity, while statistical control and randomization control give good external validity.

Statistical control produces additional information about the size of the effects of the confounding variables on the dependent variable. The other methods do not provide this information.

Balancing the various advantages and disadvantages of these three methods for controlling for confounding variables means that the researcher must be very clear about the questions the research is to answer. Is internal validity more important than external validity? Can the confounding variables be identified and measured? Is information about the relationship between the confounding variables and the dependent variable useful? Like most decisions, the choice of control is a trade-off, with costs and benefits associated with each method.

References and Additional Readings

Campbell, D. T. & Stanley, J. C. (1963). *Experimental and quasi-experimental designs for research.* Boston: Houghton Mifflin.

Cook, T. D. & Campbell, D. T. (1979). *Quasi-experimentation: Design and analysis issues for field settings.* Chicago: Rand-McNally (Chapter 9, "The Conduct of Randomized Experiments").

Kish, L. (1987). *Statistical design for research.* New York: Wiley (Chapter 1, "Representation, Randomization, and Realism").

$Chapter$ 5

Populations and Samples: The Principle of Generalization

The remaining major component of the scientific method to be discussed is the process of scientific or statistical generalization. Generalization is a very common human process. We all draw conclusions about reality from a limited amount of experience. This saves us effort, but it can mislead us, because our experiences may be so limited or selective that the conclusions drawn from them are quite wrong. If I purchase an automobile that breaks down frequently, I might tell all my friends that "all Belchfires are pieces of junk." But maybe only *my* Belchfire is a piece of junk, and all the others are very high quality. Another person may have a wonderful experience with a Belchfire and conclude that Belchfires are the finest automobiles made.

As anyone who has participated in a wine tasting will tell you, you pronounce a wine to be dry, oaky, acid, or fruity on the basis of a single sip. And when you make such a statement, you are not really talking only about that sip (a limited observation), but your pronouncements are really about the remaining untasted wine in the bottle (and perhaps, all the other bottles of the same type produced by that vineyard that year). In a similar vein we can look at dating. It starts with limited observation (spending a few evenings at the movies, going to parties, perhaps studying together), which is followed by a decision to either continue seeing this person or to break off the relationship. The decision is based on (and reflects) a generalization from the limited past experiences with this person to what future and unobserved experiences with him or her would be like. And who has not watched the first five minutes or so of a situation comedy, only to turn it off, vowing never to tune in again?

Each of these examples relies on the judgment of a single individual, using whatever criteria the person deems appropriate. In contrast, science uses mathematics and statistics to standardize the generalization process, and provide some ways to describe the trustworthiness of a generalization. The same rules of observation and decision are used by different individuals, so the process does not depend on the whims of any individual. As we've mentioned before, scientific truth must be objective and capable of being shared among the whole scientific community. Statistical generalization provides this common ground for agreement.

Statistical generalization is the process where the scientist takes his or her conclusions, which are based on the observation of a limited number of cases, and extends these conclusions to cover all the other unobserved cases that fit in the same category. The set of limited observations is called the *sample* and the total number of cases is the *population* or *universe*.

Generalization is very much a part of all science, including communication science. Political polling organizations interview relatively small samples of eligible voters in order to find out what the political preferences of the voting public are, or how a particular candidate is faring. The A. C. Nielsen Company relies on observing the TV viewing behaviors of a small number of households to make statements about what the entire audience is viewing. Detroit auto manufacturers pull a small number of cars off the assembly line and test them to get a measure of the quality of all the cars produced during a particular time period.

Advantages and Disadvantages of Generalization

Why do we generalize? Probably the best reason we can give is that it is efficient. It saves us a lot of time, effort, and money. Look at the examples above in the light of efficiency. Perhaps political pollsters would really like to interview every registered voter and ask each one how he or she feels about a particular candidate, and for whom he or she plans to vote in the next presidential election. However, the amount of time and money required to carry out such a task would be enormous. Furthermore, the information obtained would probably be useless by the time it was available. Suppose that a candidate for political office is interested in finding out whether a change in political advertising strategy is necessary in the remaining two weeks before an election. Spending a couple of days interviewing a sample of prospective voters will yield an answer quickly enough so that changes can be made before the election. It is highly doubtful that a canvass of all prospective voters could yield the needed information in time. Similarly, before we could ask all television households in the United States about the shows that they watch, the current television season would be long past.

However, there are also other reasons for generalizing to a large group from a smaller number of observations, such as the lack of an alternative. To determine how long light bulbs really last, a bulb manufacturer chooses a selection of bulbs from a particular production run, and measures the number of hours each bulb lasts before it burns out. The average lifetime of the tested bulbs then will be ascribed to the remaining untested bulbs in the same production run. In this case, the manufacturer generalizes because there is no alternative. To test the entire set of products would leave nothing to sell. This illustrates another reason for generalizing from a limited sample to a full population: Sometimes the process of observation is destructive of the actual cases being observed. Fortunately, this is infrequently the case in communication research, although the research process can sometimes disrupt the very phenomenon that is being studied (see Chapter 13).

The above examples point out the advantages of studying only a limited number of cases and generalizing to the others. But there are also problems introduced by generalization.

One problem lies in generalizing from a limited set of observations to the larger set, when the limited set is not representative of the larger set. A sip of wine from a bottle that has been exposed to heat and sunlight would provide a taste experience which might not be representative of an entire production run. To interview only middle-class males about their family communication patterns will yield an inaccurate picture of the communication patterns of the entire population. To generalize from any sample which is not representative will usually result in an incorrect characterization of the population.

What do we mean by representative? Basically, that all the characteristics in a sample drawn from a population are present in the same proportion as they are in the original population. If the population of the United States is 52 percent female, the proportion of females in a national sample should be approximately 52 percent. Likewise, if 10 percent of the population is below the poverty level, 10 percent of the sample should also fall in ' this region, and so forth for every other relevant characteristic of the population.

For the average person acting as a naive scientist, the problem of the representativeness of observations is often not a particularly pressing one. Also, it may be very difficult to determine whether a set of observations is indeed representative. However, to the scientist the problem of representativeness is a key problem. Consequently the scientific method contains a number of prescriptions for selecting cases for observation which helps assure representative samples.

Samples and Populations

As we've seen, a scientist formulates a theory about a phenomenon and uses it to generate specific hypotheses. For instance, he or she may predict that personal income increases are associated with increases in newspaper readership, or that female gender is associated with greater sensitivity to nonverbal cues, or that increases in environmental uncertainty is associated with decreased centralization of communication in organizations. In formulating these predictions, the scientist is implicitly stating that the predictions made by the hypothesis will hold for all members of the population, not just for the sample being observed to test the hypothesis. That is, the predictions are general statements.

To be totally confident that any findings are really general statements about the population, we would have to inspect the entire population. We would have to say that all males were tested for nonverbal sensitivity, as were all females, and that the predicted difference indeed held up; that income and readership were measured in all newspaper subscribing households, etc. If we look at every case in the population, we can be completely confident that we've described the relationships correctly.

But this is usually impossible. It is obvious that a scientist will hardly ever be in a situation where the whole population can be scrutinized. We will never be able to contrast all the males in the United States to all the females, or, for that matter, to ask every registered voter who his or her favorite candidate for the presidency is. Since hypotheses generally cannot be tested on populations, the scientist has to be content with selecting a subset from the population. The hypotheses can then be tested on this subset from the population and the results of the test generalized to the population.

Such a subset is the sample. It is considered to be representative of the population. Notice we did not say that the sample actually *is* representative of the population, merely that it is *thought* to be so. It must be selected in such a way that any conclusions drawn from studying the sample can be generalized.

The scientist is fully aware that generalizations to the population will be made, and that is why it is so critical that the scientist follow certain rules to assure that the sample on which the test was carried out can be considered to be representative of the population. These rules have been devised to prevent biases from creeping in. The introduction of any biases would make samples unrepresentative, and the conclusions not generalizable.

Sample Bias

There are two major sources of sample bias: *selection bias* and *response bias*. Selection bias is introduced by the actions of the researcher; response bias is introduced by the actions of the units (such as individuals) being sampled.

Selection Bias

This type of bias is introduced when some potential observations from the population are excluded from the sample by some systematic means. For example, if we were to carry out research on political information seeking by conducting in-house interviews, we might be tempted to systematically avoid those houses with "Insured by Smith & Wesson" signs, houses at the end of long muddy driveways, apartments on the fourth floor of rickety tenement buildings, and all the haunted-looking houses on Elm Street. By avoiding these places we would be selecting nice, reliable-looking houses, probably inhabited by nice, reliable people (like us, incidentally). As nice as this sample might be, it's probably not very representative of the population of voting citizens. If we try to generalize the conclusions of hypothesis tests from this sample to the whole population, we're probably going to be wrong.

To be a bit formal, a sample contains selection bias whenever each unit in the population does not have an equal probability of being chosen for the sample. The idea of having an equal probability of selection for all units in the population is called the *equal likelihood principle*.

Response Bias

Response bias is difficult to avoid. It occurs when the cases chosen for inclusion in the sample systematically exclude themselves from participation in the research. For instance, in studying the relationship between the kinds of job rules in an organization and certain aspects of subordinate-superior communication, we will need to observe a large number of organizations. But it is quite likely that those organizations which consent to having employees interviewed are different in many respects (other than cooperativeness) from those organizations which decline to participate. These differences may affect the hypothesis being tested. After all, those companies that consented to have interviewers come in may have done so because they have no serious organizational problems. If we assume that other companies may have turned us down because they have problems which they don't want to air, then we see the potential for error. In our biased sample we may find that the imposition of restrictive job rules does not affect the amount of superior-subordinate communication. But in the unobserved organizations, more job rules may lead to decreased communication. To generalize to all organizations from our biased sample will simply yield the wrong conclusions.

Randomization

Sample bias can result from either the action of the scientist (selection bias) or from the units of the sample (response bias). The scientist must take steps to avoid both types of bias, so that the study results can be safely generalized to the population. The rules the scientist must follow in drawing samples are designed to counteract or defuse the often unconscious tendencies to select or overlook certain observations in favor of others (selection biases), or to detect and deliberately compensate for response biases.

The method of avoiding selection bias is quite simple: Base the selection process on pure chance. This process is called *random sampling*. Randomness can be defined as the inability to predict outcomes. If we select street addresses by pulling street names and house numbers out of a hat containing all street names and numbers, we'll not be able to predict which houses will be selected for our sample. Further, each house will have exactly the same probability of being selected, which satisfies the equal likelihood principle. It then follows that we will not be able to predict whether any person selected in our political information seeking study is a nice, middle-class person or is a member of some other socioeconomic class. All socioeconomic classes should therefore be represented in the sample in their correct proportions, rather than being systematically excluded. The final sample should then have nonmiddle-class observations proportional to the number of nonmiddle-class persons in the population, and we can safely generalize our findings to the whole population.

Unfortunately, random selection will not help us avoid response bias. We can select the sample randomly, but if respondents eliminate themselves, the result is a biased sample. But there are a number of techniques to detect response bias and to compensate somewhat for it. In general, sample bias is estimated by comparing known characteristics of the population, such as age and income levels obtained from the U. S. census, to the same variables measured in the sample. If these values are highly discrepant, then the sample is probably biased. This bias can be partially overcome by sampling techniques like oversampling (deliberately selecting additional cases similar in the known characteristics to those who refused to respond) and weighting (treating some observations as more important than others). These techniques violate the equal likelihood principle, but they do so in a way that partially compensates for known sample biases. In essence, they introduce a canceling bias that produces a final sample that is closer to one which adheres to the equal likelihood principle. Oversampling and weighting are covered in more detail in the next chapter.

**TABLE 5-1   Actual Number of Conversations
Between Mother and Child**

Mother A: 5
Mother B: 6
Mother C: 7
Mother D: 8
Mother E: 9

Sampling Error

Even an unbiased sample can be less than a completely accurate representation of the population. The degree to which the value of an estimate calculated from the sample deviates from the actual population value is called *sampling error*. If we select observations for a sample randomly, we still might get an unrepresentative sample by simple bad luck, just as we might draw ten consecutive losing hands at blackjack. It's improbable, but it can happen. For example, even if we choose house addresses randomly, we might get all middle-class households. This is improbable, but it's possible.

It is important to understand that the error in an unbiased sample is qualitatively different from the error in a biased sample. Sampling error in an unbiased sample is not systematic, and it becomes less and less with each additional observation added to the sample, as it's less and less likely that we'll continue to pick improbable units, and more and more likely that we'll pick units which cancel out the error in our previous observations (we'll talk more about this below). If we continue to add house addresses to our political information sample, it is increasingly unlikely that the sample will include only middle-class families.

Sampling error is not systematic, that is, it is random. This means that we are just as likely to make too high estimates as we are to make too low estimates. This makes sampling error different from sample bias, where the estimates will always be systematically too high or too low. If we draw a number of biased samples from a population, we will always tend to get an estimate that is systematically too high or too low. But if we draw a number of unbiased samples, the sample estimates will be about equally spread between too high and too low ones.

An Illustration of Sampling Error

One of the best ways of illustrating the concept of sampling error is through a simple numerical example.

To keep the example simple, let us assume that we have a population with only five persons, all mothers of school-aged children. We are going to use samples to estimate the number of conversations about schoolwork these mothers have had, on the average, with their children in the past week, and generalize this sample estimate to the entire population. The actual number of conversations each person has had in the past week is shown in Table 5-1.

One way to describe the communication about schoolwork that occurs in this population is to compute the average of these five scores to provide a single index that characterizes the population as a whole, without enumerating all the individual cases as in

TABLE 5-2   All Possible Samples of $N = 2$ and Their Associated Means

Sample Values	$\overline{X}$	Sample Values	$\overline{X}$	Sample Values	$\overline{X}$	Sample Values	$\overline{X}$	Sample Values	$\overline{X}$
5, 5	5.0	6, 5	5.5	7, 5	6.0	8, 5	6.5	9, 5	7.0
5, 6	5.5	6, 6	6.0	7, 6	6.5	8, 6	7.0	9, 6	7.5
5, 7	6.0	6, 7	6.5	7, 7	7.0	8, 7	7.5	9, 7	8.0
5, 8	6.5	6, 8	7.0	7, 8	7.5	8, 8	8.0	9, 8	8.5
5, 9	7.0	6, 9	7.5	7, 9	8.0	8, 9	8.5	9, 9	9.0

Sampling with replacement from a population consisting of the values 5, 6, 7, 8, and 9 (see Table 5-1).

Table 5-1. We'll call this average M, short for mean. Its value is:

$$M = (5 + 6 + 7 + 8 + 9)/5 = 7.00$$

The "average" member of the population talks about schoolwork with her child seven times per week.

Now let us take all the possible samples of two individuals ($N = 2$) from this population. We'll do this in a special way called "sampling with replacement." We randomly select the unit to measure, then we replace that unit in the population before we select the next unit. Why would we do this? Because each unit must have an identical probability of being selected for the sample—the equal likelihood principle. Since we have five cases in the population, each case has a chance of selection of one out of five, or 20 percent.

If we select one case and don't replace it in the population, the chance of any of the remaining four being selected into the sample is now one out of four, or 25 percent. This violates the equal likelihood principle of random sampling, because the probabilities of being selected into the sample are not the same for all the units in the population. By returning any unit to the population before choosing the next unit to observe, the odds of any unit (including the one chosen in the first observation) being chosen for the second observation in the sample then remains at one out of five, or 20 percent.

This kind of sampling is almost never done in communication research. Normally our population is so large that the probability differences between sampling with replacement and without replacement (where any unit chosen in the sample is not eligible for later inclusion in the sample) are trivial. For example, if our population is 10,000, the first observation has a probability of being chosen of $\frac{1}{10,000}$ or .0001000. The probability of any of the remaining units being chosen next is $\frac{1}{9999}$ or .00010001, which is very close to the same probability as the first observation. Such small violations of equal likelihood do not bias the sample to any important extent. But with a small population, like the one in this example, we have to sample with replacement, or the sample will be seriously biased.

Choosing all possible samples of two observations from the population of five gives us the values for mean conversations per week shown in Table 5-2. Notice that in this table we use the symbol $\overline{X}$ to represent the mean of the variable for a sample.

TABLE 5-3   Means and Their Frequencies of Observation for All Possible Samples of $N = 2$

	$\overline{X}$	Frequency	Proportion
	5.0	1	1/25 = .04
	5.5	2	2/25 = .08
	6.0	3	3/25 = .12
	6.5	4	4/25 = .16
True Population Mean →	7.0	5	5/25 = .20
	7.5	4	4/25 = .16
	8.0	3	3/25 = .12
	8.5	2	2/25 = .08
	9.0	1	1/25 = .04
		25	1.00

Values taken from a population consisting of the values 5, 6, 7, 8, and 9 (see Tables 5-1 and 5-2).

Notice that our sampling procedure generates 25 different samples, but it generates fewer than 25 different means. If you look closely at Table 5-2, you'll see that only nine different values of the mean were observed. These means and the number of times that each was generated are presented in Table 5-3. This table is important. If we select observations randomly, then we are equally likely to see any one of the pairs of values in Table 5-2. But five of the 25 combinations (20 percent) have a mean of 7.0, 16 percent have means of 6.5 and 7.5, and so on. That means that if we draw any sample of $N = 2$ from the population, the most probable value which we are likely to get from the sample is 7.0, which is exactly the population mean! That's just what we want from a sample, since if we generalize that value to the population, we'll be exactly right. Furthermore, if we get (by chance) one of the next most probable values (6.5 or 7.5), we'll be in error by only .5 conversations per week. The further the estimated sample value is from the true population value (in other words, the more it is in error), the less likely we are to observe it when we randomly select a sample.

Put another way, small under- or overestimates occur more frequently than large under- or overestimates. That is, when we sample randomly we are more likely to obtain samples that are representative of the population (or close to it) than we are to get samples that are less representative. The odds are with us. But samples that are not representative of the population (ones with substantial sampling error) nonetheless *do* occur, and we can't discount them totally.

There are other important patterns in Tables 5-2 and 5-3. First of all, the observed sample means are just as likely to overestimate the true population mean as they are to underestimate it. Sample means of 5.0, 5.5, 6.0, and 6.5 all underestimate the population mean; in the aggregate they were found for ten combinations of two sampled observations (Table 5-2). The sample mean values 7.5, 8.0, 8.5, and 9.0 all overestimate the population mean of 7.0; they, too, occur ten times in total.

Second, overestimates and underestimates of the same magnitude occur with equal frequency. Consider the sample mean of 5.0, an underestimate of 2.0 (7.0 − 5.0). This sample mean occurs only once in the 25 combinations, so it will be seen only 4 percent of the time in a random sample of $N = 2$. A sample mean that overestimates by the same amount (the value 9.0, 2.0 conversations per week above the true population value) was also observed only once. Similarly, overestimates of .5 (means of 7.5) and underestimates of the same size (means of 6.5) each will occur four times, or in 16 percent of the random samples; under- and overestimates of 1.0 will each occur 12 percent of the time, and so on.

The third observation, which follows naturally from the first two, is that all the overestimates and underestimates cancel one another, so that across a large number of samples we can obtain an accurate estimate of the population value of any variable. If we keep sampling, we'll tend to get a better picture of the population.

The ideas contained in this simple example are fundamental and can be expressed in very elegant mathematical proofs. But, for our purposes, it's enough to remember these simple principles: Although there is error associated with the process of random sampling, the *most likely* sample value which we will obtain is the correct population value. And the more observations we make, the more likely we are to arrive at (or near) this value. The value obtained from a random sample is unbiased, as one cannot predict whether error is likely to be above or below the population value, and so we will not systematically under- or overestimate the true population value. We can thus use the sample value to generalize to the population in an unbiased way.

But the above example assumes that we have not introduced any sample bias during our sampling procedures. Sample biases produce systematic errors in our estimates. The following example shows what happens when the sample is biased.

An Example of Sample Bias

Using the same procedures as we did in the previous example, we will introduce a rather severe form of bias in sampling: We will give Mother E no chance of being selected into the samples of $N = 2$ that will be drawn from the population. Perhaps those who spend large amounts of time discussing schoolwork with their children are too busy to cooperate with our interviewer, so response bias is introduced. Or perhaps our interviewer has interviewed professional women who have less time to interact with children, thus introducing a selection bias. In either case, the result is the same: the values 5, 6, 7, and 8 will each have a 1 in 4 chance of being included in the sample (25 percent), and the value 9 will have no probability of being included (0 percent).

Table 5-4 contains all the different samples and sample means we obtain when we sample with this bias. This table differs from the one presented in Table 5-2 only by the elimination of any sample which contains the value 9.

Only 16 different combinations of values are observed now. The resulting distribution of sample means and the frequency with which they are obtained is shown in Table 5-5.

If we contrast the pattern of sample means we observed while sampling with a bias (Table 5-4) to the pattern of those found in an unbiased sample (Table 5-2), an important difference emerges.

TABLE 5-4   All Possible Biased Samples of $N = 2$ and Their Associated Means

Sample Values	$\overline{X}$	Sample Values	$\overline{X}$	Sample Values	$\overline{X}$	Sample Values	$\overline{X}$
5, 5	5.0	6, 5	5.5	7, 5	6.0	8, 5	6.5
5, 6	5.5	6, 6	6.0	7, 6	6.5	8, 6	7.0
5, 7	6.0	6, 7	6.5	7, 7	7.0	8, 7	7.5
5, 8	6.5	6, 8	7.0	7, 8	7.5	8, 8	8.0

Values and their associated means computed when sampling with replacement from a population consisting of the values 5, 6, 7, 8, and 9 with the value 9 (number of conversations for Mother E) excluded from the samples.

TABLE 5-5   Means and Their Frequencies of Observation from Biased Samples of $N = 2$

	$\overline{X}$	Frequency	Proportion
	5.0	1	1/16 = .0625
	5.5	2	2/16 = .1250
	6.0	3	3/16 = .1875
	6.5	4	4/16 = .2500
True Population Mean⟶	7.0	3	3/16 = .1875
	7.5	2	2/16 = .1250
	8.0	1	1/16 = .0625
		16	1.0000

The most probable value for the mean that we will likely find using such a biased sample is 6.5, and this is *not* the true population mean of 7.0. The observed sample means are also less likely to overestimate than they are to underestimate the true population mean. Sample means of 5.0, 5.5, 6.0, and 6.5 which underestimate the population mean are observed in 10 of the 16 samples. The only sample mean values that overestimate the population mean of 7.0 are 7.5 and 8.0, and together they occur only three times. For example, consider the sample mean of 5.0, which represents an underestimate of 2.0 (7.0 − 5.0). This sample mean was observed once. A sample mean which would have overestimated by the same amount (a sample mean of 9.0) was never observed. Overestimates and underestimates of the true population are not equal, and they do not cancel one another, even if a large number of samples are drawn. When we have a biased sample in which all the units in a population do not have an equal chance of being selected into a sample, overestimates will fail to cancel underestimates, and we will either consistently overestimate or underestimate the population characteristic being observed. Figure 5-1 shows this bias graphically.

This simple example illustrates the danger of generalizing from biased samples. If we generalize from this sample, we will probably make an incorrect statement about the number of conversations that the "average" mother has with her child. And drawing more

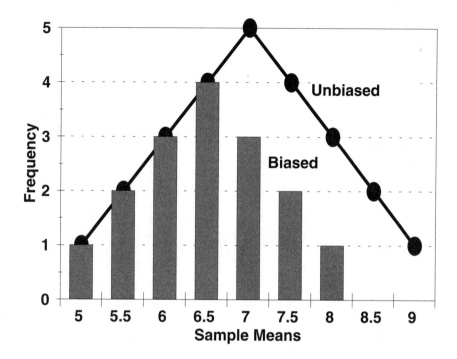

FIGURE 5-1   **Distributions of Means from Biased and Unbiased Random Sampling with All Possible $N = 2$ Samples**

samples will not help, as we will, for this example anyway, consistently underestimate the true population value. As long as bias is present, we will get incorrect results.

Sample Size

The last example in this chapter shows the effect of collecting more observations in a random sample. We've seen that a random sample without bias will tend to give the correct population value, but that most samples will probably contain some error in estimating this value. In Table 5-3, for example, we see that 80 percent of the samples will have some error in their estimate of the true population value. Since the name of the game is to obtain a sample with the least possible discrepancy between sample characteristics and population characteristics, we want to improve the accuracy of a sample by increasing the number of observations. We will carry out the same sampling process as before, except that now we will select unbiased samples of three observations ($N = 3$), rather than $N = 2$ as before.

If we look at Table 5-6, one of the consequences of increasing sample size is rather dramatically obvious: The number of different samples that can be obtained when we take samples of $N = 3$ has risen to 125, in contrast to the 25 different samples that are possible

TABLE 5-6   All Possible Samples of $N = 3$ and Their Associated Means

Sample Values	$\overline{X}$	Sample Values	$\overline{X}$	Sample Values	$\overline{X}$	Sample Values	$\overline{X}$	Sample Values	$\overline{X}$
5,5,5	5.00	5,6,5	5.33	5,7,5	5.66	5,8,5	6.00	5,9,5	6.33
5,5,6	5.33	5,6,6	5.66	5,7,6	6.00	5,8,6	6.33	5,9,6	6.66
5,5,7	5.66	5,6,7	6.00	5,7,7	6.33	5,8,7	6.66	5,9,7	7.00
5,5,8	6.00	5,6,8	6.33	5,7,8	6.66	5,8,8	7.00	5,9,8	7.33
5,5,9	6.33	5,6,9	6.66	5,7,9	7.00	5,8,9	7.33	5,9,9	7.66
6,5,5	5.33	6,6,5	5.66	6,7,5	6.00	6,8,5	6.33	6,9,5	6.66
6,5,6	5.66	6,6,6	6.00	6,7,6	6.33	6,8,6	6.66	6,9,6	7.00
6,5,7	6.00	6,6,7	6.33	6,7,7	6.66	6,8,7	7.00	6,9,7	7.33
6,5,8	6.33	6,6,8	6.66	6,7,8	7.00	6,8,8	7.33	6,9,8	7.66
6,5,9	6.66	6,6,9	7.00	6,7,9	7.33	6,8,9	7.66	6,9,9	8.00
7,5,5	5.66	7,6,5	6.00	7,7,5	6.33	7,8,5	6.66	7,9,5	7.00
7,5,6	6.00	7,6,6	6.33	7,7,6	6.66	7,8,6	7.00	7,9,6	7.33
7,5,7	6.33	7,6,7	6.66	7,7,7	7.00	7,8,7	7.33	7,9,7	7.66
7,5,8	6.66	7,6,8	7.00	7,7,8	7.33	7,8,8	7.66	7,9,8	8.00
7,5,9	7.00	7,6,9	7.33	7,7,9	7.66	7,8,9	8.00	7,9,9	8.33
8,5,5	6.00	8,6,5	6.33	8,7,5	6.66	8,8,5	7.00	8,9,5	7.33
8,5,6	6.33	8,6,6	6.66	8,7,6	7.00	8,8,6	7.33	8,9,6	7.66
8,5,7	6.66	8,6,7	7.00	8,7,7	7.33	8,8,7	7.66	8,9,7	8.00
8,5,8	7.00	8,6,8	7.33	8,7,8	7.66	8,8,8	8.00	8,9,8	8.33
8,5,9	7.33	8,6,9	7.66	8,7,9	8.00	8,8,9	8.33	8,9,9	8.66
9,5,5	6.33	9,6,5	6.66	9,7,5	7.00	9,8,5	7.33	9,9,5	7.66
9,5,6	6.66	9,6,6	7.00	9,7,6	7.33	9,8,6	7.66	9,9,6	8.00
9,5,7	7.00	9,6,7	7.33	9,7,7	7.66	9,8,7	8.00	9,9,7	8.33
9,5,8	7.33	9,6,8	7.66	9,7,8	8.00	9,8,8	8.33	9,9,8	8.66
9,5,9	7.66	9,6,9	8.00	9,7,9	8.33	9,8,9	8.66	9,9,9	9.00

Sampling with replacement from a population consisting of the values 5, 6, 7, 8, and 9.

when $N = 2$. But only 13 different sample means are obtained from these 125 samples. These sample means and the frequency with which they were observed are presented in Table 5-7.

To compare the accuracy of these samples of $N = 3$ with the $N = 2$ samples, we'll look at the percentage of means which come relatively close to the actual population value. For this example, let's look at means that fall within plus or minus 1.0 from the population mean of 7.0. The sample means that fall within this error bracket are, relatively speaking, close to the true population mean and reflect small amounts of sampling error. Those outside the bracket reflect more sampling error. The greater the proportion of means inside the bracket, the less the degree of sampling error.

As Table 5-8 shows, the proportion of sample means that fall within 1.0 of the true population mean is 76 percent when $N = 2$, and 84 percent when $N = 3$. Another way of stating this finding is this: If we were to take a sample of 2 observations from this

TABLE 5-7 Means and Their Frequencies of Observation for All Possible Samples of $N = 3$

	$\overline{X}$	Frequency	Proportion
	5.00	1	1/125 = .008
	5.33	3	3/125 = .024
	5.66	6	6/125 = .048
	6.00	10	10/125 = .08
	6.33	15	15/125 = .12
	6.66	18	18/125 = .144
True Population Mean ⟶	7.00	19	19/125 = .152
	7.33	18	18/125 = .144
	7.66	15	15/125 = .12
	8.00	10	10/125 = .08
	8.33	6	6/125 = .048
	8.66	3	3/125 = .024
	9.00	1	1/125 = .008
		125	1.000

Sampling with replacement from a population consisting of the values 5, 6, 7, 8, and 9.

TABLE 5-8 Effect of Sample Size on Sampling Error

$N = 2$		$N = 3$	
Means within ± 1.0 of Population Mean	Proportion	Means within ± 1.0 of Population Mean	Proportion
6.00	.12	6.00	.08
		6.33	.12
6.50	.16	6.66	.144
		7.00	.152
7.00	.20	7.33	.144
		7.66	.12
7.50	.16	8.00	.08
8.00	.12		
	.76		.84

population, we would have a 76 percent chance of getting an estimate that is within 1.0 of the true population value. If we increase the sample size to 3, the odds of observing a discrepancy of 1.0 or less improves to 84 percent. Looking at it negatively, when $N = 2$, we have a 24 percent chance of having sampling error greater than 1.0; when $N = 3$ this chance is reduced to 16 percent.

The general conclusion to be drawn from this exercise is that increased sample size is associated with decreases in sampling error. An increased sample size increases the representativeness of samples and makes generalization safer. Unfortunately, as we will see later, the relationship between sampling error and sample size is not a simple proportional one. As we increase the sample size more and more, we will always get improved accuracy, but the reductions in sampling error get smaller and smaller with each added observation. There are diminishing returns associated with adding observations to the sample, so there comes a point where it is not cost effective to add any more observations to a sample. We will also discuss ways to determine the appropriate sample sizes in Chapter 12.

Summary

The process of statistical generalization is an integral part of the scientific process. From a limited number of observations, called the *sample*, we extend conclusions to a whole *population*, which contains all the units which we could observe. We sample and generalize for reasons of cost efficiency, speed in obtaining information, or because our observations interfere with the phenomenon being studied.

Statistical generalization requires that samples be drawn in an unbiased fashion, or our conclusions will be in error. There are two types of bias against which the communication scientist must guard: *selection biases* in which each member of the population does not have an equal probability of being chosen for a sample; and *response biases* in which the member of the population chosen does not participate in the research. Both biases violate the *equal likelihood principle,* which requires that all members of the population have an identical probability of being included in the sample. To meet the equal likelihood principle, some random procedure for selecting samples is typically used.

Even with pure random selection, there is still *sampling error* to contend with. By chance alone, we may select an unrepresentative sample from the population. However, the probability of selecting unrepresentative samples goes down as the size of the sample is increased. Larger samples are less likely to contain large sampling errors than are smaller samples, as the error introduced by new observations will tend to cancel previously introduced error. However, larger sample sizes will not correct sample bias. Biased samples will give systematically incorrect results.

Only when we are confident that whatever we observe in the sample is also true for the population can we make reasonable generalizations. For this reason, the researcher must guard against sample biases, and include as many observations in the sample as is practically reasonable, in order to reduce sampling error.

References and Additional Readings

Cochran, W. G. (1983). *Planning and analysis of observational studies.* New York: Wiley (Chapter 2, "Statistical Induction").

Hogben, L. (1970). Statistical prudence and statistical inference. In D. E. Morrison & R. Henkel (Eds.) *The significance test controversy: A reader* (pp. 22–56). Chicago: Aldine.

Loether, H. J. & McTavish, D. G. (1974). *Inferential statistics for sociologists: An introduction.* Boston: Allyn & Bacon (Chapter 1, "Descriptive and Inferential Statistics").

Part II

Basic Tools of Research: Sampling, Measurement, Distributions, and Descriptive Statistics

*When you can measure what you are speaking about, and express it in numbers,
you know something about it; but when you cannot measure it, when you cannot
express it in numbers, your knowledge is of a meager and unsatisfactory kind:
it may be the beginning of knowledge, but you have scarcely, in your thoughts,
advanced to the stage of science.—WILLIAM THOMSON, LORD KELVIN
BRITISH PHYSICIST [1824–1927]*
POPULAR LECTURES AND ADDRESSES [1891–1894]

*Things added to things, as statistics, civil history, are inventories. Things used
as language are inexhaustibly attractive.—RALPH WALDO EMERSON
AMERICAN AUTHOR [1803–1882]*

*He uses statistics as a drunken man uses lampposts: for support rather than
illumination.—ANDREW LANG
SCOTTISH SCHOLAR AND POET [1844–1912]*

*All science is dominated by the idea of approximation.—BERTRAND RUSSELL
BRITISH PHILOSOPHER AND MATHEMATICIAN [1872–1970]*

*Numerical precision is the very soul of science.—MIGUEL DE UNAMUNO
SPANISH PHILOSOPHER [1864–1936]*
ON GROWTH AND FORM *(1917)*

*unless statistics lie he was more brave than me:more blond than you.
—e e cummings
AMERICAN POET [1894–1962]*
I SING OF OLAF GLAD AND BIG *(1935)*

Chapter 6

Sampling

As we saw in the previous chapter, statistical generalization requires a representative sample. In this chapter, we will look at some ways to construct such a sample. But first we must define some basic terms and ideas.

Basic Ideas

Population or Universe

A population is the full set of all the possible units of analysis. The population, also sometimes called the universe of observations, is defined by the researcher, and it determines the limits of statistical generalization.

Suppose you wish to study the impact of corporate image advertising in large corporations. You might define the unit of analysis as the corporation, and the population as "*Fortune* 500 Corporations" (a listing of the 500 largest corporations in the United States compiled by *Fortune* magazine). Any generalizations from your observations would be valid for these 500 corporations, but would not necessarily apply to any other corporations. Alternatively, you might define the universe as "*Fortune* 1000 Corporations." This includes the first 500, but expands the universe, and your generalizations, by adding an additional 500 corporations that are somewhat smaller.

When all the members of the population are explicitly identified, the resulting list is called a *sampling frame*. The sampling frame is a document that can be used with different selection procedures to create a subset of the population for study. This subset is the *sample*. A sampling frame for voters in a precinct would be the voter registration listing, for example.

The table of the 1000 largest corporations in *Fortune* magazine is the sampling frame for large corporations. Each entry on the sampling frame is called a *sampling unit*. It is one instance of the basic unit of analysis, like an individual or corporation. In our example, each corporation is a sampling unit of the population. By applying some choice procedure to get a smaller subset of units, we "draw a sample."

All observations of variables occur in the population. Each variable has one operational value for each observation. In our corporate advertising project, suppose we define "column inches of newspaper advertising last year" as a variable in the advertising study, when the population is defined as *Fortune* 1000 corporations. Then there will be exactly 1000 numbers (obtained from our operational definition of the theoretical concept) representing the universe of observations for this variable.

Census

If we actually measure the amount of advertising for each of 1000 corporations, we will be conducting a census of the variable. In a census, any statements about the variable (advertising column inches, in this case) are absolutely correct, assuming that the measurement of the variable is not in error. Suppose we conduct a census of image advertising done by *Fortune* 1000 corporations in two different years. To summarize the advertising done in each year, we calculate the average number of column inches of advertising done each year (by adding together all 1000 measurements for a year together, and dividing the sum by 1000). If this figure is 123.45 column inches for the first year and 122.22 column inches for the second year, we can say, *with perfect confidence*, that there was less image advertising done in the second year. The difference may be small, but it is trustworthy because all units (corporations) in the population are actually observed. Thus, when we examine every member of a population, any difference we observe is a real one (although it may be of trivial size).

Sampling

But you may not want to actually observe each unit in the population. Continuing with our example, suppose we only have time and resources to measure the advertising of 200 corporations. Which 200 do we choose? As we saw in Chapter 5, we need a representative sample if we want an unbiased estimate of the true values in the population, and a representative sample requires that each unit of the population have the same probability of being chosen. If you are unfamiliar with the idea of probability, see Exhibit 6-1.

We'll now examine several kinds of sampling, discuss the strengths and weaknesses of each, and describe the typical procedures used to draw the sample. Figure 6-1 on page 87 illustrates the relationships among population and types of samples.

What Are Random Choice Processes?

There are a number of ways of drawing a sample. The method chosen depends largely on the size and nature of the population, the existence of a sampling frame, and the resources of the researcher. But the basic requirement of a sample is outlined in Chapter 5: It must

EXHIBIT 6-1   Probability

Probability can be defined as the ratio of the frequency of a single outcome to the total number of possible outcomes. As an example, suppose we toss a coin. Two outcomes are possible: The coin comes up heads or tails. The probability of obtaining heads (one outcome) is the ratio of that single outcome to the two possible outcomes, or 1 : 2, or $\frac{1}{2}$, or .50, or 50 percent. If the coin is balanced, the probability of obtaining tails is exactly the same as that of obtaining heads—it is also .50.

If we roll a single die, six possible outcomes can occur: The spots can come up as 1, 2, 3, 4, 5, or 6. The probability associated with each individual outcome is therefore equal to $\frac{1}{6}$ or .1667.

In the simple examples above, each outcome has an identical probability of occurring (i.e., each has *equal likelihood*). The balanced physical structure of the coin or die does not favor heads over tails, or 1 over 6, or 2 over 5, and so on. But the individual probabilities within a set of outcomes are not always equal. Let's look at what happens when you throw two dice. Since each die can come up with 1 to 6 spots showing, we have 11 sums that represent the outcome of throwing two dice: the numbers 2 (1 + 1), 3 (2 + 1), 4 (1 + 3 or 2 + 2), ...11, 12. But the probability of getting each number is not equal to $\frac{1}{11}$, since there are differing numbers of combinations of values of the dice that may produce a number. Table 6-1 shows all the combinations.

If you count the different combinations that the dice might show, you'll see that there are 36 unique pairs of values. Each of these pairs are equally probable, since they are the result of the action of two independent dice, each of which possess equally probable individual outcomes. Since each pair of numbers represents a unique outcome, we can divide the number of unique outcomes (1) by the total number of possible outcomes (36) to get the probability of any single pair of numbers.

But we can get this result more easily than listing all combinations. Let's consider a specific What is the probability of getting the pair that has a [3] on Die 1 and a [5] on Die 2? If we throw one die, we know the probability of getting a [3] is $\frac{1}{6}$. So, we will expect to have to throw the dice six times in order to get the first number of the pair on Die 1. If we

then consider Die 2, we will expect to get a [5] (or any other given number) only on one of every six throws. So it should take us 6 times 6, or 36 throws before we can expect Die 1 to come up [3] and Die 2 to come up [5]. This is the same probability ($\frac{1}{36}$) that we find if we list all possible combinations, but we can find it by simply multiplying two simple probabilities. This is called the *multiplicative rule* of probabilities, and it can be stated like this:

> *The probability of two independent events occurring jointly (i.e., within the same observation) is the product of the individual probabilities of each event.*

Using the multiplicative rule, we don't have to list all 36 pairs of outcomes to compute the probability of a particular outcome. We know the probability of Die 1 coming up [3] is $\frac{1}{6}$ and of Die 2 coming up [5] is $\frac{1}{6}$, so we can just compute:

$$\text{Prob of [3 \& 5]} = \frac{1}{6} \times \frac{1}{6} = \frac{1}{36}$$

We can use the multiplicative rule to compute other probabilities. For example, what is the probability of throwing four heads in a row with a coin?

$$\text{Prob [4 heads]} = \frac{1}{2} \times \frac{1}{2} \times \frac{1}{2} \times \frac{1}{2} = \frac{1}{16}$$

Now let's look at another question that can be answered by looking at Table 6-1: What is the probability of the sum of the dice being 5? If we look at the table, we see that there are four combinations of Die 1 and Die 2 values that sum to 5. Since there are 36 unique pairs of values, the probability of getting a sum of 5 is $\frac{4}{46}$, or $\frac{1}{9}$. We expect to get a sum of 5 about once in every nine throws of the two dice.

We can compute this another way by using the *additive rule* of probabilities. This rule states:

> *The probability that one of a set of independent outcomes will occur is the sum of the probabilities of each of the independent outcomes.*

Applying this rule to the simple question above, we get:

Continued

EXHIBIT 6-1   *Continued*

Table 6-1   Dice Combinations and Probabilities

Die 1	Die 2	Outcome (Sum of dice)	Number of Ways to Get This Number	Probability of Outcome
1	1	2	1	1/36 = .0278
1	2	3	2	2/36 = .0556
2	1			
1	3	4	3	3/36 = .0833
2	2			
3	1			
1	4	5	4	4/36 = .1111
2	3			
3	2			
4	1			
1	5	6	5	5/36 = .1389
2	4			
3	3			
4	2			
5	1			
1	6	7	6	6/36 = .1667
2	5			
3	4			
4	3			
5	2			
6	1			
2	6	8	5	5/36 = .1389
3	5			
4	4			
5	3			
6	2			
3	6	9	4	4/36 = .1111
4	5			
5	4			
6	3			
4	6	10	3	3/36 = .0833
5	5			
6	4			
5	6	11	2	2/36 = .0556
6	5			
6	6	12	1	1/36 = .0278
			36 combinations	36/36 1.0000

Continued

EXHIBIT 6-1 *Continued*

Prob[sum of 5] = Prob [1 & 4] + Prob [2 & 3] +
$$= \text{Prob } [3 \& 2] + \text{Prob } [4 \& 1]$$

$$= \frac{1}{36} + \frac{1}{36} + \frac{1}{36} + \frac{1}{36}$$

$$= \frac{4}{36} = \frac{1}{9}$$

Another example: "What is the probability of getting either a sum of 5 or a sum of 6?"

Prob[sum 5 or sum 6] = Prob[sum 5] + Prob[sum6]

$$= \frac{4}{36} + \frac{5}{36}$$

$$= \frac{9}{36} = \frac{1}{4}$$

Restated, we expect to get a sum of 5 or 6 about one-fourth of the time.

The rules can be combined to compute the probability of complex situations. For example, we might ask this question while we are constructing a sample: "What is the probability that a middle- or upper-middle-class female from Connecticut will be selected in a sample from the population of the entire United States?" From census figures we find that Connecticut has 2 percent of the U.S. population, that 52 percent of the U.S. population is female, that 40 percent of the population is middle-class and 20 percent is upper-middle-class.

Using the additive rule first, we compute:

Prob[middle or upper-middle] = .40 + .20 = .60

Stated in words, the probability that we will choose a middle- or upper-middle class person from the U.S. population (regardless of sex or state) is 60 percent.

Then using the multiplicative rule, we calculate the probability of selecting a female who is also from Connecticut:

Prob[Conn, female] = .02 .52 = .0104

Finally, combining the results to get the probability of selecting a middle- or upper-middle-class female from Connecticut, we get:

Prob of selection = .60 .0104 = .00624

If we select a sample of 1000 from the U.S. population, we would expect to find about 6 middle- or upper-middle-class females from Connecticut in it.

be unbiased. This means that the selection of units for the sample must be based on a process that is *random*.

But what is a random choice? It is common for the naive scientist to confuse *unsystematic* choices with *random* choices, and this is a serious error. In a random choice procedure, three conditions must hold:

1. Every unit in the population must have an equal probability of being chosen. This is the equal likelihood principle mentioned earlier. We'll call this the *chance* probability *p*. This requirement ensures that the sample will have (within the limits of sampling error, as described in Chapter 5) the same makeup as the population. If 52 percent of the population is female, the sample will have (again, within sampling error limits) 52 percent females.
2. There must be no way for an observer to predict which units are selected for the sample with any greater accuracy than the chance probability *p*. This is another way of saying that random choices are not predictable.
3. We must be able to draw a sample that includes every possible combination of units from the sampling frame, no matter how improbable the combination. This condition eliminates any bias that might result from the systematic exclusion of some units.

Rolling an honest die results in a number between 1 and 6 which cannot be predicted by having any knowledge of the dice thrower, the time of day, the results of previous dice

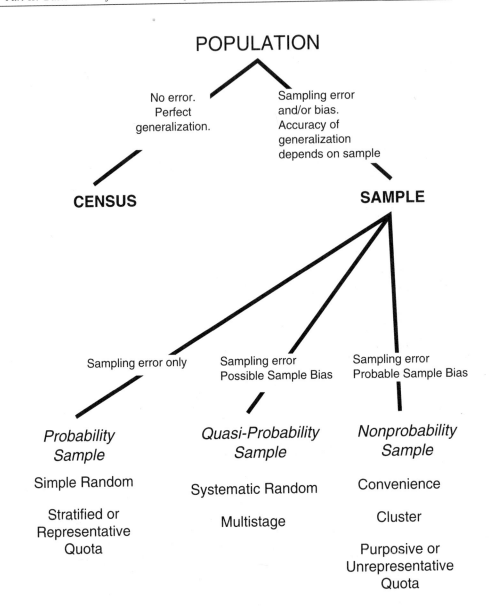

FIGURE 6-1   Types of Samples

throws, or the need of the dice thrower's children for new shoes. Each number between 1 and 6 will come up an approximately equal number of times if many throws are made, and any predictions made by an observer will be right only $\frac{1}{6}$ of the time (the chance probability).

But true random outcomes like this are hard to come by. Asking someone to think of a random number between 1 and 6 *will not* result in a random choice, for example. People will say "three" much more frequently than they will say "five" or "one." Thus an observer who always guesses "three" will be correct about 1 time in 6 when the outcome is determined by a throw of a die, but will be correct more often when a person determines the outcome. The observer's knowledge provides an edge in predicting the outcome, and this is never the case in a true random choice.

It is important to distinguish between haphazard or unsystematic choice processes and true random choice processes. Just because no systematic rule for selection is employed does not mean that a choice is random. If I walk down a mid-city street at noon, close my eyes, twirl around three times, point, then interview the person I've pointed to, I still have not collected a random sample of the general population. Persons on a downtown city street at noon are much more likely than average to be office workers rather than factory workers, to be adults rather than adolescents, to be middle-class and not receiving public assistance, and so on. In other words, three things about my sampling procedure conspire to make it non-random: first, every unit (person) does not have an equal chance of being selected—I've biased my sample toward selecting middle-class office workers; second, an observer can predict who will be selected at better than the chance probability by having knowledge of the choice procedure—the observer can predict that school children will not be selected, for instance; and third, by my choice of sampling locale, I have systematically excluded some combinations of persons in the sample, since certain persons in the population are not present on the street at the time of selection.

Aids for Drawing Random Samples

Random choice procedures involve some kind of process that generates unpredictable outcomes. Frequently these outcomes are in the form of random numbers, which are then used to designate the units in the population to be included in the sample. Units in the sampling frame are numbered, and then random numbers are used to select the units that are to be in the sample. Printed random number tables such as the one shown in Table 6-2 have been constructed which contain sequences of numbers that are truly unpredictable.

A random numbers table has sequences of numbers that have been shown to have no predictable structure, that is, to be just as unpredictable as if they were chosen from a hat. Even if all the numbers in the table except one are known, an observer will still not be able to predict the last number at any better than the chance probability level.

To use a random numbers table, some true random starting point is chosen (e.g., a row in the table equal to the current temperature and a column number equal to the sum of the digits in the researcher's birth date). Some systematic procedure for choosing entries in the table is also selected, such as every third entry in a column. It does not matter what procedure is chosen, as long as a different one is used each time the random numbers table is used. This is to avoid choosing identical sequences of numbers in different samples.

Mechanical procedures are also often used to make random selections. Some state lotteries use a number of balls that are carefully matched for size and weight so that no ball has any mechanical advantage in being chosen over any other ball. The balls are mixed up in a drum by a mechanical "stirrer," or by a jet of air. When a random choice is needed, one of the mixed balls is allowed to fall into a selection slot. There is no way to predict which ball will be nearest the slot when the choice is made, and as all balls are equally likely to be near the slot, the selection will be random.

Computers are also sometimes used to generate random numbers. This is actually difficult to do, since computers are constructed to give predictable results, not unpredictable ones. Good random number procedures for computers rely on some mechanical or electronic process for a random starting point. For example, the computer program might look at the computer system's clock when the request for a random choice is made. The milliseconds (a millisecond is $\frac{1}{1000}$ of a second) reading will spin between 000 and 999 each second, and the exact instant at which the computer program asks for the number is probably not predictable (at least to the nearest $\frac{1}{1000}$ of a second). This random "seed" is used to construct, via systematic mathematical procedures (which are *not* random), a random sequence of digits.

This is a general principle. Any procedure that starts with a true random choice will produce a random result, even if systematic procedures for selection are subsequently

TABLE 6-2   A Sample Random Numbers Table

TO USE THE TABLE:

1. Select a random row, by any means. For example, choose the row number closest to the current time in minutes past the hour. If this is larger than the row number at the bottom of the page, continue counting by going back to the top row.

2. Select a random column by a different means. For example, the number of seconds past the current minute.

3. Choose some arbitrary rule to select individual digits. Do not just read left to right. The intent is to get a different sequence of digits each time you use the table, even if your starting point is the same. As an example, you might choose every third digit from right to left, or you might go diagonally down the table left to right, then diagonally back across right to left, etc.

4. To create multidigit random numbers within a range, choose each digit sequentially from the table by the above procedure. If the resulting number is out of range, you should ignore it and select the next one, using the same rule. For example, if you wish to create random numbers between 01 and 50, first select the left-most digit. If it is 6–9, you can ignore it (as that would create a random number between 60 and 99, i.e., out of range). After selecting a valid left-most digit, select the right digit. If the resulting number is in range, write it down. If it is out of range (00 or 51, for example), ignore the whole number and start creating a new one.

Continued on page 91

NOTE: This table should not be used for serious research studies. It does not contain a sufficient number of random digits to ensure complete randomness. Use a larger random number table, such as those published in some standard volume, such as the Beyer *Basic Statistical Tables* (see References and Additional Readings at the end of this chapter).

TABLE 6-2 (Continued)

COLUMN	5	10	15	20	25	30	35	40	45	50
ROW	↓	↓	↓	↓	↓	↓	↓	↓	↓	↓
1-	81452	99891	74461	20636	79165	08583	39324	36228	37144	89726
2-	70303	19459	25002	28942	76839	48790	29530	47744	60002	10498
3-	52800	32227	95542	19916	84500	97239	88319	70443	88400	09684
4-	75197	18820	69546	57111	35268	55007	86339	77447	15530	21391
5-	91644	83953	90888	64999	61829	45781	88919	84238	80636	12637
6-	78834	17367	35169	80520	57512	45179	50177	69765	06604	58541
7-	20457	18141	59316	82368	64026	73218	96632	24768	21715	53400
8-	54564	46089	02584	01454	43725	50708	59875	08001	95823	52875
9-	39455	67007	78612	32439	25522	56210	59615	47484	92475	43489
10-	16483	98421	60059	30865	10106	71968	44899	50234	58560	23167
11-	43683	01213	76549	99609	44919	75226	57017	87094	52428	20723
12-	75722	69110	11929	13976	33486	61306	31004	71133	58490	29089
13-	00610	47034	17172	72154	04504	94336	45536	58072	45524	96408
14-	24693	60487	64372	73191	72793	03564	37212	16269	03874	26006
15-	30509	33920	45374	75079	13832	66671	33359	68053	20655	40137
16-	67518	55619	62840	64373	46406	42228	34913	11311	58687	10141
17-	21784	32628	17404	22605	00067	23884	42471	37624	08654	91083
18-	99133	10573	18060	45124	31698	41269	01075	91682	09936	78302
19-	92637	14268	93559	61023	25164	23112	97139	94092	24449	83049
20-	08479	59778	42341	76517	84435	91167	01190	89230	51149	39969
21-	41899	58160	09106	43882	58968	71042	35408	45162	84468	33744
22-	59263	22895	85536	00420	09297	08060	97074	22517	92059	71084
23-	93240	51332	87765	37420	53253	97080	82370	91507	61161	85543
24-	99241	57256	31396	59440	93464	49764	21613	99890	82405	61077
25-	16297	89781	83155	08817	26674	08373	89479	69881	77802	02122
26-	40886	56419	27746	60953	64457	22380	84703	04819	94568	51104
27-	17549	09217	20113	54701	71241	39117	07176	93911	81817	43462
28-	11476	00112	61831	33931	64446	72739	02924	76653	46506	32645
29-	85913	82007	93303	17369	94597	98964	61518	35242	12887	85278
30-	25694	32998	40794	60839	79324	14011	69236	51929	36371	75454
31-	82295	63810	02239	58034	58058	55555	93909	94947	93657	18799
32-	28883	91723	38991	88714	70219	28139	44669	05869	37983	60503
33-	46553	40760	65586	62802	58070	03224	19176	53216	86922	39646
34-	23889	85187	68597	98724	04891	27962	40263	40241	26395	17881
35-	50230	67824	04884	19372	82351	01321	40355	99086	91630	74552
36-	15038	79291	78888	56221	17443	73341	20216	47746	62091	90530
37-	33913	76152	57478	01053	63783	64188	01119	20000	66098	69944
38-	27000	91866	35019	16478	96227	28305	55606	27791	92231	35092
39-	64112	56357	16268	79742	18564	33724	60778	11856	68018	14424
40-	76210	67435	57131	61636	74110	64168	56437	10396	06431	85715
41-	89631	18109	91389	20564	96030	84372	49214	94226	70297	31352
42-	09271	90186	68422	50454	61260	01053	97246	81909	41355	90138
43-	16720	96078	24374	24427	05468	65022	53403	85957	72094	99232
44-	19135	22613	17057	54150	40203	05598	51308	29896	06817	93414
45-	67850	58840	27110	06140	41253	38904	44898	79765	14818	30841

used. That is the basis for using a random starting point in a printed random numbers table. Since the starting point is random, and the number sequences themselves are random, the resulting systematic selection still produces a random sequence of numbers.

Each entry chosen by a random procedure designates a unit in the sampling frame. For example, if we want to sample from the *Fortune* 500 companies, we could assign the numbers 1 to 500 to each company in the list. Then by choosing random numbers from a table, we can select companies to include in the sample. Numbers drawn from the table that are not used to label a unit in the sampling frame (numbers which are greater than 500, for example), are just discarded.

True Probability Samples

There are two types of true representative samples that meet the three requirements for a random choice: simple probability samples and stratified probability samples. The simple probability sample is the standard to which all other procedures must be compared.

Simple Probability Sample

If a sampling frame is available, drawing a representative probability sample is quite easy. You simply select units from the list by using some truly random process like a random numbers table or computer program, so that every entry on the list has exactly the same probability of being chosen. A clear example of a simple random probability sample is drawing a single name from a hat: the sampling frame (a list of names defining the universe) is torn up into equally sized slips of paper, placed in a hat, mixed up (randomized), and then a name is picked from the hat. All names have equal probability of being picked, and the mixing process ensures that no systematic bias in selecting a name enters. Once again, there is no way to predict whose name will be drawn. Any name can be chosen, and all names have the same chance probability of being drawn (1 divided by the number of names in the hat).

If no sampling frame is available, it is still sometimes possible to create a random probability sample. An example of this is *random digit telephone number sampling*. In this technique, a telephone number consisting of random digits is created, usually by a computer program. Many of the numbers created by the computer will not correspond to working numbers, but numbers that do work will all have an equal probability of being selected.

The penalty for not having a sampling frame of telephone numbers is the effort which is subsequently required to determine if the random telephone number is a legitimate part of the population. If the population is residential households, all unassigned numbers, business numbers, special service numbers (toll-free 800 numbers), and so on, must be eliminated. Some of these illegitimate numbers might be eliminated by restricting the geographic area being sampled to that served by a small set of known exchange prefixes (the first three digits of the number). A random digits computer program can then restrict its random selections to the known working prefixes for a particular city or state, for example. The program can also reject all known nonresidential numbers (555, 800, and

---

Simple Probability Sample

Strengths of this Type of Sample

A simple random sample will have no selection bias. Care should be taken to avoid response bias.

Very simple to draw, if the population is small and has an existing sampling frame.

Weaknesses of this Type of Sample

Time-consuming to use on large populations, even with a sampling frame, unless the sampling frame can be used with a computer program to automatically draw the sample.

Adds to data collection cost, if there is no sampling frame, as each potential unit must be screened to ensure that it is a member of the population.

Best Use

When there is a complete and accurate sampling frame.

When the sample can be drawn by computer program.

When sample bias is a critical issue and must be avoided, even at additional data collection cost.

Examples of Use

Experiments on student populations, where the sampling frame is an enrollment list.

Surveys that use commercial random digits dialing computer programs.

---

900 prefixes, for example). But interviewers are likely to have to screen the remaining numbers to determine if they are part of the population, and this adds to the cost of data collection.

On the positive side, random digit dialing will create unlisted numbers that do not appear in a telephone book. Using a telephone book as a sampling frame would result in a biased sample, since over one-third of the residential telephones in the United States are unlisted. There is a moral here: A bad sampling frame, like a telephone book, may produce serious bias, and it may be better to ignore it. If the sampling frame is clearly incomplete, as the telephone book is, it is better to use sampling procedures that do not require a sampling frame, even if they demand more effort.

If a choice of sampling procedures is available, a simple probability sample is almost always preferable, as it produces a true representative sample. If you remember, we defined external validity in Chapter 4 as our ability to generalize from the results of a research study to the real world. If our sample is biased, this will impair our ability to generalize. This is another argument for using true probability samples whenever possible. Any sampling method that produces bias reduces the external validity of our study.

Stratified or Known Quota Sample

If we draw a simple random probability sample, we expect to find that the characteristics of the sample are identical to those of the population. If 75 percent of the persons in the population are high school graduates, we will expect to find that about 75 percent of the persons in the simple probability sample will also be high school graduates. But we probably won't get *exactly* 75 percent in any single sample. Due to sampling error, we might get 72 percent or 81 percent high school graduates, just as we might throw a coin 10 times and get 7 heads and 3 tails, rather than the expected value of 5 heads and 5 tails.

If some particular characteristics are critical to our research, and if we have prior information about the proportion of the characteristic present in the population, we can take some steps to eliminate this sampling error. The information is used to guide the sample selection. If it is done properly, sample error can be reduced.

If we know the exact proportions of one or more characteristics of the population (i.e., we have prior census information about the population), we can sample so as to ensure that the exact proportions of the known characteristic are included in the sample. We do this by randomly sampling a known quota of units within defined strata, or categories, of the population. Each quota is proportional to the size of the stratum. In essence, each stratum becomes a subpopulation from which a simple probability sample is chosen.

For example, suppose we want to draw a probability sample of 100 undergraduates from a university for a study of the effect of professor-student communication patterns on student grades. Figures from the university records state that 65 percent of the students are majoring in liberal arts. We know, then, that a representative sample should include 65 liberal arts majors and 35 majors in other fields. So we begin by separating the registrar's student list (the sampling frame) into two strata: the liberal arts majors and the non-liberal arts majors. We then draw a random sample of 65 from the liberal arts stratum and another random sample of 35 from the non-liberal arts stratum.

The result is an unbiased sample in which there is no sampling error on the stratifying variable (academic major). The sample has exactly the same proportion of liberal arts/non-liberal arts majors as does the population. Of course, other unstratified variables in the sample are still subject to sampling error.

This procedure is somewhat more complicated to use when a sampling frame does not provide information about the stratifying variable. In general, we will have to get some information about the stratifying variable from each unit chosen for the sample, in order to place it in its correct stratum. To see how we might do this, let's go back to the example of a region that has 75 percent high school graduates, as described by the U. S. census figures. Assume that we wish to telephone interview a representative sample of 100 persons from this region. We will first generate a random probability sample by creating a set of random digit telephone numbers. Unfortunately, this list will tell us nothing about the educational status of each respondent (the strata), so we'll have to ask each respondent a *screening or qualifying question* about his or her high school graduation status, probably something like "are you a high school graduate?"

Suppose we randomly select and interview the first 90 persons in our hypothetical research study, recording each response to the screening question. At this stage of the study, we find that we have 25 high school nongraduates included in the sample. From this point on, we will not complete the interview with any respondents who indicate on the screening question that they have not graduated from high school. But we will keep interviewing all high school graduates until we have 75 included in the sample. At the end of the interviewing, we will have exactly 75 randomly chosen high school graduates and 25 randomly chosen nongraduates, just as if we had known their strata during the drawing of the sample.

Stratified or Known Quota Sample

Strengths of this Type of Sample

A stratified random sample will have no sampling bias. Care should be taken to avoid response bias. A stratified random sample will have no sampling error on the variable(s) used for stratifying.

Weaknesses of this Type of Sample

The sampling frame must have population information, or a set of screening questions must be added to assign each unit in the sample to its appropriate stratum.

Adds to data collection cost, as some selected units must be rejected from the sample if the quota for their stratum is full.

Best Use

When there is detailed information about the characteristics of the population.

When the cost of contacting and screening units for inclusion in the sample is low.

When sampling error is a critical issue and must be avoided, even at additional data collection cost.

Examples of Use

Political communication studies, where the proportions of membership in all parties are known from voter registration rolls.

Marketing communication studies, where the target consumer population is defined and can be stratified by sex, age, income, or other demographic variables.

Quasi-Probability Samples

Quasi-probability samples produce results that approximate those from a simple random sample, but they may contain some sample bias. These procedures should be chosen only when drawing a true probability sample is not practical.

Systematic Random Sample

This procedure is a variation of the simple random sampling procedure. It relies on the fact that any systematic choice procedure which begins with a random choice will produce a sample that is close to truly random. This procedure is often used when the sampling frame is very large, and numbering each entry would be too time consuming, or where sequential selection (from a computer tape, for example) is required. A systematic sample is not precisely random, as we'll see below, because certain combinations of units from the population cannot appear in any sample. In a true random sample, *any* combination of units might occur as a result of the random choice procedure.

Suppose you want to conduct a survey of political communication in a community that has 100,000 registered voters. The sampling frame can be defined as the voter registration list obtained from the city clerk's office. To draw a sample of 500 voters, you could just place a number next to each of the 100,000 names, use a random numbers table to construct 500 random numbers, then interview the 500 persons on the sampling frame who had the corresponding numbers next to their names. The result would be a simple probability sample.

The alternative to this time-consuming procedure is to draw a systematic random probability sample, by choosing a random starting point, then systematically selecting every kth entry in the sampling frame, as in the following example:

1. Since you wish to interview 500 of 100,000 voters, compute the proportion of the population that will be interviewed:

$$\text{Prop.} = \frac{500}{100,000} = \frac{1}{200}$$

2. If you interview every two-hundredth voter on the list, you will have a sample of the proper size. But you cannot just start with the first voter and interview every two-hundredth person, as all persons on the list will not have an equal probability of being chosen for the sample. (The first person has a probability of being included of 1.00, the second, third, fourth, etc., a probability of 0.00). Instead, use a random numbers table to create a random starting point between 1 and 199. Suppose the random number comes up 102.

3. Count down 102 persons on the list, and interview this person. Then count 200 more, interview that person, and then continue interviewing every two-hundredth person in the rest of the list. This would be very easy to do with a simple computer program if the voter registration list is stored as a sequential file on tape or disk. Even if the list is printed, you might measure the distance between 200 printed names, and then just measure the printed list to determine the sampled names (every 23 inches, for example), rather than counting each name.

This example illustrates the basics of a systematic random sample: a random starting point, followed by some systematic selection rule. The selection rule can be a simple one, as illustrated above, or it can be very complex. It does not matter as long as the starting point is truly random.

The resulting sample is quasi-random: Initially, each unit (person) in the population has the same probability of being chosen ($\frac{1}{100,000}$). But after the initial random starting point is selected, all 199 persons who fall between the sampling intervals have a zero probability of being chosen, while those at the sampling intervals have a 1.0 probability of being chosen. This can result in some sample bias (selection bias). No matter how many samples we draw from this population, we will never have a sample that includes persons whose names are closer to each other than 200 entries on the sampling frame. But a truly random sample might occasionally include two, three, or more persons from a block of 200 names, even though the most probable number of persons selected from this block would be one. The assumptions we make about statistical distributions (as will be explained further in Chapter 9) rely on the fact that we expect to observe these less probable samples a known percentage of the time. But when we use systematic random samples, we can never actually get these less probable samples, so our statistical assumptions are not entirely correct.

Systematic Random Sample

Strengths of this Type of Sample

Quick and easy to draw sample.

Easy to use with large sampling frames stored in computer files.

Weaknesses of this Type of Sample

A systematic random sample will have some sample bias due to selection procedures.

Best Use

In very large populations where a full sampling frame is available.

Examples of Use

An organizational communication study that uses the employee list of a large corporation as the sampling frame.

A study of the effectiveness of a health information campaign conducted by a group medical practice, that uses the patient records as the sampling frame.

The bias introduced by systematic random sampling is usually small, so in practical situations this procedure is frequently used. However, if it is possible to draw a simple random sample rather than a systematic random sample, one should always do so.

Multistage Sample

Multistage sampling is used when the sampling frame is huge, and does not exist as a single list. Drawing a sample from the population of a country is an example of this situation. There is no single list of the residents of the United States, and if there were, drawing a simple probability sample from such a large list would be difficult, even with the aid of a computer.

In a multistage sampling procedure, the unit is not sampled directly from the population, but is determined indirectly by a series of selections from different sampling frames. We'll call these "super frames." Super frames have units that encompass large aggregates of the basic unit. The first sampling stages eliminate most of the population. When the number of units has been reduced to a manageable size, we can then choose the final sample by using one of the previously described sampling procedures.

For example, to collect a national sample of voters, we might first sample from the super frames of states (e.g., randomly select five states), then counties (e.g., randomly select eight counties from each of the five states), and finally sample individual persons from the county voter registration list. At the first stage of sampling, a huge number of individual units are eliminated (the residents of most states), at the next stage a large number are also subsequently eliminated (the residents of most counties in the state), and so forth, until the number of units is small enough that simple random selection procedures can be used.

The challenge in multistage sampling is to make sure that each individual in the population has an equal probability of being chosen. If any of the super frames contain disproportionate numbers of the population, and we fail to take this into account, we will get a biased sample. For example, suppose we do a multistage sampling procedure to choose a representative sample of U.S. citizens. We will first choose from the super frame of "states of the United States" (Stage 1), then do a simple probability sample of the state's citizens by doing random digit dialing for all the telephone exchanges in the state (Stage 2).

The super frame has 50 state names, but if we choose a simple random sample from it, where each state has an equal probability of being chosen $(\frac{1}{50})$, we *will not* get a sample of states that will subsequently yield a representative sample of individuals. This is because the number of individuals in each state varies. If we choose all states with equal probability, we will be giving Rhode Island and California an equal chance of being chosen. But suppose Rhode Island has a population of about 2,000,000 persons and California has 30,000,000 persons.[1] The Stage 2 selection process gives each individual in Rhode Island a chance of $\frac{1}{2,000,000}$ to be selected, while a California resident has a much lower probability of $\frac{1}{30,000,000}$. Using the multiplicative rule for probabilities, we see that individuals in Rhode Island do not have the same probability of being chosen as those in California, and so we have a biased sample:

$$\text{Prob[RI]} = \frac{1}{50} \times \frac{1}{2,000,000} = \frac{1}{100,000,000} = .0000001$$

and

$$\text{Prob[CA]} = \frac{1}{50} \times \frac{1}{30,000,000} = \frac{1}{1,500,000,000} = .00000000067$$

To correct this problem, we must adjust the probability of choosing each unit from the super frame so that it is proportional to the population within each super frame unit. Suppose the population of the United States is 250,000,000[1] persons. Rhode Island thus has $\frac{2,000,000}{250,000,000} = \frac{1}{125} = .008$ (0.8 of 1 percent) of the U.S. population, while California has $\frac{30,000,000}{250,000,000} = .12$, or 12 percent of the population. To make sure that the sample is representative, our Stage 1 random choice procedure must be over 12 times more likely to choose California than Rhode Island.

If we set the probability of choosing a super frame unit proportional to the population, the probabilities of choosing any individual are:

$$\text{Prob[RI]} = .008 \times \frac{1}{2,000,000} = .000000004$$

and

$$\text{Prob[CA]} = .12 \times \frac{1}{30,000,000} = .000000004$$

The probabilities of selecting a Rhode Islander and a Californian are now the same and we now have the equal selection probability required for an unbiased sample of individuals.

How would we actually go about accomplishing this unequal probability sampling from the super frame in practice? One way would be to construct a (very large) die with 1000 sides. On 8 of the sides we would place the name Rhode Island, so that 0.8 percent of the sides would contain that name. On 120 (12 percent) of the sides we would place the name California, and on the other sides we would similarly place state names proportional to their population. When we rolled the die, the state names would come up with the correct probabilities. In reality, we would probably use a computer program that produces random numbers according to a set of probabilities that are defined according to the population of each state.

We can extend this probability adjustment process for each subsequent stage in a multistage sampling process. If we wish to sample counties at the next stage after sampling states, we must find the population of each county, and choose counties based on probabilities proportional to the population size of the county.

If we know all the probabilities for each super frame, we can theoretically construct a completely unbiased sample. But in reality, the exact probabilities are often not known, and we are forced to make assumptions. If we sample blocks in a neighborhood (sometimes called an *area sample*), for example, it is likely that each block will have a differing number of houses, and thus a differing population size. To select a completely unbiased sample, we would have to select blocks based on the number of people who live on each block. But we are unlikely to have the population information for each block, and we will then be forced to sample blocks on an equal probability basis. By doing this, we would be assuming that every block has the same number of residents, even though this may introduce some sample bias. Because of all the possible sources of error in estimating the sampling probabilities and the likelihood of not having all the necessary information about some of the super frame probabilities, we will consider the results of multistage sampling as being a quasi-probability sample.

Nonprobability Samples

Nonprobability samples produce results that can be generalized to the population only by making some strong assumptions. The truth of the conclusions drawn from observing nonprobability samples depends completely on the accuracy of the assumptions. This type of sampling should be avoided if at all possible.

Convenience Sample

This sampling procedure is described by its name: Units are selected because they are convenient. This type of sample is also sometimes called an "accidental" or "opportunity" sample.

Typical kinds of convenience samples include:

Multistage Sample

Strengths of this Type of Sample

Reduces the sampling complexity for very large populations.

Can be used where no sampling frame exists, without the need for qualifying or screening questions.

Best Use

With populations that are organized into groups, like national and local political boundaries; large organizations that are divided into departments; classrooms within a school system.

Weaknesses of this Type of Sample

Relies on extensive information about different units in different super frames.

Because of limited information, multistage sampling will likely have some sample bias due to selection procedure.

Examples of Use

A study of the effectiveness of computer conferences in high technology industries across the United States.

National public opinion polling to determine the audience response to televised presidential campaign debates.

Person-on-the-street samples

Units are selected from public places in a haphazard, but not random, fashion. These are often used to represent the entire population, but are biased because of geographic restrictions, and the lack of a true random selection process.

Shopping mall intercept samples

These are a kind of person-on-the-street sample, but the population is restricted to people who are probably best described as consumers. These samples are often used in marketing and marketing communication research. While persons in a shopping mall are quite likely to be consumers, they are not necessarily representative of *all* consumers, so the resulting sample will probably contain some bias. This can be reduced somewhat by conducting sampling at different malls (reducing geographic bias) and at different times of day (to get at different lifestyles of the population— stay-at-homes and night shift workers are more likely to be in the malls during the day, with office and factory workers showing up during the evenings). Selection procedures can be randomized somewhat too. For example, a random numbers table can be used to count the number of persons who must pass by the intercept location before the next person is selected for the sample. While these techniques can reduce sample bias, they cannot eliminate the central problem: All members of the population are not available for sampling, so the equal likelihood principle is violated.

Intact group samples

These are already-formed groups, such as church groups, political organizations, service groups, or classrooms of students. No selection procedure is used, but the entire group is used to represent some larger population. The validity of results from this kind of sample is determined by the process by which the group was formed. A classroom containing 100 freshmen in a required introductory course is more likely to represent all college students, for example, than is a classroom that has 25 senior philosophy majors.

Fortuitous samples

These are persons, such as friends and neighbors of the investigator, who are used because they are available (rather than because they accurately represent the population). These samples are generally not useful for any purpose except for trying out research procedures (often referred to as pilot testing), as any person's set of acquaintances are unlikely to accurately represent any research population (except maybe the population of friends of communication researchers).

Although the danger in generalizing from nonprobability samples cannot be overstated, there are still some times that such a sample is justified. There is one paramount condition that should hold before you use a convenience sample: The convenience sample should not be obviously different from the population *in any characteristic that is thought to affect the outcome of the research.*

If we are studying the attention patterns of children to Saturday morning cartoons, we might justify using an intact group of children in a suburban daycare center, arguing that their age is representative of the population in which we are interested, and that the geographic location of their homes and the income levels of their parents, while not representative of the general population, will not affect their attention spans. But if there is a suspicion that these latter factors *are* important, then this intact group should not be used. This illustrates the essential problem with a nonprobability sample: We must rely on arguments that are not based on actual observations to justify the sample as being representative, rather than relying on the impersonal and objective laws of random choice used to create a probability sample. This permits critics of our research to challenge our view of reality by challenging our arguments. If our assumptions are weak, so will be the quality of our research.

Cluster Sample

Depending upon how it is done, a cluster sample could be considered either a quasi-probability or a nonprobability sample. We have chosen to discuss it as a nonprobability sample, as there are many substantial possibilities for serious sample bias in this procedure.

Cluster sampling is similar to multistage sampling in its use of a super frame to draw the initial sample of aggregate units like states, cities, or blocks. But it differs from multistage sampling in the fact that the final selection of the sample is not a probability

---

Convenience Sample

Strengths of this Type of Sample

Inexpensive and easy to obtain the sample.

Does not require a sampling frame.

Weaknesses of this Type of Sample

A convenience sample will have unknown sample bias both in terms of the amount as well as the direction. The amount of bias can be large.

The validity of statistical generalization will depend on assumptions about the representativeness of the sample, and hence cannot be ascertained.

Best Use

Where the social or personal characteristics of the sampled units are not thought to be involved in the process being studied. For example, studies involving some basic physiological or nonconscious responses may be less susceptible to sample bias. Basic perceptual, reasoning, and memory processes may be so universal that sample bias is not a problem.

Examples of Use

Brain wave (EEG) measurements of processing of communications.

A study of the long-term recall of the content of interpersonal communications.

---

sample. In cluster sampling, every unit in the aggregate unit selected from the super frame is included in the sample.

Cluster sampling is often used to cut costs for interviewing research participants in person. As an example, suppose an organizational communication researcher wishes to interview 100 middle-level managers about their communication with subordinates. The researcher collects the personnel lists from all corporations with more than 50 employees in a large Midwestern city and defines this as the universe. (This decision might be criticized, if the results of the research are to be generalized outside that city. The critic would ask: "Are these corporations really representative of all corporations in the United States, or are there some unique geographic or economic conditions in this city that might influence the results?")

At this point, the researcher might draw a simple probability sample from the sampling frame. But to do this would require visiting a large number of different corporate headquarters spread out all over the urban area. Instead, one can list all the corporations in a super frame, and draw a simple probability sample of 10 corporations from this frame. Then *all* middle-level managers in each corporation can be interviewed.

This procedure results in a biased sample, since each middle-level manager in the city does not have an equal probability of being included in the sample. Managers from larger corporations are less likely to be included, since small corporations are just as likely to be chosen from the super frame as are large corporations, and there are likely to be many more small corporations. Also, interviewing large "clusters" of managers in a few corporations will exaggerate any peculiar characteristics of the chosen corporations. These will show

Cluster Sampling

Strengths of this Type of Sample

Cluster sampling cuts data collection costs, particularly for research that requires in-person data collection.

Weaknesses of this Type of Sample

Requires some information to construct the super frame.

A cluster sample will have unknown sample bias. This can be large.

The validity of statistical generalization will depend on assumptions about the representativeness of the sample, and hence cannot be ascertained.

Best Use

When interviewing costs are high.

When the sampled units are hard to contact.

When the clusters correspond to collections of observations that are useful in the research, such as departments in organizations, families, and so on.

Examples of Use

A study of the individual factors that affect family communication patterns. Extended families can be cluster sampled, and each family member included in the sample.

A study of the use of cable television services by apartment dwellers. Apartment buildings can be cluster sampled, and each resident interviewed.

up in the sample more frequently than they would if only a few managers from each of a larger number of corporations were interviewed, as would be the case if the researcher had used a simple probability sample.

On the positive side, the researcher's interviewing costs are now affordable. As with other quasi- or nonprobability sampling techniques, one must balance the costs of sample bias against the benefits of the (biased) information.

Sample bias in cluster sampling can be reduced by making the number of sample units in each cluster as small as possible. If a researcher randomly selects houses in a city, then interviews two persons in each house (two units in each cluster), the sample will have less bias than if he or she selects city blocks, then interviews each person on the block (possibly 50 persons in each cluster).

Unrepresentative Quota Sample

This sample is sometimes also called a "purposive" sample. In this sampling, quotas are not chosen to be representative of the true proportions of some characteristic in the population, but are chosen by the researcher on some other basis.

For example, a communication researcher interested in contrasting the political knowledge of television viewers with nonviewers would probably not use a probability sample, as less than 1 percent of the population watches no television at all. To find even 100 nonviewers in a simple probability sample, the researcher would have to interview over 10,000 persons in a random sample drawn from the general population. This is probably going to be too expensive. So the researcher might set a quota of 100 nonviewers and 100 viewers. The sample of viewers might be drawn as a simple random probability sample, using random digit dialing. The nonviewers sample might be solicited via response to a newspaper ad, or it might be screened from a probability sample by using an initial (and quick) qualifying question about television usage.

In either event, the resulting sample will be far from representative of the total population, as it will contain 100 times more nonviewers than would be found by a simple random choice procedure. Furthermore, if a nonrandom choice procedure like newspaper solicitation is used, the nonviewers sample is not even representative of the population of nonviewers due to response bias. As a result, generalization to the population of nonviewers is not warranted.

But if the purposive sample of the nonviewers can be assumed to be representative of the population of nonviewers, as it would be if qualifier questions were used to screen units from a probability sample of the general population, the quotas can be recombined to form a representative sample. Generalizing from the recombined sample is much more valid.

This general procedure is called *oversampling and weighting*, and it depends upon some census knowledge about the population. If we know that nonviewers make up 1 percent of the general population, we can take our two quota samples and multiply each observation so that it represents the correct proportional amount of the population. In the above example, we would multiply the value of each variable in the viewers sample by .99, as these individuals represent 99 percent of the population, and we would count each observation as .99, rather than 1.0 observation. Likewise we would multiply each value in the nonviewers sample by .01, and count each observation as .01 observation, to represent 1 percent of the population. The resulting sample that combines the two quotas would have an equivalent of 100 observations (.99 × 100 viewers + .01 × 100 nonviewers), and the value of each variable in the combined and weighted sample would be corrected for the true population proportions.

Oversampling and weighting is valid only when each of the combined quota samples is randomly chosen, using one of the probability sampling procedures (as would be the case with a telephone screening question, but not the case with respondents solicited from newspaper ads). The technique is useful when one wants to investigate small subpopulations, but also wants to use the observations from these subpopulations in a representative sample of the whole population. Most statistical packages now make this weighting procedure easy.

How Big Should the Sample Be?

This is a very common question. But it is also one that is very difficult to answer with anything other than the frustrating phrase "it depends." To adequately answer this question, we have to refer to some new ideas like distributions, statistical error, and statistical power. We'll get to these later in this book, but for now we'll have to be content with some general statements and rules of thumb.

Unrepresentative Quota Sample

Strengths of this Type of Sample

Oversampled quotas provide information about small subpopulations in the general population.

Subpopulations of particular interest can be studied.

Weaknesses of this Type of Sample

The sample is not representative of the population, so it cannot be used for generalization without additional weighting procedures.

Weighting requires knowledge of census values.

Best Use

When targeted information about small subpopulations is needed.

When the number of potential observations are limited or hard to obtain.

When the population is small, and a nonrandom sample can include a substantial proportion of the total population.

Examples of Use

A study of marital communication patterns of convicted spouse abusers.

A study of exposure to cable television commercials by purchasers of Blinding White toothpaste.

The basic reason for drawing a sample is to be able to make accurate statements about the population without having to conduct a census. But as we saw in the last chapter, using a sample will introduce some sampling error, and the governing principle is this: The greater the number of observations in the sample, the less the sampling error.

But, as we will see in more detail later, there is a diminishing return associated with each additional unit included in a sample. If you have sampled only 50 units, you will get much more reduction in error by adding an additional observation than you will get when you have already sampled 500. Since obtaining additional observations adds progressively less and less value to the sample in the form of reduced error, there is some point at which it is uneconomical to make the sample larger. In this perspective, the best sample size comes from a trade-off between the cost of collecting additional observations and the sampling error.

To choose the size of the sample, a researcher might set a range of sampling error values (say, sample means that are likely to be within 1 percent, 5 percent, and 10 percent of the real population means) and use these values to calculate the number of observations required to meet each particular error criterion. (We'll see how to do this calculation in Chapter 10.) The researcher then chooses the sample size that is both economically affordable and that gives an acceptably low error.

Another way of choosing sample size is to consider *statistical power*. This is a somewhat complicated statistical idea that is covered in detail in Chapter 11. In very simple terms, increasing the sample size has three effects: (1) it decreases the probability of falsely concluding that two variables are related to each other, when there is really no relationship between them; (2) it decreases the probability of falsely concluding that there is no relationship between two variables, when there is in fact a relationship; and

(3) it allows the detection of weaker relationships between two variables. Sample size can be determined by choosing error levels for (1) and (2), and by choosing the size of the smallest relationship which we wish to detect (3). These values are used to look up the appropriate sample size in a statistical power table.

Regardless of the method used to choose the sample size, there is one basic fact that you must remember: The accuracy of the results obtained from a sample depends on the *absolute number* of observations, NOT on the percentage of the population that is being sampled. Although it seems contrary to common sense, the accuracy that you can obtain by sampling 100 units out of a population of 1000 is exactly the same as the accuracy you get by sampling 100 units from a population of 100,000,000. Sampling a tiny percentage of a population can give quite accurate results. Political pollsters often quite accurately predict the behavior of 80,000,000 voters from samples of 2000 persons.

Detecting Error or Bias in a Sample

After choosing a sample, it is natural to ask, "How do I know if it's a good one?" There is no absolute answer to this question, but there are some ways you can investigate the likelihood of having drawn an unbiased sample. These are kinds of consistency checks you can do after collecting data for the research variables in the sample.

Checking Against Census Values

If you have census information about one or more of the variables, you can compare the census values to the sample values for the same variables. For example, if you have drawn a simple probability sample of 100 persons from a general population, you know from census information that you should have about 52 females in your sample. Because of sampling error, it is unlikely that you will have exactly 52, but the sample value should be near the census value. If you find only 35 females, you can conclude that one of two things has happened: either, purely by luck, you have drawn a very improbable sample (it's possible—a coin *can* come up heads 10 times in a row, but it's very unlikely), or you have accidentally introduced some source of sample bias. You must investigate your sampling procedures to find out which is the most likely case. If you can find no obvious source of sample bias, you may want to draw a supplementary sample to see if you just drew a very improbable set of units.

Checking Against Known Relationships

Prior research studies can be examined for consistent relationships between some of the variables. If you fail to find such well-established relationships, you should critically examine your sampling procedures. For example, hundreds of studies have shown a negative relationship between the number of hours spent watching television and the income of an individual. If this relationship is not present, there may have been some problem with sample selection.

Summary

A *population* (or "universe") contains all the units to which the researcher wants to generalize. A listing of all the units in the population is called a sampling frame. If data are collected from all units in the population, a *census* has been conducted, and the results can be generalized to the whole population with perfect confidence.

The cost and difficulty of conducting communication research force most researchers to select a small subset of the population for study. This is called a *sample.* Because not all units in the population are observed, a sample may produce results that contain some error. There are two major types of error introduced by sampling: *sample bias*, which can be due to some systematic inclusion or exclusion process due to selection method (selection bias) or due to respondents "opting out" of the sample (response bias); and *sampling error*, which results from random chance during the sample selection.

If random choice procedures are used in selecting the sample, the sampling error will be reduced with increasing size of the sample. In other words, the accuracy of the statistical generalization will increase with more observations. Sample bias, however, will not decrease with larger samples. It must be reduced by selecting the proper sampling procedures.

To select the sample that gives the best statistical generalization, the researcher must eliminate selection bias, and ensure that only the minimum random selection error is present. To eliminate selection bias, the researcher must ensure that all units in the population have the same probability of being chosen for the sample. This is the *equal likelihood principle.* The researcher must also ensure that the selection process is random. This means that there is no way that anyone can predict, at better than chance probability ("pure guess") levels which units of the population will be chosen. Finally, the sample selection process must permit any combination of units in the population to be chosen.

All sampling procedures are constructed so that they approach these goals as nearly as possible. A *simple probability sample* and a *stratified or known quota sample* achieve the goals, but they sometimes require more effort or information about the population than the researcher possesses.

Quasi-probability samples like *systematic random samples* and *multistage samples* approach these goals, but introduce some sample bias. However, their ease of construction sometimes makes their use a favorable choice.

Nonprobability samples like *convenience samples, cluster samples*, and *unrepresentative quota samples* introduce the most sample bias. They should be used only in very restricted circumstances when either wide generalization is not required, or when the communication process being studied is considered to be so universal that selection biases are not important.

In general, sample sizes should be as large as possible to reduce sampling error. However, there are diminishing returns in error reduction for each addition to the sample. The practical cost of collecting information places some ceiling on the size of the sample. At some point, the reduction of additional sampling error is not worth the cost of collecting more information. It is important to remember that the amount of sampling error is determined by the size of the sample, and not by the size of the population. You will get the same accuracy from a sample of 1000 in a population of 10,000 or 10,000,000.

Notes

^{1} These are not the actual population figures, but are simpler numbers which make the calculations clear.

References and Additional Readings

Babbie, E. R. (1992). *The practice of social research* (6th ed.). Belmont, CA: Wadsworth (Chapter 8, "The Logic of Sampling").

Barnett, V. (1991). *Sample survey principles and methods*. New York: Oxford University Press (Chapter 2, "Simple Random Sampling"; Chapter 5, "Stratified Populations and Stratified Random Sampling"; Chapter 6, "Cluster and Multi-Stage Sampling").

Beyer, W. H. (Ed.). (1971). *Basic statistical tables*. Cleveland, OH: Chemical Rubber Company.

Hays, W. L. (1981). *Statistics* (3rd. ed.). New York: Holt, Rinehart & Winston (Chapter 2, "Elementary Probability Theory").

Kerlinger, F. N. (1986). *Foundations of behaviorial research* (3rd ed.) New York: Holt, Rinehart and Winston (Chapter 7, "Probability"; Chapter 8, "Sampling and Randomness").

Moser, C. A. & Kalton, G. (1972). *Survey methods in social investigation* (2nd ed.). New York: Basic Books (Chapter 4, "Basic Ideas of Sampling"; Chapter 5, "Types of Sample Design").

Slonim, M. J. (1960). *Sampling*. New York: Simon and Schuster.

Smith, M. J. (1988). *Contemporary communication research methods*. Belmont, CA: Wadsworth (Chapter 5, "Sampling Methods").

Thompson, S. (1992). *Sampling*. New York: Wiley. (Chapter 1, "Simple Random Sampling"; Chapter 11, "Stratified Sampling"; Chapter 12, "Cluster and Systematic Sampling"; Chapter 13, "Multi-Stage Designs").

Chapter 7

Measurement

Measurement is the foundation of scientific inquiry. In order to test our hypotheses, we must observe our theoretical concepts at the operational level. In simple words, we must measure what we have defined. But there are different levels of measurement, which provide differing amounts of information about the theoretical construct. We must also address some basic issues about the adequacy of measurement.

Levels of Measurement

Depending on our operational definition, a measurement can give us differing kinds of information about a theoretical concept. However, at the minimal level a measure must provide the ability to detect the presence or absence of the theoretical construct. All levels of measurement give this ability, or they wouldn't be measurements at all. If the presence or absence of a theoretical construct is the only information that the measurement provides, we call the measure *nominal*. A second level of measurement adds the idea of quantity, or an underlying dimension, to the measure's ability to detect. At this level, we can not only detect the presence of the theoretical construct, but we can also make comparative statements about its quantity, like "more of ..." or "higher than ...." If the measurement contains only detection and comparative ordering information, we call it *ordinal*. At the next higher level, a measurement adds the idea of units, so that we can make absolute (rather than simple comparative) statements about the similarity or difference between measurements. That is, we can state the number of units by which observations are measured to be different. This level of measurement is called *interval*. Finally, if the measure is interval, but also contains an absolute zero category or scale point, we can make statements of proportion ("only one-half of") or ratios ("twice as much ...") about the magnitude of our measurements. We call this highest level of measurement *ratio-level*.

Nominal Measurement

A nominal measure makes only a single, simple distinction: between the *presence* or *absence* of the theoretical concept within the unit of analysis. It's a simple black-or-white kind of view that we will use to categorize the observed units. For instance, we might operationally define the theoretical concept "gender of participant" by classifying all participants in an experiment as either male or female.

Let us carefully analyze what we actually do when we assign these labels. We choose to ignore all gradations of masculinity or femininity. We will merely characterize every subject as having "present" or "absent" the characteristic maleness, OR as having "present" or "absent" the characteristic femaleness. What we actually do then is to measure the participant on one of two nominal variables—Maleness or Femaleness. We only need to rate the participant as absent or present on one of the two, because present on the characteristic maleness, for instance, implies absence on the characteristic femaleness, and vice versa. Because absence on maleness implies presence on femaleness, the categories in a nominal measure (or any other level of measurement, for that matter) are called *mutually exclusive.* This means that it must not be possible for any single unit of analysis to be a member of more than one category. Furthermore, the categories in any variable at any level of measurement must be *exhaustive*: Every unit of analysis we encounter must be able to be assigned to one of the nominal categories. Mutual exclusivity and exhaustiveness therefore constitute the minimal requirements for measurement, whether measurement be nominal, ordinal, interval or ratio. Observe also that there is no ordering of the two categories—female is not bigger or smaller than male, and male is not greater than or less than female—they are simply mutually exclusive.

Gender of participant is an example of the simplest nominal measurement, called *dichotomous* or *binary* measurement. In this kind of operational definition, the variable may take on only one of two possible values.

Of course, theoretical concepts can have more than two nominal response categories. If so, the construct is properly called a *nominal factor,* as it really consists of a number of simple nominal variables. Again, an example is probably the best way to explain this. Suppose we are conducting a political communication study, and we want to determine the political affiliation of each respondent. We can define the theoretical concept "political party affiliation" as a nominal factor with the response categories of Democrat, Republican, and Independent. These three categories actually require that we characterize each respondent as absent or present on two nominal variables to correctly represent each person's political affiliation. We'll call the nominal variables Democratic party membership and Republican party membership. A respondent's party affiliation is then described as the particular combination of presence or absence of each of these two variables, as is shown in Table 7-1.

If a person is scored as absent on the nominal variable Democratic party membership *and* also as absent on the variable Republican party membership, it is implied that the person is an "Independent." Present on either one of these implies membership in that party. Again notice how this measurement scheme is mutually exclusive. Furthermore, it is exhaustive as all observations that are not assigned to Democrat or Republican will

TABLE 7-1   **Nominal Components of the Factor Political Party Affiliation**

	Nominal Variables	
Nominal Category	Democratic Party Membership	Republican Party Membership
Democratic	Present	Absent
Republican	Absent	Present
Independent	Absent	Absent

logically be assigned to the category Independent. Again, there is no underlying order to these three categories of party affiliation.

We can extend this idea to theoretical concepts with any number of nominal categories. We will always need $G-1$ nominal variables to represent a nominal factor with G categories.

In general, we recommend that nominal measurements be avoided, as they provide the least amount of information about the theoretical concept, and they can be quite cumbersome to analyze if you define a nominal factor with a large number of categories. But sometimes they are the only realistic possibility. It is very easy to measure the gender of subject by categorizing each subject as either male or female; it is much harder to determine the degree of masculinity or femininity. We may not have the time to administer a complicated psychological gender scale to each participant in our research, so we may decide to settle for the nominal male-female distinction. Other times it may appear that we do not have any choice but to use nominal variables for concepts such as party affiliation. Later on in this chapter we will provide an example of how we may well be able to replace such nominal variables with variables at higher levels of measurement and obtain more information about the concept being measured.

Ordinal Measurement

As we just saw, the categories in a nominal variable cannot be arranged in any order of magnitude. But if we add this idea of ordering by *quantity* to the definition of the categories, we can improve the sensitivity of our observations.

Let's look at another simple example. Suppose we wish to measure the theoretical concept "age" using a dichotomized variable. Every unit in our sample will be categorized as either "old" or "young." This measurement of age is an example of an ordinal-level measurement. In addition to viewing the old and the young categories as mutually exclusive and exhaustive, we can also think of the young category as lesser in age than the old category. Furthermore, if we want to add the category "middle-aged," we can place it in between young and old with some justification. Contrast this with the situation of adding a new category called Socialist to the set of categories in the political party concept discussed in the previous section. This new category can be slotted anywhere in the set of already existing categories, which indicates that political party is truly a nominal factor, with no inherent quantities which can be used to arrange the order of the categories. But for the category middle-aged there is only one position that makes sense: right between young and old.

Ordinal measurements allow us to make comparative distinctions between observations along some dimension. For instance, suppose we ask participants in an interpersonal communication experiment to rank the physical attractiveness of a number of conversational partners by sorting a stack of photographs so that the most attractive partner is on top and the least attractive is on the bottom. We can now say that second photograph in the pile is *more* attractive to the subject than all the photos in the pile below it, but *less* attractive than the photo on the top of the pile. We can assign an "attractiveness" score to each photograph by numbering it, starting at the top of the pile (1 = most attractive, 2 = second most attractive, etc.). This is called a rank-order measurement. This measurement takes on *comparative degrees* of difference, and this distinguishes an ordinal measure from a nominal one, in which we have only a single distinction of difference (in nominal measurement, an observation is the *same* as others in its category, and *different* from all other categories).

This feature allows us to introduce the general idea of comparative similarity in observations. In the photo ranking example, we can conclude that adjacent photographs in the sorted pile are similar to each other in attractiveness, and that photos near the top of the pile are very different in attractiveness from those at the bottom of the pile. This distinction gives us more information about attractiveness than a nominal measurement scheme. This information can be used to great advantage during statistical tests which establish relationships between ordinal variables.

But one thing which we cannot do with ordinal data is determine the absolute distance between adjacent categories. For example, suppose we knew the "real" attractiveness score of each photograph for two subjects, that is, the actual amount of attractiveness each photograph has for each subject. In Figure 7-1, we've placed the photos on the "real" attractiveness scale according to each subject's true evaluation. Although each subject's "real" evaluation of the conversational partners is quite different, each will rank the partners' comparative attractiveness identically.

An ordinal measurement will give us only relatively fuzzy comparative distinctions among observations. To get truly sensitive measurement, we must add absolute measurement units to the operational definition. These units add more information to the measurement, in the form of *magnitudes* between adjacent categories. If we can do this, we are measuring at the interval level.

Interval Measurement

When we can not only rank order observations, but can also assign them numerical scores which register the *degree* of distance between observations or points on the measurement scale, we have improved the level of measurement to *interval*. In interval measurement, equal numerical distances imply equal dissimilarity.

In the example shown in Figure 7-2, for Subject 1, Jane is one unit more attractive than Bill, and John is one unit more attractive than Ann. We conclude that the difference between Jane and Bill's attractiveness is identical to the difference between John and Ann's, as the interval between each of the pairs is identical: one unit. Furthermore, we see

Subject 1's "real" perceptions

| Jane   Bill   Mary   John Ann |
| _____+_____+_____+_____+____+_____ |
| More   Less
| Attractive   Attractive

Subject 2's "real" perceptions

| Jane   Bill   Mary   John   Ann |
| _____+_____+_____+_____+_____+_____ |
| More   Less
| Attractive   Attractive

Subject 1's	1 - Jane		Subject 2's	1 - Jane
Ordinal	2 - Bill		Ordinal	2 - Bill
Ranking	3 - Mary		Ranking	3 - Mary
	4 - John			4 - John
	5 - Ann			5 - Ann

FIGURE 7-1   "Real" Scores Versus Ordinal Measurements

that Mary is equidistant between Jane and Ann for Respondent 2, and that the difference in attractiveness between Ann and Jane is twice as large as the difference between Mary and Jane. And we can compare Jane's attractiveness to each of the subjects, and see that Subject 1 found her more attractive (gave her 12 units) than did Subject 2 (who only gave her 10 units), although both ranked her as the most attractive partner.

Once again, the additional information provided by interval measurement will make it easier to detect relationships between variables. But there are still some statements that cannot be made with an interval measurement. We cannot say, for example, that Mary (with 6 attractiveness units) is three times more attractive than Ann (who received 2) for Subject 2. To make comparative statements based on ratios, we must move to yet another higher level of measurement.

Ratio Measurement

If the measurement classes include an absolute zero point, corresponding to the complete absence of the theoretical concept, we have the highest level of measurement: measurement at the *ratio* level. A survey respondent's age, expressed in "number of years since birth," is a good example of a ratio measurement. The classes of that variable contain a zero (if this year is the year of birth), and we can make statements like "Tom is twice as old as Vanessa" if the ratio of their ages is 2:1, or 2.0. It is important to point out that interval level measurement classes may also contain a zero. In this case the zero is an "arbitrary" zero; it does not denote the absence of whatever characteristic is being observed. For instance, the Fahrenheit scale for measuring temperature has a zero-point which does not, however, indicate the "absence" of heat. So if today's temperature is 60 degrees and yesterday's was 30, we cannot say that it is twice as warm today as it was yesterday.

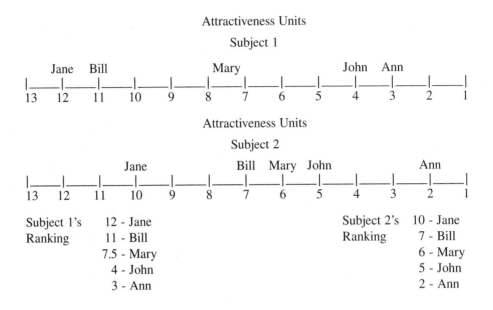

FIGURE 7-2   Interval Measurements

Ratio-level measurements are the most desirable, as they contain the most information about each observation of the theoretical construct.

In the social and behavioral sciences, it is customary to treat interval-level measurements as if they are ratio-level. Normally, this does not distort observations, as long as the theoretical concepts include the implication of an absolute zero point, even if it is not part of the actual operational definition. The attractiveness scale used in the example above does not have an actual zero-point on the scale, but we can visualize a zero-point for attractiveness (no attractiveness whatsoever). Being able to treat variables as ratio variables gives us access to many extremely useful statistics (which we will discuss later) that assume ratio-level measurement in their computations.

Choosing the Level of Measurement

This choice is easy: Always construct your operational definition at the highest level of measurement that is practically possible. This will give the maximum sensitivity in your measurement, and you can use more powerful statistics to test your hypotheses.

The first thing to keep in mind when you construct an operational definition is this: Use a measurement definition that is interval or ratio, if at all possible. It is often tempting to "simplify" measurement of a theoretical concept by dropping down a level of measurement or two. A simple example will illustrate the dangers in succumbing to this temptation. Let's look at several ways of measuring the concept of age.

The best way is to simply request that the experimental subject or survey respondent report the number of years since their birth. This is a ratio-level measurement. It preserves very small differences between observations, and permits both comparative and quantitative comparisons of observations or groups of observations. But we might ask the age question in another way. Suppose we ask the respondent to categorize his or her age in this way:

What is your age?
a. under 18
b. 18–21
c. 22–29
d. 30–39
e. 40–64
f. 65 or above

This is a common method of requesting age information. But it has reduced the level of measurement from ratio to ordinal. The category boundaries are not equal in range, so we can't infer the magnitude of differences in age by category membership.

Suppose two respondents differ by one category. How different are their ages? If the categories are (b) and (c), the average age difference will be the difference between the midpoints of each category, or $25.5 - 19.5 = 6$ years. But if the categories are (d) and (e), the average difference will be $52 - 34.5 = 17.5$ years. This varying difference between category boundaries makes quantitative comparisons useless. We can certainly say that the person in the higher age category is *older* than the person in the lower category, but we can't say *how much* older.

The difference in size of the categories also means that there may be more variation in age within a category (all of whose members are considered identical in age) than there is between categories. Persons could differ by up to 24 years in category (e), while they could differ by only 3 years in category (b). Having wide boundaries for the categories also means that we've lost sensitivity in expressing age differences—a 40-year-old respondent will be considered identical in age to a 64-year-old. Categorizing age this way reduces the precision of measurement and thereby reduces our ability to detect relationships between our theoretical concepts. And finding relationships is the basic reason that we're conducting research.

We can do even more damage to our ability to accurately observe the theoretical concept by again "simplifying" the measurement of age to the following question:

Are you a(n)
a. Child
b. Adolescent
c. Adult

Now, not only are the categories different in size, as they were in the previous example, but we have also added fuzzy boundaries between the categories. We would consider this measurement to still be ordinal-level, since it is possible to order the categories along a single dimension. But the ordering is weak, as the boundary between adolescent and adult, for example, is not clear. One 18-year-old might consider herself an adult, while another 18-year-old might classify himself as an adolescent.

Why would we ever use this form of measurement? As mentioned above, the primary reason is for convenience. But before using this kind of measurement, we should make an attempt to move up to interval- or ratio-level measurement if at all possible.

One way to do this is to consider the real nature of the theoretical concepts we're measuring, and see if we're expressing the central ideas of our investigation. Often there is a tendency to use simple nominal categories that describe the surface features of a concept, rather than the more specific dimensions that truly matter. Whenever possible, we must specify the theoretical constructs in a way that will allow us to use the highest level of measurement.

Let's look at an example. Suppose that we initially think that the political affiliation of survey respondents may be associated with their readership of particular magazines. The almost reflexively obvious way to measure these concepts is to ask each respondent these questions:

> To which political party do you belong?
> a. Democratic
> b. Republican
> c. Neither

and

> Which one of these magazines do you regularly read?
> a. *Time*
> b. *Newsweek*
> c. *U.S. News and World Report*
> d. *Commentary*
> e. *New Republic*
> f. None of the above

Both theoretical concepts (party affiliation and magazine readership) are measured at the nominal level, so we receive the minimum amount of information about each. For example, we know that Democrats can range from very conservative to very liberal, and that the political beliefs of some Republicans are almost identical to those of some Democrats, but none of this information will be captured. Furthermore, we can't be sure how a respondent will define a magazine that is "regularly read." One respondent might consider glancing at the headlines each week as regular reading, while another might decide that only magazines which are read cover-to-cover qualify. Such a difference will result in substantial amounts of error in the reporting of actual exposure to the content of these magazines.

The problem can be solved by considering the details of the theoretical process that we are investigating. As we consider these, perhaps we will realize that what we are really trying to understand is something more specific than general party affiliation and simple magazine readership. We might conclude that we *really* want to investigate the relationship between political liberalism or conservatism and exposure to political news and commentary. We can then replace the nominal political party categories with a set of questions about political views. If these questions are expressed as scales, as described in the next section, we then have measurement at ordinal or interval level to replace the nominal political party categories. Similarly, we might replace the nominal checklist of magazines with a measurement question like, "How many hours in an average week do you devote to reading political news and commentary?" This is a ratio-level measurement which is much more sensitive than the nominal categories. As a result, we can use more sensitive statistics which require interval-level measurement, rather than simpler nominal-level statistics.

In the process of defining higher-level measurement, we have also honed our theoretical thinking. It is often true that improvements in defining theoretical concepts lead to better measurements, as well. As we saw in Chapter 2, there is a strong interplay between the "verbal world" of theoretical concepts and the "measurement world" of operational definitions. Insightful thinking about theoretical or operational definitions will probably result in improvements to both.

Scaling

Scaling is a term used to describe the way that an operational definition can be conceptualized to provide numerical measurement. Usually the term is applied only to ordinal- or interval-level measures, as nominal scaling is really just a matter of classification within a set of categories, as we saw above. There are a vast number of different scaling techniques and procedures, and scaling represents a whole area of study by itself. Here, we'll just outline some of the more common types of scaling.

Counting Frequencies

Perhaps the simplest scaling involves *natural measures* like the counting of instances of occurrence of events. Such occurrence is absolute in nature and can be measured in terms of its *frequency*. Scales reflecting measures of frequency are at the ratio level of measurement, and thus are very desirable. Typical operational definitions might involve counting the number of different cartoons presented by a network on Saturday morning; counting the number of times (the frequency) that an employee communicates with the boss in a week; measuring the frequency with which stories on a particular topic appear in a newspaper; counting the number of retrieval requests for a particular document in an electronic database.

We can also use *established metrics* such as temperature scales and electrical units like volts and ohms (these are often useful in physiological measurements), measurements of sound amplitude in the decibel scale, distances in miles or meters, measures of time, such as hours and minutes, and so forth. These units of measurement are arbitrary in nature, rather than absolute. When we count the number of "inquiries" to a database, the unit of measurement is an "inquiry"—we count the number that occur. However, when the unit of measurement is arbitrary we need to establish first what the unit of measurement is going to be. To measure distance, for instance, we need to agree upon some arbitrary way of expressing that distance: in terms of meters or yards, kilometers or miles. These units are not absolute, but their definitions have been established over a long time period, are

"I communicate with my mother …"

1   2   3   4   5   6   7
Infrequently   Frequently
_____

"There is too much violence on television"
1. Strongly agree
2. Agree
3. Neither agree nor disagree
4. Disagree
5. Strongly disagree
_____

"If George Washington represents 100 and Adolf Hitler
represents 0 on a scale of democratic leadership, where
does our current president fall?"   _____

FIGURE 7-3   Examples of Magnitude Scales

widely accepted, and they are standardized so that reliable measurement is possible. They are usually ratio scales, too. Although these metrics are attached to theoretical concepts of their own (like "displacement in space" for distance metrics), they can be used as partial indicators of more abstract communication concepts. For example, distance may be used to measure (at least partially) the degree of difficulty in obtaining information from a library, as in this question:

> *How many miles do you have to drive or walk to obtain a book from your nearest public library?* _____

The skin's resistance to electrical currents can be measured in ohms; as a consequence, arousal due to, for instance, exposure to erotic video programs, is often measured in terms of changes in skin resistance as measured in ohm units. In both of these examples we would measure the amount of the arbitrarily defined units.

Measuring Magnitude

Some scaling procedures are associated more specifically with behavioral research. Perhaps the most common of these are the *magnitude* types of scales, of which the *Likert* scale is a typical example. In this measurement procedure, verbal "anchors," which define the extremes of the dimension being measured, are provided to allow a range of responses to some specific question. The experimental subject or respondent is then provided with a statement and is asked to choose some point on the scale which represents his or her judgment of magnitude. Figure 7-3 contains some examples of different magnitude scales.

In the three examples in Figure 7-3, "Infrequently" and "Frequently," "Strongly Agree" and "Strongly Disagree," "George Washington" and "Adolf Hitler" represent the extreme poles or anchors of the underlying dimensions of, respectively, frequency of communication, agreement, and democratic leadership.

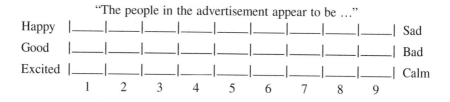

FIGURE 7-4　**Semantic Differential Scales**

If the scale anchors are a set of adjectives that are antonyms (adjectives that are logical opposites), the resulting set of scales, such as shown in Figure 7-4, is sometimes called a *semantic differential* scale.

It is a mistake to assume that the measurement obtained from magnitude scales such as these are at the interval or ratio level because we have no way of determining that the distances between adjacent scale points are really equal. In fact, there is considerable evidence that the "psychological distance" between scale points in the middle of magnitude scales is smaller than it is near the end points. There is a general reluctance on the part of respondents to use the extreme ends of magnitude scales. While the difference between the adjacent scale points representing "neutral" and "mildly agree" (scale points 5 and 6 on a 9-point scale) might be seen as slight, the distance between "agree" and "strongly agree" (scale points 8 and 9) is perceived as much greater, even though these are also adjacent scale points.

If magnitude scales are analyzed with ordinal statistics like those described later in this book, this lack of interval distances makes no difference. But magnitude scales are frequently selected to measure theoretical concepts which require analysis with statistics that assume at least interval data. Research on magnitude scales has shown that the assumption of interval-level measurement does not give seriously incorrect results in most cases. To handle the more severe noninterval problem at the end points of the scales, some researchers add extra scale points to either end of the scale, and then collapse the two end points into a single value. For example, to minimize the problem in a scale with 7 points, a researcher would use a 9-point scale, then consider responses 1 and 2 as identical, and 8 and 9 as identical. The result is a 7-point scale (going from 2 to 8) which is closer to interval-level.

There are scaling methods which directly address the problem of constructing scales with equal intervals between adjacent points. *Thurstone scaling* is a procedure in which the scale consists of a series of questions to which the subject responds with yes–no or agree–disagree answers. The questions are chosen so that they represent a set of intervals that appear similar in magnitude to respondents. A set of Thurstone scale questions to measure the degree of "reliance on informal communication" in an organization might look like the ones depicted in Exhibit 7-1.

If such a scale is well-constructed, a respondent's position on the dimension being measured can be determined by the scale value of the question at which the respondent switches from agreement to disagreement.

EXHIBIT 7-1   Example of Thurstone Scaling

---

1. "Most of what I know about what happens in management comes from rumors."

[Agree]   [Disagree]

(This question represents scale point 3, representing high reliance on informal communication.)

2. "Information about our company's long-term decisions is just as likely to be passed down in conversation with friends in management as it is to show up in the company newsletter."

[Agree]   [Disagree]

(Represents scale point 2, reliance on *both* formal and informal communication)

3. "We have a very efficient system of meetings, newsletters, and briefings which management uses to keep us fully informed about the business decisions that they make."

[Agree]   [Disagree]

(Scale point 1, low reliance on informal communication)

The questions used on a Thurstone scale are selected from a much larger set of potential questions by a rather laborious procedure which is too detailed to discuss here. (See the References and Additional Readings section for some readings which detail scaling procedures.) For much communication research, the improvement in measurement represented by equal-appearing interval scales does not justify the extra effort, so Thurstone scales are seen only rarely.

Guttman or cumulative scales use a similar format in which the scale consists of a series of questions. But Guttman scaling also provides a way of determining if the scale is unidimensional, that is, if it is measuring only a single theoretical concept. If the statements are ordered in magnitude, we should see a consistent pattern of responses in which all questions that are below a critical magnitude for the respondent are answered in the same way, and all questions above this point are answered in the opposite fashion. Exhibit 7-2 contains a hypothetical set of questions to measure the threshold of what constitutes pornography for three subjects, and shows how these three subjects could have responded to the questions.

EXHIBIT 7-2   Example of Guttman Scaling

A: Consistency in Responses

"I think the following contains pornographic material"	Subject A	B	C	Scale Value
Adult movies rated XXX	[Yes]	[Yes]	[Yes]	4
Playboy magazine	[Yes]	[Yes]	[No]	3
Lingerie advertisements	[Yes]	[No]	[No]	2
New York Times	[No]	[No]	[No]	1

B: Inconsistencies in Responses

"I think the following contains pornographic material"	Subject A	B	C	Scale Value
Adult movies rated XXX	[Yes]	[Yes]	[Yes]	4
Playboy magazine	[Yes]	[No]	[Yes]	3
Lingerie advertisements	[Yes]	[Yes]	[No]	2
New York Times	[No]	[No]	[Yes]	1

C: Coding Inconsistencies

"I think the following contains pornographic material"	Subject A	B	C	Scale Value
Adult movies rated XXX	(+)	(+)	(+)	4
Playboy magazine	(+)	(+)	(+)	3
Lingerie advertisements	(+)	(-)	(+)	2
New York Times	(+)	(+)	(-)	1

Exhibit 7-2(A) shows how we can score responses: Subject A would receive a score of 2 on this scale, Subject B a score of 3, and Subject C would score 4. Subject C would be thought to have the highest threshold for pornography of these three individuals.

But suppose the subjects responded as in Exhibit 7-2(B). This kind of response is possible if the scale is not unidimensional, or if the scale language is not being interpreted the same by each respondent, or if the respondents are simply not responding in a reliable manner. Person B, for instance, would not be expected to rate lingerie advertisements as pornographic once *Playboy* magazine has been rated as not pornographic. To do so might mean that another dimension, such as accessibility by minors, plays a role in these judgments. In that case the scale would not be just measuring the single dimension of a person's threshold for pornography, which is what we would expect the scale to do. Instead the scale might be measuring that person's threshold for pornography depending upon whether minors do or do not have access to the content, so it would not be unidimensional.

Cumulative scaling provides a statistic, called the *coefficient of reproducibility* (CR), which indicates the degree to which the pattern of responses is consistent with what would be expected in a perfect unidimensional scale. Its formula is:

$$CR = 1.0 - (\text{Number of inconsistencies/Number of choices})$$

In the example in Exhibit 7-2 there are 12 choices (3 subjects × 4 questions). The inconsistencies are marked in part C of that figure as (−). For person B, the inconsistency lies in the fact that after rating *Playboy* as nonpornographic, lingerie ads are rated as pornographic again. Similarly, C rates the *New York Times* as pornographic after having said that lingerie advertisements are not. Using the data from part C we determine the value of the coefficient of reproducibility to be:

$$CR = 1.0 - \left(\frac{2}{12}\right) = .8333$$

The higher this coefficient, the more confident you can be that the scale is measuring only a single theoretical concept (that is, that every respondent is interpreting the language similarly) and that the respondents are replying in a reliable and logical fashion.

Thurstone and Guttman procedures can be combined to create an equal-appearing interval, unidimensional scale. But the amount of effort required to create such a scale would probably only be expended where measurement is critical. In many cases Likert-type magnitude scales are sufficient to meet typical measurement demands.

Reliability

Establishing the reliability of the measurement is critical to good scientific observation and allows us to increase confidence in our findings.

Remember that one of the basic requirements of science is that independent observers measuring the same theoretical concept will always see the same thing, regardless of when or where the measurements are made. While some concept like "freedom" may mean many things to many people, this should never be the case with measurement of a scientific concept. All measurements have to exhibit two basic characteristics: *stability* and *consistency*. To the degree that they do, we call them reliable measures.

Stability

A stable measure will yield identical measurement results whenever it is applied to an identical amount of the theoretical concept. To illustrate this, let's consider a thermometer scale which is a measure of the theoretical concept "temperature." If the measurements of a thermometer are stable, the thermometer will give identical results whenever it encounters the same temperature. To test this stability, we'll take the thermometer and place it in a jar of ice water for several minutes, then record its scale reading. Suppose the thermometer reads 0 degrees Celsius. Then we'll take the thermometer out of the water and let it return to room temperature. After a while, we'll again place it in the ice water, let it remain a few minutes, and read the scale once more. If the thermometer scale is a reliable measure of temperature, it will read 0 degrees once again. But suppose it now reads 2 degrees C instead of zero. If we repeat the procedure several times, we find that the thermometer reads −1 degree C., 3 degrees C., 0 degrees C., and −2 degrees C., on subsequent trials. This thermometer is exhibiting some instability in measurement, and thus it is somewhat unreliable.

Any measure used in communication research can also be tested for stability in a similar fashion. This procedure is often called *test-retest reliability*. Suppose we have a measurement instrument which quantifies the theoretical concept "communication apprehension," defined as the amount of fear or nervousness a person experiences before giving a public presentation. We would expect the measure to give identical results if it was given to the same person on two consecutive days (or some similar short time interval within which we can be fairly sure that nothing happened to change the amount of apprehension). To test the stability of the measure, we might select a random sample of college students, and give them the test in two consecutive class meetings. Each person will then have two scores, one for the first response to the instrument and one for the second. If the two scores are identical for all persons, the measure is perfectly reliable (from the standpoint of stability).

But since perfect reliability is a very unusual situation in behavioral research, we need to use some mathematical way of expressing the amount of stability shown by a measure. One way would be to simply take the difference between the two scores for each person, and average this difference over all persons. The resulting "average stability error" will give some indication of the test reliability, expressed in the same units as are used by the measurement. More commonly, stability is computed with a correlation coefficient (described in Chapter 19) which ranges from +1.0 for perfect reliability to 0.0 when no consistent pattern of relationship can be found between the second measurement and the first. This reliability index has the virtue of being *standardized*—that is, of having the same range and meaning for any measurement instrument, regardless of its actual measurement units, be they temperature degrees, apprehension scale points, or any other metric.

Some kinds of measures have characteristics that make test-retest reliability checks inappropriate. Usually this happens when there is something about the first measurement that affects the second. In the case of the communication apprehension scale, it is possible that during the retest subjects might remember the scale questions and their answers from the first test administration. The consistency in answers introduced by memory will falsely inflate the stability estimate. In these cases, a *multiple sample* (sometimes called a dual sample or split sample) check may be used.

We already know that two (or more) random probability samples drawn from the same population will have the same characteristics (subject to some sampling error, which decreases as the number of observations in the samples increases). A stable measuring instrument applied to each sample should give identical readings, at least within the range of expected sampling error. We can thus apply the measure to two or more random samples from the same population, and compare the results.

Describing the actual statistics for quantifying the degree of multiple sample stability will have to wait until we introduce the ideas of sampling distributions and inferential tests for differences between two or more samples in much more detail in later chapters.

Consistency

Stability is only one characteristic of reliable measurement. Reliability, in addition, demands that our operational definition describe a measurement procedure which behaves in a consistent fashion. There are two major kinds of consistency.

Interjudge or *intercoder reliability* determines the consistency with which the measurement rules, categories, or procedures defined in the operational definition are applied by human judges. In a content analysis of newspaper stories, for example, we might want to determine the amount of coverage devoted to a content category called "positive economic news." The amount of coverage is to be measured by calculating the number of square inches devoted to this type of coverage in each newspaper in our sample. However, the nature of "positive economic news" is open to interpretation by the person doing the measurement. To the extent that two coders differ in their judgment of ambiguous stories, the measure will be unreliable.

To assess the amount of unreliability, we can give two or more coders the same stories to measure. The reliability of the positive economic news variable can then be determined by finding the extent of agreement among the coders. The average correlation among the coders might be used to characterize the intercoder reliability.

We might set some lower limit like .80 for reliability as a limit below which we will not consider the measurement of the variable as reliable enough to be useful. If the reliability figure is 1.0, the variable positive economic news is perfectly reliable, and we can trust the observations made with this operational definition. But if it is .65, we will have to take some corrective action. The first thing we can do is to improve the operational definition. This can be accomplished by being more specific in what, to us, constitutes positive economic news. This will make it easier for the coders to recognize the concept being measured and thus to agree upon its presence and amount. A second thing we can do is to improve our measurement procedure. For instance, we might train coders more thoroughly to improve their ability to recognize "positive economic news." Or we might use more diligent persons as coders.

Another kind of consistency is important when a measure is made up of more than one item, indicator, or question. This is the *internal consistency* of the indicator items. If the items are all supposed to be measuring the same theoretical concept, they should perform in predictable ways. To the degree that they do not, the measure constructed from them is unreliable.

We have already shown an example of one kind of internal consistency test in our discussion of the coefficient of reproducibility in Guttman scaling. Since each test item is supposed to be measuring a different magnitude of the same concept, we can predict the pattern of responses which we should see, and use a numerical measure to compute the degree to which we actually see the pattern.

One common way to combine measurement indicators is simply to add scale scores. Suppose we wished to measure a concept called "positive facial expression" in a nonverbal

EXHIBIT 7-3   Examples of Likert Scaling

			Pleasant			
1	2	3	4	5	6	7
Very					Not at all	
			Happy			
1	2	3	4	5	6	7
Very					Not at all	
			Appealing			
1	2	3	4	5	6	7
Very					Not at all	
			Favorable			
1	2	3	4	5	6	7
Very					Not at all	

communication experiment. We ask the subjects in an experiment to rate a number of photographs on a series of Likert-type scales, such as the ones in Exhibit 7-3.

To compute the measure of overall positive facial expression, our operational definition instructs us simply to sum all the scale values. We expect that each of these items should be answered similarly; that is, photographs scoring high on one scale should score high on the others, since all scales indicate similar aspects of the theoretical concept. If we see experimental subjects consistently rating photographs in the "very happy" range at the same time they rate them as "not at all appealing," we lack internal consistency within the items.

There are a number of ways to measure internal consistency, some of them requiring very sophisticated statistical procedures. They are discussed extensively in some of the texts we've listed at the end of this chapter. We'll mention some to guide you in your search. A very common indicator of internal consistency is *Cronbach's Alpha*. One can also use correlation coefficients or factor analysis to determine the degree of similarity in scale responses.

A note of caution: It is *not* always necessary to have internal consistency in measurement items in order to have a reliable measure. Internal consistency is required only when a series of individual items is used to measure a common aspect of a theoretical construct. If each item measures a different aspect of the concept, then the series of items does not necessarily have to be answered in a consistent pattern. In the example above, if we consider "happy" and "favorable" as somewhat independent components of positive facial expression, it would not be necessary for the subjects to rate the photographs similarly on each scale. A expression could be simultaneously happy and unfavorable or favorable and unhappy. This would mean that measures of internal consistency could be low.

However, if the items are actually independent, as in the above example, we probably should not be simply adding together the scale values. To do so is to add possibly unrelated units (apples to oranges), which may give us misleading/distorted results (Is one unit of "happy" really equal to one unit of "favorable"?). Low internal consistency figures may indicate that we should examine our theoretical definition, to make sure that it truly is

TABLE 7-2   Increasing Reliability with Multiple Items

	Subject 1	Subject 2	Subject 3	Subject 4
Pleasant	6	5	5	7
Happy	5	6	6	6
Appealing	6	6	7	5
Favorable	4	4	3	3
Positive Facial Expression (Sum)	21	21	21	21

unidimensional. If it is not, we'd be well advised treating the concept as a multidimensional construct.

The perceptive reader may wonder why we would bother with internal consistency at all, since it just measures the similarity of response to duplicate measurement items. Why not just get rid of the duplication and use a single item? Instead of using four scales to measure positive facial expression, why not use one scale that just asks for the amount of such expression?

The reason is simple—using multiple items increases reliability. Any single item may be somewhat unreliable by itself, but in conjunction with a number of similar items, may produce a reliable measure. Two different subjects in our experiment may rate a photograph slightly differently on the "happy" scale and also slightly differently on the "favorable" scale, etc., but these small differences will tend to cancel over the whole set of scales. Table 7-2 shows that, although the different subjects have somewhat different ratings of the photograph on the individual scales, their overall summed ratings of the positiveness of facial expression are identical.

Reliability may also increase with multiple indicators because each item can be described or defined in much more concrete terms than a single operational measure of the overall concept. For example, it is more specific to ask to what degree the photograph shows a "happy," a "favorable," or a "pleasant" expression than to ask for "positive" expressions. Providing multiple items increases our ability to obtain accurate responses as the respondents do not have to define "positive" for themselves. Requiring each respondent to make such a definition might introduce a large amount of difference in responses because of differences in individual interpretations.

Validity

Our measurement must be not only reliable, it must also be valid. As we saw in Chapter 2, the degree to which the operational definition reflects the same meaning as the theoretical definition determines the most critical kind of validity, *measurement validity*. (This is also sometimes called *empirical validity*.) The amount of measurement validity cannot be determined by any numerical method. It relies on a self-evident overlap between "verbal world" theoretical definitions and "measurement world" operational definitions. Furthermore, the self-evident overlap must be generally agreed upon by independent observers. It is not enough that an operational definition shows measurement validity to the researcher who constructs it; it must also exhibit the same measurement validity to other researchers and critics.

Some kinds of validity can be inferred by observing the pattern of relationships between measurements. The basic logic of these kinds of validity tests is explained below.

Concurrent Validity

If my operational definition provides valid measurement, the results it gives should covary strongly (or agree) with the results given by other operational definitions of the same concept or measures of a related concept. This is called *concurrent* or *convergent validity*. If I construct a measure of "reading ability," I expect that it will correlate highly with a high-school student's SAT-Verbal score which reflects general verbal ability. If it does not, there is some reason to question the validity of my measurement.

Valid measurements may not correlate perfectly with other measures of the same concept, however, for two reasons other than a mismatch between the theoretical and operational definitions: First, the measurements of the concepts being compared are probably not perfectly reliable. An unreliable measure cannot correlate perfectly with *any* measure, as it contains some random "noise." Second, the two theoretical definitions of the concept may differ somewhat. My definition of verbal ability may emphasize vocabulary, while the SAT-Verbal definition may emphasize logical relationships in language. Since the verbal world of the two theoretical definitions does not overlap perfectly, the measurement world of their respective operational definitions cannot overlap perfectly either. Because of these limitations, we usually expect to find a moderate, but not perfect, convergent validity.

Discriminant Validity

If my operational definition provides valid measurement, the results it gives should NOT covary strongly with the results given by measures of different concepts. This is called *discriminant validity*. My measure of verbal ability should not correlate strongly with a student's SAT-Math scores. If the relationships between my verbal ability measure and the SAT-Verbal and the SAT-Math scores are comparable in size, I can conclude that I have an indiscriminate measure, and thus one which is at least partially invalid. Perhaps my operational definition really measures intellectual abilities of all kinds, and thus is only partially a valid measure of verbal ability.

Construct Validity

The object of assessing convergent and discriminant validity is to determine that an operational definition provides measurement of only the defined concept, *and not* measurement of any other concept. But the degree of measurement of the target concept can vary. That is, it is possible that an operational definition measures only part of the meaning outlined in the theoretical definition. The degree to which the operational definition taps the full meaning of the theoretical definition is called *construct validity*. This is obviously closely related to measurement validity, and the two terms are sometimes used interchangeably. However, we will consider construct validity as a quantifiable idea, like convergent validity.

One way to assess construct validity is by means of multiple indicators. If the meaning of the theoretical concept or construct is somewhat abstract, one way to measure it is by operationally defining a number of different measurement indicators which get at different parts of the meaning. In Chapter 2 we saw an example of this in the definition of "source credibility." This concept was defined as a combination of formal education, experience, job title, mode of dress, objectivity, and other more concrete concepts. If we operationally define these concepts, so that they are measured as separate indicators of source credibility, we can combine them to form a measurement of the more abstract concept of source credibility. The question of construct validity then becomes this: How well do my indicators, when combined, represent the full meaning of the theoretical concept? To answer this question, I can ask a sample of respondents to rate a number of communication sources on the above indicators, and also on a summary scale of source credibility. The covariance between the total set of indicators and the summary scale is an estimate of the construct validity. The statistical methods necessary to calculate this estimate will be addressed much later in this book. They involve multiple correlation and other advanced statistics.

Figure 7-5 graphically illustrates the relationships between theoretical meanings and operational measurement which have been outlined here. The bold boxes in each part of the figure represent the overlap between each of the boxes immediately above and below.

Summary

Chapter 2 of this book provided an introduction to the explication of theoretical concepts: the process of producing theoretical and operational definitions. In this chapter we have extended this discussion of operational definitions to include detailed descriptions of how different strategies in operationalization will yield different levels of measurement, how these levels of measurement can be quantified by the different types of scaling methods, and how we can assess the adequacy of measurement.

The level of measurement is an important topic due to the varying amounts of information provided by the different levels of measurement. *Nominal* measurement represents the lowest form of measurement: The various categories in a nominal factor are merely mutually exclusive and exhaustive. An observation assigned to a given category is considered identical to all the other observations in that category and not identical to the observations in other categories. *Ordinal* measurement adds to the dimension of magnitude: The categories in an ordinal variable can be ordered as representing "more" or "less" of a particular attribute. *Interval* measurement adds to this the notion of equal intervals of some metric, be they of an absolute or of an arbitrary nature. The presence of equal intervals allows us to extend statements of "more" to "How *many units* more?" Finally, *ratio* measurement incorporates an explicit or implicit absolute zero indicating the absence of whatever it is we attempt to measure. The presence of a zero unit means that different observations can be compared in statements such as "twice as much as" or "only half as much as."

The process of converting ordinal or better levels of measures to numerical measurement is called *scaling*. We distinguished between two general categories of scaling: measurement in terms of natural or established metrics which requires either interval or ratio measurement, and the scaling of magnitude, which applies generally to

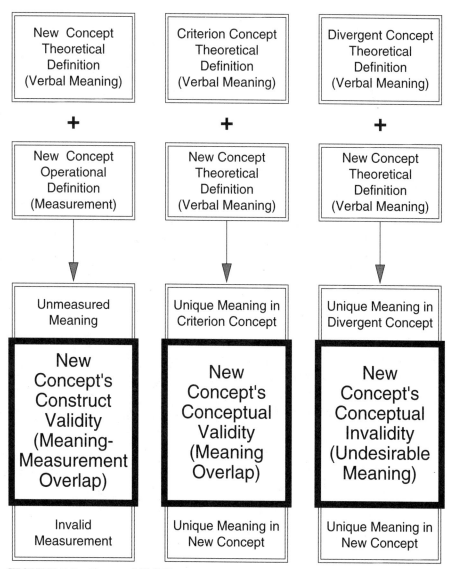

FIGURE 7-5 Types of Validity

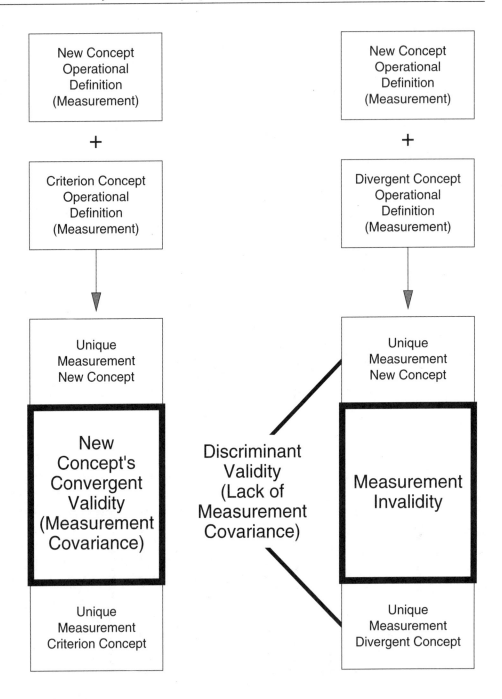

FIGURE 7-5 *Continued*

measurement that is inherently ordinal in nature. Specific examples of *magnitude scaling* are Likert scales and the semantic differential scale. The Thurstone and Guttman types of scales can be considered to be attempts to introduce equal or nearly equal intervals in what is essentially ordinal measurement.

Regardless of level of measurement, the most important criterion of evaluation of any measurement scheme has to be the adequacy of measurement. This adequacy can be evaluated in terms of two different dimensions: the *reliability* of measurement and the *validity* of measurement.

The reliability of measurement refers to how well a measurement scheme works, and its ability to operate properly can be expressed in terms of its *stability* and its *consistency*. A measure is considered to be stable if it gives identical results whenever an identical observation is encountered. A stretchable latex ruler used to measure a board repeatedly would not be stable, as it would likely stretch differently on each application. A steel ruler, however, would give stable results. The latex ruler would also not be consistent; different people using this ruler would probably observe different results. The steel ruler, again, would yield identical measures for different users. Internal consistency is another aspect of reliability that can be determined whenever multiple scales are used to assess a single theoretical construct. Internal consistency refers to the extent to which items in scales yield similar results when applied to the same observation.

In addition to assessing how reliably we can make measurements, we should also be concerned about *validity*: whether we indeed measure what we intend to measure. One way to assess validity is through *measurement validity* or empirical validity. There is no quantitative index for this type of validity; it is based on agreement by independent observers that there is sufficient overlap between the meaning contained in the theoretical definition and the measures of the operational definition. In addition, some quantitative measures of validity exist. *Convergent validity* measures the extent to which our measurement agrees with other measures that purport to measure the same meaning. Measures of *discriminant validity,* on the other hand, are based on the premise that our measurement should disagree with other measures that purport to measure some other, different concept.

References and Additional Readings

Babbie, E. R. (1992). *The practice of social research* (6th ed.). Belmont, CA: Wadsworth (Chapter 5, "Conceptualization and Measurement"; Chapter 7, "Indexes, Scales, and Typologies").

Campbell, D. T. & Fiske, D. W. (1959). Convergent and discriminant validation by the multitrait-multimethod matrix. *Psychological Bulletin, 56,* 81–105.

Gorden, R. (1977). *Unidimensional scaling of social variables-concepts and procedures.* New York: Free Press (Chapter 1, "Scaling Theory").

Guttman, L. (1974). The basis for scalogram analysis. In G. M. Maranell (Ed.), *Scaling: A sourcebook for behavioral scientists.* Chicago: Aldine.

Kerlinger, F. N. (1986). *Foundations of behavioral research* (3rd ed.). New York: Holt, Rinehart and Winston (Chapter 29, "Objective Tests and Scales").

Likert, K. (1974). The method of constructing an attitude scale. In G. Maranell (Ed.), *Scaling—A sourcebook for the behavioral sciences* (pp. 233–243). Chicago: Aldine.

Miller, D.C. (1983). *Handbook of research design and social measurement* (4th ed.). New York: Longman (Part 4, "Selected Sociometric Scales and Indexes").

Oppenheim, A. N. (1966). *Questionnaire design and attitude measurement.* New York: Basic Books (Chapter 4, "Checklists, Rating Scales, and Inventories"; Chapter 6, "Attitude-Scaling Methods").

Osgood, C. E., Suci, G. J. & Tannenbaum, P. H. (1957). *The measurement of meaning.* Urbana, IL: University of Illinois Press.

Smith, M. J. (1988). *Contemporary communication research methods.* Belmont, CA: Wadsworth (Chapter 4, "Collecting and Measuring Data").

Thurstone, L. & Chave, E. (1929). *The measurement of attitude.* Chicago: University of Chicago Press.

Torgerson, W. S. (1958). *Theory and method of scaling.* New York: Wiley (Chapter 1, "The Importance of Measurement in Science"; Chapter 2, "The Nature of Measurement"; Chapter 3, "Classification of Scaling Methods").

Chapter 8

Describing Data: Measures of Central Tendency and Dispersion

In the previous chapter we discussed the various levels of measurement that can be used to describe the extent of a particular theoretical construct present in an individual observation. Such a description is referred to as a *datum*. An example of a datum could be how many conversations a person initiates in a given day, or how many minutes per day a person spends watching television, or how many column inches of coverage are devoted to labor issues in the *Wall Street Journal*. Multiple observations of a particular characteristic in a population or in a sample are referred to as *data*.

After we collect a set of data, we are usually interested in making some statistical summary statements about this large and complex set of individual values for a variable. That is, we want to describe a collective such as a sample or a population in its entirety. This description is the first step in bridging the gap between the "measurement world" of our limited number of observations, and the "real world" complexity. We refer to this process as describing the *distribution* of a variable. There are a number of basic ways to describe collections of data.

Describing Distributions

Description by Enumeration

One way we can describe the distribution of a variable is by enumeration, that is, by simply listing all the values of the variable. But if the data set or distribution contains more than just a few cases, the list is going to be too complex to be understood or to be communicated effectively. Imagine trying to describe the distribution of a sample of 300 observations by listing all 300 measurements.

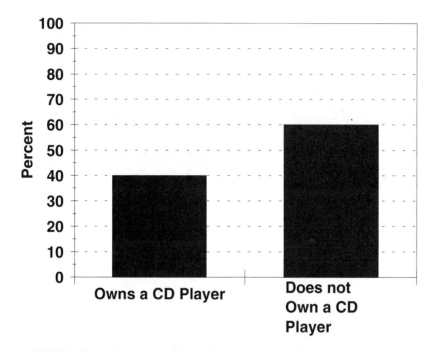

FIGURE 8-1   Representation of Data in a Bar Chart

Description by Visual Presentation

A frequently used alternative is to present the data in some visual manner, such as with a bar chart, a histogram, a frequency polygon, or a pie chart. Figures 8-1 through 8-5 give examples of each of these, and the examples suggest some limitations that apply to the use of these graphic devices.

The first limitation that can be seen in Figure 8-1 is that the data for *bar charts* should consist of a relatively small number of response categories in order to make the visual presentation useful. That is, the variable should consist of only a small number of *classes* or categories. The variable CD Player Ownership is a good example of such a variable. Its two classes (Owns a CD Player and Does not Own a CD Player) lend themselves readily to presentation via a bar chart.

Figure 8-2 gives an example of the presentation of data in a *histogram.* In a histogram the horizontal axis shows the values of the variable (in this case the number of CD discs a person reports having purchased in the previous year) and the vertical axis shows the frequencies associated with these values, that is, how many persons stated that they purchased, for instance, 8 CDs.

In histograms or bar charts, the shape of the distribution can convey a significant amount of information. This is another reason why it is desirable to conduct measurement at an ordinal or interval level, as this allows you to organize the values of a variable in some meaningful sequence. Notice that the values on the horizontal axis of the histogram are ordered from lowest to highest, in a natural sequence of increasing levels of the theoretical

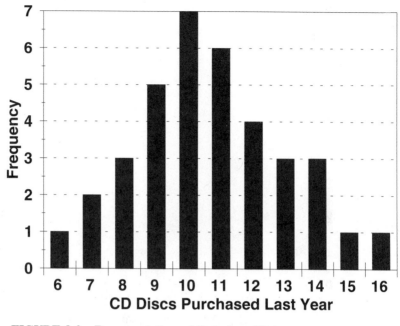

FIGURE 8-2   Representation of Data in a Histogram

concept (compact disc purchasing). If the variable to be graphed is nominal, then the various classes could be arranged visually in any one of a large number of sequences. Each of these sequences would be equally "natural," since nominal categories contain no ranking or ordering information, and each sequence would convey different and conflicting information about the distribution of the variable. The shape of the distribution would convey no useful information at all. Bar charts and histograms can be used to compare the relative sizes of nominal categories, but they are more useful when the data graphed are at the ordinal or higher level of measurement.

Figure 8-3 gives an alternative to presenting data in a histogram. This method is called a *frequency polygon*, and it is constructed by connecting the points which have heights corresponding with the frequencies on the vertical axis. Another way of thinking of a frequency polygon is as a line which connects the midpoints of the tops of the bars in the histogram.

Notice that the number of response categories that can be represented in the histogram or frequency polygon is limited. It would be very difficult to accommodate a variable with many more classes. If we want to describe a variable with a large number of classes using a histogram or a frequency polygon, we would have to collapse categories, that is, combine a number of previously distinct classes, such as the classes 0, 1, 2, and so on, into a new aggregate category, such as 0 through 4, 5 through 9, 10 through 14, etc. Although this process would reduce the number of categories and increase the ease of presentation in graphical form, it also results in a loss of information. For instance, a person who purchased 0 CDs would be lumped together with a person who purchased as many as 4 CDs in the 0–4 class, thereby losing an important distinction between these two

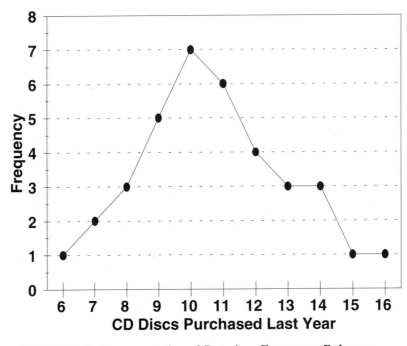

FIGURE 8-3   Representation of Data in a Frequency Polygon

individuals. Figure 8-4 illustrates the results of such a reclassification or recoding of the original data from Figure 8-3.

Yet another way of presenting data visually is in the form of a *pie chart*. Figure 8-5 shows a piechart that presents the average weekly television network ratings during prime time.

Pie charts are appropriate for presenting the distributions of nominal variables, since the order in which the values of the variable are introduced is immaterial. The four classes of the variable as presented in this chart are: tuned to ABC, tuned to NBC, tuned to CBS and, finally, tuned to anything else or not turned on. There is no "one way" in which these levels of the variable can or should be ordered. The sequence in which these shares are listed really does not matter. All we need to consider is the size of the "slice" associated with each class of the variable.

Descriptive Statistics

Another way of describing a distribution of data is by reducing the data to some essential indicator that, in a single value, expresses information about the aggregate of all observations. Descriptive statistics do exactly that. They represent or epitomize some facet of a distribution.

These descriptive statistics allow us to go beyond the mere description of a distribution. They can also be used for statistical inference, which permits generalizing from the limited

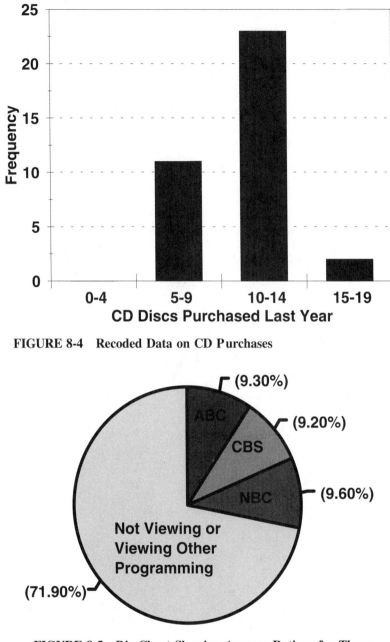

FIGURE 8-4   Recoded Data on CD Purchases

**FIGURE 8-5   Pie Chart Showing Average Ratings for Three
Networks**

number of observations in a sample to the whole population. We explained in Chapter 5 that this is a major goal of scientific endeavors. This fact alone makes descriptive statistics preferable to either enumeration or visual presentation. However, descriptive statistics are often used in conjunction with visual presentations.

Descriptive statistics can be divided into two major categories: *measures of central tendency* and *measures of dispersion or variability*. Both kinds of measures focus on different essential characteristics of distributions. A very complete description of a distribution can be obtained from a relatively small set of central tendency and dispersion measures from the two categories.

Measures of Central Tendency

The measures of central tendency describe a distribution in terms of its most frequent, typical, or average data value. But there are different ways of representing or expressing the idea of typicality. The descriptive statistics most often used for this purpose are the *mean* (the average), the *mode* (the most frequently occurring score), and the *median* (the middle score).

Mean

The mean is defined as the *arithmetic average* of a set of numerical scores, that is, the sum of all the numbers divided by the number of observations contributing to that sum.

$$\text{Mean} = \overline{X} = \text{sum of all data values/number of data values}$$

or, more formally,

$$\overline{X} = \frac{\sum_{i=1}^{N} X_i}{N}$$

which is the formula to be used when the data are in an array, which is simply a listing of a set of observations, organized by observation number. An example of data in an array can be found in Table 8-1.

Before we proceed, a few words about notation. The subscript i (in X_i) in the above formula represents the fact that there will be a number of values of the variable X, one for each observation: X_1 is the value of X for observation one (the first subject or respondent), X_2 is the value of X for the second observation, and so on, all the way to X_N, which is the value of X for the last observation (there are N observations in the sample). If we observe 25 college students and ask them how many compact discs they have bought over the last year, the response of the first person will be X_1; the second person's response will be X_2; and the last, or Nth response, will be X_{25}. The symbol $\sum$ in the formula instructs us to sum all these values of X, beginning with X_1 ($i = 1$) and continuing to do this until the last observation (N, or 25 in the example) has been included. We will encounter this notation regularly in the chapters to come.

TABLE 8-1 Organization of a Data Set

Data organized in a DATA ARRAY

i Observation Number	X_i Observation Value	i Observation Number	X_i Observation Value
1	7	28	6
2	5	29	8
3	9	30	7
4	6	31	6
5	7	32	5
6	8	33	9
7	5	34	7
8	7	35	8
9	8	36	5
10	6	37	9
11	7	38	6
12	6	39	6
13	5	40	7
14	8	41	5
15	7	42	8
16	9	43	7
17	6	44	7
18	8	45	6
19	5	46	5
20	7	47	5
21	5	48	8
22	6	49	6
23	9	50	9
24	6	51	7
25	7	52	6
26	5	53	8
27	7	54	7

$$N = 54 \qquad \sum_{i=1}^{N} X_i = 364$$

$$\overline{X} = \frac{\sum_{i=1}^{N} X_i}{N} = \frac{364}{54} = 6.74$$

Data organized in a FREQUENCY DISTRIBUTION

X_i	f (Frequency)	Cumulative Frequency	Cumulative Percentage	$f \cdot X_i$
5	11	11	20.37%	$5 \cdot 11 = 55$
6	13	$11 + 13 = 24$	44.44	$6 \cdot 13 = 78$
7	15	$24 + 15 = 39$	72.22	$7 \cdot 15 = 105$
8	9	$39 + 9 = 48$	88.88	$8 \cdot 9 = 72$
9	6	$48 + 6 = 54$	100.00	$9 \cdot 6 = 54$
	$N = 54$			$\sum f \cdot X_i = 364$

$$\overline{X} = \frac{\sum f \cdot X_i}{N} = \frac{364}{54} = 6.74$$

The reason why the sum of all the observations' values is divided by N (the number of observations) is probably intuitively clear. Computing the mean is something you have likely done innumerable times. It may, however, be informative to explain why the simple sum of a set of observations does not have much utility for describing distributions. The reason is that its value is dependent upon two factors: the *values* of the individual observations *and* the *number* of observations.

A given sum can be obtained in many different ways: four individuals who each watch 5 hours of television per day, watch, among them, 20 hours of television. The same total would also be obtained from 20 individuals who each watch 1 hour per day. These are the same sums, but they are obtained from very different data distributions. By knowing that the group as a whole watched 20 hours, we cannot draw any conclusions about how much each individual watched without knowing how many individuals were in the group. When we compute the mean we *standardize* the simple sum by spreading it evenly across all observations. The mean then represents, in our example, the "average viewing hours per person" and the information contained in the mean can be interpreted without having to know the number of individual observations in the distribution.

The mean can also be interpreted as the "balance point" or the "value center" of the distribution. Referring to the mean this way has its basis in physics, as is illustrated in Table 8-2. If we look at a data distribution as if it were a seesaw, then the mean can be taken as that point where the fulcrum keeps the board perfectly balanced. At the top of Table 8-2 the two observations (distribution values 6 and 2) are both 2 units away from the mean of 4, and 4 is the point where the distribution is balanced. Another way of stating this is to say that 6 has a deviation of +2 from the mean, and that 2 has a deviation of −2 from the mean. At the bottom of Table 8-2, the value 6 again has a deviation of +2, but now this deviation is offset by the two values of 3 which are each 1 unit away (for a total deviation of two) in the opposite direction. Here too the mean "balances out" the values on both sides of it within the data distribution. This characteristic of the mean is also known as the *zero-sum principle*; in *any* distribution, regardless of size, shape or anything else, the deviations of scores from the mean will cancel one another out, or sum to 0.00, as can be seen in Table 8-2. We will encounter the zero-sum principle again later on in this chapter.

In addition to being ordered in the form of a simple array, data can also be organized in a *frequency distribution*, as is also shown in Table 8-1. A frequency distribution is merely a convenient way of listing all the observations in a distribution by taking advantage of the fact that the observed values usually have multiple occurrences. Instead of listing, for instance, the value 5 eleven times, we create a table which lists the observed value as well as the number of times (or f, the abbreviation for frequency) the value was observed.

When data are in the form of a frequency distribution, the formula for the mean changes to take that into consideration:

$$\overline{X} = \frac{\sum f \cdot X_i}{N}$$

TABLE 8-2 Mean As the Balance Point of a Distribution

Distribution values: 6 and 2
Mean value = 4

X_i	$X_i - \overline{X}$
—	
6	+2.00
2	−2.00
—	
	0.00

← +2.00 →← −2.00 →

X_1 X_2

6   5   4   3   2

↑
Mean

Distribution values: 6, 3 and 3
Mean value = 4

X_i	$X_i - \overline{X}$
—	
6	+2.00
3	−1.00
3	−1.00
—	
	0.00

              X_3

X_1 X_2

6   5   4   3   2

↑
Mean

which instructs us to sum a set of products $(f \cdot X_i)$ and to divide that sum by the number of observations. Multiplying the value of a class in a frequency distribution by the class frequency has the same effect as adding it the same number of times when we compute the mean in the simple data array. For example, the value "5" appears 11 times in the data array. If we compute the mean by adding all the observed values in the array, we will add the value "5" to the total sum 11 times. Multiplying 5 by 11 and adding it to the total sum has the same result.

Mode

The mode is simply *the most frequently occurring* score in a distribution. The mode can be determined by observation, and its value is most easily determined in a classified frequency distribution. All we need to do is to find the highest frequency of occurrence in the frequency (f) column and note the observed value that occurred with that frequency. In the example shown in Table 8-1, the highest frequency is associated with the value 7; it is the mode for this distribution. A distribution such as this one is called a *unimodal distribution* as it only has one mode.

Suppose that the value 6 (or some other value) also had occurred 15 times. In this case there would have been two modes, and the distribution would then be called a *bimodal distribution*. It is in fact possible to have any number of modes in a distribution, although the usefulness of the mode as a descriptive measure decreases in distributions where there are many modes.

Since the mode represents the most frequently occurring score in a distribution, the mode is also often referred to as the "probability" center of the distribution. If we were to randomly select one single observation out of the distribution, the modal value is the one that we would be most likely to observe, since it occurs more often in the data than any other value.

Median

The median is the *middle* score in a distribution, determined after all the values in a distribution have been rank-ordered from lowest to highest, or vice versa. The median can also be defined as that point in a distribution above which and below which lie 50 percent of all the cases or observations in the distribution. The median is also called the *visual center* of the distribution.

We will use the data from Table 8-1 to show a method for determining the median for a frequency distribution. This frequency distribution shows a total of 54 observations of X_i divided over 5 different values. The median is to be located in such a way that 50 percent of the cases are below it, and 50 percent above. This means that the median will lie between the twenty-seventh and the twenty-eighth case, so there will be 27 cases below the median (cases 1 through 27) and 27 cases (28 through 54) above the median. This places the median somewhere between 6 and 7 in the distribution.

How do we determine the precise location? Consider the following logic. The value category 5 contains the 11 cases that are the lowest scores (20.37 percent of all observations). We find these 11 cases also in the column headed by "cumulative frequency." In passing through category 6 we find an additional 13 cases, for a cumulative frequency (so far) of 24 cases (which constitute 44.44 percent of all the cases in the distribution)—but we have not encountered the median yet; the median is not in category 6. In passing through category 7, we count an additional 15 cases, for a total of 39, or 72.22 percent of the total number of observations. Now we are above the 50 percent mark, indicating that the median is located somewhere *after* we get out of class 6 but *before* we get out of class 7.

Note that we have no data value exactly at the median in this distribution, as the median lies somewhere in the middle of class 7. But we can construct a value to represent the real meaning of the median as the center score by estimating (through interpolation) some fraction within class 7.

In order to do this we have to recognize that the categories we have labeled as 5, 6, 7 ... actually contain a range of values. In fact, by rounding, we say that all the numbers between 6.50000... and 7.49999... will fall within the category we have called 7. The real lower limit of the value 7 is then 6.5000.

We can interpolate a value for the median by using the following formula which is based on this lower limit:

$$\text{Median} = L + \frac{N/2 - cf}{f(\text{class})} \quad (I)$$

where

L is the true lower limit of the class in which we
expect to find the median (in this case, 6.5)

N is the total number of observations in the distribution
(here 54)

cf is the cumulative frequency UP TO but NOT INCLUDING the
class in which we expect the median to fall (in this
case, 24)

f(class) is the number of cases in the class in which we
expect the median to fall (in this case, 15), and

I is the width or size of the class or interval (in this
case equal to 1.0, for instance, from 6.5 to 7.5)

For this data set the median is calculated to be:

$$\text{Median} = 6.5 + \frac{54/2 - 24}{15} \quad (1)$$
$$= 6.5 + \frac{27 - 24}{15} \quad (1)$$
$$= 6.5 + \frac{3}{15} \quad (1)$$
$$= 6.5 + .2(1) = 6.7$$

If we look closely at the formula we can see its logic: $N/2$ is the number of cases at the 50 percent mark, so if we subtract from this number (27) the cumulative number of cases observed up to the lower limit of the interval (24), the difference gives the number of additional cases needed (3) in the interval in which the median occurs. Since this interval holds 15 cases (and has a range of 1), we need to go $\frac{3}{15}$ of the range into the interval. Adding this $\frac{3}{15}$, or .2, to the lower limit of the interval (6.5), gives us the final value of the median.

Comparing Mean, Mode and Median

The information obtained from these three measures of central tendency in a data distribution is similar in the sense that all reflect some aspect of the data values which is "typical" of the whole distribution. But they differ in the *kind* of "typicality" which they report and in how sensitive they are to changes in the values of the observations.

The mean represents the balance point, or center of gravity of the distribution. Its value will change when there is a change in any of the data values in the distribution.

The mode represents the most frequent or probable single value in the distribution. If the value of a datum in the distribution changes from a nonmodal value to the modal

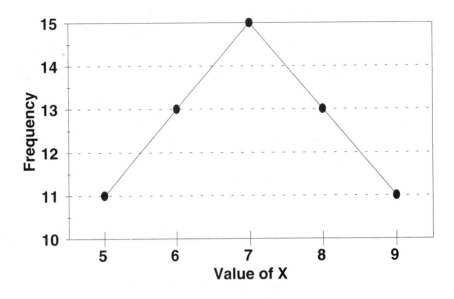

FIGURE 8-6   Example of a Symmetrical Distribution

value, the value calculated for the mode remains the same, even though the mean would (and the median might) change.

The median represents the middle score of the distribution. If the value of a datum is changed so that its position relative to the magnitude of the other values is not changed, the median will remain the same, even though the mean would, and the mode might, change.

To illustrate the differences in these measures' sensitivity to changes in the data, consider what would happen if the 6 observations of the value 9 were to change to 6 observations of the value 19. The effect on the mode and the median is nil, but the value of the mean increases from 6.74 to 7.85.

Shape of the Distribution: Skewness

There is one important situation in which all three measures of central tendency are identical. This occurs when a distribution is symmetrical, that is, when the right half of the distribution is the mirror image of the left half of the distribution. In this case the mean will fall exactly at the middle of the distribution (the median position) and the value at this central point will be the most frequently observed data value, the mode. An example of such a distribution is shown in Figure 8-6.

If the values of the mean, the mode, and the median are identical, a distribution will always be symmetrical. To the extent that differences are observed among these three measures, the distribution is asymmetrical or *skewed.*

Asymmetry will occur whenever the distribution contains one or more observations whose deviation from the mean is not matched by an offsetting deviation in the opposite

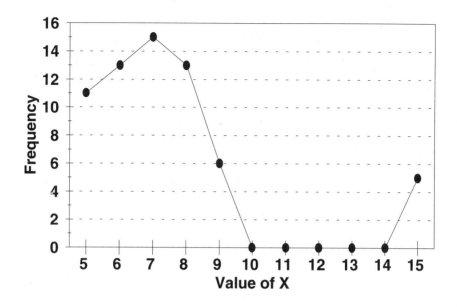

FIGURE 8-7   Example of a Skewed Distribution

direction. Figure 8-7 gives an illustration of a mildly skewed distribution, where we have simply changed some of the values shown in Figure 8-6.

This distribution contains some values on the high end of the distribution which are very far from the mean, and are not matched by corresponding values on the low end of the distribution. Consequently, the value of the mean has increased (from 7.00 to 7.46) and is drawn away from the center of the distribution toward the side of the distribution where the extreme values occurred. Note that the value of the median and the mode have not changed. Had the extreme cases been located at the low end of the distribution, then the mean would have been drawn in that direction. The degree of discrepancy between the median and the mean can then be interpreted as an indicator of skewness, or the lack of symmetry. If these two indices are identical, the distribution is symmetrical. If the mean is greater than the median, the extreme values (or "outliers") are located at the high end of the distribution and the distribution is said to be "positively skewed"; when the outliers are at the low end of the distribution, the mean will be less than the median and the distribution is said to be "negatively skewed."

Measures of Dispersion

The measures of central tendency focus on what is typical, average, or in the middle of a distribution. The information provided by these measures is not sufficient to convey all we need to know about a distribution. Figure 8-8 gives a number of examples of distributions which share the same measures of central tendency, but are radically different from one

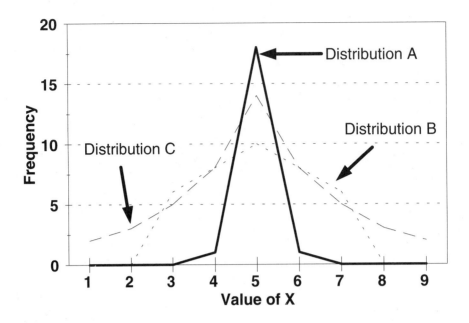

FIGURE 8-8   **Distributions with Identical Measures of Central Tendency and Varying Degrees of Dispersion**

another in another aspect, that is, how the observations are distributed (or *dispersed*) around these measures of central tendency.

For simplicity's sake we have presented these three distributions as symmetrical distributions, and from the preceding sections you will recall that the mean, median, and mode are all equal in such a case. All similarity ends there, however. When we inspect distribution A, we see that the values in that distribution all equal 5 with the exception of single instances of the values 4 and 6. Distribution B shows a pattern of greater dispersion: the values 3 and 4 and 6 and 7 occur repeatedly in this distribution, but not as frequently as the value 5. The greatest degree of dispersion is observed in distribution C: Here values as small as 1 and as large as 9 are observed.

The main point to remember from these examples is that knowing the mean, the median, or the mode (or all of these) of a distribution does not allow us to differentiate among distributions A, B, and C in Figure 8-8. We need additional information about the distributions. This information is provided by a series of measures which are commonly referred to as measures of dispersion. These measures of dispersion can be divided into two general categories: *between-points* measures of dispersion and *around-point* measures of dispersion.

Between-Points Measures of Dispersion

One way of conceptualizing dispersion is to think of the degree of similarity-dissimilarity in a distribution. There is dispersion when there is dissimilarity among the data values. The greater the dissimilarity, the greater the degree of dispersion. Therefore a distribution in which the values of all the observations are equal to one another (and where the value of each observation then is equal to the value of the mean) has no dispersion. If the values are not equal to one another, some will be larger than the mean and some will be smaller. Measuring the distance between the highest and lowest values will then provide us with a measure of dispersion. The description "between-points" is used, since the measure of dispersion refers to the end points of the distribution.

Crude Range and Range

Based on this logic are two commonly used measures of dispersion: the *crude range* and the *range*.

The former is defined as follows:

$$\text{Crude range} = \begin{array}{c}\text{highest}\\\text{observed}\\\text{value}\end{array} - \begin{array}{c}\text{lowest}\\\text{observed}\\\text{value}\end{array}$$

For the examples in Figure 8-8, the crude range for the three distributions is:

$$\text{Distribution A:} \quad 6 - 4 = 2$$
$$\text{Distribution B:} \quad 7 - 3 = 4$$
$$\text{Distribution C:} \quad 9 - 1 = 8$$

The range is defined as

$$\text{range} = \begin{array}{c}\text{highest}\\\text{observed}\\\text{value}\end{array} - \begin{array}{c}\text{lowest}\\\text{observed}\\\text{value}\end{array} + 1$$

which therefore equals the crude range plus 1.

For the examples in Figure 8-8 this formula gives Distribution A a range of 3, Distribution B a range of 5, and Distribution C a range of 9.

The range can be interpreted as the number of different value classes between the highest and the lowest observed values, including the highest and lowest classes themselves. But this does not mean that observations were in fact found in all the classes between these extremes. The weakness of the range (and of the crude range) is that its value is only sensitive to the highest and lowest valued observations in the distribution. This can be misleading.

Distribution C in Figure 8-8 has a range of 9, indicating that there were 9 classes of values, and, in fact, cases were observed in all nine classes. But consider the following distribution which also has a range of 9:

X_i	f
1	1
4	14
5	20
6	14
9	1

The range for this distribution is also equal to $9(9-1+1)$, but the dispersion of values is very different from that found in Figure 8-8. The distribution could more accurately be described as consisting of the values 4, 5, and 6, with two extreme values, 1 and 9. These infrequently occurring extreme values (sometimes called "outliers"), in fact determine the value of the range in this case. For this reason we should be very careful in interpreting the value of the range, as it will be affected by rarely occurring extreme values that may occur because of measurement error.

Around-Point Measures of Dispersion

The second category of measures of dispersion is based on the same conceptualization of dispersion as explained above, but with some different logic in its calculation. Instead of looking at the extreme instances of data values as we did in computing the range, the around-point measures of dispersion look at differences between individual data values and the mean of the set of values.

Because these methods are based on comparing data values (located around the mean) with the mean, we call them "around-point" measures of dispersion. Dispersion is measured by calculating the extent to which each data value is different from that point in the distribution where the mean is located. We call this difference the *deviation from the mean*. For this deviation we will use the following notation:

$$(X_i - \overline{X})$$

Table 8-3 gives an example of two distributions with varying degrees of dispersion. For each value of X, the deviation from the mean has been computed. To determine the degree of dispersion in each distribution, it would appear that we would merely need to sum the individual deviations, like this:

$$\sum f \cdot (X_i - \overline{X})$$

However, because of the zero-sum principle we will quickly find that the sums of the deviations will equal zero for *any* distribution, regardless of the degree of dispersion. It follows that the average deviation also has to be zero. For this reason sums of deviations (and thus average deviations) are useless for comparing the dispersion of these distributions.

Squaring the Deviations
However, we can readily overcome the zero-sum principle by squaring the deviations from the mean. This process is illustrated in Table 8-4. Squaring a deviation rids us of the

TABLE 8-3   Deviations and Sums of Deviations from the Mean in Two Distributions

A				B			
X_i	f	$(X_i - \overline{X})$	$f \cdot (X_i - \overline{X})$	X_i	f	$(X_i - \overline{X})$	$f \cdot (X_i - \overline{X})$
3	6	−2	−12	1	2	−4	−8
4	8	−1	−8	2	3	−3	−9
5	10	0	0	3	5	−2	−10
6	8	+1	+8	4	8	−1	−8
7	6	+2	+12	5	14	0	0
		$\sum f(X_i - \overline{X}) = 0$		6	8	+1	+8
				7	5	+2	+10
				8	3	+3	+9
				9	2	+4	+8
						$\sum f \cdot (X_i - \overline{X}) = 0$	

sign of the deviation, because squaring a positive deviation yields a positive value (or, more precisely, an unsigned one); and squaring a negative deviation gives the same result. Summing the squared deviations will then produce a non-zero sum under *all conditions but one*: In a distribution with *no* dispersion (when all the values in a distribution are equal to one another and therefore equal to the mean), all the deviations from the mean will equal zero, will remain equal to zero when squared, and will sum to zero.

The Sum of Squared Deviations

Below is the notation for computing the squared deviation from the mean:

$$(X_i - \overline{X})^2$$

Based on the squared deviation, the sum of the squared deviations for a classified frequency distribution is then computed as follows:

$$\sum f \cdot (X_i - \overline{X})^2$$

Table 8-4 illustrates the computation of the sum of squared deviations (also often referred to as the sum of squares) for the two distributions A and B from Table 8-3.

For Distribution A, the distribution with the smaller dispersion, the sum of the squared deviations is equal to 64, for Distribution B the sum of squares equals 174.

Variance

If we want to compare distributions with differing numbers of observations, the sum of squared deviations needs to be standardized to the number of observations contributing to

TABLE 8-4   Computing Around-Point Measures of Disperson: Sums of Squared Deviations, Variance, and Standard Deviation.

	Distribution A				Distribution B		
X_i	f	$(X_i - \overline{X})^2$	$f \cdot (X_i - \overline{X})^2$	X_i	f	$(X_i - \overline{X})^2$	$f \cdot (X_i - \overline{X})^2$
3	6	4	24	1	2	16	32
4	8	1	8	2	3	9	27
5	10	0	0	3	5	4	20
6	8	1	8	4	8	1	8
7	6	4	24	5	14	0	0
				6	8	1	8
				7	5	4	20
$\overline{X} = 5$				8	3	9	27
$N = 38$				9	2	16	32

$\overline{X} = 5$

$N = 50$

$$\sum f \cdot (X_i - \overline{X})^2 = 64$$

$$\text{Variance} = \frac{64}{38} = 1.68$$

Standard deviation $= \sqrt{1.68}$

$= 1.30$

$$\sum f \cdot (X_i - \overline{X})^2 = 174$$

$$\text{Variance} = \frac{174}{50} = 3.48$$

Standard deviation $= \sqrt{3.48}$

$= 1.87$

that sum. To do this, we compute the *average squared deviation*, which is more frequently referred to as the *variance*. The formula for determining a distribution's variance is as follows:

$$\text{Variance} = \frac{\sum f \cdot (X_i - \overline{X})^2}{N}$$

Applying this formula to the sums of squares of distributions A and B yields variances of 1.68 and 3.48, respectively, as illustrated in Table 8-4. The value of the variance is interpreted as the average squared deviation of all observations and can be used to compare different-sized distributions. Our conclusion from comparing the variances of A and B is that the scores in Distribution B are more dispersed than are those in Distribution A.

Standard Deviation

Remember that we squared an observation's deviation from the mean in order to overcome the zero-sum principle. The sum of squared deviations and the variance we obtained are therefore squared versions of the original deviations from the mean. To return to the magnitude of the original units of measurement we simply reverse the distortion introduced from squaring an observation's deviation from the mean by taking the square root of the variance. This produces another measure of dispersion, which is referred to as the *standard*

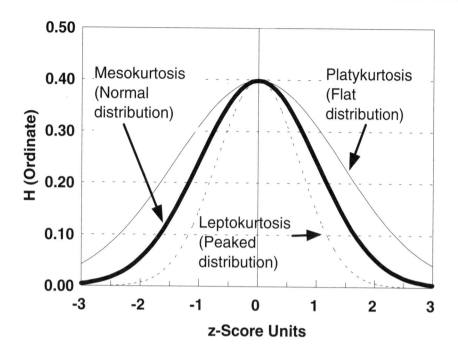

FIGURE 8-9   Shapes of Distributions: Kurtosis

deviation. The formula for determining the value of the standard deviation is defined as follows:

$$\text{Standard deviation} = \sqrt{\frac{\sum f \cdot (X_i - \overline{X})^2}{N}}$$

This description of dispersion can now be expressed in the original units of measurement. If the X_i values in Table 8-4 are the number of conversations with children per day, then we can say that the standard deviation of Distribution A is 1.30 conversations, while that of Distribution B is 1.87 conversations.

Shape of a Distribution: Kurtosis

Earlier in this chapter we discussed skewness, the degree to which a distribution deviates from symmetry. Another way in which a distribution can be characterized is in terms of kurtosis, or whether a distribution can be described as relatively flat, or peaked, or somewhere in between. Different shapes of distributions have different labels, and some of them are shown in Figure 8-9.

A leptokurtic distribution is a relatively tall and narrow distribution, indicating that the observations were tightly clustered within a relatively narrow range of values. Another way of describing a leptokurtic distribution would be to say that it is a distribution with

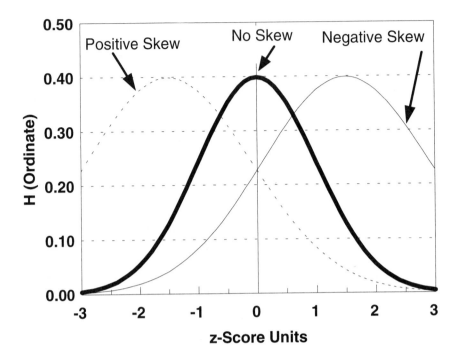

FIGURE 8-10   Shapes of Distributions: Skew

relatively little dispersion. A mesokurtic distribution reveals observations to be more distributed across a wider range of values, and a platykurtic distribution is one where proportionately fewer cases are observed across a wider range of values. We could also say that mesokurtic and platykurtic distributions are increasingly flatter, and have increasingly greater dispersions.

Figure 8-10 shows another example of skew in a normal distribution. None of the distributions in Figure 8-10 vary in kurtosis. All are mesokurtic.

Measurement Requirements for Measures of Central Tendency and Measures of Dispersion

The choice of descriptive measures depends entirely on the level of measurement for a particular variable. To refresh your memory, the levels of measurement are:

TABLE 8-5   Appropriateness of Measures of Central Tendency and Dispersion for Different Levels of Measurement

	Mode	Median	Mean	Variance/ Standard Deviation
Nominal	yes	no	no	no
Ordinal	yes	yes	no	no
Interval/Ratio	yes	yes	yes	yes

Nominal measurement	merely a set of mutually exclusive and exhaustive categories.
Ordinal measurement	as in nominal, but with the addition of an underlying dimension which allows comparative statements about a larger or smaller quantity of the property being measured.
Interval measurement	as in ordinal, with the addition of equal sized value intervals separating each of the value classes. Values are continuous, i.e., fractional values of intervals are meaningful.
Ratio measurement	as in interval, but the scale includes an absolute zero class.

The measures of central tendency require different minimum levels of measurement. Table 8-5 indicates appropriate central tendency statistics, for a given level of measurement.

As we mentioned in Chapter 7, the measurement decisions made while specifying the operational definition for a concept will have consequences. For instance, operationally defining a dependent variable at the ordinal level denies the possibility of computing a mean for the variable. This is important, because a statistical test that contrasts means can't be used to establish a relationship between this variable and another one; a test that contrasts medians, however, would be appropriate. The most sensitive measure of central tendency is the mean, and it can be meaningfully computed only for interval- or ratio-level data. This argues for making every attempt to obtain interval or ratio levels of measurement for variables. With interval/ratio data the widest range of statistics, and those most sensitive to subtle differences in data distributions, can be used.

The basis for computing the sum of squared deviations, the variance, and the standard deviation is an observation's deviation from the mean. The level of measurement required for these measures of dispersion is therefore identical to the level of measurement required for computing means, i.e. interval/ratio measurement. If the theoretical concept is measured at the nominal or ordinal levels, these descriptions of dispersion are meaningless.

Central Tendency and Dispersion Considered Together

There are a number of reasons why it is useful to consider the descriptions of central tendency and dispersion together.

The first one is the ability to fully describe distributions. The computation of *both* measures of central tendency *as well as* measures of dispersion allows us to describe distributions with sufficient detail to visualize their general dimensions; neither the measures of central tendency nor the measures of dispersion alone allow us to do this. For instance, Distribution A in Table 8-4 is characterized by a mean, mode, and median of 5, as is Distribution B. This just tells us that the two distributions are symmetrical, and have the same central values. But adding the information that Distribution A has a standard deviation of 1.30, as compared to B's standard deviation of 1.87, tells us that the latter has a more dispersed distribution; that is, it is "wider" in appearance than Distribution A.

Z-score

A second, and extremely useful, way in which measures of central tendency and dispersion can be used together is in the *standard score*, also known as the *z-score*. A standard or *z*-score represents an observations's deviation from the mean, expressed in standard deviation units:

$$z_i = \frac{X_i - \overline{X}}{\text{Standard Deviation of } X}$$

By dividing by the standard deviation, we can compare data values from distributions which vary widely in dispersion. For very dispersed distributions, the standard deviation will be large, and thus a very large deviation from the mean is required before the *z*-score becomes large. For distributions with data values tightly clustered around the mean (i.e., with very small standard deviations), a very small deviation from the mean can give the same standard score. Standard scores thus tell us how far a data observation is from the mean—relatively, where it is positioned in the distribution.

Z-scores are useful in a number of different ways. First, from the formula it can be readily seen that the *z*-score is a *signed value*, that is, a non-zero *z*-score has either a negative or a positive value. If the score to be "standardized" is larger than the mean, the deviation will be a positive one and the value of the *z*-score will be positive. If the score to be standardized is smaller than the mean, the resulting *z*-score will be negative. The sign of a *z*-score thus tells us immediately whether an observation is located above or below the mean. The position of an unstandardized (or "raw") data value relative to the mean can only be determined if we know the mean, but a *z*-score communicates this information directly.

Second, the *magnitude* of the *z*-score communicates an observation's relative distance to the mean, as compared to other data values. A *z*-score of +.10 tells us that an observation has a positive, though relatively small, deviation from the mean, as compared to all the other data values in the distribution. It is only one-tenth of a standard deviation above the mean. On the other hand, an exam grade which standardizes to a *z*-score of −2.30 indicates that the unfortunate recipient of that grade turned in one of the poorest performances. It's not only below the mean (a negative *z*-score), but it's also a very large deviation, compared to the deviation for the average student. This is indicated by the large *z*-score value obtained after dividing the student's deviation from the mean by the standard deviation, i.e., making the student's deviation from the mean proportional to the "average" deviation.

TABLE 8-6   Standardizing a Distribution

	Raw Scores				Raw Scores Converted to Standard Scores		
X_i	f	$(X_i - \overline{X})^2$	$f \cdot (X_i - \overline{X})^2$	z_i	f	$(z_i)^2$	$f \cdot (z_i)^2$
3	6	4	24	−1.54	6	2.37	14.20
4	8	1	8	− .77	8	.59	4.73
5	10	0	0	0.00	10	0.00	0.00
6	8	1	8	+ .77	8	.59	4.73
7	6	4	24	+1.54	6	2.37	14.20

$\sum f \cdot (X_i - \overline{X})^2 =$ 64

$\overline{X} = 5$
$N = 38$
Variance = 1.68

Standard deviation = 1.30

$\sum f \cdot (z^2) =$ 37.86

$\overline{X} = 0.00$

Variance = 37.86/38 = .996
(rounds to 1.00)
Standard deviation = $\sqrt{.996}$ = .998
(rounds to 1.00)

Again, the same interpretation could be given to a raw score only if it was accompanied by both the mean and the standard deviation.

Third, we can use z-scores to standardize entire distributions. By converting each score in a distribution to a z-score we obtain a standardized distribution. Such a standardized distribution, regardless of its original values, will have a mean of 0.0 and a variance and standard deviation of 1.0. Table 8-6 shows an example of a standardized distribution.

Table 8-6 shows that the sum of the squared deviations in the standardized distribution is equal to N (excluding rounding error), and hence that the variance and the standard deviation of a standardized distribution are equal to 1.00.

By standardizing entire distributions, we can compare very dissimilar distributions, or observations from dissimilar distributions. For instance, we can't directly compare a student's score on a 100 point exam, on which the class performance varied widely, to the same student's score on a 20 point quiz, on which all the class members performed in very similar fashion. Such a comparison would be inappropriate because the central points of the two distributions are different, and so are the dispersions of the scores. By converting the exam score and the quiz score to z-scores, the two scores become comparable because the two distributions have become comparable: both have a mean of 0.00 and a standard deviation of 1.00. Assume that the student's score on a 100 point exam was 70 and that the student also got 9 points on a 20-point quiz. Did the student perform differently on the two tasks? If we know, furthermore, that the class mean for the exam was 65, with a standard deviation of 15, and that the quiz mean and standard deviation, respectively, were 12 and 4, we can answer that question by computing the z-scores z_{exam} and z_{quiz}. These z-scores are:

$$z_{exam} = \frac{70 - 65}{15} = +.33$$

$$z_{quiz} = \frac{9 - 12}{4} = -.75$$

The *z*-scores indicate that although the student scored a little above the mean on the exam, performance on the quiz was a substantial distance below the class mean.

As another example, imagine that we are interested in determining whether a person is more dependent on television than on newspapers for news, compared to the dependence of other respondents in a survey. We can contrast that person's time spent with television news, converted to a *z*-score, to newspaper-reading time *z*-score. If the television *z*-score were to be the greater, dependence on television news would be thought to be higher.

The fourth reason why *z*-scores are useful is because they can be mathematically related to probabilities. If the standardized distribution is a normal distribution (a "bell-shaped curve") we can state the probability of occurrence of an observation with a given *z*-score. The connection between probability and *z*-scores forms the basis for statistical hypothesis testing and will be extensively discussed in the next three chapters.

Summary

In this chapter we have presented the most commonly used ways for describing distributions. Of these methods, visual representations of data appear to be relatively limited in their utility from a data-analytic point of view. Furthermore, the use of these methods is significantly constrained by the level of measurement of the data to be described.

Of particular interest to the communication researcher are the descriptive statistics which use mathematics to summarize a particular aspect of a data distribution. These aspects essentially center on what is typical or common in a distribution and on the amount of variability of data in the distribution. The first set of measures is called *measures of central tendency*; the second is called *measures of dispersion.*

Neither set of measures is sufficient by itself if we wish to have a complete visualization of a data distribution. For instance, contrasting the *mean* and the *median* will allow us to determine the degree of symmetry in a distribution, but we will also need such indicators as the *variance* or the *standard deviation* to fully describe the shape of the data distribution.

Of particular importance in this chapter is the *z-score* or *standard score,* which brings together both a measure of central tendency and a measure of dispersion. Not only does the *z*-score allow for the comparison of cases from dissimilar distributions (with differing mean and standard deviation) but it is also basic to the process of hypothesis testing and statistical inference, as it provides the link, based on probability, between a limited set of observations and other unobserved cases in the population.

The next several chapters will provide an extensive introduction to the process of statistical inference by introducing the types of distributions we'll need to consider and the role these distributions play in classical hypothesis testing. For these reasons it is imperative that you have a strong grasp of the materials that have been presented in this chapter.

References and Additional Readings

Annenberg/CPB (1989). *Against all odds.* [Videotape]. Santa Barbara, CA: Intellimation.

Hays, W. L. (1981). *Statistics* (3rd. ed.). New York: Holt, Rinehart & Winston (Chapter 4, "Central Tendency and Variability").

Kachigan, S. K. (1986). *Statistical analysis: An interdisciplinary introduction to univariate and multivariate methods.* New York: Radius Press (Chapter 4, "Central Tendency"; Chapter 5, "Variation").

Kerlinger, F. N. (1986). *Foundations of behavioral research* (3rd ed.) New York: Holt, Rinehart and Winston (Chapter 6, "Variance and Covariance").

Loether, H. J. & McTavish, D. G. (1974). *Descriptive statistics for sociologists: An introduction.* Boston: Allyn & Bacon (Part II, "Descriptive Statistics: One Variable").

Chapter 9

Distributions: Population, Sample, and Sampling Distributions

In the three preceding chapters we covered the three major steps in gathering and describing distributions of data. We described procedures for drawing samples from the populations we wish to observe; for specifying indicators that measure the concepts in the sample observations; and, in the last chapter, ways to describe a set of data, or a distribution.

In this chapter we will expand the idea of a distribution, and discuss different types of distributions and how they are related to one another. Let us begin with a more formal definition of the term *distribution*:

> *A distribution is a statement of the frequency with which units of analysis (or cases) are assigned to the various classes or categories that make up a variable.*

To refresh your memory, a variable can consist of a number of classes or categories. The variable "gender," for instance, usually consists of two classes: male and female; "marital communication satisfaction" might consist of the satisfied, neutral, and dissatisfied categories, and "time spent viewing TV" could have any number of classes, such as 25 minutes, 37 minutes, or any other integer value. The definition of a distribution simply states that a distribution tells us how many cases or observations were seen in each class or category.

For instance, a sample of 100 college students can be distributed in two classes which make up the variable "ownership of a CD player." Every observation will fall either in the owner or non-owner class. In our example, we might observe 40 students who own a CD player and a remaining 60 students who do not own a CD player. These two statements describe the distribution.

There are three different types of distributions that we will use in our basic task of observation and statistical generalization. These are the *population distribution*, which represents the distribution of all units (many or most of which will remain unobserved during our research); the *sample distribution,* which is the distribution of the observations that we actually make, after drawing a sample from the population; and the *sampling distribution,* which is a description of the accuracy with which we can make statistical generalization, using descriptive statistics computed from the sample observations.

Population Distribution

We've already defined a population as consisting of all the units of analysis for our particular study. A population distribution is made up of all the classes or values of variables which we would observe if we were to conduct a census of all members of the population. For instance, if we wish to determine whether voters approve or disapprove of a particular candidate for president, then all individuals who are eligible voters constitute the population for this variable. If we were to ask every eligible voter his or her voting intention, the resulting two-class distribution would be a population distribution. Similarly, if we wish to determine the number of column inches of coverage of *Fortune* 500 companies in the *Wall Street Journal,* then the population consists of the top 500 companies in the United States as determined by the editors of *Fortune* magazine. The population distribution is the frequency with which each value of column inches occurs for these 500 observations. Here is a formal definition of a population distribution:

> *A population distribution is a statement of the frequency with which the units of analysis or cases that together make up a population are observed* or are expected to be observed *in the various classes or categories that make up a variable.*

Note the emphasized phrase in this definition. The frequency with which units of analysis are observed in the various classes of the variable is not always known in a population distribution. *Only* if we conduct a census and measure every unit of analysis on some particular characteristic (that is, actually observe the value of a variable in every member of the population) will we be able to directly describe the frequencies of this characteristic in each class. In the majority of cases we will not be in a position to conduct a census. In these cases we will have to be satisfied with drawing a representative sample from the population. Observing the frequency with which cases fall in the various classes or categories in the sample will then allow us to formulate *expectations* about how many cases would be observed in the same classes in the population.

For example, if we find in a randomly selected (and thus representative) sample of 100 college undergraduates that 40 students own CD players, we would expect, in the absence of any information to the contrary, that 40 percent of the whole population of college undergraduates would also have a CD player. The implications of making such estimates will be detailed in following chapters.

The distribution that results from canvassing an entire population can be described by using the types of descriptive indicators discussed in the previous chapter. Measures of central tendency and dispersion can be computed to characterize the entire population distribution.

When such measures like the mean, median, mode, variance, and standard deviation of a population distribution are computed, they are referred to as *parameters*. A parameter can be simply defined as a summary characteristic of a population distribution. For instance, if we refer to the fact that in the population of humans the proportion of females is .52 (that is, of all the people in the population, 52 percent are female) then we are referring to a parameter. Similarly, we might consult a television programming archive and compute the number of hours per week of news and public affairs programming presented by the networks for each week from 1948 to the present. The mean and standard deviation of this data are population parameters.

You probably are already aware that population parameters are rarely known in communication research. When we do not know population parameters we must try to obtain the best possible estimate of a parameter by using statistics obtained from one or more samples drawn from that population. This leads us to the second kind of distribution, the sample distribution.

Sample Distribution

As was discussed in Chapter 5, we are only interested in samples that are representative of the populations from which they have been drawn, so that we can make valid statistical generalizations. This means that we will restrict our discussion to randomly selected samples. These random probability samples were defined in Chapter 6 as samples drawn in such a way that each unit of analysis in the population has an equal chance of being selected for the sample.

A sample is simply a subset of all the units of analysis which make up the population. For instance, a selected group of voters who approve or disapprove of a particular presidential candidate constitute a small subset of all those who are eligible voters (the population). If we wanted to determine the actual number of column inches of coverage given to *Fortune* 500 companies in the *Wall Street Journal* we could draw a random sample of 50 of these companies. Below is a definition of a sample distribution:

> *A sample distribution is a statement of the frequency with which the units of analysis or cases that together make up a sample are actually observed in the various classes or categories that make up a variable.*

If we think of the population distribution as representing the total information which we can get from measuring a variable, then the sample distribution represents an *estimate* of this information. This returns us to the issue outlined in Chapter 5: how to generalize from a subset of observations to the total population of observations.

We'll use the extended example from Chapter 5 to illustrate some important features of sample distributions and their relationship to a population distribution. In that example, we assumed the population consisted of only five units of analysis: five mothers of school-aged children, each of whom had differing numbers of conversations about schoolwork with her child in the past week.

TABLE 9-1   **Parameters of a fictitious population of $N = 5$ cases**

Person	X_i	$(X - M)$	$(X - M)^2$
A	5	-2	4
B	6	-1	1
C	7	0	0
D	8	1	1
E	9	2	4
	$\sum X = 35$	$\sum(X - M) = 0$	$\sum(X - M)^2 = 10$

Parameter mean $= M = \sum X/N = 35/5 = 7$

Parameter variance $= \dfrac{\sum(X - M)^2}{N} = \dfrac{10}{5} = 2$

Parameter standard deviation $= \sqrt{2} = 1.41$

The population parameters are presented in Table 9-1, along with the simple data array from which they were derived. Every descriptive measure value shown there is a parameter, as it is computed from information obtained from the entire population. But we know that any sample will contain a certain amount of sampling error, as we saw in Chapter 5. For a refresher, see Table 5-6 in that chapter for a listing of all the samples and their means that would be obtained if we took samples of $N = 3$ out of this population. Table 9-2 shows just three of the 125 different sample distributions that can be obtained when we do just this.

Since the observed values in the three samples are not identical, the means, variances, and standard deviations are different among the samples, as well. These numbers are not identical to the population parameters shown in Table 9-1. They are only *estimates* of the population values. Therefore we need some way to distinguish between these estimated values and the actual descriptive values of the population.

We will do this by referring to descriptive values computed from population data as parameters, as we did above. We'll also use the term *statistics* to refer specifically to descriptive indicators computed from sample data. The meaning of the term statistic is parallel to the meaning of the term parameter: They both characterize distributions. The distinction between the two lies in the *type* of distribution they refer to. For sample A in Table 9-2, for instance, the three observations are 5, 6, and 7; the statistic mean equals 6.00 and the statistic variance is .67. However, the parameter mean and parameter variance are 7.00 and 2.00, respectively. In order to differentiate between sample and population values, we will adopt different symbols for each as shown in Table 9-3.

One important characteristic of statistics is that their values are always known. That is, if we draw a sample we will always be able to calculate statistics which describe the sample distribution. In contrast, parameters may or may not be known, depending on whether we have census information about the population.

TABLE 9-2   Some Samples of $N = 3$ and Their Associated Means, Variances, and Standard Deviations[a]

Sample	$\overline{X}$	$(X - \overline{X})$	$(X - \overline{X})^2$
A	5	−1.00	1.00
	6	0.00	0.00
	7	1.00	1.00
		$\sum(X - \overline{X})^2 =$	2.00

Sample mean $= \overline{X} = 6$

Sample variance $= var = 2.00/3 = .67$

Sample standard deviation $= sd = \sqrt{.66} = .82$

Sample	$\overline{X}$	$(X - \overline{X})$	$(X - \overline{X})^2$
B	5	−2.00	4.00
	8	1.00	1.00
	8	1.00	1.00
		$\sum(X - \overline{X})^2 =$	6.00

$\overline{X} = 7$

$var = 6.00/3 = 2.00$

$sd = \sqrt{2.00} = 1.41$

Sample	$\overline{X}$	$(X - \overline{X})$	$(X - \overline{X})^2$
C	7	.33	.11
	8	1.33	1.77
	5	−1.66	2.76
		$\sum(X - \overline{X})^2 =$	4.64

$\overline{X} = 6.67$

$var = 4.64/3 = 1.56$

$sd = \sqrt{1.55} = 1.25$

[a]Samples taken with replacement from a population consisting of the values 5, 6, 7, 8, and 9.

One interesting exercise is to contrast the statistics computed from a number of sample distributions with the parameters from the corresponding population distribution. If we look at the three samples shown in Table 9-2, we observe that the values for the mean, the variance, and the standard deviation in each of the samples are different. The statistics take on a range of values, i.e., they are variable, as is shown in Table 9-4.

TABLE 9-3   Symbols for Population and Sample Descriptive Measures

	Population	Sample
Mean	M	$\overline{X}$
Variance	σ^2	*var*
Standard Deviation	σ	*sd*

TABLE 9-4   Descriptive Statistics from Three Samples of the Same Population

	Mean	Variance	Standard Deviation
Population	$M = 7$	$\sigma^2 = 2.00$	$\sigma = 1.41$
Sample A	$\overline{X} = 6$	*var* = .67	*sd* = .82
Sample B	$\overline{X} = 7$	*var* = 2.00	*sd* = 1.41
Sample C	$\overline{X} = 6.67$	*var* = 1.56	*sd* = 1.25

The difference between any population parameter value and the equivalent sample statistic indicates the error we make when we generalize from the information provided by a sample to the actual population values. This brings us to the third type of distribution.

Sampling Distribution

If we draw a number of samples from the same population, then compute sample statistics for each, we can construct a distribution consisting of the values of the sample statistics we've computed. This is a kind of "second-order" distribution. Where the population distribution and the sample distribution are made up of data values, the sampling distribution is made up of values of *statistics* computed from a number of sample distributions.

Probably the easiest way to visualize how one arrives at a sampling distribution is by looking at an example. We'll use our running example of mothers' communication with children in which samples of $N = 3$ were selected. Figure 9-1 illustrates a model of how a sampling distribution can be obtained.

Figure 9-1 illustrates the population which consists of a set of scores (5, 6, 7, 8, and 9) that distribute around a parameter mean of 7.00. From this population we can draw a number of samples. Each sample consists of three scores which constitute a subset of the population. The sample scores distribute around some statistic mean for each sample. For sample A, for instance, the scores are 5, 6, and 7 (the sample distribution for A) and the

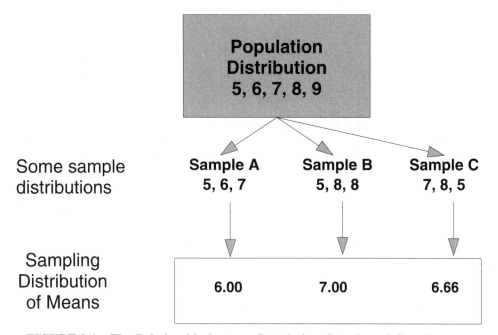

FIGURE 9-1   The Relationship between Population, Sample and Sampling Distributions

associated statistic mean is 6.00. For sample B, the scores are 5, 8, and 8, and the statistic mean is 7.00. Each sample has a different statistic mean.

The statistics associated with the various samples can now be gathered into a distribution of their own. The distribution will consist of a set of values of a *statistic*, rather than a set of observed values. This leads to the definition for a sampling distribution:

> *A sampling distribution is a statement of the frequency with which values of statistics are observed or are expected to be observed when a number of random samples are drawn from a given population.*

It is extremely important that a clear distinction is kept between the concepts of sample distribution and of sampling distribution. A sample distribution refers to the set of scores or values that we obtain when we apply the operational definition to a subset of units chosen from the full population. Such a sample distribution can be characterized in terms of statistics such as the mean, variance, or any other statistic. A sampling distribution emerges when we sample *repeatedly* and record the statistics that we observe. After a number of samples have been drawn, and the statistics associated with each computed, we can construct a sampling distribution of these statistics.

The sampling distributions resulting from taking all samples of $N = 2$ as well as the one based taking all samples of $N = 3$ out of the population of mothers of school-age children are shown in Table 9-5. These sampling distributions are simply condensed versions of the distributions presented earlier in Tables 5-2 and 5-6. In the first column we see the various means that were observed. The frequency with which these means were observed is shown in the second column. The descriptive measures for the sampling distribution are computed next and they are presented at the bottom of the sampling distribution.

The first such measure computed is a measure of central tendency, the mean of all the sample means. This is frequently referred to as the *grand mean,* and it is symbolized like this: $\overline{\overline{X}}$

From the values in the sampling distribution we can also compute measures of dispersion. Using the difference between any given statistic mean and the grand mean, we can compute the variance and the standard deviation of the sampling distributions, as illustrated in columns 4, 5, and 6 of Table 9-5. In the fourth column we determine the difference between a given mean and the grand mean; in column five that difference is squared in order to overcome the zero-sum principle, and in column six the squared deviation is multiplied by f to reflect the number of times that a given mean (and a given difference between a statistic mean and the grand mean, and the squared value of this difference) was observed in the sampling distribution.

As you see, the descriptive measures in a sampling distribution parallel those in population and sample distributions. To avoid the confusion that may be caused by this similarity we will use a set of special terms for these descriptive measures. The variance of a sampling distribution will be referred to as *sampling variance* and the standard deviation of the sampling distribution will be called the *standard error*. Table 9-6 provides a listing that allows for a ready comparison of the three main types of distributions, what the distributions consist of, and the labels of the most frequently used descriptive measures.

Maintaining these different symbols and labels is important. Whenever we see, for instance, $M = 4.3$, we know that 4.3 is the mean of a population, and *not* the mean of a sample or sampling distribution. Furthermore, whenever the term *sd* is used we know that the measure refers to the variability of scores from a sample; whenever the term *std error* is encountered we know that reference is being made to dispersion within a distribution of statistics.

Utility of a Sampling Distribution

By now it should be clear how a sampling distribution might be constructed. However, questions about the utility of doing so may remain. Why do we bother to construct sampling distributions, particularly sampling distributions of means? There are three reasons for constructing sampling distributions of means. In a nutshell, these sampling distributions give us insight into sampling error; they give insight into probability; and they allow us to test hypotheses.

Sampling Distributions as Distributions of Sampling Error

In Chapter 5 we encountered the term sampling error when we discussed random sampling. When we draw random samples from a population there are no guarantees that the sample will indeed be exactly representative of the population. As seen earlier in this chapter, it is

TABLE 9-5 Sampling Distributions of Means from Samples of $N = 2$ and $N = 3$[a]

Sample Size = 2

(1) $\overline{X}$	(2) f	(3) $f \cdot (\overline{X})$	(4) $(\overline{X} - \overline{\overline{X}})$	(5) $(\overline{X} - \overline{\overline{X}})^2$	(6) $f \cdot (\overline{X} - \overline{\overline{X}})^2$
5.0	1	5.00	−2.00	4.00	4.00
5.5	2	11.00	−1.50	2.25	4.50
6.0	3	18.00	−1.00	1.00	3.00
6.5	4	26.00	−.50	.25	1.00
7.0	5	35.00	.00	.00	.00
7.5	4	30.00	.50	.25	1.00
8.0	3	24.00	1.00	1.00	3.00
8.5	2	17.00	1.50	2.25	4.50
9.0	1	9.00	2.00	4.00	4.00
	25	175.00			25.00

Mean of means: $\overline{\overline{X}} = 175/25 = 7.00$

Sampling variance: $25/25 = 1.00$

Standard error: $\sqrt{1.00} = 1.00$

Sample Size = 3

(1) $\overline{X}$	(2) f	(3) $f \cdot (\overline{X})$	(4) $(\overline{X} - \overline{\overline{X}})$	(5) $(\overline{X} - \overline{\overline{X}})^2$	(6) $f \cdot (\overline{X} - \overline{\overline{X}})^2$
5.00	1	5.00	−2.00	4.00	4.00
5.33	3	15.99	−1.67	2.79	8.37
5.66	6	33.96	−1.34	1.79	10.74
6.00	10	60.00	−1.00	1.00	10.00
6.33	15	94.95	−.67	.45	6.73
6.66	18	119.88	−.34	.12	2.16
7.00	19	133.00	0.00	0.00	0.00
7.33	18	131.94	.34	.12	2.16
7.66	15	114.90	.67	.45	6.73
8.00	10	80.00	1.00	1.00	10.00
8.33	6	49.98	1.34	1.79	10.74
8.66	3	25.98	1.67	2.79	8.37
9.00	1	9.00	2.00	4.00	4.00
	125	875.00			84.00

Mean of means: $\overline{\overline{X}} = 875/125 = 7.00$

Sampling variance: $84/125 = .672$

Standard error = $\sqrt{.672} = .819$

[a]Observations drawn randomly with replacement from a population consisting of the values 5, 6, 7, 8, and 9

TABLE 9-6   Units of Observation and Descriptive Measures for Three Types of Distributions.

	Distribution Type		
	Population Distribution	Sample Distribution	Sampling Distribution
Distribution consists of	Individual observations	Individual observations	Statistics
	X	X	e.g., $\overline{X}$
Central Tendency	M (parameter)	$\overline{X}$ (statistic)	$\overline{\overline{X}}$ (statistic of statistics)
Dispersion	Population variance (parameter) σ^2	Sample variance (statistic) *var*	Sampling variance of means (statistic of statistics) *sampling var*
	Population standard deviation (parameter) σ	Sample standard deviation (statistic) *sd*	Standard error of means (statistic of statistics) *std error*

quite possible that there will be differences between sample characteristics and population characteristics. In fact, *sampling error* can be defined as the discrepancy between the parameter of a population and the corresponding statistic computed for a sample drawn randomly from that population.

One way of looking at Table 9-5 is as an illustration of sampling error. It shows a listing of all the sample statistic means that were computed when all possible samples of a given size were drawn from the population. Most of these different statistic means show a certain amount of discrepancy with the population mean; some means show larger discrepancies, others show smaller ones (see column 4). The sampling distribution that results when we take all samples from a given population is therefore also the distribution of the amounts of sampling error that we encountered as we drew those samples.

Sampling Error and the Standard Error

We know that sampling error is unavoidable, even when we sample randomly. However, let us assume for a moment that we could randomly sample without committing sampling error. In that case, for all the samples that we would draw from a population, there would be no discrepancy between the statistic computed for each sample and the population parameter. Each sample mean would be exactly equal to the population mean. Since all the entries in the sampling distribution would be identical, the sampling distribution would have a mean equal to the population mean. The sampling variance and the standard error are measures of dispersion of a set of statistics about the mean of the sampling distribution of those statistics. As all entries in this distribution are exactly equal to the mean, it follows that under these conditions we would observe the sampling variance and standard error to be equal to zero. A zero standard error indicates that there is no sampling error, which is correct, given our original assumption of sampling without error.

If we assume small amounts of sampling error, the observed statistics will be quite similar to one another, but not identical. This means that they will be quite similar to the population parameter. As a consequence, the resulting sampling distribution would have a non-zero sampling variance and standard error, but both will be quite small, since all statistics will be similar to the population parameter. As increasing amounts of sampling error are introduced, the differences between the individual sample statistics and the population parameter will increase, and the sampling variance and standard error will be larger.

Factors Affecting Sampling Error

The preceding section makes it quite clear that the amount of sampling error encountered determines the size of the sampling variance and the standard error, making the standard error a convenient way of estimating sampling error. But another question arises. What determines the size of the sampling error itself? Briefly, sampling error is determined by (1) the population variance and (2) the sample size.

Population Variance. The larger the population variance, the larger the sampling error. If you think about it for a moment, you'll probably see why this is the case. A population distribution with a small variance has its scores more tightly clustered around the population mean. This means that any random sample drawn from this population is likely to contain many observed values which are close to the population mean. The mean of such a sample (and the means of others like it) will then be close to the population mean, and there will be little sampling error.

The effect of population variance on sampling error can be demonstrated by contrasting the sampling distributions associated with three different populations A, B, and C, which have different variances. These population distributions, along with their parameters and the resulting sampling distributions, are shown in Table 9-7.

Population A has the smallest parameter variance; all the scores are closely lumped together. Consequently the sampling distribution shows little variability. The mean of any sample drawn from Population A cannot be smaller than 6, nor can it be larger than 8. It follows, then, that all other sample means have to be between these two extremes and that they also must be quite similar to the true population parameter. The fact that the means are close to one another and close to the population mean is reflected in the standard error value of .44.

In the sampling distribution associated with Population B the sample means are somewhat more dispersed. The highest and lowest possible sample means in this population

TABLE 9-7 Population Variance, Sampling Error, and Standard Error: Three Examples

Population A		Population B		Population C	
Values 6,7,7,7,8		Values 5,6,7,8,9		Values 3,5,7,9,11	

PARAMETERS

Population A		Population B		Population C	
$M = 7.00$		$M = 7.00$		$M = 7.00$	
$\sigma^2 = .40$		$\sigma^2 = 2.00$		$\sigma^2 = 8.00$	
$\sigma = .63$		$\sigma = 1.41$		$\sigma = 2.83$	

SAMPLING DISTRIBUTIONS

Population A		Population B		Population C	
Sample $\overline{X}$	f	Sample $\overline{X}$	f	Sample $\overline{X}$	f
6.0	1	5.0	1	3	1
6.5	6	5.5	2	4	2
7.0	11	6.0	3	5	3
7.5	6	6.5	4	6	4
8.0	1	7.0	5	7	5
	25	7.5	4	8	4
		8.0	3	9	3
		8.5	2	10	2
		9.0	1	11	1
			25		25

$(\overline{X} - M)$	$f \cdot (\overline{X} - M)^2$	$(\overline{X} - M)$	$f \cdot (\overline{X} - M)^2$	$(\overline{X} - M)$	$f \cdot (\overline{X} - M)^2$
−1.00	1.00	−2.00	4.00	−4.00	16.00
−.50	1.50	−1.50	4.50	−3.00	18.00
0.00	0.00	−1.00	3.00	−2.00	12.00
.50	1.50	−.50	1.00	−1.00	4.00
1.00	1.00	0.00	0.00	0.00	0.00
		.50	1.00	1.00	4.00
		1.00	3.00	2.00	12.00
		1.50	4.50	3.00	18.00
		2.00	4.00	4.00	16.00
$\sum f \cdot (X - M)^2$	5.00		25.00		100.00

SAMPLING VARIANCE

Population A		Population B		Population C	
$5.00/25 = .20$		$25.00/25 = 1.00$		$100.00/25 = 4.00$	

STANDARD ERROR

Population A		Population B		Population C	
$\sqrt{.20} = .44$		$\sqrt{1.00} = 1.00$		$\sqrt{4.00} = 2.00$	

are 5 and 9, reflecting a maximum sampling error of −2.00 or +2.00, respectively. The standard error for this distribution is 1.00. The third population distribution has the greatest dispersion of scores; the scores here range from 3 to 11. Its sampling distribution reveals the greatest dispersion of sample means and consequently the greatest standard error of 2.00.

Sample Size.   The second factor that determines the magnitude of the sampling error is the size of the sample drawn from the population. The general rule of statistical generalization that we developed in Chapter 5 is that increased sample size reduces the sampling error, all other things remaining equal. Again, this phenomenon can be illustrated simply with an example. If we go back to Table 9-5, we can see the sampling distributions that result when we take samples of two different sizes. If we look at the various sample means that are observed when $N = 2$ and when $N = 3$, we see that, as sample size increases, a larger proportion of the sample means will fall near the true population mean.

Let us look, for instance, at the proportion of sample means that have a discrepancy from the parameter mean which does not exceed +1.00 or −1.00. Column 2 in Table 9-5 shows that, when $N = 2$, 19 of the 25 samples have means that fall within this range. These 19 sample are 76 percent of the possible sample means. When $N = 3$, however, the proportion of samples with means that fall within the same range is equal to 105/125, or 84 percent. As sample size increases, a greater proportion of sample means will fall closer to the true parameter.

Table 9-5 also contains the sampling statistics for these two sampling distributions. These are simply a more precise way of stating the same information: When $N = 2$, the sampling variance equals 1.00, as does the standard error. When $N = 3$, the sampling variance equals .672 and the standard error is .819, reflecting the increased clustering of sample means around the population mean, and thus less sampling error.

Yet another way of illustrating this phenomenon is through a graph, as in Figure 9-2. The curve representing the sampling distribution based on samples of $N = 2$ is a distribution with relatively "thick" tails, indicating that, proportionally, sample means with large deviations from the population mean occur relatively frequently; certainly proportionally more frequently than they do in the sampling distribution based on samples of $N = 3$ which has clearly "thinner" tails. Again, these shapes reflect that, when $N = 2$, only 76 percent of the sample means will be between 6 and 8 inclusive; when $N = 3$, 84 percent fall within this interval.

If we take into consideration *both* population variance *and* sample size, then it is relatively easy to understand that sampling error will be minimized in large samples taken from populations that have little variability. Relatively larger amounts of sampling error can be expected as sample size decreases and/or the population variance is larger.

Figure 9-2 also illustrates an important point that has already been presented in Chapter 5. The two sampling distributions depicted in this figure are symmetrical distributions. Recall that a symmetrical distribution means that overestimates of the population statistic of a particular size or magnitude are just as likely to occur as underestimates of the same size. The important implication of this phenomenon is that sample means are considered to be *unbiased* estimators of the population mean. This means that the most probable value for the sample statistic is the population statistic, regardless of the amount of sampling error.

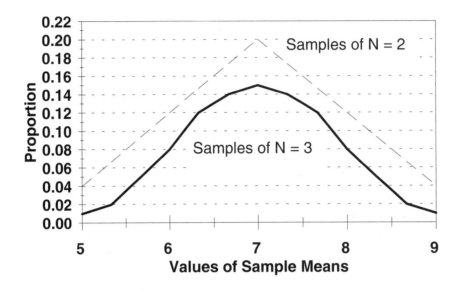

FIGURE 9-2   Proportional Occurrence of Sample Means

Figure 9-2 illustrates this clearly. Both sampling distributions have 7.00, the population *M*, as their most frequently occurring sample mean.

Sampling Distributions as Distributions of Probability

Perhaps *the* most important reason for constructing sampling distributions is that they can be interpreted in terms of the probability associated with the various statistics that are obtained when we sample randomly.

Table 9-8 presents the two sampling distributions we have encountered earlier, along with the probabilities associated with the various means. For the first sampling distribution, based on samples of $N = 2$, we can note that a total of nine different means were observed. A mean of 5.00 was observed only once, 5.50 was observed twice, and so on. Once we sum all the occurrences of the various outcomes we note that there were a total of 25 occurrences associated with 9 different outcomes. The probability of any outcome is simply the ratio of that outcome's frequency to the total frequency, so we divide the frequency of each of the outcomes by 25 to get the 9 probabilities associated with each value of the mean. For example, the probability of obtaining a mean of 5.00 is computed by dividing its one occurrence by 25, giving a probability of .04. By the same reasoning the probability of observing a mean of 7.00 would be equal to 5 out of 25, or .20.

In addition to predicting the probability of obtaining a single outcome, we can also predict the probability of obtaining a range of outcomes by simply summing the probabilities of the individual outcomes contained within that range (see the section on "Probability" in Chapter 6). For example, the probability of obtaining a sample mean not more than one point away from the true population mean of 7.00 when we take samples of $N = 2$ (that is,

TABLE 9-8   Sampling Distributions and Probability

Sample Size $N = 2$			Sample Size $N = 3$		
$\overline{X}$	f	probability	$\overline{X}$	f	probability
5.0	1	1/25 = .04	5.00	1	1/125 = .008
5.5	2	2/25 = .08	5.33	3	3/125 = .024
6.0	3	3/25 = .12	5.66	6	6/125 = .048
6.5	4	4/25 = .16	6.00	10	10/125 = .08
7.0	5	5/25 = .20	6.33	15	15/125 = .12
7.5	4	4/25 = .16	6.66	18	18/125 = .144
8.0	3	3/25 = .12	7.00	19	19/125 = .152
8.5	2	2/25 = .08	7.33	18	18/125 = .144
9.0	1	1/25 = .04	7.66	15	15/125 = .12
	25	1.00	8.00	10	10/125 = .08
			8.33	6	6/125 = .048
			8.66	3	3/125 = .024
			9.00	1	1/125 = .008
				125	1.000

$\overline{\overline{X}} = M = 7.00$ $\overline{\overline{X}} = M = 7.00$

to obtain a mean of 6.00, 6.50, 7.00, 7.50, or 8.00) would have an associated probability of .12 + .16 + .20 + .16 + .12 = .76.

For the sampling distribution based on samples of $N = 3$, the probability of obtaining a sample mean within the same range would be equal to .08+.12+.144+.152+.144+.12+.08, = .84. This means that if we were to take a sample of $N = 3$ out of the population consisting of the values 5, 6, 7, 8, and 9, we would have an 84 percent chance of drawing a sample whose mean would be within 1.0 point of the true population mean, *and* that we would have a 16 percent chance of observing a sample mean *more than* 1.0 away from M.

Sampling Distributions and Hypothesis Testing

The ability to assign probabilities to the various values of sample statistics is extremely important. It means that we can make a probabilistic statement about the amount of sampling error that we may have obtained in drawing any single sample. For instance, if we were to draw a sample of 2 observations out of the population and if we then obtained a mean of 5.00 from this sample, we would consider that a relatively unusual event. Why? Because according to the sampling distribution based on samples of this size, a mean of 5.00 had only a 4 percent chance of occurring. We would have expected to observe a value like 6.5, or 7, or 7.5, because these outcomes are much more likely. If we obtain a mean of 5.00, we can say that it is relatively *unlikely* (but not impossible) that the population mean is really 7.0.

This kind of probability statement will be of critical importance when we begin to test hypotheses. As we saw in Chapter 3, one way that we can test a relationship is to observe differences in a variable between two groups (a comparative hypothesis). As an example, let us assume that we have a research hypothesis (H_A) that mothers in rural communities communicate with their children about school with a *different* frequency than do urban mothers.

The associated null hypothesis (H_0) is that the two populations of mothers communicate with *equal* frequency. We will also assume that we know the population mean for the communication variable among urban mothers (an unlikely event, but bear with us). But we do not know the variable's mean for rural mothers. So we will have to draw a sample from that population and compute a sample mean to serve as our best estimate of the unknown population parameter for rural mothers. If the urban and rural populations communicate equally frequently, we expect the mean of the sample drawn from the population of rural mothers to be equal or nearly equal to the population mean for the urban mothers.

If we find a sample mean for rural mothers that is near the population mean for urban mothers, we will conclude that the null hypothesis appears to be a fair description of reality—the urban/rural distinction does not seem to produce differences in communication frequency beyond those that can *likely* be attributed to sampling error in the rural sample. The key word in the previous sentence is *likely*. This is a probability statement, and the evidence for making it can be obtained from a sampling distribution.

But suppose the sample mean for rural mothers is quite different from the population mean for urban mothers. There are two reasons why this might occur. The first is sampling error—perhaps the population means for both rural and urban mothers are really the same, but because of sampling error we've gotten one of the improbable sample means. The second reason is that the population means themselves are really different. In this case, we've gotten a reasonable (i.e., *probable*) estimate of the population mean for rural mothers, and it happens to be different from the population mean for urban mothers. This situation would argue for our rejection of the null hypothesis, or, put another way, it would provide evidence in favor of our research hypothesis.

How do we decide which one is really the true situation? Unfortunately, we have no direct way of telling, so we are forced into a kind of betting game. What we will do is figure the odds of being right or wrong, and when these odds (that is, probabilities) are sufficiently unfavorable to the null hypothesis, we will reject the null hypothesis. As the difference between the population mean and the sample mean increases, the probability of the difference being due to sampling error decreases. At some arbitrary point we will conclude that it's just too improbable that sampling error was the cause of the difference, and conclude that something else must be causing the difference between the sample mean for rural mothers and the population mean for urban mothers. If all other things are equal (and they will be, if we have drawn a good, unbiased, random sample of rural mothers), then the urban/rural difference must be the cause of the difference in the amount of communication.

We'll investigate hypothesis testing in much more detail in Chapter 12. For right now, the important thing to remember is that the sampling distribution gives us the basic probability information that we need to distinguish between the null and the research hypotheses.

**TABLE 9-9   Sampling Distribution of Sample Variances
Based on Samples of $N = 2^a$**

Sample	$\overline{X}$	var	Observed Variances	Freq.	Prob.
5 − 5	5.0	.00	0.00	5	.20
5 − 6	5.5	.25	.25	8	.32
5 − 7	6.0	1.00	1.00	6	.24
5 − 8	6.5	2.25	2.25	4	.16
5 − 9	7.0	4.00	4.00	2	.08
6 − 5	5.5	.25			
6 − 6	6.0	.00			
6 − 7	6.5	.25			
6 − 8	7.0	1.00			
6 − 9	7.5	2.25			
7 − 5	6.0	1.00			
7 − 6	6.5	.25			
7 − 7	7.0	.00			
7 − 8	7.5	.25			
7 − 9	8.0	1.00			
8 − 5	6.5	2.25			
8 − 6	7.0	1.00			
8 − 7	7.5	.25			
8 − 8	8.0	.00			
8 − 9	8.5	.25			
9 − 5	7.0	4.00			
9 − 6	7.5	2.25			
9 − 7	8.0	1.00			
9 − 8	8.5	.25			
9 − 9	9.0	.00			

[a]Observations drawn with replacement from a population consisting of the values 5, 6, 7, 8 and 9

Other Sampling Distributions

Any statistic that we compute from sample observations is part of a sampling distribution for that statistic; we don't need to restrict ourselves to sampling distributions of means. For example, we could compute sample variances and construct a sampling distribution of variances. An example of such a sampling distribution is presented in tabular form below in Table 9-9, and in graphic form in Figure 9-3.

The sampling distribution that results when we collect the sample variances of these 25 samples is different in a dramatic way from the sampling distribution of means computed from the same samples. The sampling distribution of variances is *not* a symmetrical distribution. The distribution is positively skewed. If we compute the mean of all the observed sample variances we obtain an average of 1.00, well below the true population variance of 2.00. This lack of symmetry tells us that sample variances are biased estimators of population variance. The average variance is *not* the most probable variance found in the sampling distribution.

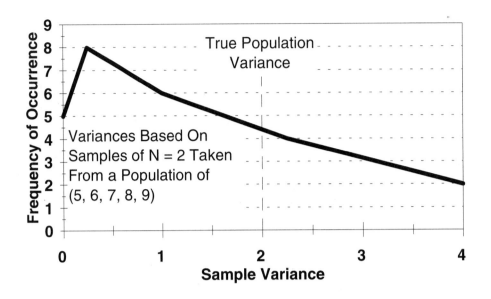

FIGURE 9-3   Sampling Distribution of Sample Variances

Furthermore, we can see that the nature of the bias is to underestimate the population variance. An inspection of Figure 9-3 and Table 9-9 illustrates this point: Sample variances that underestimate the true population variance occur with greater frequency than those that overestimate the population variance.

In the process of carrying out communication research we will frequently estimate a population's mean and variance with sample statistics. The sample mean will be an unbiased estimator of the population parameter, but we will have to "adjust" for the sample variance's tendency to underestimate. Again, we'll defer the details of how to do this until a later chapter.

The difference between the sampling distributions for the mean and for variance illustrates two things: First, all sampling distributions are not identical; second, we have to know the "shape" (actually, the mathematical formula) of the sampling distribution so that we can see if it is biased, and to correct for any bias that is present.

Summary

In this chapter we have presented a discussion of three important and related distributions. The reason for discussing them is that they feature prominently in hypothesis testing. The first of these three distributions is the *population distribution*, which is made up of all units of analysis in the population, and represents the frequency of occurrence of every value of a particular variable in the whole population, whether it is actually observed by a researcher or not. The population distribution is described by *parameters*.

The second type of distribution is the *sample distribution*, which is made up of a sampled subset of units from the population. The values in the sample distribution are actually observed by the researcher. Descriptive values are called *statistics* when they are computed from a sample distribution. Sample distributions are subject to *sampling error*, which is random in nature, but which produces, purely by chance, differences of varying magnitude between sample statistics and the corresponding population parameters.

The third type of distribution results when all possible samples from a population are drawn, and a descriptive statistic such as a mean or a variance is computed for each sample. Such a distribution of statistics is called a *sampling distribution*. This distribution can be used to compute estimates of the sampling error based on the dispersion of the sample statistics, such as the *standard error* of a statistic.

The sampling distribution can also be used to compute the probability of finding a statistic different from a given population parameter, simply as a result of sampling error. This probability information can be used to test hypotheses.

Sampling distributions can thus be seen as central to hypothesis testing. However, constructing sampling distributions following the method outlined in this chapter may be almost impossible under conditions normally encountered in hypothesis testing. Therefore, the next chapter will introduce a methodology which greatly facilitates description of sampling distributions.

References and Additional Readings

Annenberg/CPB (1989). *Against all odds*. [Video-tape]. Santa Barbara, CA: Intellimation.

Hays, W. L. (1981). *Statistics* (3rd. ed.). New York: Holt, Rinehart & Winston (Chapter 5, "Sampling Distributions and Point Estimation"; Chapter 6, "Normal Population and Sampling Distributions").

Kachigan, S. K. (1986). *Statistical analysis: An interdisciplinary introduction to univariate and multivariate methods*. New York: Radius Press (Chapter 7, "Sampling Distributions").

Kerlinger, F. N. (1986). *Foundations of behavioral research* (3rd ed.). New York: Holt, Rinehart and Winston (Chapter 11, "Purpose, Approach, Method").

McNemar, Q. (1969). *Psychological statistics* (4th ed.). New York: Wiley (Chapter 7, "Small Sample or t-technique").

$$C \; h \; a \; p \; t \; e \; r \quad 10$$

Sampling Distributions and the Central Limit Theorem

In the previous chapter we explained the differences between sample, population, and sampling distributions, and we showed how a sampling distribution can be constructed by repeatedly taking random samples of a given size from a population.

A quick look back at Table 9-8 shows the outcome of the process. To summarize, when all possible samples of $N = 2$ are taken from a population with the values 5, 6, 7, 8, and 9, a total of 25 different samples with 9 different means can be observed. When the sample size is increased to 3, 125 different samples with 13 different means are produced. If we were to take samples of $N = 4$ from this same population of values, we would find that 625 distinct combinations of 4 numbers could be observed. It is quite obvious that constructing a sampling distribution by the method we used in the preceding chapter becomes extremely laborious as soon as the population size is larger than 10. In fact, the number of different samples (S) of any given size (N) taken from a population of size (P) when we sample with replacement can be expressed by the following equation:

$$S = P^N$$

For populations of 5 units ($P = 5$) like our example, this yields the number of samples that were illustrated in Chapter 9:

$$\text{For } N = 2, \; S = 5^2 = \;\; 25$$
$$\text{For } N = 3, \; S = 5^3 = 125$$
$$\text{For } N = 4, \; S = 5^4 = 625$$

Imagine constructing a sampling distribution by drawing samples of $N = 5$ students out of a population of 50 students in an undergraduate communication research methods class. If we sample with replacement, the number of different samples is 50 raised to the power 5, or $50 \times 50 \times 50 \times 50 \times 50$ or 312,500,000 different samples. Computing the mean, sampling variance, and standard error of such a sampling distribution would be a monumental assignment. Furthermore, determining the probabilities associated with each of the various sample means would be an equally enormous task. But we need these probabilities to make a valid statistical generalization from a random sample. We obviously need to use another approach to obtaining these probabilities. Fortunately such an approach exists.

Central Limit Theorem

The central limit theorem provides us with a shortcut to the information required for constructing a sampling distribution. By applying the theorem we can obtain the descriptive values for a sampling distribution (usually, the mean and the standard error, which is computed from the sampling variance) and we can also obtain probabilities associated with any of the sample means in the sampling distribution.

The mathematics which prove the central limit theorem are beyond the scope of this book, so we will not discuss them here. Instead we will focus on its major principles. They are summarized below:

If we randomly select all samples of some size N out of a population with some mean M and some variance σ^2, then

- *The mean of the sample means $(\overline{\overline{X}})$ will equal M, the population mean.*
- *The sampling variance will be $\dfrac{\sigma^2}{N}$ (the population variance divided by N, the sample size). The standard error will equal the square root of the sampling variance.*
- *The sampling distribution of sample means will more closely approximate the normal distribution as N increases.*

We'll discuss each of these points separately in the following sections of this chapter. But before we do, let us be sure to emphasize the three assumptions of the central limit theorem: We know what size sample (*N*) we would like to draw from the population, and, more importantly, that we know the two population parameters *M* and σ^2.

Mean of the Sampling Distribution of Means: Parameter Known

According to the central limit theorem, the mean of the sampling distribution of means is equal to the population mean. We have already observed this in the examples given in the previous chapter. Our population, consisting of the values 5, 6, 7, 8, and 9, has a mean of 7. When we took all samples of $N = 2$ or $N = 3$ out of this population, the mean of all the resulting sample means $(\overline{\overline{X}})$ in the two sampling distributions were both equal to 7.

TABLE 10-1   Sampling Distribution Variances Computed from Population Variance

X_i	$(X_i - M)^2$
5	4
6	1
7	0
8	1
9	4
	$\overline{10} = \sum(X_i - M)^2$

$$\sigma^2 = \frac{10}{5} = 2.00, \text{ population variance}$$

	$N = 2$	$N = 3$	$N = 4$
sampling variance $= \dfrac{\sigma^2}{N} =$	$\dfrac{2}{2} = 1.00$	$\dfrac{2}{3} = .672$	$\dfrac{2}{4} = .50$
standard error $=$	$\sqrt{1.00} = 1.00$	$\sqrt{.672} = .819$	$\sqrt{.500} = .707$

Therefore, if we know the parameter mean, we can set the mean of the sampling distribution equal to M. This allows us to avoid two massively difficult steps: (1) calculating sample means for all possible samples that can be drawn from the population and (2) calculating the sampling distribution mean from this mass of sample means.

Variance of the Sampling Distribution of Means: Parameter Known

According to the theorem, the variance of the sampling distribution of means equals the population variance divided by N, the sample size. The population variance (σ^2) and the size of the samples (N) drawn from that population have been identified in the preceding chapter as the two key factors that influence the variability of the sample means. As we saw in the examples in that chapter, the larger the variance of the values in the population, the greater the range of values that the sample means can take on. We also saw that the sample size was inversely related to the variability of sample means: The greater the sample size, the narrower the range of sample means. The effect of both factors is thus captured by computing the value of the sampling variance as σ^2/N. If we know the variance of the population as well as the sample size, we can determine the sampling variance and the standard error.

This aspect of the theorem can be illustrated by using our running example. As you can see in Table 10-1, the variance of the population equals 2.00.

Applying the central limit theorem to sample sizes of $N = 2$ and $N = 3$ yields the sampling variances and standard errors shown in Table 10-1. For $N = 2$ and $N = 3$, these are exactly the same values for the sampling variance and standard error that were computed from the full set of sample means shown in Table 9-5. Table 10-1 also shows the sampling variance and standard error for a sampling distribution based on a sample size of $N = 4$ drawn from the same population. Had we calculated these values from the set of 625 sample means, we would have obtained exactly the same results for the variance and standard error.

But what do we do when the population parameters are unknown? For example, assume that we are interested in studying the population of newly married couples. Specifically, we are interested in the amount of time they spend talking to each other each week about their relationship. It is highly unlikely that any parameters for this population would be available. As we have already mentioned several times, the absence of known parameters is very common in communication research. How are we to proceed under these conditions?

In the absence of known parameters we will have to make do with reliable estimates of these parameters. Such reliable estimates can be obtained when we take random samples of sufficient size from the population.

Suppose we draw a random sample of $N = 400$ from this population. After measuring the amount of time these newlyweds spend talking to one another about their relationship we observe the mean to be 2 hours per week and the sample standard deviation is 1 hour per week. We can use this information to estimate the mean, the variance, and the standard error of the sampling distribution.

Mean of the Sampling Distribution of Means: Parameter Unknown

Since we have only a single sample mean, we can't compute the mean of the means. But we can make a simple assumption, based on probability, that will allow us to work from the results of this single sample.

We know that the most probable mean found in the sampling distribution is the true population mean (you can see this in Table 9-5 in the previous chapter), and that this mean is at the center of the sampling distribution. So if we have only one sample from a population, the assumption that the value of the sample mean is the same as the value of the population mean is more likely to be correct than any other assumption we could make. When we do this, we place the center of the sampling distribution right at the sample mean. That is, we arrange our sampling distribution around the computed value of our sample mean (see Figure 10-1). It is important to note that the sample mean of 2.0 is the best estimate of the unknown population (or true) mean. But we have to realize that there is also the possibility that the true population mean is somewhat higher or lower than that figure. We can use the sampling distribution to describe how probable it is that the real population mean falls somewhere other than the computed sample mean. We will return to this point once we are able to fully describe the sampling distribution.

Variance of the Sampling Distribution of Means: Parameter Unknown

The sampling variance (and hence the standard error) can be estimated from the sample variance if we are willing to make the same assumption about the population variance as we did with the population mean—namely, that the most probable value for this unknown parameter is the one that we have computed from our single sample. After we make this

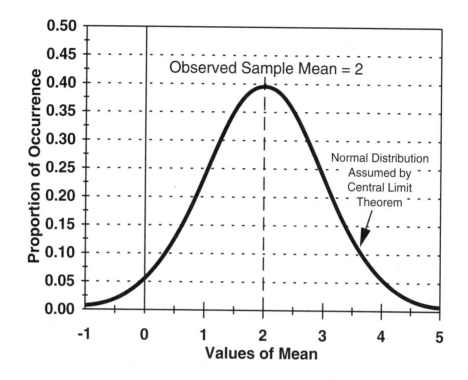

FIGURE 10-1 **Central Tendency of the Sampling Distribution**

assumption, we can estimate the measures of dispersion by the same method as we did in Table 10-1.

$$\text{Sampling Variance} = var/N = 1/400 = .0025$$
$$\text{Std Error} = \sqrt{var/N} = \sqrt{1/400} = .05 \text{ Hours, or}$$
$$\text{Std Error} = sd/\sqrt{N} = 1/\sqrt{400} = 1/20 = .05 \text{ Hours}$$

We now have a complete description of the sampling distribution, constructed from the information provided by a single random sample.

Once the sampling distribution has been identified, either by using known parameters or by using estimates of these parameters obtained from samples, we can now use this distribution to carry out the next important step: computing the probabilities of observing different means in the sampling distribution. We need these probabilities to be able to make statements about the likelihood of the truth or falsity of our hypotheses, as we've already mentioned in the previous chapter.

Whether the sampling distribution was derived from known parameters or from estimates matters little in terms of the remainder of the discussion in this chapter, as long as one condition is met: If estimates are used, the sample from which the estimates are derived should be sufficiently large. A violation of this condition does not alter the logic, but requires some computational adjustments. Any statistics text will explain how to carry out these adjustments whenever small samples are encountered.

Sampling Distribution of Means and Probability

The most important reason we need to construct sampling distributions is to obtain the probabilities associated with varying amounts of sampling error. We can use this information for statistical generalization and for testing our hypotheses.

Recall that the sampling distribution of means, constructed as in the previous chapter, yields a number of means, along with the frequency with which these means were observed. From such a table of means we can determine, for any given amount of sampling error, the likelihood of occurrence of such a sampling error. This likelihood is determined by dividing the frequency with which a given sampling error occurred by the total number of samples.

The central limit theorem enables us to directly compute the mean, variance, and standard error of the sampling distribution without going to the trouble of drawing all possible samples from the population. But we still need a way to describe the shape of the distribution of sample means. Fortunately, we can do this by using the third principle of the central limit theorem. This principle states that the sampling distribution of means will tend to look like a *normal distribution*, when we select samples that contain relatively large numbers of observations.

What does this mean? Just this: If we were able to compute the thousands or millions of means from every different sample in a population, then collect these means into a frequency distribution, we would see that the distribution has the characteristics of the standard normal distribution. But we don't have to do this. We can simply *assume* a normal distribution (a "bell-shaped curve") will result, as the central limit theorem tells us that we're going to find this distribution *if our samples are large enough*.

A standard normal distribution like our sampling distribution can be described by the following equation:

$$H = \frac{1}{\sqrt{2\pi}} e^{-z^2/2}$$

In this equation, the quantity H is known as the ordinate (or height) of the curve at any point. This computation involves two mathematical constants (e, which equals 2.7183 and π, which equals 3.1416) and a quantity called "z," which is the standard score as defined and discussed in Chapter 8. A standard score defines any data point (which can be either a data value or a statistic) in terms of the number of standard deviation units (or standard error units) that the point is from the mean. For a given value of z (such as the value marked *a* in Figure 10-2), the height of the normal distribution can then be computed from the above formula.

Why do we need to know this? Because the height of the normal distribution represents the frequency of occurrence in the sampling distribution of a mean that is some distance

z from the center of the distribution occurs. We can use the frequency to compute probabilities, as we did in Chapter 9. A mean with a large z value is distant from the center of the distribution, and it has a small H (i.e., frequency). This implies that a mean with a large z value has a low probability of occurring in a random sample. The most probable mean (the largest H value) appears when $z = 0$. Furthermore, when we compute the height of the curve at two points with different values of z, then the two heights will define an area under the curve which will include a certain proportion or percentage of the means in the sampling distribution, which is the same as saying that it defines a certain proportion of the total area under the curve, as can be seen in Figure 10-2.

Normal Distribution and Areas Under the Curve

Determining the magnitude of the proportion of means in a given area under the curve is quite straightforward. It is based, essentially, on the mathematical procedure for determining the area of a rectangle: Multiply the length of the rectangle by its width. Remember that the formula for the standard normal distribution allows us to compute H, or the height of the curve, for any point z on the baseline. Figure 10-2 shows the values for $z = 0.0$ and $z = 1.0$, a range in which we might be interested.

When $z = 0.00$, the value of H is .3989; when $z = 1.00$, the value of $H = .2420$. The areas of two rectangles can now be computed. The first rectangle is the area defined by the product of these two dimensions: .3989 (or b, the height of the curve at $z = 0.0$ and the length of the rectangle) and 1.00 (a, the difference between $z = 0.00$ and $z = 1.00$, and the width of the rectangle), or ($a \times b$), which equals .3989. The second rectangle has the dimensions .2420 and 1.00 (or a and c, the height at $z = +1.00$), giving an area of .2420.

The first rectangle ($a \times b$) obviously covers more than the area under the curve we are interested in; a certain amount of area in the rectangle is not under the curve. The second rectangle does not cover all the area under the curve: There is a certain amount of area under the curve which is not included in the rectangle. However, it would appear from Figure 10-2 that the overestimate of the first rectangle and the underestimate of the second rectangle might cancel. Taking the average of the two rectangles yields $(.3989 + .2420)/2 = .3205$, which, as we shall see below, is quite close to the actual figure for the portion of the area under the normal curve between that point where the mean is located and another point one standard deviation from the mean.

We could also compute the area under the curve between the points $z = +1.00$ and $z = +2.00$. At $z = +2.00$, H equals .0540. Following the same averaging procedure as we carried out above, we'd obtain $(.2420 + .0540)/2 = .1480$ as an estimate of the area under the curve between $z = +1.00$ and $z = +2.00$. Since the right half of the distribution contains .50 of the total area under the normal curve, this crude method of determining areas under the curve leaves $.50 - (.3205 + .1480) = .0315$ as the size of the area beyond $z = +2.00$.

Also, we already know that the normal distribution is symmetrical and so half of the area under the curve falls to the left of the mean, the other half to the right. Consequently, the same proportions for areas under the curve hold for the left-hand side of the distribution.

In Figure 10-2, neither the rectangle $a \times b$ nor the rectangle $a \times c$, nor even their average, is a completely satisfactory estimate of the area under the curve. It is obvious

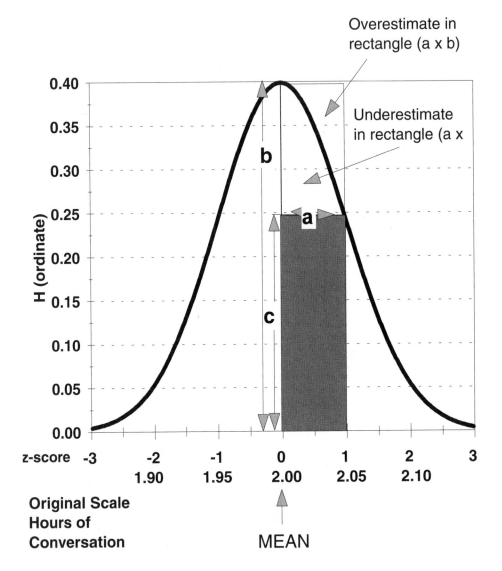

FIGURE 10-2   Estimates of Areas Under the Normal Curve

that a better approximation of the area under the curve between the mean ($z = 0.0$) and $z = 1.00$ could be obtained by dividing the baseline in tenths (or even smaller parts) of a standard deviation, then computing the area of a larger number of rectangles. The total area could then be obtained by adding together the areas calculated from the larger number of smaller rectangles. Students familiar with elementary calculus will recognize this as the basic process involved in integration of the normal distribution function between two

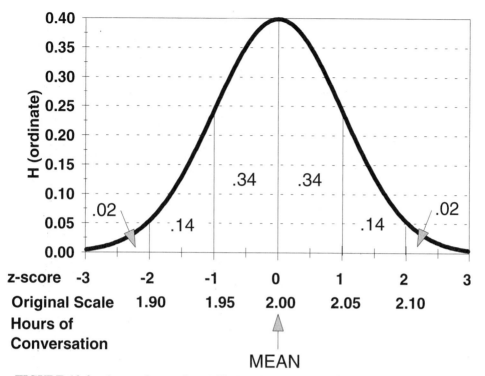

FIGURE 10-3   Approximate Areas Under the Normal Distribution

limits. By making the rectangle bases smaller and smaller, and summing the resulting areas, we will get more and more accurate estimates of the true area between any two z-score limits.

Figure 10-3 illustrates the result of the calculus of integrals. It shows the broad outline of the relationship between standard scores and areas under the curve. In a normal distribution approximately .34 (or 34 percent) of the area under the curve lies between the mean (0.00) and one standard unit in either direction. An additional 14 percent will be observed between 1.00 and 2.00 standard units. Note that these proportions are quite similar to the values obtained by our rough method of taking the averages of the areas of the various rectangles. This means that between −1.00 and +1.00 standard units, we will find approximately 68 percent of all the observations in the normal distribution. Between −2.00 and +2.00 standard deviations—roughly 96 percent of the observations in the distribution—will occur. That is, an additional 28 percent (14 percent + 14 percent) are observed between 1 and 2 standard units from the mean. The remaining 4 percent of cases can be found in each tail (2 percent in the positive tail, and 2 percent in the negative tail). These represent the cases that are two or more standard deviations away from the mean of the distribution. Also notice that the .34, .14, and .02 in each half of the distribution sum to the .50 probability that we expect.

Earlier in this chapter we wondered about the probability that the true population mean was either higher or lower than the observed sample mean of 2.00. From the sampling distribution we can find the probability that the true population lies between any two values in the sampling distribution by determining the area under the curve between these two values. For instance, there is a .34 probability that the true population mean lies somewhere between 2.00 hours of conversation and 2.05 hours. The symmetry of the distribution allows us to double that proportion to get the probability that the population mean lies somewhere between 1.95 hours and 2.05 hours. This means that we have better than 2:1 odds that the population mean lies within .05 hour (or one standard error) of the sample mean. The probability is .96 that the population mean lies between 1.90 and 2.10 hours of conversation. This example illustrates the way we can use a sampling distribution to quantify our confidence in the results that we get from a random sample.

Table of Areas Under the Normal Curve

Because of the widespread use of the normal distribution, tables have been prepared which show percentages of area under the normal distribution function very accurately for a wide range of z-values. Tabled values for areas under the curve of the normal distribution can be found in Appendix A. We'll reproduce a portion of that table here to illustrate how to interpret it. Use the numbers above the various columns in the table to refer to areas under the curve.

In row (a) of the table under Figure 10-4, the z-score is located exactly on the mean ($z = 0.0$), and therefore the mean-to-z area is equal to 0.0. The fact that this z-score is located on the mean also implies that the area under the normal curve is divided into two equal parts; thus the "larger" and the "smaller" areas are equal to one another (and also equal to .50). Finally, column 5 gives the height of the curve at that point as .3989.

In row (b) we see a z-score of .75, a location three-fourths of a standard unit away from the mean. The area under the curve from the mean to this value of z is approximately .27 (or 27 percent). The larger area is now equal to .50 plus .27, or .77. This means that the smaller portion under the curve is equal to $1.00 - .77 = .23$.

Rows (c) and (d) illustrate what happens when the z-score becomes larger, that is, when we move farther away from the mean of the normal distribution. The area between the mean and the z-value becomes larger, the "larger" portion becomes larger, the "smaller" portion becomes smaller, and the height of the curve decreases. For instance, row (d) indicates that when $z = 2.50$, the values in the "larger" portion of the distribution (i.e., those with lower z-values) constitute 99.38 percent of all cases in the distribution. Cases that have values that are 2.50 standard units *or further* from the mean constitute only the remaining .62 percent of all the cases in the distribution.

Since the normal distribution is symmetrical, the results for negative z-scores are the same as those of the positive z-values. In order to use the tables for negative z-scores, you need only look up the corresponding positive z-score. With negative z-scores the "smaller area" under the curve will be located in the left-hand side of the curve; the "larger area" will be on the right. The "mean-to-z" and "ordinate" values are the same for negative z-scores.

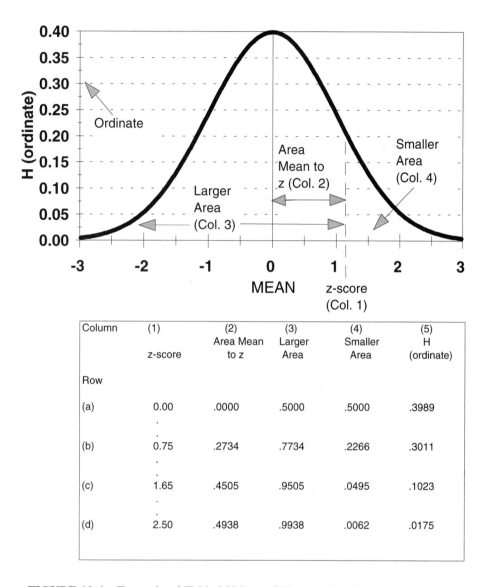

Column	(1)	(2)	(3)	(4)	(5)
		Area Mean	Larger	Smaller	H
	z-score	to z	Area	Area	(ordinate)
Row					
(a)	0.00	.0000	.5000	.5000	.3989
(b)	0.75	.2734	.7734	.2266	.3011
(c)	1.65	.4505	.9505	.0495	.1023
(d)	2.50	.4938	.9938	.0062	.0175

FIGURE 10-4   Example of Tabled Values of Normal Distribution

Sampling Distribution of Means and the Sample Size

We know from the examples in Chapters 5 and 9 that increasing the sample size will decrease the sampling error. By using sampling distributions based on the normal curve, constructed from a single sample with the mean and variance estimates provided by the central limit theorem, we can see the effects of sample size even more clearly. Figures 10-5a, b, and c

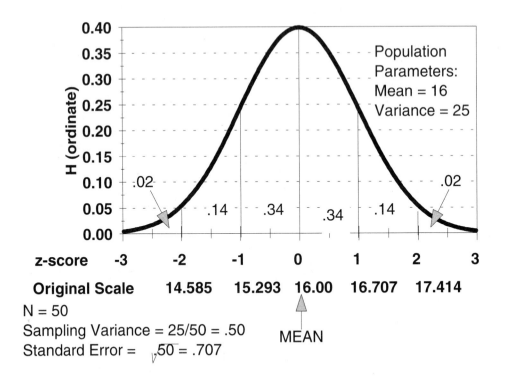

FIGURE 10-5A   Sampling Distribution of the Mean ($N = 50$)

illustrate sampling distributions constructed from samples of different size which were drawn from a population with a mean of 16 and a variance of 25.

First, a general observation. Figures 10-5a, b, and c show us how the normal distribution can be used to associate probabilities with certain sample means. For instance, the first sampling distribution (Figure 10-5a) shows that when we take samples of $N = 50$ from this population we would expect 96 percent of all the sample means to fall between 14.585 and 17.41, inclusive. Only 2 percent of the sample means would be expected to be larger than 17.41 (or smaller than 14.585). In other words, applying the normal distribution to the sampling distribution allows us to distinguish between "likely" and "unlikely" sample means when sampling from a given population. The ability to do this is of key importance in hypothesis testing and this topic will be taken up again later.

There are several items in Figures 10-5a, b, and c you should pay close attention to. First, all sampling distributions have the same mean, since they are centered at the population mean. Further, since all are based on a normal curve, the z-values for each band of probabilities are the same. But these are the only things the three distributions have in common. Although each distribution has the same central tendency and is symmetrical, the dispersion differs. This can be seen by looking at the distribution as a function of the expected sample means, rather than the standard scores. The same ranges of z-values

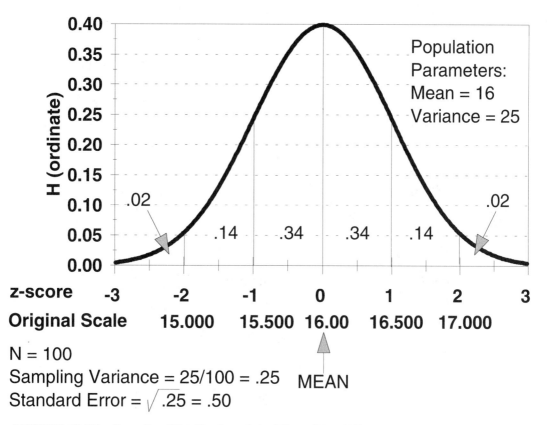

FIGURE 10-5B Sampling Distribution of the Mean ($N = 100$)

are associated with an increasingly narrower range of sample means. The sample means become more tightly clustered around the population mean when the sample size increases.

Thus the general observation that we can draw from Figure 10-5a, b, and c is that increases in N are associated with decreases in sampling variance and standard error. That is, the sample means that we will obtain will be better estimates of the true value of the population mean as we increase the number of observations.

When we plot the sample sizes and the values of the standard error, as in Figure 10-6, we see that the relationship between sample size and the size of the standard error is nonlinear. That is, for each *identical* further increase in sample size we obtain a *smaller* reduction in the standard error.

When $N = 50$, the standard error was equal to .707. Doubling N to 100 (an increment of 50) brings the standard error down to .50, for a reduction of .207. An additional increment of 50 in N (to a total of 150) brings the standard error to .408, for a reduction of .092. The reduction in the standard error for the second increment is less than half of that of the first increment. Were we to increase N to 200, the new standard error would be .354, a reduction of .054, which is only one-fourth of the reduction in the standard error

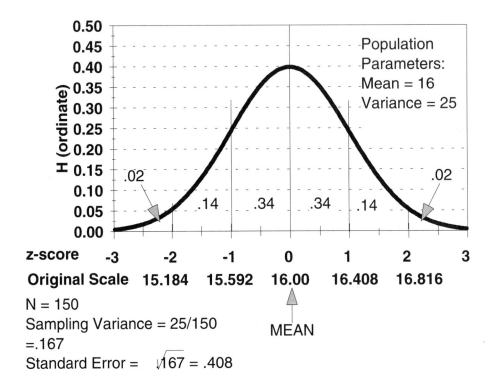

FIGURE 10-5C   Sampling Distribution of the Mean (*N* = 150)

obtained from the first increment of 50 in the sample size. Since subsequent increases in sample size will yield increasingly smaller reductions in sampling error, it clearly is not worth our while to continue increasing sample size indefinitely. In our current example, for instance, there doesn't seem to be much point in increasing the sample size beyond 150.

Another point about the relationship between sample size and sampling error is less evident, but just as important. Note that none of our discussion about sampling distributions and sampling error has involved the size of the population. Only the size of the *sample* has been shown to have an effect on sampling error. This seems counter-intuitive, but it's correct: Sampling error in a true random sample is a function *only of sample size*. It doesn't matter if we sample from a population with 1000 members or with 100,000,000. The standard error depends only on the number of observations that we actually make.

Often communication or public opinion research is criticized for generalizing to huge populations on the basis of sample sizes that are small, relative to the total size of the population. For example, people often ask "How can the TV ratings services describe what's going on in 100,000,000 households when they only collect information in 1200 homes?" The answer to this question is contained in this chapter: The error in measurement due to sampling is determined solely by the sample *N* of 1200, and the total population

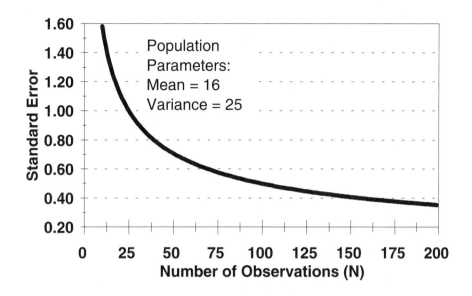

FIGURE 10-6   Relationship Between Sample Size and Standard Error

size is irrelevant. A sample of 1200 in a single city with only 10,000 houses will be just as accurate (or inaccurate) as a national sample of the same size.

Summary

In this chapter, we demonstrated how the *central limit theorem* can eliminate the need to construct a sampling distribution that examines all possible samples that might be drawn from a population. The central limit theorem enables us to determine the sampling distribution by using the parameter mean and variance values or estimates of these obtained from a single sample. In particular, the theorem tells us that the estimated sampling distribution has a mean which is the same as the population mean, or our best estimate, a sample mean, and that the variance of the sampling distribution can be determined from either the population parameter variance or its sample estimate.

The third contribution of the central limit theorem is that it tells us that the shape of the sampling distribution can be approximated by a *normal curve*. The normal curve can be described as a function of standard or z-scores. Using the normal curve allows us to describe sampling error in terms of probabilities, which are represented as areas under the curve. Standard tables which describe the areas under the normal curve have been constructed to aid in making probability statements. We can use these tables to see what the likelihood is that samples with means a certain distance from the true population mean will be observed.

When the sample size is increased, we see that the range of values that correspond to a fixed probability level under the normal curve decreases, indicating a corresponding decrease in sampling error. The decrease in sampling error is a simple function of sample size, and is not related to the size of the population. Furthermore, increases in sample size and decreases in sampling error are related by a law of diminishing returns, making it inefficient to increase samples beyond a certain size.

With the tools provided by the central limit theorem, we can proceed to the next task in communication research: testing hypotheses about the relationships between our theoretical constructs. In order to do this we will need to use the sampling distributions and the probability statements that they give us.

References and Additional Readings

Annenberg/CPB (1989). *Against all odds*. [Video-tape]. Santa Barbara, CA: Intellimation.

Hays, W. L. (1981). *Statistics* (3rd. ed.). New York: Holt, Rinehart & Winston (Chapter 6, "Normal Population and Sampling Distributions").

Kerlinger, F. N. (1986). *Foundations of behaviorial research* (3rd ed.). New York: Holt, Rinehart and Winston (Chapter 12, "Testing Hypotheses and the Standard Error").

Moore, D. S. & McCabe, G. P. (1989). *Introduction to the practice of statistics*. New York: Freeman (Chapter 6, "From Probability to Inference").

C h a p t e r 11

Describing Bivariate Relationships

In Chapter 8 we looked at a number of ways to describe the univariate data (data obtained from a single variable) drawn from a sample or population. In that chapter we presented visual methods of describing data, such as pie charts, bar graphs, and frequency polygons, but we were much more extensive in our discussion of mathematical ways of describing data, particularly the measures of central tendency and the measures of dispersion. In this chapter, we will use these univariate descriptive statistics to build descriptive measures of *relationships* between pairs of variables. By coupling these descriptions of relationships to the ideas of sampling distributions and probabilities (which we discussed in the preceding chapters), we will have the necessary tools to test hypotheses, as we'll see in the next chapter.

The purpose of this chapter is to outline the basic techniques for describing the relationship between two variables. Not all the statistics that can be used to measure relationships will be presented here. However, before we get to statistics, it is important that we cover some basic ideas about formal hypothesis testing.

First, we want to introduce the general strategy for detecting relationships. This strategy is based on the discrepancy between what we *actually* observe in the data, versus what we would *expect* to observe if there were no relationship between two variables. The logical method for detecting a relationship between variables is by contradiction: If we find a result that should not be there if no relationship existed, we conclude that there is probable cause to conclude that the relationship really exists.

This conceptual strategy brings the research and null hypotheses discussed in Chapter 3 squarely back on center stage. The null hypothesis states that no relationship exists between two variables. If we can visualize what data would look like if the null hypothesis was true, then we can interpret deviations from this picture as evidence supporting the research hypothesis which states that a relationship between the two variables does in fact exist.

There are two steps in determining if a relationship exists. The first step is to describe the magnitude of the relationship; the second is to determine if this magnitude is large enough to be considered unlikely to have happened by chance alone. This chapter focuses

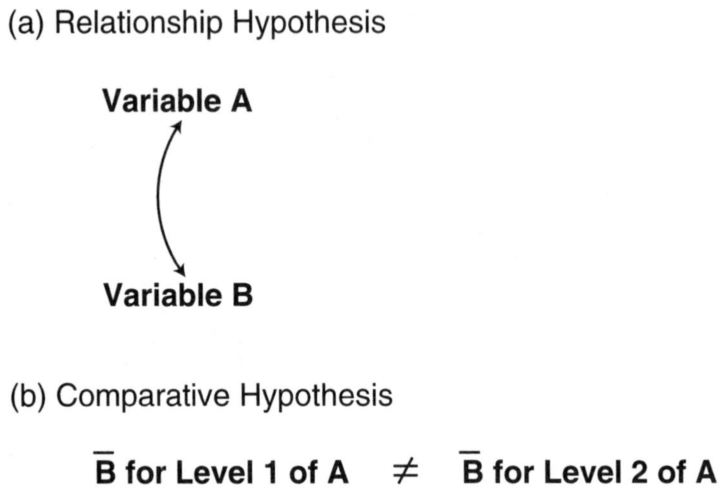

(a) Relationship Hypothesis

Variable A

Variable B

(b) Comparative Hypothesis

$$\overline{B} \text{ for Level 1 of A} \quad \neq \quad \overline{B} \text{ for Level 2 of A}$$

FIGURE 11-1 **Diagraming a Relationship**

only on the first step, outlining some general ways that we can describe relationships. The next chapter will outline the second step of the process, which is the formal decision-making process for testing whether the null hypothesis or the research hypothesis has the better probability of being correct. In Chapter 19, we will present a general guide to methods for testing for the presence of relationships under different conditions of measurement and in different research settings.

We will start with the fact that the level of measurement determines our choice between two fundamentally different methods that can be used to describe relationships between variables: Contrasting groups versus measuring relationships directly.

Relationships and Levels of Measurement

If you remember, in Chapter 3 we presented an extensive discussion about the nature of relationships between variables. Figures 3-1 and 3-6 showed the various ways a relationship between two variables can be diagramed. Figure 11-1 shows a nondirectional covariance relationship in abstract form.

Both notations in Figure 11-1 really represent the same relationship. Different levels of Variable B will be observed whenever different levels of Variable A are observed, and the levels of Variable A and Variable B will be associated in some non-random fashion (that is, they will covary).

In order to say that a relationship between some variable A and another variable B indeed exists, the following criteria need to be met:

1. Variable B must be observed under at least TWO levels of variable A.

TABLE 11-1   Levels of Measurement and Types of Hypotheses

		Independent Variable		
		Nominal	*Ordinal*	*Interval/ Ratio*
Dependent Variable	*Nominal*	Comparative	Comparative	Comparative
	Ordinal	Comparative	Relationship Comparative	Relationship Comparative
	Interval/ Ratio	Comparative	Relationship Comparative	Relationship Comparative

> 2. *The observed levels of variable B must be coordinated with the different levels of variable A, so that the levels of Variable A can be used to* predict *the levels of variable B (and possibly vice versa). Criterion (2) is another way of stating that the variables must covary in a nonrandom fashion.*

The level of measurement forces us to choose between two different ways of stating the nature of the relationship. As you recall from Chapter 3, one way to distinguish types of hypotheses is by separating them into the following two groups: (1) *relationship hypotheses*, those hypotheses that use expressions of the amount of covariance between the independent variables and the dependent variable as their basis, and (2) *comparative hypotheses*, which use statements of dependent variable differences among two or more groups which have different levels of the independent variable. These two types of hypotheses are presented in Figure 11-1 as (a) and (b), respectively.

Whenever we formulate a hypothesis about the relationship between two variables, we will need to consider the level of measurement of the two variables. Table 11-1 shows the various permutations of levels of measurement that might occur when we are examining the relationship between any two variables. From this table, we can see that for some combinations of levels of measurement, only comparative hypotheses can be used to describe the predicted relationship between the two variables. For other combinations, however, relationship hypotheses are appropriate. And as is illustrated in Table 11-1, whenever relationship hypotheses are appropriately used, comparative hypotheses can also be stated.

Looking at Table 11-1, it is apparent that a comparative hypothesis is the only possible alternative whenever *either* the independent variable *or* the dependent variable is measured as a nominal variable.

The reason is quite simple. Nominal measurement does not possess an underlying dimension that implies "more" or "less," while the other three levels of measurement do have this characteristic. The classes or categories of a nominal factor merely state that the observations which are assigned to the different categories are "different." In contrast, the classes in ordinal, interval, and ratio variables add to this distinction the idea that the theoretical concept may be present to some *degree*, i.e., that measurement may show the presence of more or less of the quantity indicated by the concept.

An important consequence of this distinction is that a relationship involving at least one nominal variable cannot be characterized as, for instance, a positive or negative relationship. For example, gender is a nominal variable, which means that we cannot say that gender is positively related to frequency of initiation of intimate conversations. We can't say it because it doesn't make any sense. Although the frequency of initiation of intimate conversations variable clearly has an underlying dimension which allows us to translate "positive" to changes in the "more" direction, the variable gender certainly does not have this characteristic. The nominal factor gender has two classes: male and female. Which one should we call "positive" or "more" and which one "negative" or "less"?

The only option we have is to state relationships involving nominal factors in terms of the *groups that are defined by the various classes* that make up the nominal factor. For instance, we may represent the relationship between gender and frequency of initiation of intimate conversations with some statement like "Males will initiate such conversations less often than will females." To describe the magnitude of this hypothetical relationship, we will contrast males (one class of the independent variable) and females (the other class of the independent variable) on their frequency of initiation of intimate conversations (the interval-level dependent variable). This contrast method forms the basis for a number of techniques for describing the degree of relationship between a nominal independent variable and other dependent variables at whatever level of measurement.

Describing Relationships by Comparing Nominal Groups

A hypothesis involving a nominal independent variable will have some statement about how two (or more) groups, representing two (or more) classes of that independent variable, are expected to differ from one another on some dependent variable. Such a difference is described as a contrast between an appropriate univariate descriptive statistic for one group and the equivalent descriptive statistic for the other group or groups.

The kind of group contrast and the descriptive statistics involved are determined by the level of measurement of the dependent variable and by the number of groups to be contrasted.

Comparisons and the Level of Measurement

In Chapter 8 we discussed the appropriateness of different univariate descriptive measures of central tendency and dispersion for different levels of measurement. Our discussion is summarized in Table 11-2.

If a relationship is to be described by contrasting two or more groups on some dependent variable, then such a contrast should be done with a statistic that is appropriate to the level of measurement of the dependent variable.

For instance, nominal measurement will allow us to contrast two groups in terms of proportions observed in the various classes of the dependent variable. Interval and ratio variables are appropriately represented by the proportion too. However, we have argued before (and we will continue to remind the reader regularly) that important information will be "thrown away" if we treat interval/ratio measurement as if it were nominal or ordinal measurement. Such underuse of available information would occur if we were to contrast groups in terms of their proportions or medians when the level of dependent

TABLE 11-2   Levels of Measurement and Descriptive Statistics

		Descriptive Statistics			
		Proportion	Mode	Median	Mean
Measurement	*Nominal*	yes	yes	no	no
	Ordinal	yes	yes	yes	no
	Interval/ Ratio	yes	yes	yes	yes

Yes = statistic is appropriately applied at this level
No = statistic is inappropriate

variable measurement was appropriate for contrasts of means. The information contained in a measurement should be exploited to the fullest extent possible, by using descriptive statistics at the highest level warranted by the data. We'll later give some examples to illustrate how contrasts between groups can be carried out at the highest level appropriate for each level of measurement of the dependent variable.

Number of Groups to Be Contrasted

The second factor to consider when choosing an appropriate way to conduct such a contrast is the number of groups to be compared. This is determined by the number of classes or categories that constitute the nominal factor. The variable "newspaper subscriber" has only two classes: "yes" and "no," and the test of a relationship between this variable and, for instance, knowledge of local political affairs, would require comparing the knowledge of subscribers and nonsubscribers. But nominal factors may have more than two classes. For instance, we may wish to describe a relationship between political party affiliation and the frequency of exposure to news coverage of politics. To describe such a relationship we will have to make contrasts of the frequency of exposure among groups of Republicans, Democrats, Communists, Socialists, Unaffiliateds, and others. Again, in Chapter 19 we will provide a guide to statistical methods for comparing multiple groups, regardless of level of measurement. We'll try to keep it as simple as possible in this chapter, but the importance of the number of nominal classes to the correct choice of descriptive statistic should not be lost.

Nominal Group Contrasts with a Nominal Dependent Variable

When the criterion or dependent variable (the variable on which the groups are to be compared) is a nominal variable, the appropriate statistic is the proportion. We can multiply this by 100 (i.e., move the decimal point two places to the right) to convert this to the familiar statistic called "percentage." The size of a relationship between the independent and the dependent variable is detected by looking at the proportions of cases assigned to different classes of the dependent variable, for each of the groups which

EXHIBIT 11-1   Testing a Comparative Hypothesis: Group Contrast with Nominal Dependent Variable

An experiment is carried out to determine whether there is a relationship between the gender of a speaker and audience members' evaluations of that speaker.

Two students, one a female, the other a male, are audio taped while reading identical passages from a book. The two tapes are played to two groups of 50 male students. The first group listens to the tape of the male reader, and the second group listens to the tape of the female reader. After listening, the participants are asked to fill out a questionnaire about the presentation. Among other questions, they are asked whether they thought that the person whose voice they just heard came from an "urban" or a "rural" background.

represent the different classes of the nominal independent variable. We'll illustrate this with the example described in Exhibit 11-1.

In this exhibit the independent variable is gender (of the speaker), which is a nominal factor with the classes "male" and "female." The dependent variable, origin, is also a nominal factor which consists of the classes "urban" and "rural." The hypothesis of no relationship can be stated like this:

H_0: *The proportion of listeners who think the male speaker is "urban" is the same as the proportion of listeners who think that the female speaker is "urban."*

Note that this H_0 implies that the proportion of listeners who think that the male speaker is rural should also equal the proportion who think that the female speaker is rural.

The corresponding nondirectional research hypothesis is as follows:

H_R: *The proportion of listeners who think the male speaker is "urban" is NOT the same as the proportion of listeners who think that the female speaker is "urban."*

If there is no relationship between gender and place of origin, the female speaker and the male speaker should be equally likely to be identified as being from an "urban" background. If there are differences in the proportion of listeners to the male and female speakers who identify the speaker as "urban," then we would be more likely to believe that a relationship exists.

We will have to do a formal test of this belief, to establish our confidence in its truth, but this will be discussed in the next chapter. From what we see in Table 11-3 it appears that the female speaker is somewhat more likely to be identified as "urban" than is the male speaker.

How can we describe the relationship more accurately? Essentially, we must look at the pattern of proportions predicted by the null hypothesis, and contrast that with the pattern of proportions that we actually observe. But how do we determine the pattern of proportions that we would observe if the hypothesis of no relationship is true?

TABLE 11-3   Group Contrast with Nominal Dependent Variable Observed Frequencies in Cells

		Speaker		
		Male	Female	
	Urban	25	35	60
Origin				
	Rural	25	15	40
		$N = 50$	$N = 50$	Total $N = 100$

We know from our results (Table 11-3) that of the 100 people who participated in the experiment, 60 (a proportion of .60, or 60 percent) identified the speaker as "urban" and 40 (or .40, 40 percent) did not. If the gender of the speaker did not matter (that is, the null hypothesis is true), then we would expect that 60 percent will call the speaker "urban" and 40 percent will call the speaker "rural," regardless of whether the speaker is male or female. Since 50 people listened to the male speaker, we would expect that .60 of these 50 listeners (or 30 listeners) will characterize the male speaker as "urban." Likewise, the proportion of subjects who characterize the male speaker as "rural" will be the remaining .40 of these 50, which would be 20 individuals. Since the null hypothesis states that gender does not matter, an identical pattern should hold for the female speaker. For the male speaker *as well as* the female, the proportion who'd call the speaker urban and the proportion who'd call the speaker rural should be .60 and .40, respectively. The frequencies associated with these proportions, the 30 who would call the speaker urban and the 20 who would call the speaker rural, are called the *expected frequencies*. These are the frequencies that are expected, *if* the null hypothesis is true. We can then contrast the expected frequencies with the actual *observed frequencies*, as shown in Table 11-4.

The statistical test we'd apply would focus on the difference between these two frequencies. Generally speaking, the greater the difference between the two sets of frequencies, the greater the magnitude of the relationship and the lower the probability that the difference was due to a chance occurrence.

Nominal Group Contrasts with a Discrete Ordinal Dependent Variable

When the dependent or criterion variable (the variable on which the groups are to be compared) is an ordinal variable, a number of descriptive statistics are appropriate for contrasting the groups representing the different classes of the independent variable.

Because ordinal measurement can take two forms, two different statistics can be used for making contrasts. The statistic encountered in the previous example, the proportion or percentage, can also be used here, as we'll see. The other statistic appropriately used with data at this level of measurement is the median. And whether we would use the proportion or the median as the statistic of choice depends on the type of ordinal measurement being used. In Exhibit 11-2 we expand the previous example to explain this further.

TABLE 11-4   Group Contrast with Nominal Dependent Variable, Observed and Expected Frequencies for Two Nominal Variables

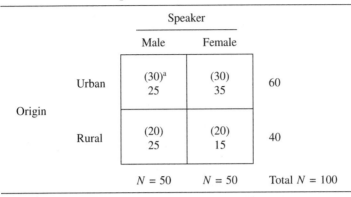

		Speaker		
		Male	Female	
Origin	Urban	(30)ᵃ 25	(30) 35	60
	Rural	(20) 25	(20) 15	40
		N = 50	*N* = 50	Total *N* = 100

ᵃExpected Frequencies are in parentheses.

EXHIBIT 11-2   Testing a Comparative Hypothesis: Group Contrast with Discrete Ordinal Dependent Variable

After the research participants listened to the either the tape of the male or of the female speaker, they were asked to use a scale to indicate their degree of liking of the speaker. The scale used was the following:

The research participants were asked to place a check mark in the space on the scale which most closely represented their feelings about the speaker.

Like very much	Like	Neither Like nor Dislike	Dislike	Dislike very much

---

The level of measurement associated with the dependent variable is ordinal; there is an underlying dimension (amount of liking) associated with the variable, but the dimension is divided into a set of five *discrete* categories which the respondents were requested to use. Discrete refers to the fact that there is no possibility of finer distinctions in categorization. Respondents have to either choose "dislike" or "dislike very much"; they cannot choose a location in between these two.

The results, presented in Table 11-5, indicate that, of all those who listened to the male speaker, 2 indicated that they liked him very much, 10 said that they liked him, and so on. The analysis necessary to determine whether the gender and liking variables are

TABLE 11-5   Group Contrast with Discrete Ordinal Dependent Variable

		Speaker		
		Male	Female	
Liking	Like Very Much	2 (10)[a]	18 (10)	20
	Like	10 (15)	20 (15)	30
	Neither Like nor Dislike	10 (10)	10 (10)	20
	Dislike	18 (10)	2 (10)	20
	Dislike Very Much	10 (5)	0 (5)	10
		$N = 50$	$N = 50$	Total $N = 100$

[a]Expected Frequencies are in parentheses.

related is analogous to the procedure outlined above for contrasting groups on nominal dependent variables.

The H_0 to be tested is the following:

The respondents who listened to the male speaker and the respondents who listened to the female speaker will use the response categories in the same proportions.

Associated with the H_0 is the following nondirectional H_R:

The respondents who listened to the male speaker and the respondents who listened to the female speaker will use the response categories in different proportions.

Again, from our results we know that of the 100 people who participated in the experiment, 20 (or .20) liked the speaker "very much," 30 percent "liked" the speaker, and so on. By applying the same procedures as in the previous example, we can calculate the expected frequencies for each cell in the table. Once again, these frequencies (those expected under the null hypothesis) are presented between parentheses in the cells of the table. Note that the discrete ordinal dependent variable in this example was treated as if it was a nominal factor. The results in Table 11-5 indicate that the female speaker was liked to a greater degree than would be expected if the null hypothesis were true.

Nominal Group Contrasts with a Continuous Ordinal Dependent Variable
Ordinal measurement, however, does not necessarily result in a discrete variable. Another way in which an ordinal variable can appear is as a *continuous* measure. This kind of

---

EXHIBIT 11-3   Testing a Comparative Hypothesis: Group Contrast with Continuous Ordinal Dependent Variable

Imagine that the research participants in our study had been requested to use a different scale to evaluate the speaker. Assume that they had been asked to do the following:

Please rate the speaker you have just heard on a scale from 1 to 10, where 10 means that you liked the speaker very much, and where 1 means that you did not like the speaker at all.

Every listener will use this scale to rate the speaker, and the result of this process will be two frequency distributions, one for each of the speakers:

	Speaker			
	Male		Female	
Score	Frequency		Score	Frequency
1	6		1	0
2	4		2	0
3	8		3	1
4	10		4	1
5	5		5	4
6	5		6	6
7	6		7	8
8	4		8	12
9	2		9	10
10	0		10	8
	$N = 50$			$N = 50$

---

variable potentially has an infinitely large number of classes or categories (even if all these classes do not appear in the operational definition of the variable).

In Exhibit 11-3 we present another variation on our current example, but this time with a continuous ordinal variable as the dependent variable.

The data that we have obtained are continuous ordinal data. The system of measurement is ordinal because the numbering system merely represents more or less liking. We are not assuming that the measure is interval, as there is no standard amount that separates a single unit of "liking." The amount of distance between 1 and 2 may be much smaller than the amount between 9 and 10. But the measurement is continuous in that any one of a potentially infinitely large number of values between 1 and 10 could have been selected by a respondent. Respondents could reply "1.5" or even "2.32145."

Data at this level of measurement opens some options in the computation of the descriptive statistics. By the logic laid out in Table 11-2, the frequencies obtained here can be readily converted to proportions, and we could revert to treating the ordinal responses as if they were nominal. A better alternative, however, is to compute the median and use this statistic to contrast the two groups.

There is some logic behind using the median as a descriptive statistic for contrasting groups. If the independent variable gender does not have an effect on the speaker evaluation, then the frequency distributions of ratings for each gender should have the same value for the median and this median should be equal to the median of the *combined* frequency distributions.

As discussed in Chapter 8, the value of the median is the one which divides a distribution in half, so if the null hypothesis is true, .50 of all cases in each distribution

TABLE 11-6 Group Contrast with Continuous Ordinal Dependent Variable

Combined Frequency Distribution

Score	Frequency	Cumulative Frequency
1	6	6
2	4	10
3	9	19
4	11	30
5	9	39
6	11	50
7	14	64
8	16	80
9	12	92
10	8	100
	$N = 100$	

Using the formula for the median from Chapter 8:

$$\text{Median} = \text{TLL} + \frac{N/2 - cf}{F}(I)$$

$$= 5.5 + \frac{100/2 - 39}{11}(1)$$

$$= 5.5 + 1 = 6.5$$

should be above the median of the two groups combined, and the remaining .50 of cases should be below that median. The computation of the median for the combined frequency distribution is illustrated in Table 11-6.

We can use this median to test the H_0:

The proportion of scores above *the combined median in the frequency distribution associated with male speaker should be equal to the proportion of scores* above *the combined median for the frequency distribution associated with the female speaker and should equal .50;*

which is simply a very explicit restatement of

$$\text{Median}_{\text{Male}} = \text{Median}_{\text{Female}}.$$

The associated nondirectional H_R is:

The proportion of scores above *the combined median in the frequency distribution of the male speaker should NOT be equal to the proportion of scores above the combined median for the frequency distribution of the female speaker and should NOT equal .50.*

TABLE 11-7   Group Contrast with Continuous Ordinal Dependent Variable

	Male	Female	
Above Median	(25)[a] 12	(25) 38	50
Combined Median = 6.5			
Below Median	(25) 38	(25) 12	50
	$N = 50$	$N = 50$	Total $N = 100$

[a]Expected Frequencies are in parentheses.

which could be restated simply as: $\text{Median}_{\text{Male}} \neq \text{Median}_{\text{Female}}$.

Since the median of the combined frequency distributions equals 6.5, we will observe 50 of the 100 liking scores to be above 6.5, and the remaining 50 to be below 6.5. Likewise, under a true H_0, we would expect 25 of the 50 ratings (50 percent) of the male speaker to be above 6.5, and 25 to be below that value. The same pattern of responses would be expected for the female speaker's ratings, as can be seen in Table 11-7. In that table the frequencies expected under the true H_0 (seen there in parentheses) can then be contrasted with the frequencies of scores actually observed. We simply go through the two frequency distributions and find the number of scores greater than, and those less than, 6.5. Again, the same logic for finding evidence of a relationship prevails. A relationship will be reflected by a discrepancy between the values expected, given a true null hypothesis, and those actually observed. Since the female speaker had more ratings above the median than would be the case if there was no effect of gender, it appears as if gender is related to the liking variable.

Nominal Group Contrasts with an Interval/Ratio Dependent Variable

When the criterion variable is an interval or ratio variable, the descriptive statistic that is most appropriate for contrasting the groups which represent the different classes of the independent variable is the mean. This statistic exploits all the measurement characteristics in these levels of measurement, in which the classes of the dependent variable carry not only the idea of "more" and "less," but also have equidistant units of measurement which separate the classes.

We'll expand our running example in Exhibit 11-4 to look at this situation. The recall data are ratio (and thus interval) in nature, which allows for the computation of the mean as the descriptive statistic. We can use the mean to contrast groups who heard the male and female speakers. Although contrasts using proportions or medians are also possible with interval/ratio measurement, such practices are not recommended because they are less sensitive and therefore likely to be less accurate.

The H_0 associated with the relationship described in Exhibit 11-4 is the following:

EXHIBIT 11-4   Testing a Comparative Hypothesis: Group Contrast with Interval/Ratio Dependent Variable

After the research participants rated the speakers in terms of liking, they also filled out a brief questionnaire to measure their recall of factual information provided in the book passage which was read to them by the male and female speakers.

A series of 15 questions were prepared and each listener was assigned a recall score reflecting the number of questions he or she could correctly answer. The following results were obtained.

	Speaker		
	Male		Female
	Number Correct	Frequency	Number Correct	Frequency
	6	3		
	7	4		
	8	8	8	3
	9	10	9	1
	10	5	10	4
	11	5	11	7
	12	6	12	7
	13	4	13	11
	14	4	14	9
	15	1	15	8
		$N = 50$		$N = 50$

$$\overline{X} \text{ Recall}_{\text{Male speaker}}$$
$$= \frac{\sum f \cdot x_i}{N}$$
$$= \frac{500}{50} = 10.0$$

$$\overline{X} \text{ Recall}_{\text{Female speaker}}$$
$$= \frac{\sum f \cdot x_i}{N}$$
$$= \frac{623}{50} = 12.46$$

H_0: *The mean recall of information of subjects who listened to the male speaker is equal to the mean recall of information of subjects who listened to the female speaker, or:*

$$\overline{X} \text{ Recall}_{\text{Male speaker}} = \overline{X} \text{ Recall}_{\text{Female speaker}}$$

and the associated nondirectional H_R is:

H_R: *The mean recall of information of subjects who listened to the male speaker is NOT equal to the mean recall of information of subjects who listened to the female speaker, or:*

$$\overline{X} \text{ Recall}_{\text{Male speaker}} \neq \overline{X} \text{ Recall}_{\text{Female speaker}}$$

The logic for determining what should be observed if the H_0 were true is very simple indeed. If the gender of the speaker is not related to recall of information provided by that speaker, then the average level of recall should be the same for both groups of listeners. Consequently, a true H_0 ought to yield the following:

$$\overline{X} \text{ Recall}_{\text{Male speaker}} - \overline{X} \text{ Recall}_{\text{Female speaker}} = 0$$

The greater the difference between the two means, the more likely it is that a relationship between the two variables exists, and the less likely that such a difference was due to sampling error. The means calculated in Exhibit 11-4 show some relationship between gender and recall, as the research participants recalled an average of 10 items after listening to the male speaker, and 12.46 after listening to the female speaker.

Describing Relationships by Comparing Groups Created from Ordinal or Interval Variables

An independent variable does not necessarily have to be a discrete nominal or ordinal variable to be used in a comparative hypothesis. Any continuous independent variable— either ordinal, interval, or ratio—also lends itself to this type of hypothesis. However, a continuous variable must be reduced to a set of discrete classes, before the techniques described above can be applied. The general strategies described above merely require that the independent variable consist of at least two classes, each represented by one group. Whether these groups have an underlying dimension is quite immaterial to the analysis. We can choose to ignore the additional information supplied by the underlying dimension, if we wish.

The process of defining groups by collapsing ranges of a continuous independent variable is not recommended, since doing so forces a very large number of potential differences to fit in a relatively small number of nominal classes. As we've explained previously, this will cause us to lose some of the information contained in the data.

We might accept this loss and choose to categorize ordinal or interval independent variables, however, if the dependent variable is a nominal variable and we want to use proportional comparison procedures. But if the dependent variable is also a continuous ordinal or interval variable, then establishing whether a relationship exists can be much more efficiently handled by techniques that measure relationships directly without ignoring available information in the data. These techniques measure the degree to which there is simultaneous variation of both continuous variables and will be introduced in the next part of this chapter.

Describing Relationships by Measures of Association

The methods for *directly* assessing a relationship between variables assume that both the independent and the dependent variable are ordinal, interval, or ratio in nature. In this section of this chapter we will outline, in general terms, the various ways of determining directly whether a relationship exists. We will present two variations on a conceptual approach to the measurement of the degree and the nature of association between variables which are at least ordinal. Once again we will see that the choice of procedures is dependent upon the level of measurement of the independent and dependent variables. The specific computations required to use these statistics can be found in any statistics text and we'll defer descriptions of the computations until later in this book. Here we'll focus on the logic behind the procedures.

Measures of Association and Relationship Hypotheses

Direct measures of relationships are appropriate when we have formulated a *relationship* hypothesis. When two non-nominal variables are thought to be related to one another, changes in the magnitude of one of the variables should be associated with changes in magnitude of the other variable. There are two general strategies for determining whether a relationship exists, and the choice between them depends on the level of measurement of the two variables thought to be covarying.

The presence of an underlying dimension is shared by both ordinal measurement and interval/ratio measurement. Both categories of measurement convey a sense of magnitude. Interval and ratio measurement, in addition, are characterized by equal intervals between classes or categories. This characteristic is critical to this discussion because of the constraints it imposes on the use of measures of association between variables that do not share the same level of measurement. Let us first turn our discussion to a measure of relationship between ordinal variables, which do not have equal intervals between classes.

Relationships Between Ordinal Variables

The general strategy for measuring relationships between two ordinal variables is based on agreement/disagreement in observations' rankings on both the independent and the dependent variable. The ordinal nature of measurement will allow the N observations of the independent variable to be arranged in order of increasing or decreasing magnitude.

To these ordered observations we can then assign the rank numbers 1 through N (or N through 1). Observations' scores on the dependent variable can be ordered and have ranks assigned in the same way as they were for the independent variable. Let us look at a new example in Exhibit 11-5.

If the ranks largely agree with one another—that is, we see that each organization has similar ranks on both variables—we infer that a positive relationship exists between degree of change and reliance on hierarchical communication. In fact, if the rank numbers for both the X and the Y variable are identical, we have a perfect positive relationship. Conversely, in the event we observe totally *dis*similar rank pairs we draw the conclusion that a perfect negative relationship exists. In this case, high ranks on one variable would always be associated with low ranks on the other variable. Inconsistent results (for instance, high ranks on one variable are observed to be associated with both high and low ranks on the other variable) are indicative of a null relationship.

The directional H_R regarding the relationship between degree of change and reliance on hierarchical communication is the following:

EXHIBIT 11-5   Testing a Relationship Hypothesis: Ordinal Measurement for Both Variables

A researcher is interested in establishing the relationship between the "degree of change" confronting an organization and that organization's "reliance on hierarchical communication." Degree of change is measured by presenting key informants in the organization with a number of statements about change in organizations (e.g., "There is something different to do every day"). The informants rate how true these statements are for their organization on a seven-point scale ranging from 1 (not at all true) to 7 (completely true). Reliance on hierarchical communication is measured using a set of similar statements (e.g., "I have to ask my boss before I do almost anything") and uses the same rating scale.

For every organization a total degree of change score is computed by adding all the scales, as is a total reliance on hierarchical communication score.

However, the researcher is not willing to assume that the measurement scales have equal intervals, so the resulting scores are to be considered as ordinal data.

The following results were obtained.

Scores

Org.	Degree of Change (X)	Reliance on Hierarchical Communication (Y)	Rank X	Rank Y	Difference in Rank
A	53	27	1	7	−6
B	50	25	2	8	−6
D	47	32	3	6	−3
G	43	38	4	4	0
F	36	45	5	2	3
H	35	53	6	1	5
E	30	42	7	3	4
C	23	35	8	5	3

$$H_R: \text{Degree of change} \xrightarrow{\;-\;} \text{Reliance on hierarchical communication}$$

This hypothesis reflects the reasoning that increased change requires that decisions be made at lower levels in the organization, without communicating with higher-ups. The associated H_0 is:

$$H_0: \text{Degree of change} \qquad \text{Reliance on hierarchical communication}$$

The first step in determining whether the variables are related is the conversion of the variable raw scores to ranks, as is shown above in Exhibit 11-5. The next step is to determine, for any given organization, the discrepancy or difference in rank numbers between its rank on the X variable and its rank on the Y variable. We then look at the pattern of these discrepancies across the whole set of observations. In Exhibit 11-5 we see that the pattern of differences between these ranks in our data is quite revealing:

TABLE 11-8 **Example of Differences in Ranks of Variables for a Null Relationship**

Observation	Variable *X* Rank	Variable *Y* Rank	*D*
A	1	7	−6
B	2	1	+1
C	3	6	−3
D	4	5	−1
E	5	4	+1
F	6	3	+3
G	7	8	−1
H	8	2	+6

High ranks on the degree of change variable tend to be associated with low ranks on the hierarchy of communication variable. This indicates some support for our research hypothesis.

It is instructive to compare these results with the kind of results that we would see if the null hypothesis was correct. Table 11-8 shows a set of ranks and their differences typical of an absence of a relationship.

Notice that the observations which have a high rank on the *X* variable (e.g., A and B) have both a high rank (B) and a low rank (A) on the *Y* variable. The same can be said for all observations with low ranks on the *X* variable. They are associated with both high and low *Y* ranks. The ranking of *Y* cannot be predicted by knowing the rank on *X*. This lack of predictive power indicates that the two variables are not related.

We focus on the extent to which a pattern of rank differences deviates from a random pattern to tell us the extent to which the variables are related (the patterning of ranks) *and* the direction of the relationship.

Relationships between Interval/Ratio Variables

Interval and ratio level variables share the characteristic of equal intervals between classes in the variables. This characteristic has two significant consequences. First, equal intervals in measurement allow for the computation and inspection of the mean as the key descriptive statistic. Second, we can conceptualize covariation differently from the way we conceptualize covariation among ordinal variables. With ordinal variables, we are restricted to talking about variation in ranks, without considering the distances between adjacent ranks (as these may be quite different, for different rank numbers). With interval level data, these distances become part of the definition of the dispersion of the variable, as we saw in Chapter 8. We can then develop another conceptualization of *covariation*.

In the context of interval/ratio variables covariation is defined as the coordinated, simultaneous deviation of an observation from the means of two distributions. Positive covariation occurs when either observations that are above the mean for the *X* variable are also above the mean for the *Y* variable *by similar distances*, or when observations for which the *X* value falls below the mean also have *Y* values that fall similar distances below

EXHIBIT 11-6   Testing a Relationship Hypothesis: Interval/Ratio Measurement for Both Variables

Let us look again at the degree of change occurring in an organization to see how this variable might be related to the degree of communicated formalization in the organization. Communicated formalization refers to the extent to which job descriptions and functions have been explicitly made available for employees.

For the same eight organizations used in the previous example, we define the degree of change as the number of new products that have been introduced by the organization in the past year. Communicated formalization is defined as the percentage of positions in the organization for which written job descriptions exist.

The following results were obtained from the eight organizations.

			Deviations from Means	
		Percent		
	No. of	of Jobs		
	New	with	New	Job
Organization	Products	Descriptions	Prod.	Descr.
A	6	20	+1.625	−18.12
B	5	25	+.625	−13.12
C	3	35	−1.375	−3.12
D	5	32	+.625	−6.12
E	3	50	−1.375	+11.88
F	4	45	−.375	+6.88
G	4	40	−.375	+1.88
H	5	60	+.625	+21.88
	$\Sigma = 35$	$\Sigma = 307$		

$\overline{X}_{\text{No. of New products}}$ $\quad = 35/8 \;= 4.375$

$\overline{Y}_{\text{Percent with job descriptions}}$ $\quad = 307/8 = 38.12$

the mean. This pattern of similar deviations defines a positive relationship. The reverse is true for negative relationships: X values above the mean are associated with Y values below the mean, and vice versa.

In this conceptualization of covariation, we retain the idea that two variables can be related in either a positive or negative direction. This idea was introduced with ordinal variables, but another requirement is added. Observations' distances from their respective means for the X and Y variables must also be coordinated, in order to define a relationship. This is a more stringent requirement, and it gives us a better description of the relationship between the variables.

When the direction of the deviation for one variable is observed in conjunction with both positive and negative deviations of the other variable, or if large deviations on one variable are seen in conjunction with both large and small deviations of the other variable, then we conclude that there is no relationship between the variables. In interval/ratio covariance *both* the direction *and* the magnitude of the deviation from the means must be coordinated before we conclude that there is a relationship. Exhibit 11-6 shows an example of a relationship that is being investigated using variables at the interval/ratio measurement level.

We will propose the following directional research hypothesis about the relationship between these variables:

$$H_0: \text{No. of New} \longleftrightarrow \text{Positions with}$$
$$\text{Products} \qquad \text{Job Descriptions (\%)}$$

based on the theoretical linkage that the greater the change occurring in an organization, the less sense it makes to define jobs, as they are bound to undergo change. The associated H_0 is:

$$H_0: \text{No. of New} \qquad \text{Positions with}$$
$$\text{Products} \qquad \text{Job Descriptions (\%)}$$

In Exhibit 11-6 we see the extent to which the data reveal a pattern of "simultaneous deviation" from the means of the two data distributions. Marking the individual organizations' locations on these two distributions with + signs for positive deviations and − signs for negative deviations reveals a fairly consistent pattern of negative association between the two variables. Positive deviations on the new products variable are associated with negative deviations on the job description variable, and vice versa. Furthermore, the larger deviations in the X variable tend to be associated to some degree with larger deviations in the Y variable.

Mixed-Measurement Relationships

Mixed-measurement relationships occur whenever the variables we expect to be related are measured at different levels. Such a situation could easily occur in the last few examples. Imagine, for instance, that we are interested in exploring the relationship between reliance on hierarchical communication and communicated formalization.

Recall that the measurement we used for reliance on hierarchical communication was ordinal, while the communicated formalization measurement was interval. To determine the degree of association between these two variables we will have to use the measure of association that is appropriate for describing both variables. This will always be the measure of association that is appropriate for the variable characterized by the *lowest level* of measurement.

Since the variable reliance on hierarchical communication was operationalized at the ordinal level, it does not allow the computation of means. So, for example, using a method of establishing relationships based on deviations from means (like that described in the last example) would be inappropriate. The only option that remains is to treat the interval/ratio variable as if it were merely an ordinal variable and to determine its relationship with the true ordinal variable (reliance) by using the method based on agreement-disagreement between ranks. This will work, but we will lose the magnitude information contained in the interval variable. Not to be tedious, but once again, this points out the importance of creating operational definitions that are at the highest level of measurement possible.

Summary

In this chapter we have outlined the interdependency that exists among measurement, descriptive statistics for characterizing the size of relationships, and the basic procedures used for detecting relationships between variables. Students (and some communication researchers) sometimes tend to draw a line between communication theory construction and research design on the one hand, and data analysis on the other, considering them to be almost unrelated activities. We hope we have shown in this and in previous chapters that there is an uninterrupted path from the theoretical definition of concepts to the operational definition, with its associated level of measurement, to the detection and testing of hypothetical relationships. The way in which an independent variable is operationalized will dictate whether *comparative hypotheses* or *relationship hypotheses* will be appropriate. Decisions that are made when the dependent variable is operationalized will determine what descriptive statistic must be used. Decisions regarding measurement should always be made with intended analysis procedures explicitly considered.

We have outlined very basic strategies for describing relationships at the measurement level. The fundamental strategy consists of comparing the observed pattern of some descriptive statistic with the pattern which we would expect to find if no relationship existed. Deviations from the null relationship pattern are taken as evidence for the existence of a relationship. The greater the deviation, the greater the presumed strength of the relationship.

The kind of contrast that we can make is determined by the lowest level of measurement of either the independent or the dependent variable. We can always reduce a higher level of measurement to a lower one and use contrast procedures appropriate for the lower level. But when we do so, we lose information and statistical sensitivity. In describing relationships and testing hypotheses, we should always strive to operate at the highest level of measurement possible, as this will give us the most powerful way of scrutinizing our theoretical statements.

In future chapters we will explore in greater detail some variations on the basic strategies for describing and testing relationships that we have outlined here.

References and Additional Readings

Buchanan, W. (1984). Nominal and ordinal bivariate statistics: The practitioner's view. In H. Asher, H. F. Weisberg, J. H. Kessel & W. Phillips Shively (Eds.), *Theory building and data analysis in the social sciences* (pp. 189–210). Knoxville: University of Tennessee Press.

Loether, H. J. & McTavish, D. G. (1974). *Descriptive statistics for sociologists: An introduction.* Boston:
Allyn & Bacon (Part III, "Descriptive Statistics: Two Variables").

Weisberg, H. F. (1984). Fundamentals of data analysis. In H. Asher, H. F. Weisberg, J. H. Kessel & W. Phillips Shively (Eds.), *Theory building and data analysis in the social sciences* (pp. 151–188). Knoxville: University of Tennessee Press.

Chapter *12*

Testing Hypotheses

The previous chapters have provided us with the basic tools and strategies needed to test hypotheses. In this chapter, we will combine the statistics for describing relationships between variables with their sampling distributions to test hypotheses. This is the point at which our "verbal world" of theory meets the "measurement world" of empirical verification.

The process of hypothesis testing is a general one, and one that underlies virtually all the methods for analyzing data that have been introduced in the previous chapters, as well as ones that will be encountered in greater detail later. All these procedures have the same basic idea—the comparison of one outcome to an alternative outcome, stated as a probability.

As long as we are sampling from a population, we can never be absolutely sure that our results are not due to random error, so all true/false statements are really "probably true/probably false" statements. Computing the probability of truth and using this value to decide between competing hypotheses is the process that we'll focus on in this chapter.

It is very important to have a clear understanding of the different types of hypotheses before proceeding (see Chapters 3 and 4). You should know the differences between comparative and relationship hypotheses; directional and nondirectional hypotheses; and alternative or research hypotheses versus null hypotheses. Table 12-1 outlines the basic kinds of hypotheses, as described in Chapter 3.

Notice that all hypotheses compare one situation to another. In relationship hypotheses, covariances for the research hypothesis are compared to covariances in the opposite direction (non-null competing hypothesis) or zero covariance (null hypothesis). In comparative hypotheses, a descriptive measure (such as the mean or the proportion) for one group is compared to the same descriptive measure for another group. The competing hypotheses here are differences in the opposite direction (non-null competing hypothesis) or zero differences (null hypothesis).

However, since relationship and comparative hypotheses differ only in the level of measurement of the independent variable, we can treat both in the same way. In fact,

TABLE 12-1   Types of Hypotheses

A: Relationship Hypotheses

	Relationship Between Variables X and Y		
	Directional		Nondirectional
Research Hypothesis	$X \xrightarrow{+} Y$	$X \xrightarrow{-} Y$	$X \xrightarrow{+\text{ or }-} Y$
Competing Hypotheses:			
Non-null Hypotheses	$X \xrightarrow{-} Y$	$X \xrightarrow{+} Y$	
Null Hypothesis	$X \quad Y$	$X \quad Y$	$X \quad Y$

B: Comparative Hypotheses

	Difference between Groups A and B of Independent Variable X on Dependent Variable Y		
	Directional		Nondirectional
Research Hypothesis	$\overline{Y}_{Gr\,A} > \overline{Y}_{Gr\,B}$	$\overline{Y}_{Gr\,A} < \overline{Y}_{Gr\,B}$	$\overline{Y}_{Gr\,A} \neq \overline{Y}_{Gr\,B}$
Competing Hypotheses:			
Non-null Hypotheses	$\overline{Y}_{Gr\,A} < \overline{Y}_{Gr\,B}$	$\overline{Y}_{Gr\,A} > \overline{Y}_{Gr\,B}$	
Null Hypothesis	$\overline{Y}_{Gr\,A} = \overline{Y}_{Gr\,B}$	$\overline{Y}_{Gr\,A} = \overline{Y}_{Gr\,B}$	$\overline{Y}_{Gr\,A} = \overline{Y}_{Gr\,B}$

we refer to either as "research hypotheses." When you see this term, recognize that the hypothesis being discussed can be either a comparative or relationship hypothesis, and it really doesn't matter whether we are talking about differences between the means (or other statistics) of two groups, or about the relationship between two continuous variables.

We can similarly simplify the discussion of competing hypotheses. The competing hypothesis can either be a null hypothesis (no covariance, or no difference between groups) or a non-null hypothesis which states that the direction of the covariance or of the group difference is in the opposite of that predicted by the hypothesis. From the standpoint of the procedures that follow, this distinction is not relevant. General hypothesis testing involves testing the value of a statistic against a competing value, and it really doesn't matter if the competing value is zero (null), or something else that is not in the expected direction.

In most discussions of hypothesis testing, the null hypothesis is used as the competing explanation to the research hypothesis. As we saw in the previous chapter, this is a natural

---

EXHIBIT 12-1   Testing a Nondirectional Comparative Hypothesis

The owner of a medium-sized corporation receives a request from an officer of a local charity, asking her to persuade her employees to increase their contributions. Through an inspection of payroll records she determines that her employees make donations to this fund that amount to, on the average, $150 per year, and that these donations have a variance equal to 3600. Before writing a personal letter to all employees she consults an employee communications consultant who warns her that the consequences of such a letter might be twofold: The letter can either increase contributions, as employees may feel flattered by hearing from the boss; or contributions may decrease, as it is possible that employees might see the letter as an intrusion into what they consider a private matter. Given the uncertainty regarding the outcome, the owner holds off sending a letter to all employees and decides instead to test for the effect of the letter by writing to a randomly selected sample of 50 employees to see how their contributions change. A reasonable time after sending the letter, the payroll records of the random sample will be inspected and this data will be used to determine the specific effect, if any, of the campaign.

---

comparison, since the null hypothesis describes a situation in which there is no relationship between the independent and dependent or criterion variable, while the research hypothesis describes the competing situation in which there is a relationship. We'll also use the null hypothesis as the primary competing hypothesis, but again urge the reader to keep in mind that any other competing hypothesis value could also be used. The logic for testing the null competing hypothesis (we'll start shortening this to "null hypothesis") is quite simple and can be easily illustrated in an example.

Testing a Comparative Hypothesis

In the example presented in Exhibit 12-1, we want to establish whether a relationship exists between two variables. The independent variable—the attempt to persuade through a communication campaign—has two levels: absent or present. The test of the effect of the persuasion attempt will consist of contrasting the donations of two groups: the donations of the whole work force (those who donated prior to the letter writing campaign—in the absence of a communication campaign) and the donations of the sample (those who received the boss' letter and were possibly affected by the communication). The amount of donation is the dependent variable, and it is measured at the ratio level. Since we will be contrasting the average donations of the two groups (those who received the communication and those who did not), we will use a comparative hypothesis.

The rationale given above for the effectiveness of the letter implies that we need a nondirectional research hypothesis, since we don't know whether the letter writing campaign, if it is effective, will increase or decrease donations:

$$H_R: M_{\text{before letter}} \neq \overline{X}_{\text{after letter}}$$

If the letter is irrelevant, we have the following null hypothesis:

$$H_0: M_{\text{before letter}} = \overline{X}_{\text{after letter}}$$

Another way of stating the null hypothesis is this: If the letter writing campaign does not affect donations, then the average donations of employees who have received the letter will be the same as the average donations made by employees prior to the letter.

This statement has a very important implication. If the null hypothesis is true, then we expect that the group who received the encouraging letter (the sample of 50 employees) is the same in all respects to the group who did not receive a letter. This implies that the population parameters (the mean and variance of donations) are identical to those of the sample. Testing the null hypothesis is thus a fairly simple procedure, because we know what descriptive values we should find in the sample, if the null hypothesis is correct.

Null Hypothesis and the Sampling Distribution of Means

Assume then that the null hypothesis is correct. If the sample of 50 employees is representative of the population (and it should be, if we have drawn an unbiased probability sample), then we know that we should find a sample mean of $150 and a sample variance of 3600. We can further state that the mean of this sample will be part of a sampling distribution of means that would be obtained if we were to take all random samples of $N = 50$ out of this population. Such a sampling distribution can be completely described by the application of the central limit theorem, which generates the following statements:

- The mean of the sampling distribution ($\overline{\overline{X}}$) will be equal to M, the mean of the population, or $150.
- The variance of the sampling distribution will be equal to σ^2/N, where σ^2 is the population variance (3600), and N is the sample size (50). Hence, the sampling variance will be equal to 3600/50 = 72.00.
- The standard error will then equal $\sqrt{\text{sampling variance}} = \sqrt{72.00} = \$8.48$.
- The sampling distribution of means will tend toward a standard normal distribution if N is sufficiently large (50 is large enough to make this assumption).

The sampling distribution that would result from taking all samples of $N = 50$ from this population is shown in Figure 12-1. Remember that a sampling distribution of means provides us with two pieces of information. First, the sampling distribution of means is a distribution of sampling error. It shows us the size of the discrepancies between statistics and parameters that we should expect to observe, if we take samples of N out of a population with known parameters. Second, since we can assume the standard normal distribution, the sampling distribution of means also becomes a distribution of the probabilities of observing any particular size of sampling error. The sampling distribution

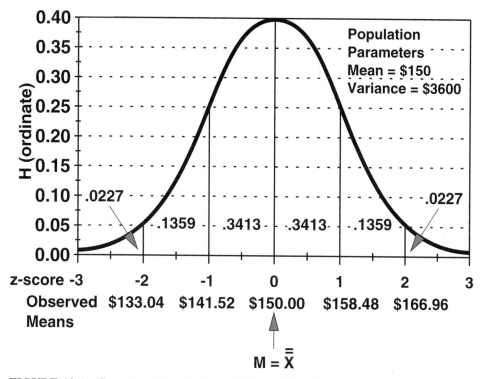

FIGURE 12-1   **Sampling Distribution of Means ($N = 50$)**

shows the probabilities associated with the various sample means, or, to put it in another way, shows the likelihood of occurrence of various amounts of sampling error.

The sampling distribution shown in Figure 12-1 indicates that if we were to take all possible samples of $N = 50$ out of this population, we would observe that 68.26 percent of all the sample means would be between \$141.52 and \$158.48 ($\overline{\overline{X}} \pm 1$ standard error, or \$150.00 ± \$8.48). Furthermore, our chances of observing any of the sample means of less than \$133.04 would be .0227, the same as our chances of observing any sample mean over \$166.96.

If the null hypothesis is true, and if we could sample from the population without incurring sampling error, we would find the sample mean exactly equal to the parameter, or \$150. However, sampling error *will* occur. The intervention of purely random events means that we should reasonably expect some difference between the parameter and the statistic, even if the null hypothesis is true. However, we expect the value of the statistic to be fairly close to the value of the parameter.

As Figure 12-1 shows, we have roughly a two-out-of-three chance (68.26 percent probability, to be exact) of observing a sample mean between \$141.52 and \$158.48, when the true population mean is \$150.00. If we observe a sample mean within this range—that is, one which is reasonably close to the center of the sampling distribution associated with the null hypothesis—we can safely assume that the null hypothesis is probably correct, and that the difference between the population parameter and the sample mean is probably due to random error.

Null Hypothesis and the Region of Rejection

The last sentence of the previous section contains a key idea: As long as we observe a *negligible* difference between the mean donation made by the receivers of the letter, and the population mean observed before the letter writing campaign began, we can remain confident that the H_0 is probably true. But what happens to our confidence in the null hypothesis as the difference between the sample mean and the population mean increases? As the sample mean deviates further from the center of the sampling distribution, its probability of occurrence under the null hypothesis is lower. It becomes increasingly unlikely that it occurred simply by random chance. Our confidence in the truth of the null hypothesis will wane accordingly.

If the mean of the sample of employees was found to be located in one of the extreme tails of the distribution, we would have very little confidence in the H_0, because if the null hypothesis was correct, we should have observed a sample mean that was much closer to the expected value at the center of the sampling distribution.

Just as we have less confidence in the truth of the null hypothesis when the sample mean deviates widely from the center of the sampling distribution, we simultaneously have increasing confidence that the nondirectional research hypothesis is probably correct, since only one of the two alternatives can be right.

Figure 12-2 illustrates how our confidence in either hypothesis varies as a consequence of the location of the sample mean. As we move further into the tail of the sampling distribution for the null hypothesis, we will eventually arrive at some point where the degree of confidence we have in the null hypothesis simply is not sufficient to consider that hypothesis as a reasonable explanation of the actual situation. At that point we will "fail to accept the H_0," leaving us no alternative but to consider the H_R (the research hypothesis) as probably true.

The problem lies in determining when we have reached the point where we no longer feel confident that the null hypothesis is true. To make this determination we must convert the continuously varying probabilities into a true/false dichotomy. This is akin to converting varying shades of gray into "black" and "white" by using a criterion paint chip for comparison: darker than the chip is "black," lighter than the chip is "white." The decision to reject (or fail to accept) the null hypothesis is made by employing a similar criterion. The application of this decision rule involves setting up a *region of rejection* in the sampling distribution. To do this, we set a *critical value* of the statistic located at some distance from the center of the sampling distribution. Statistics that are closer to the center of the distribution than the critical value are considered to be close enough to the value predicted by the null hypothesis that we cannot reject H_0. Values further from the center than the critical value are considered improbable enough for us to reject H_0, and accept the research hypothesis.

But where in the sampling distribution should we place the critical value? Remember that values of the test statistic representative of a true null hypothesis will be observed at or near the center of the sampling distribution. Those sample means that are observed

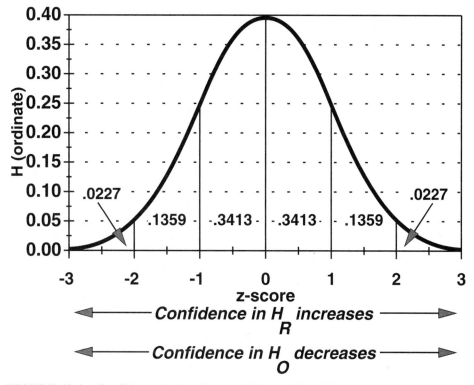

FIGURE 12-2 **Confidence in the Truth of H_R and H_0 with a Nondirectional Hypothesis**

further away (in the tails of the distribution) are considered as less representative of null conditions. Accordingly, the region of rejection will be located somewhere in the tail(s) of the distribution. The region of rejection (the range of means in which we can reject H_0) will be located in one or both tails of the sampling distribution, depending on whether the research hypothesis is directional or nondirectional. If the sample statistic that we observe is within the region of rejection, we will reject the null hypothesis. Observing a value for the test statistic not in the region of rejection will allow us to accept the null.

Size of the Region of Rejection

The size of the region of rejection is determined by the amount of confidence that we wish to place in our decision to accept or reject the null hypothesis. We saw in Chapter 10 how to translate an area under the normal curve that describes the sampling distribution to a probability. As we saw there, this probability can be interpreted as a sampling error probability. Stating such an error probability, such as .05 (5 percent), or .01 (1 percent), is also referred to as setting the *level of significance*. The probability level is commonly abbreviated to *p* and is also referred to as the *alpha level* or α for testing the null hypothesis.

When we set the level of significance at $p = .05$, we set aside an area under the tail or tails of the sampling distribution which contains the most extreme 5 percent of the values of the test statistic. This area is 5 percent of the total area under the normal curve, and the test statistics falling in this area or areas together constitute .05 (or 5 percent) of all possible sample statistics in the sampling distribution. We then know that there is only a 5 percent chance that a sample statistic will fall in this area due to sampling error, when the actual population value is the one predicted by the null hypothesis. If our sample statistic then falls in the region of rejection, we can be confident that there is only a 5 percent chance of the null hypothesis being true, and a 95 percent chance that the research hypothesis is true.

As we'll see below, when we set the level of significance, we automatically set the critical value of the test statistic, since only one value (or two, if the hypothesis is nondirectional, and the region of rejection lies under both tails of the sampling distribution) of the test statistic will delimit 5 percent of the area under the normal curve.

The size of the region of rejection is selected with an eye on the consequences of our decision about whether to accept or reject the null hypothesis. These consequences will be discussed later in the section on various errors in testing hypotheses.

Where to Locate the Region of Rejection: Directional and Nondirectional Hypotheses

Whether or not the alternative hypothesis is directional (and if so, in which direction) is critical in determining the location of the region of rejection. Returning to the communication campaign example presented in Exhibit 12-1, assume that we decide to test the H_0 at $p = .10$. We will then set aside a region of rejection equal to 10 percent of the area under *both tails* of the sampling distribution. Figure 12-3 shows this graphically.

The nondirectional research hypothesis requires that the region of rejection be located in both tails of the distribution, since we are not predicting whether the effect of the communication will be to increase or to decrease donations. Therefore the total error probability (.10) is divided over both tails, with an area equal to .05 in each tail. In the table of the normal distribution in Appendix A, we find that .05 of the area under the curve remains in the tail of a distribution when the standard score z equals ± 1.65. Another way of stating this is to say that between $z = -1.65$ and $z = +1.65$ lies 90 percent of the total area under the curve.

If our sample mean is in the region of rejection, it will have to be at least 1.65 standard errors (in either direction) away from the mean of the sampling distribution, which is centered around the expected null value. That means that the critical value of z in this case is ± 1.65.

Whether a sample mean in fact falls in the region of rejection can be determined by computing a *z-statistic*. For the differences between a sample and a population mean, the following formula is used:

$$z = \frac{\overline{X} - M}{\text{standard error}}$$

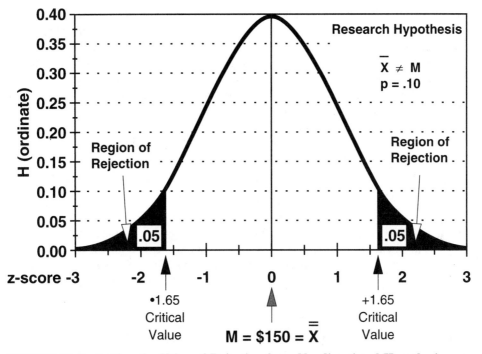

FIGURE 12-3   Setting the Value of Rejection for a Nondirectional Hypothesis

Notice that this formula is the exact analog of the standard score, or z-score that we have been using. The z-statistic represents the *deviation of a statistic* (the sample mean) from the mean of that set of statistics (the population or grand mean) under a normal curve, in the sampling distribution of statistics. The z-score represents the *deviation of a data value*, also under a normal curve, in the sample distribution. A similar deviation statistic can be computed for other test statistics, as we'll see later when we test a relationship hypothesis.

The computed value of the z-statistic is evaluated against the critical value to see if it meets or exceeds the minimal value required to be in the region of rejection. Let's see how this operates within our example:

> *Three months after the letters are mailed, the payroll records for the employees in the random sample are checked. The average payroll deduction, prorated for a year, is found to be $170.00.*

The computed z-statistic is then equal to:

$$z = \frac{\$170 - \$150}{\$8.48} = \frac{+\$20}{\$8.48} = +2.36$$

As $z_{observed} \geq z_{critical}$, the observed sample mean is within the region of rejection. Consequently, we will reject the null hypothesis which states that the encouragement to donate will have no effect. Rejecting this hypothesis then implies its logical alternative—that encouragement *did* have an effect. More specifically, by inspecting the value of the mean of the sample, we conclude that its effect was to increase contributions to charity.

But suppose we have a more specific theoretical linkage which states a *direction* to the expected effect if the research hypothesis is true. A directional research hypothesis implies that the region of rejection is located in only one of the two tails of the distribution, namely the tail that is in the direction stated by the research hypothesis.

Let us return to our example. Assume that the theoretical linkage we develop states that employees will be honored to have this donation request directed at them by their boss, and therefore they will increase their payroll deductions. The H_R will then be:

$$M_{\text{before letter}} < \overline{X}_{\text{after letter}}$$

In other words, based on our theoretical linkage we expect that the observed mean of the sample will be GREATER than the population value measured before the communication campaign began. Logically associated with this research hypothesis is the H_0:

$$M_{\text{before letter}} \geq \overline{X}_{\text{after letter}}$$

The research hypothesis states that the mean of the sample will be GREATER than the population mean. This H_R then dictates that we locate the region of rejection (equal to .10 of the area under the normal curve) in the *right-hand tail* of the sampling distribution which contains all of the sample means that are greater than the population mean M. Note that the H_0 is really two competing hypotheses in this case: (1) The population mean is equal to the sample mean; and (2) the population mean is greater than the sample mean. But since the truth of either implies that we have found no evidence for our research hypothesis, we will follow the standard practice of referring (somewhat confusingly) to both competing hypotheses as the null hypothesis. Figure 12-4 shows this hypothesis graphically.

A quick reference to the table in Appendix A indicates that the sample means in the region of rejection equal to .10 of the area under the curve are at least +1.28 standard errors above the mean of the sampling distribution. In other words, the critical value of z for the directional hypothesis has only one value, +1.28. The observed sample mean of $170.00, with an associated z-statistic of +2.36 is larger than this critical value, and is located in the region of rejection. Again, we can reject the null hypothesis.

A different theoretical linkage might produce a different alternative research hypothesis, however. Suppose our theory leads us to the conclusion that writing a letter to employees will be viewed by the recipients as an invasion of privacy and this will result in reduced donations. The research hypothesis would then be:

$$M_{\text{before letter}} > \overline{X}_{\text{after letter}}$$

Based on this different theoretical linkage we would expect that the mean of the sample to be observed to be LESS than M. Logically associated with this research hypothesis is

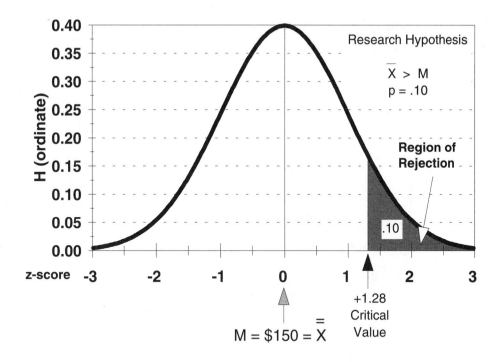

FIGURE 12-4   Setting the Region of Rejection for a Positive Directional Hypothesis

the following H_0:

$$M_{\text{before letter}} \leq \overline{X}_{\text{after letter}}$$

Figure 12-5 illustrates the decision rule: We will reject the H_0 only if the observed sample mean is located in the region that makes up the extreme 10 percent of all sample means in the left-hand tail of the sampling distribution. In this case the critical value of the z-statistic is -1.28, or 1.28 standard errors *below* the mean of the sampling distribution. An observed sample mean of $170, and its associated z-statistic of $+2.36$, will not be located in the region of rejection. We will therefore fail to reject the null hypothesis which states that the sample mean will be equal to or greater than the population mean. Although the sample mean is a substantial distance away from the mean of the sampling distribution, it is in the wrong direction, so it does not support our research hypothesis.

Testing a Relationship Hypothesis

We can use the same ideas developed above to test relationship hypotheses. We'll use an example from the previous chapter to illustrate how to test the significance of a statistic called a correlation coefficient. In this example, completely described in Exhibit 11-6 in the

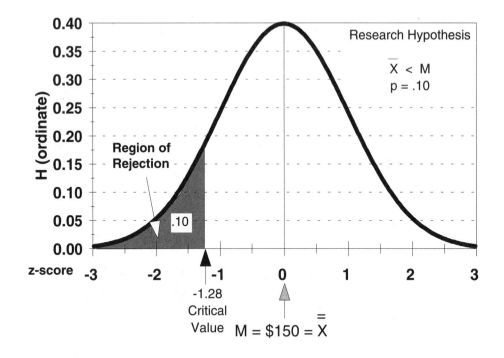

FIGURE 12-5 **Setting the Region of Rejection for a Negative Directional Hypothesis**

previous chapter, we are looking at a possible relationship within organizations between two variables: "degree of change" and "communicated formalization." The degree of change variable is defined by the number of new products that have been introduced by the organization in the past year. The variable communicated formalization is defined as the percentage of positions in the organization for which written job descriptions are available. The hypothetical data set and some necessary computations are in Table 12-2.

Because the level of measurement is interval for *both* the independent *and* the dependent variable, the Pearson product moment correlation coefficient will be used to compute the degree of relationship between the two variables in this sample. This correlation coefficient will be equal to +1.00 in case of a perfect positive relationship; −1.00 if there is a perfect negative relationship and will equal 0 when there is no relationship between two variables.

Based on the theoretical linkage that the greater the change occurring in an organization, the less sense it makes to define jobs, as they are bound to undergo change, the following research hypothesis is proposed:

$$H_R: \text{No. of New} \longrightarrow \overset{-}{\text{Positions with}}$$
$$\text{Products} \qquad \text{Job Descriptions (\%)}$$

TABLE 12-2 Hypothetical Data for Testing a Relationship Hypothesis with Pearson Correlation Coefficient.[a]

Org.	No. of New Products	Positions with Job Descriptions (%)			
	X	Y	X^2	Y^2	XY
A	6	20	36	400	120
B	5	25	25	625	125
C	3	35	9	1225	105
D	5	32	25	1024	160
E	3	50	9	2500	150
F	4	45	16	2025	180
G	4	40	16	1600	160
H	5	60	25	3600	300
	$\sum X = 35$	$\sum Y = 307$	$\sum X^2 = 161$	$\sum Y^2 = 12999$	$\sum XY = 1300$

$$r = \frac{N \cdot \sum XY - (\sum X) \cdot (\sum Y)}{\sqrt{[N \cdot \sum X^2 - (\sum X)^2] \cdot [N \cdot \sum Y^2 - (\sum Y)^2]}}$$

$$r = \frac{8 \cdot 1300 - (35) \cdot (307)}{\sqrt{[8 \cdot 161 - (35)^2] \cdot [8 \cdot 12999 - (307)^2]}}$$

$$= \frac{10400 - 10745}{\sqrt{[1288 - 1225] \cdot [103992 - 94249]}}$$

$$= \frac{-345}{\sqrt{[63] \cdot [9743]}} = \frac{-345}{783.46} = -.44$$

[a]Note: For reasons of simplicity in calculation and to save space the data set presented above is extremely small. The strategy for testing the significance of a correlation coefficient presented in this section assumes sample sizes far larger than the one used here, typically $N > 100$.

along with its associated H_0:

$$+ \text{ or } 0$$

H_0: No. of New $\longrightarrow$ Positions with
Products   Job Descriptions (%)

Null Hypothesis of No Relationship and the Sampling Distribution of the Pearson Product-Moment Correlation Coefficient

If the null hypothesis of no relationship is true, then the correlation coefficient between the number of new products and percentage of positions with written job descriptions should be equal to 0.0. Furthermore, the correlation coefficient observed in this sample should be part of a sampling distribution of correlation coefficients which would be obtained if

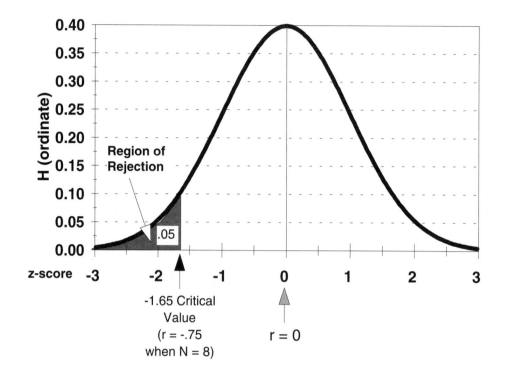

FIGURE 12-6   Sampling Distribution of a Correlation Coefficient

we were to take all samples of this size N out of the population of organizations. That sampling distribution is shown in Figure 12-6.

The sampling distribution shows the various correlation coefficients that could be obtained if H_0 is true, when samples of a given size N are taken. If the null hypothesis is in fact the true hypothesis, we would expect to observe a correlation coefficient of 0.0, or very close to 0.0, in our sample. If we do observe a correlation coefficient that is close to zero, we will consider the H_0 to be probably true. If the correlation differs a great deal from zero, we will consider H_0 to be probably false.

Because the H_R predicts that a negative relationship between the two variables will be observed, we have a directional hypothesis, and the region of rejection will be established in the left-hand tail of the sampling distribution. For this example we have selected a region of rejection equal to .05 (or 5 percent) of the area under the curve. The table in Appendix A showing the areas under the normal distribution shows us that .05 of the area under the curve will remain in the tail of the distribution that is −1.65 or more standard errors away from the mean of the distribution.

To determine whether or not the null hypothesis can be rejected requires two steps. The first step is the computation of the Pearson correlation coefficient, which describes the size of the relationship between the two variables. (We'll expand futher on the correlation coefficient in Chapter 19.) The second step is to find out how far, in standard errors, that this correlation deviates from the zero value predicted by the null hypothesis.

The actual computation of the Pearson product-moment correlation coefficient takes place by means of a rather cumbersome looking formula:

$$r = \frac{N \cdot \sum XY - (\sum X) \cdot (\sum Y)}{\sqrt{[N \cdot \sum X^2 - (\sum X)^2] \cdot [N \cdot \sum Y^2 - (\sum Y)^2]}}$$

As you can see in Table 12-2, the calculated Pearson correlation coefficient between the two variables is $-.44$. This describes the size of the relationship. But is this far enough from the value predicted by the null hypothesis that we can reject the null? To answer this question, we have to see whether the observed correlation coefficient is located in the region of rejection. This means that it must be at least -1.65 standard errors away from the mean of the sampling distribution.

To determine this we will compute a z-statistic. If we assume the sample size to be sufficiently large (see the note in Table 12-2) the formula for z is:

$$z = \frac{r - 0}{\frac{1}{\sqrt{N}}}$$

In this formula the numerator $(r - 0)$ represents "how far" the observed correlation coefficient is away from 0, the expectation under the null hypothesis, and where

$$\frac{1}{\sqrt{N}}$$

is the standard error of the sampling distribution of correlation coefficients. The formula for the standard error tells us that the larger the number of observations, the smaller will be the standard error. If $N = 25$, the standard error would be $\frac{1}{5} = .20$; if $N = 100$, the standard error would be $\frac{1}{10} = .10$, and so on.

The computed z-statistic for our example is then

$$z = \frac{-.44 - 0}{\frac{1}{\sqrt{8}}} = \frac{-.44}{.3536} = -1.244$$

As $z_{observed}(-1.244) > z_{critical}(-1.65)$, the computed correlation coefficient is NOT within the region of rejection. Consequently, we will accept the null hypothesis that states that there is no relationship between the variables as the probably true hypothesis. We conclude that we have no convincing evidence for systematic parallel change (covariance) in these two variables.

TABLE 12-3   Error Types and Correct Conclusions in Hypothesis Testing

		True Situation	
		Null Correct	Null False
Researcher's Conclusion	Null False	*ERROR* Type 1 or α Error	*CORRECT* Relationship Power, or $(1 - \beta)$
	Null Correct	*CORRECT* No Relationship $(1 - \alpha)$	*ERROR* Type 2 or β Error

Errors and Power in Hypothesis Testing

In the information campaign example, we tested the null hypothesis that the letter writing campaign had no effect. The statistical test produced a z-statistic of $+2.36$, that, when contrasted with a critical value of z, enabled us to reject the nondirectional null hypothesis. We concluded that the null hypothesis is probably false, and that the research hypothesis is probably true. It needs to be emphasized once again that we speak in terms of "probably true" and "probably false," because we can never be completely sure that the null hypothesis in fact is not the true hypothesis.

The reason we are never sure is because in contrasting the null hypothesis and the research hypothesis, it is possible to make two kinds of errors, along with two correct inferences. These four situations arise out of the decisions the researcher makes about the null hypothesis—to reject the H_0 versus failure to reject—combined with the true situation that exists within the population—the null hypothesis is actually true or the null hypothesis is actually false. These combinations are summarized in Table 12-3.

Type 1 Error and the Correct Conclusion of No Relationship

The probability of correctly accepting or rejecting the null hypothesis is based on the area under the normal curve that is associated with the sampling distribution for the null hypothesis. This curve is centered around the expected value for the null hypothesis, and its "width" (actually the dispersion or standard error of the sampling distribution) is determined by the number of observations and the dispersion of the original data (see Chapter 9). This curve is the left one in Figure 12-7.

If the researcher rejects the H_0, when in fact it is the true hypothesis, *Type 1 error* is committed. The researcher will erroneously conclude that the research hypothesis is probably true, when actually there is no relationship between the independent and dependent variables.

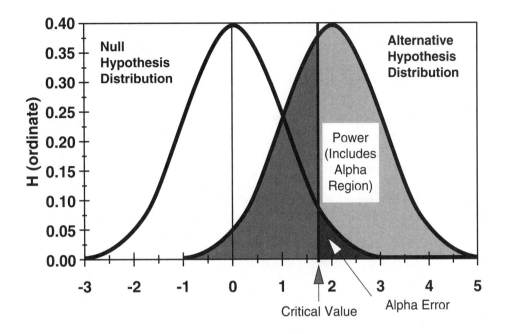

FIGURE 12-7   Errors in Hypothesis Testing and Statistical Power

The probability of this error occurring is determined by the size of the region of rejection, as we can see in Figure 12-7. This probability is stated by the level of significance (e.g., $p = .05$). The level of significance is just another way of stating the probability of making a Type 1 or α error.

If we find a value of the sample statistic that does indeed fall into the region of rejection, we consider that its occurrence by chance is highly unlikely, and hence the sample statistic is indicating the probable falsehood of the null hypothesis. However, it is very important that we remember that even though the sample result was very *unlikely* under the null hypothesis, it is not *impossible* to obtain such results by pure chance. Sample statistics in the region of rejection have a finite probability of occurrence, even when the null hypothesis is true. This probability, which is equal to the area under the normal curve within the region of rejection, is the probability of committing a Type 1 error. The larger the region of rejection, the more likely it is that we will reject the null hypothesis, and thus the more likely we are to commit a Type 1 error. This can be seen by contrasting the α error in Figure 12-8 with that in Figure 12-7.

The farther the critical value is from the center of the sampling distribution which is centered around the null hypothesis expected value, the lower is the probability that a sample statistic of the critical magnitude (or greater) will occur by chance. So decreasing the region of rejection (e.g., from .05 to .025) makes it harder to reject the null hypothesis, and therefore decreases the risk of committing Type 1 error. It also improves the chances of making a correct no relationship decision. The probability of making this correct decision is $(1 - \alpha)$, so it increases as α decreases. However, this decision has an impact on Type 2 error, as we'll see below.

Type 2 Error and Statistical Power

The probability of correctly detecting or failing to detect a true relationship is based on the area under the normal curve that is associated with the sampling distribution for the research or alternative hypothesis. The shape of this curve (its standard error) is the same as that of the null hypothesis distribution, but it is centered at some non-null value. This curve is on the right in Figure 12-7.

When the researcher accepts the H_0 when in fact it should have been rejected, *Type 2 error* is committed. Here, the researcher incorrectly concludes that there is no relationship between the independent and dependent variables, when one actually exists. The researcher has erroneously accepted the null hypothesis. The probability of making this error is indicated by the area under the tail of the sampling distribution for the research hypothesis that exceeds the critical value, in the direction of the expected value for the null hypothesis, as shown in Figure 12-7.

The probability of correctly rejecting the null hypothesis is indicated by the remaining area under the non-null sampling distribution. This area $(1 - \beta)$ is also sometimes called the "statistical power," since it represents the probability that a researcher will be able to correctly conclude that a relationship exists from examining the sample data.

Effect Size and the Expected Value for the Research Hypothesis

How do we determine the expected value of the alternative research hypothesis? While the value for expected value of the null hypothesis is usually self-evident (no difference between means; a zero correlation, etc.), there is no such easily obtained value for a research hypothesis. If we're not even sure that a relationship exists, how can we state an expected value? The answer lies in realizing that the expected value for the research hypothesis is essentially an arbitrary decision made by the researcher. It is not just a number pulled out of a hat, however. There are several motives that a researcher might have for assigning a particular expected value to the research hypothesis.

One way to set the research hypothesis expected value is to set this effect size at some minimum but meaningful value. In the communication campaign example described earlier, the researcher might decide that any communication campaign that produces less than an average additional $10 per year donation is not worth the effort of implementing. Since the population mean before the campaign was $150 (the null hypothesis expected value), adding the minimum effect size of interest ($10) gives a research hypothesis expected value of $160.

Another way of setting the expected value is by examining prior research. If a number of studies have indicated that the average correlation between the number of new products produced by an organization, and the number of jobs with a written description is $-.35$, we might set the research hypothesis expected value at $-.35$.

Once we have set the expected value, we can begin to talk about error in terms of *effect size*. The difference between the expected value for the null hypothesis and for the research hypothesis is the effect size. In essence, it summarizes the size of the difference between the situation of no relationship (the null hypothesis) and a significant relationship (the research hypothesis) that we are trying to detect.

Alpha (α) and Beta (β) Error, Effect Size, and the Number of Observations

There is an interactive relationship among the levels of α error, β error, the effect size, and the standard error of the sampling distribution. Changing any of these values has some effect on the others. A researcher who understands this interplay can adjust the values to get the maximum value from the research.

Changes in the standard error of the sampling distribution can be made by changing the number of observations (N) in the sample. The standard error has been defined earlier within the context of the central limit theorem as:

$$\sqrt{\frac{\sigma^2}{N}} \text{ or } \frac{\sigma}{\sqrt{N}}$$

Since the dispersion of the data distribution for the population is a constant, and is not affected by any action that the researcher may take, only the N is involved in determining the dispersion of the sampling distribution.

The α and β error levels are arbitrary values set by the researcher. By tradition, the α level, or significance level, is frequently set at 5 percent ($p = .05$). Likewise, the conventional level for β is .20. There are no real reasons for these values—they've just emerged because a large number of people have used them in the past. But the intelligent researcher will set both error values according to the rewards and penalties for making each type of error, rather than deferring to tradition. An example will help to illustrate the value of considering both error types.

Suppose a researcher in health communication has devised a counseling program for recent heart attack victims. This program uses group sessions, printed brochures with advice about diet and exercise, and periodic monitoring to convince patients to modify their behavior toward more healthful practices. Two groups are randomly chosen. One will receive the communication program after discharge from the hospital, and the other will not. The long-term survival rate of patients is used as the dependent variable.

As this is an expensive communication program, the researcher will want to be sure that it works before recommending implementation of the program for all patients. This will require that a fairly low α error level be used, since the researcher will not want to falsely conclude that the program works, when it actually works no better than no intervention at all (Type 1 error). But there is a penalty for making a Type 2 error, too. If the program really works, the researcher will certainly not want to conclude that it is ineffective. So the β error level must be set reasonably low, also. As we'll see below, this will be a demanding situation.

Contrast this situation with a similar communication program which just periodically mails brochures to recent heart attack patients. This is a low-cost program, so making a Type 1 error carries a far lower economic penalty. Here, we may increase the α level,

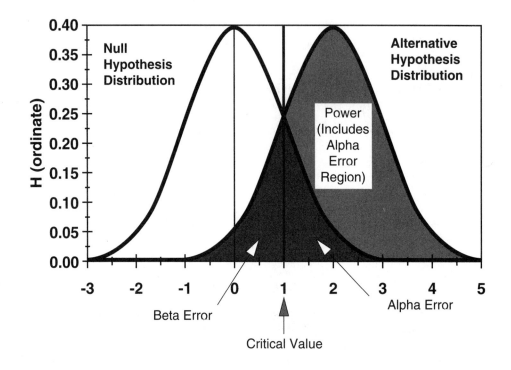

FIGURE 12-8   Effect of Increasing Alpha Error Level

since making a Type 1 error is fairly inexpensive, while making a Type 2 error (concluding the program has no effect, when it actually works) will be very expensive, as it will fail to save lives by abandoning a working communication program.

As we mentioned above, the effect size is also an arbitrary value set by the researcher. Likewise, the number of observations is determined by the researcher, but since data collection requires time and monetary resources, the researcher will usually want to keep the N at as small a value as possible. Since α, β, effect size, and number of observations interact, we can often trade off the settings of one or more of these values for the setting of another. At the end of this process, the researcher will want the optimum settings that will detect the smallest meaningful effect size with the smallest number of observations and with the smallest possible α and β error levels.

Figures 12-8, 12-9, and 12-10 show the effects of changing some of these values. Each figure should be compared to Figure 12-7, to see the difference that changing one of the values has on the others.

Figure 12-8 illustrates the effect of increasing the α level of significance, which moves the critical value closer to the null hypothesis expected value. If the α is increased, the size of region of rejection is increased, and the probability of making a Type 1 error is increased. But the probability of making a Type 2 (β) error is *decreased*. This illustrates the inverse nature of Type 1 and Type 2 error. If all else remains constant, a reduction in

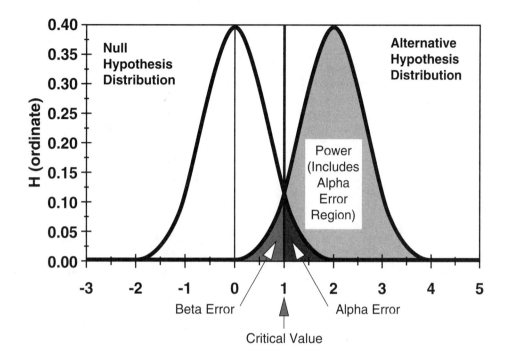

FIGURE 12-9   Effect of Increasing Number of Observations (*N*)

the probability of making a Type 1 error will be associated with an increased probability of making a Type 2 error, and vice versa.

Figure 12-9 illustrates the effect of increasing the *N*. With more observations, the standard error of the sampling distribution is reduced, and *both* α and β error probabilities are reduced for the same critical value. Alternatively, the α value may be fixed at the same level, and this will decrease the probability of β error even more dramatically. Increasing *N* is obviously a good way to reduce error, but it is also frequently the most expensive decision the researcher can make.

Figure 12-10 illustrates a way to reduce β error without increasing the α error or the number of observations. But this also carries a cost. In this figure, the effect size is increased, by moving the research hypothesis expected value further from the null hypothesis value. Since the sampling distribution for the null hypothesis is not affected, the α error remains constant. But the center of the research hypothesis sampling distribution is shifted to the right, and the critical value that determines the β error level falls further out on the tail of this non-null distribution. In effect, we have improved the β error, but only for stronger relationships, that is, those in which the sampling distribution for the research hypothesis is assumed to be centered further from the sampling distribution of the null hypothesis.

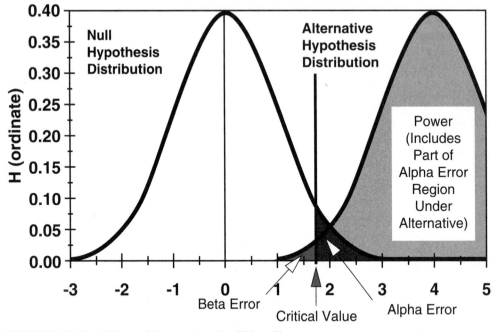

FIGURE 12-10   Effect of Increasing the Effect Size

Power Analysis

Since the α, β, effect size, and N are functionally related, setting the values for any three of the four will determine exactly the value of the fourth. This fact can be used in designing research and in analyzing research results. We'll illustrate two typical uses of "power analysis," which is the generic term for investigating the tradeoffs of error, effect size, and sample size.

One of the most useful ways to use power analysis is to determine the number of observations needed to test a hypothesis. If we collect too few observations, the standard error of the sampling distributions will be large, and we'll have large α and/or β errors for anything except very large effect sizes. If we collect too many observations, we are wasting time and money by going beyond the error levels with which we would usually feel comfortable in drawing conclusions, or by having trivial effect sizes.

To determine the number of observations, we must set the α level, the β level (or its complement, the power $(1 - \beta)$), and the effect size. Once we have set these values, we can determine exactly the number of observations that we must have in our sample.

Using the health counseling example, suppose we decide that the cost of the extensive program means that we want 100:1 odds that any significant effect we detect in the sample is really present in the population, and is not due to random sampling error. So we set the α level of significance at .01. Next, we determine that the value of saving lives with this program means that we want no more than a 5 percent chance of missing a real effect of the communication program, if it is present in the population. This sets the β error level at .05

and the power at .95. Finally, we wish to see at least a 10 percent improvement in patient mortality as a result of the program. We will not worry about detecting improvements smaller than this with the same error levels, as they are probably not justified by the cost of the program. This sets the effect size.

By referring to standard tables of statistical power, such as those found in Cohen (1977) or Kraemer and Thiemann (1987), we can now find the *N* required to meet these conditions. An abbreviated power table is shown in Appendix B.

The standard deviation of the survival rate of patients is already known from published health statistics. Assume it is 50 percent. Using the procedure in Appendix B, we look down the $\alpha = .01$ column and across the Power = .95 row to get the standardized effect, $z_{\text{diff}} = 3.971$. Using the computational formula in Appendix B,

$$N = \left(\frac{z_{\text{diff}} \cdot sd}{\overline{X}_1 - \overline{X}_2} \right)^2 = \left(\frac{3.971 \cdot .50}{.10} \right)^2 = 394$$

We will need about 394 observations in order to be confident that we will have only a 1 in 100 chance of falsely concluding that a communication effect exists when it does not; and only a 1 in 20 chance of missing a 10 percent or greater improvement in patient mortality.

Another common use of power analysis occurs when we fail to reject a null hypothesis. We might fail to reject the hypothesis for two reasons: There really isn't a relationship; or we do not have enough statistical power $(1 - \beta)$ to detect the relationship with any confidence.

Looking at the organizational change and formalization example from Table 12-2 again, we found that the correlation between the number of new products and the percentage of jobs with written specifications (−.44) did not fall in the region of rejection. Possibly there is no real relationship between the two variables, and that's why we failed to find a correlation beyond the critical value. But it is also possible the relationship exists, and that the number of observations was so low that we missed getting a large enough correlation simply because of random sampling error.

The level of significance (α error) was set to .05 in that example, and the *N* was 8. If we set the effect size at −.44 (the observed size of the relationship), we can use the power tables to find the β error probability, and the statistical power $(1 - \beta)$. As we can see from the tables for the power of *r* (one-tailed) in Appendix B, the power is less than 30 percent, which means that our β error probability is 70 percent! We will incorrectly conclude that there is a null relationship, when the relationship size is actually $r = -.45$ or some smaller negative correlation, about 7 times in 10! We obviously do not want to accept the null hypothesis under these conditions. We are better off withholding judgment until more observations can be collected.

Summary

The process of hypothesis testing establishes the probable truth or probable falsehood of the hypothetical statements developed during theory construction. The general logic of hypothesis testing is to contrast the predictions of our research hypothesis H_R with the predictions of a competing hypothesis which states that there is no relationship (the null hypothesis H_0.)

To make the comparison, a sampling distribution is constructed, centered around the value of the statistic we expect to occur, if the null hypothesis is correct. Next, we set a *level of significance* for the hypothesis test. This level states the Type I error probability we are willing to accept. For example, we may set the probability at .05, meaning that we will reject the null hypothesis if our results indicate that there is only a 5 percent or less chance of this decision being incorrect.

This error level (called α or *Type 1 error*) corresponds to an area under the normal curve that represents the sampling distribution for the null hypothesis. By converting this area to a critical value, we have a criterion for comparison with our sample statistic. If the value of the sample statistic is beyond the critical value, we can reject the null hypothesis, and accept the alternative research hypothesis.

Both comparative and relationship hypotheses can be tested using this approach. Sampling distributions can be created for group difference statistics like the difference between means, or for covariance statistics like correlation coefficients. The procedure for contrasting research and null hypotheses is the same in both cases.

While the α error level, or level of significance, describes the probability of falsely concluding that a relationship exists, when there really is no relationship, β *or Type 2* error describes the probability of concluding that there is no relationship, when one really exists. The probability of this error depends on the *effect size*, which is the distance between the expected value of the research hypothesis and the expected value of the null hypothesis, and on the number of observations.

Power analysis examines the tradeoffs among α error, β error, effect size, and the N. It can be used to determine the number of observations which are required to achieve suitably low error levels, to determine tradeoffs between Type 1 and Type 2 error, or to examine null results to find out if they were possibly nonsignificant because of too few observations.

References and Additional Readings

Cohen, J. (1977). *Statistical power analysis for the behavioral sciences*. New York: Academic Press (Chapter 1, "The Concepts of Power Analysis").

Cohen, J. & Cohen, P. (1983). *Applied multiple regression/correlation analysis for the behavioral sciences*. (Chapter 2, "Bivariate correlation and regression"). Hillsdale, NJ: Lawrence Erlbaum Associates.

Hays, W. L. (1981). *Statistics* (3rd. ed.). New York: Holt, Rinehart & Winston (Chapter 7, "Hypothesis Testing").

Keppel, G. (1982). *Design and analysis: A researcher's handbook*. Engelwood Cliffs, NJ: Prentice-Hall (Chapter 2, "Specifying Sources of Variability").

Kerlinger, F. N. (1986). *Foundations of behavioral research* (3rd ed.). New York: Holt, Rinehart and Winston (Chapter 11, "Purpose, Approach, Method"; Chapter 12, "Testing Hypotheses and the Standard Error").

Kraemer, H. C. & Thiemann, S. (1987). *How many subjects: Statistical power analysis in research*. Newbury Park, CA: Sage.

Part III

Research Designs, Settings and Procedures

Observation is a passive science, experimentation an active science.
—CLAUDE BERNARD
FRENCH PHYSIOLOGIST [1813–1878]
INTRODUCTION À L'ÉTUDE DE LA MÉDECINE EXPERIMENTALE [1865]

Aristotle could have avoided the mistake of thinking that women have fewer teeth than men by the simple device of asking Mrs. Aristotle to open her mouth.
—BERTRAND RUSSELL
BRITISH PHILOSOPHER AND MATHEMATICIAN [1872–1970]

The great tragedy of science: the slaying of a beautiful theory by an ugly fact.
—THOMAS HENRY HUXLEY
ENGLISH BIOLOGIST [1825–1895]

The progress of science is strewn, like an ancient desert trail, with the bleached skeletons of discarded theories which once seemed to possess eternal life.
—ARTHUR KOESTLER
ENGLISH WRITER [1905–1983]

Chapter *13*

Principles of Research Design

Research designs can be classified into three broad categories, depending on the amount of control the researcher maintains over the conduct of the research study. The three general categories are *experimental research, field research,* and *observational research.* Each category varies on two important characteristics: *internal validity* and *external validity.*

Research Design and Internal and External Validity

The terms internal and external validity must not be confused with measurement validity, which was discussed in Chapter 7. Instead, these terms refer to the overall validity of a research study as discussed in Chapter 4, not to the measurement of the concepts used in the research.

Internal validity describes the ability of the research design to unambiguously test the research hypothesis. An internally valid design accounts for all factors which might affect the outcome of hypothesis tests, including those that are not directly specified in the theory being tested. It ensures that these factors do not confound the results.

Since it is impossible for any single research design to account for all such potentially confounding factors, we must speak of better or worse internal validity, not of perfect validity. But designs with higher internal validity will, for example, control or account for the actions of variables that might produce spurious relationships. They will use representative samples, so that subject or group differences will not be confused with the action of independent variables. In general, they will eliminate more of the alternative explanations of research findings (those that contradict the theory being tested) than will research designs with weak internal validity.

External validity refers to the *generalizability* of the research, that is, the ability of its conclusions to be validly extended from the specific environment in which the research study is conducted to similar "real world" situations. The results of an externally valid study can be used to predict the behavior of the theoretical constructs outside the laboratory or data center. Externally valid research with generalizable conclusions is obviously more valuable than externally invalid research, whose conclusions are restricted to specific research settings.

Experimental Research

The first category that we will examine is experimental research. In this kind of research study, the researcher controls the setting in which the research is conducted (the "laboratory"), manipulates the levels of the independent variable or variables, and follows this by observation of the corresponding changes in the dependent variable or variables.

By controlling the surroundings in which the research is conducted, the researcher can eliminate some environmental conditions that might confuse the results. This control improves the internal validity of the research study. For example, a researcher studying the effects of music on children's learning from educational videotapes would probably want to show the tapes to the experimental subjects in a quiet room. Furthermore, it is likely that he or she will use the same, or very similar, rooms, equipped with similar furniture, lighting, and potentially distracting items like books and toys. Ensuring that all subjects see the tapes under the same conditions eliminates the possibility that learning (or lack of learning) is due to factors other than the experimental videotapes. If the same tapes were shown in uncontrolled settings like individual homes, learning for some children might be disrupted by distracting brothers and sisters, the presence of toys, etc. The effects that these environmental factors have on learning will obscure the effects that are the result of the use of music. These are the effects that the researcher really wants to observe.

By directly manipulating the levels of the independent variables in an experimental design, the researcher can meet all the conditions for establishing a relationship between variables, as outlined in Chapter 3. This manipulative control will also improve the internal validity of the study, as it allows the experimenter to predetermine the time sequence of events, and to ensure that the independent variable takes on a wide enough range of values (i.e., has enough variance) that an unambiguous test of the hypothesized relationships can be made.

Suppose the researcher studying children's learning creates two videotapes, one using music at critical points in the presentation, and a second that does not use music, but is otherwise identical. The nominal independent variable (presence or absence of music) is manipulated, while other possibly confounding factors are controlled. By using the same tape for both groups, with only the music track modified, the effects of other content features of the tapes, like the narrator, the script, or the illustrative visuals, are constant for viewers of both tapes. These factors will then produce identical effects on viewers of either version of the tape, so the effects of these features will not be confused with the effects of music.

The researcher then selects two different groups of children, using appropriate random sampling techniques, and shows one of the tapes to each group. Several days later, the children's recall of the material on the tape is measured. Using some variant on the basic statistical methods outlined in the previous chapters, the researcher tests a directional comparative hypothesis which states that "Material presented with a musical background will be recalled at higher levels than will the same material presented without music."

In this simple experiment, the researcher has met the basic requirements for testing a hypothesis:

1. The independent variable is present in at least two levels (presence and absence of music).

2. The two groups can be treated as equivalent within the limits of sampling error, since their members were chosen randomly. This eliminates any systematic effect from variables that were not measured as part of the research, like the effect of differing academic abilities or attention spans for different children. Since the groups are randomly chosen, each should contain a similar number of high ability and low ability children, children with long and with short attention spans, and so on.

3. The researcher can conclude that any difference seen in the dependent variable for the two groups must have been produced by the different levels of the independent variable. This establishes covariance.

4. Since the dependent variable is observed after the presentation of the independent variable, temporal priority between the cause variable (independent variable) and the effect variable (dependent variable) is established by the researcher.

5. Since the unit of analysis is the individual child, the requirement for spatial contiguity is satisfied.

6. If the researcher has provided a good theoretical linkage that relates the presence/absence of music to recall, the final condition for causality, necessary connection, is established.

The control that an experimental study affords a researcher helps to establish strong evidence for causal connections between the independent and dependent variables. But it can also cause some problems in generalizing the results of the research to the outside world. The very strong control that improves the internal validity of the experiment can sometimes damage its external validity.

Suppose the experiment described above shows that children recall more of the material from the videotape that used music. Most of the factors that could produce a spurious relationship between music use and recall are controlled by the experiment. The program content is constant in both groups, the groups are equivalent because of random assignment, the level of distraction from the environment is constant for both groups, etc. This is an experiment that is strong on internal validity. It is therefore very tempting to generalize its results to all educational videotapes for children, and to prescribe the use of music to enhance learning.

Unfortunately, this experiment happens to be somewhat weak in external validity, so such a prescription may not be warranted. The conditions under which the children actually watch television in their homes are very different from the experimental conditions. For example, children often have low levels of attention to television when they are viewing at home. In the experimental setting, the attention level may have been much higher, due to the experimental instructions given by a high-authority figure (the adult researcher says "please watch this tape"), or by the lack of familiar distractions like favorite toys or

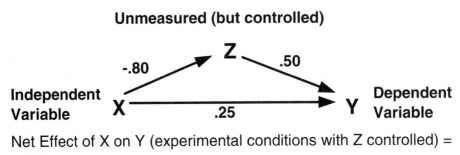

Net Effect of X on Y (experimental conditions with Z controlled) =
+.25

Net Effect of X on Y (realistic conditions with Z uncontrolled) =
.25 + (-.80 x .50) = .25 - .40 = -.15

FIGURE 13-1   Effects of Experimental Control on External Validity

siblings. As a result, learning from tapes which use music may be very similar to learning from tapes which do not use it, if overall attention levels are low—that is, not much will be recalled from *either* kind of tape. If this is the case, adding music to educational tapes will be a waste of money, even though, under the right conditions (like those in the experimental setting), the researcher can show a positive effect of music.

The experiment also uses the tape of a single educational presentation. While the conclusions about the use of music may be correct for this presentation (and probably are, because of the high internal validity of the experiment), the results may not generalize to other teachers, or other topics. Again, the control that can be exerted over the experimental material by making sure it is identical in all experimental conditions carries the cost of limiting the external validity of the conclusions.

The issue here is one of the costs and benefits of controlled observation. A good experimental design will control for potentially confounding factors, *whether they are explicitly identified or not.* In the videotape experiment, the researcher does not have to define all the possible variables that might affect recall (such as attention, distraction, the inherent appeal of the material) because it can be assumed that they are all present in equal amounts in both experimental groups. Since their effects are equal, they can't bias the results.

But these variables *do* affect recall in realistic situations. The control that experimental designs impose over these outside variables may actually obscure the realistic operation of the system of variables in the real world. Figure 13-1 illustrates how this can happen. Variables X and Y are investigated in an experiment, which controls for the effect of an outside variable Z. This variable is negatively related to X and positively related to Y. The numbers represent the strength of relationships (they might be correlation coefficients, for example).

In the experiment, the direct effect of X on Y is found to be +.25. The variable Z will not enter into this finding, since its effect will be controlled by the experimental design. But in the realistic situation, X will affect Z at a −.80 level, and Z will then affect Y at a +.50 level. So in addition to the direct +.25 effect of X on Y, a 1.0 unit change in X makes a −.80 unit change in Z. Half (.50) of this −.80 unit change is passed on to Y, making the contribution of this path of influence equal to −.40. The total effect of X on Y, in the realistic situation, is then made up of two components: the +.25 direct effect, and the −.40 indirect effect via variable Z. The net effect of X on Y is then −.15 in reality, while the experimental results will indicate that the effect of X on Y is +.25! And the experimental conclusion of a +.25 effect *is* correct. However, the +.25 effect is not generalizable, and thus the experiment has exhibited poor external validity due to the very control which produces good internal validity.

The solution to this situation is to *identify* and explicitly include the relevant variables in the experiment. If Z is theoretically and operationally defined and is included as part of the experimental design (with the addition of two new hypotheses: $X \rightarrow Z$ and $Z \rightarrow Y$), then the correct net effect of X on Y can be found. This solution calls for measuring or manipulating all relevant variables. Of course, this will increase the complexity and cost of the research, once again illustrating the fundamental truth that obtaining higher-quality information requires added costs and added effort.

In an alternative approach, described in the next section, the variables are observed as they operate in the "real world." External validity is improved without substantially increasing the complexity of the research, but only at the expense of decreasing the internal validity.

Field Research

The second major category of research is *field research*. In this kind of research setting, the researcher retains control over the independent variables, but conducts the research in a natural setting, without any control over environmental influences.

For instance, suppose that a researcher is interested in the ability of a communication training program to reduce communication anxiety in persons who must give speeches or public presentations. The researcher, who is employed by a large corporation, creates two randomly selected groups of subjects by drawing samples from a sampling frame which is a list of all employees of the organization. Each person in both groups is asked to fill out a questionnaire. The questionnaire contains the information for operationalizing the dependent variable "communication anxiety." It asks for self-reports of the person's apprehension immediately before giving a recent presentation and the discomfort felt while speaking at that time.

The independent variable, "training program," is operationalized by creating a program of study and practice in public speaking and use of audiovisual materials. This variable then has two levels (presence or absence of training), and each level is applied to one of the groups. That is, one group receives the training program, while the other does not. This latter group is often called a *control group*.

The directional comparative hypothesis being tested is this: "Those who receive communication training will have reduced levels of communication anxiety compared to those who did not receive communication training." If the subsequent mean anxiety level for the group that received training is significantly lower than the mean for the control group, the researcher will conclude that the hypothesis was supported.

The researcher waits until the end of the training program, and then asks each group to again fill out the same questionnaire. It is presumed that both groups will have made some public presentations during the interval. If the training program worked, those in the group receiving the training should have felt more comfortable in speaking than those in the control group.

Note the difference between this kind of research setting and an experimental setting. In field research, the conditions under which the effects of the independent variable are observed are not under the researcher's control. Although the researcher still exerts control over the independent variable (by creating the training program and controlling who is exposed to it), there is no control of the setting in which the independent variable exerts an effect on the dependent variable. Different subjects may have had very different public communication experiences. One may have had to give a large number of presentations during the months between the two administrations of the questionnaire, while another may have had few or no opportunities to put the training into practice; some persons may have had to give presentations to large audiences, while others spoke only to small groups. Because of this variation, the researcher must expect that some variation in the dependent variable is due to uncontrolled factors in the field research setting. These variations should not bias the results, however, as the randomly selected groups should both have equivalent numbers of persons with frequent and infrequent presentations, large audience and small audience experiences, and so on. But the strength of covariance between the independent and dependent variables will be reduced by the random error that is introduced, and this will make it harder to confidently state that the condition of covariance has been met—that is, to obtain statistically significant relationships between the independent and dependent variables. This is because there are variables other than the independent variable acting on the dependent variable, and their effects may mask the effect of the independent variable.

Given this penalty, why would a researcher ever choose to do field research, rather than experimental research? The basic reason has to do with the generalizability or external validity of the research. Field research, because it occurs under natural conditions, is often more informative than pure experimental research.

The researcher in our example could have used an experimental design, by requiring that all persons in each of the groups give a presentation on the same subject, to the same audience, in the same room. This control over the research setting would remove the random error due to differences in subjects' public communication experiences, and would enhance the researcher's ability to answer the relatively narrow question posed by the research hypothesis. As we saw in the previous section, this kind of control improves the internal validity of the research.

But the researcher probably wants to know more than simply whether the hypothesis is supported or not; he or she also wants to know if the effect that was hypothesized works under realistic conditions—those conditions outside the rigid control of the experimental laboratory. For this reason, a researcher might trade some of the research power of an experiment for the more general test of the hypothesis in the setting to which the results are eventually to be generalized.

In the example, the researcher might find that the training program significantly reduces communication anxiety in the experimental setting. But the experiment only tests the effect of communicator training for a single kind of presentation, to a single kind of audience. To generalize the results of the experiment to all kinds of presentations, with all kinds and sizes of audiences, requires some strong assumptions: (1) all presentations are equivalent to the one required in the experimental procedure; and (2) that all audiences, regardless of size or makeup, are equivalent. The researcher may be quite reluctant to make these assumptions.

Of course, the researcher could modify the experimental design to add different conditions that better represent the complexities of the real setting. Subjects might be asked to give different kinds of presentations to different sizes of audiences, speak in large and small halls and conference rooms, and so on. But the research design would then be much more complex, and possibly too expensive to complete. And there would still be no assurance that the researcher had adequately reproduced all the conditions that a large number of public speakers were likely to encounter in the real world.

The researcher can regain some of the lost sensitivity to the effect of the independent variable in a field experiment by measuring the "outside" variables and using statistical control (this is covered in more detail in Chapter 4). The researcher still manipulates the independent variable, but uses statistical techniques (mentioned in Chapter 19) to isolate or control the effects of measured "outside" variables, and that removes them from the category of unknown error. This is illustrated in Figure 13-2. If the researcher does not measure variable Z, its effect is lumped with all others in the composite group called E. When Z is explicitly included in the field experimental design, its effect can be isolated from that of X and of all other E variables. This gives a more accurate estimate of the true strength of the $X \rightarrow Y$ relationship.

Observational Research

There are many instances in which the researcher can control neither the independent variable nor the research setting. In this situation, the researcher is limited to *measuring*, rather than *manipulating*, the independent variable. Like field research, observational research designs exert no control over the setting in which the hypothetical process occurs.

In one class of observational research called retrospective research, this lack of control occurs because the exploration is being carried out sometime after the actual process being researched has actually occurred. For example, a researcher interested in family communication patterns might ask a group of adults to describe their recollections of communications with their parents during their childhood, and then relate the types of communication to the adults' current achievements, relationships with spouses and children, or other independent variables.[1] In this case, the independent variable (types of parent-child communications) cannot be manipulated, as the communication occurred many years in the past. And obviously the setting for this process will have been different for each subject, so no control over it can be exerted years later. But it is still quite possible

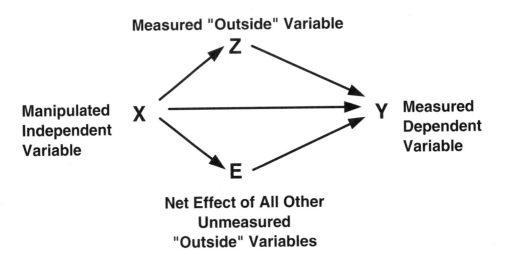

FIGURE 13-2   Manipulated and Statistical Control in Field Research

to find covariance between the different types of family communication that took place in the past, and current levels of achievement, satisfaction with current relationships, and so on.

Observational research may also be required when it is impossible to manipulate the independent variable, or when it would be unethical to do so. A researcher studying the impact of newspaper editorial endorsements on voter behavior will not be able to systematically manipulate the endorsements given by newspapers, and even if possible, would probably have ethical qualms about interfering with the political process (even for such a noble purpose as communication research).

A third reason for conducting observational research involves the use of secondary data—that is, data collected by some agency other than the researcher, possibly for some purpose other than communication research. For example, a researcher might use census data that includes information about the number of telephones and television sets and radios in different countries to study the effect of the availability of communication technology on national development. Obviously the researcher can manipulate neither the amount of communication technology (unless he or she is fabulously wealthy) nor the gross national product of countries. It is necessary to use an observational design.

Other secondary data sources such as the public opinion polling archives maintained in the Institute for Social Research at the University of Michigan and the Roper Center for Public Opinion Research at the University of Connecticut can be very economical sources of data for observational research. These archives maintain research data from a number of studies done over many years. By selecting a set of poll questions, observational data about many different social phenomena can be obtained. In addition, media content summaries and programs are preserved by the Television Archives at Vanderbilt University, the Presidential Campaign Commercial Archives at Oklahoma University, the *New York*

Times Index, and other sources. We'll cover the use of these sources in more detail in Chapter 18.

Natural Manipulations and Confounding Variables

Quite a few communication phenomena involve concepts and variables that do not lend themselves to being manipulated by the researcher. If this is the case, the researcher must rely on "natural manipulations." In both experimental and field research, variance in the independent variable is deliberately introduced by the researcher. This is the experimental manipulation. But in observational research, variance in the independent variable occurs as a consequence of the natural operation of the real world.

It is important to recognize that it makes no difference whether the independent variable varies because of experimental manipulation or because of natural manipulations. In either case, statistical methods to detect covariance between the independent and dependent variables are used. But observational research does require that the researcher give up control over the temporal priority of the cause-and-effect variables. In both experimental and field research, the fact that the researcher manipulates the independent variable, and then observes the dependent variable, means that the time ordering between the hypothesized cause and effect is known. This is not the case for observational research. Since both independent and dependent variables are measured, there is nothing to ensure that the independent variable (the presumed cause) precedes the dependent variable (the presumed effect) in time. Without time ordering, the conditions of causality cannot be met.

Some people would argue that this means that causal relationships can only be investigated using experimental or field research designs. But this is not necessarily true. Within family communication research, for example, it does not require any great leap of faith to assert that the independent variable (different types of communication with parents when the respondent was a child) precedes in time the dependent variable (the state of current relationships). Of course, establishing covariance and temporal priority does not rule out the possibility that this time-ordered relationship between the independent and dependent variables might be the spurious result of common relationships with confounding variables, as we mentioned in Chapter 4.

The establishment of scientific relationships in observational research requires that the researcher do two things: first, determine the temporal priority of the independent and dependent variable; and second, account for the effect of all relevant confounding variables.

Establishing temporal priority often can be done by making reasonable assumptions about the time ordering of the variables. The emphasis is on *reasonable*. Arbitrary time ordering will produce incorrect scientific conclusions. A conservative rule of thumb is this: If you have any doubts about the correct time order of the independent and dependent variables, do not make any assumption. This will mean reducing the relationship from a causal one to the weaker covariance relationship (see Chapter 3), but without a strong temporal ordering of the variables, a covariance relationship may be all that is warranted.

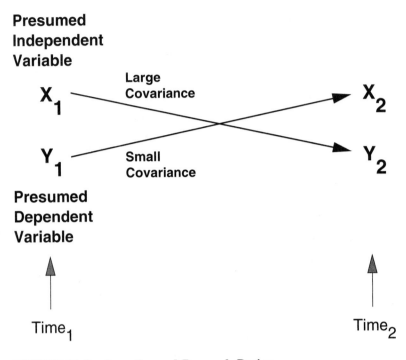

FIGURE 13-3   Cross-Lagged Research Design

An alternative way of establishing temporal order is to design a study that provides some evidence for the time order of the independent and dependent variables. Except in some special circumstances that we'll not address here, this will involve measurement at two or more points in time. Even then, the evidence for temporal ordering may not be completely unambiguous.

There are a number of ways to test temporal ordering in an observational research study. One typical way is through the use of cross-lagged correlations. In cross-lagged correlations, the independent variable and dependent variable are measured at two or more points in time. The test for temporal order is made by examining the covariance of the presumed independent variable at Time 1 with the presumed dependent variable at Time 2, and contrasting this value with the covariance between the presumed dependent variable at Time 1 and the presumed independent variable at Time 2 (see Figure 13-3).

If the presumed time ordering is correct, we should observe that the independent variable at an earlier time (Time 1) covaries with the dependent variable at a later time (Time 2). But the *temporal asymmetry principle* which states that changes in the cause variable will produce later changes in the effect variable, *and not vice versa*, predicts that the covariance between the dependent variable at an earlier time and the independent variable later should be near zero.

A classic example of analysis by cross-lagged correlation is provided by Lefkowitz, et al. (1972).[2] At issue was the relationship between children's viewing of violent television programs and their aggressiveness levels. The temporal ordering of these two variables is not clear. Viewing violent programs may be theoretically linked to higher levels of aggression in viewers by processes involving modeling of aggressive acts, by desensitization of the viewer to violence, by legitimization of violence as a solution to conflict, or by some other process in which television viewing precedes aggression. In this case, violent TV viewing is the cause variable and aggressiveness is the effect variable. On the other hand, one can reasonably link the two variables in the reverse time order by stating that naturally aggressive persons will seek to view programming that is consistent with their personal approach to conflict. In this formulation, levels of aggression precede in time the viewing patterns of individuals. Level of aggression is then the cause variable, and violent TV viewing is the effect variable.

A related extended example shown in the next chapter illustrates an experimental approach to the same problem. The Bandura study summarized there used an experimental design which manipulated the subjects' exposure to communications, and thus controlled the temporal order of the independent and dependent variables (children were always exposed to communications before measurement of their behaviors). But many media researchers reject the experimental approach on the basis of external validity. They feel that exposure to communications in an experimental setting is artificial, and so distant from how people are really exposed to media messages, that it is not valid to generalize from experimental studies to the real world. In particular, some believe that repeated exposure to messages over a period of years is necessary before meaningful change in audience behavior can be observed. This means that a retrospective, observational research study is going to be required, since it is unreasonable to think that a researcher can control the communication exposure of a sample over a period of months or years. Rather, the researcher must rely on natural manipulations to produce variance in the independent variable, and must also rely on the ability of the research subjects to accurately report the level of the independent variable, after the fact.

However, the Lefkowitz study actually measured viewing habits and aggression levels of the same persons at a ten-year time interval. It was not a retrospective study. The variables were first measured when the subjects were children in the third grade. The same variables were measured a second time when the subjects were recent high school graduates. If viewing violent television causes higher levels of aggression, Lefkowitz should have observed a significant correlation between viewing habits in the third grade and the aggressiveness of the same students after they graduated from high school. At the same time, the correlation between the aggressiveness levels of third graders and later television viewing should not have been significant. If the reverse time ordering of cause and effect is true, and aggressive predispositions predict television viewing, the data should show a reversed pattern of significant correlations.

The results of the Lefkowitz study are shown in Figure 13-4. As the diagram shows, this study found evidence for television viewing affecting later levels of aggressiveness, but none for levels of aggressiveness affecting later television viewing. This is very good evidence for the time ordering of these two variables, and helps to establish both the conditions of covariance (the significant correlation between television viewing in third grade and post-high school aggressiveness) and temporal priority (viewing predicts aggression, and not vice versa).

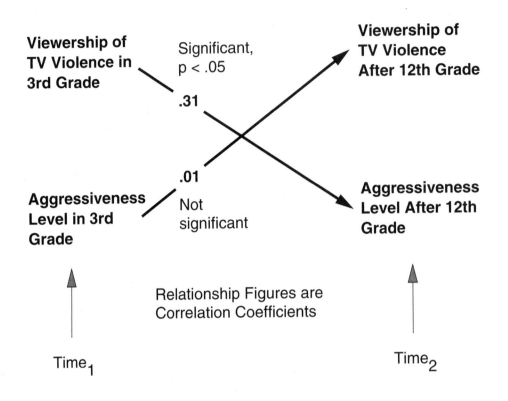

FIGURE 13-4   Results of the Lefkowitz, et al. Study

The second requirement that observational research designs must meet is the control of all variables that may cause a spurious relationship between the independent and dependent variables. As we mentioned in Chapter 4, control of these variables may be achieved through manipulation, or through statistical control based on direct measurement of the confounding variables. Experimental designs control confounding variables through manipulation, but still require that they be identified and included in the design if the experiment is to achieve good external validity. Field research designs do not require that they be included in the design, but the strength of the statistical tests is improved if they are. In observational designs, the researcher *must* identify and measure potentially confounding variables, or the internal validity of the study will decrease. And without internal validity, conclusions about relationships are incorrect, and any generalization, regardless of the level of external validity, is meaningless.

Viewed this way, the requirement of identification and measurement of all outside variables which might jointly affect the independent and dependent variables is absolute in the case of observational research, as both internal and external validity will be compromised by the failure to statistically control for these variables. It is almost as important in experimental designs, as failure to identify and include such variables in the research design will limit external validity, although internal validity will not be affected. Identification of outside variables is least important in field research, as both internal and external validity will be maintained, although the sensitivity of statistical tests will be reduced. Not surprisingly, field research is usually the most difficult and expensive research setting.

Threats to Internal and External Validity

Although we've identified some general ways that research designs may fail to achieve internal and external validity, we need to talk in more detail about some of the specific types of problems in research design validity. For both internal and external validity, we'll discuss threats that occur when measurement takes place over a time span, and threats that occur at single time points.

This will not be a completely exhaustive list of the threats to validity. Specific research designs, subject populations, or research procedures may be vulnerable to other threats. What follows is a brief discussion of some of the most common threats. Any research design should be critically reviewed by the researcher, looking not only for the following threats to validity, but for any other way by which the action of the independent variable on the dependent variable might be confused with other factors, or by which the nature of the research may fail to generalize to the population being studied.

Single-Time Point Issues in Internal Validity

Instrumentation Reliability and Validity
We've already discussed these problems in Chapter 7. Without reliable measurement, we may falsely conclude that the independent and dependent variable do not covary, when in reality our measurements just can't be trusted to be accurate. Likewise, if we are not measuring the theoretical concept that we think we are, the validity of our conclusions will be negligible. The solution to this problem is outlined in the early chapters of this book: Pay significant attention to accurate conceptualization and operationalization, and check the reliability of measurement instruments.

Sampling
Again, we've discussed this threat to validity in an earlier chapter. In an experiment, field, or observational study, if the subjects or respondents in differing research groups are not randomly chosen, we may confuse differences in the individuals who make up the groups with the effect of the different experimental treatments. The methods of random selection outlined in Chapter 6 provide a way to avoid this threat to internal validity.

Instrument Obtrusiveness
Good internal validity depends upon measurement that does not disrupt or direct the processes being investigated. To the extent that measurement intrudes on the communication process that is being studied, we can expect to be led to incorrect conclusions. A questionnaire which annoys respondents with insensitive or leading questions ("How many hours of mindless television do you watch each week?"), or which is so long that

respondents can't fill it out without collapsing with fatigue, is simply not going to give the accurate measurement that good internal validity requires. Likewise, an experimental measurement of the satisfaction with interpersonal conversation in which the experimenter interrupts the conversation every 15 seconds to ask the participants to fill out a scale rating their satisfaction will so disrupt conversation and tip off participants to the nature of the experiment that valid conclusions will be impossible to make.

Researchers can avoid this kind of threat to validity by pretesting their procedures. In the pretest, the obtrusiveness of the measurements are directly discussed with pretest subjects who have completed the research procedures, and changes to the procedure are made when it appears that this problem exists.

Manipulation Effectiveness

In experimental and field research, the researcher must be assured that the intended manipulation of the independent variable actually did produce enough difference in the levels of that variable that good tests of covariance with the dependent variable are possible. Meeting the covariance test to establish a relationship is only possible if both the independent and dependent variable have some real variance. Generally, the greater the variance in the independent variable, the easier it is to observe a significant relationship.

There are three general ways to establish the effectiveness of an experimental manipulation. The first is by *observation and assumption*: The manipulation is so obvious that anyone can see that it was effective. If a researcher studying the effect of paper color on readership of brochures prints one brochure on blue paper and another on white, it is probably sufficient to say that color was manipulated successfully.

The second way to establish effectiveness is by a *manipulation check*. This is a measurement made during or after the primary experimental procedure, to establish that the manipulation had its intended effect. Suppose a researcher was experimentally studying the effects of having negative information about a person prior to interacting with the person. To manipulate this independent variable, the researcher writes two paragraphs, one for each of two experimental groups. In one paragraph, the person's background is described positively and in the other paragraph mainly negative information is included. In this case, it is probably not sufficient to assume that the paragraphs will have the effect desired by the researcher. The researcher should include some measurement of the positive-negative evaluation of the person by the subject. For example, the researcher might use a questionnaire at the end of the experimental procedure which has the question:

Before you began talking to your partner, what was your general feeling about his/her abilities?

1	*2*	*3*	*4*	*5*	*6*	*7*	*8*	*9*
Very								*Very*
Negative								*Positive*

By checking the means of the responses to this question in each experimental group, the researcher can present some evidence for the effectiveness of the manipulation of the independent variable. If the two groups are not statistically significantly different from one another in their responses to this question, there is no evidence that the manipulation actually worked, and thus the internal validity of the experiment is poor.

The third, and probably the best, way to establish manipulation is to *measure* the independent variable using some real metric. A researcher studying the effects of violence viewing on children can count the number of acts of violence in the videotapes shown to each experimental group, and possibly weight each act by some "severity" weight (aggressive yelling = 1; slapping = 2; shooting with assault rifle = 10, etc.). To make this measurement will require the researcher to provide an operational definition for the independent variable, something that is sometimes given short shrift in experimental research. But it should not be ignored. Operationally defining the independent variable, even in the simple case where only two experimental groups are involved, will usually improve the researcher's thinking about that concept. And it will surely improve the ability of the researcher to ensure that an effective manipulation has been made.

Over-Time Issues in Internal Validity

When measurements are made at two or more points in time, such as in experiments which use before- and after-manipulation designs, some serious threats to internal validity can appear. The basic presumption in multiple time point measurement is that the only thing that differs between the first and the second or subsequent time points is the level of the independent variable. But this may not be true, and the researcher must take care not to confuse other factors that may affect later measurements with the effect of the independent variable.

History
Significant social or personal events may intrude between the first measurement and subsequent measurements. If the proper research design is not used, these events can produce changes in the dependent variable which will be confused with the effect of the independent variable. This problem increases in magnitude when there is a longer time span between measurements. A researcher who uses an observational design to study the reaction of the public's image of corporations to corporate advertising over a period of years will have to separate the effects of advertising from the effects produced by ups and downs in the economic climate, the appearance of banking scandals, the jailing of security traders, and so on. A research design that uses a comparison group (such as a before manipulation-post manipulation design with control group, described in the next chapter) is often used to account for the effects of history.

Maturation
A related over-time problem is produced by growth and changes that occur within the research subjects. Children and adults change in many ways simply due to the passage of time. Children develop new abilities, adolescents expand their intellectual horizons, and the value systems of adults change over time. An internally valid research design must not confuse these changes with the changes produced by the independent variable. A researcher studying the effect of a classroom program to increase the time elementary school children spend reading out of school will have to use a design that accounts for

the fact that children's reading ability improves dramatically in their early years. Such designs usually involve the use of a control group made up of equivalent research subjects. Since maturation effects should be identical in both the experimental and control groups, the comparison between them is insensitive to maturation effects.

Measurement Sensitization

There is a danger that the measurement instrument itself, when it is applied at the first time point, may affect the subject in ways that bias subsequent measurement. For example, a researcher who is interested in relating newspaper readership to political knowledge might use a questionnaire that poses a number of questions about the political process, as well as about newspaper readership. But by filling out this questionnaire, the respondent may become self-conscious about his or her newspaper reading, and particularly about reading political news. In the period of time between the first measurement and subsequent measurements, the respondent may increase readership, pay more attention to political events, and so on, in order to "perform better" on the next questionnaire. Just the fact of being involved in a research project may cause the subject to be much more interested in the topic of the research and to modify behavior accordingly. This difference in performance between the first and the second or subsequent measurements can be confused with the effect of the independent variable.

Using control groups with research designs can deal with this problem to some degree, as both the experimental group and the control group behavior will be modified to the same extent, and thus comparisons between them will reflect only the effect of the independent variable. But it is often more effective to disguise the intent of the measurement. In the above example, the researcher might "pad" the questionnaire with other questions not related to the political process, and make sure the instructions do not directly mention this as the intent of the research. The respondent might be told only that the questionnaire involves questions about "lifestyle." This kind of disguise can pose some ethical problems. An alternative way to deal with extreme cases of measurement sensitization is to use research designs which do not employ multiple measurements. The post-manipulation only design described in the next chapter is an example. The decision to use such a design carries some penalty in the power of the statistical tests to detect relationships, as we'll see.

Measurement Instrument Learning

If the same measurement instrument is used for multiple measurements of the same subject, there is a danger that subsequent performance on the instrument may be affected by simple learning of the experimental task or items on questionnaires. It is a well-known fact that students who repeatedly take general achievement tests like the Scholastic Aptitude Test tend to improve their performances, even though they have probably not learned a substantial body of new material in the intervening time. This improvement in performance can be confused with effects of the independent variable, if the proper design is not used. Control group designs which use only a post-test may be used to account for this learning effect.

Another approach to controlling for learning at multiple measurement points is to use equivalent, rather than identical, measurement instruments. However, establishing that two different measurement instruments give reliably equivalent scores is often difficult. Establishing this equivalence usually requires a research study of its own.

Learning can occur within a single measurement procedure too. For example, a measurement instrument may request a whole series of judgments about communications on a series of scales such as semantic differentials. Initially, these scales are unfamiliar. But as the subject gains more familiarity with them, they may begin to be used in a different fashion. This shift will give a systematic difference between ratings given at the beginning of the procedure and ratings given at the end. And this shift will be unrelated to the actual items being rated.

To guard against this kind of learning, items or experimental tasks must be randomized or arranged in a counterbalanced fashion (more about this below), so that items or tasks appear at the beginning of the procedure for some subjects, in the middle for others, and at the end for still others. Although this will not remove the learning effect, it will diminish its effect so it is less likely to be confused with the effect of the independent variable.

Measurement Instrument Instability

This is an issue in measurement reliability. If the measurement instrument "drifts" over time, different results will be obtained at different time points. Such drift can be confused with the action of the independent variable over the same time period. Whether such drift in fact exists can be determined by establishing the level of test-retest reliability. To avoid this threat, only measures with high test-retest reliability should be used.

Subject Mortality

Although this phrase conjures up horror movie images of Transylvanian castles and research assistants named Igor, it actually refers to the loss of some subjects from a research study between the first measurement and later measurements. If random selection procedures are used to select subjects or construct the research groups, the resulting sample will initially be representative of the population from which it was drawn. But any loss of subjects from this sample between two measurement points may cause systematic differences in dependent observations that are not due to the independent variable. Subject mortality is rarely random, so this difference can be systematically confused with the effect of the independent variable.

As an example, consider an experiment in which a representative sample of city residents are chosen to study the effects of a health communication program aimed at sickness prevention. Booklets, videotapes, and in-home counseling sessions are provided for the experimental group, while the control group receives none of these communications. Periodically, the subjects are asked to report to a clinic for a checkup, and to report any health problems that have occurred since the last checkup. The results of a checkup are converted, via a formula for combining the various measures, into a single index of "healthiness" which is the dependent variable.

To assess the impact of a communication campaign such as this, observations of the dependent variable must be made over long time spans—probably years. During this time, some of the sample will move out of town, some will just stop coming for checkups, and some will *really* die. None of these events is random. Respondents in the lower economic classes may be more likely to move, those in the higher economic classes may be more likely to ignore the researcher's request to visit the clinic regularly, older subjects are more likely to die than younger subjects, and so on.

This nonrandom deletion of subjects will result in a loss of internal validity that will bias the results. If subject mortality occurs as speculated above, the researcher will end up comparing a representative sample which contains young and elderly, high- and low-income subjects at the first measurement point with a sample that is heavily skewed toward younger, middle-class subjects at the end of the experiment. Since both poorer and older subjects can be expected to have more health problems, the final measurement will probably produce a higher mean "healthiness" than the first measurement, even if the communication campaign is completely ineffective.

The best way to deal with subject mortality is to take every possible step to ensure that the minimum number of subjects are lost during the duration of the research project. Research procedures that provide some incentive to continue participation are particularly desirable. The researcher who has funds might pay the research participants, or appeal to their sense of responsibility in contributing to important research, or offer them the valuable results of the study, as incentives to help in completing the project.

Control group designs are useful in avoiding gross errors in inference, as subject mortality in both the experimental and control groups should be the same. While this will allow valid comparisons between groups, subject mortality will still result in inaccurate measurement of the absolute levels of the dependent variable. Control groups improve internal validity, but still leave problems with external validity, as we'll discuss below.

Subject Fatigue

Any research procedure that requires more than a tiny amount of time or thought may be vulnerable to problems of subject fatigue or boredom. A very long questionnaire, a procedure that requires the subject to write long responses, or that requires long stretches of focused attention may produce this threat to internal validity. The basic problem is that the subject's responses at the end of the procedure are not the same as they were at the beginning, and this shift in responses can be confused with the action of the independent variable.

There are two solutions to this problem. The first is self-evident: Make the tasks or measurements as simple as possible. But meaningful measurement may require enough effort from the subject that fatigue is inevitable. In that case, steps must be taken to ensure that the effects of fatigue do not get confused with the effects of the independent variable.

The problem of fatigue is similar to the problem of measurement instrument learning discussed above. The solution to both these problems lies in the arrangement of measurement tasks or procedures. If measurements are placed at all time points during the research procedure, each measurement will be made under conditions of low, medium, and high fatigue. Since all measurements will occur under all fatigue conditions, fatigue will not be related systematically to measurement of the dependent variable, and so it will not introduce an error in inference.

As a simple example, suppose experimental subjects are rating the emotional content of four magazine advertisements, which we'll call ads A, B, C, and D, on a set of 50 Likert scales. This is a demanding task, and we can expect both fatigue and instrument learning effects. Both these effects are related to the position in the research procedure at which

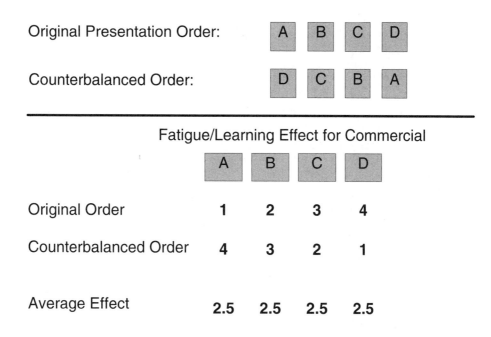

FIGURE 13-5   **Reversed Counterbalancing to Counter Fatigue and Learning**

the ad is scored. Ads measured earlier will be rated by subjects who are less fatigued and who have less experience with the scales, while later ads will be rated by subjects who are tired, bored with the procedure, and experienced in using the scales.

The simplest control for learning and fatigue is reverse counterbalancing, in which the order of measurement is simply reversed. If we assume that fatigue and learning increase linearly (at each position the incremental increase in fatigue and learning is identical), we can assign sequential "fatigue/learning" scores to each position in the presentation. As Figure 13-5 shows, the average for each commercial in the reversed counterbalancing is identical, thus removing the effect of fatigue and learning from consideration. However, learning and fatigue are not necessarily linear, and more complex counterbalancing may be required, such as the scheme discussed in the next section.

Treatment or Measurement Order Effects
This threat to internal validity stems from the fact that earlier experimental treatments (manipulations of the independent variable) or earlier measurements of the dependent variable may affect later measurements.

The example described above provides a typical situation. Suppose advertisement B contains a blatant sexual appeal (a cologne ad with two intertwined nude bodies) and ads A and C contain mild sexual appeals (attractive men and women in swimsuits on a beach). The contrast between ad B and the one which follows it (ad C in the original order and ad A in the reversed order) may cause ads A and C to be rated lower on the emotional scales related to sexual appeals, since they are so much tamer than B. Exposure to ad B changes the way that subjects rate the following ads. Without being preceded by ad B, both A and C would score higher on these scales.

This effect may also be produced in experimental or field designs that present multiple manipulations of the independent variable to a single subject. For example, experimental subjects presented with a persuasive message justifying censorship in times of war, followed by one advocating First Amendment freedoms, can be expected to show different amounts of attitude change than subjects who are first presented with a message praising the founding fathers, then one concerning the First Amendment. Experimental treatment effects often persist indefinitely, and the effects of earlier treatments must not be confused with the effects of later treatments.

Counterbalancing of treatments or measurements is prescribed for this threat to internal validity. The simple reversal counterbalancing suggested for fatigue and learning is not sufficient in this situation, as there are only two systematic patterns of presentation.

Using Figure 13-5, we can see that ad A will strongly affect the response to ad B, since it is adjacent to no other ad. Ad B will affect ads C and A, but not D; C will affect only D and B, not A, and so on. This unequal balance of effects means that we must use another type of counterbalancing to account for order effects. Specifically, we want one that does a better job of placing each ad next to all the other ads. Figure 13-6 shows such a counterbalancing, called a *Latin Square* design. Note that this counterbalancing also will control learning and fatigue effects, as each ad appears in each presentation slot once (Orders 1 and 4 are actually the same as the reverse counterbalancing described above). In fact, the requirement that learning and fatigue effects be linear is not present in this arrangement.

While the Latin Square counterbalancing will give complete control for all sequences of two, it will not completely counterbalance sequences of three or higher, as the right-hand columns of Figure 13-6 show. Some higher-order sequence effects are still possible. In fact, to control for all possible sequence effects of K treatments or measurements will require $K!$ (K factorial) sequences. In the case of four measurements, this will require $4 \times 3 \times 2 \times 1 = 24$ different orders of presentation.

In many cases, a large number of different presentation orders is not reasonable. For example, to completely counterbalance eight treatment groups would require 8! or 40,320 sequences of presentation!

The researcher must either choose a lower level of control (such as using a Latin Square design which controls only for the effects of adjacent treatments or measurements) or present the treatments or measurements in a random order to each respondent. This would randomize the error introduced by order effects, but not completely control for it.

Counterbalancing may also be necessary within measurement instruments. A very long questionnaire may introduce fatigue effects that affect items appearing nearer the end of the questionnaire, or may contain sensitive items that might affect subsequent responses. In these cases, counterbalancing of items within the questionnaire is a good practice.

The subject of counterbalancing is a complex one, and the interested communication researcher should consult one of the many textbooks and handbooks on research design to find more details about the alternatives.

Presentation Order 1:   A   B   C   D

Presentation Order 2:   B   D   A   C

Presentation Order 3:   C   A   D   B

Presentation Order 4:   D   C   B   A

Sequence	Frequency
A-B	1
A-C	1
A-D	1
B-A	1
B-C	1
B-D	1
C-A	1
C-B	1
C-D	1
D-A	1
D-B	1
D-C	1

This list contains all possible pairs of sequences

Sequence	Frequency
A-B-C	1
A-B-D	0
A-C-B	0
A-C-D	0
A-D-B	1
A-D-C	0
etc.	

This list contains a partial listing of 3-sequences

FIGURE 13-6   Latin Square Counterbalancing

Single-Time Point Issues in External Validity

Representativeness of the Sample

Sampling bias can cause problems in external validity as well as in internal validity. We covered many of the problems of a nonrepresentative sample in Chapter 6. In particular, groups that are self-selected can cause problems. Persons who volunteer for research projects can be expected to be very different from the typical person (who does not usually volunteer). Convenience samples pose the same problems. For example, much communication research is done on college and university undergraduates. The results of this research is open to questions of external validity, unless the phenomenon being investigated is not related to the social background, age, intelligence, economic status, or race of the research subject. These are variables on which undergraduates are substantially different from the general population, and unfortunately, most communication processes involve one or more of these variables.

To account for this threat, the researcher must either justify the generalizability of the sample (for example, physiological responses of students to communications are not likely to differ from those of the rest of the population, because of any differences in social variables), or limit generalization (the results apply only to white, upper-income, educated young adults).

Reactive Effects of Setting

The research setting itself can produce responses in subjects that limit their generalizability. Participants in communication research are often exposed to communications in an artificial setting which enhances their attention to messages, their motivation to process and/or act on the contents of the messages, and so on. The effects of these deviations from real world conditions limit the generalizability of the results.

To limit reactive setting effects, which affect both internal and external validity, the researcher must try to simulate the real environment to which the research is being generalized, and to be as unobtrusive as possible. For instance, laboratory television viewing should be done in as natural a setting as is possible. This may mean providing the laboratory with couches and chairs and subdued lighting, removing laboratory equipment from sight and introducing alternative targets of attention such as magazines. Or it might mean viewing with family members or friends, rather than alone. An interpersonal communication study of conversations should use a lounge-like setting, rather than a sterile classroom.

Observation and measurement should be as hidden as possible. Nonverbal measurement might be done with concealed video cameras, observations of group interaction could be made from behind one-way mirrors, and so on. The researcher must critically examine the physical research setting and use all creative means to make it as natural as possible.

Multiple Treatment Interference

Just as sequencing, fatigue, and learning from multiple treatments or multiple measurements can affect the internal validity of a research study, they can also affect the external validity. Counterbalanced designs can improve the internal validity, but they do little to counter the multiple treatment effects on external validity. Counterbalancing controls for *systematic* effects by spreading them over all treatment conditions equally, but it does not *remove* the effects. As a result, the "unrealistic" treatment effects may produce findings in research settings that are not reproduced in real world settings.

If this threat to external validity appears to be substantial, the researcher must use a research design which does not involve multiple treatments or measurements taken from a single subject. This increases the number of subjects necessary, but will remove this threat to validity.

Over-Time Issues in External Validity

Reactive Sensitization (to externals)

Behavioral changes can be introduced by measurement and experimental manipulations, as discussed above in the measurement sensitization sections. Subjects who leave controlled settings between measurement sessions may react differently to communications and other environmental stimuli, as a result of their participation in the research.

A control group design can help with the internal validity problem. But the external validity problem remains, since both the experimental group and the control group will change in unpredictable ways. Looking again at the political communication example, if we find that a structured program of newspaper reading improves the political knowledge of the experimental group by 15 percent, compared to the control group, we must temper our conclusions with the knowledge that *both* the experimental and the control group's newspaper reading behavior have been modified. The experimental group's behavior was modified by the initial measurement, which may have increased its receptiveness to political news, and also by the manipulation of its reading habits; the control group's behavior was modified only by the initial measurement. The difference between the groups is due to the structured program. But we must be careful in concluding that we will see this difference if we introduce the program to the general public *without* the sensitizing effect of the initial measurement.

A research design that uses only after-the-fact (post-manipulation) measurement may be required to answer this threat to external validity.

Subject Mortality

The loss of subjects over time introduces a similar problem in external validity. Since the beginning and the finishing samples are different in makeup, due to mortality, it is difficult to determine exactly how much of the difference that occurs over time was due to mortality, and how much was due to the independent variable. It is thus difficult to generalize the effect observed in the research to the unmeasured population. This situation is much worse in those observational designs without a control or comparison group. In this case, subject mortality can be fatal to external validity.

The solutions to this problem are the same as those described in the section on subject mortality as a threat to internal validity. Keep as many subjects within the research program as is possible.

Summary

In this chapter we have distinguished among three major types of research: *experimental research*, in which the independent variable or variables are manipulated and the environmental conditions or the setting of the research is controlled; *field research*, in which the independent variable is manipulated, but the setting is uncontrolled; and *observational research*, in which the independent variable is measured under different levels that are the result of natural manipulations, and the setting is uncontrolled.

Each of these types of research has problems with both internal and external validity. *Internal validity* is the ability of the research design to provide support for claims about the presence of a relationship between the independent and dependent variables. *External validity* is the generalizability of the results to nonresearch or "real world" settings. In general, experimental research is high on internal validity and low on external validity, observational research is low on internal validity and high on external validity, and field research has medium levels of both types of validity.

Factors which pose threats to internal and external validity can occur at single time points, when measurements or experimental manipulations are made, and they can occur over time, when multiple measurements are part of the research design. Many of the threats can be answered with appropriate sampling, research design, treatment and measurement counterbalancing, and forethought in preparing the research setting, manipulations, and measurement instruments. But all research designs involve some compromise between validity and practicality, so no single design is free from all threats to validity. As a communication scientist, you must weigh the options, and design your research to ensure the fewest and least damaging threats are present.

Notes

[1] For an example of retrospective research in family communication patterns, see Chaffee, S. H., McLeod, J. M., & Wackman, D. B. (1973). Family communication patterns and adolescent political participation. In J. Dennis (Ed.), *Socialization to politics.* New York: Holt, Rinehart & Winston.

[2] Lefkowitz, M. M., Eron, L. D., Walder, L. O., & Huesmann, L. R. (1972). Television violence and child aggression: A follow-up study. In G. Comstock & E. A. Rubenstein (Eds.), *Television and social behavior: Television and adolescent aggressiveness* (Volume 3). Washington, DC: Government Printing Office, U.S. Dept. of Health, Education, and Welfare.

References and Additional Readings

Campbell, D. T. & Stanley, J. C. (1966). *Experimental and quasi-experimental designs for research.* Chicago: Rand-McNally.

Drew, C. J. & Hardman, M. L. (1985). *Designing and conducting behavioral research.* New York: Pergamon Press (Part II, "Basic Design Considerations").

Kerlinger, F. N. (1986). *Foundations of behavioral research* (3rd ed.). New York: Holt, Rinehart and Winston (Chapter 17, "Research Design: Purpose and Principles"; Chapter 18, "Inadequate Designs and Design Criteria"; and Chapter 19 "General Designs of Research").

Kidder, L. H. (1981) *Selltiz, Wrightsman and Cook's research methods in social relations.* New York: Holt, Rinehart and Winston. (Chapter 2: "Causal Analysis and True Experiments").

Chapter *14*

Controlled Environments: Experimental Research

In the previous chapter we outlined the three basic types of research design (experimental, field, and observational), along with the relative strengths and weaknesses of each. In this and the following two chapters, we will look at each of the three types more closely. We'll first present some typical research designs, and then we will look at and evaluate some actual research studies using some of these designs.

Typical Experimental Designs

We will first have to introduce some shorthand notation to clarify and speed up our presentation. This notation is outlined in Table 14-1.

Case Studies and Single-Group Designs

The first two designs we will discuss are not strong, and in fact are not classified as experimental designs by some writers (cf. Campbell and Stanley, 1966), as they have significant threats to internal and external validity. As Table 14-2 shows, there are very few threats to validity for which these designs actually provide benefits, other than those provided by random sampling and single-time measurement.

These designs are extremely weak and should be avoided, as using them is likely to lead to incorrect or insupportable results. Many factors other than the experimental manipulation may be responsible for change in the dependent variable. For example, results of case studies may be due to subjects' reactions to measurement, or to reactive effects of the experimental setting. Since the effects of the measurement and of the research setting

TABLE 14-1   Notation for Research Designs

Y	Measurement of the dependent or effect variable
X	Measurement of the independent or cause variable
MX	Manipulation of independent variable
R:	Random assignment or selection of units of analysis
+	The design is more susceptible to this threat to validity
−	The design is less susceptible to this threat to validity
?	This threat to validity is not affected by the design under discussion. The threat may be more or less prevalent, depending on other steps taken by the researcher.

Example: *R: Y   MX   Y*   Single Group Design

(Random assignment or sampling, premanipulation measurement of dependent variable, manipulated independent variable, post-manipulation measurement of dependent variable)

Threats to Validity	*Single-Group Design*	
History	+	(this design is susceptible to this threat)
Selection	-	(not susceptible)
Instrumentation Obtrusiveness	?	(susceptibility depends on factors other than design)

cannot be isolated from the effects of the experimental manipulation of the independent variable, it is impossible to draw strong conclusions from a case study design.

Single-group designs are particularly susceptible to invalidity created by over-time measurement. The effects of the manipulation cannot be separated from history and maturation effects, sensitization created by the measurement, and so on. If these effects are strong, the researcher will likely reach completely incorrect conclusions.

Both these designs may have some utility in the early stages of an investigation. Their results may suggest hypotheses which later can be tested under more controlled circumstances. But these designs by themselves are not very useful for establishing relationships which meet the requirements of causality.

Premanipulation/Postmanipulation Control Group and Postmanipulation Only Control Group Designs

These designs are the most basic and widely used experimental designs. They provide control for many of the threats to internal validity by providing a comparison or control group. The control group's experiences are identical to the experimental groups, with one exception: They are exposed to a different level of the manipulated independent variable. Often this level is "absence," so that the control group receives no manipulation at all. But as we'll see below, this is not a necessary condition for an experiment. The control group

TABLE 14-2   Threats to Validity: Case Study and Single-Group Designs

Case Studies:	(a)		*MX*	*Y*	
	(b)	*R*:	*MX*	*Y*	
Single Group:	(a)		*Y*	*MX*	*Y*
	(b)	*R*:	*Y*	*MX*	*Y*

	Case Study		Single Group	
	(a)	(b)	(a)	(b)
INTERNAL VALIDITY				
Instrumentation Reliability and Validity	?	?	?	?
Selection (Sampling)	+	−	+	−
Instrument Obtrusiveness	+	+	+	+
Manipulation Effectiveness	?	?	?	?
History	−	−	+	+
Maturation	−	−	+	+
Measurement Sensitization	−	−	+	+
Measurement Instrument Learning	−	−	+	+
Measurement Instrument Instability	−	−	+	+
Subject Mortality	−	−	?	?
Subject Fatigue	+	+	+	+
Treatment or Measurement Order Effects	?	?	?	?
EXTERNAL VALIDITY				
Representative Sample	+	−	+	−
Reactive Effects of Setting	+	+	+	+
Multiple Treatment Interference	?	?	?	?
Reactive Sensitization	+	+	+	+
Subject Mortality	−	−	+	+

can actually be any comparison group that receives a different level of the independent variable, be that level "absence" or just a different type of manipulation.

Rather than looking for *absolute* levels or changes in the dependent variable, these designs look for *comparative* differences between the experimental and control groups. Since the control group will be subject to identical effects of all factors *except* that produced by the different level of the independent variable, any difference in the dependent variable detected when comparing the experimental and control groups after the experimental manipulation should be due to the action of the independent variable alone. Thus the covariance between the independent and dependent variable predicted in the research hypothesis can be separated from the effects of other confounding factors, and it can be tested for statistical significance. This design meets the conditions for a valid test of the

TABLE 14-3 Threats to Validity: Premanipulation/Postmanipulation Control Group and Postmanipulation Only Control Group Designs

Pre-Post	*R:*	*Y*	*MX*	*Y*	(Experimental Group)
	R:	*Y*		*Y*	(Control Group)
Post Only	*R:*		*MX*	*Y*	(Experimental Group)
	R:			*Y*	(Control Group)

	Pre-Post	*Post Only*
INTERNAL VALIDITY		
Instrumentation Reliability and Validity	?	?
Selection (Sampling)	−	−
Instrument Obtrusiveness	−	−
Manipulation Effectiveness	?	?
History	−	−
Maturation	−	−
Measurement Sensitization	+	−
Measurement Instrument Learning	+	−
Measurement Instrument Instability	+	−
Subject Mortality	−	−
Subject Fatigue	−	−
Treatment or Measurement Order Effects	?	?
EXTERNAL VALIDITY		
Representative Sample	−	−
Reactive Effects of Setting	?	?
Multiple Treatment Interference	?	?
Reactive Sensitization	+	−
Subject Mortality	+	−

existence of a relationship as outlined in Chapter 3. A checklist of these designs' strengths is provided in Table 14-3.

The only difference between these two designs is the presence of a premanipulation measurement in the control group design. The benefit of this feature is that it allows before-after comparisons, both within and between the experimental and control groups, rather than the single comparison between the experimental and control group provided by the postmanipulation only control group design. Each design has benefits and disadvantages which makes one or the other more appropriate, depending on the kind of research being conducted.

Suppose we are investigating the effects of a speaker's race on his or her ability to change attitudes toward minority hiring practices. To do this, we will develop a measure for the dependent variable which includes a number of statements about minority hiring practices, to which the subject replies on a nine-point Likert scale with "strongly agree/strongly disagree" at the endpoints. These statements will be combined into a single index that indicates the degree of "favorableness toward minority hiring." This is the dependent variable. This measurement will be taken before and after the subjects receive the communication, in a pre-post design.

For the experimental group, we will use a speaker of Chinese ancestry, who delivers a prepared address verbatim. For the control group, we will use a speaker of Western European ancestry, who will deliver the same speech. The speakers will be similar in age, physical appearance, and dress.

Note that our control group here receives the same message as the experimental group. This is necessary, as we are investigating the effects of the speaker's race, not of the message. It is not necessary that all exposure to communications be absent from the control group; indeed, to make sure that the control and experimental groups are equivalent in all respects, other than the levels of the independent variable, we will often have to use the same procedures in both groups. Our independent variable is a nominal one, with two levels: presence or absence of visual cues that the speaker is a member of an ethnic minority group. We've chosen, completely arbitrarily, to call the "presence" level of the independent variable the experimental group, and the "absence" level the control group. It really doesn't matter how we label them. All that is necessary is that we have two (or more) levels of the independent variable.

We expect that the initial attitudes of subjects on the topic of minority hiring practices will vary widely. Since we are randomly assigning subjects to experimental and control groups, however, we can assume that the same distribution of attitudes will be present in both groups (i.e., the groups will initially have similar means and variance on our dependent measure).

Here we see one advantage of the premanipulation-postmanipulation design. It will allow us to test this presumption. By comparing the groups on the premanipulation measurement, we can see the extent of sampling error that was present in the assignment of subjects to the groups. If the groups score similarly on the premanipulation measurement, we can be confident that our random selection procedure has operated properly.

We can also compare the difference between the pre- and postmanipulation measurements in the control group. This difference represents the combined effects of all the over-time threats to validity. This comparison is particularly useful when the control group is completely unexposed to any communications. For example, suppose two randomly selected groups of consumers participate in an experiment to test the effects of advertising on the consumer's intent to purchase the product being advertised. The experimental group receives the test advertisements, while the control group receives no advertising at all. The premanipulation to postmanipulation difference in the average intent to purchase that we see in the control group will indicate the effects of measurement sensitization, fatigue, etc. These effects are present in *both* the experimental and control groups.

The premanipulation/postmanipulation design also permits us to control for sampling error and for the effects of the over-time threats. To do this, we may use the *change* or difference of the dependent variable scores between the premanipulation and postmanipulation measurements as a single dependent variable.[1]

TABLE 14-4   Example of Premanipulation/Postmanipulation Results

EXPERIMENTAL GROUP

Subject	Premanipulation	Postmanipulation	Change
A	6	7	+1
B	3	4	+1
C	8	8	0
D	4	5	+1
Mean	5.25	6.00	+.75
Standard Error	.96	.79	.22

CONTROL GROUP

Subject	Premanipulation	Postmanipulation	Change
E	4	3	−1
F	6	7	+1
G	7	5	−2
H	4	4	0
Mean	5.25	4.75	−.50
Standard Error	.58	.66	.50

	Premanipulation	Postmanipulation	Change
Difference Between Experimental Mean and Control	0.00	1.25	1.25
Group Standard Error	.58	.58	.37

Dealing only with change scores will allow us to ignore the initial differences between subjects. This will give a more powerful indication of the effect of the independent variable, as we can focus on relatively small changes that occur within subjects, and ignore relatively large initial differences between subjects. In the example in Table 14-4, the two groups have the same premanipulation mean, indicating a good random sampling procedure, with low sampling error. The postmanipulation means and change scores differ by only 1.25 units. But the corresponding change score standard errors are smaller. This makes the change scores more easily distinguished from sampling error, and so the statistical test is more powerful.

The postmanipulation only design is less powerful, because it cannot distinguish between variance in the dependent variable that is caused by initial differences in the subjects, and the variance that is caused by the independent variable. But the design is less sensitive to internal validity threats like measurement sensitization and learning,

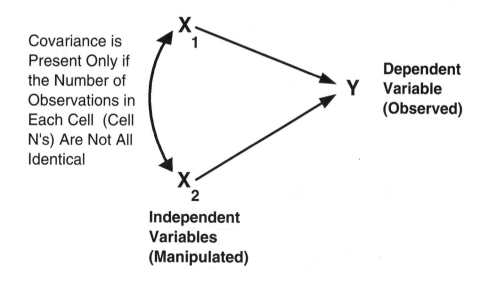

FIGURE 14-1   Factorial Designs: Multiple Independent Variables

and to external validity threats like reactive sensitization and subject mortality, since measurements are made at only one point in time.

In our example concerning the effect of race on the persuasiveness of a speaker, we would probably not use the pre-post design discussed above, but would choose the postmanipulation only design. Any premanipulation measurement of attitudes toward minority hiring would probably sensitize the subjects toward the topic. That would mean that both the experimental and the control groups would listen to the message in ways that are not typical of the way that the population would listen. Also, if only a short time elapsed between the premanipulation measurement and the postmanipulation measurement, the subjects' memory of their answers to the premanipulation measurement might affect their responses to the same postmanipulation measurement items.

Multiple Independent Variable Designs

These designs are extensions of the above designs. But instead of a single independent variable (X), there are two or more independent variables $(X_1, X_2,$ etc.) involved (see Figure 14-1). There are literally a limitless number of different research designs which involve multiple independent variables. We'll mention only one of the most common here: the factorial design.

In the factorial design, the different levels of all independent variables are presented to groups of subjects in all possible combinations. As an example, let's expand the advertising effectiveness study described above. In addition to presence or absence of advertising (X_1), we'll add another independent variable (X_2) which may cause variation in the subjects' intent to purchase the advertised product (which is the dependent variable, Y). The added

TABLE 14-5 **Factorial Research Design: Two Independent Variables**

| | X_2 | |
	No Product Sample	Product Sample
Not Exposed to Ad	Group 1 (Control Group) [Measured Purchase Intention] Y	Group 2 (Experimental Group) [Measured Purchase Intention] Y
Exposed to Ad	Group 3 (Experimental Group) [Measured Purchase Intention] Y	Group 4 (Experimental Group) [Measured Purchase Intention] Y

X_1 labels the left (Not Exposed / Exposed) dimension.

independent variable is "provision of a sample of the product." For some experimental groups, we'll provide a sample for inspection; the other groups will not receive a sample.

The resulting design looks like Table 14-5. There are four groups, each of which receives a different combination of levels of the independent variables:

Group 1: No advertising, no product sample
Group 2: Product sample only, no advertising
Group 3: Advertising only, no product sample
Group 4: Both product sample and advertising

Group 1 serves as a control group, since no manipulation is done. It can provide a baseline of the purchase intention of the population in the absence of exposure to advertising *and* the absence of a product sample. Because all levels of the independent variable are present in all their combinations, we can separate the effects of advertising (which should be present in Groups 3 and 4, and not in Groups 1 and 2) from the effects of the product sample (present in Groups 2 and 4, and not in Groups 1 and 3). We'll provide a guide to the statistical procedures needed to make the covariance tests in Chapter 19.

Let's assume that we decide to use a premanipulation/postmanipulation design. Using our shorthand notation, we can diagram this experimental design like this:

Group 1	R:	Y_{pre}			Y_{post}
Group 2	R:	Y_{pre}	MX_2		Y_{post}
Group 3	R:	Y_{pre}		MX_1	Y_{post}
Group 4	R:	Y_{pre}	MX_1	MX_2	Y_{post}

This is just a somewhat more complex version of the single independent variable pre-/postmanipulation design, with control group. All the threats to internal and external validity are the same.

Other Experimental Research Designs

The designs outlined so far are only the simplest and most common. A number of different designs have been developed to meet the specialized needs of communication and behavioral researchers. Generally they are variations on the basic theme of experimental research, which is manipulation of the independent variable and control of threats to internal validity. For further information on experimental research designs, you should consult a reference like Keppel (1982).

Units of Analysis

The basic unit that is observed and measured is called the *unit of analysis*. In communication research, three different classes of units of analysis are commonly used. The first is the individual. In studies using this unit, the variables are defined to measure characteristics or behaviors of a person: For example, we determine how different levels of the independent variable affect an individual's performance on a task, or the individual's degree of attitude change, aggressive behavior, production of messages, and so on. The *N*s in studies which use this level of analysis are equal to the number of subjects in the experiment.

The second unit of analysis is that of the social system. In this level, variables are defined by the joint action of a number of individuals. These variables might be defined for dyads, small groups, organizations or, for that matter, for societies or countries. Measurement is at the social level: We might measure the duration of time that a dyadic relationship persists, the level of performance of a group, the communication patterns of a family, the adaptability of an organization, or the ownership of VCRs in different countries. The *N*s in this kind of study are determined by the number of dyads, groups, or organizations, and not by the number of individual subjects who participated in the experiment.

The third unit of analysis is the message. While the previous units involve study of the senders or receivers of communications, this level examines the communication itself. This level is based in the study of language and symbolic information exchange. Research on media message content or frequency, nonverbal expressions or symbolic behavior, language intensity and choice of vocabulary, and similar studies will use this unit of analysis. The *N*s in studies using this unit of analysis are the number of stories, the number of utterances, the number of noun phrases, frequency of facial expressions, and so on.

Although all three units of analysis are used in communication research, the individual unit is by far the most common. Experimental research also sometimes uses social system units. But it is very rare for experimental research to involve message units of analysis. This is in contrast to observational research, in which message units of analysis are frequently used in media content analyses or interpersonal language use studies.

Measurements that relate to differing units of analysis cannot be directly mixed within a single study. A research study that uses variables based on individual characteristics as the unit of analysis cannot incorporate social system or message variables directly. This point is sometimes confusing, as it seems to imply that we cannot relate messages to individuals, or single individuals to social groups. If it is true, how can we study the communication process, in which individuals, embedded in social organizations, transmit and receive messages?

The answer lies in defining "bridging" concepts. For example, a typical study might involve content analyzing soap opera themes and relating these to the personality characteristics of viewers. This would appear to mix the message unit of analysis (with content categories which quantify themes of sex, violence, amnesia, etc.) with the individual unit of analysis (personal characteristics of dependency, strength of emotional connection to others, etc.). However, on closer examination, we see that the critical variable in relating soap opera content to personality characteristics is really the *amount of exposure* to the particular themes, not just the amount of the theme present in the message. Exposure applies to individuals, not to the message (television programs), so the study is actually relating two variables at the individual level. Exposure is a bridging concept that links the characteristics of the message to the responses of the individual.

In a similar fashion, individual level concepts can sometimes be aggregated to produce social system units of analysis. For example, we might take the average number of external telephone calls made by individuals in a corporation, and use this single number to represent the amount of "outgoing corporate telecommunications." This would be a measurement appropriate to a social systems unit of analysis, as it would apply to the corporation, and not to any individual.

We mention these distinctions here, as the examples of communication research presented in this chapter and the following chapters were chosen partly to illustrate the use of differing units of analysis. As you read them, be particularly alert to the use, or potential use, of bridging conceptualizations.

Examples of Experimental Research in Communication

We'll now move from considering experimental design in an abstract fashion to looking at some real examples of experimental communication science work. We've chosen three examples to illustrate several important similarities and differences among experimental studies.

The studies chosen for these examples do not necessarily represent the state-of-the-art in experimental research. We chose them because they are "classic," often cited studies, or because they represent an interesting or novel approach. In some cases, the conclusions have been challenged or expanded in later research.

Example of Experimental Research Using the Individual as the Unit of Analysis: The Bandura Study of Media and Child Aggression

Because of space limitations, we will synopsize the descriptions of the research projects in three exhibits. The first study, in Exhibit 14-1, involves the individual unit of analysis. In it, the response of individual children to exposure to mediated communications of violence and aggression is studied.

the other aiming and firing

The Bandura experiment uses a postmanipulation control group design, with multiple levels of the nominal independent variable (the type of mediation of the message). Random assignment to the groups is used. This is a very strong design for internal validity. However, the external validity may be somewhat suspect, as the experimental setting, the nature of the communications, and the amount of exposure are not typical of "real life" conditions. We'll cover these in more detail below.

Example of Experimental Research Using the Social System as the Unit of Analysis: The Leavitt Study of Communication Networks and Group Efficiency

The individual unit of analysis that characterizes the Bandura, Ross, and Ross study can be contrasted with the level of analysis in a study on group structure and group performance carried out by Harold Leavitt. In this study Leavitt explored the relationship that was thought to exist between the structure of a group (which determines access to the information needed in problem solving) and the speed with which a problem was solved and the number of errors that were committed in the process. In the experiment described in Exhibit 14-2, the structure of group communication patterns was manipulated by the researcher and the decision-making performance of the group was observed.

This experiment also uses a postmanipulation only design. There is no control group identified as such, but all results are drawn from comparisons among experimental groups, so the control for over-time threats to internal validity are present. Again we see high internal validity coupled with suspect external validity, due to the artificial nature of the task and the actual communication channels.

The third example illustrates a bridging concept, which transforms message-level measurements into individual units of analysis.

Example of Experimental Research Using Message Measurement and Individual Units of Analysis: The Donohue Study of Conflict and Language Use

In this study the researchers focused on how the presence of a formal procedure for making a decision affects language use, when the decision is made under conditions of conflict. This is related to the use of language to mark relational distances in dyads.

Multiple independent variables are used in this study. One, gender, is measured rather than manipulated, while the other, decision-making structure, is manipulated. The design is factorial, so there are four experimental groups: male structured, male unstructured, female structured, and female unstructured. Two dependent variables are used, so analyses are conducted twice: once for language immediacy and once for language formality.

Although the dependent variables are measured on transcripts, and thus appear to be appropriate as variables for research using the message unit of analysis, a bridging concept is actually used to define them as measures at the individual level of analysis. Rather than using utterances or syntactical units as the basic observational unit, the authors computed average scores for each subject on these language variables. This operational definition translates the measurements from being based on observations of the message alone (number of independent clauses, ratio of verbs to total words, etc.) to a basis of observations made of the individual (average number of independent clauses produced by the *individual*, etc.).

Only one of the hypotheses received support in this research, and this was found for only one of the two dependent variables. The predicted effect of decision-making structure was found for the immediacy of the language used, but not for its formality. The factorial design allowed the researchers to separate the effects of gender and decision making structure, and talk about their effects independently.

**EXHIBIT 14-1   Experimental Research: The Individual Unit of Analysis
The Effect of Modes of Exposure to Aggressive Behavior on
Children's Imitative and Nonimitative Aggressive Play**

General Topic

Bandura, Ross, and Ross designed an experiment to test a number of hypotheses about the effects of exposure to real-life and mediated aggression on the later behavior of children. They were interested in the degree to which the children would imitate the aggressive media and real-life models, as well as the amount of general aggressive behavior that occurred after exposure.

Hypotheses

The first hypothesis concerned the relationship between the realism of the portrayal and the tendency of the child to imitate the behavior he or she has seen. The researchers argued that aggressive models can be arranged on a reality-fictional dimension, with real-life models at one extreme, cartoon characters on the other extreme, and filmed human models in an intermediate position. The theoretical linkage involves the similarity and perceived closeness of the models to the children. The hypothesis predicted that the tendency to imitate the

aggressive behaviors would decrease the further the model was from "real."

The second hypothesis related aggression anxiety and aggressive behaviors. They argued that those children who generally inhibit aggressive behaviors would perform fewer imitative and general aggressive acts. An associated hypothesis was generated concerning sex differences: As aggression is generally viewed as particularly inappropriate for females and is consequently likely to be negatively reinforced, males would be more imitative of aggression than females. The fourth hypothesis predicted that exposure to aggressive behavior removes inhibitions and would trigger more general aggressive behaviors. Specifically, frustrated observers of aggressive behaviors would be more aggressive than frustrated nonobservers of aggressive behaviors, as their inhibitions against carrying out aggressive actions would be lowered by exposure.

Subjects

The subjects for this study were 48 boys and 48 girls enrolled in the Stanford University Nursery

Continued

EXHIBIT 14-1   *Continued*

School. Their ages ranged from 39 to 69 months, with a mean of 52 months. An adult male and an adult female served as models of aggression in both the "live" and filmed conditions.

General Procedure

The subjects were divided into three experimental groups and one control group, with 24 subjects per group. One group observed "live" aggressive models and a second group observed the same models on film. The third group viewed a film depicting an aggressive cartoon character carrying out the same behaviors. All groups contained equal proportions of males and females, which meant that half of the subjects in the human model conditions (the live and film groups) were exposed to models of the same sex as the subject, and half were exposed to opposite sex models. Subjects in the experimental and control groups were matched individually on the basis of ratings of their aggressiveness in social interactions in the nursery school, made by both the experimenter and the nursery school teacher.

Following the exposure, subjects were tested for the amount of imitative and general aggressive behavior. This test took place in a different setting and in the absence of the models.

Manipulations

Experimental Conditions. In the real-life aggressive condition, each subject was brought to an experimental room. While the subject was in the room receiving some instructions about an unrelated activity, the real-life model carried out a number of highly distinctive aggressive acts, and made a number of specific verbal aggressions toward a large inflated toy Bobo doll. This doll was approximately the size of the children, and would bounce back upright after being pushed over or struck.

In the human-film condition, a ten-minute motion picture was shown while the subjects were in the experimental room. The models and their behaviors were identical to those in the live condition.

In the cartoon-film condition, a film of a model costumed as a cartoon character, on a cartoon-like

set, was used to present the aggressive behaviors. This "cartoon" black cat carried out the same behaviors on the Bobo doll as had been exhibited in the other two conditions.

Aggression Instigation

The children who were exposed to the various experimental stimuli as well as the children who were part of the control group were next brought to a room containing attractive toys. Each child was initially allowed to play with these desirable toys, but once involvement with the toys was established, the child was no longer allowed to continue playing with the toys. Subsequently the child was led to a third room where he or she was allowed to play with a selection of toys which included the Bobo doll, some aggressive toys (a mallet, dart guns, etc.) as well as nonaggressive toys (crayons, a tea set, dolls, bears, etc.). The subject spent 20 minutes in this room during which his or her behavior was observed through a one-way mirror. The subject's behavior was rated on the amount of predetermined behaviors that occurred in a number of categories every five seconds.

Dependent Variable Measures

The children's behavior was classified into the following six categories:

- Imitative aggression: acts imitating the novel and specific physical and verbal aggression exhibited by the model.
- Partially imitative responses: incomplete performance of the aggression or misdirected complete aggressions. Two types were recognized:

   (1) Mallet aggression: striking objects (other than the Bobo doll) with a mallet.
   (2) Sits on the Bobo doll: sitting on the doll, but not aggressing toward it.

- Nonimitative aggression: physical acts directed toward objects other than the doll, and hostile remarks other than those uttered by the model.

Continued

EXHIBIT 14-1 *Continued*

- Aggressive gun play: shooting darts or aiming and firing imaginary shots.

Results

A partial listing of results (those relevant to the first hypothesis) is presented here. Based on the information contained in Table E14-1 and other analyses, Bandura et al. drew the following general conclusions.

In terms of overall aggression, exposing the children to aggressive models increases the probability that they will behave aggressively when instigated later. Although the three experimental conditions did not differ from one another, the children in all three experimental groups were signifi-

cantly more aggressive than those in the control group. In terms of specific categories of aggression, exposing the children to aggressive models led to increased imitative aggression relative to the control group. Live models were observed to elicit significantly more imitative behaviors than cartoonish characters, thereby lending partial support to the first hypothesis, the one linking realism of portrayal to imitative aggression. The three experimental groups did not differ from one another in partial imitative behavior. An overall evaluation of the data suggests that humans on film portraying aggression are the most influential in eliciting and shaping aggressive behaviors.

TABLE E14-1 Results of the Test for Bandura's Hypothesis 1

Dep. Variable	*Comparison of Treatment Conditions*					
	Live[a] vs Film	Live vs Cartoon	Film vs Cartoon	Live vs Control	Film vs Control	Cartoon vs Control
Overall Aggression	ns	ns	ns	a	a	a
Imitative Agression	ns	a	ns	a	a	a
Partial Imitation						
Mallet Agression[b]						
Sits on Doll	ns	ns	ns	ns	a	a
Nonimitative Aggression[b]	ns	ns	ns	ns	a	a
Aggressive Gunplay	c	ns	ns	ns	a	ns

[a]Indicates that the average value for the first named condition in the contrast was the greater one.
[b]For these dependent variables no significant overall difference was observed; further significance tests are thus inappropriate.
[c]Indicates that the average value for the first named condition in the contrast was the lesser one.
ns indicates "not significantly different."
From Bandura, Ross, and Ross (1963). Copyright 1963 by the American Psychologial Association. Reprinted (or adapted) by permission.

"Imitation of Film-Mediated Aggressive Models," Albert Bandura, Dorothea Ross, and Sheila Ross, *Journal of Abnormal and Social Psychology,* 1963, Vol. 66, No. 1, pp. 3–11.

EXHIBIT 14-2   Experimental Research: The Social System Unit of Analysis
How Group Structure Affects Group Performance

General Topic

The ways in which members of a group may be linked together to exchange information are numerous. Of all the different patterns of linkage, which are "good" patterns from the point of view of performance? Leavitt contrasts the levels of performance on a number of dependent variables of the following communication structures:

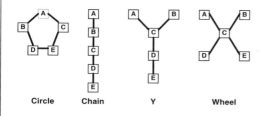

| Circle | Chain | Y | Wheel |

Hypotheses

Centrality reflects the extent to which one position is strategically located relative to other positions in a communication pattern. The position at the center of the wheel has high centrality, while the position at the end of a chain has low centrality. It is a measure of closeness to all other group members and thus it is a measure of the availability of information. Such availability should determine one's role in a problem-solving group, specifically, one's independence and responsibility. Differences in independence and responsibility should affect group performance variables such as speed and accuracy. Leavitt did not explicitly define a set of hypotheses, so we may infer that he is testing nondirectional hypotheses.

Subjects

One hundred male undergraduates from MIT were divided into 20 groups of five men each. These 20 groups were further subdivided so that five groups could be tested on each of the four communication patterns.

General Procedure

Each of the five subjects was assigned an identifying color and was given a card on which appeared a set of five (out of a possible six) symbols. Each subject's card was different from all the others: The symbol lacking on a card was different in each case. Thus, in any set of five cards there was only one symbol in common. The problem to be solved by the group was to find the common symbol that appeared on all cards.

Group members were allowed to communicate with one another by writing messages to those other members of the group with whom there was an open communication channel—that is, a link such as A-B in the chain structure, shown in Figure E14-1. Each separate written communication was considered a message.

Manipulations

Group members were seated at a round table so that each person was separated from the next by a vertical wooden partition extending from the center to 6 inches beyond the edge of the table.

To allow communication with the other men, a box with color-coded slots was built into the center of the table and the partitions. Only the slots which connected the correct links in the communication network being tested were opened by the experimenter. Members communicated with those to whom they were linked on color-coded cards. In each subject's booth were six switches, one for each of the six different symbols. If a group member thought he had determined the identity of the missing symbol, he pressed the appropriate switch. When all five members had actuated a switch, the experimenter would halt that particular trial. Each group was given 15 consecutive trials using a single communication network configuration.

The manipulated independent variable is the centrality of the communication network. Note that this variable can be defined only with collections of

Continued

EXHIBIT 14-2   *Continued*

two or more individuals. This makes the unit of analysis the social system, rather than the individual. All results are reported by referring to the performance of groups on this variable.

Dependent Variable Measures

Measurements on a number of dependent variables were obtained. We will restrict our discussion to those variables measured at the group level. These are also conceptualized at the social systems level.

The first dependent variable measured was elapsed time to obtain a solution. Two measures of time were obtained:

The first time measure was the amount of time required for all members of the network to throw the switch.

The second time measure was the fastest single trial for each group in a given network configuration.

The second dependent variable was the number of messages that were transmitted within a group, in a given trial, before the group identified the missing symbol.

The third dependent variable was the number of errors in identifying the symbol which were made by members of the group. This consisted of corrected errors (those that were corrected before the trial was over) as well as "final errors" at the end of the trial.

Results

Table E14-2 contains a partial listing of the results. From it, we can see the fastest trials occurred in the wheel and *Y* networks, which have high centrality, and the slowest were in the circle and chain, which have low centrality. More errors also tended to occur in the networks with low centrality.

TABLE E14-2   Communication Network Comparisons on Selected Dependent Variables

	Communication Network			
	Circle	Chain	Y	Wheel
Time				
Range, 15th trial (in seconds)	50–96	28–220	24–52	21–46
Fastest single trial (mean, in seconds)	50.4*	53.2	35.4	32.0*
Errors				
Mean Total Errors (last 8 trials)	7.6*	2.8	0*	0.6
Mean Final Errors	6.4*	6.2	1.6*	2.2

*Means marked with asterisk are different at $p < .05$

"Some Effects of Certain Communication Patterns on Group Performance," Harold J. Leavitt, *Journal of Abnormal and Social Psychology,* Vol. 46, 1951, pp. 38–50.

EXHIBIT 14-3 Experimental Research:
Message Measures and Individual Units of Analysis
How Problem Solving Structures Affect Utterances

General Topic

This study assessed the effects of providing a problem-solving structure to conflicting dyads on the way in which dyad members use immediate and formal language to mark their relational distance.

Hypotheses

Subjects in dyads who are initially in conflict on a decision-making task will use less immediate and more formal relational code choices when they are instructed to follow a set of decision-making rules, than will dyads who are free to reach a decision without such rules. Furthermore, females are predicted to use more immediate and informal code choices than men, regardless of the presence or absence of structure.

Subjects

Subjects were selected from 155 students enrolled in an introductory organizational communication course. Subjects were first asked to rate the importance of 10 characteristics of a hypothetical employee, to be employed as an orientation group leader. The subjects were then assigned to dyads so that individuals who maximally disagreed about the importance of the characteristics were paired together. This created 31 male dyads and 32 female dyads. Individuals were told that they were paired together because they had significant disagreement.

General Procedures

Dyads received written instructions explaining that they had 15 minutes to select one of four candidates for a job as an orientation group leader. Eighteen male and 17 female dyads served as a control group: They were instructed to deal in any way they thought appropriate with any disagreements that might arise during their interaction. The remaining 13 male and 14 female dyads were told to arrive at their choice for orientation leader following a four-step decision procedure. These experimental group members were asked to read a description of the four-step procedure. To ensure that they understood the procedure, each dyad member was tested on knowledge of the procedure prior to the actual experiment.

All dyad interactions were audio- and video-taped. The tapes were used to produce transcripts of the interactions.

Manipulation

This experiment used the pairing of maximally disagreeing individuals to create dyads in which the members stand in conflict with one another. Conflict is not a variable here as it is assumed to characterize every dyad. The variable manipulated by the experimenters is decision-making structure, which has two levels: presence and absence. The second independent variable is gender, which is a measured variable.

Dependent Variable Measures

Utterances produced by the dyads were evaluated on two variables. The first variable was "verbal formality-informality." Four measures were used to compute an overall index of this variable:

- Utterance length: the number of words, not counting interjections and hesitations
- Structural complexity: this measure is based on the number of independent clauses
- Syntactical complexity: the ratio of total number of verb forms to total words
- Gunning's Fog Index: a readability index based on the number of independent clauses

More formal language is more complex, and it indicates more social distance between the persons conversing.

The second dependent variable was "immediacy-nonimmediacy." This is a measure of the directness or intensity of the interaction. The transcripts of dyadic interaction were divided into units (simple sentences or phrases) and each of the units was rated on each of four language immediacy scales, using a

Continued

EXHIBIT 14-3 *Continued*

1 to 3 response for each scale. The scales were combined to form a single immediacy variable.

Results

The availability of a decision-making procedure had a significant effect on immediacy, but not on formality. There was no significant effect for gender. Both males and females were more immediate in the unstructured condition than in the structured condition. Table E14-3 shows the major results of the experiment.

TABLE E14-3 **Means for Four Experimental Groups on the Immediacy and Formality Indices**

	Immediacy		Formality	
Sex	Structured	Unstructured	Structured	Unstructured
Male	2.02	2.04	−.18	.58
(Std Error)	(.01)	(.01)	(.29)	(.29)
Female	2.02	2.09	−.05	−.59
(Std Error)	(.01)	(.01)	(.36)	(.27)

Donohue, W. A., Weider-Hatfield, D., Hamilton, M. and Diez, M. A., Relational distance in managing conflict. *Human Communication Research,* 1983, Vol. 11, No. 3, pp. 387–405, copyright © by Sage Publications. Reprinted by permission of Sage Publications, Inc.

"Relational Distance in Managing Conflict," William A. Donohue, Deborah Weider-Hatfield, Mark Hamilton, and Mary A. Diez, *Human Communications Research,* Vol. 11, No. 3, Spring 1985, pp. 387–405.

Similarities and Differences among the Examples

Experimental research is characterized by two major factors, control over the research setting and manipulation of the independent variables, so we'll compare the examples on these characteristics. As these issues primarily affect the internal validity of the research, we'll also compare the studies on external validity concerns.

Control over the Research Setting

Researchers must take great pains to assure that the individuals or groups who participate in the research experience conditions are as similar as possible, save for the different level of the independent variable that is applied to each experimental group. In the Bandura and the Leavitt examples we find descriptions of the efforts undertaken to exert control over the research setting.

Bandura et al. give a detailed description of the various experimental conditions that emphasizes the effort which the researchers took to assure that the physical and verbal behaviors of the models would be identical in each of the three experimental conditions. Furthermore, when the subject entered the experimental room and was allowed to play with toys, "the play material was arranged in a fixed order for each of the sessions.... (I)n order to eliminate any variation in the behavior due to mere placement of the toys in the room." The arrangement of the toys left by the preceding child could have predisposed a child to play with some toys rather than with others, and this would have affected the measurement of the dependent variable. Keeping the toys in a fixed arrangement for every session eliminated this potential source of variation in behavior.

The Leavitt study also contains references to control over the research setting. For example, the order in which the network configurations were tested was randomized. The experimenter could have chosen to run all the Y patterns first, and then to run all the circle patterns, and so on. But this would expose the research to threats to validity due to treatment or measurement order effects, measurement instrument learning, and possibly measurement sensitization. Assigning the order of the patterns randomly eliminated the possibility of confusing the effects of circumstances that appeared only early or late in the experiment (such as unfamiliarity with the experimental procedures or fatigue) with the effects of the communication network configuration. In addition, Leavitt controlled for possible effects of group members' geographical position and work station color by shifting subjects' positions for each new run. As there were five runs in each pattern and five members in each group, each subject sat in each seat, and was assigned each color once, so any systematic effect was removed.

Control over the research setting can also be used to provide assurances that the various individuals or groups in the experiment are equivalent on all variables other than the independent variable. The requirement of equivalence on all other outside variables can be satisfied in one of two ways: Either the researcher can show the groups to be equivalent on a set of relevant variables (matching); or the researcher can select participants in such a way that the groups will be assumed equivalent (random selection).

Bandura and colleagues individually matched subjects in the experimental and control conditions on the basis of ratings of their aggressive behavior in social interaction in the nursery school. The experimenter and a nursery school teacher rated the children on five-point rating scales which measured the extent to which the subjects exhibited physical aggression, verbal aggression toward inanimate objects, and aggression inhibition. By matching the children in each of the four conditions, Bandura could show that for every child with a particular pattern of aggressiveness scores in, say, the "live model" group, there was a child with a similar pattern of scores in each of the other groups. The groups are therefore identical in the extent to which group members possess traits of general aggressiveness and predispositions toward aggression.

In addition to matching subjects on the aggression variables, Bandura et al. also matched the groups on gender, so that the experimental groups were evenly split between males and females. If these variables exhaust the universe of relevant variables whose effects might be confused with the action of the independent variable, then, by controlling for their effect, Bandura and colleagues can confidently argue that any differences observed between the groups cannot be due to differences in general aggressive tendencies or gender, and must be due to the action of the independent variable.

In the Leavitt research, the references to control of individual subject variables are less clear. There are no mentions of matching subjects across groups or of random assignment of individuals to groups. However, since all subjects participated in solving a preliminary series of four problems, group differences in basic abilities should show up if the results of these preliminary tests are compared across groups. This kind of post hoc matching is sometimes used to assure that groups that were created with nonrandom procedures are actually equivalent on relevant outside variables.

In the Donohue et al. article there is also very little reference to control. Although there are two main conditions (structured decision making versus nonstructured decision making), there is no description of how dyads were assigned to these experimental conditions. Control was exerted on the creation of these dyads, by pairing subjects with maximally different scores on the employee characteristics. This is nonrandom pairing of the subjects, but if the resulting dyads were randomly assigned to experimental conditions (a procedure that was probably followed), then there is no systematic relationship between subjects and the experimental groups to which they were assigned, so this nonrandom pairing procedure will not confound the results.

Manipulation of the Independent Variables

The Bandura et al. study employed three independent variables: the degree of realism of the aggressive model, which consisted of three levels (live model, filmed model and cartoon); subject gender; and model gender. Only the first of these independent variables was manipulated. The remaining two were measured independent variables which were used in matching subjects and experimental conditions.

The Leavitt study included only one independent variable and it was manipulated. The variable was represented by four different configurations of group structure which are contrasted to one another: the circle, the chain, the Y, and the wheel. Although these categories appear to be nominal in nature, they reflect the extent to which individuals in the group have "centrality" or access to information. This centrality is least in the circle and increases as we go toward the wheel. Accordingly, the independent variable should be considered to be ordinal.

The study by Donohue and his associates reveals some interesting procedures for manipulation of the main independent variable of structure and for the establishment of the conflict condition in all groups. Conflict is operationally defined by the pairing of two individuals who have maximally different rankings on employee characteristics, and it is presumed constant for all experimental and control groups. Once a dyad was constituted following this definition, conflict was said to exist. However, the researchers had to assume that because a priori disagreement existed, conflict had to exist as well. Note that the creation of conflict is not a manipulation of the independent variable, as all experimental conditions presumably had equal levels of conflict. But the conflict was necessary to test the hypotheses, so the researchers used their control of the experimental setting to create it.

The creation of conflict was a critical control, so the researchers carried out a manipulation check. Participants were asked to rate on a scale from 1 to 5 (with 5 representing "a great amount of disagreement") the amount of disagreement they perceived in the negotiation process. The unstructured group's mean was 2.18; the structured group's mean was 2.32. This can be interpreted as low to average levels of disagreement, and it brings one of the conditions of the hypothesis test into question. If the manipulation did not truly create a high state of conflict, how confidently can it be said that this experiment constituted a fair test of the hypothesis? The extent to which the manipulation did not really produce conflict constitutes a threat to internal validity.

In sharp contrast is the manipulation check for the structure manipulation. Not only were participants tested prior to the experiment on their knowledge of the four-step decision-making procedure, but they were audio- and videotaped so that compliance to the structure could be assessed. The analysis of the tapes provides evidence that the experimental manipulation indeed was present—dyads that were supposed to use the rules indeed did use them. This knowledge of the manipulation effectiveness bolsters the internal validity.

Factors Affecting External Validity

To assess external validity, we must look at the extent to which we can generalize the results obtained in the experiment to the external world. We have encountered the topic of generalization before when we discussed sampling in Chapters 5 and 6. We stated then that the process of generalization only makes sense when we are reasonably sure that the sample that we observed is representative of the population to which we wish to generalize.

We can add to this statement another condition for experimental research: The process of generalization from the conditions of an experiment to the real world only makes sense when we are reasonably sure that the conditions under which we conducted the research are representative of the conditions which naturally occur in the real world to which we wish to generalize. The findings of an experiment will be only as externally valid as the degree to which the selections of subjects, experimental manipulations, and experimental conditions can be considered to be representative samples of real conditions from the general population.

Sample Representativeness

The usual way to obtain a representative sample is to choose randomly from the population. Robert Plutchik, in *Foundations of Experimental Research* (1983) was only partly joking when he stated that "(T)he criticism is sometimes made that a good deal of what passes as psychological fact is based upon either the white rat or the college sophomore" (p. 47). The implication of this barb is that sometimes we substantially stretch the limits of generalization when we move from experimental subjects to wider populations. And, as Plutchik also states, we too frequently overgeneralize from other aspects of experiments.

Let's look at the subjects used in the three extended examples in light of their external validity. In the Bandura study, the children participating in the research were boys and girls enrolled in the Stanford University Nursery School. There is no reference to the method of selection of these participants from the enrollment of that school. Furthermore, the extent to which we can generalize from a nursery school such as this one would greatly depend on the criteria that the children met in order to be enrolled in this school.

If parental affiliation with Stanford University is required for attendance, then the students in this school are likely to be systematically different from the population-at-large. They would probably score higher on variables such as verbal ability, income, intolerance of aggressive behaviors, and so on, than would students at a preschool with a policy of open enrollment. If such affiliation was required, then generalization of the results to nursery school students in Klamath Falls, Oregon, or Eagle, Wisconsin, or the South Bronx, in New York City, may be questionable.

The subjects in the other two extended examples were undergraduates in major research universities. An issue not discussed in either article was whether these students volunteered their participation, whether participation fulfilled a course research requirement, or whether participation was monetarily rewarded. If these conditions were present, the subjects may have been motivated to a far different degree or in a different way than persons in the general population might be. The subjects in both the Leavitt and Donohue studies were also all within the same general, but narrow, age bracket. Obvious hazards are involved in generalizing from students to middle-aged or older individuals.

Using samples of subjects who are selected for their convenience and accessibility may reduce to a very significant degree our ability to generalize. Of course, this situation is not unique to experimental research, as it can occur in field and observational research, too. But it is frequently a larger problem in experimental research, since the controlled settings of experimental research (the "laboratories") are usually not movable. Subjects must be induced to come to the research setting, and frequently this causes problems. In a sense, this problem in external validity is a consequence of the improvement in internal validity that controlled settings provide for experimental research.

So when are we justified in generalizing from our samples which were drawn from restricted populations? Generally, whenever we can say that there is no reason to think that persons outside the restricted population will react differently than persons inside this population. To generalize from the Bandura study, we must feel that "children are children," at least with regard to their learning of behaviors from models. Likewise, the Leavitt and Donohue studies can be generalized to the extent that we believe that college students use the same strategies and social rules of communication as the older population.

Representativeness of Experimental Manipulations

Experimenters

In the Bandura et al. study, a female experimenter was used in all experimental conditions. Would a male experimenter have created the same level of aggression when he told the children that they could not play with the attractive toys any more? We can expect that the sex, prestige, race, age and personality characteristics of the experimenter will influence the compliance of participants with experimental procedures.

In the Donohue et al. and Leavitt studies the identity of the experimenter(s) is not identified. It is likely, however, that faculty members or graduate students acted as experimenters. For an average undergraduate student, instructions given by such an individual will elicit different levels of compliance with experimental manipulations than instructions coming from a peer.

Communication Stimuli and Experimental Tasks

The representativeness of communication stimuli used in an experiment is a major factor in determining the level of external validity. The Bandura et al. study used the degree of realism of the model exhibiting aggressive behavior as the main independent variable. For this purpose three stimuli were defined: the actions of a live model, a filmed version of those same actions by the same live model, and a cartoon-like version of these actions. These reasonably represent real-world exposure conditions. Children will often be in situations where they can observe aggressive behaviors from adults and in the media.

However, all three versions of the stimuli shared one characteristic: The model exhibited novel and unusual aggressive behaviors. To the extent that these behaviors are novel and unusual, they are not representative of the population of aggressive acts. A consequence is that these stimuli will probably attract the attention of the research subjects. It is therefore possible that the imitative aggressive behaviors that result from stimuli of this type might not result from observing more mundane (and thus typical) acts.

The representativeness of the stimuli in the Leavitt study also affects the generalizability of findings. The independent variable, the degree of structuring of communication in groups, was manipulated by means of a rather complex arrangement of color-coded seating positions around a table divided by upright partitions which allowed only written messages to pass through slots between dividers. The resulting arrangements were hardly representative of the kinds of conditions under which people generally work or solve problems. Additionally, the experimental task (determining a missing symbol from a set of cards) is not representative of activities normally carried out by people in problem-solving groups.

In addition to determining how representative the selected communication stimuli or experimental tasks are of the universe of such stimuli or tasks, the representativeness of the number of levels of stimulus and their intensity should also be considered. Put into statistical terms, the variance of the independent variable must be representative of the real range of levels and of variance that the independent variable takes on in the real world.

An independent variable can take on a range of values, of which at least two must be selected in order to test whether the variable is related to some other dependent variable. The variable "structure of decision making," as in the Donohue study, is a variable that can take on a fairly big range of values in reality (it has lots of variance). By using only two values out of this range, the Donohue experiment leaves open the question about the generalizability of its results to *all* structured decision-making situations.

Contrast the selection of levels in that study with the selection in the Bandura et al. and the Leavitt studies. Bandura's "degree of realism" was represented by three levels; Leavitt's structuring or patterning variable was represented by five levels. It is apparent that increasing the number of levels of the independent variable is more likely to represent the full range of such a variable in the real world.

The researcher must consider not only the number of different levels, but also the intensity of these levels. To take an extreme example, suppose a researcher is interested in the effects of depictions of sexual activity on television. He or she sets up an experiment with three levels of the independent variable: an episode of "Little House on the Prairie"; an episode of "Days of Our Lives," featuring a steamy fade-out scene; and an episode from the EXXXSTACY adult cable network, featuring some fairly improbable adventures of coeds. This range of communications certainly has a wide variance, and it is likely to produce the best conditions for detecting significant relationships with dependent variables (the wider the variance of the independent variable, the easier it is to detect covariance).

But it really does not accurately represent the range of sexual depictions normally seen by real world viewers, most of whom do not view soaps, and virtually none of whom subscribe to a triple-X rated cable service. Thus the results would have dubious external validity.

Dependent Variable Measures

This issue is closely related to problems associated with defining the dependent variable. In Chapter 2 we discussed the process of defining variables. From that chapter you may recall that simple concepts are easy to define conceptually and have straightforward operational definitions. Age, for instance, can be defined as "how long someone or something has been in existence" and a reasonable operational definition might be "number of years in existence." More complex concepts often have a range of indices that claim to measure the meaning associated with the concept. Complex concepts such as group performance (as in the Leavitt study) can be measured in a number of different, and sometimes inconsistent, ways.

Leavitt measured group performance using at least three indices: the number of errors in identifying the missing symbol, the amount of time needed to arrive at a decision, and members' satisfaction with group membership. Because these indices all tap into different aspects of performance, measurement of just one of these indices would give very little justification for generalizing to the concept of performance as applied in the general population. For example, the measure of "errors in making a decision" is only one of these aspects. We would not be justified in concluding that increases in centrality, which are found to be associated with decreased probability of errors, improve "performance" in general. A narrow definition will not generalize sufficiently.

The experiment by Donohue et al. uses a wide range of measurements to get at the concept of language use. Language use is defined in terms of its "formality-nonformality," for which four different responses are coded, and "immediacy-nonimmediacy," which uses another four different response categories. The range of these measures allows the authors to make wider claims about the generality of their results.

Summary

In this chapter we have outlined some basic designs for experimental research. True experimental designs include some comparison or control group which makes the design less susceptible to various threats to validity.

Two designs are particularly useful and are in widespread use: the *premanipulation/ postmanipulation control group design*, and the *postmanipulation only control group design*. The former design uses two measurement points, one before and one after the experimental manipulation. The latter uses only one measurement point, after the experimental manipulation. The pre-post design can give powerful results, as it can be used to make before-after comparisons of the values of the dependent variable within individuals. This allows the researcher to eliminate initial differences between subjects, and focus on the change that is produced by the independent variable. But the design is also susceptible to over-time threats to validity, like measurement sensitization and learning effects and subject mortality. The post-only design is not as statistically powerful, but it is not susceptible to these threats.

Three units of analysis used in communication research are introduced: *the individual unit of analysis*, *the social system unit*, and *the message unit*. The individual unit of analysis predominates in experimental research, although some social system units can be found in interpersonal (dyads), group (collections of several individuals) and organizational (work groups or corporations) research. Message units of analysis are rarely found in experimental research in communication.

Variables appropriate to one level of analysis are often used at a different level by redefining them with *bridging concepts* like exposure (e.g., exposure to political news, which converts the message level of analysis to the individual level), or by aggregating them (averaging the responses of individuals at the individual level of analysis, to create a group score at the social system level of analysis). Variables defined at one level cannot be used at another without this redefinition.

We provided several in-depth examples of experiments on communication processes using different units of analysis. These experiments illustrated the application of experimental design. Within the context of these experiments we have shown how the experimental control, manipulation, and measurement decisions made by the researchers affected the experiment's internal validity and thus our confidence that the conclusions are correct. We also used these experiments to indicate how external validity can be affected by the research design and procedures.

While this chapter touches on some basic issues in experimental research, the serious communication researcher should consult one of the number of excellent books on experimental design listed in the references and additional readings section. The books will provide more detail about the issues presented here and will also discuss other important issues, which we are prevented from raising by space limitations.

Notes

[1] The use of change scores is recommended only for variables with high measurement reliability, as the reliability of change scores is the square of the measured variable's reliability. Thus a dependent variable with .80 reliability, which is usually considered very good, will produce a pre-post change score with a reliability of $.80^2$ or .64, which is poor. Other, more robust, ways to analyze change that occurs within a subject over time will be mentioned in Chapter 17.

References and Additional Readings

Campbell, D. T. & Stanley, J. C. (1966). *Experimental and quasi-experimental designs for research.* Chicago: Rand-McNally.

Huck, S. W., Cormier, W. H. & Bounds, W. G. (1974). *Reading statistics and research.* New York: Harper and Row (Part III: "Research Design," containing Chapters 11–14).

Keppel, G. (1982). *Design and analysis: A researcher's handbook* (2nd ed.). Englewood Cliffs,

NJ: Prentice Hall (Chapter 1, "Design of Experiments").

Kirk, R. E. (1982) *Experimental design: Procedures for the behavioral sciences.* Monterey, CA: Brooks/Cole (Chapter 1 "Introduction to Basic Concepts in Experimental Design").

Plutchik, Robert (1983). *Foundations of experimental research.* New York: Harper and Row.

Wimmer, R. D. & Dominick, J. R. (1987). *Mass media research: An introduction* (2nd Ed.). Belmont, CA: Wadsworth (Chapter 5, "Laboratory Research and Experimental Design").

$$C\ h\ a\ p\ t\ e\ r\quad \textit{15}$$

Semi-Controlled Environments: Field Research

In this chapter, we'll look at experimental designs which are applied outside the controlled environment of the laboratory. Field research uses the designs of experimental research to minimize the threats to internal validity, but applies them in realistic settings that minimize some threats to external validity. However, as we'll see, there are some tradeoffs between these two types of validity.

Typical Field Research Designs

The basic research designs are identical to those used in experimental research, and you can refer to the previous chapter to review these designs. But the threats to validity differ because of the lack of control over the setting that the researcher must accept. These threats lead to some other strategies for strengthening control that field researchers often employ. Table 15-1 contains some threats to validity for the basic experimental designs. If you compare it to the similar table for experimental research (Table 14-3), you'll see that there are more potential problems with field research designs.

First, there are often sampling problems that may affect the representativeness of the sample. In field settings, the researcher frequently has to use subjects who are available, rather than those chosen by a purely random process. For example, a researcher who is conducting a study on a city street, as in the Ellsworth, Carlsmith, and Henson study summarized in Exhibit 15-2, will have to use only the persons present on the street at the time of the study. These may be quite different in many ways from the general population, and thus it is possible that they may be a biased sample. The Ellsworth research shows the thought which a good researcher must use in developing procedures to ensure that the sample is as representative as possible.

**TABLE 15-1   Threats to Validity:
Premanipulation/Postmanipulation
Control Group and Postmanipulation
Only Control Group Designs**

Pre-Post	*R*:	*Y*	*MX*	*Y*	(Experimental Group)
	R:	*Y*		*Y*	(Control Group)
Post Only	*R*:		*MX*	*Y*	(Experimental Group)
	R:			*Y*	(Control Group)

	Pre-Post	*Post Only*
INTERNAL VALIDITY		
Instrumentation Reliability and Validity	?	?
Selection (Sampling)	+	+
Instrument Obtrusiveness	–	–
Manipulation Effectiveness	+	+
History	–	–
Maturation	–	–
Measurement Sensitization	+	–
Measurement Instrument Learning	+	–
Measurement Instrument Instability	–	–
Subject Mortality	?	?
Subject Fatigue	–	–
Treatment or Measurement Order Effects	?	?
EXTERNAL VALIDITY		
Representative Sample	+	+
Reactive Effects of Setting	–	–
Multiple Treatment Interference	?	?
Reactive Sensitization	+	–
Subject Mortality	+	–

This problem is amplified if group units of analysis are chosen, like the "community" of the Douglas, Westley, and Chaffee research summarized in Exhibit 15-1. Probability sampling from these larger units is often impossible.

A related problem is avoiding subject mortality, and thus maintaining the representativeness of the sample in pre-post designs. Subjects are not on the researcher's "home turf" (the laboratory), and it is easy for them to decline further participation in the project because of more immediate demands on their time. Or they may just disappear. The laboratory setting itself lends a certain amount of social pressure to encourage subjects to participate in research, and when this setting is missing in field research, the communication scientist must compensate.

The effectiveness of the experimental manipulation is also frequently more questionable in field research than it is in experimental research. Because the environment is not completely under the researcher's control in field research, all conditions in the experimental groups other than the manipulation are not necessarily the same, as they are in experimental research. The field researcher must take extra pains to assure that the manipulation has been effective. Often this involves an explicit measurement of the manipulation (the manipulation check).

With all these negative threats to validity, why would the researcher choose a field setting? The answer to this question can also be found in Table 15-1. One entry under the external validity heading refers to "reactive effects of setting." Field research designs are not susceptible to this threat, while experimental designs are. If you remember, this threat was discussed as a serious problem in the previous chapter. Reactive effects may cause the experimental subject to behave differently during the research than he or she would in "real life," and this will lead the researcher to erroneous generalizations of the research findings.

Field settings allow the phenomenon under investigation to operate under realistic conditions. Not only are the subjects reacting to the experimental manipulation in the same way that they would if the experimenter was not making systematic observations, but the operation of other variables in the environment is not impaired.

This point is very important. The virtue of an experimental research setting is in the control of outside variables, so that they do not confound the relationship between the cause-and-effect variables being observed. But this virtue is also a vice, when the relationship is generalized from the laboratory to the real world (we discussed this problem in detail in Chapter 4 and the previous chapter). If we use manipulative control of these outside variables, we may eliminate real and important processes in which the cause variable influences the effect variable under realistic conditions. While this will not affect the logic of our experiment (internal validity), it may lead us to the wrong predictions when we extend the results to the world outside the lab (external validity).

This is the problem that field research is designed to attack. For some communication processes, the laboratory setting produces too much reaction, or manipulatively controls too many outside variables, for the conclusions to have much utility. For example, public information or advertising campaigns are often difficult to study in the laboratory. The process of persuading or informing large and diverse audiences involves a huge number of different communication and psychological variables. Manipulative control of all of these variables except the few that are under study may give very different results from those that would be observed if these variables were allowed to operate naturally.

A good example of a type of field research which deals with the external validity problem occurs in advertising research. A common question concerns the comparative ability of two different message formats, or two different sets of product appeals to persuade the audience to purchase a product. This question lends itself to a simple postmanipulation control group design, which could be carried out either in an experimental laboratory study or in a field setting.

In this design, two groups from the target audience are randomly selected. Each is exposed to a different version of the advertising message. After exposure to the message, the product purchase amount or probability of future purchase is measured. The message that produces the highest mean value of the purchase variable is then determined to be the most effective, if its difference from the other group's mean is significantly higher.

By contrasting an experimental and a field study which both use the same basic research design, we can see why field research is often chosen to investigate this type of question. Let's be more specific, and assume that two versions of a television commercial for a headache relief medicine called Molenol are being investigated. The first features an endorsement by a "typical" white-collar worker, who lauds the product's ability to relieve headaches produced by his working conditions: demanding bosses, complaining clients, and unresponsive secretaries. The second commercial also features an endorsement by a person who uses the product to relieve work-produced headaches, but this endorser is a professional football player who complains about demanding coaches, violent linebackers, and unprotective linemen. The fundamental research question concerns whether it is better to have an endorser who is closer in social position and has problems similar to the typical audience member, or to have a more glamorous person do the endorsing.

Let us look at various ways in which the research settings produce reactivity. The first major difference between an experimental and a field investigation of this question lies in the conditions under which the subjects are exposed to the message. In the experimental study, subjects would likely be presented with the commercial in a test room. While they might not be instructed to pay close attention to the commercial, the lack of realistic alternatives might mean that the commercials are viewed with very close attention. In contrast, a field study might use a split-cable system, in which half the homes on a cable system would receive one of the test commercials inserted into a normal programming mix, while the other half receives the other commercial in the same spot. (Such split-cable systems are available to commercial researchers in several cities in the United States.) Subjects in the field test would thus be exposed to the commercials under very realistic conditions, so that their attention levels would likely be much lower than those in an experimental study.

A second critical difference is that the field study subjects might not even be aware that their response is being tested, so that they will not be sensitized to analyze the message to any degree. In contrast, the laboratory experimental subjects will know that they are being tested. This may cause them to analyze the message in much more detail than they would under normal viewing conditions.

A third difference is that the experimental study participants may feel a desire to respond positively to the nice person in the white lab coat who has convinced them to give up some of their time to participate in an important scientific study. They can do this by telling the researcher what they think he or she wants to hear (this is called a "social demand" response). Clearly, the response of experimental subjects could be very different than the response of the field research subjects.

Finally, the criterion measure of the purchase behavior is likely to be very different in the two settings. It is very difficult to accurately measure purchase behavior in a laboratory setting. Purchasing a product (like many behaviors advocated by communications) is a complex behavior which depends on many factors other than exposure to communications. One's buying habits and loyalty to competing brands, the cost and the availability of the product, and even the political position of the product's manufacturer can influence a purchase independently of communication effects. In a laboratory study, often the best one can do is ask a hypothetical purchase intention question: "How likely are you to purchase the product the next time you shop?"

This kind of question is very sensitive to "social demand" responses. Social demand refers to the tendency for research participants to respond in ways that they think the researcher wants them to respond, or ways that they believe to be socially appropriate, rather than in the way that they are most likely to respond when no one is looking. Since Molenol appears in the test commercial, subjects in the experiment may tell the researcher that they will purchase the product the next time they go to the drugstore. It's only good manners not to insult the product that the researcher is obviously interested in. But when these research subjects actually get to the drugstore, they buy the same generic aspirin that they've always bought, because it works fine, and it's cheaper (and no one is watching).

In the field study, the researcher may be able to get actual product sales information of Molenol in each of the geographic areas served by the portion of the cable which carried each version of the commercial. The researcher can then find out the net impact of each commercial on the final criterion: sales.

Note that the field researcher will have deliberately sacrificed internal validity for external validity. If there are no significant differences in sales in the two regions, this does not necessarily mean that both commercials are equally good (or poor) at convincing consumers that Molenol is a good product. The effects of the uncontrolled outside variables may actually be overwhelming the differential effects of the commercials. For example, suppose that 35 percent of the subjects who were in the area served by the cable which showed the white-collar endorsement actually purchase Molenol, while 33 percent in the area in which the pro football endorsement was shown purchase Molenol. This difference is probably not statistically significant unless huge Ns are used.

However, an experimental study with all the outside variables controlled might have shown that white-collar endorsement is actually 200 percent better at convincing subjects to purchase Molenol, *when all other factors are held constant.* The experiment will give better information about the communication process being studied, but it will do so under conditions far different from those which actually occur; it will have good internal validity and poor external validity. The field experiment will give less definitive answers about the theoretical process, but will give much better prediction about the performance of the communication under real-world conditions; it has poorer internal validity but better external validity.

It is clear that the choice of research setting must be made with some eye to the use to which the information from the study is to be put. If the researcher is interested in the more theoretical issue of the effects of endorsements in persuasive communications, a laboratory study would be preferred, because it would give a clearer answer. But the researcher who wants to select the communication that gives the largest increase in sales probably will choose a field study.

The internal validity of field studies can be strengthened by using statistical control, rather than manipulative control. With statistical control, outside variables like price and purchase habit in the above example can be measured, and their effects subtracted from the effects of the experimental variable. This allows the outside variables to operate normally while the research is in progress. But the researcher can then separate their effects from those of the manipulated variable, and so strengthen the internal validity of the research.

This is the control strategy employed in purely observational research, and we'll discuss it further in the next chapter. We'll also mention some of the statistical procedures to implement this kind of control (like partial correlation and analysis of covariance) in Chapter 19 of this book.

The external validity strengths and the care required to address internal validity weaknesses of field research designs can be seen in the following examples. These examples, once again, were chosen for their interesting features or classic status. Examples of individual units of analysis and group units of analysis are provided, but no example of a message unit of analysis appears in this section. The use of the message as the basic unit is even rarer in field research than it is in experimental research, so we will restrict our examples to the other two units of analysis.

Examples of Field Research in Communication

Example of Experimental Field Research Using the Individual as the Unit of Analysis: The Douglas, Westley, and Chaffee Study of the Effects of a Public Health Information Campaign

The example shown in Exhibit 15-1 involves the effects of a public health information campaign. Measurements were made on individuals in two communities, one of which was exposed to the information campaign and one of which was not. Although this research was conducted with individuals as the units, it could also be done with a group unit of analysis (the community) if it was replicated in a sufficient number of communities.

The Douglas, Westley, and Chaffee study points out some of the problems with representativeness of samples that can occur in field research. The communities to be studied were not chosen randomly, nor were they similar in many respects. But Douglas et al. tried to match the two communities on the characteristics whose effects they thought might be confused with the effects of the independent variable, like the educational levels, occupations, incomes, and the media use of the research subjects.

But even with matching, the two communities differed strikingly on the percentage of the original sample that consented to participate in the research. In the control community, twice as many persons refused to participate in the research. This opens the possibility that some of the effects seen might be due to systematic differences between the samples in each community, introduced because the more "uncooperative" persons were eliminated from the sample in the control community, while similar persons were not eliminated in the experimental community. If these uncooperative persons differed in their knowledge of mental retardation, or their media use, their exclusion will cause systematic differences between the experimental and control community results. These differences will be confused with the effect of the experimental manipulation.

Since the communities initially differed on the level of the dependent variable (see Table E15-1), Douglas et al. chose a research design that would allow them to look at

EXHIBIT 15-1   Experimental Field Research: Individual Units of Analysis

General Topic

A field study was carried out to determine whether a public information campaign was effective in increasing community information levels regarding mental retardation and in creating more positive community attitudes toward mental retardation. The effectiveness of the campaign was measured by contrasting the knowledge and attitude levels of individuals in an "experimental" community with those in a matched "control" community.

Hypotheses

The authors present a number of assumptions about the characteristics of the topic of mental retardation which form the basis for four hypotheses directly addressing knowledge and attitude levels.

The first characteristic assumed is a generally low level of knowledge in the population regarding mental retardation as a community problem. The second assumption is that there is a low probability that hardened attitudes toward mental retardation already exist in the population. The third assumption is that the likelihood of external events reaching the experimental and control communities during the conduct of the research (and thus confounding the results) is low. These assumed characteristics, the authors then reason, constitute optimal conditions for an information campaign to produce both knowledge and attitude change, as predicted by various media effects theories.

The first hypothesis predicted that postcampaign knowledge of information included in the campaign would be greater in the experimental community than it would be in the control community.

The second hypothesis predicted that the pre- to postcampaign increase in knowledge would be greater in the experimental community than in the control community.

The third hypothesis proposed a parallel effect on attitudes toward mental retardation: a greater positive shift from pre- to postcampaign would be observed in the experimental group than in the control group.

The fourth hypothesis proposed a positive relationship between attitude change and information gain in the experimental community.

The final two hypotheses focused on information sources. Hypothesis five predicted that, in the experimental condition, local media would be more often identified as sources of information than nonlocal media. Furthermore, in the experimental community, local media would be cited more often as sources of information than they would in the control community.

Hypothesis six proposed that "friends" would be more frequently cited as information sources in the experimental community than they would be in the control community.

Subjects

To determine the knowledge level and attitude consequences of the public information campaign, two matching towns in Wisconsin were selected. The two communities were highly comparable in population characteristics, income, occupational distribution, and median education. The only differences were that the community to be used as the control was higher in median education and had a higher proportion of professionals and managers. The experimental community was to be the setting for the information campaign; the control community was not to receive such a manipulation.

Both communities were matched on another set of attributes extremely relevant to the hypotheses to be tested. Both had locally published weekly newspapers, a weekly shopper's guide, and had local radio stations. Additionally, both communities were equidistant from the same urban center and both depended on that city's two newspapers and four television stations for external news.

Within each community a systematic random sample of households was drawn by choosing, after a random start, every tenth household on these communities' electric utility lists. This yielded 134 homes in the experimental community and 169 in the control. A single adult respondent was chosen randomly in each household.

General Procedure

Because the two communities were not equivalent in their initial involvement in mental retardation work, this field experiment was designed as a

Continued

EXHIBIT 15-1 *Continued*

"before-after" or "premanipulation-postmanipulation" study.

The before-and-after measures were separated by a period of eight months. During this period the information campaign was carried out in the experimental community; the control community was left alone. The premanipulation observation consisted of two sets of measures: One set contained items designed to measure individuals' knowledge of mental retardation, while the other measured attitudes toward mental retardation. Cooperation rates were 81 percent in the experimental community and 44 percent in the control community. The postmanipulation test contained items to measure general as well as specific knowledge levels and attitudes after the campaign had been concluded. The postmanipulation cooperation rate was 78 percent in the control community (22 percent subject mortality) versus 85 percent (15 percent subject mortality) in the experimental community, resulting in a final *N* of 85 in the experimental community and 60 in the control community.

Manipulation

A public information campaign of six months' duration was presented to the experimental community between the premanipulation and postmanipulation measurement dates. During this period, local channels of communication were used to present information about mental retardation in the experimental community. Twenty news stories, five feature stories, and a Mental Retardation Week advertisement were published in the local paper. News items were broadcast over local radio "an uncounted number of times" and were also inserted in church bulletins. Further information efforts consisted of presentations to churches, 4-H and service clubs' meetings. Finally, the local Junior Chamber of Commerce conducted a year-long project focusing on the subject.

Dependent Variable Measures

As was mentioned above, the dependent variables were measured at two points in time: precampaign and postcampaign. The researchers identified two dependent variables: knowledge about mental retardation (specific as well as general knowledge) and attitudes toward mental retardation.

Pretest Measurement

Knowledge Measurement. In the pretest, the variable was measured using a set of six items designed to measure general levels of information about retardation. The scores on the individual items were used to compute mean correct scores for each respondent and each community.

Attitude Measurement. The pretest also contained a set of 21 Likert-type items designed to measure attitudes toward retardation. Some examples:

> Mentally retarded people should never get married.
> 1   2   3   4   5   6   7
> DISAGREE   AGREE

> Our community should establish special community activities for the retarded.
> 1   2   3   4   5   6   7
> DISAGREE   AGREE

Here, too, an individual respondent's attitude was determined by computing his or her mean across all 21 attitude items, and means for each community were computed.

Postmanipulation Measurement

Knowledge Measurement. After the information campaign was concluded, the set of six general knowledge questions used in the premanipulation test was readministered. Again, individual respondent means and community means were computed.

In addition, the posttest contained an additional set of ten knowledge items covering specific information which had been presented in the information campaign. Some examples:

- How many retarded people would ordinarily be in a city of about 5000 people?
- What percentage of the mentally retarded can be trained to go out and make a living?

The answers to these questions were scored as "correct-incorrect" and for each community the percentage of respondents giving correct answers to these questions was determined.

Continued

EXHIBIT 15-1   *Continued*

Information Sources. For each of these ten specific information questions, respondents were asked to identify the source from which that specific information was obtained. They were asked to check as many responses as were appropriate from this list:

> local newspaper
> local radio
> state newspaper
> club meeting
> friends
> other _____ (what was it?)

Attitude Measurement. The posttest contained the same set of 21 Likert-type items, designed to measure attitudes toward retardation, that were on the pretest. Once again, an individual respondent's attitude was determined by computing the mean across all 21 items, and an overall mean for each community was also computed.

Results

Table E15-1 contains a partial listing of the results of this field experiment. This table contains results gleaned from various tables in the original article and does not report results relevant to all the hypotheses which were tested in this field research.

From these results the authors draw the following conclusions: The information campaign had a significant effect on specific information levels. On the average, almost one-half of the respondents in the experimental community correctly answered questions about information provided in the campaign. This proportion is almost twice as large as the proportion in the control community, where only slightly more than one-fourth of the respondents were able to answer these questions correctly.

A different conclusion is drawn about general information levels. The means for the general information items in the two communities after the campaign are not significantly different from one another, nor are they different from the pretest means. It is concluded that the information campaign did not affect knowledge levels beyond those items specifically covered in the campaign.

A final conclusion that can be drawn is that the information campaign positively affected attitudes toward mental retardation. In the experimental community, the difference between the pretest and posttest was significant; in the control condition, no significant shift was detected.

TABLE E15-1   **Knowledge and Attitude Differences Between an Experimental and a Control Community Following a Public Information Campaign**

			Experimental Community	Control Community
A:	General Information			
	Levels:	Before	1.89	2.10
		After	1.66	2.33[a]
B:	Specific Information			
	Levels Average %		48.4%[b]	28.7%
	Correct			
C:	Attitude Levels			
		Before	2.01	2.00
		After	2.16[c]	2.04

[a]Differences between before and after means are not significant.

[b]Seven of 10 items showed significant differences between experimental and control communities.

[c]Significant increase in positive attitudes from before to after.

"Response to an Information Campaign That Changed Community Attitudes," Dorothy F. Douglas, Bruce H. Westley, and Steven H. Chaffee, *Journalism Quarterly,* Autumn 1970, Vol. 47, No. 3 pp. 479–487.

change in the dependent variables, rather than at absolute levels of the dependent variables. This is a form of statistical control. Unfortunately, the premanipulation-postmanipulation design that was chosen introduced the problem of sample mortality, and worse yet, different levels of sample mortality in each community. This problem reduces the internal validity of the study, since it is possible that some of the effects seen are due to systematic attrition of certain types of research subjects (like those who learned little from information campaigns). This reduction in internal validity is the price the researchers paid for conducting their research under conditions that ensured excellent external validity.

A Second Example of Field Research Using the Individual as the Unit of Analysis: The Ellsworth, Carlsmith, and Henson Study of the Effect of Staring on Flight

In this example (Exhibit 15-2), we see how researchers go to great lengths to deal with the problem of reduced internal validity in a field setting by conducting a series of studies to eliminate possible alternative explanations for their results. These alternative explanations, which are symptomatic of poor internal validity, arise because of the inherent lack of control over the setting that field researchers must endure.

Table E15-2 shows the essential results of Experiment 4. The results of the other experiments were reported in the original article in a similar fashion.

Compared to a laboratory experiment, the Ellsworth et al. field experiment must deal with many threats to internal validity. First, there are problems with the sample and the assignment of subjects to experimental conditions.

Although painstaking randomizing procedures were used to select the subjects and to assign them to experimental or control conditions, the basic sample is still not representative of the general population. Only motorists or pedestrians who were on the street at non-rush hours could be used in the field research.

This eliminates most of the working population, who are likely to be in offices or factories at the times when the research was conducted. So while the researchers can state that there was no bias in assignment of subjects to experimental conditions, they cannot state that the subjects are representative of the general population, as there were probably many more students, housewives, retired persons, or unemployed workers used in the research than would appear in a probability sample of the general population.

But the researchers are probably not too worried about this, because it is difficult to see how overrepresentation of these kinds of subjects would change the results. Why would one expect that students or unemployed workers would react differently to a stare than other members of the general population? Although the unrepresentativeness of the sample *could* be a threat to validity, it's hard to see how it *does* obscure the results in this case. If we have no reason to suspect the sample, even though we know it's biased in some way, we can feel a little more comfortable about trusting the results. What's critical is that the bias does not appear to affect the operation of the theoretical process, or the measurement of the dependent variable.

A second noteworthy aspect of this research is the effort taken by the researchers to eliminate alternative explanations for the observed differences between the experimental

EXHIBIT 15-2 **Experimental Field Research: Individual Units of Analysis Reactions to Nonverbal Messages**

General Topic

A series of field experiments were conducted to test the idea that avoidance behavior can be created by the nonverbal communicative act of staring. It was hypothesized that a stare has negative or threatening communicative properties, and that persons who are the object of the stare will try to escape from it. If escape is temporarily impossible, tension may build up and the escape will be more dramatic.

Hypotheses

The general hypothesis tested was that the speed of withdrawal from a situation would be affected by the presence or absence of a stare by a stranger. Specifically, the speed with which a motorist or pedestrian subject crossed an intersection after a red light would be greater when the person had been the object of a stare by another motorist in an adjoining lane, or by a pedestrian standing on the curb next to the subject.

Subjects

Subjects were male and female Caucasians, ranging in age from about 16 to 70, who were driving at a busy intersection in a suburban town in northern California. Subjects were selected in both morning and afternoon hours, but not during rush hours.

General Procedure

The basic procedure involved an assistant who either drove up next to the motorist on a motor scooter, or who stood on the curb next to the driver's side on a one-way street. The assistant selected the motorist to be tested, and either stared at him or her for the duration of the red light (experimental condition) or did not stare (control condition). With a stop watch hidden in a pocket, the assistant timed the duration of the stare and the time it took the motorist to cross the intersection after the light changed. The assistant also recorded the sex and estimated the age of the driver.

Five experiments were conducted to test the basic hypothesis and to eliminate alternative explanations for any increased flight speeds in the experimental condition. Experiment 1 tested the basic hypothesis that the time to cross the intersection would be less in the experimental condition than in the control condition. In this experiment, the assistant rode up next to the driver on a motor scooter and either stared at the motorist (experimental condition) or did not stare (control condition).

Experiment 2 was conducted to test the idea that decreased time was the result of a perception by the motorist that the stare was a challenge to a race. In this experiment, the person doing the staring was on foot on the curb, but other procedures were the same.

Experiment 3 was conducted to test for effects and interactions between the sex of the assistant and the sex of the motorist, as a possible confounding factor affecting the speed of withdrawal.

In Experiment 4, the timing procedure was applied to pedestrians crossing the street, rather than motorists, to further eliminate any possibility that the effects were specific to automotive situations. Pedestrians stopped at the same red light were either stared at, or were not, and the time it took them to cross the street after the light changed was recorded. The data for Experiment 4 are given in Table E15-2.

In Experiment 5, another possible alternative explanation for withdrawal behavior was tested. The alternative explanation rested on the idea that people were withdrawing from an unknown or incongruous type of behavior, rather than reacting to the communicative properties of a stare. In this experiment, the assistant sat on the sidewalk at the intersection and began to pound the pavement with a hammer when a motorist in the experimental condition approached, but the assistant did not stare at the motorist. The motorist's transit time across the intersection was then measured. In this experiment, two additional conditions were used. One was the control condition, where no action was taken by the assistant. In the other condition, the assistant stared at the motorist, rather than pounding concrete.

Continued

EXHIBIT 15-2 *Continued*

TABLE E15-2 **Mean Crossing Time for Experiment 4:**
Eight Experimenters, Pedestrian Subjects

Stare				No Stare			
Male Experimenter		Female Experimenter		Male Experimenter		Female Experimenter	
Subject		Subject		Subject		Subject	
Male	Female	Male	Female	Male	Female	Male	Female
11.1 (23)	10.9 (10)	11.6 (16)	10.9 (17)	12.1 (17)	11.0 (14)	12.8 (17)	12.9 (14)
11.0 (33)		11.2 (33)		11.6 (31)		12.9 (31)	
11.1* (66)				12.2* (62)			

*Means are significantly different from each other. All other differences are not statistically significant. Ns for each group are in parentheses. Copyright 1972 by the American Psychological Association. Reprinted (or adapted) by permission.

Manipulation

The independent variable present in all experiments was the presence or absence of a stare, a nominal variable. In Experiment 3, the additional nominal independent variables of sex of assistant and sex of motorist were added and were systematically manipulated to test for differences between males and females for motorists and for experimental assistants, and for differences due to mixed sex conditions (the assistant and the motorist were of different sexes). In Experiment 5, a new nominal independent variable was introduced, the presence or absence of a novel or incongruous behavior (sitting on the curb and hitting the pavement with a hammer).

To assure nonsystematic assignment of subjects to conditions, the experimental assistants relied on several randomizing procedures. In Experiment 1, the assistant was given a paper with the sequence in which she was to assign the subjects to each condition. Motorists were counted each time the assistant pulled up to the traffic light. The paper, which was constructed with a random numbers table, might have said something like "Stare at the second, third, sixth, eighth, ninth,..." These motorists were the subjects in the experimental condition. The remaining subjects were not stared at, and made up the control condition.

A more elaborate procedure was used in Experiment 4:

Each experimenter had a supply of 16 jelly beans in his/her pocket, 8 each of two different colors. One color signified the stare condition, the other, the no-stare condition. When a potential subject arrived at the crosswalk, the experimenter removed 1 of the jelly beans, noted its color, and ate it. In this manner, a quasi-random assignment of subject to conditions was achieved without the experimenter attracting the attention of the subject and other bystanders by consulting a list.

Dependent Variable Measures

In each experiment, the amount of time for a motorist or pedestrian to cross the intersection was used. This variable is defined at a ratio level of measurement (time in seconds). The research design was postmanipulation only, so only a single measurement of the dependent variable was made.

Results

In all experiments, the time to cross the intersection was shorter in the "stare" conditions than it

Continued

EXHIBIT 15-2   *Continued*

was in the control conditions. This is evidence for the ability of a nonverbal communicative act to produce a flight behavior. The ability of the stare to produce this effect was present in pedestrians, as well as motorists, so it is unlikely that the stare was interpreted as an invitation to race, or in any other way connected to automobiles or the driving situation. Effects for the sex of the motorist and experimental assistant were not significant, indicating that increased speed of departure was probably not due to a desire to impress members of the same or of the opposite sex. In Experiment 5, the flight speed was significantly higher for persons stared at than it was for persons who saw the incongruous behavior of pavement pounding.

"The Stare as a Stimulus to Flight in Human Subjects: A Series of Field Experiments," Phoebe C. Ellsworth, J. Merrill Carlsmith, and Alexander Henson, Journal of Personality and Social Psychology, 1972, Vol. 21, No. 3, pp. 302–311.

and control groups. The researchers examined the possibilities that misinterpretation of the communication might be taking place (with the stare interpreted as a racing challenge or as having some sexual implication), that subjects might simply be reacting to an unusual situation, or that the reaction might occur only when automobiles were involved. By being able to reject each of these alternative explanations, the researchers strengthened the internal validity of the research.

By explicitly including variables like sex of research assistant and subject and incongruity of the situation, the researchers exerted some manipulative control over possibly confounding variables. If they could have observed other variables, they could have used statistical control procedures to remove their effects, further strengthening the internal validity of the research. In fact, in Experiments 1 and 2, the age of the subject was estimated by the research assistant, and the effect of age on flight time was tested. As the researchers found no consistent relationship of age with the dependent variable, they did not consider it in later experiments. But by measuring the variable of age and including it in the analysis, they strengthened their conclusions by eliminating another possible confounding variable.

Example of Field Research Using the Social System as the Unit of Analysis: The Fredin Study of the Effect of Interactive Telecommunication in Schools

The final example of field research (see Exhibit 15-3) illustrates a field experiment with a social system as the unit of analysis. In this research, the basic observations are made of entire school faculties. Data are collected from individuals in the schools, but the data are aggregated to provide variables that apply to schools, and not to the individuals.

It also shows the basic limitations and strengths of field research. The researcher was very constrained in the sample he could use. To try to make the experimental conditions comparable, he matched the units in each group on variables that he thought might affect the relationships that he was testing. The experimental groups are thus neither representative of all work groups, or even of all schools, since there was no random selection from either of these populations. Even assignment to the experimental groups was systematic, rather than random. This was done deliberately, to reduce the chances of random sampling error.

EXHIBIT 15-3 Experimental Field Research: Social System Unit of Analysis Telecommunications in Schools

General Topic

The effects of introducing an interactive cable television system into work groups was investigated. In particular, the role of interpersonal communication on the regulation of diversity of new ideas within the groups is examined. Interpersonal communication can either suppress or enhance the diversity of new ideas, depending upon the amount of shared information and ideas within the interpersonal communication network. Interactive telecommunication has been expected to increase the diversity of new ideas in societies, but the author argues that effects of interpersonal communication in regulating diversity of ideas make this result more complex.

In this research, the introduction of specialized two-way interactive and one-way broadcast cable technology in elementary school systems was studied. Television programs which presented new ideas or innovations in elementary school teaching were produced by the teachers themselves, and broadcast to participating schools. These broadcasts then probably served as gist for interpersonal discussion of teaching methods and materials.

Hypotheses

Because of the conflicting predictions about the ways in which interpersonal communication might regulate diversity, the researchers used a general, nondirectional hypothesis: Work groups (in this case, elementary school faculties) using an interactive cable communication system will show a different amount of "intermediation" (a characteristic of an interpersonal communication network which is defined below) than will groups not using the system.

Units of Analysis

Instead of looking at individual faculty members within each school, the researchers defined their variables at a social system or group level of analysis. The basic unit was the school. Each school was characterized on its amount of intermediation and the diversity of discussion of new ideas about teaching in the school.

Definition and Measurement of Variables

Diversity of new ideas was measured by a simple procedure: Individual faculty members in the schools were asked to fill out a questionnaire which contained the question:

> *Are there any ideas or methods you've seen or heard about during the past school year about different ways elementary school teachers might do their work?*

The responses were content analyzed (see Chapter 18 for a description of this measurement procedure), and the total number of different responses given by each faculty member was recorded.

To move this individual-level measurement to the social system level, the researchers took the average value of the individual diversity scores for each school. This aggregated value then represented the diversity of new ideas score for the basic unit of analysis, the school.

Intermediation was defined as a group property, and so it was operationally defined directly at the social system level. In groups with high levels of intermediation, most group members are involved in talking to most other group members. In groups with low levels of intermediation, only a few group members communicate with all other group members, or communication is limited to discussion within small subgroups.

The basic measurement used to detect intermediation was a variation of the sociogram. This technique asks members of a group to rate all other members of a group on some characteristic. In this case, it was the amount of communication that occurred between the person filling out the sociogram, and other members of the group:

> *I am going to hand you a list of people who work at your school. Please go through the list and put an "X" by each person you discuss teaching ideas with at least once a week.*

The data were used to compute an intermediation score for each school by a fairly complex opera-

Continued

EXHIBIT 15-3 *Continued*

tional definition. We'll reproduce it here to show how complex ideas like intermediation can be defined by mathematical operational definitions:

$$I = ((H - L) + C) \cdot M$$

Where

> H is the number of individuals in a school who were named by others two or more times more frequently than the median faculty member in the school.

> L is the number of individuals in a school who were named by others two or fewer times less frequently than the median faculty member in the school.

> C is a constant chosen so that all $(H - L)$ values are positive.

> M is the maximum value found in a school for the ratio of the number of times an individual was named by others to the total number of times he or she could have been named.

Manipulation

There were 41 schools included in this study. The schools were split into three groups: 14 schools which were provided with two-way interactive cable systems that teachers could use to view programs, respond to them, and interact with other viewers; a second group of 12 schools which received only broadcast versions of the same programs in which no interaction was possible; and the remaining 15 schools which received neither, and were the control group. Schools were matched across groups for racial makeup and for median adult education levels. Each group of schools represented a class of the nominal independent factor: the type of communication system.

Results

Support was found for the basic hypothesis. Intermediation was found to significantly decrease the diversity of new ideas in the control schools. That is, increased levels of discussion apparently produced some type of consensus which reduced the number of ideas that were actually discussed. But in both the one-way and two-way cable schools, the relationship between interpersonal communication and the diversity of ideas discussed was not statistically significant. Further tests showed that the control group correlation was significantly different from both of the cable groups' correlations, and the cable groups' correlations were not significantly different from each other. In the schools in which cable was introduced, the author speculates, the effect of introducing new ideas via television programs spurred discussion, which counteracted the negative effect of higher levels of intermediation. This produced correlations which were not significantly different from zero, as shown in Table E15-3.

According to the theoretical linkage provided by the researchers, the effects should have been greater for two-way cable than for one-way broadcasts. The correlations for these two groups were in the predicted direction, but the difference was not large enough to be significant. This may have been due to the low power of the test caused by the small number of units of analysis (small N). If you remember the discussion of power in Chapter 12, you'll recall that tests with small numbers of observations are prone to have high Type 2 (β) errors, where the researcher finds no evidence for a relationship, when one actually exists. If the researcher could have included more schools in this study, his hypothesis might have been supported more fully.

TABLE E15-3   Correlations Between Intermediation and Diversity of New Ideas

Type of Communication System					
Two-Way ($N = 14$)		One-Way ($N = 12$)		Control ($N = 15$)	
Correlation	Significance	Correlation	Significance	Correlation	Significance
.32	.14	-.25	.31	-.53	.006

"The Context of Communication: Interactive Telecommunication, Interpersonal Communication, and Their Effect on Ideas," Eric S. Fredin, *Communication Research,* 1983, Vol. 10, No. 4, pp. 553–581.

This kind of sample raises some potentially troubling questions about the internal validity of the research. Could the results be simply due to the nature of the schools assigned to each group, or to peculiarities of the schools in the single town in which the research was conducted? To the degree we are unsure of the answer to this question, we are questioning the internal validity of the study.

Limitations on the sample were amplified by the choice of the social system unit of analysis. By using whole schools as the basic unit, the researcher needed to exert much more effort to obtain a single observation, and the number of possible observations (schools) was limited by geographic and cost considerations. But since the basic theory dealt with the response of social systems (work groups) this choice of unit of analysis was warranted.

On the positive side, the experimental setting is very generalizable (at least to other schools). Teachers used the communication system in ways that were completely natural. There were no restraints on the operation of other relevant processes—teachers still had to budget their time to meet classes, grade papers, and do all their other work, so they gave no excessive amount of attention to the communication system, as they might have done in a laboratory experiment. Interpersonal communication with other teachers was also done under natural conditions.

Another typical difficulty associated with field research is illustrated in this example. Although interpersonal communication is central to the theory being tested, it is not directly observed. The researcher directly measured only the frequency of communication contacts between persons in the groups, and not content of communication. This forced him to speculate about the nature of the interpersonal communication that occurred, rather than being able to observe it and describe it.

But one thing that gives field research good external validity is the absence of an experimenter peering over the subjects' shoulders while the research is in progress. This has the negative effect of limiting the detail with which the researcher can describe the communication process, while at the same time ensuring that the process occurs naturally.

Summary

Field research uses the designs of experimental research, but applies them outside the laboratory. Changing the setting of the research generally increases the *external validity* (generalizability) of the results, but often at the expense of *internal validity*. A major problem with field research lies in the representativeness of the sample. Field research subjects are frequently chosen for pragmatic reasons, rather than with probability sampling procedures. Field researchers must often work with subjects who are available, rather than those who are clearly representative of the population. This problem is intensified when social system units of analysis are used.

Another problem lies in the *lack of control* over factors that may confound the results. Communication processes are allowed to occur under natural conditions, and sometimes these messy conditions can obscure the real relationships among research variables. The researcher often cannot observe the communication process in as much detail in a field study as would be possible in an experiment. However, part of the reason for providing a natural setting for the research lies in removing the intrusive observations or measurement that provide the researcher with more detail about the process.

These limitations are accepted by the field researcher, in return for the increased confidence in the results that the natural settings provide. This improved external validity permits the researcher to state that any relationships observed in the research study are probably true reflections of the real world.

A good field research design will attempt to minimize the problems with internal validity, while retaining the benefits of the improved external validity. Sample matching, use of random assignment procedures for experimental groups, unobtrusive observation, and measurement of relevant unmanipulated variables (for example, subjects' age and sex) are all important to good field research design.

In fact, the points soon to be made about statistical control in unmanipulated designs can also be applied to field research. In the next chapter, we'll see that measurement and statistical control of relevant variables can be used as a substitute for manipulated control. Use of these techniques in field research can alleviate to some extent the loss of internal validity which a researcher must accept in order to obtain the improved external validity provided by a field research design.

References and Additional Readings

Achen, C. H. (1986). *The statistical analysis of quasi-experiments.* Berkeley, CA: University of California Press (Chapter 1, "Experiments and Quasi-experiments").

Campbell, D. T. & Stanley, J. C. (1966). *Experimental and quasi-experimental designs for research.* Chicago: Rand-McNally.

Cook, T. D. & Campbell, D. T. (1979). *Quasi-experimentation: Design and analysis issues for field settings.* Chicago: Rand-McNally.

Fiedler, J. (1978). *Field research.* San Francisco: Jossey-Bass (Chapter 1 "Planning for Field Operations"; Chapter 2 "Research Sites and Settings").

Wimmer, R. D. & Dominick, J. R. (1987). *Mass media research: An introduction* (2nd ed.). Belmont, CA: Wadsworth. (Chapter 7, "Field Research and Related Research Methods").

Chapter *16*

Natural Environments: Observational Research

The last major class of research design that we'll examine is observational research. Designs for observational research may be used in laboratories, but they are most frequently used in natural settings. The major difference between observational research and the experimental research described in the previous two chapters lies in lack of manipulation of the independent or causal variable. The researcher relies on "natural processes" to provide different levels (variance) in the independent variable, and simply *observes* simultaneous changes in both the independent and dependent variables.

The researcher may use an observational design because there is no other choice. *Historical* or *retrospective* studies offer no possibility for manipulating the independent variable, as the variables being observed have all had their values fixed sometime in the past. For example, if a researcher wishes to relate the childhood family communication patterns of adults to their current levels of marital adjustment, an experimental design (which would systematically manipulate childhood communication) is out of the question. Ethical issues may also prohibit manipulation of the independent variable. One could not deliberately create brain lesions in subjects in order to study the effects of left-hemisphere damage on nonverbal communication.

Because the system of variables being studied is allowed to operate with no intervention, the external validity of observational designs is usually very high. On the other side of the coin, the lack of control over the independent variable (because there is no direct, systematic manipulation of the causal variable by the researcher) and the uncontrolled effects of the environment on the dependent variable (because these designs are frequently applied in the field), mean that the internal validity of observational research is often very low. Lack of control for confounding variables (as we saw in Chapter 3) may mean that it is difficult to distinguish between a true relationship and a spurious or indirect one.

This difficulty is less critical in applied research situations where the primary objective is prediction of the outcome, rather than explanation of the theoretical process. For example, suppose a researcher's primary objective is to predict the readership of a new magazine. To do this, the researcher examines the demographic characteristics of the likely audience, using variables like age, sex, geographic region, and so on, and relates these to the readership of an existing magazine with similar content. A reasonable assumption is that readers with demographic characteristics similar to the readers of the existing magazine will want to read the new magazine when it appears. By measuring the number of persons with these characteristics in the population to be reached by the new magazine, the researcher can predict its initial readership.

The demographic variables describe the kinds of persons who read the existing magazine, and enable the researcher to predict the number who are likely to choose to read the new magazine. But they will not explain *why* readers of a particular age, sex, or region choose to read either of the magazines. Perhaps older readers like the magazines because they have more experience with the topics addressed in the articles. If this is so, the relationship between age and readership is spurious, even though there is covariance between the two variables.

The true causal variable is amount of experience that the reader has had with the topics covered in the articles. If all readers were the same age, those who had more experience with the topics would be more likely to read the magazine. But if the only objective is to predict the readership in the real world, and since the population contains readers of differing ages (and thus of differing experience), this finding may not be of particular interest to the applied researcher. Age will be an adequate predictor.

But the scientist who wishes to go beyond simple prediction, and *explain* phenomena with observational designs must take pains to eliminate competing explanations of the relationship. The confidence which can be placed in the conclusions of an observational study is directly proportional to the elimination of competing explanations or spurious relationships.

It is never possible to eliminate all competing explanations for the observed changes in the dependent variable, so there is always the possibility that the covariance between two observed variables is spurious. Some people take this fact as evidence for the superiority of the experimental design, where spurious relationships can be eliminated by either manipulated control or randomization. But experiments frequently suffer from poor external validity, so there is a definite trade-off that the researcher must consider. A well-designed observational study which measures relevant confounding variables and uses statistical control to eliminate their effects could very well be superior to a tightly controlled experiment that does not generalize to the real world.

Typical Observational Research Designs

The basic research designs are very simple compared to the experimental designs outlined in the previous chapters. Fundamentally, the researcher simply observes the naturally occurring values of the independent and dependent variables, and uses statistical methods to find out whether they covary. If the observation can be done without intruding on the ordinary behavior of the research subjects, the false responses that might be introduced by the manipulative research procedures are removed. This improves the external validity.

But the problems with the internal validity of observational research that we mentioned above mean that the research designs are very susceptible to confusion between the true effect of an independent variable and the spurious effects of other uncontrolled variables. Table 16-1 shows some threats to validity for the observational designs. If you compare it with the other tables for research designs in the previous chapters, you'll see that there are more potential internal validity problems and fewer external validity problems.

The research designs described in Table 16-1 are both one-time-point, or "snapshot" designs. This is similar to the post-only experimental design described in Chapter 14, but differs from the two-time-point pre-post designs. Single time-point measurement is not susceptible to measurement learning effects, sensitization, history and maturation, subject mortality, and other threats to validity that occur over time. Multiple time-point observational research studies are somewhat more complex. These designs are covered in the next chapter. However, some of the threats to validity, like history and maturation, may confound one-time-point results, because the outside variables involved in history or maturation may produce spurious effects on the dependent variable.

The two major single-time-point designs are the simple observational design and the group comparison observational design. They differ in one fundamental way. In the simple observational design, a random representative sample is drawn from the population, and both independent and dependent variables are measured. Only a relationship hypothesis can be tested in this design. The statistic used to test the hypothesis will quantify any systematic covariance between observed levels of the independent and dependent variables. This might be a contingency table for nominal variables, or a correlation coefficient for interval or ratio variables (see Chapter 19).

In the group comparison observational design, the sample is divided into two or more groups according to the measured value of the independent variable. A comparative hypothesis is tested in this design, using a statistic that contrasts the groups on the observed levels of the dependent variable. Z- or t-tests, or analysis of variance F-ratios might be used to test these hypotheses (again, see Chapter 19 for an outline of these statistical tests).

There is a subtle, but critical, difference between the effects of random assignment of subjects in an experiment and the random selection of observations in an observational study. In an experiment, randomization ensures that the effects of outside factors are approximately equivalent among all the experimental groups, and thus eliminates any systematic effects of these outside factors. But in an observational design, the random assignment is used to ensure that the influence of the factors is the same in the study as it is in the real world. Randomization in observational designs will not remove the influence of external factors, but it will ensure that the external validity of the study is good.

The group comparison design also uses random selection of observations, but the assignment to comparison groups is then done on a nonrandom basis. This nonrandom assignment means that the comparison groups may differ on factors other than the variable used for the assignment. For example, suppose the independent variable X is age, and the dependent variable Y is the amount of usage of electronic mail. If the randomly sampled observations are assigned to two groups on the basis of age (young and old), the groups will probably be unequal on other variables that are associated with age. The older group

TABLE 16-1 Threats to Validity: Observational Research Designs

Simple Observational	R:	X	Y	(Observed Group)
		A		
		B		
		C...		[Control Variables]
Group Comparison Observational	S:	X	Y	(Observed Group)
		A		
	R:	B		
		C...		[Control Variables]
	S:	X	Y	(Control or Comparison Group)
		A		
		B		
		C...		[Control Variables]

	Simple Observational	Group Comparison Observational
INTERNAL VALIDITY		
Instrumentation Reliability and Validity	?	?
Selection (Sampling)	−	+
Instrument Obtrusiveness	?	?
Manipulation Effectiveness	−	−
History	?	?
Maturation	?	?
Measurement Sensitization	−	−
Measurement Instrument Learning	?	?
Measurement Instrument Instability	−	+
Subject Mortality	−	−
Subject Fatigue	?	?
Treatment or Measurement Order Effects	?	?
EXTERNAL VALIDITY		
Representative Sample	−	−
Reactive Effects of Setting	−	−
Multiple Treatment Interference	−	−
Reactive Sensitization	−	−
Subject Mortality	−	+

Additional Notation for Observational Research Designs
Y   Measurement of the dependent or effect variable
X   Measurement of the independent or cause variable
R: Random sampling or selection of units of analysis
S: Systematic assignment or selection of units of analysis
    based on level of the independent variable
A, B, C... Measurement of confounding variables which affect the
    dependent or effect variable

Other notation is described in Table 14-1.

will probably have a higher income (an outside variable A). This could affect electronic mail usage, since an individual with a higher income could afford the cost of the service, and is more likely to be a manager to whom quick communication is necessary. In order to avoid confounding the effects of income with those of age, the income levels in both groups must be measured and statistically controlled. Statistical control is as important in comparative designs as it is in simple observational designs.

Observational measurement is often done "unobtrusively." This means that the units of analysis (individuals, groups, organizations, etc.) are not affected by the process of observation. In fact, they may not be even be aware that the research is being conducted. When this is the case, the effects of the research setting, like reactions to the laboratory setting, social demand responses, and especially measurement instrument obtrusiveness, are removed. Some typical procedures for unobtrusive measurement are covered in Chapter 18.

In either basic observational design, it is crucial that all confounding variables be measured and controlled statistically. Statistical control is the primary form of control exerted in observational designs.

Statistical Control Requirements

As we mentioned in Chapters 4 and 13, statistical control can be used as a partial solution to the problem posed by spurious relationships. But statistical control carries a large requirement: recognition, definition, and measurement of *all* relevant variables which might confound the relationship between the independent and dependent variables. Since we can never be sure that we've recognized all the confounding variables, we can never be absolutely sure that the covariance we find between the independent and dependent variables is not spurious.

Statistical control also requires more complicated statistical analysis procedures than we've discussed so far. Instead of dealing with just two variables (the independent and dependent variables), the researcher might have to account for the effects of dozens of confounding independent variables which must be controlled. In essence, the confounding variables must be introduced into the research design as additional independent variables.

In plain words, multivariate statistical procedures are required. This opens a wide and sometimes scary world where data wizards and gurus lurk and perform feats of dazzling inference (and sometimes statistical sleight-of-hand). But all the wonderful technology and arcane vocabulary exist only to serve one purpose: control of confounding effects, so that the hypotheses that the researcher creates from theoretical reasoning can be tested and generalized.

Statistical control can sometimes be done simply by partitioning the data into sub-samples in which the confounding outside variables are held constant. In our study of use of electronic mail, we could control for the effect of income by separating the sample into several income groups—like low, middle, high—and examining the relationship between age and E-mail use within each constant income group. This is simple, but requires a large number of observations, particularly when the number of outside variables that have to be held constant is large. More complex statistics like partial correlation and regression that do the job of controlling the effects of outside variables are usually more efficient. But they also require measurement of the concepts at the interval or ratio level. Multivariate statistical control of nominal and ordinal variables is possible, but it is involved. We'll mention some of the multivariate procedures that can do the job of statistical control at different levels of measurement in Chapter 19.

The prescription for research design of observational studies is clear. Define, at the highest level possible, all the relevant variables that your theoretical reasoning says might affect the dependent variable. Then measure them at this high level (ratio or interval, if possible, rather than nominal or ordinal). The complexity of the required multivariate statistical procedures will be reduced by higher levels of measurement.

Examples of Observational Research in Communication

The following examples illustrate observational designs applied to different units of analysis. The first example is a study conducted with the individual as the unit of analysis.

Example of Observational Research Using the Individual as the Unit of Analysis: Gerbner's "Mean World" and Cultivation Analysis

The Gerbner study described in Exhibit 16-1 used a simple observational design. The variables in the study are defined as occurring within the individual: The independent variable is the amount of time spent viewing television, and the dependent variable is the similarity between the person's view of social reality and the view shown by television. The independent variable is not manipulated. It is observed directly by asking the child viewers how much time they spend with television.

between the amount of

Many factors may work to produce differences in the amount of time spent viewing. This makes random selection of the observations very important, so that sample bias is not introduced, because the factors that affect viewing time may also affect the viewer's perception of social reality. This is why Gerbner's group measured and statistically controlled for the viewer's sex, age, socioeconomic status, IQ, and so on. Each of these could be a confounding variable, and the effect of each must be removed before the researcher can attribute differing social views to the time spent with television.

Since the relationship between viewing time and having a social view which corresponded to that provided by television persisted when the competing explanations for this relationship were controlled, Gerbner concluded that television was cultivating a view of the world as being a much more violent place than it was in reality. Gerbner's critics, however, pointed to other unmeasured variables as possible confounding sources of the relationship. Because they were unmeasured, they could not be statistically controlled. This weakens somewhat the confidence which can be placed in the findings.

On the positive side, the viewing studied by Gerbner took place under natural conditions. Exposure to programming occurred before the child knew that a research project was being conducted, so the research and measurement procedures could not have modified the viewing conduct of the research subject. Viewing was done in the home, not in a laboratory, so all the real world distractions, conversations, parental restriction on program choice,

EXHIBIT 16-1   Observational Research: Individual Units of Analysis Gerbner's "Mean World" and Cultivation Analysis

General Topic

Gerbner and associates developed a theory of media effects that states that media "cultivate" a particular view of society which may differ from reality. By providing a distorted picture of society, the media cultivate a similarly distorted sense of social reality in the audience members.

In a series of studies, Gerbner used content analysis of television programming to describe the kinds of situations and social behaviors that characterized the "television world." Content analysis is a technique that uses a message unit of analysis, like the "program," rather than an individual unit of analysis. An example of a content analysis is described in Exhibit 16-3.

Gerbner's research team related media content to perceptions of social reality, in order to test the idea that the media affect the audience's general view of their society.

Hypotheses

The cultivation hypothesis for television can be stated in general terms like this:

H_R: *The greater the amount of time spent viewing television, the more similar the person's view of reality will be to the view presented by television programming as a whole.*

This hypothesis can only be tested when the events shown on television differ in frequency from those that occur in reality. If there is no difference, the viewer's perception of reality could be formed either by direct experience or by television viewing.

Operational Definition and Methods

Gerbner found a number of differences between the media depictions and the real world frequency of occurrence of acts such as violent crimes. Using this information, his research team constructed a number of questions that had a "TV answer" and a "real world answer" and asked a sample of

children to respond. A typical question might look like this:

During any given week, what are your chances of being involved in some kind of violence? About 1 in 10 or about 1 in 100.

The first answer was the TV answer as acts of violence appeared in programming far more frequently than they appear in reality (the actual probability of being involved in violence was about 1 in 200). By asking a number of these questions, and adding up the number of times the viewer gave TV answers, a variable which measured the overlap between the viewer's view of reality and the (false) TV depiction of that reality was constructed.

Time spent viewing television was measured directly by asking viewers to estimate their amount of viewing.

Results

Table E16-1 summarizes one of the tests of the general hypothesis. It also uses a partial correlation coefficient to describe the size of the relationship between viewing time and the number of TV answers given. (See Chapters 11 and 12 for details about correlation coefficients.) A partial correlation coefficient is a version of the Pearson correlation coefficient which describes the size of a relationship in which the effects of other confounding variables are held constant. This allows the researcher to eliminate these variables as potential causes.

Like the correlation coefficient, partial correlation coefficients range from -1.0 (a perfect negative relationship) to +1.0 (a perfect positive relationship), with 0.0 indicating a null relationship. Table E16-1 shows that there is a significant relationship between the amount of viewing and the tendency of children to give TV answers, rather than real world answers. The relationship persists even when the age, IQ, and sex of the child, the amount of newspaper reading done by the child, and the family's socioeconomic status are held constant. In other words, all differences due to these variables are re-

Continued

EXHIBIT 16-1   *Continued*

moved from the estimate of the size of the relationship, and it still is positive enough that we can
conclude that it is very unlikely that this result occurred simply by random sampling error. It appears

that TV viewing is related to a child's incorrect view
of reality that is consistent with the incorrect view
presented by television.

**TABLE E16-1   Relationship Between Amount of TV Viewing
and Number of "TV Answers" to Questions
About Violence and Law Enforcement Given
by Children**

Variable Controlled	Partial Correlation	Significance
None	.16	$p < .001$
Sex of Child	.15	$p < .001$
Age of Child	.16	$p < .001$
Newspaper Reading	.16	$p < .001$
Father's Education (Socioeconomic Status)	.15	$p < .001$
IQ	.13	$p < .001$
All Controls	.12	$p < .004$

$N = 466$ children in New Jersey

"TV Violence Profile No. 8: The Highlights," George Gerbner, Larry Gross, Michael F. Eleey, Marilyn Jackson-Beeck, Suzanne
Jeffries-Fox, and Nancy Signorielli, *Journal of Communication,* Spring 1977, Vol. 27, pp. 171–180.
"Cultural Indicators: Violence Profile No. 9," George Gerbner, Larry Gross, Marilyn Jackson-Beeck, Suzanne Jeffries-Fox, and
Nancy Signorielli, *Journal of Communication,* Summer 1978, Vol. 28, pp. 176–207.

and so on, were present. This gives credence to the claim that the relationship found in the
research study is also present in the general population. A laboratory experiment would
have controlled both the amount of viewing, and the conditions under which viewing took
place. This control would have strengthened the conclusions, as many additional alternative explanations could have been ruled out, but it would have also been subject to the
criticism that the effects observed would only occur under artificial laboratory conditions
and are not present in the real world.

The Gerbner study also illustrates a common and important situation in communication
research. Television programming is described with a content analysis that uses a message
unit of analysis. As an example, the results of the content analysis found that 64 percent
of TV characters were involved with violence. How can this finding about messages be
related to the individual viewers, who are the primary units of analysis?

The common way is by introducing the bridging concept of *individual exposure* to the
message. In the Gerbner study this was done indirectly, by measuring the amount of time
spent watching all TV programming. It was inferred that more time spent watching ("being
exposed to…") all programming would automatically lead to more exposure to depictions
of violence. In other studies of media violence, this exposure measurement has been done
more directly. A researcher might count the acts of violence in a number of programs (the

message unit of analysis), then ask the individual which programs he/she regularly views. A "violence viewing" score for the individual could then be constructed by adding the average number of acts of violence in each of the programs to which the subject reports being exposed. The violence viewing score is at the individual level of analysis, so it can be related to other individual level variables, such as attitudes or aggressive behaviors.

It is not possible to relate directly a variable with one unit of analysis to a variable with a differing unit of analysis. One must always use some reconceptualization device like "exposure" to bridge the different levels.

Example of Observational Research Using the Social System as the Unit of Analysis: Steeves's Study on Coorientation in Small Groups

Unlike the Gerbner research, the Steeves study described in Exhibit 16-2 uses variables that require combined measurement of two or more individuals. This makes the social system the unit of analysis. It is not possible to assign an agreement score to a single individual, as agreement is defined as the relationship between measurements made on two individuals.

Like all observational studies, there was no manipulation of the independent variable. The amount of communication was allowed to take on natural values without researcher intervention.

The basic design was the simple observational study. Although the measurements were taken over a number of weeks, time is actually being used to represent the amount of communication. If there was a direct measurement of the amount of communication made within different groups, this would be a snapshot study. However, the measurement procedure introduces some of the problems and threats to validity that occur with over-time research. These are discussed in detail in the next chapter.

Steeves apparently concluded that there were no serious confounding variables that might produce a spurious relationship, as she did not use statistical control for any outside variables in her analysis. This decision might be open to some criticism. But it is difficult to think of variables other than communication which would affect accuracy, agreement, or congruency. In the absence of plausible competing explanations for change in the dependent variables, the researcher can conclude that all relevant variables have been measured, and the likelihood of the relationship being spurious is not great.

Example of Observational Research Using the Message as the Unit of Analysis: Stempel's Study of the Prestige Press

Stempel's content analysis is a very common kind of observational study. It uses a group comparison observational design which is unobtrusive, as the coverage was measured retrospectively. Unlike the prototype design shown in Table 16-1, the units of analysis were not chosen randomly. Stempel essentially defined the prestige press as consisting of the newspapers listed in Table E16-3. He thus conducted a census of the units, so no sample bias was introduced.

EXHIBIT 16-2   Observational Research: Social System Units of Analysis Changes in Group Communication Relationships Over Time

General Topic

Coorientation variables describe some aspects of the relationship between two or more persons. The common variables are *accuracy, agreement,* and *congruency* (defined below). In the simplest form, they are obtained by comparing the answers to similar questions asked of two persons (we'll call them A and B) who have communicated about some topic (called *X*).

The amount of communication among the group members is expected to affect the coorientation variables. This study investigated the effects of communication over a time period in a small group of students working on laboratory assignments. It was essentially methodological and exploratory, but some theoretical propositions were tested.

Units of Analysis

Since the variables are defined by the relationship between the two sets of answers, the unit of analysis is not the individual, but is the dyad, or pair of participants in the communication. A or B can also be defined as social systems rather than individuals. In this research A was an individual, but B was defined as the "other members of the group," which is a social system unit. Treating a social system as if it is a composite individual is called "reifying" the group.

Definition of Variables

Accuracy is defined as the degree of similarity between the way that participant A describes participant B's view of some topic *X*, and the actual way that participant B views *X*. If A can describe B's view, A is accurate.

Agreement is the similarity between A's view of *X* and B's view of *X*. If both participants see *X* similarly, they agree.

Congruency is similarity between participant A's view of X, and participant A's description of participant B's view of *X*. If A *thinks* B views *X* the same way that A views it, there is congruency (even if A is inaccurate and B actually views *X* differently).

Hypotheses

There were several issues addressed in this study. We will focus on one: the effect of the amount of communication on the three coorientation variables.

Increases in the amount of communication are expected to improve accuracy, as both participants in the communication episode are more able to understand the other's perceptions. More communication should also increase the amount of agreement, as group members influence each other toward some common view of *X*. If the preceding two conditions are correct, communication would be expected to improve congruency, too. More communication will lead to more agreement, and to a more accurate perception of this agreement. These changes, in turn, increase congruency.

In this study, time is used as a surrogate variable for amount of communication (a surrogate variable is one that is correlated very strongly with an unmeasured variable, and is used in place of the unmeasured variable, usually because it is more convenient to measure). As time increases, it is presumed, so does the amount of communication among group members. Stated more formally in terms of time, the hypotheses are:

> H_1: *As time increases, so does the amount of accuracy in the dyad.*
> H_2: *As time increases, so does the amount of agreement in the dyad.*
> H_3: *If H_1 and H_2 are correct, as time increases, so does the amount of congruency in the dyad.*

Operational Definitions and Methods

The topics (*X*) were defined as a series of attributes of the group as a whole, like trust, initiative, intimacy, and so on. For example, to measure A's coorientation about trust, he/she would be asked two questions like this:

How trusting do you think your group is?

1	2	3	4	5	<u>6</u>	7
Very Little					Very Much	

Continued

EXAMPLE 16-2 *Continued*

How trusting do you think other members of your group think the group is?

1	2	3	4	<u>5</u>	6	7
Very Little					Very Much	

To measure agreement, person A's answer to the second question (say, 5) is compared to the average of all the other group members' responses to the first question (say, 4.3). The difference (.70) is actually "disagreement" and it can be subtracted from 7 to give an agreement score of 6.3 for person A:

$$Agreement_A = 7 - (5 - 4.3) = 6.3$$

To measure accuracy, person A's answer to the first question (6) is compared to the average of all other group members' responses to the first question, and the difference subtracted from 7:

$$Accuracy_A = 7 - (6 - 4.3) = 5.3$$

To measure congruency, person A's answer to the first question (5) is subtracted from person A's answer to the second question (6), and the difference subtracted from 7:

$$Congruency_A = 7 - (6 - 5) = 6$$

A 12-member group which met weekly for 15 weeks was used to provide data for testing the hypotheses. At each group meeting, each member was given 16 to 17 items similar to the ones shown above.

The items were varied from week to week, to minimize sensitization of the group members to particular attributes, but all attributes were measured several times during the 15-week period. Average values of accuracy, agreement, and congruency at 10 time points over the 15-week period were computed from the scales for a number of different attributes. An analysis of variance (see Chapter 19) was used to test the relationship between time (the session number, 1 to 10) and each of the coorientation variables.

Results

As hypothesized, accuracy, agreement, and congruency about the group attributes increased with time. Table E16-2 shows these results. The *F*-value, with its associated degrees of freedom, is the inferential statistic used to test for the significance of the relationship. It is related to the *z*-statistic described in Chapter 12, and, like that statistic, it is used to describe the probability that the relationship is due to sampling error. Table E16-2 shows that the probability of the relationship between time and changes in the coorientation variables being due to chance (random sampling error) is less than 5 percent.

Since the total amount of communication within the group also increased with time, it was concluded that communication produces improvements in the accuracy, agreement, and congruency of group members.

TABLE E16-2   Relationship of Time to Change in Coorientation Variables

Coorientation Variable	F-Value	Degrees of Freedom	Significance
Accuracy	9.04	1;1220	$p < .05$
Agreement	5.17	1;1297	$p < .05$
Congruency	5.40	1;1219	$p < .05$

"Developing Coorientation Measures for Small Groups," H. Leslie Steeves, *Communication Monographs,* June 1984 Vol. 51, pp. 185–192.

EXHIBIT 16-3   Observational Research: Message Units of Analysis
Newspaper Coverage of Political Campaigns

General Topic

The basic research question concerned the fairness of the coverage which the leading newspapers in the United States gave to the 1968 presidential campaign. This campaign was conducted at a time when the electorate was polarized over the Vietnam War issue and other social issues which arose from the Civil Rights movement and the Johnson administration's War on Poverty. George Wallace's American Independent Party challenged the Republican candidate, Richard Nixon, and the Democratic candidate, Hubert Humphrey.

Stempel had conducted content analyses of newspapers during the 1960 and 1964 campaigns. He found very little difference in the amount of coverage given to each of the two major party candidates in that election, even though the pattern of editorial endorsements for president was disproportionally for the Republican candidate in 1960 (Richard Nixon) and for the Democratic candidate in 1964 (Lyndon Johnson).

Stempel did not analyze the "tone" of the coverage. Rather, he measured the amount of space devoted to stories about each candidate. The addition of the Wallace candidacy in 1968, coupled with some very passionate feelings about the state of the country and some very important differences among the candidates, raised real questions about the nature of media coverage.

Hypotheses

No formal hypotheses were stated. The research question about fairness in amount of coverage did imply a null hypothesis, however: There is no difference between the mean amounts of coverage given to the Democratic and Republican candidates. The third-party candidate was not expected to have an equivalent amount of coverage. An additional research question concerned the relationship between an editorial endorsement by a newspaper,

and the amount of coverage given that candidate. The implied research hypothesis is this: The amount of newspaper coverage will be higher for endorsed candidates than for unendorsed candidates. Finally, a research question about the change in coverage over time produced this implied nondirectional null hypothesis: There will be no difference in amount of coverage in this election, as compared to past elections.

General Procedure

The newspaper (an aggregate message unit) was the unit of analysis. Amount of space in column inches (one inch of type in a standard newspaper column width) was measured for each story in the newspaper. The editorial endorsement made by each newspaper was also recorded. All stories from September 3 to November 4, 1968, in 15 major newspapers were measured.

Results

The results were presented as summary tables of descriptive statistics. A typical summary is shown in Table E16-3. The Democratic and Republican candidates received very similar amounts of coverage, and the differences from an even split were not significant. There was very little change in the percentages from election to election, so no evidence for changes in coverage proportions due to a changing political climate or the entry of a third party was seen. However, analyzing the endorsements and the amount of coverage from all three elections showed that newspapers were much more likely (29 out of 37 times) to give more coverage to candidates whom they endorsed. The difference in coverage between the endorsed and unendorsed candidate in these cases was small, but the pattern of giving more space to the candidate of choice was statistically significant (p .001).

The general conclusions were that the coverage between the major parties was well-balanced. How

Continued

EXHIBIT 16-3   *Continued*

ever, the political preference of the newspaper apparently was associated with a tendency to cover the endorsed candidate slightly more than the unendorsed candidate. This was considered a covariance relationship, and no causal inference was drawn.

TABLE E16-3   Percentage of Space for Each Party, 1960, 1964, 1968

	1960		1964		1968		
	Dem	*Rep*	*Dem*	*Rep*	*Dem*	*Rep*	*AIP*
Atlanta Constitution	60.2	39.8	53.0	47.0	36.4	34.6	29.0
Baltimore Sun	52.8	47.2	52.2	47.8	41.5	39.5	19.0
Chicago Daily News	48.8	51.6	53.9	46.1	39.0	33.9	27.1
Chicago Tribune	40.8	59.2	34.4	65.6	37.0	45.9	17.0
Christian Science Monitor	41.5	58.5	48.9	51.1	37.2	32.9	29.9
Des Moines Register	45.8	54.2	50.5	49.5	36.9	42.1	20.9
Kansas City Star	52.2	47.8	54.4	45.6	36.0	37.1	26.8
Los Angeles Times	45.2	54.8	49.9	50.1	48.1	32.7	19.1
Louisville Courier-Journal	54.5	45.5	57.8	42.2	39.4	30.2	30.4
Miami Herald	51.3	48.7	59.4	40.6	39.3	35.0	25.7
Milwaukee Journal	54.4	45.6	51.0	49.0	42.7	37.5	19.8
New York Times	50.3	49.7	57.0	43.0	43.9	38.0	18.0
St. Louis Post-Dispatch	54.6	45.4	52.0	48.0	44.2	36.6	19.2
Wall Street Journal	47.2	52.8	45.2	54.8	41.4	37.6	21.4
Washington Post	51.9	48.1	53.5	46.5	44.3	35.9	19.9
Average	50.2	49.8	51.9	48.1	41.4	36.8	21.8

Dem = Democratic
Rep = Republican
AIP = American Independent Party

"The Prestige Press Meets the Third-Party Challenge," Guido Stempel III, *Journalism Quarterly,* Winter 1969, Vol. 46, No. 4, pp. 699–706.

The independent variable (actually, a nominal factor) was the political party covered. Within each group defined by the levels of this factor, the dependent variable of amount of coverage was observed. Since this was a census, no statistical tests were required. But the research question concerning the relationship between endorsement of a party's candidate and the amount of coverage given the party was subjected to a test. In this case, Stempel is treating the selected newspapers as a sample, and is implicitly generalizing to other newspapers. If he was not doing so, he would need no statistical test, as the difference observed in this census would have no sampling error—i.e., it would be absolutely accurate.

As pointed out in the Gerbner study, a content analysis such as this that uses the message unit of analysis is frequently used in conjunction with a study using the individual unit of analysis. This linkage is one of the distinguishing hallmarks of communication research. Both message and individual qualities are observed and relationships between the two are explored. While a psychological study might concentrate on the individual, and a literary or textual analysis might concentrate on the message, good communication research designs frequently look at both.

Summary

In experimental research, the independent variable is systematically manipulated by the researcher so that it takes on different values, and the dependent variable is observed to see if it covaries. In *observational research*, the independent variable is not manipulated, but is allowed to take on different values "naturally," without the intervention of the researcher. *Both the independent and dependent variables are measured* and tested for covariance.

Because the phenomenon under study is allowed to occur naturally, the researcher has much less control over the process. This makes it harder to eliminate outside variables that might be setting up spurious relationships between the independent and dependent variables. The observational researcher must rely on *statistical control* as the major tool to prevent this.

Statistical control, however, requires that all outside variables that confound the relationship under study must be measured and used in the control procedure. Since it is difficult to state with full confidence that all confounding variables have been recognized, observational research designs are susceptible to a number of internal validity problems.

But observational designs are generally stronger in external validity than experimental designs. The lack of control over the operation of the phenomenon that decreases internal validity makes generalization to the real world easier. Adding to this external validity, observational designs are frequently used in field, rather than laboratory, settings.

There are two basic observational designs. The *simple observational design* requires measurement of the independent and dependent variables in a representative random sample. It is used to test relationship hypotheses.

In the *group comparison observational design*, sampled units are assigned to different groups according to observed (rather than manipulated) levels of the independent variable. Since this assignment is not random, the groups will differ not only on the level of the independent variable, but on any outside variables that are systematically related to the independent variable. This is unlike experimental research, where random assignment of units to experimental groups allows the researcher to assume that the groups are equivalent on all variables except the independent variable. Statistical control of outside variables is required in the group comparison observational design, as well as the simple observational design.

Observational designs must be used in retrospective research, and any research setting where manipulation of the independent variable is impossible for practical or ethical reasons. An observational design may also be preferable where the importance of external validity outweighs the additional difficulty of measuring confounding variables, and controlling their effects statistically.

References and Additional Readings

Cochran, W. G. (1983). *Planning and analysis of observational studies.* New York: Wiley.

Kidder, L. H. (1981) *Selltiz, Wrightsman and Cook's research methods in social relations.* New York: Holt, Rinehart and Winston (Chapter 16, "Survey Research Design").

Webb, E. J., Campbell, D. T., Schwartz, R. D., & Sechrest, L. (1972). *Unobtrusive measures: Nonreactive research in the social sciences.* Chicago: Rand McNally (Chapter 5, "Simple Observation").

Wimmer, R. D. & Dominick, J. R. (1987). *Mass media research: An introduction* (2nd ed.). Belmont, CA: Wadsworth (Chapter 6, "Survey Research").

Chapter *17*

━━

Over-Time Research Designs

In the first chapter of this book, we described the activities of Francine Brown, naive scientist. In the process of developing her theory, she made repeated measurements of several variables at different time points. This allowed her to distinguish among several competing explanations for the phenomenon that she was investigating. In Chapters 14 and 15, we also outlined premanipulation/postmanipulation designs that used measurements made at two time points. But dealing with research designs that require observation at two or more points in time is a more complicated process than we've admitted so far.

So why should we introduce this complication? Because communication is a process that occurs naturally over a time span (it's inherently a *dynamic process*), so making useful observations of the process will often mean that we need a design that includes multiple observations made over the time period required by the process. In this chapter, we'll focus on the opportunities and problems of making two or more observations with some time span separating them.

Panel Observations or Repeated Measurements vs. Equivalent Samples

The first distinction to consider is really fundamental: Should we make observations on the same set of units of analysis at each time point, or should we choose a new sample at each time point?

If we choose to observe the same sample at multiple time points, we have a *panel* or *repeated measures* design. The term "panel" is frequently used in observational research, while "repeated measures" is the favored terminology in experimental research. But they refer to an identical procedure: First, select a sample; then repeatedly observe the individuals, groups, or organizations in this sample at subsequent time points.

Alternatively, we may select a different sample of units of analysis to observe at each time point. This is an *equivalent samples* design. Repeated sampling from the same

TABLE 17-1   Two Basic Types of Design: Panel or Repeated Measures vs Equivalent Samples

	Time 1	Time 2	Time 3
Experimental Repeated Measures	$R: Y_{G1}$	$M_1 X_{G1} Y_{G1}$	$M_2 X_{G1} Y_{G1}$
Control Group	$R: Y_{G2}$	Y_{G2}	Y_{G2}
Experimental Equivalent Samples	$R: Y_{G1}$	$R: M_1 X_{G2} Y_{G2}$	$R: M_2 X_{G3} Y_{G3}$
Control Group	$R: Y_{G4}$	$R: Y_{G5}$	$R: Y_{G6}$
Observational Panel	$R: X_{G1} Y_{G1}$	$X_{G1} Y_{G1}$	$X_{G1} Y_{G1}$
Observational Equivalent Samples	$R: X_{G1} Y_{G1}$	$R: X_{G2} Y_{G2}$	$R: X_{G3} Y_{G3}$

NOTATION

R: Random assignment or selection of units of analysis.

X_{Gn} Measurement of the independent or cause variable in Group n.

Y_{Gn} Measurement of the dependent or effect variable in Group n.

$M_n X$ nth manipulation of the independent variable.

population produces groups which are presumed to be the same, but the individual samples taken at each time point may actually have somewhat different characteristics because of sampling error.

Some basic designs are shown in Table 17-1. The experimental design is an extension of the pre-post design described in Chapter 14, while the observational design is an extension of the snapshot designs described in the last chapter. The experimental designs incorporate a single control group in the repeated measures version, or a number of control groups in the equivalent samples design.

Each basic design has its strengths and weaknesses, as shown in Table 17-2. In general, panel or repeated measures designs are susceptible to learning, order, sensitization, and memory effects because of the multiple measurements carried out on each unit of analysis. But because all measurements are made on the same units, each unit can serve as its own comparison or "control." As we saw in Chapter 14, this allows us to separate out effects on the dependent variable that are due to differences among the sampled units (this is sometimes called "individual differences" or "subject effects") and the effects due to the independent variable. This makes the total error smaller, and makes it easier to see the true effects of the independent variable.

Equivalent samples designs do not have problems with learning, order, sensitization, or memory effects, since each sampled unit is measured at only one time point. But equivalent samples designs require sampling many more units, since they demand a fresh sample at each time point. This is expensive. Also, by using a new sample at each point, some sampling error is introduced at each new time point.

TABLE 17-2   **Strengths and Weaknesses of Panel and Equivalent Samples Observation**

	Panel or Repeated Measures		Equivalent Samples	
	Experimental	*Observational*	*Experimental*	*Observational*
INTERNAL VALIDITY				
Instrumentation Reliability and Validity	?	?	?	?
Selection (Sampling)	−	−	−	−
Instrument Obtrusiveness	−	?	−	?
Manipulation Effectiveness	?	−	?	−
History	−	+	−	+
Maturation	−	+	−	+
Measurement Sensitization	+	+	−	−
Measurement Instrument Learning	+	+	−	−
Measurement Instrument Instability	+	+	−	?
Subject Mortality	+	+	−	−
Subject Fatigue	?	?	−	−
Treatment or Measurement Order Effects	+	+	−	−
EXTERNAL VALIDITY				
Representative Sample	−	−	−	−
Reactive Effects of Setting	?	?	?	?
Multiple Treatment Interference	+	+	−	−
Reactive Sensitization	+	+	−	−
Subject Mortality	+	+	−	−
STATISTICAL POWER				
Number of Observations	Few	Few	Many	Many
Separation of Effects (Within/Between units)	Good	Good	None	None
Type 1 (α) Error susceptibility	+	+	−	−
Type 2 (β) Error susceptibility	−	−	+	+

+   The design is more susceptible to this threat to validity.
−   The design is less susceptible to this threat to validity.
?   This threat to validity is not affected by the design under discussion. The threat may be more
or less prevalent, depending on other steps taken by the researcher.

Because this sampling error occurs across different units of analysis, it cannot be estimated or controlled, as it can in repeated measures design. Variance in the dependent variable that occurs because of inherent differences in the sampled units will be indistinguishable from other sources of sampling error variance, and all error variances must be lumped together. This larger error variance makes the statistics used to test hypotheses with equivalent samples much less powerful than those used with repeated measures. Small effects of the independent variable may get lost in the error variance introduced by the effects of inherent differences between the sampled units.

So the researcher is faced with a painful decision: to use a design that contains more threats to validity, but has powerful statistical tools (repeated measures); or to use a design that is less susceptible to these threats, but requires a larger number of sampled units and has less powerful statistical tests (equivalent samples). The general rule is this: If at all possible, use a repeated measures design, since it is cheaper and the statistics are more powerful. But if the learning, sensitization, or subject mortality threats appear to threaten the validity of the results, use equivalent samples.

Contrasting Panel Designs and Equivalent Samples: Observational Studies

The best way to illustrate the differences between the two fundamental designs is to present some examples and see how they can be contrasted.

Observational Panel Design: A Political Communication Example

A researcher wants to relate the amount of interpersonal and mediated communication about political issues (the independent variable) to the likelihood that the sampled individual will vote (the dependent variable). It is hypothesized that the probability of voting will increase proportionally to the cumulative amount of communication that occurs during the campaign.

To test this hypothesis, the researcher selects a random sample from the population of a city by dialing random telephone numbers, alternately selecting the male and female head of household, and requesting participation in the study. If the person agrees, he/she is contacted each week for eight weeks by telephone for a short interview. The interview questions include estimates of the amount of time spent discussing politics with family, friends, and coworkers; the amount of time spent reading about political issues in newspapers and magazines; the amount of time spent listening to radio and television talk shows and political advertisements, and so on; and the self-reported probability that the person will vote (0–100 percent). Also collected are demographic variables like age, income, and education, which will be used as statistical control variables.

The researcher selects a sample of 200 persons. However, over the course of the study, 10 persons drop out each week. Some move away, some just get bored with the process, others go on vacation, and so on. At the end of the study, the researcher has complete data on only 120 of the sampled individuals. However, there are eight different estimates for each person's communication and voting behavior at various times in the campaign. The researcher has 960 (120 × 8) observations on 120 different individuals with which to test the hypotheses.

Observational Equivalent Samples Design: A Political Communication Example

Another researcher chooses to test the same hypothesis with a different design. To eliminate the problem of subject mortality and multiple measurement effects, an equivalent samples design is used. In each week of the measurement period, the researcher selects a new sample of 200 persons and interviews each of them, using the same questionnaire as the first researcher used. At each time point, there is a loss of 10 interviews because the person being interviewed refuses to complete the questionnaire.

At the end of the study, this researcher has 1520 observations (190×8) on 1520 different individuals. However, there are some serious limitations in the confidence which can be placed in the results with this design, too. Although the hypothesized change in voting probability occurs within individuals, there is no direct observation of this change in the equivalent samples design. At each time point the researcher can observe differences in the voting probability, but these may occur because of sampling error, since the samples are not made up of the same individuals. If the researcher does not find the hypothesized relationship, it might be because the sampling error has masked the real relationship. That is, the researcher may be making a Type 2 error.

The researcher has also expended more effort in obtaining the cooperation of 1600 individuals, rather than 200. While there are more observations, a disproportionally higher cost was paid for them.

Advantages and Disadvantages of the Panel and Equivalent Samples Observational Designs

There are some serious limitations in the confidence that can be placed in the results of the panel design because of sample bias introduced by the subject mortality. The persons who drop out of the study are likely to be different in systematic ways from those who complete the study. Those who complete the study are more likely to be stable (they don't move around as much, so they are available for the duration of the study), responsible (they finish what they start), or older (they have more time to participate). Each of these factors is probably related to the dependent variable of voting behavior, and the resulting sample bias may skew the results.

In the equivalent samples design, there is less problem with subject mortality, since individuals only have to participate for the duration of one interview. They won't move out of town before completing their part of the study. But there is still some problem with mortality and subsequent sample bias, as some people refuse to complete the interview. But it's far less of a problem than it is in the panel design.

There are also sensitizing and reactive effects introduced by the multiple measurement sessions in the panel design. The process of measurement may introduce some systematic changes in the response of individuals. By asking about political communication, the researcher may influence the participants to pay more attention than they normally would to the campaign, and to discuss it more. The repetition of political questions may influence the participant's likelihood of voting ("Since you're continually asking me if I'm going to vote, I guess I really should vote"). These effects will be picked up in subsequent measurement sessions in the panel design. Sensitization and reactivity problems are absent from the equivalent samples designs, since they occur after the measurement is completed.

All measurements of voting probability at each time point in the panel design are not independent. Each sampled unit is measured at each time point, so any sampling error present in a unit during measurement at the first time point is equally present at subsequent time points. This is both a strength and weakness of this kind of design. Measuring within the same unit leads to the introduction of systematic error. But since the error is constant, it can be estimated and removed.

For example, some persons in the sample will be highly political and spend lots of time communicating about political issues. They will also probably be more likely than others to vote. Other persons will ignore the whole campaign, and be less likely to vote. But increases in political communication may raise the voting likelihood of both persons. If we look only at the voting likelihood, we will find a large variance. Much of that variance is due to individual differences in political interest, and it makes the variance produced by differences in political communication hard to see.

Table 17-3 illustrates this point with some example data for four persons. In this table the individual effects (probably due to general interest in politics) are separated from the effects of political communication. The communication effects are identical for all of these hypothetical people. The observed value, the probability of voting, is the sum of the individual predisposition effects and the communication effects.

Since the panel measurements are taken on the same persons, we can eliminate the effect of different individual predispositions by computing a difference score between the two time points (although, as we mentioned in Chapter 14, this is not a good idea unless the measurements are highly reliable). Regardless of the individual predispositions, we see that communication produces a 10 percent gain in the probability of voting. Since this gain is the same for all individuals, it has no variance, and the standard error of the mean is zero.

The equivalent samples data shown in Table 17-3 use the same four individuals in the first sample at Time 1, but adds a different four at Time 2. The predispositions of the individuals in the second sample are different from those in the first (as a result of simple sampling error), so the variation at the second time point, as indicated by the standard deviation, is somewhat larger, although the mean is identical. But more importantly, the values for general political interest at the second time point cannot be subtracted from those obtained at the first time point, as they are from different individuals. The only way that change from Time 1 to Time 2 can be computed is by looking at the difference between the means for both time points.

In both the panel design and the equivalent samples design, the mean difference is 10 percent. But the difference in the change scores from the panel design has no error, while the standard error for the equivalent samples design is 8.29 percent, which is almost as large as the difference between the two means. We can be far less confident that the difference in voting probability observed in the equivalent samples study is real, and not due to sampling error, than we would be in finding the same difference in a panel design.

Of course, it is not likely that a researcher will actually find difference scores with a standard error of the mean of zero. But in general, the error of differences between measurement points in panel and repeated measures designs will be smaller than that in equivalent samples designs, because the effect of individual differences can be removed.

In essence, the conclusions drawn from the panel design in the example can be stated like this: "*If all units were the same at the beginning of the study*, the effect of political communication was to increase voting probability by 10 percent." By contrast, the results of the equivalent samples design can be stated like this: "*If the predispositions toward the political process of all units are permitted to vary naturally, as they do in the population,*

TABLE 17-3   Example Data for Voting Probability in Panel and Equivalent Samples Designs

	Person	Time 1		Time 2		Difference Between Times 1 and 2
Panel Data						
Individual Effects	A	50		50		0
Independent Variable		10		20		10
Observed:			60		70	10
Individual Effects	B	40		40		0
Independent Variable		10		20		10
Observed:			50		60	10
Individual Effects	C	10		10		0
Independent Variable		10		20		10
Observed:			20		30	10
Individual Effects	D	60		60		0
Independent Variable		10		20		10
Observed:			70		80	10
Mean			50		60	10
Standard Deviation			18.71		18.71	0.0
Standard Error of Mean			9.35		9.35	0.0

	Person	Time 1		Person	Time 2		Difference Between Times 1 and 2
Equivalent Samples Data							
Individual Effects	A	50		E	70		(can't be computed for
Independent Variable		10			20		individuals, since different
Observed:			60			90	persons are sampled)
Individual Effects	B	40		F	30		
Independent Variable		10			20		
Observed:			50			50	
Individual Effects	C	10		G	0		
Independent Variable		10			20		
Observed:			20			20	
Individual Effects	D	60		H	60		
Independent Variable		10			20		
Observed:			70			80	
Mean			50			60	$(60 - 50) = 10$
Standard Deviation			18.71			27.39	$\sqrt{(1400 + 3000)/8} = 23.45$
Standard Error of Mean			9.35			13.70	$23.45/\sqrt{8} = 8.29$

the effect of political communication was to increase voting probability by an average of 10 percent, *but with wide individual variation.*

Since the results in the panel design can be stated with more confidence, the researcher who chose this design will be less likely to make a Type 2 or β error (conclude that there is no relationship, when there really is one). But sensitization of subjects or other over-time threats to validity may lead to a Type 1 or α error (a conclusion that there is a relationship, when there really is none). The reverse is true for the researcher who chose the equivalent samples design. A Type 2 error is more likely to occur, since the researcher cannot control for individual differences among sampled units. But he or she is less likely to make a Type 1 error, as the other threats to validity are fewer.

Contrasting Repeated Measures and Equivalent Samples: Experimental Studies

Again, we'll contrast these designs by using two examples.

Experimental Repeated Measures Design: A Speaking Apprehension Example

A researcher is interested in the effect of training in public speaking on reduction of speaking apprehension in students. Since the training takes place over the course of the semester, it is decided to make four measurements at monthly intervals. At the beginning of the study, there is a random selection of two groups of students from a sampling frame of all students who have never taken a course in public speaking. One group is then assigned to take a course in public speaking. The other is told *not* to take such a course. The first group is the experimental group, since the independent variable (amount of training in public speaking) is systematically increased during the semester. The second group is the control group, in which the independent variable remains constant.

Each month, all members of both groups fill out a questionnaire that contains a set of standard speaking apprehension scales. These are combined to give a single apprehension score. The directional research hypothesis states that increased training will produce decreased apprehension, so the researcher expects that the scores will decline over the four measurement points.

Since apprehension should be related to experience in speaking and to maturity, as well as to formal training, the researcher expects the control group scores to decline over the semester, too, as students will be called upon to speak in other classes, and they will be maturing over the time period. However, the decline in apprehension in the control group should be less than that in the experimental group, if the hypothesis is correct.

Experimental Equivalent Samples Design: A Speaking Apprehension Example

A second researcher who disagrees with the decision to use repeated measures in this situation argues that the measurement procedure may affect the subjects in two ways. First, they may remember their responses from the prior measurement time, and thus be likely to give consistent, rather than correct, responses. Second, the scale items may provide those in the experimental group with cues to the things that they should focus on during their training, and thus may artificially intensify the effects of the training. For these reasons, the second researcher chooses to use an equivalent samples design.

At the beginning of the semester eight groups of students are randomly choosen. Four of these are assigned to take a public speaking course, and four are prohibited from taking such a course. Each month the apprehension scales are administered to a different one of the experimental groups and a different one of the control groups. In essence, this is an extension of the post-only experimental design, expanded to several time points.

Advantages and Disadvantages of the Repeated Measures and Equivalent Samples Experimental Designs

The problems and rewards of each design are essentially the same as those in the observational design. The repeated measures design requires one-fourth as many subjects, but is susceptible to sample bias because of student dropouts during the semester, reactive measurement effects, learning, memory effects, and so on. But variation in the dependent variable due to individual differences can be calculated for each subject and removed in the repeated measures design, while it must be lumped with the sampling error in the equivalent samples design.

Both experimental designs provide some control for history and maturation effects by including a control group. Both experimental researchers will test the hypothesis by contrasting decreases in the dependent variable in the experimental group with decreases in the control group. Since history and maturation effects are the same in both groups, they can be calculated and controlled for.

For example, the researchers may compute the effect of the independent variable at each time point by subtracting the mean apprehension scores for the experimental group from the mean scores for the control group at each time point. The values for the control group represent the normal history and maturation effects that occur in the population. This information, by itself, may be valuable to the researcher.

In the repeated measures design, history and maturation could be removed by using the difference between the mean *change* scores for the experimental and control group. These change scores control for individual differences, so they show less variation than the absolute apprehension scores. In the equivalent samples design, the researcher is forced to compute the difference between the absolute apprehension scores for each group, since there is no way of measuring or removing individual differences.

Decreasing Threats to Validity in Repeated Measures Designs

There are some steps that the researcher can take to diminish the threats to validity posed by repeated measurement designs. First, measurements can be made at time intervals which are as far apart as possible. This will decrease problems with learning and memory by subjects. However, it may also increase problems with subject mortality, as it gets harder and harder to retain subjects when the study goes on for long periods of time. Also, choosing a long time interval between observations may cause the researcher to miss important, but brief, dynamic processes that occur between the measurement points.

A second way that the researcher can ease measurement reactivity problems is by using unobtrusive measures. These are discussed in more detail in the next chapter.

Unobtrusive measures remove problems introduced by the measurement instrument or research setting by making the measurement invisible to the sampled units. This kind of measurement is automatic in retrospective research, and unobtrusive measurement can be achieved in many instances by using clever research procedures that hide the measurement or the intent of the researcher.

But when the research calls for measurement of concepts which reside within the minds of the research subjects, there is often little choice but to directly and obtrusively measure the variable. In these cases, the researcher must carefully weight the pros and cons of repeated measures and equivalent samples.

Using Over-time Observation to Investigate Causality and Time Lags

One of the major benefits of making multiple observations over time is that it opens up the possibility of investigating not only the covariance of the independent and dependent variables, but their temporal ordering. As you should remember from our discussion of causality in Chapter 3, one of the requirements for a causal relationship is that changes in the cause variable must precede changes in the effect variable, and not vice versa.

Experimental Designs

In an experimental design, testing temporal order is simple, although it requires two sets of observations. If the researcher is not sure whether X causes Y, or Y causes X, he or she can construct two studies, as shown in Figure 17-1. In the first study, the researcher will manipulate X and see if Y covaries in response—i.e., at a later point in time—then the researcher will manipulate Y and see if X covaries.

There are four possible outcomes, as illustrated in Figure 17-1. If X is the cause and Y the effect, then changes in X will produce corresponding changes in Y (manipulating the cause variable produces changes in the effect variable), but changing Y will not produce covariance with X (manipulating the effect variable will not produce changes in the cause variable). If Y causes X, the reverse pattern will be found.

The third case is a trivial one: Neither variable affects the other, so there is no evidence for the existence of any kind of relationship between the two variables. Finally, the researcher may find that manipulating either variable produces covariance in the other variable. This situation cues the researcher that the theory may need revision. There is not a simple causal relationship between the two variables. They are related by two different processes (the one in which X produces changes in Y, and the one in which Y produces changes in X), so that two relationships, with different temporal orderings, are being observed.

In any case, by making multiple observations of the two variables, the experimental researcher can draw some conclusions about the temporal ordering of the variables.

Observational Designs

If observational measurements are taken at a single time point, in many cases it is difficult or impossible to verify the temporal ordering of variables. Only if there is a natural time order to the variables in retrospective studies (like childhood communication preceding adult relationships) can temporal ordering be confidently specified.

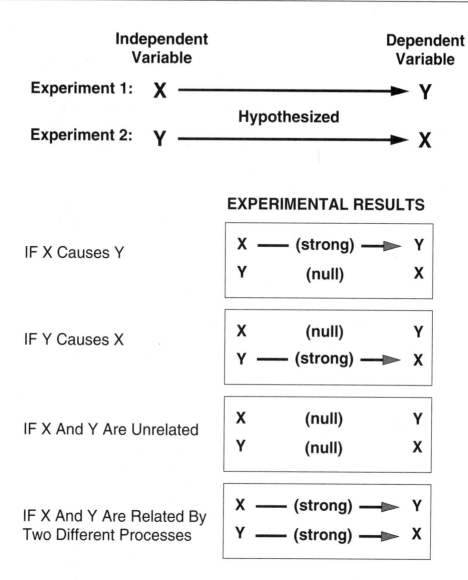

FIGURE 17-1   Determining Temporal Ordering in an Experimental Design

But the researcher who makes observations at several time points may be able to directly test the temporal ordering of variables. We'll look at some ways to do this in both panel designs and equivalent samples designs.

Time-Lagged Correlations
If a repeated measures or panel design is used, the time ordering of variables can be investigated by time-lagged correlation or regression. This procedure is sometimes called

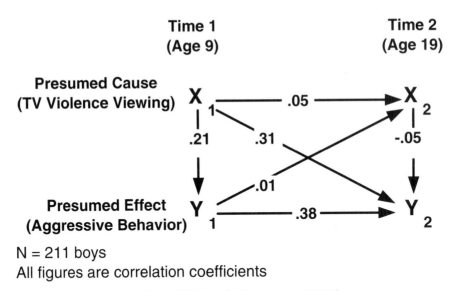

N = 211 boys
All figures are correlation coefficients

Taken from Lefkowitz, Eron, Walder, & Huesmann (1972).

FIGURE 17-2 **Cross-Lagged Correlations Between TV Violence Viewing and Aggressive Behavior**

cross-lagged correlation. The logical basis of this procedure lies in the familiar requirement that the cause produce change in the effect, and not vice versa.

Figure 17-2 reproduces the results of a frequently cited observational study which used this technique. Lefkowitz et al. (1972) measured the television viewing habits and the scores on standard psychological tests of aggression of 211 boys when they were in the third grade, and 10 years later when they had graduated from high school. The figure shows correlation coefficients to summarize the covariance between variables at different time points. Correlation coefficients range from −1.0 for a perfect negative relationship to +1.0 for a perfect positive relationship, with 0.0 indicating a null relationship.

As the figure shows, viewing of televised violence at age 9 covaried moderately (.31) with aggressiveness at age 19, but aggressiveness at age 9 did not covary (.01) with viewing violence at age 19. This pattern is consistent with a temporal ordering that states that viewing violence at an early age produces later aggressiveness, but being aggressive does not predict later violence viewing—i.e., viewing violence causes aggressiveness, and not vice versa. Although the Lefkowitz et al. study has been criticized for some methodological weaknesses (the subject mortality over 10 years was high and the reliabilities of the measures were questioned), it is a good example of the use of time-lagged correlations.

Time-Lagged Regressions
The technique of time-lagged correlations can be expanded to test not only the temporal ordering, but the actual time lag that elapses between some change in the cause variable, and

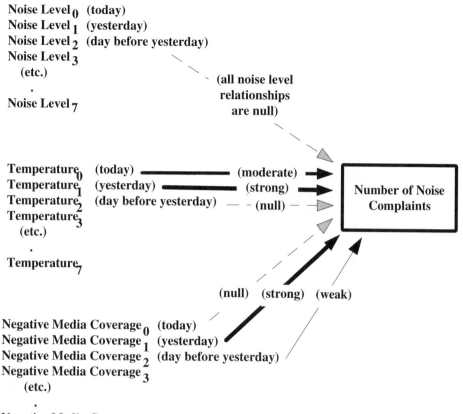

FIGURE 17-3 Time-Lagged Regressions

the corresponding response in the effect variable. A procedure called *multiple regression* is used to compute the relationship between one or more independent variables and a single dependent variable. If multiple over-time observations are taken, the independent variable can be the same concept measured at different time points, or different concepts measured at the same time points, or a combination of the two.

Figure 17-3 shows the results of a study done by Watt and van den Berg (1981). This study looked at the relationship of media coverage and other factors to the number of telephoned complaints from the public when a new, noisy jet service was introduced into two metropolitan airports. The hypotheses were that public irritation with the new service could be caused by several factors. The most obvious was the actual noise level. But the temperature might also affect the number of complaints, as windows are more likely to be open in warmer weather, exposing people to more noise. Of particular interest was the role of the media in sensitizing the public to the issue, and perhaps encouraging them to complain.

Data on temperature, noise level, and media coverage (from a content analysis of local newspapers and television news programs) were collected on a daily basis for a year. This was a simple observational study using a panel design, where the unit of analysis is the message, from the media content analyses.

There is some potential time lag in the operation of all these independent variables. For example, if a family was in the backyard Sunday afternoon grilling steaks when a very noisy jet flew over, they might subdue their irritation, eat a juicy steak, and wait until Monday morning to find the complaint line's number and make an irate call. Likewise, a person might have to read newspaper stories or see TV coverage for several days before the effect of the accumulated messages was large enough to trigger a response.

To look at this situation, each of the three independent variables was made into seven time-lagged independent variables, as shown in Figure 17-3. These 21 independent variables were related, with a multiple regression, to the dependent variable of number of complaints received in a day. Multiple regression statistically *controls* for the effect of all other independent variables, so the effect of one independent variable is not confounded with the effects of the other independent variables. This is critical in an observational study like this.

As the figure shows, the actual noise level did not covary with the number of complaints. The best predictors of the number of complaints were the current and previous day's temperature, and the previous two days' media coverage, with the major effect produced by the previous day's coverage. Coverage effects did not persist very long, however, as lags greater than two days were not related to the number of complaints.

This study illustrates the value of multiple over-time observations in understanding the dynamic nature of a communication process. We can see that communication has an effect, but that it is very transient. Single-time point data cannot show us this important fact.

ARIMA Models

There is an important kind of dynamic modeling technique that relies on multiple time point observations, usually within a repeated measures or panel design. The models are called ARIMA (*AutoRegressive Integrated Moving Average*) models, or Box-Jenkins models, after their originators.

The method for creating these models is far too complex to unravel here, but the basic idea is relatively simple. In an ARIMA model, previous values of a variable are used to predict current or future values. ARIMA models slipped into communication research from economics, where forecasting future values of a variable from past experience has a high value (often measured in dollars).

ARIMA models are usually *univariate*. They consist of multiple observations of a single variable, i.e., a time series. This limits their utility, as they cannot be used directly to establish a relationship between an independent and dependent variable. They are better suited to prediction and description of a variable's dynamic behavior than to causal explanations. However, it is possible to compare two ARIMA models of different time series variables, and look for relationships.

Let's look at a hypothetical example. Suppose a researcher is interested in the conversational patterns that occur in face-to-face situations between persons of the opposite sex. In particular, he or she wants to know if there is a relationship between comments that disclose personal, normally private, facts by one member of the dyad, and a similar

TABLE 17-4   ARIMA Models of Hypothetical Data for Self-Disclosure in Conversations

Time Point	No. Female SDs	No. Male SDs	Modeled Female SDs	Modeled Male SDs
1	0	0	1.20	1.11
2	1	0	.17	.20
3	2	1	1.03	.20
4	3	2	1.89	1.02
5	4	2	2.74	1.84
6	5	3	3.60	1.84
7	4	3	4.46	2.66
8	3	3	3.60	2.66
9	2	2	2.74	2.66
10	1	2	1.89	1.84
11	1	1	1.03	1.84
12	0	1	1.03	1.02
13	0	1	.17	1.02
14	0	0	.17	1.02
15	0	0	.17	.20
16	1	0	.17	.20
17	2	0	1.03	.20
18	2	1	1.89	.20
19	2	1	1.89	1.02
20	3	2	1.89	1.02
21	3	3	2.74	1.84
22	3	4	2.74	2.66
23	2	3	2.74	3.47
24	2	2	1.89	2.66
25	1	2	1.89	1.84
26	1	1	1.03	1.84
27	0	1	1.03	1.02
28	0	0	.17	1.02

Female Model: $SD_t = .86\ SD_{t-1}$
Male Model: $SD_t = .82\ SD_{t-1}$

self-disclosing response by the other member. Further, if such a pattern exists, which gender is more likely to initiate self-disclosure?

To do this, the researcher sets up an observational study where pairs of opposite sex students meet in a room and conduct an unstructured conversation, which is recorded. Trained coders listen to the tapes, and record the number of statements which indicate self-disclosure (SD) for each person. From this data, the researcher creates two time series that summarize the conversational behavior of each sex in the typical dyad. We'll skip over the methodological details involved in creating these two sets of data (they are formidable), and focus on the analysis. The two time series have 28 time points, and they are shown in Table 17-4.

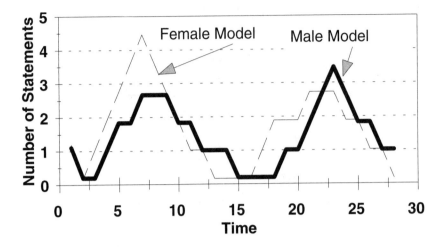

FIGURE 17-4 Hypothetical Models of Self-Disclosure

To partially answer the research questions, the researcher conducts a time-lagged regression analysis where he or she predicts the current value of male self-disclosure from the current value of female self-disclosure, the value from the previous time point, the value from the time point before that, and so on. The researcher finds that the maximum correlation occurs with this predictive equation:

$$\text{No. Male SDs}_t = .83 \cdot \text{No. Female SDs}_{t-1}$$

In words, the best way to predict the number of self-disclosing statements that the male member of the dyad will make at any time point is to multiply by .83 the number of such statements made by the female member at the time point just before this one. Males apparently follow the example of females in disclosing private details about themselves.

But this simple predictive equation does not tell the researcher much about the dynamic pattern of the conversation. To investigate this, the researcher uses a computer statistical package to explore different ARIMA models for each time series.

The best univariate model for the number of self-disclosure statements by females is very simple: To predict the number of self-disclosure statements made by females at any time point, take the number made at the previous time point and multiply by .86. The model for male self-disclosure is equally simple: Multiply value at the previous time point in the male time series by .82.

Figure 17-4 shows a plot of the two models. This plot shows clearly that there is a cycle in the conversation. Self-disclosure first increases, then decreases, then increases again, and so on. We can see that the changes occur first in the female model plot, then follow in the male model plot. This pattern reinforces the results of the time-lagged regression analysis.

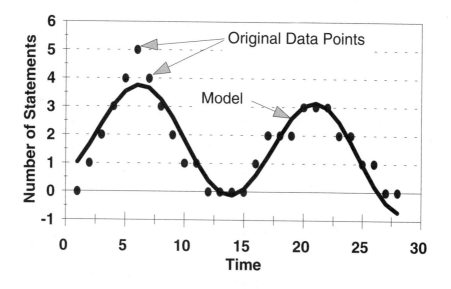

FIGURE 17-5 **Cyclical Models of Female Self-Disclosure**

The ARIMA models give the researcher a very good picture of the conversational process that occurs over time. This is their strength. However, they do not explain the nature of the process.

Fourier Analysis, Spectral Analysis, and Harmonic Models

For processes which show cycling, as did the example discussed above, there is another set of time series modeling tools. These are referred to by the terms Fourier analysis, spectral analysis, or harmonic modeling. Again, these procedures are too complex to discuss in any detail here. Conceptually, they involve finding the strongest cycles in a time series, and describing them in a simple mathematical model that relies upon sinusoids (sine or cosine functions, if you remember your high school trigonometry).

Figure 17-5 shows a harmonic (cyclical) model of the pattern of female self-disclosure obtained from a statistical package. The model is a relatively simple one with only one cosine cycle:

$$\text{No. of Female SDs} = 1.79 \cdot \cos(.427 \cdot \text{Time Point Number}/2\pi - 1.97) + 1.7$$

If you compare the plot of the ARIMA model in Figure 17-4 with the harmonic model in Figure 17-5, you can see the smoother description of the cycle which this procedure gives. Harmonic models also contain other valuable information for the researcher, such as the frequency of the cycles (periods of high self-disclosure recur every 14.7 time points), the strength or amplitude of the cycle, and other descriptive information.

TABLE 17-5   **Hypothetical Cohort Effects:**
Pure Age Effect

Age	Year			
	1960	*1970*	*1980*	*1990*
10–19	100	100	100	100
20–29	90	90	90	90
30–39	50	50	50	50
40–49	45	45	45	45
50–59	60	60	60	60
60–69	90	90	90	90

Cohort Analysis

This is a term for a number of procedures that are usually used in observational, equivalent samples designs. They are used to track data from particular groups or generations of persons ("cohorts") through multiple observations taken over some time period. A typical application would involve looking at the responses to the same questionnaire item used in a number of different surveys conducted over a time period.

As an example, suppose we are interested in determining the amount of use (in minutes per day) that "baby boomers" make of radio programming. From survey research archives, we find that this question has been asked of respondents to national surveys in 1960, 1970, 1980, and 1990.

There are several possible explanations for the amount of time a person spends with radio programming. First, the age of the person may affect the amount of time spent listening. Younger and older persons have more available free time. Second, the conditions prevailing at a time period may affect listening. There were more stations, with more diversified programming, available in 1990 than earlier. Third, the characteristics of particular cohorts may affect listening. The baby boomers made heavy use of radio in the 1960s, and so they may have a different relationship with the medium than other groups.

Table 17-5 shows the pattern in mean minutes per day that would occur if only age was associated with radio listening. In every year in which listening time was measured, each age group spent the same amount of time with radio, although the amount of time varied between age groups.

Table 17-6 shows the pattern that would occur if only the time period or "era" in which the measurement was made affected listenership. Within each time period, the amount of listening was the same, but it varied across time periods.

Table 17-7 shows the pure cohort effect. The early baby boomers, who were teenagers in 1960, were in the 20–29 age bracket in 1970, and the 30–39 age bracket in 1980, etc. By looking at the diagonal entries in the table, we can see the cohort or generational effects. Baby boomers used more radio (100 minutes per day), at all measurement points, than did the generations on either side (90 and 95 minutes).

The formal procedures for separating cohort effects from the other effects are varied, and we'll not outline them here. The researcher interested in tracing generational effects in equivalent samples data should consult a book like Glenn (1977).

**TABLE 17-6   Hypothetical Cohort Effects:
Pure Time Period Effect**

	Year			
Age	1960	1970	1980	1990
10–19	100	90	80	70
20–29	100	90	80	70
30–39	100	90	80	70
40–49	100	90	80	70
50–59	100	90	80	70
60–69	100	90	80	70

TABLE 17-7   Hypothetical Cohort Effects: Pure Cohort Effect

	Year				
Age	1960	1970	1980	1990	
10–19	100	90	80	70	
20–29	95	100	90	80	
30–39	85	95	100	90	
40–49	75	85	95	100	→ Baby Boomers
50–59	60	75	85	95	Cohort
60–69	70	60	75	85	

Other Over-Time Methods

There are a number of other analytical techniques to examine, model, and test hypotheses in data which are collected over time, but we do not have the space to outline all of them. For example, conversation and interaction researchers are likely to make use of *log-linear* or *correspondence* analysis. These methods are used to find relationships in tables that summarize the frequency with which certain events occur (contingency tables). Alternatively, the researcher might create a *Markov model* which describes a dynamic communication exchange by giving the probabilities that certain patterns of statements will appear. Each of these methods is a valuable tool for the serious communication researcher, and all rely on multiple over-time measurements.

Summary

Communication is a process that occurs naturally over some time span. Making useful observations of the process frequently requires a research design that collects information at multiple points in time.

Data can be collected over time in *repeated measures* or *panel* designs, in which the same unit sampled from the population is measured at different times, or it can be collected from *equivalent samples* in which new samples are constructed at each measurement point.

Repeated measures designs are susceptible to internal validity problems when the measurement involves people and is obtrusive. In general, panel or repeated measures designs are sensitive to learning, order, sensitization, and memory effects because of the multiple measurements which are applied to the same sampled units. But these designs are statistically powerful, as they allow separation of effects which are due to inherent differences in the sampled units from the effects of the independent variable. They are also cheap, as a single sampled unit can provide a number of data values. Some steps to reduce validity problems can be taken by selecting an appropriate time interval between measurements so that memory and sensitization effects are minimized, by using unobtrusive measures, and by creating clever research procedures which cut down on subject sensitization.

Equivalent samples designs require more subjects, since a new sample must be chosen at each time point. They are less statistically powerful, since individual differences cannot be separated from ordinary sampling error, and the resulting total error may overwhelm the effects of the independent variable. But they are less susceptible to internal and external validity threats. For this reason, equivalent samples are "conservative," i.e., the are biased toward making Type 2 or β errors. Repeated measures or panel designs, on the other hand, are biased toward making Type 1 or α errors.

Observations taken over time can be used to investigate the temporal ordering of variables. This can answer questions about the proper causal ordering of two variables that covary. In experimental designs, the temporal ordering can be reversed, and the question answered directly. In observational designs, techniques like *cross-lagged correlations* and *time-lagged regressions* can be used to explore the time ordering of variables.

Multiple observations of a single concept can be analyzed and modeled with *ARIMA* procedures or *spectral analysis*. These procedures reduce many observations of the variable to relatively simple mathematical models. The parameters of these models aid the researcher in interpreting the behavior of the variable. *Cohort analysis* can be used in equivalent samples designs to track the behavior of generational groups or cohorts over multiple time points. There are also other powerful methods for analyzing dynamic communication data that are available to the advanced communication researcher.

References and Additional Readings

Arundale, R. B. (1977). Sampling across time for communication research. In P. M. Hirsch, P. V. Miller, & F. G. Kline (Eds.), *Strategies for communication research* (pp. 257–285). Beverly Hills, CA: Sage.

Bloomfield, P. (1976). *Fourier analysis of time series: An introduction.* New York: Wiley.

Glenn, N. D. (1977). *Cohort analysis.* Sage University Paper series on Quantitative Applications in the Social Sciences, 07-005. Beverly Hills, CA: Sage.

Lefkowitz, M. M., Eron, L. D., Walder, L. O., & Huesmann, L. R. (1972). Television violence and child aggression: A follow up study. In G. Comstock & E. A. Rubenstein, (Eds.). *Television and social behavior: Television and adolescent aggressiveness* (Vol. 3). Washington, DC: Government Printing Office, U.S. Dept. of Health, Education, and Welfare.

McDowall, D., McCleary, R., Meidinger, E. E., & Hay, R. A. (1980). *Interrupted time series analysis.* Sage University Paper Series on Quantitative Applications in the Social Sciences, 07-021. Beverly Hills, CA: Sage.

Watt, J. H. & van den Berg, S. (1981). How time dependency influences media effects in a community controversy. *Journalism Quarterly, 58* (1), 43–50.

Chapter *18*

Research Procedures

In this chapter we'll discuss some major methods for measuring variables and collecting data to test hypotheses. We will present a brief introduction to the mechanics of these procedures and we will also discuss them in terms of the advantages and disadvantages they offer to the researcher. There are any number of books devoted to presenting the intricacies of interviewing, questionnaire construction, unobtrusive measurement, and so on. The serious communication researcher should refer to these sources to get more complete information about techniques, advantages, and pitfalls of the particular research procedures. Furthermore, as the measurement of communication data in many cases involves acquiring the cooperation of respondents in varying degrees, we will discuss the ethical implications of selecting different methods of gathering data.

Measurement Techniques

Behavioral Observation

Much of the measurement of communication variables falls in the category of behavioral observation. With this technique, a trained person observes a specific set of behaviors exhibited by a research subject and uses trained judgment to assign the correct values to the appropriate variables.

For instance, in the Bandura et al. experiment described in Chapter 14, if the observer sees a child from the experimental group carry out an act of physical or verbal aggression identical to that originally exhibited by the adult model, the child's act is counted in the category "imitative aggression," and not in the category called "partially imitative aggression." In the Leavitt study described in the same chapter, the observer starts a clock at the beginning of a trial, and stops the clock once all group members have thrown their switches. The number of seconds needed for completion is the value assigned to the variable "time elapsed" for that group's trial.

In both studies the observer determines the level of the variable. Because a human observer is involved, there can be large differences in the reliability of measurement. Reliability often varies according to the complexity or difficulty of the judgment required by the measurement task. The instructions issued to the observer in the Leavitt study might have read something like this:

> *Start the clock and give the signal to start the trial. Stop the clock when all five lights have been illuminated. Read the clock's elapsed time and enter the number on line 5 of the coding sheet. Reset the clock.*

This kind of behavioral observation is likely to yield highly reliable measurement. First of all, the same observer should obtain very similar results if he or she carries out the same task repeatedly under the same conditions. This is *test-retest reliability*. Second, given the simplicity and straightforwardness of the instructions, several different observers of the same trial should show very high levels of agreement on the amount of elapsed time. Such agreement is referred to as *intercoder, interexperimenter*, or *interjudge reliability*.

The greater ambiguity associated with the decision-making process in the Bandura study will probably result in lower levels of test-retest and intercoder reliability. For instance, the observer must decide to what extent a child must deviate from the model's behavior before the child's behavior is assigned to the category "partially imitative aggression" rather than to the "imitative aggression" category. If different observers evaluate the same behavior, there is likely to be some disagreement. If two different measuring instruments (the observers) give two different "readings" about the phenomenon being measured, there is measurement unreliability.

Reliability in behavioral observation can be improved in two ways: (1) Make the observation task simple and concrete; and (2) give clear, extensive instructions and training to the observers. If you ask an observer to "Count the number of nice remarks made by each person in the conversation," you are going to get some widely different answers from different observers who hear the same taped conversation, and even from the same observer redundantly coding the same conversation at a two-week interval. The instructions are too vague to produce reliable measurement.

On the other hand, if you ask the observer to "Count the number of times each person commented favorably on the clothing of the other," and "Count the number of times each person said 'thank you' to the other," you will probably get reliable results. By combining a number of such concrete observational tasks, you can measure "niceness" with much more detail and reliability than the first vague instructions could ever give.

Obtrusive and Unobtrusive Measurement

Behavioral observation can be either *obtrusive* or *unobtrusive* measurement. This distinction refers to the extent to which the respondent or subject is aware that he or she is being evaluated. As we saw in Chapter 13, this awareness can affect both the internal validity and external validity of a study. Awareness can produce sensitization to the experimental manipulation, enhanced memory effects, reactivity to the research setting, and a host of other artificial effects which will obscure true relationships.

It is almost always the goal of a communication researcher to make observation as unobtrusive as possible. This can be done with careful design of the research setting or by choosing a measurement method that is inherently unobtrusive.

Reducing Obtrusiveness.   Research settings can often be constructed so that the observer is inconspicuous or completely hidden. For example, in the Bandura study the children were observed through a one-way mirror which prevents the observed person from seeing the observer. The children may not have been aware of the purpose of a one-way mirror, but for older research participants the presence of a one-way mirror will be a dead give-away that they are being observed. This realization may affect behavior in unknown ways. But even if they realize that they are being observed from behind a mirror, there is a tendency to ignore the observer after a time, because there are no movements or noises from the observer to remind the subject that he or she is being observed.

The subject who suspects surreptitious observation may actually be more reactively sensitized than if told that someone is behind the one-way mirror. The presence of a passive mirror or a small video camera in a discreet box are easily ignored after the novelty wears off, so it is often better to inform a subject that he or she is being observed than it is to allow them to have unconfirmed suspicions. Even if it is impossible to completely hide the observer, the obtrusive effect can be reduced by placing the observer in an out-of-the-way corner of the room and instructing him or her to remain as motionless and quiet as possible, to avoid rustling the coding sheets, etc.

There is a privacy issue involved with unobtrusive measurement. It boils down to this: Should the research subject be informed that he or she is being observed, even if that information may affect behavior during the research? We'll have more to say about this in the final section of this chapter when we discuss various ethical dilemmas in communication research.

Naturally Unobtrusive Measurement.   Some types of observational measurement are inherently unobtrusive. The data are collected with little or no awareness by the sources of the data that communication research is being conducted.

For example, state and federal governments routinely collect social data. The U.S. Government collects census data which describes the population in regions as large as the whole country and as small as a few square miles. These data are often very useful for comparison with sample demographic data, and for weighting or correcting sample data to make it more representative of the population values. Census data can also be used directly when the researcher uses a social system unit of analysis like the neighborhood or region. For example, the mean income or number of telephones in urban census tracts could be useful variables for a telecommunications researcher. The U.S. Commerce Department also collects detailed data about business organizations that can be used for similar aggregate analysis purposes. Governmental data are available at many public libraries and at most university libraries.

There are also archives of individual-level data that are very useful as sources of unobtrusive communication data. Public opinion poll and marketing research data are available from archives like the Institute for Social Research at the University of Michigan and the Roper Center for Public Opinion Research at the University of Connecticut. These archives contain the data and summary results from tens of thousands of questions asked of millions of people. They are particularly useful for over-time research. Similar or identical poll questions taken from surveys conducted over a span of years provides the communication researcher with a very valuable and inexpensive source of over-time data.

For the mass communication researcher, these archives are particularly useful when their information is combined with data from media archives which collect and preserve newspaper and magazine stories, television newscasts, television and radio commercials, and other media messages. Most large libraries carry the *New York Times Index* which can be used to summarize the frequency with which newspaper stories about selected issues or topics appear. The Vanderbilt Television Archives publish an index of network television story coverage and can provide videotapes of stories about selected topics. The researcher can use a media archive to provide the material for a content analysis (described in more detail later in this chapter). The data from the content analysis, combined with data from a public opinion archive, can be used to track relationships between media messages and aggregate audience responses.

Archives of original documents like letters and manuscripts can also be a source of unobtrusive data to the researcher interested in analyzing messages. For example, the organizational researcher might gain access to electronic mail messages in a sample of corporations, and use this information to study communication patterns within different types of organizations. The researcher might also collect all the interoffice mail envelopes and code the sender's and recipient's departments to unobtrusively measure interdepartmental communication. This kind of measurement produces no social demand characteristics and no sensitization of research subjects.

Reusing the data collected by other researchers (*secondary analysis*) is often a very efficient way to collect information. This measurement may or may not be considered obtrusive. For example, an interpersonal communication researcher might be able to gain access to interviews and transcripts at a research center for family communication and therapy. Since the research subjects were probably aware that their responses were being recorded, the data will be subject to some sensitization and social demand contamination. But if the subject of the interviews was, for example, establishment of rules for adolescents, and the communication researcher is interested in the dominance of the conversation by the mother or father, the researcher's dominance measurement can be considered unobtrusive.

There are many, many other sources of data for secondary analysis. Commercial research organizations often maintain databases that they sometimes make available to academic researchers after their business value has disappeared. Electronic media ratings organizations like Arbitron and A. C. Nielsen are an example.

Self-Report Measurement

In self-report measurement, an individual respondent directly provides the value of the measured variable. There are no observers involved. This is a very different situation from behavioral observation. Self-report measurement is almost always obtrusive and subject to social demand characteristics.

In the Leavitt study in Chapter 14, data on satisfaction with group membership and individual perceptions of leadership in their group were collected directly from the research subjects. Group members were asked to respond to the question "How did you like your job in the group?" by placing a check on a rating scale that was marked "disliked it" on one end and "liked it" on the other. In this case, the individual respondent ultimately controlled the value that was assigned to the liking of the role. This type of measurement frequently occurs in communication research when subjects are asked to fill out scales (in a paper-and-pencil test) to measure their perceptions about topics or toward others who are involved in the communication process.

Self-report measurement, like behavioral observation, is subject to unreliability. Since the research subjects cannot be extensively trained, the researcher must ensure that the instructions for filling out the scales or questionnaire items are clear and unambiguous (we'll discuss this in more detail later, in the section on questionnaire design). The measurement task must be as simple as possible, too, and the measurement items should be as specific as possible. You'll get better measurement if you ask a subject a series of questions about specific behaviors, like "About how many times have coworkers asked your advice about job-related problems in the past week?" and "How many times in the past year has your employer appointed you to head work group committees?" than if you just ask the global question "How good a leader are you?"

Often self-report measurements require the research subject to remember some past information or behaviors. This was the case in the example in the previous paragraph. This kind of *retrospective* measurement is difficult to achieve because it relies on fallible human memory. As a quick example of this, consider your ability to accurately report an activity that most of you have probably spent a lot of time doing recently: Try to write down the names and the plots of all the television programs you've seen in the past week. Not too easy, is it?

One way to improve self-report in retrospective measurement is to restrict the time range that the respondent must consider. It may be better to ask "What TV programs did you watch last night?" than to ask "What TV programs have you watched this fall?" There will be more random variation in the first question, since some respondents who are normally heavy viewers will have watched no TV because they were visiting their chatty great-aunt, while other light viewers might have spent the evening as couch potatoes because they had a hard day at the office. But these uncharacteristic responses will cancel out over the entire sample, and the more specific question should lead to better recall of the actual programs viewed.

It is also easier to remember specific things than general things. Asking a respondent to estimate the number of times in the past six months that she has had a disagreement with her spouse about money that resulted in both of them shouting is better than just asking how many arguments she has had with her spouse. Once again, many specific items (like arguments about money, child care, sex) can be added together in an operational definition to give measurement of a general class of items (like arguments).

TABLE 18-1   Characteristics of Different Types of Surveys

Type of Survey	Obtaining Sample	Cooperation Rate	Cost per Respondent	Strength	Weakness
In-Person	Difficult	Medium	High	Visual & manipulative measurement, interviewer rapport	Respondent fear, expensive
Telephone	Easy	High	Medium	Fast	Limited time for interview
Mall Intercept	Easy	Medium	Medium	Fast, plus in-person advantages	Unrepresentative sample
Mail	Easy	Low	Low	Large sample is inexpensive	Unrepresentative sample, respondent errors
Computer-Administered	Difficult	High	Medium	Automatic data entry	Respondent must have computer

Surveys and Interviews

Interviews and surveys (which may or may not use an interviewer) are very commonly applied tools in communication research. These are obtrusive measurement techniques that can produce either self-report or behavioral observation data.

The term survey is usually applied to observational research which uses a questionnaire as the primary measurement instrument. The unit of analysis is almost always the individual. Surveys are frequently done at a single time point, but panel or equivalent samples designs are also used to conduct over-time research.

Surveys can be generally classified as *in-person, mail, telephone, mall intercept*, or *computer-administered*, including *disk-by-mail*. We'll discuss the characteristics of each briefly. Some of the differences among the types of surveys are summarized in Table 18-1.

In-Person Survey

In this kind of survey, the questionnaire questions are presented to the respondents by an interviewer who is speaking to them face-to-face. The interviewer records the answers.

Having an interviewer speaking to the respondent has some real advantages. A good interviewer will make a personal connection with the respondent that will increase the motivation of the respondent to answer the questions fully and truthfully. It is more difficult to refuse to cooperate with a real, live person standing in front of you than to say "no" to a voice on the telephone or throw away a letter received in the mail. It is also harder to quit cooperating in the middle of the questionnaire when the interviewer is sitting a few feet away, expectantly awaiting an answer.

In-person surveys can be used with measurement procedures that use complicated visual or measurement aids. Interviewers can show respondents photographs, videotapes, or objects like product packages or sample magazines. They can use packs of cards for ranking or sorting tasks like multidimensional scaling procedures, small poster-type displays of scale points to aid the respondent in replying to verbal questions, and other visual aids that help the respondent to provide more accurate answers.

In-person surveys have some significant disadvantages, however. The first problem is in obtaining a representative sample. Areas or households are frequently the primary sampling units, but these have real problems because of differences in housing density in different areas, different numbers of persons per household, and so on (see Chapter 6). There are also some neighborhoods or regions into which interviewers are reluctant to go. For example, inner-city tenements and sparsely populated rural areas that require lots of driving between interviews are particularly difficult areas to sample. It is hard to meet the equal likelihood requirement of a representative sample unless some complicated and expensive steps in selecting the sample (and motivating the interviewers) are used.

Selecting the units is not the only problem in obtaining a representative sample. There is a further problem in getting participation from the sampled persons. People are increasingly reluctant to allow strangers into their homes, even those who identify themselves as noncommercial communication researchers.

At one time in-person surveys had a very high cooperation rate. Cooperation rate, or *response rate*, is the proportion of sampled units who agree to complete the survey. Response rate for in-person surveys has been falling dramatically in recent years. In the 1960s, response rates near 90 percent were not uncommon, but today the figure is closer to 60 percent.

Cooperation can be improved by using any means that establishes the identity and authenticity of the interviewer. The lowest response rate will be seen when interviewers knock unannounced on a door and ask to come in for an interview. More cooperation will be achieved when the respondent is contacted in advance by mail and/or telephone, and an appointment for conducting the interview is set up. Contacting respondents by mail also provides a chance for the interviewer to present authentic credentials, like a university letterhead, which will help reassure the respondent that he or she is not opening the door to an ax murderer.

But of course contacting the respondent several times costs much more money than just knocking on the door, so there is a trade-off between cooperation and cost. In fact, the cost per completed interview for in-person surveys is the largest drawback to this research procedure. The cost of obtaining a completed interview includes a complex sampling procedure, travel time and expenses for the interviewer, incentives to go into unsafe neighborhoods, and other incidental expenses. The cost of an in-person interview is frequently two to five times as much as the cost of a telephone interview.

Telephone Survey

In a telephone survey, the interview is conducted over the telephone. This eliminates interviewer travel time and expenses. Obtaining a representative sample with techniques like random digits dialing is relatively simple, as we noted in Chapter 6. This reduces the cost of a telephone survey.

But there are drawbacks to telephone interviewing. The loss of personal face-to-face contact between the interviewer and respondent can have negative consequences for cooperation and for the accuracy of the answers. No visual aids can be used, so this kind of survey cannot be used for communication research that relies on visual judgments or responses.

Also, a telephone interview cannot be as long as an in-person interview. While an in-person interview might easily last 30 minutes or longer, the upper limit for a telephone interview is about half that time, and many experts recommend 10 minutes as the target time for a telephone interview. This is not very long, and it places a stringent limitation on the amount of information that the researcher can obtain with this kind of survey.

Cooperation rates for telephone interviews are relatively high, although they have also been falling over the years. There is not much of a fear factor in cooperating with a telephone interviewer for the respondent. But requests for telephone interviews have become more frequent, and phony telephone surveys have been used as a ploy by telemarketers and crank callers, so that the suspicions of a typical respondent may be aroused even when contacted for a legitimate survey. Both these factors have lowered the willingness of respondents to cooperate with telephone surveys. In the 1960s, response rates were typically over 80 percent, while many telephone surveys now fail to reach even a 70 percent cooperation rate.

Mall Intercept Survey

This is an in-person survey that is conducted by selecting the respondents from the persons who are present in some public place, such as a shopping mall. Respondents are randomly selected from passers-by. This eliminates the expense of complicated sampling procedures and interviewer travel, as well as the problem of dealing with bad neighborhoods and rural areas.

These advantages must be balanced against the significant drawback of obtaining an unrepresentative sample. As we mentioned in Chapter 6, the persons present in a shopping mall or a public square are not going to be typical of the entire population, so the results of this kind of survey have poor external validity when they are generalized to the general population.

For some kinds of research, however, a mall intercept provides a good approximation of a representative sample. For example, a marketing communication researcher conducting research on advertising appeals for clothing may be willing to define a population as being those people who frequent shopping malls, where most clothing is sold. In this case, if a good random sampling procedure is used at the mall intercept—people are selected using some fixed rule, like every fiftieth person who passes, interviewing is done on all days of the week, and at all times the mall is open—then the resulting sample may be quite representative of the population of consumers. But using a mall intercept for political communication research is probably unwise.

Cooperation rates for mall intercepts are somewhat better than in-person interviews, as the mall is a neutral and safe meeting ground. But the time that the interview can take is shorter. People in malls and public places are frequently pressed for time, and will literally not sit still for a very long interview. Cooperation can be improved by offering small incentives for respondents like discounts at a mall store, free ice cream cones from a nearby shop, or such. These add a little to the cost of the interview, but some businesses may provide such incentives to a researcher as a low-cost way of increasing their foot traffic.

There are practical problems with mall interviewing, too. Many malls do not permit such activity, or they may have a single commercial research firm which is licensed to conduct all survey research on the premises. Gaining permission to interview may be difficult or expensive.

Mail Survey

The mail survey is unlike the other kinds of survey discussed above in one very important way: It does not involve an interviewer. The survey is self-administered.

This introduces some significant problems. There is no interviewer who can exert subtle social pressure to convince the respondent to cooperate. If the respondent has trouble understanding the questionnaire instructions or questions, there is no one to ask for help. Since most questionnaires will be written in English, the respondent must be functionally literate in that language. This will eliminate almost 20 percent of the general population immediately.

Because of these problems, the response rate for mail surveys is usually very low. Rates of 20 percent or less for a general mailing are typical. The response rate will increase if the respondent perceives the survey as important, or holds strong opinions about the issues explored by the questionnaire, or identifies strongly with the sponsoring organization. A survey of attitudes toward guns conducted by the National Rifle Association will have a very high response rate from gun fanciers, while a survey of preferences for muffins conducted by Acme Foods will have a very low response rate from the general public.

Questionnaire design and the length of the questionnaire are very important. Long questionnaires and those with confusing instructions or complex scales will be thrown in the wastebasket. So will those with poorly written or confusing questions. The single best thing the researcher can do to increase response rate is to pay lots of attention to creating a very good, clean questionnaire.

Another way to improve response rate is to provide some incentive for the respondent. Even small incentives, like a $1 gift certificate, will help. Of course, even small incentives are expensive when they are mailed to hundreds or thousands of respondents. The researcher can sometimes provide a no-cost "psychological incentive" by stressing the value of the information for creating public good in the introduction. This works particularly well for targeted audiences. For example, a researcher studying use of public libraries by active cardholders can stress the value of the results in improving the library services being used by the respondent.

Response rates can be improved by contacting respondents who do not reply to the first mailing. A typical way to do this is to mail out a reminder postcard or a second copy of the questionnaire to those members of the sample who do not respond to the original mailing. This might be followed by a telephone call if the second mailing does not produce results. A rough rule of thumb is that each additional contact will add another 5 percent or so to the response rate.

Multiple contacts are very expensive. Say the original mailing to a sample of 1000 costs $1000 and produces a 25 percent response rate. Each completed questionnaire in this mailing costs the researcher $4. The second mailing of the complete questionnaire to the 750 people who did not return the first questionnaire will cost $750 and produce perhaps 50 more questionnaires, at a cost of $15 per questionnaire. But the extra questionnaires may be worth the cost, as the sample will be much more representative with their addition.

Multiple contacts require that the respondents be identified, so the researcher can tell who has returned the questionnaire and who has not. This can be a problem if the questionnaire deals with sensitive topics where respondent anonymity is desirable. Even innocent questionnaires with identification are avoided by some respondents who are afraid that the information might be used to target them for junk mail or sales calls.

One method to deal with this problem is to identify each questionnaire with a code number, and to include some phrase in the questionnaire introduction like "Each response is identified with a confidential code number. This number will be used for tabulation purposes only, and your responses will be kept completely private." Some researchers attach this code number to a return envelope and mention nothing about it in the questionnaire. This practice falls in an ethically gray area, and we'll discuss it further in the last section of this chapter.

Mail surveys are relatively cheap because there are no interviewer expenses. But with low return rates and multiple mailings, they may actually cost more per completed questionnaire than telephone surveys. The low return rates usually mean that the researcher cannot make a strong case for a representative sample, and so must qualify the results with cautions about the generalizability of the findings.

Computer-Administered Survey

This kind of survey relies on a computer to conduct the interview. This provides some advantages and disadvantages.

On the positive side, a very extensive set of questions can be prepared, but only a relevant subset will be asked of a given respondent. If the researcher is studying relationship communication, an early question might be "Are you married?" The respondent who answers yes might be given one set of questions; if the answer is no, there will be another set of questions aimed at unmarried persons. Because the computer can immediately analyze replies and use this information to select the correct questions, the respondent does not have to follow complex instructions on a printed questionnaire. All the respondent sees is a set of simple questions presented on a computer screen. This is called *adaptive interviewing*, and some very sophisticated computer software is available which does extensive statistical data analysis during the interview and uses the results to structure the interview.

Since the reply to the questionnaire questions is made directly on a computer keyboard, the data can be immediately analyzed. Complete data analysis can be obtained a few minutes after the end of interviewing. The cost of keying in the data is eliminated.

The largest drawback to computer-administered surveys is the lack of respondent access to computer systems. This kind of survey is not very useful for reaching a general population. It can be used in doing business related research, since most businesses, even very small ones, have personal computer systems.

TABLE 18-2 Response Rates in a Hypothetical Telephone Survey

Original Sample	1000
Disconnected Number	100
Business Number or fax machine	200
No Answer after 5 call backs	100
Answering Machine	50
No one in household over 18	25
Did not complete full interview	50
Refused to Cooperate	75
Completed Interview	400

Disk by Mail

These surveys are a combination of mail and computer-administered surveys. The respondent is mailed a computer disk with a programmed set of questions. The respondent replies to the questions using his or her own computer system, then mails the disk back to the researcher. Since computer disks can be reproduced in quantities for $1 to $2 each, the cost is not a lot higher than printed questionnaires, and the difference is offset by the elimination of data input costs.

Computer-administered surveys can also be used in in-person or mall intercept settings. The interviewer can present the respondent with a laptop computer, explain how to respond to the questions, and then stand by to help out if computer operation problems occur.

Some researchers feel that computer-administered interviews are superior to interviews conducted by humans when the questions involve very sensitive personal issues. People are surprisingly willing to reveal personal details to the very impersonal computer, apparently because it is perceived as being anonymous and not judgmental. Socially desirable responses are less frequent. Who cares what a computer thinks? The respondent can complete the survey in private (the researcher can leave the room), and embarrassing responses appear to disappear from the screen into the depths of computer memory, rather than residing rather permanently on paper.

Calculating Response Rates

We have mentioned cooperation or response rates repeatedly. They are a critical part of the decision about which survey method to use, but they are a little more complicated than we've admitted.

Let's take a telephone survey as an example. Suppose a political communication researcher wishes to study voting behavior in a state. The population is defined as all persons over the age of 18 in the state. A random digits dialing procedure is used to select a sample of 1000 telephone numbers. The results of calling these numbers are shown in Table 18-2. Only 400 of the original 1000 numbers result in a completed interview. What is the response rate?

The simplest answer is 40 percent, since that is the percentage of the original numbers that gave good data. But it's probably incorrect to consider the disconnected numbers and business numbers as part of the original population. If we eliminate them, we have a response rate of 400/700, or 57 percent.

But what about the 100 numbers that never answered? Some telephone numbers are used for computer data transmission, so they never answer. Others may be the back rooms of businesses, or be used for automatic alarm systems, or other nonpersonal uses. But they may also be the households of persons who are just not at home very often. It is very hard to guess how many persons in the universe are missed in this category. If the interviewer tried calling at different times of day on different days of the week, the researcher may be justified in eliminating these no answers from the population. The more call backs that are tried, the better the justification for eliminating the no answer numbers from the population. If they are eliminated, the response rate becomes 400/600, or 67 percent.

If an answering machine picked up the telephone every time the interviewer called back, there is probably some evidence that this number should be part of the universe. But the answering machine might be in a work-at-home office or a teenager's bedroom. Some researchers would eliminate these from the population, and increase the response rate to 400/550, or 73 percent.

The next set of persons agree to participate, but do not complete the interview, because they tell the interviewer that there is no one over 18 in the household. This eliminates them from the population, and increases the response rate to 400/525, or 76 percent.

The last two sets are clearly part of the universe. They qualify, but do not complete the interview because they either refuse at the beginning to participate, or quit part of the way through the interview. However, some of those who refuse may be under 18, so including them in the universe may underestimate the actual response rate. But there is no way to know this.

As you can see, we can get response rates ranging from 40 percent to 76 percent from the same study. Some of the differences in the response rates reported by different researchers are due to differences in the way the rate is calculated. To give the best description of the response, the researcher must consider each group that did not cooperate fully, or that did not clearly refuse to cooperate. The next step is to decide whether they are more likely to be inside or outside of the population, and adjust the calculation accordingly. It is very important that the researcher report the details of who was included and excluded in the write-up of the research, so that the reader can tell exactly how the response rate was computed.

Choosing the Type of Survey

The characteristics of each type of survey should be matched to the requirements of the research problem. For instance, if obtaining a representative sample is very important, mail surveys are ruled out. But if obtaining a large number of responses at reasonable cost is a requirement, then mail surveys may be preferable to the other types.

Generally, the combination of relatively high cooperation rate and low cost makes telephone surveys attractive for many research applications. But telephone surveys cannot be used whenever any visual aids are required, so either mail, mall intercept, or in-person surveys may be required.

The researcher must weigh the various pros and cons of each survey type carefully. Making up a more extensive matrix like that shown in Table 18-1 may help with the decision.

Interviewer Requirements

The primary rule for interviewers is this: Intrude in the research process as little as possible. This means that the interviewer should never direct the respondent toward an answer, should never be judgmental, and should not interpret the respondent's answers according to his or her own beliefs or values. The interviewer must be consistent in his or her communication style and language, so that each respondent is exposed to the same kind of measurement environment.

This is easier said than done. Some types of interviewing require judgments and decisions from the interviewer, while others do not. A telephone interview with a scripted introduction and closed-ended questions will give the interviewer little chance for interpretation or choice of language or instructions that might guide the respondent toward a particular answer. But in semi-structured interviews like focus groups (see below), the interviewer must exercise immediate judgment about the kind of question to ask next, and may ask questions differently to different respondents. This gives the interviewer the great potential to bias the results.

Even in a very structured interview, a poor interviewer can lead a respondent to particular answers by vocal inflection or by off-hand comments ("Are you SURE you want to say that TV censorship is OK?"). The only answer is training, and interviewer training is crucial in all forms of communication research that require measurement which involves interaction between the researcher and the research subject. The highest quality questionnaire or most sophisticated research design can be ruined if the researcher neglects sufficient training for the people who collect the data.

The first step in training interviewers is to give them a detailed set of instructions on how to approach the research subject and what is expected of them during the interview. The interviewer must share the researcher's appreciation for nondirection and pleasantness, and have some idea about how to start the interview and set its tone.

The next step in interviewer training is the dry-run interview. The interviewer runs through the full interview process with someone playing the part of a typical respondent, while the researcher observes the interview. The researcher then discusses the interviewer's performance, notes the areas that need improvement, and repeats the process until the researcher is convinced that the interviewer is sufficiently low-key and consistent and will not bias the results.

In-Person Interviews

There are some particular requirements for interviewers who must interact face-to-face with respondents. First, the interviewer must establish legitimacy. Showing some identification, such as a photo identification card with the name of the interviewing organization prominently shown, is often the first step. The interviewer must then gain the respondent's cooperation by being polite, but persistent. The interviewer can stress the importance of the research, its ease, and so on. This is essentially an exercise in selling. The interviewer is asking the respondent to contribute something valuable (time) and must give the respondent some persuasive reason to make this contribution.

After cooperation is obtained, the interviewer must establish a personal connection with the respondent. There is no good prescription that will spell out how to do this. Basically, the interviewer must be friendly, polite, and speak respectfully to the respondent. Some interviewers do this automatically, others must learn it, and some never achieve it. Those who do not must be eliminated as possible interviewers.

The formation of a relationship between the interviewer and the respondent carries some dangers too. The interviewer must guard against introducing any influence that might create social demand in respondents' answers. The interviewer must also strive to treat all respondents in a consistent fashion, so that any bias accidentally introduced is at least consistent across all respondents. To be clearer about this, suppose a female interviewer is able to easily establish a warm relationship with female respondents, but is rather stiff with male respondents. This might bias respondents' answers along sex lines, and introduce false conclusions about gender differences on the measured variables.

Telephone Interviews

The telephone interviewer does not have the advantage of the personal immediacy provided by face-to-face interaction. He or she must identify him- or herself very quickly, without the aid of a physical artifact like an ID card. It is necessary to also quickly assure the respondent that the interviewer is not selling something or making an obscene telephone call.

The telephone interviewer must also quickly gain cooperation from the respondent and establish some personal connection. Generally, this connection will be "cooler" than a face-to-face relationship. This actually may aid the interviewer in asking sensitive questions, but it may hinder in gaining replies to difficult or challenging questions.

The telephone interview will often generate more requests for clarification of questions from respondents, since they will have no visual aids. For example, an in-person marketing communication interviewer may show a respondent a picture of a new product, then ask questions about it. A telephone interviewer will have to describe the product verbally. The telephone respondent is then likely to ask for clarifications, like "how big is it?" The telephone interviewers must be instructed on how to reply to such questions. It is particularly critical that all interviewers apply the same rules to their replies. If one interviewer replies "I'm not allowed to say," while another replies "It weighs 4.75 pounds, comes in white and red, and it fits on your desktop," response bias will be introduced by the different interviewers.

Focus Group Interviews

One particular type of interviewing that has been used more and more extensively in recent years is the focus (or "focused") group interview. This term has been applied to a wide range of interviewing techniques and settings, so it actually refers to a class of procedures, rather than one type of interview. But we can describe a typical focus group interview process in general terms.

First, the researcher determines the topic or topics to be investigated. This may be very general ("What perceptions of my political candidate are held by the electorate?") or it may be a specific list of topics ("... perceptions of the candidate's stand on abortion; reaction to campaign commercials stressing family values; evaluation of the candidate's response to charges by staffers of sexual harassment ..."). The focus group interviewer (often called the *moderator*) uses this list to guide the interviewing process. There are usually no specific prewritten questions, so this list serves the same purpose as a questionnaire in a survey. It structures the interviewing process, but to a much lesser degree than a questionnaire. The focus group interview is more like a journalistic interview than a survey.

Second, a group of respondents is chosen. The group size is typically 4 to 10 people. The researcher often determines the characteristics of the group ("... white males over 35 ..."; "... suburban Midwest residents..."). Convenience samples are the norm in current research practice. This limits the generalizability of the results, but convenience samples are often used for pragmatic (i.e., cost) reasons. Multiple groups may be involved in the research project, but the total number of participants is usually fairly small.

Third, the group is assembled at some interviewing location where the interviewer and the group can be placed in comfortable surroundings that will encourage them to talk freely. The interview room usually is equipped with some means by which the group can be observed. This is frequently a one-way mirror, behind which observers watch or summarize the conversation of the group members. The focus group may also be audio- or videotape recorded. The group interview process often requires an hour or more. At the beginning, the group must have time to relax and warm up to the discussion, and then the discussion must be allowed to keep flowing to get at more subtle views or opinions.

In some cases the focus group interviewer also summarizes the interactions among group members, but this is generally not a good practice. The interviewer has to listen carefully to responses and allow them to lead to the next question, while still considering how to steer the discussion to cover the issues outlined by the researcher. If the interviewer also has to summarize the conversation, the flow of interaction in the group may be interrupted. This choppy discussion may give much less information.

Finally, the group's discussion must be analyzed and conclusions drawn from it. This is often done by making a transcript of the discussion from the audio- or videotape recordings. This transcript can be analyzed impressionistically by one or more judges, or it can be subjected to a formal content analysis. For exploratory research, the impressionistic procedure is often used. For formal hypothesis testing, full content analysis is often used.

Focus group interviewing is expensive. It requires highly trained interviewers, expensive or scarce facilities, and lots of time from the respondents, who often have to be paid for their participation. For this reason, focus group research often uses very small numbers of respondents, as we noted above. But it produces a very rich set of data in the transcripts. Because the researcher does not completely determine the structure of the interview beforehand, focus group interviews can produce unexpected and important results. An interview that starts discussing a political candidate's problems with his personal life may end up showing that the group is much more concerned about his stand on gun control.

Focus groups are frequently used as a first step in constructing a more formal question-naire. This is an excellent, if expensive, strategy. The strength of focus group interviewing is in the wide range of qualitative information that is produced by its lack of structure. But the small *N*s, the convenience samples, and the lack of consistency in the way questions are asked when multiple groups are interviewed makes the external validity of focus group research generally poor. (The makers of a popular soft drink who changed its formula as a result of focus group results found this out to their very expensive dismay.)

On the other hand, structured questionnaires, such as those described in the next section, can be applied to large representative samples under controlled interviewing conditions. But if the researcher asks the wrong questions on the questionnaire, the results will be poor. By using focus groups to identify the critical variables and processes that characterize a phenomenon, then using more formal quantitative techniques to test hypotheses about the phenomenon, the communication researcher can produce superior results.

Training a focus group moderator is no small task. A telephone survey interviewer might be trained in a few hours, but a focus group interviewer will require days of practice and many dry runs before his or her basic group interviewing skills are sufficiently developed. Once trained in the basic processes, the interviewer can take on subsequent focus groups more quickly. But the interviewer must have good knowledge of both the research question and of the group characteristics in order to ask relevant questions and pick up on the subtle hints that group members exhibit. Asking a young male business executive who eats most meals in restaurants to moderate a group of middle-aged female housewives discussing baking products is not going to work well. The researcher should always try to find an interviewer whose background and lifestyle matches the group's as much as possible. The interviewer must either be trained extensively about the discussion topic, or have some prior knowledge of it.

Because of the difficulty of training people to become knowledgeable moderators and of assembling groups in appropriate interviewing facilities, a number of commercial research firms specialize in providing focus group interviewing services. These firms frequently specialize in certain topics or ethnic groups. Some focus group suppliers specialize in political communication research, in consumer and marketing communication research, in Spanish-language research, and so on. Using these firms for focus group research is not cheap, but the odds of obtaining good data are usually improved.

It is not impossible for the individual researcher to use focus groups, however. But the researcher should recognize that they are quite demanding and will require extensive preparation and analysis to produce useful results. It's very easy to do a poor job, and very hard to do a good one.

Questionnaire Design

Many communication research projects rely on data collection from questionnaires. Ex-perimental, field, and observational research designs frequently use questionnaires. Public opinion surveys, political surveys, surveys of product purchases, and readership and view-ership surveys are all general examples of research which is conducted almost exclusively with questionnaires. But an interpersonal communication researcher might use questionnaires to get descriptions of the communication behavior of individuals, their demographic characteristics, and so forth. Good questionnaire design and construction is critical to a wide range of communication research.

Writing a questionnaire is a little like playing the guitar. It's easy to just jump in and do it badly, but it's very hard work to do it well. At first glance, the process looks like simplicity itself. Just ask the respondents some questions, and record their responses. But 50 years of study of questionnaire construction has shown that the way one asks questions often determines the quality of the information and may even determine the results that one gets.

Questionnaire Introduction

The first thing a questionnaire must do is convince the respondent to cooperate in answering the questions. This task is particularly demanding if self-administered questionnaires are being used. Self-administration is always the case in mail surveys, and might occur in experimental research if the dependent variables are easily operationalized with questionnaire items that can be filled out by the experimental subject.

The introduction to the questionnaire must be very clear and simple. It should state the purpose of the research and it must disarm any fears or suspicious about the motives of the researcher. It must establish a rapport with the respondent and convince him or her to cooperate. Questionnaires have been misused as sales devices, for political solicitations, and for other nonresearch purposes, and potential respondents are justifiably suspicious about them.

The introduction to a mail questionnaire might be in a cover letter, or it might be the first paragraph of the questionnaire form. For telephone or in-person interviewing, the introduction might be read or spoken to the respondent. It is best to defuse the suspicions of the respondent by immediately identifying the person or organization doing the research. For example, a telephone interview might begin with an introduction like this:

> *Hello, I'm John Jones. I'm conducting a survey of audience reactions to television advertising for the Opinion Research Institute at the University of Calisota. This is a research project, and the information will not be used for sales purposes. Your identity will not be recorded. Can you spare a few minutes to answer some questions?*

There may be times when stating the full purpose of the research or even the organization doing the research at the beginning of the interview might bias responses to later questions. Withholding information in the questionnaire introduction becomes an ethical issue, and we'll discuss this later in this chapter.

Question Wording

Writing individual question items on the questionnaire demands that the researcher pay careful attention to a number of important points.

Vocabulary and Style

Questions must be written in the simplest language possible. Use of polysyllabic words like "polysyllabic" should be avoided, as should jargon and slang. Using long sentences with many dependent clauses is also poor practice. The questionnaire writer should strive for "journalistic" prose: short declarative sentences using active tenses. If a 12-year-old can't read and understand the question, it probably should be rewritten.

Leading Questions

Items can lead respondents to a certain response by the way that they are phrased. This biases the responses, and it will probably annoy the observant respondent. Asking a question like "Do you support the efforts of the Independent Party to improve the working conditions of all Americans?" will produce no useful information. Rephrasing the question as "How would you rate the performance of the Independent Party on workplace regulation?" allows the possibility of a valid negative response.

Another way that questions can lead the respondent to an answer involves associating some response with an influential group. "Most Church leaders deplore televised violence. How do you feel about the amount of violence on television?" Obviously, the questionnaire writer must avoid this kind of question.

Leading questions are sometimes unethically used to produce the results desired by the organization which sponsors the research. A critical reader of research results will be sensitive to the way in which questions are asked, and will reject the results of any research that uses such questions. The questionnaire writer should be aware of the leading nature of some questions, and be very careful to phrase all questions in a neutral fashion that makes all responses equally easy for the respondent.

Social Desirability

The response to some questions may be biased because of prevailing ideas about "correct" opinions or behavior. Such questions are said to have *social demand characteristics*, because social norms demand that the respondent who does not see him- or herself as socially deviant (i.e., everyone) give a particular "correct" answer. The respondent then gives an answer thought to be expected or socially appropriate, rather than one that accurately represents a position. "Are you in favor of equal employment opportunities for minorities?" will be overwhelmingly answered in the affirmative by nearly all respondents, but it's unlikely that such a large number of respondents really hold that opinion. Phrasing questions that avoid demand characteristics is often difficult when dealing with emotionally charged issues.

To compensate, the questionnaire writer can sometimes reframe an issue that has demand characteristics so that a range of responses is possible. The basic strategy is to reassure the respondent that he or she is not alone in expressing an opinion at either end of the measurement scale. For example, the equal employment question in the previous paragraph might be recast like this: "Some people feel that equal employment programs have produced problems for the average worker, while others feel that they have opened up opportunities for all workers. On a 1 to 7 scale, where 1 is Strongly Unfavorable and 7 is Strongly Favorable, how would you rate your own feelings about equal employment programs?"

Vague Questions

If a questionnaire item is not phrased carefully, different respondents may interpret the question differently, and the resulting measurement will be invalid. "Would you call your relationship with your spouse good or bad?" is a very general question. Some respondents may interpret the word relationship to mean sexual relationship, while others may consider it to mean communication of private feelings, and still others will think about all the items that make up their personal definition of a relationship, and mentally average them. The researcher will actually be getting a measurement of different concepts from each of these respondents (that is, invalid measurement). To avoid this, questions must be as concrete and explicit as possible. Their meaning should be unambiguous.

Since questionnaire items are part of the operationalization of a theoretical concept, the researcher can refer to the theoretical definition (see Chapter 2) as a guide to the meaning elements that should be included in a question. In the above example, if the theoretical definition of "relationship" included both sexual compatibility and self-disclosure of personal feelings, the single vague question could be expanded to two more explicit questions about each of these elements.

Double Items

Sometimes a poorly constructed questionnaire item may really ask two or more questions. The respondent must then base a response on one of the two questions and ignore the other, or simply give up and refuse to answer. Suppose a manager is asked this question: "Are you in favor of installing computer mediated conferencing equipment in your organization, or do you think existing communication facilities are adequate?" It is quite possible that the respondent thinks existing communication facilities are poor, but does not feel that computer conferencing will solve the problem (installing additional voice mail equipment might be better). It is impossible to respond accurately to this item.

Double items must be split into simple items that measure only a single concept: "Are you in favor of installing computer mediated conferencing equipment?" and "Do you feel existing communication facilities in your organization are adequate?"

Structuring Questions

Aside from the issues of question wording discussed above, the questionnaire author must also deal with some structural issues in each question.

Complex Instructions

Some questions or measurements require explanation before the respondent can reply. These should be as short as possible, and as simple as possible. This is particularly the case with telephone or in-person interviewing, as the respondent cannot back up and reread the instructions. Even in mail and self-administered questionnaires, long and complex instructions will reduce the number of respondents who complete the item or the whole questionnaire.

Any set of instructions that has more than three or four sentences should be critically reviewed. Of course, there is a trade-off here. Respondents must clearly understand what is expected of them. But if explaining the procedure requires a long and complex set of instructions, the researcher probably should review and revise the measurement procedure. It may be too complicated to be successful.

Long Lists of Alternatives

Respondents deal best with a fairly small set of comparative judgments. Humans have trouble making more than 5 to 10 simultaneous comparisons. Questionnaire items that ask respondents to rank order 30 alternatives are going to give poor results. So are questions that force the respondent to choose from a large set of items that differ on more than a few basic dimensions.

If you present two different sample layouts for a magazine article, the respondent will have little trouble choosing the preferred one. But if you present 25 samples, you may overwhelm his or her ability to make fine distinctions and to consider all the differences among the choices. Research has shown that people presented with this situation tend to focus on just a few dimensions in order to simplify their task. Unfortunately, the dimensions they focus on may differ among respondents, so the resulting measurement may have poor validity. For example, some respondents may focus on attractive type faces in judging magazine layouts, while others may use pictures or graphics. This will give preferences that are not really comparable.

Comparisons of complicated situations or objects should be broken down to comparisons on basic dimensions whenever possible, in order to increase the validity of the judgments, and the number of comparisons reduced to the minimum possible. There are advanced methods, such as *conjoint analysis*, which address the problem of making complicated distinctions among alternative choices on a number of dimensions without overloading the respondent.

"Strange" Response Requirements

Some measurement procedures rely on responses from the research subjects that are not familiar. For example, some scaling procedures ask respondents to rate ideas or objects on unfamiliar dimensions. A semantic differential item might ask a respondent to rate another person on a scale with "hot" at one end and "cold" at the other. Or a multidimensional scaling item might request the "distance" between an apple and an orange. This is not the way most people normally make distinctions, and the researcher is going to have to take some pains in the instructions for such items to ensure that the respondent feels comfortable with such responses.

Instructions that disarm the respondent's potentially negative reaction to the measurement task are useful in these cases. Examples are usually necessary, too. The instructions might be phrased like this: "Although you may find it a little strange to fill out these scales, just check the box that seems best to you. There are no right or wrong answers. For example, ..."

Open- vs Closed-Ended Questions

Closed-ended questions require the respondent to choose from a fixed set of alternatives or to give a single numerical value. Open-ended questions allow respondents to choose their own replies. Some examples are shown in Table 18-3.

TABLE 18-3 Examples of Closed- and Open-Ended Questions with Precoding

Closed-Ended

Generally speaking, do you feel that your communication with your spouse is

1. VERY SATISFACTORY
2. SOMEWHAT SATISFACTORY
3. NEITHER SATISFACTORY NOR UNSATISFACTORY   (4:22)
4. SOMEWHAT UNSATISFACTORY
5. VERY UNSATISFACTORY

Approximately how many hours a day do you spend watching television?

__._ Hours   (4:23–26)

The people in the advertisement appear to be

Happy										Sad	(4:27)
Good										Bad	(4:28)
Excited										Calm	(4:29)

1 2 3 4 5 6 7 8 9

Of the program types listed below, mark the ONE program category that you
like to watch the most   (4:30)

__ news programs (1)   __ sports   (5)
__ movies   (2)   __ public affairs (6)
__ sitcoms   (3)   __ dramatic series (7)
__ musical/variety (4)   __ other   (8)

Open-Ended

Think back to yesterday. What topics did you discuss with your children?   (5:6–7)

Please list, as fully as you can, everything you remember about the diet soda commercial.   (5:8–11)

What is the most important issue facing the American public today?   (5:12–13)

Choosing one type of question or the other is not strictly a question of style or preference. Some measurement techniques will require scales or numerical responses, while others will require free responses.

Closed-ended questions are much easier (i.e., cheaper) to process. Responses can be precoded (the data processing codes such as (4:22) are placed right on the questionnaire) so that data entry is simplified. There is also a uniformity to the response that improves the reliability of the responses. But closed-ended questions can be restrictive. If the questionnaire author has not included all relevant alternatives, the respondent may be frustrated in trying to answer.

Open-ended questions are much harder to handle, because each must be examined by a trained coder, and the responses classified for analysis. The researcher must conduct a separate content analysis for each question. (Content analysis procedures are described later in this chapter.) Highly verbal respondents will give long replies; respondents with low levels of literacy may skip the questions entirely. But open-ended answers can provide a very rich source of information, particularly about topics that have a wider range of possible answers than the researcher can anticipate.

The general prescription is to use open-ended questions sparingly, and reserve them for measurements that have many alternatives, or for exploratory purposes. Closed-ended questions are efficient and reliable. But it's a mistake to force all questions into a closed-ended format, if open-ended will give better information.

Questionnaire Architecture

The entire questionnaire should be seen as a communication between the researcher and the respondent. Simply creating a good set of questionnaire items is not enough. The items must be placed in the questionnaire so that the whole presentation is effective.

Length and Fatigue

Filling out a questionnaire is work. Since participation in communication research is almost always voluntary, a long, demanding questionnaire can significantly cut down on the number of people willing to finish it. A questionnaire should be as short as possible, and the items as simple as possible. The fatigue that comes from filling out a long questionnaire may interfere with the responses. While a careful researcher can reverse questionnaire items on half the questionnaires (but not always—see the next section) to remove *systematic* effects of fatigue, the fatigue will still cause errors in measurement that will make it harder to detect real relationships among variables.

Although the amount of interest and commitment by the respondents will determine the length of questionnaire that they are willing to complete, any self-administered questionnaire that requires more than 15 minutes to fill out in a pilot test should be critically reviewed to see if it can't be reduced in size. A telephone questionnaire should be even shorter, about 10 minutes.

A primary rule is this: Never ask anything that your research design does not require. Novice questionnaire authors often decide to include questions "just in case" they might be useful later. Avoid this temptation! Each questionnaire item should be part of the operational definition of a theoretical concept laid out during your analysis of the research questions. If there's no theoretical variable, there doesn't need to be an operational questionnaire item. The damage done by a too-long questionnaire will far outweigh the insurance of asking questions that may not relate to any theoretical construct of interest.

Question Order

Filling out a questionnaire takes time, so different concepts are measured at different time points over a short period. Measurement of one concept at one point in the questionnaire may affect later measurement of other concepts. Sensitization effects occur within the time span of the measurement, and they may affect the results.

Suppose a researcher is interested in the public's concern about the amount of sexually oriented material on cable television. The questionnaire might begin with an open-ended question like "What do you think is the most important issue or problem facing the country today?" This can be followed by a more focused question, "What is the most important issue or problem related to the mass media?" and finally by specific questions about depictions of sexual activity in the media in general and then on cable television. By ordering the questions from general to specific, the researcher can get a measurement of the respondent's concern in the context of other issues that the respondent thinks are important. With a reversed order of the questions, the questions about cable television would probably have prompted respondents to consider this issue more strongly when they responded to the questions about mass media and about general problems faced by the country.

Many attitude or opinion questions suffer from sensitizing or context effects that are introduced by other questions or by the measurement setting itself. For example, valid measurement is sometimes impossible if the intent of the researcher is known by the respondents. Although concealing intent introduces some ethical concerns (see the final section in this chapter), it can be done by "masking" sensitive questions with questions about other issues. To do this, the questionnaire author arranges the critical questions randomly in a set of other unrelated questions. A family communication researcher who wishes to find out respondents' attitudes toward several aspects of divorce (child custody, alimony, religious prohibitions, etc.) can sprinkle questions about these issues among dozens of other questions about other political and personal matters. Placing all the questions about divorce together in a block might sensitize the respondents to the issue, and make their responses more extreme.

Another important consideration on item placement is where to put sensitive questions like those about age, income, or personal habits. In general, these are best placed near the end of the questionnaire. Respondents are more likely to cooperate in answering these questions after some rapport has been established with the interviewer during in-person and telephone interviews, or some time commitment has already been made by filling out the first part of mail or self-administered questionnaires.

Personal questions are always potentially dangerous, so they should be asked only if absolutely necessary. These questions may cause the respondent to become suspicious of the researcher's or interviewer's motives or they may be considered offensive or an invasion of privacy. If a respondent feels this way, he or she may refuse to answer any further questions, so information from questions that appear after the sensitive ones will be lost.

Question Skips

Many questionnaires require "skips," where the interviewer or respondent is instructed to skip over a set of questions, if there was a particular answer to some prior question. For example, if a marketing communication researcher is studying automotive advertisements, he or she might want to ask different sets of questions of persons who have purchased an automobile in the past year, and of those who have not:

1. Have you purchased a new or used automobile in the past 12 months?
__ Yes   __ No

→ IF YOU ANSWERED YES, SKIP TO QUESTION 4

2. Do you expect to purchase a new automobile in the next 12 months?
__ Yes   __ No

3. Please rate the importance to *you* of each of the following features of a new car

Very Important				Very Unimportant			
1	2	3	4	5	6	7	Color
1	2	3	4	5	6	7	Automatic Transmission
1	2	3	4	5	6	7	Four-wheel Drive

4. Are you a subscriber to any of the following magazines?

Yes	No	
__	__	*Road and Track*
__	__	*Car and Driver*
__	__	*Motorcar*

Skips are a necessary evil. They are a particular problem in self-administered question-naires, because the researcher cannot ensure that the respondent has answered the right set of questions. Even when an interviewer is reading the questions, skips complicate the training and slow down the interview process. Skips should be as short as possible, and the instructions should be very clear. You should avoid complicated skip patterns ("If you answered 'yes' to Question 14 and are a male who checked 6 or higher on the scale in Question 5b, skip to Question 33..."). Many skips with complex instructions will ensure many errors by respondents.

Esthetics

The appearance of a questionnaire can be very important for self-administered question-naires. Respondents are more likely to think that the research being conducted with a professional-looking questionnaire is important, and to spend the necessary time to com-plete it. Even in questionnaires filled out by interviewers, a simple layout can cut down on the number of interviewer errors.

It is important to make the questionnaire as visually simple and clean as possible. Use lots of white space in laying out the questionnaire, and space or indent the items and sections so that related sets of questions, like skip blocks, are visually offset. Adding white space may add to the number of pages in the questionnaire, so there is some trade-off, especially in the cost of postage if the questionnaire is to be mailed. But a questionnaire with tiny type and cramped response lines and boxes is much more likely to be thrown in the trash.

Desktop publishing and advanced word processing packages make the task of producing a good-looking questionnaire much less difficult than it once was. These software packages can produce very professional looking questionnaires on simple desktop computers equipped with inexpensive laser printers. The questionnaire author should strive for a consistent visual style throughout the questionnaire, and avoid "typeface diddling" with many fonts. Select a basic typeface, with one or two sparingly used alternates (like italics) for instructions, important questions, and so on.

Precoding and Data Processing

The data analysis for almost all surveys will involve entering the data into a computer file so it can be processed by a tabulation or statistical package. This is an expensive step, and the questionnaire author should consider ways to cut costs.

Responses from questionnaires are usually coded with numbers. If a scale is used, the numbers are the scale points. Numbers are arbitrarily assigned to nominal categories for questionnaire items that do not use magnitude-type measurement. These numbers are typically placed into fixed columns on one or more data lines. (These data lines are still often called "cards," because data used to be punched into IBM cards.) These data lines contain all the responses for a single questionnaire, which are collectively called an observation.

One way to cut data entry costs is through precoding the responses. Table 18-3 shows a sample of precoding. The code and location of the data are placed in parentheses right next to the item. For example, the scaled responses (1 to 5) to the question about communication with spouse are to be entered on line or card 4, in column 22 of the observation. The number of hours of television viewing is to be placed in line 4, columns 23 to 26.

The open-ended responses must be manually coded, using some content analysis scheme. The content codes are normally written by the content coder in the margin beside the written response. The questionnaire author has specified that the coded response to the question about discussions with children should be entered into line 5, columns 6 and 7, of the observation.

It is very important to reserve enough columns to enter the full range of codes, including signs and decimal points. The question about hours of television viewing reserved four columns for the response, which allows it to range from 0.00 to 24.0 (i.e., the full range). If the author had left only two columns, the response would have had to be rounded to the nearest hour (00 to 24 hours), and this would have caused lost precision when a respondent used any fractional hours in a reply, such as "$2\frac{1}{2}$ hours."

Likewise, room must be reserved for the largest number of open-ended codes that is likely to show up in the responses. Since the questionnaire author is not likely to know this number in advance, plenty of room should be left. The first open-ended question in Table 18-3 is limited to 100 categories of discussion, because the author has reserved only two columns to hold codes 00 to 99. The second open-ended question can have 10,000 categories of response because the author has reserved four columns.

In large-scale, self-administered surveys, precoding can be taken a step further by having the survey questions and responses printed on an optical scanner sheet. The respondents mark their responses in "bubbles" that the scanner can read and translate directly into a data file. This cuts the data entry costs greatly.

Pilot and Pretest Studies

All questionnaires should be pilot tested and revised before they are used in a research project. The researcher should first have a convenience sample serve as pilot subjects and fill out the questionnaire. Then the researcher should go over each instruction and question on the questionnaire and ask each pilot subject "Did you understand this?" and "What did this mean? How did you interpret it?" By probing for understanding and having the pilot subjects explain why they filled out the items as they did, the researcher can find instructions or questions that need to be rewritten, areas of misunderstanding, architectural problems that caused the pilot subject confusion, and so forth.

If at all possible, a full pretest study with a small sample from the target population should also be conducted. This test should address the same problems as the pilot test, but with a sample of persons who are similar to the persons who will participate in the full research study. It is usually harder to probe for language or question order problems in a pretest, especially if the questionnaire is used in a mail or telephone survey, but architectural problems like confusing skips will show up, as will fatigue problems.

The data from the pretest can be used to create and test data processing procedures. The best technique is to carry out all the procedures necessary to test the research hypotheses, using the pretest data. Often this will point out fatal problems like missing questionnaire items ("How could I forget to ask the respondent's age!"), or errors in the precoding scheme ("The scale goes from 1 to 10, but the coding says the response is supposed to be placed in Column 29 of the data line. It's hard to type a 10 in one column!")

Pilot and pretesting, followed by a thorough revision of the questionnaire, will produce a much better measurement instrument that will cause far fewer problems for the researcher, and will give more accurate results.

Content Analysis

Content analysis is a measurement procedure used in a wide variety of communication research. Essentially, content analysis is the measurement of constructs which can be observed within the messages produced in a communication process. It is used in almost all subdisciplines of communication research. Content analysis is used to analyze media content, the transcripts of interpersonal conversations or group discussions, persuasive messages, organizational memos, and even nonverbal interchanges.

Units of Analysis

The first task in conducting a content analysis is to define the units of analysis. In order of decreasing size, these can be the *medium*, the *message* or *story* carried by that medium, or the individual *assertions* that are found in a given story. These units can be aggregated at lower levels to produce higher-level units. That is, the content of assertions can be combined to define message content, and the content of messages can be used to define medium content.

Only mass media researchers would be likely to choose the medium as the unit of analysis. The Stempel study described in Chapter 16 is an example of this unit. The content produced by individual newspaper messages is summarized in a single observation of medium content. This unit of analysis would be used to contrast the content of different television networks, or to compare print versus television on some common aspect of content.

The message or story unit of analysis is very common. Here each observation is a complete story or intact message. In interpersonal or group communication research, this unit might be a complete conversation or meeting. In organizational communication research it might be a memo, electronic mail message, or transcript of a meeting.

The assertion is the smallest unit of analysis. It is a part of a complete message, and it may be defined as a paragraph, sentence, phrase, clause, or even an individual word. Content analysis of assertions is more difficult to conduct as the assertion unit becomes smaller, but smaller units can be used to make finer distinctions in content and they sometimes improve the reliability of measurement.

Content Categories

The next step in a content analysis is to define the *content categories*. These are the content variables which take on some value when applied to a sample of assertions or messages or media. For example, a small group communication researcher might analyze the assertions made by each person during a group discussion about alcohol use according to some set of categories like "asked question about medical effects," "provided information about alcoholism rates," "agreed with previous assertion," and so forth. By counting the number of times an assertion was made in each category, the researcher can characterize the content of the entire discussion.

An important point should be made here. If the set of categories is applied independently to each participant in the communication, the resulting set of values can be considered to be properties of the individual. Thus content analysis, which really operates at the message unit of analysis, can be shifted to the individual unit of analysis, and used in research that focuses on individual behaviors or differences.

Content categories must be *mutually exclusive* so that any content unit (assertion or message, for example) will properly fall into only one. They must be *exhaustive* so that every message unit can be placed in a category. Often the researcher will meet this requirement by providing an "other" category into which any odd message unit can be placed. The alert reader will recognize these requirements as the same ones that nominal variables must meet (see Chapter 7).

The level of measurement that these content variables take on depends upon the definition of the coding procedure. The simplest is a nominal level, in which each content category is simply marked as "present" or "absent." Coding the content of the group discussion of alcohol use in this way will give a picture of the topics that were discussed, but it will not provide any information about *how much* they were discussed. Nominal coding is quick, but it provides only minimal information about the content, as it does not distinguish between topics which dominate the discussion and those which are only mentioned in passing.

To get some measurement of the amount of content in each category, the frequency of appearance of an assertion or message in each category can be counted. This will give a ratio level of measurement for each content category. The value for each category (actually, it's now a content variable) now contains information about the amount of a particular content that is present. In the group discussion, for example, the researcher might find that the categories relating to the social effects of alcohol use are mentioned far more frequently than those relating to the medical effects, although both are mentioned at least once. This information is important in inferring the relative importance of the two areas to the group members.

The *intensity* (amount) and *valence* (evaluative direction) of message units can be coded to give even more information. Instead of just counting each message unit that falls in a category, the content coder assigns it some numerical weight that reflects the unit's intensity and possibly some positive or negative sign that reflects its valence. In the alcohol use discussion, the assertion that falls in the category "provided information about medical effects" might be coded on a 7-point scale like this:

PROVIDED INFORMATION ABOUT MEDICAL EFFECTS

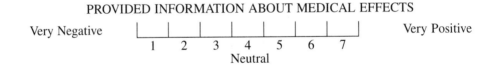

Very Negative   Very Positive
         1   2   3   4   5   6   7
                Neutral

An assertion taken from the transcript that read "… alcohol can cause death by damaging the liver …" might be coded a '1,' while an assertion that "… people who have two drinks a day are less likely to die from heart disease …" might be coded a '6.'

While this kind of coding provides more information, it relies heavily on the judgment of the content coders. This will probably reduce the reliability of the measurement. To improve measurement reliability, the categories must be as concrete as possible. Very general or vague categories will make accurate classification difficult. Categories must be clearly defined so that the content coders can be sure about the kinds of message unit that should be placed in each category. If intensity or valence scales are used, the scale end points and units should be defined as clearly as possible. Providing examples during coder training may help in this definition.

Intercoder Reliability

Human judges are almost always used in content analysis (although computer content analysis is being increasingly used for some straightforward content summaries), so the researcher must determine the amount of unreliability which is introduced by differences in judgment. A basic reliability check comes from computing an *intercoder reliability coefficient*. To compute this coefficient, a set of identical message units is coded, using the

TABLE 18-4   Calculation of Percentage of Agreement Intercoder Reliability for Nominal Categories

Message	No. of Agreements	No. of Disagreements	Agreement (%)
1	46	4	92
2	40	10	80
3	49	1	98
4	45	5	90
5	43	7	86
6	41	9	82
7	48	2	96
8	39	11	78
9	45	5	90
10	44	6	88

OVERALL AGREEMENT (%) = 440/500 · 100 = 88%

same set of categories, by two or more coders. If the measurement is perfectly reliable, every coder will produce the same results. To the extent that the results from different coders are not the same, the measurement is unreliable.

There are a number of ways to compute intercoder reliability, and they depend on the level of measurement of the content categories. If the categories are nominal, a simple percentage agreement can be computed. For example, suppose the researcher defines 50 content categories and has two coders code an identical set of 10 messages using these categories. There are 50 judgments which must be made for each message (for each of the 50 categories, the coder is answering the question "does the message contain this content?"). By dividing the number of categories about which the coders agree that the content is either present or absent by the total number of judgments, the researcher can get a reliability figure for each message, and for the entire set of messages. Table 18-4 illustrates this process.

Intercoder correlations can be computed to get the intercoder reliability for intensity and valence scales, since in this case, the categories are coded at the interval level. Table 18-5 shows how the data might be set up if the 50 categories were measured on interval scales. There are 500 judgments made by each coder (50 categories, with one scale per category × 10 messages). The correlation between the responses for Coder A and Coder B on this set of $N = 500$ observations is an indication of the reliability of the coding. If the coders give identical ratings, the correlation will be 1.00. If the coding measurement is totally unreliable, the correlation will be 0.00. (See the next chapter for details on calculating a correlation coefficient.)

Generally, the percentage agreement for a good set of content categories should be above 80 percent. Likewise, a rule of thumb for the size of an intercoder correlation that indicates acceptable reliability is .80.

TABLE 18-5 Calculation of Intercoder Correlation for Categories Coded at Interval Level

Message	Category	Coder A	Coder B
1	1	+5	+4
1	2	0	−1
1	3	+2	+1
...	...		
1	50	−4	−5
2	1	−2	−1
2	2	−6	−4
2	3	+4	+1
...	...		
2	50	+2	+5
3	1	−1	+1
3	2	0	0
3	3	+7	+7
...	...		
...	...		
9	50	−3	−5
10	1	−1	+1
10	2	0	0
10	3	+7	+7
...	...		
10	50	−2	0

Correlation between coder values: $r_{AB} = .82$

Poor reliability may indicate that the content categories are poorly defined or are too general. But it may also indicate that the content coders are not well trained. Coder training is critical to good measurement.

Coder Training

The first step in coder training is to provide the coders with detailed written definitions and descriptions of the content categories, and instructions on how to carry out the coding task. After the coders have studied this information, they should each code an identical sample of messages. From this data, the researcher should compute an intercoder reliability *for each content category*. This information will pinpoint poorly defined or vague categories. The researcher should then redefine the categories, and repeat the process until the intercoder reliabilities for the categories (and thus the overall reliability) are satisfactory.

Poor intercoder reliability might be the result of a poor coder, rather than a flaw in the coding categories or definitions. To isolate poor coders, the researcher will need more than two coders. For example, suppose three coders (A, B, and C) code the 10 messages in Table 18-5, and the intercoder correlations are:

$$r_{AB} = .80$$
$$r_{AC} = .50$$
$$r_{BC} = .40$$

Coder Cs ratings are inconsistent with those of Coder A and Coder B, but both Coder A and B produce similar ratings. Coder C may not understand the coding task, or may be unmotivated, or possibly just sloppy. Poor coders have to be retrained or eliminated from the research study so that their data do not contaminate the results.

Computer Content Analysis

As we mentioned above, some content analysis can be conducted by computer program. The computer program scans the messages, which are contained in computer text files, and produces a summary. The text might be newspaper or magazine articles or conversation transcripts which have been typed into computer files, or it might be information from databases or computer archives.

Computer content analysis is restricted to very simple content judgments. For instance, a researcher might have a computer program retrieve all the Associated Press national coverage for the past year, and count the number of times the word "Poland" appears. This would give one measurement of the amount of coverage of Poland that has appeared. Word scans can be combined to give rough definitions of more detailed content. The researcher might instruct the computer program to count the number of stories in which both "Poland" and one of the following words appear: "Communism," "Prime Minister," "Congress," "Treaty." This would give an indication of the amount of coverage of political events in Poland, and should eliminate most stories on travel or arts, or other nonpolitical events in Poland.

If you look critically at the preceding example, you can see the difficulty of computer content analysis. It is very hard to define a set of words that will clearly differentiate Polish political stories from all others, and will still include all relevant stories. Stories about U.S. relations with Poland will probably appear in the analysis, as will unrelated stories about the Polish Communist government's repression of the arts in the 1960s, and so on. Some relevant stories that do not mention Communism, prime ministers, Congress, or treaties will be missed, too.

Human coders would have no problem in dealing with these distinctions, as they have a wealth of "common knowledge" to make judgments. Computers are very thorough and very reliable, but they lack this body of common knowledge. The researcher is essentially trading expensive, sophisticated judgment (which may be somewhat unreliable) for very reliable, cheap, but simple computer analysis.

Ethical Issues

Communication research practices often raise ethical issues. Some of these are easy to handle, while others require some difficult decisions.

The primary ethical imperative for the researcher is this: "Tell the truth." This immediately instructs the researcher to refrain from fabricating data, or from deliberately structuring a research study so that demand characteristics or social pressure will produce the results that the researcher wants for some personal or political reason. It also demands that the researcher interpret the data objectively, and report all results accurately, whether they are good or bad (from the perspective of the researcher).

But there are other ethical issues raised by particular communication research procedures that are less clearly resolved. One of these issues involves concealing the researcher's intent from the research subject. "Tell the truth" cuts both ways on this issue. In order to avoid sensitizing effects that will distort the results, the researcher may have to conceal something from the subject. In other words, in order to tell the truth (about the phenomenon), the researcher must avoid telling the truth (about the research study).

It is usually ethical to withhold some information from a research subject *if* two important conditions are met: (1) The subject is not deliberately misled about anything that could cause stress or damage; (2) the subject is fully informed about the research project at the end of the measurement procedure, when there is no further danger of sensitization. This is sometimes called *debriefing* the research subject.

There is an ethical continuum at work. Very few people would have any problem with a researcher masking the intent of a set of questionnaire items by mixing them with a set of dummy items. There is no direct attempt to mislead the research subject.

Withholding the identity of the organization conducting the research is somewhat less acceptable. However, if knowing that identity is likely to bias the response, it is probably acceptable to avoid mentioning the organization's name, and, if the respondent asks, to say that "I can't tell you that, because it might affect your answers."

Another ethically gray area is identification of respondents in surveys. Again, the policy is to tell the truth, but not necessarily the whole truth. For example, if the respondent's identity must be recorded (so that a second interview can be conducted at a later time, or follow-up mailings can be made), you must not explicitly promise that the survey responses are anonymous. But it is probably ethical to code the response envelopes and not mention the subject of anonymity in the cover letter. But there is a fine line between being somewhat vague in explaining the research procedures and being misleading, and the researcher must consider the question very carefully.

Concealed observation of research subjects is also an area of ethical concern. An individual's privacy should not be invaded without consent. But in some areas of research, such as nonverbal communication, a subject's knowledge that he or she is being observed will completely invalidate the measurements. What should the ethical researcher do in order to make unobtrusive behavioral observations?

First, recognize the difference between observations made in public places and those which invade privacy. A person who walks down the street is expecting to be observed, and has tacitly given up a right to privacy. In this case, the researcher can make unobtrusive observations without ethical concern. But a person does not expect to be observed in a private home, so using a telescope to peer through someone's windows is clearly unethical. Even quasi-public places provide some expectations of privacy that a researcher must respect. In one infamous case, a social psychologist made hidden observations of persons using a public rest room. This was generally condemned as an unethical practice. Even though the rest room was open to the public, there was a general expectation that one's behavior there was private.

In laboratory settings, there is also an implied consent by the research subject that behavior can be observed and recorded. But it is always better to make this explicit. For example, the subject may be asked to sign a consent form which contains some language like "... Your actions and behaviors may be observed as part of the research...." By signing such a form, the subject consents to be unobtrusively observed, so there is no problem with placing a research assistant behind a one-way mirror to record behavior, for example.

Permanent recording of behavior on audio- or videotape adds another wrinkle. The implied or direct consent to be observed by the subject probably covers taping, but most researchers would feel more comfortable if the subjects consented directly to the recording. Keeping a permanent record seems to be one step beyond mere observation. If the research design will not be damaged by revealing that the recording is taking place, the prescription is clear: Ask in the consent form for the subject's permission to make recordings.

But in many cases, the knowledge that cameras are rolling will make subjects self-conscious or overly formal in their behavior, and this may affect the measurements. A possible compromise used by some researchers is to secretly tape the research sessions, then *after* the measurement is completed, ask for permission to keep the recordings. If the subject refuses, the tapes are immediately erased.

Further along the ethical continuum is deliberate deception of research subjects. It is usually not ethical to deliberately mislead or lie to the subject. We can't be categorical about this, however. Some kinds of research require that the subject be led to believe that something is true when it is not. For example, a "conversational partner" may actually be a research assistant who is deliberately behaving in some fashion to introduce an experimental manipulation. The assistant must be presented to the subject in a false light. That's a polite way of saying that the researcher must lie to the subject. And this fact must be made clear to the respondent during debriefing.

The extent of the deception and the magnitude of its impact on the subject probably determines its ethical status. A "white lie" about a research assistant is not too bad, if the subject is told the truth at the end of the measurement. But an interviewer who identifies himself as an FBI agent before asking a series of personal questions is probably acting unethically, even if he reveals his true identity at the end of the interview.

Once again, the two conditions mentioned above must hold before deception can ever be considered to be within the bounds of acceptability: The subject cannot be damaged by the deception, and must be informed about the deception at the end of the measurement. Even then, deliberately misleading research subjects should be a last resort. The positive benefits of the research must be weighed carefully against the negative ethical cost of misleading another person.

At the far end of the continuum is research that carries the possibility of physical or mental damage to the subject. Fortunately, this occurs infrequently in communication research. But it is not unheard of. Researchers studying effects of pornography or graphic violence, for example, must consider the possibility that the material may have a damaging impact on subjects. In these cases it is absolutely mandatory to fully inform the subject about the kinds of material or procedures to which they will be exposed. Subjects must have all pertinent information so they can make an informed decision about whether or not to participate in the research.

Most academic institutions have a Human Subjects Committee which reviews research procedures that involve individuals. These committees normally require that subjects be informed about the research procedures, and that they sign a consent form to indicate that they have been fully informed and have decided to participate. These committees usually take a dim view of deception, and require detailed justification of its necessity before they will approve such a procedure. They usually require that a subject be told that participation can be declined and that participation can be ceased at any time. While these instructions may dismay the researcher who is trying to obtain a representative sample of subjects, they are necessary to protect individuals.

Professional organizations such as the American Association for Public Opinion Research, the American Marketing Association, the American Psychological Association, and others have guidelines for the ethical treatment of research subjects. The communication researcher should consult these when considering ethical issues.

Summary

Measurement techniques can be classified in several ways. One major type of measurement is *behavioral observation*. This kind of measurement relies on a human observer to assign values to variables. Behavioral observation can be either *obtrusive* or *unobtrusive*. In obtrusive measurement, the research subject is aware of being observed, while the opposite is true in unobtrusive measurement.

Obtrusiveness increases the possibility of interference between the measurement or research setting and the natural operation of the phenomenon being studied. It may also introduce sensitization that distorts research subjects' behaviors or their responses to measurement. The researcher must always strive to reduce measurement obtrusiveness whenever possible.

Behavioral observation introduces questions about measurement reliability, as the basic measurement instrument relies on human observation and judgment. Measurement procedures must be designed to make the observer's judgments as easy as possible. Clear instructions, behavioral variables that are concrete and clearly defined, and observer training all help to improve measurement reliability.

In contrast to behavioral observation, *self-report measurements* do not rely on the judgment of trained observers. The research subject directly provides the information that assigns values to variables. Self-report measurements can be either obtrusive or unobtrusive, but are normally the latter, since the subject is directly involved in the measurement procedure. An important exception involves naturally unobtrusive measurements, such as those obtained from archives, libraries, or databases.

Surveys and interviews are commonly used communication research measurement techniques. Surveys can be generally classified as *in-person, mail, telephone, mall intercept,* or *computer-administered*. Each has different characteristics such as *response rate* and *cost*, and the selection of the appropriate type of survey must be matched to the research problem being investigated.

Interviewers for in-person or telephone surveys must be trained carefully. *Focus group* interviewers require even more training, as they do not have a questionnaire to structure the interview. Focus group interviews can range freely about many topics, so they are particularly useful for exploratory research. The data from a focus group is unlike the coded data from a survey. It is usually a transcript which is summarized by judges or content coders.

Surveys use *questionnaires* as their primary research tool. Writing a good questionnaire is a demanding task. The author must construct an *introduction* which convinces the respondent to cooperate and must be very sensitive to issues like question wording, vocabulary, leading questions, questions which produce socially desirable responses, vague questions, and double item questions.

The *presentation and type of questions* must be considered too. Complex instructions and long lists of alternative answers must be avoided. "Strange" measurement procedures must be explained clearly. The author must choose between *open-ended questions* whose responses must be classified and coded after respondents have replied to them, and *closed-ended questions* which have a fixed set of alternative responses. Open-ended questions allow more freedom of response, but they are harder to analyze, while closed-ended questions restrict responses but are easy to analyze.

The *questionnaire architecture* as a whole must also be considered. The author must keep the questionnaire short enough that respondent fatigue is not a factor. The sensitizing effects of question order must be considered, and question skips must be constructed so that respondents are not confused. The physical appearance of the questionnaire must be such that respondents are not confronted with a confusing or ugly document. Questionnaires must be tested before being used on the final research sample.

Content analysis is another major communication research procedure. Content can be analyzed according to the units of analysis of medium, message or story, or assertion within a message. Mutually exclusive and exhaustive *content categories* are first defined, and the content of a sample of units is measured by coding the appearance, frequency, or intensity and valence of the units that fall in each category.

Since content analysis, like behavioral observation, relies on human judgment, it is important to assess the reliability of measurement. This is done by computing *intercoder reliability coefficients*. These summarize the agreement among content coders about the presence or amount of content in each category. During the development of the content coding categorical scheme and the training of coders, these coefficients are particularly useful in detecting poor categories or problems with individual coders.

In many communication research procedures, the researcher must confront *ethical decisions*. The primary ethical concerns of telling the truth, protecting the privacy of individuals, and protecting them from harm, may conflict with the desire to conduct communication research that is free from the spurious effects introduced by the research setting or measurement procedures. The latter desire may require withholding information, or even outright deception of research subjects.

While subjects should always be informed as much as possible about research procedures, it may be ethical to temporarily withhold information or mislead subjects, *if* the subject is not damaged, and if the subject is fully informed of the truth at the end of the measurement procedure. Informed consent for taping observations is desirable. For participation in research studies which have some potential for long-term negative effects, this consent is mandatory.

References and Additional Readings

Babbie, E. R. (1992). *The practice of social research* (6th ed.). Belmont, CA: Wadsworth (Chapter 10, "Survey Research").

Beauchamp, T. L., Fadden, R. R., Wallace, R. J., & Walters, L. (1982). *Ethical issues in social science research.* Baltimore: Johns Hopkins University Press (Chapter 2, "Ethical Issues in Different Social Science Methods").

Converse, J. M. & Presser, S. (1986). *Survey questions: Handcrafting the standardized questionnaire.* Sage University Paper Series on Quantitative Applications in the Social Sciences, 07-063. Beverly Hills, CA: Sage.

Greenberg, B. S. (1981). Ethical issues in communication research. In G. H. Stempel & B. H. Westley (Eds.), *Research methods in mass communication* (pp. 255–277). Englewood Cliffs, NJ: Prentice Hall.

Hsia, H. J. (1988). *Mass communications research methods: A step-by-step approach.* Hillsdale, NJ: Lawrence Erlbaum Associates (Chapter 7, "Questionnaire Construction"; Chapter 8 "Mail and Telephone Surveys"; Part IV, "Historical, Qualitative, and Secondary Research").

Lavrakas, P. J. (1987). *Telephone survey methods: Sampling, selection, and supervision.* Beverly Hills, CA: Sage.

Moser, C. A. & Kalton, G. (1972). *Survey methods in social investigation* (2nd ed.). New York: Basic Books.

Oppenheim, A. N. (1966). *Questionnaire design and attitude measurement.* New York: Basic Books (Chapter 2, "Problems of Questionnaire Construction").

Reynolds, P. D. (1982). *Ethics and social science research.* Englewood Cliffs, NJ: Prentice Hall.

Stempel, G. H., III (1981). Statistical designs for content analysis. In G. H. Stempel & B. H. Westley (Eds.), *Research methods in mass communication* (pp. 132–143). Englewood Cliffs, NJ: Prentice Hall.

Webb, E. J, Campbell, D. T., Schwartz, R. D., & Sechrest, L. (1972). *Unobtrusive measures: Non-reactive research in the social sciences.* Chicago: Rand McNally.

$$Chapter \quad 19$$

Selecting Statistical Tests

After selecting the appropriate procedures to collect data, we arrive at the point of choosing the appropriate statistics to test hypotheses. In several earlier chapters we talked in general terms about the necessity of inferring that two variables covary, as part of establishing that a causal or covariance relationship exists between them. And in Chapters 11 and 12 we described the basic outlines of how this is accomplished.

Covariance is determined through the use of inferential statistical tests, but there are hundreds of these statistical tests. How should you select the ones to use?

The Six Questions

To answer this general question, we'll have to back up a little and talk about the character-istics of your research design and variable measurement that you need to consider. These will guide you toward the appropriate statistical test.

We'll try to simplify this by posing a set of six questions that apply to your research design and variables. The pattern of answers to the questions will point toward the appropriate statistical test. The six questions are:

1. *How many independent variables covary with the dependent variable?* If the answer is "one," you will use *bivariate* statistical tests. If it is more than one, you will need *multivariate* statistical tests.

2. *At what level of measurement is the independent variable?* If the independent vari-able is conceptualized as a nominal variable, the hypotheses will be comparative, and you will need a statistical test that compares two or more groups, where each group represents one level of the independent variable. There are some tests which work only if the independent variable consists of two levels (groups), while others work for more than two groups.

If the independent variable is conceptualized as an interval or ratio variable, the hypotheses usually will be relationship hypotheses, and you will need a statistical test that summarizes the covariance between the independent and dependent variables within each unit of analysis.

If the independent variable is measured at the ordinal level, your hypothesis may be either comparative (if the ordinal variable is considered as a set of categories) or relationship (if it is considered as an ordered set of continuously varying classes).

3. *What is the level of measurement of the dependent variable?* Different statistics will be required if the dependent variable is measured at the interval/ratio, ordinal, or nominal level.

4. *Are the observations* independent *or* dependent? The answer to this question is rooted in research design. It arises out of two fundamentally different ways in which observations can be made.

Independent observations are made when each group or sample contains a different set of sampled units of analysis. With independent observations, *completely different* persons, dyads, organizations, messages, or other units of analysis, are observed in each of the two or more groups used to test a comparative hypothesis. In testing a relationship hypothesis with independent observations, the dependent variable is measured only once for each sampled unit.

Dependent observations are made when selection of the first sample or group determines the composition of the second or subsequent samples. With dependent observations, *the same or related* persons, dyads, organizations, or messages are observed in each of the two or more groups used in testing a comparative hypothesis. In testing a relationship hypothesis, the same dependent variable is measured multiple times within the same (or related) units.

Dependent observations come about in two different ways. The first of these consists of letting the members of the first group also be the members of the second group. Observations of the same units are made in all of the groups which represent the two or more levels of the independent variable. This might occur when measurements are made on the same units at two time points, as in a panel design in observational research or in a pre-post experimental design.

This is a situation we discussed when we covered over-time research designs in Chapter 17. The observations in an equivalent samples research design are independent, since a new sample is drawn at each time point, while those in a repeated measures or panel research design are dependent because the same set of persons, organizations, or other units of analysis are measured at each time point. In a repeated measures design, a subject is exposed to first one level of the independent variable, then subsequently to a second level (and possibly third, fourth, etc., level), and the dependent variable is measured within the same subject after each exposure.

The second major way that dependent observations are obtained is via *matched samples*. In a matched sample, each member to be included in the second sample is selected so as to provide, on a number of relevant variables, as perfect a match as possible to a member which has already been selected into the first sample. Although different units of analysis appear in each group, the characteristics of the members of the first sample determine the characteristics of the members of the second sample, so the observations made in these samples are dependent.

5. *Is the hypothesis being tested a comparative or relationship hypothesis?* The fifth question comes from the kind of hypotheses that you have derived. If your independent variable is a set of nominal or ordinal categories, only comparative hypotheses can be stated. But if it is a continuous ordinal or interval/ratio variable, it is possible to test either kind of hypothesis.

6. *Are you comparing populations to populations, a sample to a population, or are you making comparisons between two or more samples?* Since a population parameter has no error variance, different techniques are needed to compare a sample statistic to a population value than are needed to compare two sample statistics, both of which are subject to sampling error.

If dependent observations are made, the population to population and population to sample comparisons use tests identical to those used in independent observations. There is either no sampling error at all (population to population tests) or a single source of sampling error (population to sample tests), so there is no nonrandom error—the sampling error distributions are identical to those found in independent observation tests.

But sample to sample comparisons need different statistical tests which account for the nonrandom error that occurs whenever dependent observations are made on the same or related units. These tests remove error due to individual subjects (which appears systematically in all groups or repeated measurements, since it comes from the same or matched subjects) from other random error.

In Table 19-1, we've listed some statistical tests that are appropriate for each combination of answers to the six questions posed above. These are not the only statistical tests that are appropriate for each situation, but they are commonly used. You'll need to refer to standard statistics books and manuals (like Hays, 1981; Bruning & Kintz, 1977; Norusis, 1992) for details about most of these tests.

We'll sidestep the Herculean task of describing each of the different statistical tests, and instead focus on a few of the most common statistics used in communication research. These will illustrate the general logic of using statistics to test hypotheses. We'll give a brief description of how they work and how we can use them to test hypotheses.

TABLE 19-1   Choosing the Appropriate Statistical Test

Independent Variable Measurement	Number of Independent Variables	Dependent Variable Measurement	Type of Observations	Hypothesis Type	Statistical Test
				Comparative Hypothesis	
Nominal	1	Nominal	Independent	Population to Population Population to Sample Sample to Sample	Inspection of percentages One-Sample Chi-Square test Contingency table Chi-Square Log-Linear models
Nominal	1	Nominal	Dependent	Population to Population Population to Sample Sample to Sample	Inspection of percentages One-Sample Chi-Square test McNemar test Cochran's Q test
				Relationship Hypothesis	
					Phi Coefficent Contingency Coefficient
				Comparative Hypothesis	
Nominal	1	Ordinal (categorical)—see Nominal dependent variable immediately above			
		Ordinal (continuous)	Independent	Population to Population Population to Sample Sample to Sample	Inspection of medians One-sample median test Two-group median test Kruskal-Wallis ANOVA by ranks
Nominal	1	Ordinal (continuous)	Dependent	Population to Population Population to Sample Sample to Sample	Inspection of medians One-sample median test Sign test for dependent samples Friedman ANOVA
				Relationship Hypothesis	
		(categorical ordinal dependent variable)			Phi Coefficent Contingency Coefficient
				Comparative Hypothesis	
Nominal	1	Interval/Ratio	Independent	Population to Population Population to Sample Sample to Sample	Inspection of means One-sample t-test One-sample ANOVA Two-sample t-test ANOVA (Analysis of Variance)
Nominal	1	Interval/Ratio	Dependent	Population to Population Population to Sample Sample to Sample	Inspection of means One-sample t-test One-sample ANOVA Dependent t-test Repeated measures ANOVA
				Relationship Hypothesis	
					Correlation ratio (eta^2) Point-biserial correlation

(continued)

TABLE 19-1 *Continued*

Independent Variable Measurement	*Number of Independent Variables*	*Dependent Variable Measurement*	*Type of Observations*	*Hypothesis Type*	*Statistical Test*
				Comparative Hypothesis	
Nominal	2 or more	Nominal	Independent	Population to Population Population to Sample Sample to Sample	Inspection of percentages Multiple one-sample Chi-Square Contingency table Chi-Square Log-Linear models
Nominal	2 or more	Nominal	Dependent	Population to Population Population to Sample Sample to Sample	Inspection of percentages Multiple one-sample Chi-square Log-Linear models
				Relationship Hypothesis	
					Log-Linear models
				Comparative Hypothesis	
		Ordinal-(categorical)— see Nominal dependent variable immediately above			
Nominal	2 or more	Ordinal (continuous)	Independent	Population to Population Population to Sample Sample to Sample	Inspection of medians Multiple One-sample median test Multiple-group median test
Nominal	2 or more	Ordinal (continuous)	Dependent	Population to Population Population to Sample Sample to Sample	Inspection of medians Multiple One-sample median test Multiple-group median test
				Relationship Hypothesis	
			(categorical ordinal dependent variable)		Log-Linear models
				Comparative Hypothesis	
Nominal	2 or more	Interval/Ratio	Independent	Population to Population Population to Sample Sample to Sample	Inspection of means Multiple one-sample t-tests Factorial ANOVA
Nominal	2 or more	Interval/Ratio	Dependent	Population to Population Population to Sample Sample to Sample	Inspection of means Multiple one-sample t-tests Repeated measures factorial ANOVA
				Relationship Hypothesis	
					Correlation ratio (eta^2)
				Comparative Hypothesis	
Ordinal (categorical)	1	Nominal	Independent	Population to Population Population to Sample Sample to Sample	Inspection of percentages One-Sample Chi-Square test Contingency table Chi-Square Log-Linear models
Ordinal (categorical)	1	Nominal	Dependent	Population to Population Population to Sample Sample to Sample	Inspection of percentages One-Sample Chi-Square test McNemar test Cochran's Q test
				Relationship Hypothesis	
					Phi coefficient Contingency coefficient

(continued)

TABLE 19-1   *Continued*

Independent Variable Measurement	Number of Independent Variables	Dependent Variable Measurement	Type of Observations	Hypothesis Type	Statistical Test
				Comparative Hypothesis	
Ordinal (categorical)	1	Ordinal-(categorical)—see Nominal dependent variable immediately above			
		Ordinal (continuous)	Independent	Population to Population	Inspection of medians
				Population to Sample	One-sample median test
				Sample to Sample	Two-group median test
					Kruskal-Wallis ANOVA by ranks
Ordinal (categorical)	1	Ordinal (continuous)	Dependent	Population to Population	Inspection of medians
				Population to Sample	One-sample median test
				Sample to Sample	Sign test for dependent samples
					Friedman ANOVA
				Relationship Hypothesis	
				(Two categorical ordinal variables)	Phi coefficient
					Contingency coefficient
					Gamma
				(Two continuous ordinal variables)	Spearman Rank-Order Correlation
				Comparative Hypothesis	
Ordinal (categorical)	1	Interval/Ratio	Independent	Population to Population	Inspection of means
				Population to Sample	One-sample t-test
				Sample to Sample	Two-sample t-test
					ANOVA (Analysis of Variance)
Ordinal (categorical)	1	Interval/Ratio	Dependent	Population to Population	Inspection of means
				Population to Sample	One-sample t-test
				Sample to Sample	Dependent t-test
					Repeated measures ANOVA
				Relationship Hypothesis	
				(with categorical ordinal variable)	Correlation ratio (eta^2)
				(with continuous ordinal variable)	Spearman Rank-Order Correlation
				Comparative Hypothesis	
Ordinal (categorical)	2 or more	Nominal	Independent	Population to Population	Inspection of percentages
				Population to Sample	Multiple one-sample Chi-Square
				Sample to Sample	Contingency table Chi-Square
					Log-Linear models
Ordinal (categorical)	2 or more	Nominal	Dependent	Population to Population	Inspection of percentages
				Population to Sample	Multiple one-sample Chi-square
				Sample to Sample	Log-Linear models
				Relationship Hypothesis	
					Log-Linear models

(continued)

TABLE 19-1 *Continued*

Independent Variable Measurement	Number of Independent Variables	Dependent Variable Measurement	Type of Observations	Hypothesis Type	Statistical Test
				Comparative Hypothesis	
		Ordinal (categorical)—see Nominal dependent variable immediately above			
Ordinal (categorical)	2 or more	Ordinal (continuous)	Independent	Population to Population	Inspection of medians
				Population to Sample	Multiple One-sample median test
				Sample to Sample	Multiple-group median test
Ordinal (categorical)	2 or more	Ordinal (continuous)	Dependent	Population to Population	Inspection of medians
				Population to Sample	Multiple One-sample median test
				Sample to Sample	Multiple-group median test
				Relationship Hypothesis	
				(Two continuous ordinal variables)	Spearman Rank-Order Correlation
				(Two categorical ordinal variables)	Gamma
				Comparative Hypothesis	
Ordinal (categorical)	2 or more	Interval/Ratio	Independent	Population to Population	Inspection of means
				Population to Sample	Multiple one-sample t-tests
				Sample to Sample	Factorial ANOVA
Ordinal (categorical)	2 or more	Interval/Ratio	Dependent	Population to Population	Inspection of means
				Population to Sample	Multiple one-sample t-tests
				Sample to Sample	Repeated measures factorial ANOVA
				Relationship Hypothesis	
				(Categorical ordinal variable)	Correlation ratio (eta^2)
				(Continuous ordinal variable)	Spearman Rank-Order Correlation
				Comparative Hypothesis	
Interval/Ratio	1	Nominal	Independent	Population to Population	Inspection of means
				Population to Sample	One-sample t-test
				Sample to Sample	Two-sample t-test
					ANOVA (Analysis of Variance)
Interval/Ratio	1	Nominal	Dependent	Population to Population	Inspection of means
				Population to Sample	One-sample t-test
				Sample to Sample	Dependent t-test
					Repeated measures ANOVA
				Relationship Hypothesis	
					Discriminant analysis
					Logistic regression
					Point-biserial correlation

(continued)

TABLE 19-1 *Continued*

Independent Variable Measurement	Number of Independent Variables	Dependent Variable Measurement	Type of Observations	Hypothesis Type	Statistical Test
				Comparative Hypothesis	
Interval/Ratio	1	Ordinal (categorical)	Independent	Population to Population Population to Sample Sample to Sample	Inspection of means Multiple one-sample *t*-tests ANOVA
Interval/Ratio	1	Ordinal (categorical)	Dependent	Population to Population Population to Sample Sample to Sample	Inspection of means Multiple one-sample *t*-tests Repeated measures ANOVA
				Relationship Hypothesis	
				(continuous ordinal variable)	Spearman Rank-Order Correlation
				Comparative Hypothesis	
Interval/Ratio	1	Interval/Ratio	Independent	Population to Population Population to Sample Sample to Sample	Comparative hypotheses generally not used here unless one (or both) variable were recoded to a categorical variable—then see above
Interval/Ratio	1	Interval/Ratio	Dependent	Population to Population Population to Sample Sample to Sample	
				Relationship Hypothesis	
					Pearson Product-Moment Correlation Regression Coefficients
				Comparative Hypothesis	
Interval/Ratio	2 or more	Nominal	Independent	Population to Population Population to Sample Sample to Sample	Recode the Independent variables to Categorical variables—then see above
Interval/Ratio	2 or more	Nominal	Dependent	Population to Population Population to Sample Sample to Sample	
				Relationship Hypothesis	
					Multiple Discriminant Analysis
				Comparative Hypothesis	
Interval/Ratio	2 or more	Ordinal (categorical)	Independent	Population to Population Population to Sample Sample to Sample	Recode the Independent variables to Categorical variables—then see above
Interval/Ratio	2 or more	Ordinal (categorical)	Dependent	Population to Population Population to Sample Sample to Sample	
				Relationship Hypothesis	
				(Continuous ordinal variable)	Spearman Rank-Order Correlation

(continued)

TABLE 19-1   *Continued*

Independent Variable Measurement	Number of Independent Variables	Dependent Variable Measurement	Type of Observations	Hypothesis Type	Statistical Test
				Comparative Hypothesis	
Interval/Ratio	2 or more	Interval/Ratio	Independent	Population to Population Population to Sample Sample to Sample	Comparative hypotheses generally not used here unless one or both variables were recoded to
Interval/Ratio	2 or more	Interval/Ratio	Dependent	Population to Population Population to Sample Sample to Sample	categorical variables—then see above
				Relational Hypothesis	
					Multiple Correlation Multiple Regression Partial Correlation Semi-partial Correlation

Common Statistical Tests

The Contingency Table and Chi-Square

Although they are the least sensitive forms of measurement, nominal variables are very common in communication research. Exhibit 19-1 describes a typical kind of research project that will produce nominal independent and dependent variables. In this kind of design, the statistical test to be used is a simple contingency table that cross-tabulates the levels of the nominal independent variable with the levels of the nominal dependent variables.

In Exhibit 19-1, the independent variable is a nominal factor called academic program type, of which there are three levels: BA only, BA plus MA, and the BA, MA, and PhD program. The dependent variable (book adoption) also is a trichotomy: The instructors may adopt the text, may not adopt the text, or may wish to reserve judgment. The data are collected into a contingency table, as shown in the Table E19-1. The null hypothesis associated with this problem is that educational setting has no effect on adoption decisions:

H_0: *Adopters will constitute the same proportion of the population in all three educational settings, as will nonadopters and those who defer judgment.*

The alternative hypothesis states that there are differences, or

H_A: *Not H_0*

The region of rejection for the null hypothesis will be set at $p = .05$.

If H_0 is correct, then the number of observations that appear in any cell of the contingency table is determined by random chance. We can estimate this chance value by computing the *expected frequency* in the cell:

$$E_{rc} = \frac{R_{total}}{N} \cdot \frac{C_{total}}{N} \cdot N = \frac{R_{total} \cdot C_{total}}{N}$$

where E_{rc} is the expected frequency of the cell at row r and column c

R_{total} is the total frequency observed in row r

C_{total} is the total frequency observed in column c

N is the total number of observations.

This formula represents the probability of an observation appearing in a particular cell as the probability of being in the particular row (total frequency in a row divided by the total number of observations) multiplied by the probability of the observation being in the particular column (total frequency in the column divided by N). When this joint probability is multiplied by the total number of observations, it gives the number of observations that should appear in a cell as the result of random chance. This is the value that would be expected if the null hypothesis is correct.

If the alternative hypothesis is correct, the observed frequency will differ from this random expected frequency. The hypothesis is appropriately tested by means of Chi-square (Chi^2), using the formula

$$Chi^2 = \sum_{i=1}^{nc} \sum_{j=1}^{nr} \frac{(O_{ij} - E_{ij})^2}{E_{ij}}$$

where O is the observed frequency in a cell of the contingency table

E is the expected frequency in a cell

nr is the number of rows (categories in the dependent variable)

nc is the number of columns (groups in the independent variable)

In Table E19-1, the expected frequencies are shown in parentheses. The resulting value of Chi^2 is:

$$Chi^2 = \frac{-6.58^2}{24.57} + \frac{-3.85^2}{28.85} + \frac{10.42^2}{24.58} + \frac{7.88^2}{15.12} + \frac{6.25^2}{17.75} +$$
$$\frac{-14.12^2}{15.12} + \frac{-1.30^2}{6.30} + \frac{-2.40^2}{7.40} + \frac{3.70^2}{6.30}$$
$$= 1.76 + .51 + 4.42 + 4.10 + 2.20 + 13.19 + .27 + .78 + 2.17 = 29.40$$

Determining the significance of Chi-square

The first step is to determine the correct degrees of freedom for the statistical test. Degrees of freedom are an index of the number of observations in a distribution which are free to vary (or deviate from the mean). For example, in a single series of numbers (such as the data for a t-test), $N-1$ numbers are free to change. Once $N-1$ have been identified, along

EXHIBIT 19-1   Nominal Independent and Dependent Variables

The Contingency Table and Chi-Square

A publisher of communication textbooks is interested in determining whether a text that is currently in the planning stages will have different levels of adoption in different educational settings. An evaluation package containing a sample chapter and outline of the text is mailed to a random sample of 200 instructors in communication who are asked to indicate whether they (a) would adopt the text, (b) would not adopt the text, or (c) wish to reserve judgment until they can see the whole book. Of the instructors who received the package, 146 return the evaluation form. These respondents are classified according to characteristics of the communication program where they teach: BA only; BA plus MA; and BA, MA, and PhD. The data are shown in Table E19-1.

TABLE E19-1   Contingency Table Data

		Academic Program Type			
		BA only	*BA+MA*	*BA, MA, and PhD*	
	Adopt	18 (24.58)	25 (28.85)	35 (24.58)	78
Adoption Decision	Do Not Adopt	23 (15.12)	24 (17.75)	1 (15.12)	48
	Defer	5 (6.30)	5 (7.40)	10 (6.30)	20
		46	54	46	*N* = 146

Observed frequencies are shown in each cell. The corresponding frequencies expected computed from the formula are shown in parentheses.

with a mean, the last observation is fixed, i.e., not free to change value. Degrees of freedom differ for different arrangements of the data and for different statistical tests. They are essentially a replacement for N that gives the correct alpha and beta error probabilities in a statistic's distribution. A complete statistics text should be consulted for more information about degrees of freedom.

The degrees of freedom for a contingency table is equal to (columns − 1) · (rows − 1), or $(3 - 1) \cdot (3 - 1) = 4$. Looking in Appendix C, we see the critical value of Chi^2 for $p = .05$ and 4 d.f. is 9.49. Values higher than this occur fewer than 5 times in 100 by chance alone.

The observed value of Chi^2 is 29.40, sufficiently large to reject the null hypothesis. Consequently, we conclude that educational setting probably does affect instructors' decisions about text adoption.

The t-Test

A very common situation in communication research arises when we have the independent variable represented by two nominal levels such as "male/female," "viewers/nonviewers," or "purchasers/nonpurchasers." If the dependent variable is measured at the interval/ratio level, the *t*-test is an appropriate statistical test.

Two-Sample t-test for Independent Observations

Exhibit 19-2 illustrates a typical situation. The directional research hypothesis H_A being tested is:

$$\overline{X} \text{Accuracy}_{One\ year\ or\ less} < \overline{X} \text{Accuracy}_{Greater\ than\ one\ year}$$

The competing null hypothesis H_0, to be tested at $p = .05$ is:

$$\overline{X} \text{Accuracy}_{One\ year\ or\ less} \geq \overline{X} \text{Accuracy}_{Greater\ than\ one\ year}$$

We know that if H_0 is true, taking a separate sample from each population should give us this result:

$$\overline{X} \text{Accuracy}_{One\ year\ or\ less} - \overline{X} \text{Accuracy}_{Greater\ than\ one\ year} \geq 0$$

The statistical test will contrast the observed difference between the two sample means to a difference of 0.0, which is expected if H_0 is true. This difference is evaluated by means of the *t*-test for two independent samples:

$$t = \frac{(\overline{X}_1 - \overline{X}_2) - 0.0}{\sqrt{\frac{\sum_{i=1}^{N_1}(X_{1i} - \overline{X}_1)^2 + \sum_{i=1}^{N_2}(X_{2i} - \overline{X}_2)^2}{N_1 + N_2 - 2} \cdot \left(\frac{1}{N_1} + \frac{1}{N_2}\right)}}$$

Where

$\overline{X}_1$	is the mean of the first group (i.e. those married one year or less)
$\overline{X}_2$	is the mean of the second group (those married for more than one year)
0.0	is the mean of the sampling distribution of differences between means in the null distribution
$\sum_{i=1}^{N_1}(X_{1i} - \overline{X}_1)^2$	is the sum of the squared deviations of the group married one year or less
$\sum_{i=1}^{N_2}(X_{2i} - \overline{X}_2)^2$	is the sum of the squared deviations of the group married more than one year
N_1 and N_2	are the number of observations in the first and the second group, respectively

EXHIBIT 19-2 Nominal Independent Variable with an Interval/Ratio Dependent Variable: Two Independent Groups

The t-test Between Independent Samples

A researcher is interested in determining how the length of time people have been married to one another affects the accuracy with which partners perceive one another's positions on a number of public and private issues. After all, the researcher reasons, the longer people have been married, the more opportunity they have had to communicate with one another and to assess one another's attitudes and beliefs. This leads the researcher to expect that people who have been married longer should have more accurate assessments of their partner.

A university maintains a housing complex for married students and the researcher turns to the administrators of this housing unit for help. Tenant application records are used to determine how long a couple has been married. The tenants are then divided into two groups: those married less than one year, and those married for more than one year.

From each of these two groups a random sample of 50 couples is drawn.

The researcher prepares a list of 15 issues (having children early in marriage, prayer in school, public funding for private education, etc.) on which one partner's opinion will be obtained. This partner will be asked to state whether he or she is, or is not, in favor of the particular act or issue. The other partner will then be asked to provide an estimate of that opinion: Is your partner in favor of, or not in favor of (this act or issue), or don't you know? For each couple, a flip of the coin is used to determine whether the wife or the husband will be asked to provide estimates of the other's positions on these issues.

A response is considered accurate when the position ascribed to one of the partners matches the position actually stayed by that partner. Accuracy is thus measured by the number of correct estimates, ranging from 0 to 15.

TABLE E19-2 Data for Independent *t*-test

				Length of Marriage				
		One Year or Less				*More than One Year*		
Score	*f*	$(X - \bar{X}_1)^2$	$f \cdot (X - \bar{X}_1)^2$		*Score*	*f*	$(X - \bar{X}_2)^2$	$f \cdot (X - \bar{X}_1)^2$
6	3	16	48					
7	4	9	36					
8	8	4	32		8	2	25	50
9	10	1	10		9	1	16	16
10	5	0	0		10	2	9	18
11	5	1	5		11	5	4	20
12	6	4	24		12	7	1	7
13	4	9	36		13	8	0	0
14	4	16	64		14	13	1	13
15	4	25	25		15	12	4	48

$\sum f \cdot X = 500$

$\bar{X}_1 = 500/50 = 10.00$

$\sum_{i=1}^{N} f \cdot (X_i - \bar{X}_1)^2 = \qquad 280.0$

$\sum f \cdot X = 650$

$\bar{X}_2 = 650/50 = 13.0$

$\sum_{j=1}^{N} f \cdot (X_i - \bar{X}_2)^2 = \qquad 172.0$

The numerator of this formula is the difference between the sample means, and the denominator is the pooled standard error (due to sampling error) from both sample means. The standard error of the sampling distribution of differences between means is estimated from the two unbiased variance estimates.

Using the data shown in Table E19-2,

$$t = \frac{(10 - 13) - 0}{\sqrt{\dfrac{280 + 172}{50 + 50 - 2} \cdot \left(\dfrac{1}{50} + \dfrac{1}{50}\right)}}$$

$$= \frac{-3.00}{.430} = -6.98$$

Determining the significance of t for independent samples. The degrees of freedom associated with this t-test are determined by $(N_1 + N_2) - 2$, or $50 + 50 - 2 = 98$. The t_{critical} from the table of t-values in Appendix D for these d.f. and $p = .05$, one-tail (for a directional hypothesis), is 1.661. Since the t_{observed} is much greater in magnitude and in the correct (negative) direction, we can conclude that the longer people have been married, the more accurately they perceive their partner's stance on issues.

Two-Sample t-test for Dependent Observations

Often a researcher will want to measure the change in a sampled group at two times, to find out if any significant shift in the dependent variable has occurred. Exhibit 19-3 illustrates this kind of situation. The narrative suggests this directional research hypothesis:

$$H_A : \overline{X}_{t_2 - t_1} > 0$$

Competing is the null hypothesis of no effect or opposite effect:

$$H_0 : \overline{X}_{t_2 - t_1} \leq 0$$

The dependent t-test will contrast the mean difference in the dependent variable between time$_1$ and time$_2$ to the mean difference expected when the null hypothesis H_0 is true. This difference is 0.0. We will use the data from Table E19-3 to test the null at $p = .01$, one-tail.

The value of t is computed by:

$$t = \frac{(\overline{X}_{2-1}) - 0}{\sqrt{\dfrac{\sum\limits_{i=1}^{N} (X_{2-1i} - \overline{X}_{2-1})^2}{N - 1} \cdot \dfrac{1}{N}}}$$

$$t = \frac{1.5 - 0}{.462} = +3.24$$

EXHIBIT 19-3   Nominal Independent Variable with an Interval/Ratio Depen-Dependent Variable: Two Dependent Groups

The t-test Between Dependent Samples

The management of a public library is interested in increasing grade schoolers' use of library resources by combining efforts with a local cable television system. The cable television company agrees to locally produce an educational children's program on a wide range of topics, using a variety of experts living in the community. After each program segment, an announcement will inform viewers that the library has books, videotapes, and other materials that provide more in-depth information on the topic. The library hopes to attract new users, as well as increase the use of the library by current users. To

evaluate the effect of this program on current users, a research study is designed.

The library keeps records on its individual card holders and their borrowing behaviors, so it is possible to draw a random sample of $N = 25$ of grade school age children from this list. The records allow the researcher to determine how many books and other materials were borrowed by the members of this sample during the two-month period preceding the beginning of the cable program.

Three months after the first airing of the program, records of these same student card holders are pulled again to determine borrowings during the preceding two months.

TABLE E19-3   Data for a *t*-test between Two Dependent Samples

Student	X_1 Before Campaign	X_2 After Campaign	X_{2-1i}	$(X_{2-1i} - \bar{X}_{2-1})^2$
		Number of Items Borrowed		
A	6	7	1	.25
B	8	9	1	.25
C	8	4	−4	30.25
D	8	8	0	2.25
E	9	9	0	2.25
F	9	11	2	.25
G	9	8	−1	6.25
H	9	14	5	12.25
I	10	11	1	.25
J	10	12	2	.25
K	10	9	−1	6.25
L	10	14	4	6.25
M	10	10	0	2.25
N	10	12	2	.25
O	10		moved to another town	
P	10	15	5	12.25
Q	10	16	6	20.25
R	11	13	2	.25
S	11	10	−1	6.25
T	11	14	3	2.25

Continued

TABLE E19-3   *Continued*

Student	X_1 *Before* *Campaign*	X_2 *After* *Campaign*	X_{2-1i}	$(X_{2-1i} - X_{2-1})^2$
U	11	12	1	.25
V	12	12	0	2.25
W	12	14	2	.25
X	12	15	3	2.25
Y	14	17	3	2.25

$$\sum_{i=1}^{N} X_{2-1i} = 36.00$$

$$\sum_{i=1}^{N} (X_{2-1i} - \overline{X}_{2-1})^2 = 118.00$$

$$\text{Mean change} = \overline{X}_{2-1} = \frac{\sum_{i=1}^{N} X_{2-1i}}{N} = \frac{36.00}{24} = 1.5$$

Note that the standard error of the sampling distribution of the differences is based on an unbiased estimate of the variance of the sample of difference scores around the mean of the set of difference scores.

Determining the significance of *t* for dependent samples.   The data for this test consist of 24 difference scores, so the degrees of freedom are $(N - 1)$ or 23. The critical value of *t* is found by entering the *t*-table at $p = .01$, one-tail and 23 degrees of freedom. The observed value of *t* (3.24) is larger than the critical value of *t* (2.50). We fail to accept the H_0, and conclude that the alternative research hypothesis is supported.

Analysis of Variance

In this section we will focus on those cases where the independent variable has *more than* two levels, so that three or more groups will be compared on an interval/ratio dependent variable.

One-Way ANOVA for Independent Observations

From the narrative in Exhibit 19-4 we derive the following H_0 to be tested at $p = .05$.

$$H_0 : \overline{X}_{\text{tastes good}} = \overline{X}_{\text{rich and creamy}} = \overline{X}_{\text{no preservatives}}$$

The alternative research hypothesis asserts that the appeals will differ in their effectiveness:

$$H_A : NOT\ H_0$$

indicating that all appeals will not necessarily produce the same levels of sales.

One way to test the multiple group differences is to conduct a series of t-tests, and compare all pairs of means. *This is a bad idea.* Multiple t-tests increase the probability of making a type 1 error, since the probabilities sum. For example, if we did 20 t-tests at $p = .05$, we would *expect* that one of the 20 tests would be significant simply by random sampling error.

Instead we'll test the null hypothesis with an F-ratio. The F-ratio is computed by the following formula:

$$F = \frac{variance_{between}}{variance_{within}}$$

The formula indicates that the focus of the statistical test is on variance. More specifically, it is the ratio of two estimates of population variance. This explains why the process of analyzing differences among multiple means is also referred to as *analysis of variance* or ANOVA.

If H_0 is true, the means of the three appeal conditions will differ from one another by no more than can be accounted for by sampling error. In fact, the central limit theorem suggests that under a true H_0, the variance of the set of sample means can be used to estimate a population variance. Note that by rewriting the computation of sampling variance as:

$$sampling\ variance = \sigma^2/N$$

we can compute the population variance:

$$\sigma^2 = N \cdot (sampling\ variance)$$

We'll call this estimate of the population variance the $variance_{between}$, as it comes from differences between the means of the groups which represent the different levels of the independent variable.

The variance of scores in a sample can be used as an estimate of the unknown population variance. The variances of multiple samples can also be combined into a single estimate of the population variance, as we did for the two-sample t-test. We'll extend the idea in this section and refer to this estimate as $variance_{within}$, as it comes from within samples.

When the H_0 is true, these two variance estimates should be equal, and the ratio of the variances, called the F-*ratio*, should be equal to 1.0. If the H_0 is not true, that is, if the different appeals had an effect and produced sample means that are different from one another, the $variance_{between}$ estimate should be quite a bit larger than the $variance_{within}$ estimate and F should be greater than 1.0. The greater the value of F, the greater the likelihood that H_0 is not the true hypothesis:

EXHIBIT 19-4   Nominal Independent Variable with an Interval/Ratio Dependent Variable: Three Independent Groups

Analysis of Variance for Independent Samples

A researcher for a large food products company wants to test the comparative effectiveness of three different appeals for persuading shoppers to buy its brand of salad dressing. The choice in the three strategies centers on whether to emphasize taste (tastes good!), texture (rich and creamy!) or preparation (no preservatives!)

A decision is made to run a test using one of the three appeal types (tastes good, rich and creamy, and no preservatives) in the company's advertising in three equivalent urban areas, so that a different appeal will be used in each city. Within each city nine supermarkets are randomly selected. The measure of the effectiveness of the different messages (the dependent variable) will be the percentage of salad dressing sales in each supermarket which are accounted for by our researcher's product.

In this example the independent nominal factor (appeal type) has three levels. The dependent variable (percentage of salad dressing sales) is a ratio variable. The observed data are shown in Table E19-4.

TABLE E19-4   Data for One-Way ANOVA

	Appeal Type			
	Tastes Good!		*Rich and creamy*	*No Preservatives*
	15,16,17		16,19,20	22,23,23
	18,19,20		21,21,21	25,26,27
	21,22,23		22,23,26	29,29,30
	$\bar{X}_{tg} = 19$		$\bar{X}_{rc} = 21$	$\bar{X}_{np} = 26$
			$\bar{\bar{X}} = 22$	

	Appeal Type				
	Tastes Good!		*Rich and creamy!*		*No Preservatives!*
X_i	$(X_i - \bar{X}_{tg})^2$	X_i	$(X_i - \bar{X}_{rc})^2$	X_i	$(X_i - \bar{X}_{np})^2$
15	16	16	25	22	16
16	9	19	4	23	9
17	4	20	1	23	9
18	1	21	0	25	1
19	0	21	0	26	0
20	1	21	0	27	1
21	4	22	1	29	9
22	9	23	4	29	9
23	16	26	25	30	16
$\bar{X}_{tg} = 19$		$\bar{X}_{rc} = 21$		$\bar{X}_{np} = 26$	
$N_{tg} = 9$		$N_{rc} = 9$		$N_{np} = 9$	
$\sum\limits_{i=1}^{N_g} (X_i - \bar{X}_g)^2 =$	60		60		70 Sum of Squared Group Deviations

These data were collected after the advertising campaign was completed. The figures refer to the percentage of total salad dressing sales accounted for by the particular brand.

If H_0 is false:

$$F = \frac{\text{variance}_{\text{between}}}{\text{variance}_{\text{within}}} > 1.0$$

From the data in Table E19-4 we obtain the estimates of the population variance. In computing the variance$_{\text{between}}$, the first step is to compute the sampling variance as an unbiased estimate:

$$\text{Sampling variance} = \frac{(\overline{X}_{tg} - \overline{\overline{X}})^2 + (\overline{X}_{rc} - \overline{\overline{X}})^2 + (\overline{X}_{np} - \overline{\overline{X}})^2}{\text{d.f.}}$$

$$= \frac{(19 - 22)^2 + (21 - 22)^2 + (26 - 22)^2}{\text{d.f.}}$$

$$= \frac{9 + 1 + 16}{2} = 13.00$$

$$\text{degrees of freedom (d.f.)} = \text{Number of groups} - 1$$

The first unbiased estimate of the population variance then is:

$$\sigma^2 = N \cdot (\text{sampling variance})$$

$$= 9 \cdot (13) = 117 = \text{variance}_{\text{between}}.$$

For variance$_{\text{within}}$ for the three groups, the first step is to compute the sum of squares for each of the three sample distributions (see Table E19-4). After that we'll add the three sums together and divide that sum by the sum of the degrees of freedom. From the data:

$$\text{variance}_{\text{within}} = \frac{\sum_{i=1}^{N_i}(X_i - \overline{X}_{tg})^2 + \sum_{j=1}^{N_j}(X_j - \overline{X}_{rc})^2 + \sum_{k=1}^{N_k}(X_k - \overline{X}_{np})^2}{(N_i - 1) + (N_j - 1) + (N_k - 1)}$$

$$= \frac{60 + 60 + 70}{24} = \frac{190}{27}$$

$$= 7.92$$

The F-ratio is then computed as:

$$F = \frac{\text{variance}_{\text{between}}}{\text{variance}_{\text{within}}} = \frac{117}{7.92} = 14.78$$

Determining the significance of F.   In order to determine the critical level of F in the table in Appendix E, three pieces of information are needed: the level of significance of the statistical test (the Type 1 or α error); the degrees of freedom associated with the numerator (d.f. for the variance$_{\text{between}}$) and the degrees of freedom associated with the denominator (d.f. for the variance$_{\text{within}}$). For this example these are .05, 2, and 24, respectively. We find that 3.40 is the critical value of F. As the F-ratio we observed (14.77) is greater than the critical value of F, we can reject the null hypothesis of no difference due to communications appeal, and conclude that different appeals covary with different levels of sales (with less than a 5 percent chance that this finding is due to sampling error).

The Alternative Hypothesis Revisited: Post hoc tests.   The statement that the null hypothesis is not true *does not* imply this alternative hypothesis:

$$H_{A1}: \overline{X}_{\text{tastes good}} \neq \overline{X}_{\text{rich and creamy}} \neq \overline{X}_{\text{no preservatives}}$$

Although this hypothesis—that all means are not equal to one another—*might* be true, there are additional hypotheses that might also be true when the F-ratio falls into the region of rejection of the null hypothesis. In fact, there are seven ways in which the group means might differ from the null hypothesis. For example, two of these ways are:

$$H_{A2}: \overline{X}_{\text{tastes good}} > \overline{X}_{\text{rich and creamy}} = \overline{X}_{\text{no preservatives}}$$

and

$$H_{A3}: \overline{X}_{\text{tastes good}} = \overline{X}_{\text{rich and creamy}} < \overline{X}_{\text{no preservatives}}$$

These hypotheses assert that two of the three means are equal to one another, but differ from the remaining third. As all are alternatives to the H_0, the H_A is stated simply as "Not H_0."

Post hoc tests are used to investigate the differences among various group means. These tests account for some of the problems associated with increased Type 1 error when multiple tests are conducted. Discussions of these tests can be found in Hays (1981), McNemar, (1969) and in Kerlinger (1986).

Correlation

If we have defined both the independent and dependent variables at the interval/ratio level, we can use correlation to describe the relationship between the variables. The sampling distribution of the correlation statistic is then used to test the hypothesis relating the independent to dependent variable.

Table 19-2 shows seven observations of individuals' age and the number of minutes each day that each spends reading newspapers. The first step in examining two variables for a linear relationship is to determine where each observation's value is located relative to the mean of all the observations for that variable. This step is seen in columns 3 and 4 of Table 19-2. The plus and minus signs associated with these deviations show a fairly clear pattern which indicates that these two variables are positively related. Positive deviations of x are associated with positive deviations of y, and negative deviations of x and y also occur together.

Crossproducts
A way of combining the simultaneous deviations from the two means is shown in column 5 of Table 19-2. This column displays the product of the two deviations for each observation.

TABLE 19-2   Covariation as Simultaneous Deviation from Two Means

Observation	*(1)* Age (X)	*(2)* Time/ Newspapers (mins) (Y)	*(3)* $(X - \overline{X})$	*(4)* $(Y - \overline{Y})$	*(5)* $(X - \overline{X}) \cdot (Y - \overline{Y})$
A	20	20	−17	−10	+170
B	46	35	+9	+5	+45
C	63	40	+26	+10	+260
D	19	15	−18	−15	+270
E	38	35	+1	+5	+5
F	25	25	−12	−5	+60
G	48	40	+11	+10	+110

$$\sum(X) = 259 \qquad \sum(Y) = 210 \qquad \sum(X - \overline{X}) = 0 \qquad \sum(Y - \overline{Y}) = 0$$

$$\overline{X} = 37 \qquad \overline{Y} = 30 \qquad \qquad \sum(X - \overline{X}) \cdot (Y - \overline{Y}) = 920$$

$$\text{Std.Dev.}_X = 15.29 \quad \text{Std.Dev.}_Y = 9.26$$

Observation	Standard Scores Age z_x	Time z_y	Cross- Product $z_x z_y$
A	−1.11	−1.08	1.20
B	.59	.54	.32
C	1.70	1.08	1.84
C	−1.18	−1.62	1.91
E	.07	.54	.04
F	−.78	−.54	.42
G	.72	1.08	.78

$$\sum z_x z_y = +6.51$$

$$r_{xy} = \frac{\sum_{i=1}^{N} z x_i z y_i}{N}$$

$$= \frac{6.51}{7} = .93$$

It is frequently referred to as the *crossproduct* of the two deviations. Because of the strong positive relationship between these variables, each crossproduct has a positive value. Across all observations the *sum of crossproducts* equals +920, where the sign of the sum of crossproducts indicates the positive direction of the relationship.

A negative relationship between the two variables would be seen when the positive deviations from the mean of the age variable are associated with negative deviations from the mean of the time variable. If this was the case, the crossproducts would have a negative sign, and a negative sum.

What pattern of simultaneous deviations from the mean would be observed if two variables are not systematically related? In such a case we'd see that for any given observation, the deviation from the mean on the age variable would be equally likely to be associated with either a negative or a positive deviation from the mean of the time variable. As a consequence, the crossproducts will tend to cancel one another out when they are summed. When two variables are not related to one another, the sum of crossproducts will be zero, plus or minus some sampling error.

Factors Affecting the Sum of Crossproducts

The sum of crossproducts is a summary description of the linear relationship between the two variables. Its sign indicates whether the relationship is positive or negative. On first glance it would appear that the size of the sum should indicate the size of the relationship. But the size of sum of the crossproducts is affected by two additional factors: the units of measurement of the independent (X) and the dependent (Y) variables, and by the number of observations contributing to the sum of crossproducts. To be a useful description that can be applied to any two variables with any sample size, these two factors have to be removed.

To remove the effect of the unit of measurement we standardize the two distributions. The z-scores or standard scores convert the values in the two data distributions into two sets of scores that have a mean of 0.0 and a standard deviation of 1.0, regardless of the original unit of measurement. The z-score was described in Chapter 8.

Using the means and standard deviations for the variables age and time with newspapers we can compute z-scores for the two variables, then calculate the crossproducts of the two z-scores. These z-scores and their crossproducts are also shown in Table 19-2. The important fact to remember is that a sum of crossproducts obtained from z-scores is completely independent of the original units of measurement.

The second factor that contributes to the size of the sum of crossproducts is the number of observations. The sum of crossproducts can be standardized for the number of observations contributing to the sum by simply dividing by the number of observations, i.e., computing the average or mean crossproduct.

Pearson Product Moment Correlation Coefficient

Once the average crossproduct has been computed, we have arrived at the formula for the Pearson correlation between variables X and Y, commonly referred to as "r_{XY}":

$$r_{XY} = \frac{\sum_{i=1}^{N} zx_i zy_i}{N}$$

For the example data the correlation coefficient between variables X and Y is +.93. Other formulas to compute the Pearson r are frequently used. We will present one of these formulas in a moment.

We have already seen that the sum of the crossproducts (as well as the value of the Pearson r) will be zero if there is no relationship between the two variables. We also know that for a non-null relationship the correlation coefficient's sign indicates the direction of the relationship. What, however, are the limits of the values for the correlation coefficient?

These limits are relatively easy to establish once we realize what is meant by a perfect linear relationship between two variables. In such a relationship, every observation of X and Y, if plotted, would fall exactly on top of a straight line. By knowing the value of X, we could predict exactly the value of Y from the simple formula for a straight line:

$Y = MX + B$, where M is the slope of the line and B is the Y-axis intercept. From the standpoint of hypothesis testing, this would represent perfect covariance of X and Y, with no error.

We can see one perfect linear relationship by looking at the relationship of any variable with itself, that is, by making $Y = X$. If we were to compute the correlation coefficient between a variable and itself we would obtain the index of a perfect positive relationship. (Of course, the coefficient computed between a variable and its inverse would be the index of perfect negative relationship.) For any set of values (and you may want to determine this with either the age variable or the time variable), the correlation between a variable and itself is equal to +1.00, and it is −1.00 between a variable and its inverse. These are the upper and lower limits for the correlation.

Testing Relationship Hypotheses With Correlation Coefficients

In Exhibit 19-5 we describe a fictitious research study of the relationship between two independent variables and one dependent variable. We will be concerned only with the relationship between the number of new products introduced (NPRO) and the percentage of co-workers named as communication partners (PPART). The directional alternative research hypothesis associated with this relationship is:

$$H_A: r_{\text{NPRO–PART}} > 0$$

The associated H_0 is then

$$H_0: r_{\text{NPRO–PART}} \leq 0$$

Our basic test of the H_0 is then a test that the sample correlation coefficient equals the population correlation coefficient, which equals 0.00. This is a sample statistic (the observed r) to population parameter contrast, where the population r is assumed to be equal to 0.00. For this example, we will test the H_0 at $p = .01$.

If we reject the H_0, we must also eliminate the following alternative hypothesis before we can claim support for our directional research hypothesis:

$$r_{\text{NPRO–PART}} < 0$$

If the computed correlation is less than zero, we will accept H_0. The formula we will use for computing the value of r for this data set is a relatively simple computational equivalent to the conceptual formula that we developed earlier in this chapter. It is just an algebraic combination of the z-score and average crossproducts formulas. While it looks complex, calculating it is really just a matter of computing the various squares and crossproducts and summing them up.

$$r = \frac{N \cdot \sum XY - \sum X \cdot \sum Y}{\sqrt{[N \cdot \sum X^2 - (\sum X)^2] \cdot [N \cdot \sum Y^2 - (\sum Y)^2]}}$$

EXHIBIT 19-5   Interval/Ratio Independent Variable with an Interval/ratio Dependent Variable

Correlations Between Interval/Ratio Variables

A researcher is interested in identifying factors that affect communication among coworkers in organizations. More specifically, the researcher is interested in determining why it is that some employees consistently communicate on work-related topics with a broad range of coworkers, where in other organizations individual communication tends to be more specialized among a smaller set of coworkers.

It is theorized that work-related communication behavior is likely to be affected by the amount of change confronting the organization and by the amount of information that can be provided by coworkers in an organization. The researcher argues that the greater the change confronting the organization, the less the likelihood that any particular coworker will be informed enough to be consistently the main source of information. Furthermore, the greater the number of knowledgeable

coworkers, the greater the potential range of communication partners.

From a sample of 17 equally sized for-profit organizations three measures are obtained. The first measure is the number of new products introduced by that organization in the preceeding year (NPRO). This number indicates the amount of change facing the organization. The second measure is the percentage of members of each organization who are identified by at least three coworkers as a consistent communication partner (PPART). The greater this percentage, the more communication is distributed across the entire organization. The third measure is the percentage of subordinates in the organization who have advanced academic degrees in areas relevant to the organization's mission (PAVD). The greater this percentage, the greater the available information.

The data obtained for the 17 organizations is shown in Table E19-5.

TABLE E19-5   Data for Computing the Correlation Coefficient

Organization	No. of New Products per Year (NPRO)	Members Identified as a Target (%) (PPART)	Members with Advanced Degrees (%) (PAVD)
A	6	80	37
B	5	75	48
C	3	45	20
D	5	58	35
E	3	50	40
F	4	45	20
G	4	60	35
H	5	50	40
I	6	85	47
J	5	70	40
K	3	55	40
L	5	78	47
M	3	40	35
N	4	60	40
O	4	63	50
P	5	57	25
Q	4	60	40
	$\overline{X}_{\text{NPRO}} = 4.353$	$\overline{X}_{\text{PPART}} = 60.647$	$\overline{X}_{\text{PAVD}} = 37.588$
	Std.Dev._NPRO = .967	Std.Dev._PPART = 12.751	Std.Dev._PAVD = 8.650

TABLE 19-3   Computing the Pearson Correlation Coefficient: Raw Score Formula

Org.	New Products (NPRO) (X)	% of Co-workers (PPART) (Y)	X^2	Y^2	XY
A	6	80	36	6400	480
B	5	75	25	5625	375
C	3	45	9	2025	135
D	5	58	25	3364	290
E	3	50	9	2500	150
F	4	45	16	2025	180
G	4	60	16	3600	240
H	5	50	25	2500	250
I	6	85	36	7225	510
J	5	70	25	4900	350
K	3	55	9	3025	165
L	5	78	25	6086	390
M	3	40	9	1600	120
N	4	60	16	3600	240
O	4	63	16	3969	252
P	5	57	25	3249	285
Q	4	60	16	3600	240
	74	1031	338	65291	4652
	$\sum X$	$\sum Y$	$\sum X^2$	$\sum Y^2$	$\sum XY$

$$r = \frac{N \cdot \sum XY - \sum X \cdot \sum Y}{\sqrt{[N \cdot \sum X^2 - (\sum X)^2] \cdot [N \cdot \sum Y^2 - (\sum Y)^2]}}$$

$$r = \frac{17(4652) - (74)(1031)}{\sqrt{[17(338) - (74)^2] \cdot [17(65293) - (1031)^2]}} = \frac{2790}{\sqrt{[270] \cdot [46986]}}$$

$$= \frac{2790}{\sqrt{12686220}} = \frac{2790}{3561.77} = .783$$

$$t = \frac{r - 0}{\sqrt{\dfrac{1 - r^2}{N - 2}}} = \frac{.783}{\sqrt{\dfrac{1 - (.783)^2}{15}}} = \frac{.783}{\sqrt{\dfrac{.387}{15}}}$$

$$= \frac{.783}{.161} = 4.86$$

The various steps associated with this computational process are laid out in Table 19-3. As it indicates, the value of r in this set of observations is +.783.

Determining the Significance of the Correlation Coefficient. The null hypothesis of no relationship between X and Y is

$$H_0: r_{XY} = 0$$

If we were to draw many samples of size N from a population where the parameter $r = 0.00$, we would obtain a symmetrical sampling distribution of r where 0.00 is the mean, median, and mode. If N was extremely large, this sampling distribution of r would approximate the standard normal distribution (see Chapter 10). Since sample sizes are usually far smaller than infinity, the sampling distribution of r is more properly approximated by the t-distribution. The test of the H_0 is therefore carried out by t-test, using this computational formula:

$$t = \frac{r - 0}{\sqrt{\dfrac{1 - r^2}{N - 2}}}$$

The numerator of this formula is the difference between the sample and the population values for r, with the population value set at the null value of 0.00. The critical value of t is established with $N - 2$ degrees of freedom. Why $N - 2$? Since two observations define a straight line, computing a correlation coefficient using only two observations will *always* result in a perfect linear relationship with a value of r of $+1.0$, or -1.0. The correlation is not free to vary. This means that in any set of observations, only $N - 2$ observations will be free to vary and to determine the value of the correlation coefficient.

The critical value of t for our study (from Appendix D) is 2.602. The correlation coefficient of .783 has an associated t-value of 4.89. Since this is beyond the critical value of t, we will reject the H_0. As the sign of the obtained correlation is in the predicted positive direction, we can accept the H_A and conclude that a substantial positive relationship exists between NPRO and PPART.

Summary

The choice of the correct statistical test depends upon the definition of the variables, and particularly upon their level of measurement. It also depends upon the research design used, and the nature of the hypotheses.

The answers to six questions will isolate the correct statistical test:

1 How many independent variables covary with the dependent variable?
2 At what level of measurement is the independent variable?
3 What is the level of measurement of the dependent variable?
4 Are the observations independent or dependent?
5 Is the hypothesis being tested a comparative or relationship hypothesis?
6 Are you comparing populations to populations, a sample to a population, or are you comparing two or more samples?

Using the answers to the six questions in conjunction with Table 19-1 will point you in the direction of the correct statistical procedures.

We've shown some examples of statistical tests commonly used in communication research. In examining relationships between nominal variables, *contingency table Chi²* tests can be used. If the dependent variable is interval, and the independent variable is a nominal variable with two classes, a *t-test* is appropriate. A *t*-test can be used to contrast two different samples (*t*-test for independent observations) or to contrast the same units at two different times (*t*-test for dependent observations).

If the independent variable is a nominal factor with more than two classes, and the dependent variable is interval/ratio, *analysis of variance (ANOVA)* can be used to test hypotheses. Finally, if both independent and dependent variables are measured at the interval/ratio level, a *Pearson correlation coefficient* can be used to describe the size of the relationship, and to compute a *t*-statistic that will test the null hypothesis.

The competent communication researcher will need a background in statistical procedures that goes well beyond what we've been able to include in this book. That might include an introductory statistics course, and it most certainly includes using a good statistics textbook as a natural companion to this book.

References and Additional Readings

Bruning, J. L. & Kintz, B. L. (1977). *Computational handbook of statistics* (2nd ed.). Glenview, IL: Scott, Foresman.

Capon, J. A. (1988). *Elementary statistics for the social sciences.* Belmont, CA: Wadsworth.

Cohen, J. & Cohen, P. (1983). *Applied multiple regression/correlation analysis for the behavioral sciences* (2nd ed.). Hillsdale, NJ: Lawrence Erlbaum Associates (Chapter 2, "Bivariate Correlation and Regression").

Hays, W. L. (1981). *Statistics* (3rd. ed.). New York: Holt, Rinehart & Winston.

Healey, J. F. (1993). *Statistics: A tool for social research.* Belmont, CA: Wadsworth.

Kerlinger, F. N. (1986). *Foundations of behavioral research* (3rd ed.). New York: Holt, Rinehart and Winston.

McNemar, Q. (1969). *Psychological statistics* (4th ed.). New York: Wiley (Chapter 8, "Correlation: Introduction and Computation").

Norusis, M. J. (1992) *SPSS/PC+ base system user's guide* (Version 5.0). Chicago: SPSS, Inc.

Williams, F. (1992). *Reasoning with statistics: How to read quantitative research* (4th ed.). Fort Worth, TX: Harcourt Brace Jovanovich.

Chapter *20*

Qualitative Research Methodologies

Paul L. Jalbert

Authors' Note:

In the preceding 19 chapters we have presented a fairly detailed description of a philosophy of science and its corresponding methods. We believe this approach is extremely useful and productive in extending our knowledge of the world. However, the approach to "fixing belief" that we have advocated in these pages is by no means the only current philosophy of science. Competing philosophies exist and they are used by communication researchers as well as other social scientists. These *qualitative alternatives*, as they are often called, are based on assumptions which differ sharply from the ones we have embraced so far, and they utilize research methodologies which also differ significantly from those we have outlined. In order to present you with an overview of current alternative philosophies of science and a different perspective and set of approaches to communication research, we asked a colleague, who has conducted a number of qualitative research projects, to prepare this chapter.

Introduction

In the preceding chapters, you have been introduced to some of the major elements of quantitative research methods employed by social scientists who study human communication. Major assumptions, concepts, and procedures, in the quantitative research area have been presented and illustrated. This chapter is concerned with presenting and exemplifying some of the major features of a set of *qualitative* research methodologies.

We shall begin by reviewing some of the differences in the assumptions and philosophical groundings of each strategy. It should be noted at the outset that both quantitative and qualitative methodologies share one assumption: Members of a culture share a common experience available in and through one (or several) common language(s) and it is within this common experience that any analysis of communication is possible at all.

Because the overall methodological programs of quantitative and qualitative research are so different, we will not try to map categories of features relevant to one method onto those of the other. There is no one-to-one relationship between the features of one set of methods and the other. Each method presents a wholly different set of features necessary for its use. Qualitative and quantitative approaches are truly conceptually different kinds of research strategies.

The Matter of Assumptions

Quantitatively based approaches to the analysis of communicative phenomena project the existence of an "objective reality" independent from the beliefs and orientations of participant agents. Only if one accepts the existence of an objective realm of phenomena can one aspire to apply quantitative methods of research to such phenomena. One basis for such an assumption is the argument that what people *believe* to be the case and what actually is the case often diverge. In other words, a sharp distinction is made between people's perspectives, beliefs and claims about reality, and the actually independent structure of that reality. The latter may be investigated primarily through the application of scientific methods, among which quantitative research techniques are prominent. Indeed, to some theorists and researchers, scientific methods equal quantitative methods. This idea, and its accompanying assumptions, are not beyond contention, and many researchers reject them. In particular, the idea that a truly scientific approach *must* involve quantification is far from universally shared.

Another leading assumption of much quantitative work in the field is the argument that explanation necessitates prediction. That is to say, if one has truly explained some phenomenon, one must have in one's hands the means to predict that phenomenon (or certain of its defining properties). The model here is drawn from classical physics. For example, a scientist who maintains that there is a good explanation for the behavior of a gas, must be able to predict changes in its temperature, volume, and pressure under specifiable conditions. In our domain, explaining communicative phenomena, the comparable goal has been to develop models that enable one to assign predictive *probabilities* to certain forms of communicative behavior or its interpretation.

The *apparatus* of quantitative research consists of the following, among other things:

- Operational definitions of concepts (especially those amenable to formulation in terms of measurable indices).
- Sampling of units of analysis, and collection of data based upon such operationalizations.
- Established procedures for testing hypotheses about variables, using the relationships between such operationally defined variables, using sampled observations.
- The application of statistical methods of reasoning and "confirmation."
- Detecting relationships among the variables from which predictions or causal explanations may be made.

Much information, and a range of theoretically interesting claims, can be obtained employing such methods. However, they are by no means the exclusive methods employed by researchers exploring human communicative phenomena; and they cannot be thought of as the only proper contenders for the title of *scientific inquiry* in the field. In what follows, we shall discuss several of the most rigorous strategies deployed by communication analysts. These depart significantly from the assumptions, procedures, and philosophies of quantitative communications research.

No attempt will be made here to characterize all modes of nonquantitative research: It should be noted that qualitative investigators are not necessarily in harmony about the best qualitative strategies to employ for given problems. The do not even agree as to what should count as the most interesting or important problems in the field. However, most qualitative investigations in the communication sciences *do* share a minimum common range of epistemological commitments (philosophical positions about what should count as a defensible assumption about obtaining knowledge or a warrantable finding).

Some Major Modes of Nonquantitative Research

We mention only some of the major modes here to provide the student with some sense of the variety of approaches established for the study of human communication. One point we make from the start is that these research modes are not "methodologies" as such, but rather modes of research targeting certain features of communication which interest the practitioners of those modes of inquiry.

For example, content analysts consider part of their research program to involve the investigation of semantic features or issues of meaning (including contextual features and relational features among a variety of social phenomena). While these have a qualitative flavor, their *methodological* orientation is *quantitative*, that is, statistical. Much information is gained from this approach, and it is a very popular type of research in communication. However, *content analysis* is based on the assumptions and procedures of quantitative methodologies and not qualitative ones.

A popular qualitative approach is *semiotics*. Semioticians investigate the meaning of signs and symbols and their attendant features. They are not interested in quantitative descriptions and do not operate with a particular set of qualitative methods to produce their analyses. Rather, they seek to develop strategies for understanding current and historical treatments of both established and new sign and symbol systems.

Yet another approach is called *pragmatics*. Much of what its practitioners investigate are the *inferential* features of communication, such as issues of presupposition, referential functions, and implication in the communication process. They do not use quantitative procedures, nor do they operate within qualitative methods. Essentially, semiotics and pragmatics are informed by methods used in *linguistics* and *semantics*. These represent a rigid set of often formulaic procedures designed to organize usages of language into a stylized form, almost a mathematical model. While these influences are clear, practitioners in semiotics and pragmatics do not hold as rigidly to these patterns as their colleagues in linguistics.

Cultural studies researchers also investigate the usages of human communication. Many studies about television, radio, popular culture, and music videos have been produced under this label. Much has been gained through these analyses to enlighten our understandings about changes in our culture. This mode of research is not necessarily informed by any particular method, either quantitative or qualitative, although there is some leaning toward qualitative insights.

While these modes of analysis yield important and interesting insights into the features of human communication, and occasionally borrow a quantitative insight here and a qualitative one there, they are not fundamentally based on any set of qualitative methods as discussed in the following sections. To express this fact is not, in any way, to show any lack of appreciation for their contributions, only to distinguish between approaches which are informed by specific methodological commitments and those which are not. A library catalog search of these topics will give the interested student ample references to pursue any investigation into these approaches.

Elements of Qualitative Communication Research Methods

One of the basic concerns in the development of qualitative methodologies was, and remains, the adoption of a particular theoretical attitude to the points of view perspectives or orientations of members of a communication community in deciding what is to constitute the nature of an objective phenomenon. Indeed, in contrast to the realist or objectivist assumption underpinning a good deal of quantitative work in the field, most qualitative communications researchers adopt the view that what counts as real or objective is a function of the reasoning, concepts, and orientation of the members of a communication community.

Developed within the social sciences, the idea of "reality construction" has been a major feature of an increasingly influential set of approaches, from *symbolic interactionism* (with its emphasis on how actors "define" the situations in which they find themselves) to *phenomenology* (with its interest in how people make sense of the manifold "appearances" of their environments and thereby transform such appearances to "phenomena") to *ethnomethodology* (with its focus on how members of a communication community create and use methods for determining the intelligibility and orderliness of the world in all of its aspects). In particular, social reality is treated as social interactions which are primarily *communicative* in nature. Not only does language structure our experience(s) of phenomena, but interpersonal communication is the primary medium through which social reality is constructed.

Symbolic Interactionism

One of the major figures in the formation of the symbolic interactionist approach within qualitative social research was Herbert Blumer (1969). Blumer, following G. H. Mead

(1934), was concerned about researchers who used the methods of the natural sciences to study social phenomena. His now classic essay regarding "variable analysis" details his concerns (Blumer 1967). In it, he argued that variable analysis relied upon the identification and specification of a relationship between two or more "variables."

To illustrate this procedure, we cite the previously mentioned case of a gas and its varying properties: pressure (the independent variable) and temperature (the dependent variable). They are variables because their values can increase or decrease. The claim (hypothesis) is that pressure varies directly (*i.e.,* in the same direction) with temperature. Hence any increase/decrease in pressure produces an increase/decrease in temperature. If researchers can show that this occurs consistently (that is, the variables covary), they have not only identified and specified the relationship between these two variables, but their results are even more elegant because they are able to measure these parameters to the point where they can determine the exact change that occurs in this cause-effect relationship. However, for Blumer, it is unacceptable to import this kind of analysis into the domain of the social sciences. He argues:

> *The conventional procedure in variable analysis is to identify something which is presumed to operate on group life and treat it as an independent variable, and then to select some form of group activity as the dependent variable. The independent variable is put at the beginning part of the process of interpretation and the dependent variable at the terminal part of the process. The intervening process is ignored, or what amounts to the same thing, taken for granted as something that need not be considered. (Blumer, 1969, p. 133)*

One way to illustrate this point is to consider the popular analysis of the effects of viewing television violence by children and their resulting propensity toward violence. The hypothesis often goes like this: Television violence viewed by children *leads* to violent behavior in children. While the content of this kind of proposition looks very much like the delineation of the relationship between the independent and the dependent variables, the form looks very much like: Stimulus *leads* to response. Blumer was not arguing that this kind of approach cannot produce correlational findings which may be very interesting and suggestive. However, these "findings" can never get at the heart of what it is that human beings do and what it takes for them to do it. The reason for this is that the complexity of human activities and their accompanying features is not genuinely reducible to a computer or mathematical model. Even if relationships are found to exist by these procedures, Blumer argues that, as researchers, we

> *... do not know the run of their experiences which induced an organisation of their sentiments and views, nor do we know what that organisation is; we do not know the social atmosphere or code in their social circles; we do not know the reinforcements and rationalisations that come from their fellows; we do not know the defining process in their circles; we do not know the pressures, the incitants, and the models that come from their niches in the social structure; we do not know how their ethical sensitivities are organized and so what they would tolerate.... (Blumer, 1969, p. 131)*

It is not that these features have been left out of the analysis by an inattentive researcher and that, if they are now included, the analysis has been corrected. Not so. *It is that they are not includable!* To continue with the example, the expansion of findings cannot operate to produce correct results, such that

- A decrease in children's exposure to television violence *and*
- An increase in parental responsibility with regard to children television viewing practices *and*
- An increase in the fostering of nonviolent means to solve problems
- automatically *lead* to a decrease in the propensity of violence in children

To enumerate a multitude of variables does not solve the problem raised by Blumer. If a decreased exposure to television violence by children indicates a decrease in violence in children, it is not because children react automatically to the decrease in exposure. Any change in their behavior relies upon the complexity of attitudes, values, beliefs, and so on, of their living circumstances. Perhaps it is to these circumstances of people's lives that researchers can turn in order to arrive at their explanations.

According to Blumer and his successors (among them Strauss and Becker (1956) and Becker (1963), a preferred qualitative strategy for inquiring into the complexities of peoples's actual life circumstances is *participant field observation*. This approach involves the researcher's actual participation in communicative activity and interaction by which he or she can develop a rich appreciation for the contingencies which actually, recurrently, and consequentially shape the actors' relevances, categories of understanding and usage, and structure their social worlds.

Nonetheless, aside from detailed ethnographic reportage (or what Geertz (1973), following Ryle, referred to as "thick description"), no truly rigorous *methodology* emerged from this school. Novel ethnographic research strategies and altered philosophical assumptions were developed, much excellent descriptive work was done (particularly by the representatives of the Chicago School), but no genuinely *scientific* procedures were advanced. The Iowa School's efforts to codify and operationalize G. H. Mead's concept of "the self" through questionnaire instruments have long ago faded into obscurity. (Kuhn, 1967)

Research as Unfolding the "Drama"

Erving Goffman, something of a maverick in the tradition of qualitative interactionist research, produced many brilliant observational studies (1959, 1961) but his "data" were largely illustrative scenarios, anecdotes, and snippets of media reportage bound together by masterly metaphorical glosses. His "methods" are more readily comparable to those of the literary critic and documentary journalist than the communication scientist. Only in his last book (Goffman, 1981), did he address himself *technically* to the details of communicative phenomena, and then in a manner inspired by (and critical of) the work of his former student, Harvey Sacks. We shall return to consider Sacks' contribution in more detail further on.

The Phenomenological Turn

Building upon the primarily *theoretical* accomplishments of the symbolic interactionist tradition were the phenomenologists. Alfred Schutz (1971) was the foremost social phenomenologist who drew inspiration from the contributions of G. H. Mead and other precursors of symbolic interactionism and from Max Weber's (Weber, 1966) earlier "interpretive" or *verstehende* sociology). Schutz was a student and follower of the founder of "phenomenology," Edmund Husserl (1913, 1970), but he rejected the pure "subjectivism" of Husserl (according to whom all phenomena are given meaning only by acts of "consciousness"). He placed the concept of "*inter*subjectivity" at the center of his (later) work, which became influential, and helped to shape the ideas of Peter Berger and Thomas Luckmann (1967) in their seminal book, *The Social Construction of Reality.*

According to Schutz, "understanding the meaning of actions" is not only the prerogative of the professional analyst of social relations. To Schutz, understanding the meaning of actions, utterances, and interactions was a prerequisite for *any* person's social existence. Moreover, by virtue of their constant interpretive work, social actors deciphered the nature of reality *relevant* to their ongoing projects. "Reality" became a function of agents' "structures of relevance" in everyday life. Schutz argued that social researchers of *any* kind must begin inquiries into the social world by determining and classifying these structures of relevance, the categories, concepts, expressions, interpretive schemes, stocks of knowledge, and so on) *actually used by and shared among* members of a communication community. Thus, social research was inevitably a "second-order" enterprise, in which the researcher has to develop models of the subjects' systems of concepts and "relevancies" as these become observable in their everyday existence.

The phenomenologists after Schutz (like Husserl before him) rejected any goal of prediction as part of a science of social, experiential, and communicative phenomena. For them, "explanation" was not symmetrical with "prediction." Only for those phenomena for which a *causal* explanation was possible was prediction a proper objective. And, they argued, given the interpretive and contextual nature of human activities, deterministic accounts cannot be made to work like they work in the natural-scientific realm.

However, explanation is not restricted to causal accounts. In Schutz's conception of a phenomenological social science, explanation consists of analyzing *how* communicative and other social interaction phenomena are achieved.

Another methodological point of departure, made by the phenomenologists was the rejection of operational definitions in the conduct of research. At first, this seems strange. After all, how can one hope to study complex communicative phenomena if one does not define one's concepts and give them observable indices?

Within quantitative research, operationalizations are essential requirements. For the *non*quantitative researcher and analyst, such is not the case. How, then, can rigorous research proceed in the absence of operational definitions of "variables"? Phenomenologists, like symbolic interactionists, are not at all in the business of trying to explain *why* people do what they do. Rather, they are interested in explaining *how* people do what they do; according to what constructs they manage to organize their daily lives, especially their communications between each other. As causal explanation and prediction is not the goal of research in this field, it does not require operationalizations of the sort needed for such projects. In fact, the phenomenologists reject operationalism for additional reasons. They argue that people themselves manage to get along in their routine affairs, manage to make sense of each other's activities and utterances, manage to interpret the phenomena in their environments and contexts of action by using the rich resources of their language and culture. Instead of *re-defining* their common sense concepts, as operationalism necessitates, qualitative analysts must *clarify the rules of their use*.

Communication as Practical Action: Ethnomethodology

As we have discussed, the qualitative approach is concerned with *how* human communication works by explaining the properties and features of the interactions themselves. We shall now begin to present some of the ethnomethodological analytic procedures for explicating these features of communication interaction. We shall consider the foundational work of Harold Garfinkel, who coined the term "ethnomethodology" ("members' methods"), which sets forth a whole new attitude toward formal analysis of communication phenomena. We shall move on to the work of Harvey Sacks, whose attention to the logic of "categorization practices" has opened up a new terrain of formal investigation into the workings of communication practices. Then we consider, in some detail, the formal structure of everyday language use in the form of simple conversations, emphasizing the structural components of the "adjacency-pair," as developed by Sacks and Schegloff. Following these is a discussion of some of the most important conceptual contributions in this kind of research: Sacks' notion of "category-boundedness" and Coulter's "disjunctive category-pairs."

One of the first features researchers encounter is the consistent orderliness of human conduct, in general, and communicative activity in particular. This orderliness of activities is a product of the very process of actions on the part of members of a communication community.

Harold Garfinkel (1967) identified his task to be one of describing and explicating the methods that members of a communication community employ in order to make sense of their world. Garfinkel [after Wittgenstein (1969) and as described by Coulter (1986)], adopted the attitude that the analyst's "job basically is not to reconstruct the world in order to analyze it, but to analyze the world." Garfinkel explained that ways of sense-making consist

> *of members' uses of concerted everyday activities as methods with which to recognize and demonstrate the isolatable, typical, uniform, potential repetition, connected appearance, consistency, equivalence, substitutability, directionality, anonymously describable, planful—in short, the rational properties of indexical expressions and indexical actions. (1967:10)*

Indexical expressions and activities are those whose understandings are made available or achieved by the circumstances of their use. And for Garfinkel, *all* expressions and activities are indexical. The meanings that emerge out of communication activities are a result of the multiplicity of features present in that context, of which the actual use of language is a part. Hence, meanings can change in different contexts, according to the different features available to the participants including whatever they bring to the interaction, e.g., their activities, including speech acts, their nonverbal communication, their background knowledge, their moral orientations and belief-commitments, and so on. Accordingly, Garfinkel suggests that we explicate the features of naturally occurring communication interaction, and so outline the *logic* of sense-making.

Garfinkel noticed that members managed their interactional engagements through what he called "the documentary method of interpretation." This is a members' method which allows them to analyze and assess what is going on in vivo, *here* and *now*. Members select *tacitly* the elements of the continuously produced "document" of their interaction, what is significant, what should be changed or repaired, what should the practical upshot(s) of the interaction be, and so on. For members, the tacit use of this method of analysis enables them to manage and understand the taken-for-granted world in which they live. This method enables ethnomethodologists to investigate the common-sense workings of the unproblematic orderliness of everyday social life.

Garfinkel recommended that analysts study the ways in which members perform daily activities in collaboration with one another. The explication of the methods which members use to accomplish these familiar and unremarkable activities will yield insight into the complexity and sophistication of competence required of all members of a communication community (Cuff and Payne, 1984).

How, then, can communications researchers "get at" the actual methods used by members of a communication community to produce and comprehend their communicative constructions? This question takes us directly to the issue of data: What is to count as data for ethnomethodological analysis? And what is the relevance of sampling, if any, in such an inquiry?

Categorization Practices

Harvey Sacks, a close, early collaborator with Garfinkel, developed a unique approach to the problem of data. For Sacks, the development of audio and videotape recorders particularly served the purposes of qualitative investigators, and became qualitative researchers' equivalent to computer technology in quantitative work. Recordings of communicative processes of any kind, from courtroom trials (Atkinson and Drew, 1975) to psychiatric interviews (Coulter, 1973), from routine telephone conversations (Schegloff, 1979) to police interrogations (Watson, 1983) and from interactions in school classrooms (Meehan, 1979; Heap, 1985; McHoul, 1985) to news broadcasts (Heritage and Greatbatch, 1991; Jalbert, 1989, 1992) facilitated the production of an "objectively reproducible record" of events in the form of a detailed transcription. Sacks' colleague, Gail Jefferson, produced a notation system for transcribing real-world, communicative processes which has become standard for the field (Jefferson, 1978). She has also made many independent contributions to ethnomethodological work on the organization of interpersonal communication. (Jefferson, 1974, 1988, 1992)

Communication as "Formal Structures"

One of Sacks' innovations was to identify the basic methods whereby communicative interaction between conversational partners is organized. He discovered that members of any communication community arrange their contributions to discourse according to specific organizational rules of "turn-taking" and "sequential logic" (Sacks, 1992). For example, most questions get answers, most summonses get answers, most greetings get returned. He coined the notion of "adjacency pairing" to capture the apparent regularity in the sequential arrangement of these types of "turns at talk"; and then proceeded to locate "anomalies"—sequences in which questions are *not* answered in adjacent turns, greetings are *not* returned immediately—to see what might be discovered about these apparently "deviant" cases.

Through this he became aware of a structure of communication which is not a *statistical* property, but a *logical one*. Garfinkel and Sacks (1970) were to refer to such a structure as a "formal" structure of practical action. And we shall also discuss, a little further on, the broader methodological significance of this for qualitative investigations into human communication.

Adjacency pairing involves the following features: There are two utterances, comprising distinctive speech-acts (e.g., requesting and granting the request). These component utterances have adjacent positions; different speakers produce each utterance, and two parts of the adjacency pair are ordered (first parts precede second parts—e.g., questions conventionally precede answers). A crucial feature is the existence of *discriminative relations* between the parts (i.e., the pair type of which a first pair part is a member is relevant to communication partners in selecting among possible second pair parts). (Schegloff and Sacks, 1974)

The importance of discriminative relations is this: If a pair type second part is *not* produced, it will be heard as a *noticeable* absence; and if a silence ensues after a first pair-part, it will be attributable to the second speaker as *his or her* silence. Moreover, exactly *what* is *not* being communicated by the second speaker will be detectable (he is *not* "answering my question," she is *not* "returning my greeting," he is *not* "responding to my summons"). Human beings are the only beings who can exploit this silence to tell specifically what one of their number is *not* doing or saying.

There are further complications, however. Adjacency pairs can come in two forms: simple and complex. Simple adjacency pairs are those with unique second pair-parts (thus, *questions* make answers relevant and not summonses). Complex adjacency pairs are those with (minimally) two *alternative* second pair-parts (thus, invitations are paired with acceptances *or* rejections; offers call for acceptances *or* rejections; requests call for grants *or* denials; accusations call for concessions *or* defeats, excuses *or* justifications, etc.).

Sacks noted that, for complex adjacency pairs, there is a *preference* ordering operating on second pair-parts such that, for example, invitations prefer acceptance (that is their purpose), and, even when someone makes an invitation which he or she *as a person* would prefer *not* be accepted, it is done knowing that invitations themselves *project* acceptance as their point. (Thus, we have phenomena such as modified or hedged forms of "invitation"; and delayed and "concessionary" rejections, since rejections are *dispreferred* over acceptances).

In addition, Sacks observed that complex adjacency pairs permit "pre-sequence expansions." If a complex adjacency pair first-part is produced by a speaker, like, "Would you like to come to the movies with me tonight?" (invitation), a usable device is to *preface* such an actual invitation with a pre-sequence, like: "Are you doing anything tonight?" (Pre-invitation). The response to a pre-invitation can take the form of a "solicit" (e.g., "No. What d'ya have in mind?") and then the base sequence can be produced by both parties (e.g., "A trip to the mall?" [invitation] "Oh, that'd be great!" [acceptance]).

The following is an example of this kind of structure:

PRE-INVITATION: E.g., A: Are you busy tonight?

SOLICIT: E.g., B: Nope.

INVITATION: E.g., A: How about taking in a movie?

ACCEPT (preferred selection from alternates Accept/Reject): E.g., B: Let's go!

The categories identifying the structural components (e.g., Invitation, Solicit, etc.) become the abstractions of any next set of naturally occurring utterances (hence the "E.g.," inserted before the actual utterances). The pre-sequence is itself an adjacency pair comprising pre-item and solicit, the base sequence (produced in tandem) comprising the base first pair-part and the base second pair-part. Note that, having produced a solicit in the "opportunity space" following a pre-item, speakers are constrained to produce the preferred second pair-part. If the *dispreferred* is actually offered (e.g., the invitation is rejected after the pre-sequence has been run through), it is conventionally produced with the reason or account, whereas simple acceptances (the preferred second pair-parts) never call for any such account. (One does not have to supply reasons for accepting invitations made directly, whereas rejecting one, especially after having produced a solicit, requires one, makes one legitimately requestable, etc.). Consider this example of a pre-sequence expansions, a pre-offer:

PRE-OFFER: E.g., A: We finally got some of those cookies you like!

SOLICIT: E.g., B: Yuh did!!

BASE OFFER: E.g., A: Want one?

BASE ACCEPTANCE: E.g., B: You bet!

Here is an example of a pre-request sequence:

PRE-REQUEST: E.g., A: Do you know anything about making omelettes?

SOLICIT: E.g., B: I'm an expert on omelettes!

REQUEST: E.g., A: Could you make us some for breakfast?

ACCEPTANCE: E.g., B: Sure.

Here is an example of a pre-announcement sequences (a favorite among young children):

PRE-ANNOUNCEMENT: E.g., A: Guess what?

SOLICIT: E.g., B: What?

ANNOUNCEMENT: E.g., A: I got an "A" on my paper!

ASSESSMENT: E.g., B: That's terrific! Congratulations!

Sacks further observed that complex adjacency pairs permit "insertion expansions." Thus, within any one complex adjacency pair, another (simple) one can be inserted. Consider the following (deliberately simple) insertion sequence example. This is a request sequence:

REQUEST: E.g., A: Can I borrow your tapes?

Insert QUESTION: E.g., B: Do you need them this very minute?

Insert ANSWER: E.g., A: No, it can wait awhile.

GRANT: E.g., B: Okay, send Joe up for them in ten minutes.

And here is an offer sequence:

OFFER: E.g., A: Want to borrow some bread?

Insert QUESTION ONE: E.g., B: When do you need it back?

Insert ANSWER ONE: E.g., A: No hurry, whenever you can.

Insert QUESTION TWO: E.g., B: What's the interest?

Insert ANSWER TWO: E.g., A: Eighteen percent.

REJECTION: E.g., B: That's too steep. I can do better at the bank.

Of course, not all interchanges between communicators run off as smoothly as these scenarios depict. Sacks turned his attention to a detailed analysis of what he called "repair operations" in communication, the study of breakdowns and the methods by which these are/can be managed by co-present communicators. Although there is considerable complexity to his investigation of these phenomena, in what follows we shall keep matters as fundamental as possible.

Any utterance can turn out to be a source of trouble for its hearer. (We shall omit any discussion of speaker *self-repair* here.) Thus, communicative "repairable items" are potentially ubiquitous and not determinable in advance of actual conditions of production. If, then, someone orients to a prior turn as a "repairable item," he or she can signal both *that* it has caused a problem and *what about it* that has caused the problem. So, for example, if someone were to say: "What made you do it?" and the hearer did not hear or understand it fully, the hearer can produce one of two kinds of next turn repair initiators (NTRIs): a nontargeted one (such as: "Huh? What? Say again..." or any comparable token) or a targeted one (such as, in this case, "What made me WHAT?," where the upper case WHAT targets the specific component of the prior turn which has caused the problem of hearing or comprehension). After an NTRI has been produced, the initial speaker is enjoined to produce a candidate repair ("candidate" because an utterance is only a genuine repair if it satisfies the interlocutor). A typical repair sequence runs as follows:

REPAIRABLE ITEM: E.g., A: What time did they leave Bridgeport?

NTRI (Nontargeted): E.g. B: Huh?

CANDIDATE REPAIR: E.g., A: When did they head out for home?

ACKNOWLEDGEMENT: E.g., B: Oh, yeah… uhh, around ten.

There are three forms of candidate repairs: full repeats of prior, reformulations of prior, and partial repeats (such as: "What time did they leave" [omitting "Bridgeport"]). The example above is one of a reformulation of the prior. The repeat form addresses issues of hearing or mishearing, but not misunderstanding (since a mere repeat will not solve a problem of comprehension even though it may solve a problem of hearing), while reformulations (though they *may* be used generically) are primarily designed to handle possible comprehension problems.

Arguments, diagnostic interviews, therapy sessions, military planning sessions, and so on, exist in such structures. Joined to the two basic methods for taking turns in interpersonal communication (current speaker selects next, or next speaker self-selects), sequential logic constrains and enables persons to make sense of their interactive worlds together.

From here, an entire domain of analysis was opened up: the formal analysis of the methods by which people communicate with and understand each other. Where does "sampling" figure in this mode of analysis? Would one need to alter one's analysis if "more data" or "representative" data were gathered? But what could we mean by a "representative sample" of communication in this domain? There is not a finite universe of empirically occurring communications: the domain is strictly *indefinite*, being ever expanded. However, one does not have to study N games of chess before being able to decipher the rules of procedure of the game, and, by similar reasoning, one does not need N cases or instances of recorded communications in order to decipher the rules of procedure for properly circumscribed modalities of discourse. Sacks' findings comprise some *a priori* methods of procedure (see Coulter, 1983) for conducting conversational exchanges between two parties that has been elaborated to encompass multiparty exchanges. In a further study (Sacks, 1974), required only *one single instance* of an utterance in order to (begin to) appreciate the operative methods of what he called "the categorization of persons." This famous example was culled from an infant story-telling exercise in a school. A child had written: "The baby cried. The mommy picked it up." Sacks asked the following questions:

1. What relationship(s) do we hear or read as existing between the categories "baby" and "mommy"; and according to what rule(s)?
2. Why did the mommy pick up the baby? Is there a rule for reasoning this through the resources provided in this simple, two-sentence "story?"
3. To what or to whom does "it" refer in the story?
4. What does "picked … up" mean here; and how can we tell?

In answering the first question using only his communicative *common sense* (and not trying to incur a scientific "amnesia" for this essential resource!), Sacks noted that we would see the relationship as one of "members of a family," and, more specifically, "members of the *same* family." But how to account for this? Moreover, Sacks proposed, we can tell, quite unproblematically, that the mommy's action of picking the baby up was not just an unrelated second occurrence, but an action done *because* of the action reported as having occurred first (the baby's crying). How so? Further, Sacks remarks that our use of "it" to mean the baby is unproblematic. But why? And finally, Sacks observes that we can right away tell that what the mommy "picked up" " was *the baby*, and not, say, the baby's crying sound, in that "picking up" here means "physically lifting the infant up" and *not* "hearing it cry." Again, how is this to be procedurally accounted for?

The Logic of Categories

Sacks' analytical apparatus, designed to handle the details of these common-sense "hearings" became extendible to more and more complex cases. It is the foundation of what has come to be known as "membership categorization logic." (Jayyusi, 1984)

There are three procedural bases for the kind of hearing of the above mini-story which operate in countless other domains as well. They are the (1) consistency rule, (2) duplicative organization provision, and (3) category boundedness rule.

Consistency Rule

"If some population of persons is being categorized, and if a category from some device's collection has been used [e.g., "baby" from the device "family" or the device "stage-of-life"] to categorise a first member of the population, then that category or other categories [e.g., "mommy"] of the same collection *may* be used to categorize members of the population ... this is a "relevance" rule." (Sacks, 1974:219). This accounts for our hearing the "baby" as indexing "family member," given the subsequent use of "mommy," rather than as indexing only "stage-of-life."

Duplicative Organization Provision

"When a [duplicatively organised] device is used on a population, what is done is to take its categories, treat the set of categories as defining a unit and place members of the population into cases of the unit. If a population is so treated, one counts not numbers of daddies, numbers of mommies, and numbers of babies but numbers of families." Thus, "if some population has been categorised from some device whose collection has the 'duplicative organization' property, and a member is presented with a categorized population which can be heard as 'coincumbents' of a case of that device's unit, then: Hear it that way." (Sacks, 1974, p. 221) This accounts for our hearing that the mommy and the baby belong not just to a family, but to the *same* family. In other words, the "mommy" is heard to be the mommy of *that* baby, not any other one.

Category-Boundedness Rule

"Many activities are taken by members to be done by some particular categories of members where the categories are categories from membership categorization devices."

EXHIBIT 20-1   Example of Category-Boundedness

Set I

He sentenced him to ten years' imprisonment.
  (He = Judge)

She diagnosed her condition as diabetes melitus.
  (She = Physician)

He arrested them for drunken driving.
  (He = Police Officer/Cop)

She married them at four o'clock last Tuesday.
  (She = Justice of the Peace/Priest/Vicar/
    Captain of Ship)

Set II

He committed suicide. (He = ?)

She complained bitterly. (She = ?)

They kept on interrupting me. (They = ?)

(Sacks, 1974, p. 222). Since crying is categorially tied to "babies" and "picking up crying babies" and also categorially tied to their mommies, the easy connection is that the mommy *physically lifted her* baby ("picked it up"), rather than that the mommy *caught the sound* of someone's baby crying ("picked it up"). This also accounts for our intuitive sense that the mommy picked the baby up *because* it was crying, and not simply as a disconnected operation or merely subsequent (and maybe unmotivated) occurrence.

Each of these rules has application elsewhere. For example, in introducing oneself by title plus last name and profession ("I am Dr. Jones, resident cardiologist"), one anticipates (and *tries to hear*) subsequent categories used in the return as derived from the same devices (title plus last name and profession), such that if someone then says: "Oh, how do you do? Dr. Smith, pediatrics," it is understood that "pediatrics" is the professional specialization. Indeed, one may hear a possibly unknown descriptor in such cases and intelligibly (even if incorrectly) *infer* that it is the name of professional affiliation, about which one may then inquire, as in:

A: I'm Dr. Jones, resident cardiologist.

B: Pleased to meet you. Dr. Smith, positron emissions tomography.

A: Oh…I'm not acquainted with that specialty. Tell me something about it….

There has been a great deal of analytical work done in this field exploiting Sacks' major insight about the category-boundedness of whole domains of human action. Consider the ease with which we can supply the correct and relevant categories in Exhibit 20-1 from simply noting the actions attributed to the pronomially designated persons in set I, and the impossibility of doing so for set II.

Of course, there are borderline or undecidable cases; but they come close to being decidable by reference to categorially bound activity-types, such as: "They carried them out of the burning building before it collapsed." "They" here *could* be, but need not be, fire-fighters. (Perhaps they were simply co-family members or heroic passers-by.). However, in our own communication community, the references in set I are *all* quite determinate. In set II, *none* of them are.

EXHIBIT 20-2   Example of Membership Categorization

Peter Eglin and Stephen Hester (1992) have shown how the comprehension of newspaper reportage can be seen to be organized by facets of the logic of membership categorization. They use as their basic example the following headline: ENGAGEMENT WAS BROKEN—TEMPERAMENTAL YOUNG MAN GASSED HIMSELF. How is it that we know that the "engagement" was for marriage and not for dinner? How do we tell that the young man was the one engaged, and not someone else? How can we discern that the engaged parties were engaged to each other and not to others? That the broken engagement was the young man's, not another's? That the gassing was a *suicide* and not an accident? That the gassing happened *because of* the broken engagement? That it happened due to desperation arising out of the loss?

None of these connections and reasons are actually made *explicit* in the headline, but they are easily available to us and organize our expectations for reading what is to follow in the newspaper's text.

Among the analytical arguments they introduce, Eglin and Hester remark:

> *As an action, "committing suicide" also has its conceptual grammar, its* category-tied predicates. *It is done for conventional reasons, in certain psychological states, arising out of conventional interactional and structural social circumstances, with conventional methods, and so on. Why would a fiance(e) commit suicide? Because of the loss of the (other) fiance(e). For whom would the loss of a fiance(e) be a reason for suicide? The (other) fiance(e). (Thus our assumption above.) What might a fiance(e) do over the loss of the fiance(e)? Among a range of grammatical possibilities, narrowed by "temperamental" considerations, commit suicide." (1992, p. 245, emphasis added).*

Implications through Contrastive Category-Sets

This kind of explication of the features of intelligibility is what ethnomethodologists are in the business of doing. The process of clarifying these taken-for-granted properties of communication creates a window into the workings of everyday language use. Another analytical construct, also developed by Sacks (1972), which deals with pairs of a different kind, shed light upon how members refer to one another when making distinctions is important. He noticed that certain sets of categories come together in ways which indicate a pairing. Sacks called these *standardized relational pairs.* These standardized relational (S-R) pairs can either be symmetrical or asymmetrical. Symmetrical S-R pairs display common rights and obligations, binding them together (e.g., friend/friend, sister/brother, husband/wife, father/mother, etc.), such that the invocation of one pair part of an S-R pair makes the use of the other pair part *programmatically relevant.* In other words, within a communicative discourse, when one category such as "wife" is invoked, the category "husband" is programmatically relevant because the existence of one requires the existence of the other, otherwise they are not properly used. Hence one cannot be a wife without being paired with a husband and *vice versa.* This kind of analytical point can help us to understand the logical grammars (rules for proper use) of the concepts we employ so unproblematically every day.

Asymmetrical S-R pairs do not display common rights and obligations, but rather a noncontingent and/or mutually exclusive bond (*e.g.,* doctor/patient, parent/child, employer/employee, master/slave). The specification of this analytical construct has yielded significant insight into the workings of contrastive categorization practices and their accompanying features. Just as in symmetrical S-R pairs, when categorizing members of different groups of people, the use of one category of an asymmetrical S-R pair makes the use of other contrastive categories programmatically relevant.

For example, consider the pair "government"/"junta." The category "junta" elicits a *negative* implication of "dictatorship," "totalitarianism" and "militarism." On the other hand, the category "government" elicits a *positive* (or at least "neutral") implication of "legitimacy," "democracy," and "constitutionality." The use of contrastive categories of this kind, especially when a contrast category is known to those communicating when they describe social phenomena such as persons, places, institutions, collectivities of people, and objects, *makes available to the recipients the beliefs of the user of the category.* Coulter (1979) describes this phenomenon as involving the use of *disjunctive category-pairs.*

> *At the level of the social organization of their use, we can speak of the categories "belief" and "knowledge" as forming a* disjunctive category-pair....*Other such pairs would include vision/hallucination; telepathy/trickery and ideology/science. Where one part of these pairs is invoked to characterize some phenomenon seriously,* the speaker's belief-commitment may be inferred, and the structure of subsequent discourse may be managed in terms provided for by the programmatic relevance of the disjunctive category-pair relationship. *Thus, to the nonbeliever, Joan of Arc suffered hallucinations; to the believer, divine visions. To the nonbeliever, Uri Geller was a sophisticated conjurer; to the believer, a telepath and tele-kineticist, and so on. (1979, p. 181)*

To illustrate this kind of analysis, consider the use of the aforementioned disjunctive category-pair: junta/government. When these categories are employed to categorize a country's leadership, not only do they provide a means to describe it, they also make available to listeners or viewers the asymmetrical character of these categories and provide insight into the views, attitudes and beliefs or values of the speaker of the particular category. When the mass media, during the Carter administration, were referring to the El Salvadoran regime by employing the category junta, certain inferences were made available to audiences about the attitudes of the U.S. administration toward the leadership of El Salvador. When President Reagan was elected, the mass media changed and selected the category government, making certain *different kinds* of inferences available.

When it is desired to present persons, collectivities of persons, and their activities in a negative light, the use of one component of a disjunctive category-pair is most effective. The tacit manner in which such a negative view is accomplished is through the use of the *non-self-avowable category*; that is, that category which *conventionally* would not be self-avowed by a person or member of the collectivity being categorized. Consider, for example, the disjunctive category-pair "terrorist"/"freedom-fighter," within the context of the Arab-Israeli conflict: From the standpoint of Israeli combatants, they are the freedom-fighters and the Palestinians are terrorists; from the standpoint of the Palestinian combatants, they are the freedom-fighters and the Israelis are the terrorists. Note how each group takes on the self-avowable category and ascribes the non-self-avowable one to the others. This practice is so common that the following observation is worth mentioning:

> *A logical point of continuity, endogenous to these structures, is that when people are reported to have* self-avowed *a disavowable [conventionally non-self-avowable] category, it is often expressed in those very terms*, e.g., "He is a self-avowed racist." *The report is marked or flagged because it is an* unconventional *form of avowal. (Jalbert, 1989, p. 240)*

This kind of analysis explicates the logico-grammatical properties of concepts and their accompanying categorization practices.

Summary

In this chapter we have presented an overview of contemporary ideas and research strategies prominent in qualitative research in communication sciences. We have traced the intellectual development of the strategies from the *symbolic interactionist* tradition, most notably the work of Herbert Blumer, whose concern was to develop a methodological framework for the social sciences separate and distinct from that of the natural sciences, one which is qualitative rather than quantitative (statistical) in kind. Erving Goffman's work brought this tradition closest to what we consider to be a methodological contribution.

Alfred Schutz's brand of *phenomenology* brought the concept of "intersubjectivity" into prominence in the context of the construction of reality. This was important because the notion of an "objective" reality was challenged as an element in the formation of a methodological apparatus. Through the work of Berger and Luckmann, reality was understood as a social construction and achievement.

The notion of "prediction" was also deemed to be inappropriate to analysis of *social* phenomena. Rather, the routine patterns of "social conventions" are what allow members of a culture (and analysts) to form expectations in their everyday lives.

Upon these foundational contributions Harold Garfinkel and Harvey Sacks built a qualitative methodology for the social sciences: *ethnomethodology*. Their contributions include analyses of conventional social and communicative interactions routinely undertaken by members of our culture in their unproblematic sense-making of everyday life.

Some of the formal structures discussed in this chapter are: the turn-taking system; sequential logic; the adjacency pair in several of its manifestations (e.g., OFFER, REQUEST, SUMMONS, INVITATION, etc.); repair logic; the procedural bases of categorization logic (i.e. the consistency rule, the duplicative organization provision, and the category-boundedness rule); programmatic relevance and the logic of asymmetrical and symmetrical, including disjunctive category-pairs. All of these distinct analytical constructs, and many others, allow the ethnomethodologist and other qualitative analysts to use a formal set of procedures and constructs for outlining those taken-for-granted structures of routine communication.

The ethnomethodological perspective discussed here differs quite radically from the kind of work commonly found in the quantitative research literature. It asks and tries to answer different *kinds* of questions, ones sometimes considered basic for studies of interpersonal and mass media communication. There are perhaps stronger ties between this mode of qualitative analysis and research conducted in logic and linguistics than to research in the other social sciences.

The power of these ways of conceiving of communicative phenomena may be discovered by examining lengthier explanations, as suggested in the references and additional readings section.

References and Additional Readings

Atkinson, J. M. & Drew, P. (1979). *Order in court: The organization of verbal interaction in judicial settings.* London: MacMillan and Humanities Presses.

Becker, H. S. (1963). *Outsiders: Studies in the sociology of deviance.* Glencoe, IL: Free Press.

Benson, D. & Hughes, J. A. (1983). *The perspective of ethnomethodology.* New York: Longman.

Berger, P. & T. Luckmann, (1967). *The social construction of reality.* Garden City, NY: Anchor Books.

Blumer, H. (1967). "Sociological analysis and the variable" in J. G. Manis & B. N. Meltzer (Eds.), *Symbolic interactionism: A reader in social psychology.* Boston: Allyn & Bacon.

Blumer, H. (1969). *Symbolic interactionism: Perspective and method.* Englewood Cliffs, NJ: Prentice-Hall.

Boden, D. & Zimmerman, D. H., Eds. (1991). *Talk and social structure: Studies in ethnomethodology and conversation analysis.* Berkeley, CA: University of California Press.

Coulter, J. (1973). *Approaches to insanity: A philosophical and sociological study.* New York: Wiley Interscience.

Coulter, J. (1979). "Beliefs and practical understanding" in G. Psathas (Ed.), *Everyday language: studies in ethnomethodology.* New York, Irvington Publishers.

Coulter, J. (1983). "Contingent and *a priori* structures in sequential analysis," *Human Studies*, 6, (4). 361–376

Coulter, J. (1986). "Mentalistic and sociological models of mind," Colloquium, Department of Psychology, Tufts University.

Cuff, E. C. & Payne, G. C. F., Eds. (1984). *Perspectives in sociology.* London: George Allen & Unwin.

Eglin, P. & Hester, S. (1992). "The pragmatics of practical action" *Semiotica*, Vol. 88, Nos. 3/4.

Garfinkel, H. (1967). *Studies in ethnomethodology.* Englewood Cliffs, NJ: Prentice-Hall.

Garfinkel, H. & Sacks, H. (1970). "On formal structures of practical actions," in F. C. McKinney & E. A. Tiryakian (Eds.), *Theoretical sociology: Perspectives and developments.* New York: Appleton-Century-Crofts.

Geertz, C. (1973). *The interpretation of cultures.* New York: Basic Books; and Ryle, G. (1949, 1963). *The concept of mind.* London: Hutchinson & Co.

Goffman, E. (1959). *The presentation of self in everyday life.* New York: Doubleday Anchor.

Goffman, E. (1961). *Asylums.* New York: Doubleday Anchor.

Goffman, E. (1981). *Forms of talk.* Philadelphia: University of Pennsylvania Press.

Heap, J. L. (1985). "Discourse in the production of classroom knowledge: Reading lessons" *Curriculum Inquiry*, 15(3); p. 245–279.

Helm, D. et al., Eds. (1989). *The interactional order: New directions in the study of social order.* New York: Irvington Publishers.

Heritage, J. & Greatbatch, D. (1991). "On the institutional character of institutional talk: The case of news interviews," in Boden, D. and Zimmerman, D. (Eds.). *Talk and social structure: Studies in ethnomethodology and conversation analysis.* Berkeley, CA: University of California Press.

Husserl, E. (1913). *Ideas.* London: George Allen & Unwin.

Husserl, E. (1970). *The crisis of European sciences and transcendental phenomenology* (Trans. D. Carr). Evanston, IL: Northwestern University Press.

P. L. Jalbert (1989). "Categorization and beliefs: News accounts of Haitian and Cuban refugees," in Helm, D. et al. (Eds.). *The interactional order: New directions in the study of social order.* New York: Irvington Publishers.

Jalbert, P. L. (1992). "Charting the logical geography of the concept of 'cease-fire'" *Human Studies*, 15, 2–3 p. 265–290

Jefferson, G. (1974). "Error correction as an interactional resource," *Language and Society*, 3,(2); 181–199.

Jefferson, G. (1978). "Explanation of transcript notation" in Schenkein, J. *Studies in the organization of conversational interaction.* New York: Academic Press.

Jefferson, G. (1988). "On the sequential organization of troubles talk in ordinary conversation," *Social Problems*, 35 (4). 418–442.

Jefferson, G. (1992). "Side sequences" in Sudnow, D. (Ed.). *Studies in social interaction.* Glencoe, IL: Free Press.

Jayyusi, L. (1984). *Categorization and the moral order.* Boston: Routledge and Kegan Paul.

Kuhn, M. (1967). "Major trends in symbolic interactionist theory in the past twenty-five years," in Manis, J. G. & Meltzer, B. N. *Symbolic interactionism: A reader in social psychology.* Boston: Allyn & Bacon.

Manis, J. G. & Meltzer, B. N. (1967). *Symbolic interactionism: A reader in social psychology.* Boston: Allyn & Bacon.

McHoul, A. W. (1985). "Two aspects of classroom interaction, turn-taking and correcting: A research report," *Australian Journal of Human Communication Disorders*, 13, p. 53–64.

McKinney, F. C. & Tiryakian, E. A., Eds. (1970). *Theoretical sociology: Perspectives and developments.* New York: Appleton-Century-Crofts.

Mead, G. H. (1934). *Mind, self, and society.* Chicago: University of Chicago Press.

Mead, G. H. (1964). *On social psychology: Selected papers*, Strauss, A. (Ed.). Chicago: University of Chicago Press.

Meehan, H. (1979). *Learning lessons: Social organization in the classroom.* Cambridge: Harvard University Press.

Psathas, G. (1979). *Everyday language: Studies in ethnomethodology.* New York: Irvington Publishers.

Sacks, H. (1972). "An initial investigation of the usability of conversational data for doing sociology," in D. Sudnow (Ed.). *Studies in social interaction.* Glencoe, IL: Free Press.

Sacks, H. (1974). "On the analyzability of stories by children," in R. Turner (Ed.). *Ethnomethodology.* Harmondsworth Penguin.

Sacks, H. (1992). *Lectures on conversation.* 2 Volumes, Edited by G. Jefferson. Oxford, Basil Blackwell.

Schegloff, E. (1979). "Identification and recognition in telephone conversation openings" in Psathas, G. (Ed.). *Everyday language: Studies in ethnomethodology.* New York: Irvington Publishers.

Schegloff, E. & Sacks, H. (1974). "Opening up closings," in R. Turner (Ed.). *Ethnomethodology.* Harmondsworth Penguin.

Schenkein, J. (1978). *Studies in the organization of conversational interaction.* New York: Academic Press.

Schutz, A. (1971). *Collected papers I: Problems of social reality.* the Hague: Martinus Nijhoff.

Strauss, A. L. & Becker, H. S. (1956). "Careers, personality and adult socialization," *American Journal of Sociology*, Vol. LXVII, November.

Sudnow, D., Ed. (1992). *Studies in social interaction.* Glencoe, IL: Free Press.

Turner, R., Ed. (1974). *Ethnomethodology.* Harmondsworth, England: Penguin.

Watson, D. R. (1983). "The presentation of victim and offender in discourse: The case of police interrogations and interviews." *Victimology*, 8(1 and 2). pp. 31–52.

Weber, M. (1966). "The theory of social and economic organization" Edited by Parsons, T. Glencoe, IL: Free Press.

Wittgenstein, L. (1969). *Philosophical investigations.* New York: MacMillan Publishing Co.

Appendix *A*

Table of Areas Under the Standard Normal Curve

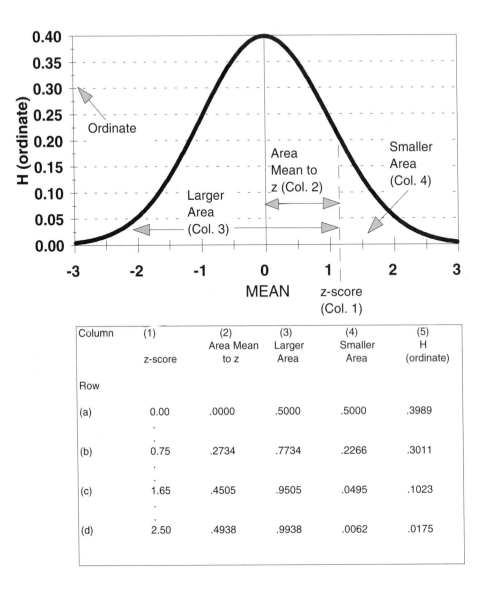

Column	(1) z-score	(2) Area Mean to z	(3) Larger Area	(4) Smaller Area	(5) H (ordinate)
Row					
(a)	0.00	.0000	.5000	.5000	.3989
	.				
	.				
(b)	0.75	.2734	.7734	.2266	.3011
	.				
	.				
(c)	1.65	.4505	.9505	.0495	.1023
	.				
	.				
(d)	2.50	.4938	.9938	.0062	.0175

Column 1 gives the z-score, or the number of standard deviations away from the mean of the distribution. Column 2 gives the area under the curve between the mean and z, a given location on the baseline. Notice also that the line drawn up from the point marked "z-score" divides the total area under the curve into two parts. In the curve shown, this would mean a "larger" part (under the curve, but to the left of z), and a "smaller" part to the right of z. The "larger area" can be found in Column 3 (which can also be thought of as consisting of the 50 percent of the area under the curve in the left-half of the distribution plus the area between the mean and z); the smaller area can be found in Column 4. Finally, Column 5 contains the value of H, the height of the curve, at the given value of z.

(1)	(2) Area Mean to z	(3) Larger Area	(4) Smaller Area	(5) H (ordinate)
z-score				
0.00	0.0000	0.5000	0.5000	0.3989
0.01	0.0040	0.5040	0.4960	0.3989
0.02	0.0080	0.5080	0.4920	0.3989
0.03	0.0120	0.5120	0.4880	0.3988
0.04	0.0160	0.5160	0.4840	0.3986
0.05	0.0199	0.5199	0.4801	0.3984
0.06	0.0239	0.5239	0.4761	0.3982
0.08	0.0319	0.5319	0.4681	0.3977
0.09	0.0359	0.5359	0.4641	0.3973
0.10	0.0398	0.5398	0.4602	0.3970
0.11	0.0438	0.5438	0.4562	0.3965
0.12	0.0478	0.5478	0.4522	0.3961
0.16	0.0636	0.5636	0.4364	0.3939
0.17	0.0675	0.5675	0.4325	0.3932
0.18	0.0714	0.5714	0.4286	0.3925
0.19	0.0753	0.5753	0.4247	0.3918
0.20	0.0793	0.5793	0.4207	0.3910
0.21	0.0832	0.5832	0.4168	0.3902
0.22	0.0871	0.5871	0.4129	0.3894
0.23	0.0910	0.5910	0.4090	0.3885
0.24	0.0948	0.5948	0.4052	0.3876
0.25	0.0987	0.5987	0.4013	0.3867
0.27	0.1064	0.6064	0.3936	0.3847
0.29	0.1141	0.6141	0.3859	0.3825
0.31	0.1217	0.6217	0.3783	0.3802
0.32	0.1255	0.6255	0.3745	0.3790
0.33	0.1293	0.6293	0.3707	0.3778
0.34	0.1331	0.6331	0.3669	0.3765
0.35	0.1368	0.6368	0.3632	0.3752
0.36	0.1406	0.6406	0.3594	0.3739
0.37	0.1443	0.6443	0.3557	0.3725
0.38	0.1480	0.6480	0.3520	0.3712
0.39	0.1517	0.6517	0.3483	0.3697
0.40	0.1554	0.6554	0.3446	0.3683
0.41	0.1591	0.6591	0.3409	0.3668
0.42	0.1628	0.6628	0.3372	0.3653
0.43	0.1664	0.6664	0.3336	0.3637
0.44	0.1700	0.6700	0.3300	0.3621
0.45	0.1736	0.6736	0.3264	0.3605
0.46	0.1772	0.6772	0.3228	0.3589
0.47	0.1808	0.6808	0.3192	0.3572
0.48	0.1844	0.6844	0.3156	0.3555
0.49	0.1879	0.6879	0.3121	0.3538
0.50	0.1915	0.6915	0.3085	0.3521
0.51	0.1950	0.6950	0.3050	0.3503
0.53	0.2019	0.7019	0.2981	0.3467

(Continued)

(1) z-score	(2) Area Mean to z	(3) Larger Area	(4) Smaller Area	(5) H (ordinate)
0.54	0.2054	0.7054	0.2946	0.3448
0.55	0.2088	0.7088	0.2912	0.3429
0.57	0.2157	0.7157	0.2843	0.3391
0.58	0.2190	0.7190	0.2810	0.3372
0.59	0.2224	0.7224	0.2776	0.3352
0.62	0.2324	0.7324	0.2676	0.3292
0.63	0.2357	0.7357	0.2643	0.3271
0.64	0.2389	0.7389	0.2611	0.3251
0.65	0.2422	0.7422	0.2578	0.3230
0.66	0.2454	0.7454	0.2546	0.3209
0.67	0.2486	0.7486	0.2514	0.3187
0.68	0.2517	0.7517	0.2483	0.3166
0.69	0.2549	0.7549	0.2451	0.3144
0.70	0.2580	0.7580	0.2420	0.3123
0.71	0.2611	0.7611	0.2389	0.3101
0.72	0.2642	0.7642	0.2358	0.3079
0.73	0.2673	0.7673	0.2327	0.3056
0.74	0.2703	0.7703	0.2297	0.3034
0.75	0.2734	0.7734	0.2266	0.3011
0.76	0.2764	0.7764	0.2236	0.2989
0.77	0.2793	0.7793	0.2207	0.2966
0.78	0.2823	0.7823	0.2177	0.2943
0.79	0.2852	0.7852	0.2148	0.2920
0.80	0.2881	0.7881	0.2119	0.2897
0.81	0.2910	0.7910	0.2090	0.2874
0.82	0.2939	0.7939	0.2061	0.2850
0.83	0.2967	0.7967	0.2033	0.2827
0.84	0.2995	0.7995	0.2005	0.2803
0.85	0.3023	0.8023	0.1977	0.2780
0.86	0.3051	0.8051	0.1949	0.2756
0.87	0.3078	0.8078	0.1922	0.2732
0.88	0.3106	0.8106	0.1894	0.2709
0.89	0.3133	0.8133	0.1867	0.2685
0.90	0.3159	0.8159	0.1841	0.2661
0.91	0.3186	0.8186	0.1814	0.2637
0.92	0.3212	0.8212	0.1788	0.2613
0.93	0.3238	0.8238	0.1762	0.2589
0.94	0.3264	0.8264	0.1736	0.2565
0.95	0.3289	0.8289	0.1711	0.2541
0.96	0.3315	0.8315	0.1685	0.2516
0.97	0.3340	0.8340	0.1660	0.2492
0.98	0.3365	0.8365	0.1635	0.2468
0.99	0.3389	0.8389	0.1611	0.2444
1.00	0.3413	0.8413	0.1587	0.2420
1.01	0.3438	0.8438	0.1562	0.2396
1.02	0.3461	0.8461	0.1539	0.2371
1.06	0.3554	0.8554	0.1446	0.2275
1.07	0.3577	0.8577	0.1423	0.2251

(Continued)

(1)	(2) Area Mean to z	(3) Larger Area	(4) Smaller Area	(5) H (ordinate)
z-score				
1.08	0.3599	0.8599	0.1401	0.2227
1.09	0.3621	0.8621	0.1379	0.2203
1.10	0.3643	0.8643	0.1357	0.2179
1.14	0.3729	0.8729	0.1271	0.2083
1.15	0.3749	0.8749	0.1251	0.2059
1.16	0.3770	0.8770	0.1230	0.2036
1.17	0.3790	0.8790	0.1210	0.2012
1.18	0.3810	0.8810	0.1190	0.1989
1.19	0.3830	0.8830	0.1170	0.1965
1.23	0.3907	0.8907	0.1093	0.1872
1.24	0.3925	0.8925	0.1075	0.1849
1.25	0.3943	0.8943	0.1057	0.1826
1.26	0.3962	0.8962	0.1038	0.1804
1.27	0.3980	0.8980	0.1020	0.1781
1.28	0.3997	0.8997	0.1003	0.1758
1.29	0.4015	0.9015	0.0985	0.1736
1.30	0.4032	0.9032	0.0968	0.1714
1.31	0.4049	0.9049	0.0951	0.1691
1.32	0.4066	0.9066	0.0934	0.1669
1.33	0.4082	0.9082	0.0918	0.1647
1.34	0.4099	0.9099	0.0901	0.1626
1.35	0.4115	0.9115	0.0885	0.1604
1.36	0.4131	0.9131	0.0869	0.1582
1.37	0.4147	0.9147	0.0853	0.1561
1.38	0.4162	0.9162	0.0838	0.1539
1.39	0.4177	0.9177	0.0823	0.1518
1.40	0.4192	0.9192	0.0808	0.1497
1.41	0.4207	0.9207	0.0793	0.1476
1.42	0.4222	0.9222	0.0778	0.1456
1.43	0.4236	0.9236	0.0764	0.1435
1.44	0.4251	0.9251	0.0749	0.1415
1.45	0.4265	0.9265	0.0735	0.1394
1.46	0.4279	0.9279	0.0721	0.1374
1.47	0.4292	0.9292	0.0708	0.1354
1.48	0.4306	0.9306	0.0694	0.1334
1.49	0.4319	0.9319	0.0681	0.1315
1.50	0.4332	0.9332	0.0668	0.1295
1.51	0.4345	0.9345	0.0655	0.1276
1.52	0.4357	0.9357	0.0643	0.1257
1.53	0.4370	0.9370	0.0630	0.1238
1.54	0.4382	0.9382	0.0618	0.1219
1.55	0.4394	0.9394	0.0606	0.1200
1.56	0.4406	0.9406	0.0594	0.1182
1.57	0.4418	0.9418	0.0582	0.1163
1.58	0.4429	0.9429	0.0571	0.1145
1.59	0.4441	0.9441	0.0559	0.1127
1.60	0.4452	0.9452	0.0548	0.1109

(Continued)

(1) z-score	(2) Area Mean to z	(3) Larger Area	(4) Smaller Area	(5) H (ordinate)
1.61	0.4463	0.9463	0.0537	0.1092
1.62	0.4474	0.9474	0.0526	0.1074
1.63	0.4484	0.9484	0.0516	0.1057
1.64	0.4495	0.9495	0.0505	0.1040
1.65	0.4505	0.9505	0.0495	0.1023
1.66	0.4515	0.9515	0.0485	0.1006
1.67	0.4525	0.9525	0.0475	0.0989
1.68	0.4535	0.9535	0.0465	0.0973
1.69	0.4545	0.9545	0.0455	0.0957
1.70	0.4554	0.9554	0.0446	0.0940
1.71	0.4564	0.9564	0.0436	0.0925
1.72	0.4573	0.9573	0.0427	0.0909
1.73	0.4582	0.9582	0.0418	0.0893
1.74	0.4591	0.9591	0.0409	0.0878
1.75	0.4599	0.9599	0.0401	0.0863
1.76	0.4608	0.9608	0.0392	0.0848
1.77	0.4616	0.9616	0.0384	0.0833
1.78	0.4625	0.9625	0.0375	0.0818
1.79	0.4633	0.9633	0.0367	0.0804
1.80	0.4641	0.9641	0.0359	0.0790
1.81	0.4649	0.9649	0.0351	0.0775
1.82	0.4656	0.9656	0.0344	0.0761
1.83	0.4664	0.9664	0.0336	0.0748
1.84	0.4671	0.9671	0.0329	0.0734
1.85	0.4678	0.9678	0.0322	0.0721
1.86	0.4686	0.9686	0.0314	0.0707
1.87	0.4693	0.9693	0.0307	0.0694
1.88	0.4699	0.9699	0.0301	0.0681
1.89	0.4706	0.9706	0.0294	0.0669
1.90	0.4713	0.9713	0.0287	0.0656
1.91	0.4719	0.9719	0.0281	0.0644
1.92	0.4726	0.9726	0.0274	0.0632
1.93	0.4732	0.9732	0.0268	0.0620
1.94	0.4738	0.9738	0.0262	0.0608
1.95	0.4744	0.9744	0.0256	0.0596
1.96	0.4750	0.9750	0.0250	0.0584
1.97	0.4756	0.9756	0.0244	0.0573
1.98	0.4761	0.9761	0.0239	0.0562
1.99	0.4767	0.9767	0.0233	0.0551
2.00	0.4772	0.9772	0.0228	0.0540
2.02	0.4783	0.9783	0.0217	0.0519
2.03	0.4788	0.9788	0.0212	0.0508
2.04	0.4793	0.9793	0.0207	0.0498
2.05	0.4798	0.9798	0.0202	0.0488
2.07	0.4808	0.9808	0.0192	0.0468
2.09	0.4817	0.9817	0.0183	0.0449
2.11	0.4826	0.9826	0.0174	0.0431

(Continued)

(1) z-score	(2) Area Mean to z	(3) Larger Area	(4) Smaller Area	(5) H (ordinate)
2.12	0.4830	0.9830	0.0170	0.0422
2.13	0.4834	0.9834	0.0166	0.0413
2.14	0.4838	0.9838	0.0162	0.0404
2.16	0.4846	0.9846	0.0154	0.0387
2.18	0.4854	0.9854	0.0146	0.0371
2.20	0.4861	0.9861	0.0139	0.0355
2.21	0.4864	0.9864	0.0136	0.0347
2.23	0.4871	0.9871	0.0129	0.0332
2.25	0.4878	0.9878	0.0122	0.0317
2.27	0.4884	0.9884	0.0116	0.0303
2.28	0.4887	0.9887	0.0113	0.0297
2.29	0.4890	0.9890	0.0110	0.0290
2.30	0.4893	0.9893	0.0107	0.0283
2.32	0.4898	0.9898	0.0102	0.0270
2.34	0.4904	0.9904	0.0096	0.0258
2.36	0.4909	0.9909	0.0091	0.0246
2.37	0.4911	0.9911	0.0089	0.0241
2.38	0.4913	0.9913	0.0087	0.0235
2.39	0.4916	0.9916	0.0084	0.0229
2.41	0.4920	0.9920	0.0080	0.0219
2.43	0.4925	0.9925	0.0075	0.0208
2.45	0.4929	0.9929	0.0071	0.0198
2.46	0.4931	0.9931	0.0069	0.0194
2.48	0.4934	0.9934	0.0066	0.0184
2.50	0.4938	0.9938	0.0062	0.0175
2.52	0.4941	0.9941	0.0059	0.0167
2.53	0.4943	0.9943	0.0057	0.0163
2.54	0.4945	0.9945	0.0055	0.0158
2.55	0.4946	0.9946	0.0054	0.0154
2.56	0.4948	0.9948	0.0052	0.0151
2.57	0.4949	0.9949	0.0051	0.0147
2.58	0.4951	0.9951	0.0049	0.0143
2.59	0.4952	0.9952	0.0048	0.0139
2.60	0.4953	0.9953	0.0047	0.0136
2.61	0.4955	0.9955	0.0045	0.0132
2.62	0.4956	0.9956	0.0044	0.0129
2.63	0.4957	0.9957	0.0043	0.0126
2.64	0.4959	0.9959	0.0041	0.0122
2.65	0.4960	0.9960	0.0040	0.0119
2.66	0.4961	0.9961	0.0039	0.0116
2.67	0.4962	0.9962	0.0038	0.0113
2.68	0.4963	0.9963	0.0037	0.0110
2.69	0.4964	0.9964	0.0036	0.0107
2.70	0.4965	0.9965	0.0035	0.0104
2.71	0.4966	0.9966	0.0034	0.0101
2.72	0.4967	0.9967	0.0033	0.0099
2.73	0.4968	0.9968	0.0032	0.0096

(Continued)

(1) z-score	(2) Area Mean to z	(3) Larger Area	(4) Smaller Area	(5) H (ordinate)
2.74	0.4969	0.9969	0.0031	0.0093
2.75	0.4970	0.9970	0.0030	0.0091
2.76	0.4971	0.9971	0.0029	0.0088
2.77	0.4972	0.9972	0.0028	0.0086
2.78	0.4973	0.9973	0.0027	0.0084
2.79	0.4974	0.9974	0.0026	0.0081
2.80	0.4974	0.9974	0.0026	0.0079
2.81	0.4975	0.9975	0.0025	0.0077
2.82	0.4976	0.9976	0.0024	0.0075
2.83	0.4977	0.9977	0.0023	0.0073
2.84	0.4977	0.9977	0.0023	0.0071
2.85	0.4978	0.9978	0.0022	0.0069
2.86	0.4979	0.9979	0.0021	0.0067
2.87	0.4979	0.9979	0.0021	0.0065
2.88	0.4980	0.9980	0.0020	0.0063
2.89	0.4981	0.9981	0.0019	0.0061
2.90	0.4981	0.9981	0.0019	0.0060
2.91	0.4982	0.9982	0.0018	0.0058
2.92	0.4982	0.9982	0.0018	0.0056
2.93	0.4983	0.9983	0.0017	0.0055
2.94	0.4984	0.9984	0.0016	0.0053
2.95	0.4984	0.9984	0.0016	0.0051
2.96	0.4985	0.9985	0.0015	0.0050
2.97	0.4985	0.9985	0.0015	0.0048
2.98	0.4986	0.9986	0.0014	0.0047
2.99	0.4986	0.9986	0.0014	0.0046
3.00	0.4986	0.9986	0.0014	0.0044
3.01	0.4987	0.9987	0.0013	0.0043
3.02	0.4987	0.9987	0.0013	0.0042
3.03	0.4988	0.9988	0.0012	0.0040
3.04	0.4988	0.9988	0.0012	0.0039
3.05	0.4989	0.9989	0.0011	0.0038
3.06	0.4989	0.9989	0.0011	0.0037
3.07	0.4989	0.9989	0.0011	0.0036
3.08	0.4990	0.9990	0.0010	0.0035
3.09	0.4990	0.9990	0.0010	0.0034
3.10	0.4990	0.9990	0.0010	0.0033
3.11	0.4991	0.9991	0.0009	0.0032
3.12	0.4991	0.9991	0.0009	0.0031
3.13	0.4991	0.9991	0.0009	0.0030
3.14	0.4992	0.9992	0.0008	0.0029
3.15	0.4992	0.9992	0.0008	0.0028
3.16	0.4992	0.9992	0.0008	0.0027
3.17	0.4992	0.9992	0.0008	0.0026
3.18	0.4993	0.9993	0.0007	0.0025
3.19	0.4993	0.9993	0.0007	0.0025
3.20	0.4993	0.9993	0.0007	0.0024

(Continued)

(1) z-score	(2) Area Mean to z	(3) Larger Area	(4) Smaller Area	(5) H (ordinate)
3.21	0.4993	0.9993	0.0007	0.0023
3.22	0.4994	0.9994	0.0006	0.0022
3.23	0.4994	0.9994	0.0006	0.0022
3.24	0.4994	0.9994	0.0006	0.0021
3.25	0.4994	0.9994	0.0006	0.0020
3.26	0.4994	0.9994	0.0006	0.0020
3.27	0.4995	0.9995	0.0005	0.0019
3.28	0.4995	0.9995	0.0005	0.0018
3.29	0.4995	0.9995	0.0005	0.0018
3.30	0.4995	0.9995	0.0005	0.0017
3.31	0.4995	0.9995	0.0005	0.0017
3.32	0.4995	0.9995	0.0005	0.0016
3.33	0.4996	0.9996	0.0004	0.0016
3.34	0.4996	0.9996	0.0004	0.0015
3.35	0.4996	0.9996	0.0004	0.0015
3.36	0.4996	0.9996	0.0004	0.0014
3.37	0.4996	0.9996	0.0004	0.0014
3.38	0.4996	0.9996	0.0004	0.0013
3.39	0.4997	0.9997	0.0003	0.0013
3.40	0.4997	0.9997	0.0003	0.0012
3.41	0.4997	0.9997	0.0003	0.0012
3.42	0.4997	0.9997	0.0003	0.0012
3.43	0.4997	0.9997	0.0003	0.0011
3.44	0.4997	0.9997	0.0003	0.0011
3.45	0.4997	0.9997	0.0003	0.0010
3.46	0.4997	0.9997	0.0003	0.0010
3.47	0.4997	0.9997	0.0003	0.0010
3.48	0.4997	0.9997	0.0003	0.0009
3.49	0.4998	0.9998	0.0002	0.0009
3.50	0.4998	0.9998	0.0002	0.0009
3.51	0.4998	0.9998	0.0002	0.0008
3.52	0.4998	0.9998	0.0002	0.0008
3.53	0.4998	0.9998	0.0002	0.0008
3.54	0.4998	0.9998	0.0002	0.0008
3.55	0.4998	0.9998	0.0002	0.0007
3.56	0.4998	0.9998	0.0002	0.0007
3.57	0.4998	0.9998	0.0002	0.0007
3.58	0.4998	0.9998	0.0002	0.0007
3.59	0.4998	0.9998	0.0002	0.0006
3.60	0.4998	0.9998	0.0002	0.0006
3.61	0.4998	0.9998	0.0002	0.0006
3.62	0.4999	0.9999	0.0001	0.0006
3.63	0.4999	0.9999	0.0001	0.0005
3.64	0.4999	0.9999	0.0001	0.0005
3.65	0.4999	0.9999	0.0001	0.0005
3.66	0.4999	0.9999	0.0001	0.0005
3.67	0.4999	0.9999	0.0001	0.0005

(Continued)

(1) z-score	(2) Area Mean to z	(3) Larger Area	(4) Smaller Area	(5) H (ordinate)
3.68	0.4999	0.9999	0.0001	0.0005
3.69	0.4999	0.9999	0.0001	0.0004
3.70	0.4999	0.9999	0.0001	0.0004
3.71	0.4999	0.9999	0.0001	0.0004
3.72	0.4999	0.9999	0.0001	0.0004
3.73	0.4999	0.9999	0.0001	0.0004
3.74	0.4999	0.9999	0.0001	0.0004
3.75	0.4999	0.9999	0.0001	0.0004
3.76	0.4999	0.9999	0.0001	0.0003
3.77	0.4999	0.9999	0.0001	0.0003
3.78	0.4999	0.9999	0.0001	0.0003
3.79	0.4999	0.9999	0.0001	0.0003
3.80	0.4999	0.9999	0.0001	0.0003
3.81	0.4999	0.9999	0.0001	0.0003
3.82	0.4999	0.9999	0.0001	0.0003
3.83	0.4999	0.9999	0.0001	0.0003
3.84	0.4999	0.9999	0.0001	0.0003
3.85	0.4999	0.9999	0.0001	0.0002
3.86	0.4999	0.9999	0.0001	0.0002
3.87	0.4999	0.9999	0.0001	0.0002
3.88	0.4999	0.9999	0.0001	0.0002
3.89	0.4999	0.9999	0.0001	0.0002
3.90	0.5000	1.0000	0.0000	0.0002
3.91	0.5000	1.0000	0.0000	0.0002
3.92	0.5000	1.0000	0.0000	0.0002
3.93	0.5000	1.0000	0.0000	0.0002
3.94	0.5000	1.0000	0.0000	0.0002
3.95	0.5000	1.0000	0.0000	0.0002
3.96	0.5000	1.0000	0.0000	0.0002
3.97	0.5000	1.0000	0.0000	0.0002
3.98	0.5000	1.0000	0.0000	0.0001
3.99	0.5000	1.0000	0.0000	0.0001
4.00	0.5000	1.0000	0.0000	0.0001

Power Tables

Approximate Power for two-sample t-test, one-tailed (directional hypothesis $N_1 + N_2 > 100$.

Table entries are standardized effect sizes:

$$z_{\text{diff}} = \frac{\text{difference in means}}{\text{pooled standard error}} = \frac{X_1 - X_2}{\dfrac{\text{pooled sd}}{\sqrt{N_{\text{tot}}}}}$$

$$= \frac{X_1 - X_2}{\sqrt{\dfrac{\displaystyle\sum_{i=1}^{N}(X_{li} - \overline{X}_1)^2 + \sum_{i=1}^{N}(X_{2i} - \overline{X}_2)^2}{N_1 + N_2 - 2}\left(\dfrac{1}{N_1} + \dfrac{1}{N_2}\right)}}$$

Where $\overline{X}^1$ is the mean of the first group.

$\overline{X}_2$ is the mean of the second group

$\displaystyle\sum_{i=1}^{N}(X_{1i} - \overline{X}_1)^2$ is the sum of the squared deviations of group 1

$\displaystyle\sum_{i=1}^{N}(X_{2i} - \overline{X}_2)^2$ is the sum of the squared deviations of group 2

N_1 and N_2 are the number of units in the first and the second group, respectively;

To solve for N:

1. Set α and β error levels. Power = 1 - β.
2. Get standardized difference (z_{diff}) from table below.

3. Estimate pooled sd of data distributions from prior research, pilot study, or assumption.
4. Set meaningful difference between means in raw measurement units.
5. Solving above equation,

$$N = \left(\frac{z_{diff} \cdot sd}{\overline{\overline{X}}_1 - \overline{\overline{X}}_2} \right)^2$$

Table entries are z_{diff}. For two-tailed (nondirectional hypothesis), double the α level.

			α		
Power	*.10*	*.05*	*.02*	*.01*	*.001*
.10	0.000	0.363	0.772	1.045	1.806
.15	0.245	0.608	1.017	1.290	2.051
.20	0.440	0.803	1.212	1.485	2.246
.25	0.607	0.970	1.379	1.652	2.413
.30	0.757	1.120	1.529	1.802	2.563
.35	0.896	1.260	1.668	1.941	2.702
.40	1.028	1.392	1.800	2.073	2.834
.45	1.156	1.519	1.928	2.201	2.962
.50	1.282	1.645	2.054	2.326	3.088
.55	1.407	1.771	2.179	2.452	3.213
.60	1.535	1.898	2.307	2.580	3.341
.65	1.667	2.030	2.439	2.712	3.473
.70	1.806	2.169	2.578	2.851	3.612
.75	1.956	2.319	2.728	3.001	3.762
.80	2.123	2.486	2.895	3.168	3.929
.81	2.159	2.523	2.932	3.204	3.965
.82	2.197	2.560	2.969	3.242	4.003
.83	2.236	2.599	3.008	3.280	4.042
.84	2.276	2.639	3.048	3.321	4.082
.85	2.318	2.681	3.090	3.363	4.124
.86	2.362	2.725	3.134	3.407	4.168
.87	2.408	2.771	3.180	3.453	4.214
.88	2.457	2.820	3.229	3.501	4.263
.89	2.508	2.871	3.280	3.553	4.314
.90	2.563	2.926	3.335	3.608	4.369
.91	2.622	2.986	3.394	3.667	4.428
.92	2.687	3.050	3.459	3.731	4.493
.93	2.757	3.121	3.529	3.802	4.563
.94	2.836	3.200	3.608	3.881	4.642
.95	2.926	3.290	3.699	3.971	4.732
.96	3.032	3.396	3.804	4.077	4.838
.97	3.162	3.526	3.934	4.207	4.968
.98	3.335	3.699	4.107	4.380	5.141
.99	3.608	3.971	4.380	4.653	5.414

Power of Correlation Coefficient

$\alpha = .10$ *(two-tailed) / .05 (one-tailed)*
Population Correlation (r)

N	.10	.20	.30	.40	.50	.60	.70	.80	.90
4	.061	.075	.091	.111	.137	.171	.218	.292	.431
5	.066	.087	.114	.148	.193	.253	.338	.464	.669
6	.071	.098	.134	.181	.244	.328	.443	.602	.817
7	.074	.108	.152	.213	.292	.398	.536	.710	.903
8	.078	.117	.170	.243	.338	.462	.616	.792	.950
9	.081	.125	.188	.272	.382	.521	.684	.852	.975
10	.084	.134	.204	.300	.424	.575	.742	.896	.988
11	.087	.142	.221	.328	.464	.624	.791	.928	.994
12	.090	.150	.237	.354	.501	.668	.831	.951	.997
13	.092	.158	.253	.380	.537	.708	.864	.966	.999
14	.095	.165	.268	.405	.570	.743	.891	.977	.999
15	.097	.173	.283	.430	.602	.775	.913	.985	>.999
16	.100	.180	.298	.453	.631	.804	.931	.990	>.999
17	.102	.188	.313	.476	.659	.829	.945	.993	>.999
18	.105	.195	.328	.498	.685	.851	.957	.995	>.999
19	.107	.202	.342	.520	.710	.870	.966	.997	>.999
20	.109	.209	.356	.541	.732	.887	.973	.998	>.999
21	.111	.216	.370	.561	.754	.902	.979	.999	>.999
22	.114	.223	.384	.580	.773	.916	.984	.999	>.999
23	.11	.230	.397	.599	.792	.927	.987	.999	>.999
24	.118	.237	.410	.617	.809	.937	.990	>.999	>.999
25	.120	.244	.423	.634	.824	.946	.992	>.999	>.999
26	.122	.251	.436	.651	.839	.953	.994	>.999	>.999
27	.124	.257	.449	.667	.852	.960	.995	>.999	>.999
28	.126	.264	.461	.682	.865	.966	.996	>.999	>.999
29	.129	.271	.473	.697	.876	.971	.997	>.999	>.999
30	.131	.277	.485	.711	.887	.975	.998	>.999	>.999
31	.133	.284	.497	.725	.896	.978	.998	>.999	>.999
32	.135	.290	.509	.738	.905	.982	.999	>.999	>.999
33	.137	.297	.520	.750	.914	.984	.999	>.999	>.999
34	.139	.303	.531	.762	.921	.987	.999	>.999	>.999
35	.141	.309	.542	.774	.928	.989	.999	>.999	>.999
36	.143	.316	.553	.785	.935	.990	>.999	>.999	>.999
37	.145	.322	.564	.795	.940	.992	>.999	>.999	>.999
38	.147	.328	.574	.806	.946	.993	>.999	>.999	>.999
39	.149	.334	.584	.815	.951	.994	>.999	>.999	>.999
40	.150	.340	.594	.824	.955	.995	>.999	>.999	>.999
41	.152	.346	.604	.833	.959	.996	>.999	>.999	>.999
42	.154	.352	.613	.842	.963	.996	>.999	>.999	>.999
43	.156	.358	.623	.850	.966	.997	>.999	>.999	>.999
44	.158	.364	.632	.857	.969	.997	>.999	>.999	>.999
45	.160	.370	.641	.864	.972	.998	>.999	>.999	>.999
46	.162	.376	.650	.871	.975	.998	>.999	>.999	>.999
47	.164	.382	.658	.878	.977	.998	>.999	>.999	>.999
48	.166	.388	.667	.884	.979	.999	>.999	>.999	>.999
49	.167	.394	.675	.890	.981	.999	>.999	>.999	>.999
50	.169	.399	.683	.896	.983	.999	>.999	>.999	>.999

(Continued)

$\alpha = .10$ *(two-tailed) / .05 (one-tailed)*
Population Correlation (r)

N	.10	.20	.30	.40	.50	.60	.70	.80	.90
55	.178	.427	.721	.920	.990	>.999	>.999	>.999	>.999
60	.187	.455	.756	.940	.994	>.999	>.999	>.999	>.999
65	.196	.481	.786	.955	.996	>.999	>.999	>.999	>.999
70	.205	.506	.813	.966	.998	>.999	>.999	>.999	>.999
75	.214	.530	.837	.974	.999	>.999	>.999	>.999	>.999
80	.222	.553	.858	.981	.999	>.999	>.999	>.999	>.999
85	.231	.576	.877	.986	>.999	>.999	>.999	>.999	>.999
90	.239	.597	.893	.989	>.999	>.999	>.999	>.999	>.999
95	.247	.618	.907	.992	>.999	>.999	>.999	>.999	>.999
100	.256	.638	.920	.994	>.999	>.999	>.999	>.999	>.999
110	.272	.674	.940	.997	>.999	>.999	>.999	>.999	>.999
120	.288	.708	.956	.998	>.999	>.999	>.999	>.999	>.999
130	.304	.739	.967	.999	>.999	>.999	>.999	>.999	>.999
140	.319	.767	.976	>.999	>.999	>.999	>.999	>.999	>.999
150	.334	.792	.982	>.999	>.999	>.999	>.999	>.999	>.999
160	.349	.815	.987	>.999	>.999	>.999	>.999	>.999	>.999
170	.364	.835	.991	>.999	>.999	>.999	>.999	>.999	>.999
180	.378	.854	.993	>.999	>.999	>.999	>.999	>.999	>.999
190	.393	.870	.995	>.999	>.999	>.999	>.999	>.999	>.999
200	.406	.885	.997	>.999	>.999	>.999	>.999	>.999	>.999
300	.534	.968	>.999	>.999	>.999	>.999	>.999	>.999	>.999
400	.638	.992	>.999	>.999	>.999	>.999	>.999	>.999	>.999
500	.723	.998	>.999	>.999	>.999	>.999	>.999	>.999	>.999
600	.790	>.999	>.999	>.999	>.999	>.999	>.999	>.999	>.999
700	.842	>.999	>.999	>.999	>.999	>.999	>.999	>.999	>.999
800	.883	>.999	>.999	>.999	>.999	>.999	>.999	>.999	>.999
900	.913	>.999	>.999	>.999	>.999	>.999	>.999	>.999	>.999
1000	.936	>.999	>.999	>.999	>.999	>.999	>.999	>.999	>.999

α = .05 *(two-tailed)* / .025 *(one-tailed)*
Population Correlation (r)

N	.10	.20	.30	.40	.50	.60	.70	.80	.90
4	.032	.039	.049	.062	.079	.103	.137	.195	.313
5	.035	.047	.064	.087	.118	.164	.232	.342	.549
6	.037	.054	.077	.110	.157	.224	.324	.477	.722
7	.039	.060	.090	.133	.195	.283	.411	.594	.838
8	.041	.066	.102	.156	.232	.341	.492	.690	.909
9	.043	.072	.115	.178	.269	.397	.565	.768	.950
10	.045	.077	.127	.201	.306	.450	.631	.828	.974
11	.047	.083	.139	.223	.342	.500	.689	.874	.986
12	.049	.088	.151	.245	.378	.548	.740	.909	.993
13	.050	.094	.163	.268	.412	.592	.783	.935	.996
14	.052	.099	.175	.289	.445	.633	.820	.954	.998
15	.053	.104	.187	.311	.477	.670	.852	.968	.999
16	.055	.110	.199	.333	.508	.705	.878	.977	>.999
17	.057	.115	.211	.354	.538	.737	.901	.984	>.999
18	.058	.120	.223	.375	.567	.766	.919	.989	>.999
19	.060	.125	.235	.395	.594	.792	.934	.993	>.999
20	.061	.130	.247	.416	.620	.815	.947	.995	>.999
21	.063	.136	.259	.435	.645	.837	.957	.997	>.999
22	.064	.141	.271	.455	.668	.856	.966	.998	>.999
23	.065	.146	.282	.474	.690	.873	.972	.998	>.999
24	.067	.151	.294	.493	.711	.888	.978	.999	>.999
25	.068	.156	.306	.511	.731	.902	.982	.999	>.999
26	.070	.162	.317	.529	.750	.914	.986	>.999	>.999
27	.071	.167	.329	.546	.768	.924	.989	>.999	>.999
28	.072	.172	.340	.563	.784	.934	.991	>.999	>.999
29	.074	.177	.351	.579	.800	.942	.993	>.999	>.999
30	.075	.182	.363	.595	.814	.950	.995	>.999	>.999
31	.077	.187	.374	.611	.828	.956	.996	>.999	>.999
32	.078	.193	.385	.626	.841	.962	.997	>.999	>.999
33	.079	.198	.396	.641	.853	.967	.997	>.999	>.999
34	.081	.203	.406	.655	.864	.971	.998	>.999	>.999
35	.082	.208	.417	.669	.874	.975	.998	>.999	>.999
36	.083	.213	.428	.682	.884	.978	.999	>.999	>.999
37	.085	.218	.438	.695	.893	.981	.999	>.999	>.999
38	.086	.223	.449	.708	.901	.984	.999	>.999	>.999
39	.087	.229	.459	.720	.909	.986	.999	>.999	>.999
40	.089	.234	.469	.731	.916	.988	>.999	>.999	>.999
41	.090	.239	.479	.743	.923	.990	>.999	>.999	>.999
42	.091	.244	.489	.754	.929	.991	>.999	>.999	>.999
43	.093	.249	.499	.764	.935	.992	>.999	>.999	>.999
44	.094	.254	.509	.774	.940	.993	>.999	>.999	>.999
45	.095	.259	.518	.784	.945	.994	>.999	>.999	>.999
46	.097	.264	.528	.793	.950	.995	>.999	>.999	>.999
47	.098	.269	.537	.802	.954	.996	>.999	>.999	>.999
48	.099	.274	.546	.811	.958	.996	>.999	>.999	>.999
49	.100	.279	.555	.819	.961	.997	>.999	>.999	>.999
50	.102	.284	.564	.828	.965	.997	>.999	>.999	>.999

(Continued)

$\alpha = .05$ *(two-tailed)* / *.025 (one-tailed)*
Population Correlation (r)

N	.10	.20	.30	.40	.50	.60	.70	.80	.90
55	.108	.309	.607	.863	.977	.999	>.999	>.999	>.999
60	.115	.334	.647	.892	.986	.999	>.999	>.999	>.999
65	.121	.358	.683	.916	.991	>.999	>.999	>.999	>.999
70	.127	.382	.717	.934	.994	>.999	>.999	>.999	>.999
75	.134	.405	.747	.949	.997	>.999	>.999	>.999	>.999
80	.140	.428	.775	.961	.998	>.999	>.999	>.999	>.999
85	.147	.451	.800	.970	.999	>.999	>.999	>.999	>.999
90	.153	.472	.823	.977	.999	>.999	>.999	>.999	>.999
95	.159	.494	.843	.982	>.999	>.999	>.999	>.999	>.999
100	.166	.515	.862	.987	>.999	>.999	>.999	>.999	>.999
110	.178	.555	.893	.992	>.999	>.999	>.999	>.999	>.999
120	.191	.592	.917	.996	>.999	>.999	>.999	>.999	>.999
130	.203	.627	.937	.998	>.999	>.999	>.999	>.999	>.999
140	.216	.660	.952	.999	>.999	>.999	>.999	>.999	>.999
150	.229	.691	.963	.999	>.999	>.999	>.999	>.999	>.999
160	.241	.719	.972	>.999	>.999	>.999	>.999	>.999	>.999
170	.254	.745	.979	>.999	>.999	>.999	>.999	>.999	>.999
180	.266	.770	.985	>.999	>.999	>.999	>.999	>.999	>.999
190	.278	.792	.988	>.999	>.999	>.999	>.999	>.999	>.999
200	.291	.812	.991	>.999	>.999	>.999	>.999	>.999	>.999
300	.409	.937	>.999	>.999	>.999	>.999	>.999	>.999	>.999
400	.516	.981	>.999	>.999	>.999	>.999	>.999	>.999	>.999
500	.609	.995	>.999	>.999	>.999	>.999	>.999	>.999	>.999
600	.688	.999	>.999	>.999	>.999	>.999	>.999	>.999	>.999
700	.755	>.999	>.999	>.999	>.999	>.999	>.999	>.999	>.999
800	.809	>.999	>.999	>.999	>.999	>.999	>.999	>.999	>.999
900	.852	>.999	>.999	>.999	>.999	>.999	>.999	>.999	>.999
1000	.887	>.999	>.999	>.999	>.999	>.999	>.999	>.999	>.999

α = .02 (two-tailed) / .01 (one-tailed)
Population Correlation (r)

N	.10	.20	.30	.40	.50	.60	.70	.80	.90
4	.013	.017	.022	.029	.038	.051	.072	.110	.197
5	.015	.021	.030	.042	.061	.089	.136	.220	.403
6	.016	.024	.037	.056	.085	.130	.205	.336	.588
7	.017	.027	.044	.070	.110	.174	.277	.449	.732
8	.018	.031	.051	.084	.136	.219	.349	.552	.833
9	.019	.034	.058	.099	.163	.265	.420	.642	.900
10	.020	.037	.066	.114	.191	.311	.487	.719	.942
11	.021	.040	.073	.130	.220	.357	.550	.783	.967
12	.021	.043	.081	.146	.249	.402	.609	.834	.982
13	.022	.046	.089	.162	.278	.447	.661	.874	.990
14	.023	.049	.097	.178	.307	.489	.709	.906	.995
15	.024	.052	.105	.195	.336	.530	.751	.930	.997
16	.025	.055	.113	.212	.365	.569	.788	.949	.999
17	.026	.059	.121	.229	.393	.605	.821	.963	.999
18	.026	.062	.130	.246	.421	.640	.849	.973	>.999
19	.027	.065	.138	.264	.449	.672	.873	.981	>.999
20	.028	.068	.147	.281	.475	.702	.894	.986	>.999
21	.029	.071	.155	.298	.502	.731	.912	.990	>.999
22	.029	.075	.164	.316	.527	.756	.927	.993	>.999
23	.030	.078	.173	.333	.552	.780	.940	.995	>.999
24	.031	.081	.182	.350	.576	.802	.950	.997	>.999
25	.032	.085	.191	.367	.599	.822	.959	.998	>.999
26	.033	.088	.200	.384	.621	.841	.967	.998	>.999
27	.033	.091	.209	.401	.642	.858	.973	.999	>.999
28	.034	.095	.218	.418	.663	.873	.978	.999	>.999
29	.035	.098	.227	.434	.682	.886	.982	.999	>.999
30	.036	.102	.236	.450	.701	.899	.985	>.999	>.999
31	.036	.105	.246	.466	.719	.910	.988	>.999	>.999
32	.037	.108	.255	.482	.736	.920	.990	>.999	>.999
33	.038	.112	.264	.498	.752	.929	.992	>.999	>.999
34	.039	.116	.273	.513	.768	.937	.994	>.999	>.999
35	.039	.119	.282	.528	.783	.945	.995	>.999	>.999
36	.040	.123	.292	.543	.796	.951	.996	>.999	>.999
37	.041	.126	.301	.557	.810	.957	.997	>.999	>.999
38	.042	.130	.310	.571	.822	.962	.997	>.999	>.999
39	.043	.134	.319	.585	.834	.967	.998	>.999	>.999
40	.043	.137	.329	.599	.845	.971	.998	>.999	>.999
41	.044	.141	.338	.612	.855	.974	.999	>.999	>.999
42	.045	.145	.347	.625	.865	.977	.999	>.999	>.999
43	.045	.148	.356	.638	.874	.980	.999	>.999	>.999
44	.046	.152	.365	.650	.883	.983	.999	>.999	>.999
45	.047	.156	.374	.662	.891	.985	>.999	>.999	>.999
46	.048	.159	.383	.674	.899	.987	>.999	>.999	>.999
47	.048	.163	.392	.686	.906	.988	>.999	>.999	>.999
48	.049	.167	.401	.697	.913	.990	>.999	>.999	>.999
49	.050	.171	.410	.708	.919	.991	>.999	>.999	>.999
50	.051	.175	.419	.718	.925	.992	>.999	>.999	>.999

(Continued)

$\alpha = .02$ *(two-tailed) / .01 (one-tailed)*
Population Correlation (r)

N	.10	.20	.30	.40	.50	.60	.70	.80	.90
55	.055	.194	.462	.767	.949	.996	>.999	>.999	>.999
60	.058	.213	.504	.808	.966	.998	>.999	>.999	>.999
65	.062	.233	.544	.844	.977	.999	>.999	>.999	>.999
70	.066	.252	.582	.873	.985	>.999	>.999	>.999	>.999
75	.070	.272	.618	.898	.990	>.999	>.999	>.999	>.999
80	.074	.292	.652	.918	.994	>.999	>.999	>.999	>.999
85	.078	.312	.683	.934	.996	>.999	>.999	>.999	>.999
90	.082	.332	.712	.948	.997	>.999	>.999	>.999	>.999
95	.086	.351	.740	.959	.998	>.999	>.999	>.999	>.999
100	.090	.371	.765	.968	.999	>.999	>.999	>.999	>.999
110	.099	.409	.809	.980	>.999	>.999	>.999	>.999	>.999
120	.107	.447	.847	.988	>.999	>.999	>.999	>.999	>.999
130	.116	.483	.877	.993	>.999	>.999	>.999	>.999	>.999
140	.125	.519	.903	.996	>.999	>.999	>.999	>.999	>.999
150	.134	.552	.923	.998	>.999	>.999	>.999	>.999	>.999
160	.143	.585	.940	.999	>.999	>.999	>.999	>.999	>.999
170	.152	.615	.953	.999	>.999	>.999	>.999	>.999	>.999
180	.161	.645	.963	>.999	>.999	>.999	>.999	>.999	>.999
190	.170	.672	.972	>.999	>.999	>.999	>.999	>.999	>.999
200	.179	.698	.978	>.999	>.999	>.999	>.999	>.999	>.999
300	.275	.878	.999	>.999	>.999	>.999	>.999	>.999	>.999
400	.372	.957	>.999	>.999	>.999	>.999	>.999	>.999	>.999
500	.464	.986	>.999	>.999	>.999	>.999	>.999	>.999	>.999
600	.550	.996	>.999	>.999	>.999	>.999	>.999	>.999	>.999
700	.626	.999	>.999	>.999	>.999	>.999	>.999	>.999	>.999
800	.694	>.999	>.999	>.999	>.999	>.999	>.999	>.999	>.999
900	.751	>.999	>.999	>.999	>.999	>.999	>.999	>.999	>.999
1000	.800	>.999	>.999	>.999	>.999	>.999	>.999	>.999	>.999

Appendix *C*

Table of Chi Square

			α		
d.f.	*.10*	*.05*	*.02*	*.01*	*.005*
1	2.71	3.84	5.41	6.64	7.88
2	4.61	5.99	7.82	9.21	10.59
3	6.25	7.82	9.84	11.34	12.84
4	7.78	9.49	11.67	13.28	14.86
5	9.24	11.07	13.39	15.08	16.75
6	10.64	12.59	15.03	16.81	18.55
7	12.02	14.07	16.62	18.48	20.27
8	13.36	15.51	18.17	20.09	21.95
9	14.68	16.92	19.68	21.66	23.59
10	15.99	18.31	21.16	23.21	25.19
11	17.28	19.68	22.62	24.72	26.75
12	18.55	21.03	24.05	26.22	28.29
13	19.81	22.36	25.47	27.69	29.81
14	21.06	23.68	26.87	29.14	31.32
15	22.31	25.00	28.26	30.58	32.80
16	23.54	26.30	29.63	32.00	34.27
17	24.77	27.59	30.99	33.41	35.72
18	25.99	28.87	32.35	34.81	37.16
19	27.20	30.14	33.69	36.19	38.58
20	28.41	31.41	35.02	37.57	40.00
21	29.62	32.67	36.34	38.93	41.40
22	30.81	33.92	37.66	40.29	42.80
23	32.01	35.17	38.97	41.64	44.18
24	33.20	36.41	40.27	42.98	45.56
25	34.38	37.65	41.57	44.31	46.92
26	35.56	38.89	42.86	45.64	48.29
27	36.74	40.11	44.14	46.96	49.64
28	37.92	41.34	45.42	48.28	50.99
29	39.09	42.56	46.69	49.59	52.33
30	40.26	43.77	47.96	50.89	53.67
31	41.42	44.98	49.23	52.19	55.00
32	42.58	46.19	50.49	53.48	56.33
33	43.75	47.40	51.74	54.77	57.65
34	44.90	48.60	53.00	56.06	58.96
35	46.06	49.80	54.24	57.34	60.27
36	47.21	51.00	55.49	58.62	61.58
37	48.36	52.19	56.73	59.89	62.88
38	49.51	53.38	57.97	61.16	64.18
39	50.66	54.57	59.20	62.43	65.48
40	51.81	55.76	60.44	63.69	66.77

Appendix D

Table of t-values

d.f.	$\alpha = $ 2-tail / 1-tail				
(N − 1)	.20/.10	.10/.05	.05/.025	.02/.01	.01/.005
1	3.078	6.314	12.706	31.821	63.657
2	1.886	2.920	4.303	6.965	9.925
3	1.638	2.353	3.182	4.541	5.841
4	1.533	2.132	2.776	3.747	4.604
5	1.476	2.015	2.571	3.365	4.032
6	1.440	1.943	2.447	3.143	3.707
7	1.415	1.895	2.365	2.998	3.499
8	1.397	1.859	2.306	2.896	3.355
9	1.383	1.833	2.262	2.821	3.250
10	1.372	1.812	2.228	2.764	3.169
11	1.363	1.796	2.201	2.718	3.105
12	1.356	1.782	2.179	2.681	3.054
13	1.350	1.771	2.160	2.650	3.012
14	1.345	1.761	2.145	2.624	2.977
15	1.341	1.753	2.131	2.602	2.946
16	1.337	1.746	2.120	2.583	2.921
17	1.333	1.740	2.110	2.567	2.898
18	1.330	1.734	2.101	2.552	2.878
19	1.328	1.729	2.093	2.539	2.861
20	1.325	1.725	2.086	2.528	2.845
21	1.323	1.721	2.080	2.518	2.831
22	1.321	1.717	2.074	2.508	2.819
23	1.319	1.714	2.069	2.500	2.807
24	1.318	1.711	2.064	2.492	2.797
25	1.316	1.708	2.060	2.485	2.787
26	1.315	1.706	2.056	2.479	2.779
27	1.314	1.703	2.052	2.473	2.771
28	1.313	1.701	2.048	2.467	2.763
29	1.311	1.699	2.045	2.462	2.756
30	1.310	1.697	2.042	2.457	2.750
31	1.309	1.696	2.039	2.453	2.744
32	1.309	1.694	2.037	2.449	2.738
33	1.308	1.692	2.035	2.445	2.733
34	1.307	1.691	2.032	2.441	2.728
35	1.306	1.690	2.030	2.438	2.724
36	1.306	1.688	2.028	2.434	2.719
37	1.305	1.687	2.026	2.431	2.715
38	1.304	1.686	2.024	2.428	2.711
39	1.304	1.685	2.023	2.426	2.708
40	1.303	1.684	2.021	2.423	2.704

(Continued)

d.f. (N − 1)	.20/.10	.10/.05	.05/.025	.02/.01	.01/.005
			α = 2-tail / 1-tail		
41	1.303	1.683	2.020	2.421	2.701
42	1.302	1.682	2.018	2.418	2.698
43	1.302	1.681	2.017	2.416	2.695
44	1.301	1.680	2.015	2.414	2.692
45	1.301	1.679	2.014	2.412	2.690
46	1.300	1.679	2.013	2.410	2.687
47	1.300	1.678	2.012	2.408	2.684
48	1.299	1.677	2.011	2.407	2.682
49	1.299	1.677	2.010	2.405	2.680
50	1.299	1.676	2.009	2.403	2.678
51	1.298	1.675	2.008	2.402	2.676
52	1.298	1.675	2.007	2.400	2.674
53	1.298	1.674	2.006	2.399	2.672
54	1.297	1.674	2.005	2.397	2.670
55	1.297	1.673	2.004	2.396	2.668
56	1.297	1.673	2.003	2.395	2.666
57	1.297	1.672	2.002	2.394	2.665
58	1.296	1.672	2.002	2.392	2.663
59	1.296	1.671	2.001	2.391	2.662
60	1.296	1.671	2.000	2.390	2.660
61	1.296	1.670	2.000	2.389	2.659
62	1.295	1.670	1.999	2.388	2.657
63	1.295	1.669	1.998	2.387	2.656
64	1.295	1.669	1.998	2.386	2.655
65	1.295	1.669	1.997	2.385	2.654
66	1.295	1.668	1.997	2.384	2.652
67	1.294	1.668	1.996	2.383	2.651
68	1.294	1.668	1.995	2.382	2.650
69	1.294	1.667	1.995	2.382	2.649
70	1.294	1.667	1.994	2.381	2.648
71	1.294	1.667	1.994	2.380	2.647
72	1.293	1.666	1.993	2.379	2.646
73	1.293	1.666	1.993	2.378	2.645
74	1.293	1.666	1.993	2.378	2.644
75	1.293	1.665	1.992	2.377	2.643
76	1.293	1.665	1.992	2.376	2.642
77	1.293	1.665	1.991	2.376	2.641
78	1.292	1.665	1.991	2.375	2.640
79	1.292	1.664	1.990	2.374	2.639
80	1.292	1.664	1.990	2.374	2.639

(Continued)

d.f. (N − 1)	α = 2-tail / 1-tail				
	.20/.10	.10/.05	.05/.025	.02/.01	.01/.005
81	1.292	1.664	1.990	2.373	2.638
82	1.292	1.664	1.989	2.373	2.637
83	1.292	1.663	1.989	2.372	2.636
84	1.292	1.663	1.989	2.372	2.636
85	1.292	1.663	1.988	2.371	2.635
86	1.291	1.663	1.988	2.370	2.634
87	1.291	1.663	1.988	2.370	2.633
88	1.291	1.662	1.987	2.369	2.633
89	1.291	1.662	1.987	2.369	2.632
90	1.291	1.662	1.987	2.368	2.632
91	1.291	1.662	1.986	2.368	2.631
92	1.291	1.662	1.986	2.368	2.630
93	1.291	1.661	1.986	2.367	2.630
94	1.291	1.661	1.986	2.367	2.629
95	1.291	1.661	1.985	2.366	2.629
96	1.290	1.661	1.985	2.366	2.628
97	1.290	1.661	1.985	2.365	2.627
98	1.290	1.661	1.984	2.365	2.627
99	1.290	1.660	1.984	2.365	2.626
100	1.290	1.660	1.984	2.364	2.626
101	1.290	1.660	1.984	2.364	2.625
102	1.290	1.660	1.983	2.363	2.625
103	1.290	1.660	1.983	2.363	2.624
104	1.290	1.660	1.983	2.363	2.624
105	1.290	1.659	1.983	2.362	2.623
106	1.290	1.659	1.983	2.362	2.623
107	1.290	1.659	1.982	2.362	2.623
108	1.289	1.659	1.982	2.361	2.622
109	1.289	1.659	1.982	2.361	2.622
110	1.289	1.659	1.982	2.361	2.621
111	1.289	1.659	1.982	2.360	2.621
112	1.289	1.659	1.981	2.360	2.620
113	1.289	1.658	1.981	2.360	2.620
114	1.289	1.658	1.981	2.359	2.620
115	1.289	1.658	1.981	2.359	2.619
116	1.289	1.658	1.981	2.359	2.619
117	1.289	1.658	1.980	2.359	2.618
118	1.289	1.658	1.980	2.358	2.618
119	1.289	1.658	1.980	2.358	2.618
120	1.289	1.658	1.980	2.358	2.617
>120 (normal distribution)	1.282	1.645	1.960	2.326	2.576

Table of F-values

Numerator degrees of freedom (d.f.)

Denom d.f.	1	2	3	4	5	6	7	8
1	161.400							
2	18.510	19.000						
3	10.130	9.552	9.277					
4	7.709	6.944	6.592	6.388				
5	6.608	5.786	5.407	5.189	5.046			
6	5.987	5.143	4.757	4.532	4.386	4.282		
7	5.591	4.737	4.347	4.120	3.971	3.865	3.786	
8	5.317	4.459	4.066	3.837	3.687	3.580	3.500	3.438
9	5.117	4.256	3.863	3.633	3.481	3.374	3.292	3.229
10	4.964	4.103	3.708	3.478	3.326	3.217	3.135	3.071
11	4.844	3.982	3.588	3.357	3.204	3.095	3.012	2.948
12	4.747	3.885	3.490	3.259	3.106	2.996	2.913	2.848
13	4.667	3.805	3.411	3.179	3.025	2.915	2.832	2.767
14	4.600	3.739	3.344	3.112	2.958	2.848	2.764	2.699
15	4.543	3.682	3.288	3.056	2.901	2.790	2.707	2.641
16	4.494	3.634	3.239	3.007	2.852	2.741	2.657	2.591
17	4.451	3.591	3.195	2.965	2.810	2.699	2.614	2.548
18	4.414	3.555	3.158	2.926	2.771	2.660	2.575	2.509
19	4.381	3.522	3.126	2.893	2.739	2.627	2.542	2.476
20	4.351	3.493	3.097	2.865	2.710	2.598	2.513	2.446
21	4.325	3.467	3.071	2.839	2.684	2.572	2.487	2.419
22	4.301	3.443	3.048	2.815	2.660	2.548	2.463	2.396
23	4.279	3.422	3.027	2.794	2.639	2.527	2.441	2.374
24	4.260	3.403	3.008	2.775	2.620	2.507	2.422	2.354
25	4.242	3.385	2.990	2.758	2.602	2.490	2.404	2.336
26	4.225	3.369	2.974	2.742	2.586	2.473	2.388	2.320
27	4.210	3.354	2.959	2.727	2.571	2.458	2.372	2.305
28	4.196	3.340	2.946	2.713	2.557	2.445	2.359	2.291
29	4.183	3.328	2.933	2.700	2.545	2.432	2.346	2.278
30	4.171	3.316	2.921	2.689	2.533	2.420	2.334	2.266
31	4.160	3.305	2.910	2.678	2.522	2.409	2.323	2.254
32	4.149	3.295	2.900	2.668	2.512	2.398	2.312	2.244
33	4.139	3.285	2.891	2.658	2.502	2.389	2.302	2.234
34	4.130	3.276	2.882	2.649	2.493	2.380	2.293	2.225
35	4.121	3.267	2.873	2.641	2.484	2.371	2.285	2.216
36	4.113	3.259	2.865	2.633	2.477	2.363	2.277	2.208
37	4.105	3.252	2.858	2.625	2.469	2.356	2.269	2.200
38	4.098	3.245	2.851	2.618	2.462	2.349	2.262	2.193
39	4.091	3.238	2.844	2.612	2.455	2.342	2.255	2.186
40	4.085	3.232	2.838	2.605	2.449	2.335	2.249	2.180
45	4.055	3.203	2.811	2.578	2.422	2.308	2.221	2.152
50	4.033	3.182	2.789	2.557	2.400	2.286	2.199	2.130
55	4.015	3.164	2.772	2.539	2.382	2.268	2.181	2.112
60	4.000	3.150	2.758	2.525	2.368	2.254	2.166	2.097
65	3.987	3.137	2.745	2.513	2.356	2.241	2.154	2.084
70	3.976	3.127	2.735	2.502	2.345	2.231	2.143	2.073
80	3.959	3.110	2.718	2.485	2.328	2.214	2.126	2.056
90	3.946	3.097	2.705	2.473	2.315	2.201	2.113	2.043
100	3.935	3.087	2.695	2.462	2.305	2.190	2.102	2.032
110	3.926	3.078	2.687	2.454	2.297	2.182	2.094	2.023
120	3.919	3.071	2.680	2.447	2.290	2.175	2.087	2.016
300 or more	3.872	3.025	2.635	2.401	2.244	2.129	2.040	1.969

(Continued)

$$\alpha = .05$$
Numerator degrees of freedom (d.f.)

Denom d.f.	9	10	11	12	13	14	15	16
9	3.179							
10	3.020	2.978						
11	2.896	2.854	2.818					
12	2.796	2.753	2.717	2.687				
13	2.714	2.671	2.635	2.604	2.577			
14	2.646	2.602	2.565	2.534	2.507	2.484		
15	2.588	2.544	2.507	2.475	2.448	2.424	2.403	
16	2.538	2.493	2.456	2.425	2.397	2.373	2.352	2.333
17	2.494	2.450	2.413	2.381	2.353	2.329	2.308	2.289
18	2.455	2.410	2.374	2.342	2.314	2.290	2.269	2.250
19	2.422	2.377	2.339	2.307	2.279	2.255	2.233	2.214
20	2.392	2.347	2.309	2.277	2.249	2.224	2.202	2.183
21	2.365	2.320	2.282	2.249	2.221	2.197	2.175	2.155
22	2.341	2.296	2.258	2.225	2.197	2.172	2.150	2.131
23	2.319	2.274	2.236	2.203	2.174	2.150	2.128	2.108
24	2.299	2.254	2.216	2.183	2.154	2.129	2.107	2.087
25	2.281	2.236	2.197	2.164	2.136	2.111	2.088	2.069
26	2.265	2.219	2.180	2.147	2.119	2.093	2.071	2.051
27	2.250	2.204	2.165	2.132	2.103	2.078	2.055	2.035
28	2.235	2.189	2.151	2.117	2.088	2.063	2.041	2.021
29	2.222	2.176	2.137	2.104	2.075	2.050	2.027	2.007
30	2.210	2.164	2.125	2.092	2.063	2.037	2.014	1.994
31	2.199	2.153	2.114	2.080	2.051	2.025	2.003	1.982
32	2.188	2.142	2.103	2.069	2.040	2.014	1.992	1.971
33	2.178	2.132	2.093	2.059	2.030	2.004	1.981	1.961
34	2.169	2.123	2.083	2.050	2.020	1.995	1.972	1.951
35	2.160	2.114	2.075	2.041	2.011	1.985	1.963	1.942
36	2.152	2.106	2.066	2.032	2.003	1.977	1.954	1.933
37	2.144	2.098	2.058	2.024	1.995	1.969	1.946	1.925
38	2.137	2.090	2.051	2.017	1.987	1.961	1.938	1.918
39	2.130	2.084	2.044	2.010	1.980	1.954	1.931	1.910
40	2.124	2.077	2.037	2.003	1.973	1.947	1.924	1.903
45	2.095	2.048	2.009	1.974	1.944	1.918	1.895	1.874
50	2.073	2.026	1.986	1.951	1.921	1.895	1.871	1.850
55	2.055	2.008	1.967	1.933	1.902	1.876	1.852	1.831
60	2.040	1.992	1.952	1.917	1.887	1.860	1.836	1.815
65	2.027	1.980	1.939	1.904	1.874	1.847	1.823	1.802
70	2.016	1.969	1.928	1.893	1.863	1.836	1.812	1.790
80	1.999	1.951	1.910	1.875	1.844	1.817	1.793	1.771
90	1.985	1.937	1.897	1.861	1.830	1.803	1.779	1.757
100	1.975	1.927	1.886	1.850	1.819	1.792	1.767	1.746
110	1.966	1.918	1.877	1.841	1.810	1.783	1.758	1.736
120	1.959	1.910	1.869	1.834	1.802	1.775	1.750	1.728
300 or more	1.911	1.862	1.821	1.784	1.753	1.725	1.700	1.677

(Continued)

$\alpha = .05$
Numerator degrees of freedom (d.f.)

Denom d.f.	20	25	30	35	40	50	60	70
20	2.123							
21	2.095							
22	2.070							
23	2.047							
24	2.026							
25	2.007	1.955						
26	1.989	1.937						
27	1.973	1.921						
28	1.958	1.905						
29	1.944	1.891						
30	1.931	1.878	1.841					
31	1.919	1.866	1.828					
32	1.908	1.854	1.816					
33	1.897	1.843	1.805					
34	1.887	1.833	1.795					
35	1.878	1.824	1.785	1.757				
36	1.869	1.815	1.776	1.748				
37	1.861	1.806	1.768	1.739				
38	1.853	1.798	1.759	1.731				
39	1.846	1.790	1.752	1.723				
40	1.839	1.783	1.744	1.715	1.693			
45	1.808	1.752	1.712	1.683	1.660			
50	1.784	1.727	1.687	1.657	1.634	1.599		
55	1.764	1.707	1.666	1.636	1.612	1.577		
60	1.748	1.690	1.649	1.618	1.594	1.559	1.534	
65	1.734	1.676	1.634	1.603	1.579	1.543	1.518	
70	1.722	1.664	1.622	1.591	1.566	1.530	1.505	1.486
80	1.703	1.644	1.602	1.570	1.545	1.508	1.482	1.463
90	1.688	1.629	1.586	1.554	1.528	1.491	1.464	1.445
100	1.676	1.616	1.573	1.541	1.515	1.477	1.450	1.430
110	1.667	1.606	1.563	1.530	1.504	1.466	1.439	1.418
120	1.659	1.598	1.554	1.521	1.495	1.456	1.429	1.408
300 or more	1.606	1.543	1.497	1.462	1.435	1.398	1.368	1.346

Numerator degrees of freedom (d.f.)

Denom d.f.	1	2	3	4	5	6	7	8
1	4052.000							
2	98.500	98.950						
3	34.120	30.810	29.470					
4	21.200	18.000	16.690	15.980				
5	16.260	13.270	12.060	11.390	10.965			
6	13.750	10.920	9.760	9.147	8.745	8.465		
7	12.250	9.546	8.443	7.846	7.460	7.191	6.992	
8	11.260	8.649	7.587	7.006	6.632	6.371	6.177	6.029
9	10.560	8.021	6.990	6.422	6.057	5.802	5.613	5.467
10	10.040	7.559	6.552	5.994	5.636	5.386	5.200	5.057
11	9.646	7.204	6.216	5.668	5.316	5.069	4.886	4.744
12	9.330	6.925	5.953	5.411	5.063	4.819	4.638	4.498
13	9.074	6.700	5.740	5.204	4.861	4.619	4.440	4.301
14	8.862	6.514	5.564	5.035	4.694	4.455	4.277	4.139
15	8.683	6.358	5.417	4.893	4.555	4.318	4.141	4.004
16	8.531	6.226	5.280	4.772	4.437	4.201	4.026	3.889
17	8.400	6.111	5.175	4.669	4.336	4.101	3.926	3.791
18	8.285	6.012	5.083	4.579	4.248	4.014	3.840	3.705
19	8.185	5.925	5.002	4.500	4.170	3.938	3.765	3.630
20	8.096	5.849	4.931	4.430	4.102	3.871	3.699	3.564
21	8.017	5.780	4.867	4.369	4.042	3.812	3.639	3.505
22	7.945	5.719	4.810	4.313	3.988	3.758	3.587	3.453
23	7.881	5.663	4.759	4.263	3.939	3.710	3.539	3.406
24	7.823	5.613	4.713	4.218	3.895	3.667	3.496	3.363
25	7.770	5.568	4.670	4.177	3.855	3.627	3.457	3.324
26	7.721	5.526	4.632	4.140	3.818	3.591	3.421	3.288
27	7.677	5.488	4.596	4.105	3.785	3.558	3.388	3.256
28	7.636	5.453	4.564	4.074	3.754	3.527	3.358	3.226
29	7.598	5.420	4.534	4.045	3.725	3.499	3.330	3.198
30	7.562	5.390	4.506	4.018	3.699	3.473	3.304	3.173
31	7.530	5.362	4.480	3.993	3.674	3.449	3.281	3.149
32	7.499	5.336	4.456	3.969	3.652	3.427	3.258	3.127
33	7.471	5.312	4.433	3.948	3.630	3.406	3.238	3.106
34	7.444	5.289	4.412	3.927	3.610	3.386	3.218	3.087
35	7.419	5.268	4.393	3.908	3.592	3.368	3.200	3.069
36	7.396	5.248	4.374	3.890	3.574	3.351	3.183	3.052
37	7.373	5.229	4.357	3.873	3.558	3.334	3.167	3.036
38	7.353	5.211	4.340	3.857	3.542	3.319	3.152	3.021
39	7.333	5.194	4.325	3.842	3.528	3.305	3.137	3.006
40	7.314	5.178	4.310	3.828	3.514	3.291	3.124	2.993
45	7.234	5.110	4.249	3.767	3.454	3.232	3.066	2.935
50	7.170	5.057	4.199	3.719	3.408	3.186	3.020	2.890
55	7.119	5.013	4.159	3.681	3.370	3.149	2.983	2.853
60	7.077	4.977	4.126	3.649	3.339	3.119	2.953	2.823
65	7.041	4.947	4.098	3.622	3.313	3.093	2.928	2.798
70	7.011	4.922	4.074	3.600	3.291	3.071	2.906	2.777
80	6.963	4.881	4.036	3.563	3.255	3.036	2.871	2.742
90	6.925	4.849	4.007	3.535	3.228	3.009	2.845	2.715
100	6.895	4.824	3.984	3.513	3.206	2.988	2.823	2.694
110	6.871	4.803	3.965	3.495	3.188	2.970	2.806	2.677
120	6.851	4.786	3.949	3.480	3.174	2.956	2.792	2.663
300 or more	6.720	4.677	3.848	3.382	3.079	2.862	2.699	2.571

(Continued)

$\alpha = .01$
Numerator degrees of freedom (d.f.)

Denom d.f.	9	10	11	12	13	14	15	16
9	5.351							
10	4.942	4.849						
11	4.632	4.539	4.462					
12	4.387	4.296	4.220	4.155				
13	4.190	4.099	4.024	3.960	3.904			
14	4.029	3.939	3.863	3.800	3.745	3.697		
15	3.894	3.804	3.729	3.666	3.611	3.564	3.522	
16	3.780	3.691	3.616	3.552	3.498	3.450	3.409	3.372
17	3.682	3.593	3.518	3.455	3.400	3.353	3.311	3.275
18	3.597	3.508	3.434	3.370	3.316	3.269	3.227	3.190
19	3.522	3.434	3.359	3.296	3.242	3.195	3.153	3.116
20	3.456	3.368	3.294	3.231	3.177	3.129	3.088	3.051
21	3.398	3.310	3.236	3.173	3.119	3.071	3.030	2.993
22	3.346	3.257	3.184	3.121	3.067	3.019	2.978	2.941
23	3.299	3.210	3.137	3.074	3.020	2.973	2.931	2.894
24	3.256	3.168	3.094	3.032	2.977	2.930	2.889	2.852
25	3.217	3.129	3.056	2.993	2.939	2.892	2.850	2.813
26	3.182	3.094	3.020	2.958	2.904	2.856	2.815	2.778
27	3.149	3.062	2.988	2.926	2.871	2.824	2.783	2.746
28	3.119	3.032	2.958	2.896	2.842	2.795	2.753	2.716
29	3.092	3.004	2.931	2.868	2.814	2.767	2.726	2.689
30	3.066	2.979	2.906	2.843	2.789	2.742	2.700	2.663
31	3.043	2.955	2.882	2.819	2.765	2.718	2.677	2.640
32	3.021	2.933	2.860	2.798	2.743	2.696	2.655	2.618
33	3.000	2.913	2.840	2.777	2.723	2.676	2.634	2.597
34	2.981	2.894	2.820	2.758	2.704	2.657	2.615	2.578
35	2.963	2.876	2.803	2.740	2.686	2.639	2.597	2.560
36	2.946	2.859	2.786	2.723	2.669	2.622	2.580	2.543
37	2.930	2.843	2.770	2.707	2.653	2.606	2.564	2.527
38	2.915	2.828	2.755	2.692	2.638	2.591	2.549	2.512
39	2.901	2.814	2.741	2.678	2.624	2.577	2.535	2.498
40	2.888	2.801	2.727	2.665	2.611	2.563	2.522	2.484
45	2.830	2.743	2.670	2.608	2.553	2.506	2.464	2.427
50	2.785	2.698	2.625	2.562	2.508	2.461	2.419	2.382
55	2.748	2.662	2.589	2.526	2.472	2.424	2.382	2.345
60	2.718	2.632	2.559	2.496	2.442	2.394	2.352	2.315
65	2.693	2.607	2.534	2.471	2.417	2.369	2.327	2.289
70	2.672	2.585	2.512	2.450	2.395	2.348	2.306	2.268
80	2.637	2.551	2.478	2.415	2.361	2.313	2.271	2.233
90	2.611	2.524	2.451	2.389	2.334	2.286	2.244	2.206
100	2.590	2.503	2.430	2.368	2.313	2.265	2.223	2.185
110	2.573	2.486	2.413	2.350	2.296	2.248	2.206	2.168
120	2.559	2.472	2.399	2.336	2.282	2.234	2.192	2.154
300 or more	2.467	2.38	2.307	2.244	2.190	2.142	2.099	2.060

$\alpha = .01$
Numerator degrees of freedom (d.f.)

Denom. d.f.	20	25	30	35	40	50	60	70
20	2.938							
21	2.879							
22	2.827							
23	2.780							
24	2.738							
25	2.699	2.604						
26	2.664	2.569						
27	2.632	2.536						
28	2.602	2.506						
29	2.574	2.478						
30	2.549	2.453	2.386					
31	2.525	2.429	2.362					
32	2.503	2.406	2.340					
33	2.482	2.386	2.319					
34	2.463	2.366	2.299					
35	2.445	2.348	2.281	2.231				
36	2.428	2.331	2.263	2.213				
37	2.412	2.315	2.247	2.197				
38	2.397	2.299	2.232	2.182				
39	2.382	2.285	2.217	2.167				
40	2.369	2.271	2.203	2.153	2.114			
45	2.311	2.213	2.144	2.093	2.054			
50	2.265	2.167	2.098	2.046	2.007	1.949		
55	2.228	2.129	2.060	2.008	1.968	1.910		
60	2.198	2.098	2.028	1.976	1.936	1.877	1.836	
65	2.172	2.072	2.002	1.950	1.909	1.850	1.808	
70	2.150	2.050	1.980	1.927	1.886	1.826	1.785	1.754
80	2.115	2.015	1.944	1.890	1.849	1.788	1.746	1.714
90	2.088	1.987	1.916	1.862	1.820	1.759	1.716	1.684
100	2.067	1.965	1.893	1.839	1.797	1.735	1.692	1.659
110	2.049	1.947	1.875	1.821	1.778	1.716	1.672	1.639
120	2.035	1.932	1.860	1.806	1.763	1.700	1.656	1.622
300 or more	1.940	1.836	1.761	1.705	1.660	1.602	1.555	1.519

Index